The Economics of Association Football
Volume II

Wherever possible, the articles in these volumes have been reproduced as originally published using facsimile reproduction, inclusive of footnotes and pagination to facilitate ease of reference.

For a list of all Edward Elgar published titles visit our site on the World Wide Web at www.e-elgar.com

The Economics of
Association Football
Volume II

Edited by

Bill Gerrard

Professor of Sport Management and Finance
Leeds University Business School, University of Leeds, UK

An Elgar Reference Collection
Cheltenham, UK • Northampton, MA, USA

Published by
Edward Elgar Publishing Limited
Glensanda House
Montpellier Parade
Cheltenham
Glos GL50 1UA
UK

Edward Elgar Publishing, Inc.
136 West Street
Suite 202
Northampton
Massachusetts 01060
USA

A catalogue record for this book is available from the British Library.

ISBN-10: 1 84376 941 7 (2 volume set)
ISBN-13: 978 1 84376 941 5 (2 volume set)

Printed and bound in Great Britain by MPG Books Ltd, Bodmin, Cornwall.

Contents

Acknowledgements

The editor and publishers wish to thank the authors and the following publishers who have kindly given permission for the use of copyright material.

Blackwell Publishing Ltd for articles: Peter J. Sloane (1971), 'The Economics of Professional Football: The Football Club as a Utility Maximiser', *Scottish Journal of Political Economy*, **XVIII** (2), June, 121–46; Peter F. Pope and David A. Peel (1989), 'Information, Prices and Efficiency in a Fixed-Odds Betting Market', *Economica*, **56** (223), August, 323–41; Mark J. Dixon and Stuart G. Coles (1997), 'Modelling Association Football Scores and Inefficiencies in the Football Betting Market', *Journal of the Royal Statistical Society, Series C: Applied Statistics*, **46** (2), 265–80; Stephen Dobson and John Goddard (1998), 'Performance, Revenue, and Cross Subsidization in the Football League, 1927–1994', *Economic History Review*, **LI** (4), November, 763–85; Thomas Hoehn and Stefan Szymanski (1999), 'The Americanization of European Football', *Economic Policy*, **28**, 205–33, references; Michael Cain, David Law and David Peel (2000), 'The Favourite-Longshot Bias and Market Efficiency in UK Football Betting', *Scottish Journal of Political Economy*, **47** (1), February, 25–36; David Forrest and Robert Simmons (2000), 'Making Up the Results: The Work of the Football Pools Panel, 1963–1997', *Journal of the Royal Statistical Society, Series D: The Statistician*, **49** (2), 253–60; Ruud H. Koning (2000), 'Balance in Competition in Dutch Soccer', *Journal of the Royal Statistical Society, Series D: The Statistician*, **49** (3), 419–31; Stefan Szymanski (2001), 'Income Inequality, Competitive Balance and the Attractiveness of Team Sports: Some Evidence and a Natural Experiment from English Soccer', *Economic Journal*, **111** (469), February, F69–F84; Martin Crowder, Mark Dixon, Anthony Ledford and Mike Robinson (2002), 'Dynamic Modelling and Prediction of English Football League Matches for Betting', *Journal of the Royal Statistical Society, Series D: The Statistician*, **51** (2), 157–68; Stephen Dobson and John Goddard (2004), 'Revenue Divergence and Competitive Balance in a Divisional Sports League', *Scottish Journal of Political Economy*, **51** (3), August, 359–76.

Elsevier for article: David Forrest and Robert Simmons (2000), 'Forecasting Sport: The Behaviour and Performance of Football Tipsters', *International Journal of Forecasting*, **16**, 317–31.

Human Kinetics Publishers for article: Bill Gerrard (2005), 'A Resource-Utilization Model of Organizational Efficiency in Professional Sports Teams', *Journal of Sport Management*, **19**, 143–69.

Sage Publications, Inc. for articles: Stephen Dobson, John Goddard and Carlyn Ramlogan (2001), 'Revenue Convergence in the English Soccer League', *Journal of Sports Economics*, **2** (3), August, 257–74; Jaume García and Plácido Rodríguez (2002), 'The Determinants of

Football Match Attendance Revisited: Empirical Evidence From the Spanish Football League', *Journal of Sports Economics*, **3** (1), February, 18–38; Stephen Hall, Stefan Szymanski and Andrew S. Zimbalist (2002), 'Testing Causality Between Team Performance and Payroll: The Cases of Major League Baseball and English Soccer', *Journal of Sports Economics*, **3** (2), May, 149–68; Roger G. Noll (2002), 'The Economics of Promotion and Relegation in Sports Leagues: The Case of English Football', *Journal of Sports Economics*, **3** (2), May, 169–203; Manuel Espitia-Escuer and Lucía Isabel García-Cebrián (2004), 'Measuring the Efficiency of Spanish First-Division Soccer Teams', *Journal of Sports Economics*, **5** (4), November, 329–46.

Taylor and Francis Ltd (http://www.tandf.co.uk/journals) for articles: N. Jennett and P.J. Sloane (1985), 'The Future of League Football: A Critique of the Report of the Chester Committee of Enquiry', *Leisure Studies*, **4** (1), January, 39–56; John A. Cairns (1987), 'Evaluating Changes in League Structure: The Reorganization of the Scottish Football League', *Applied Economics*, **19**, 259–75; Stefan Szymanski and Ron Smith (1997), 'The English Football Industry: Profit, Performance and Industrial Structure', *International Review of Applied Economics*, **11** (1), January, 135–53; S.M. Dobson and J.A. Goddard (1998), 'Performance and Revenue in Professional League Football: Evidence from Granger Causality Tests', *Applied Economics*, **30**, 1641–51; Tim Kuypers (2000), 'Information and Efficiency: An Empirical Study of a Fixed Odds Betting Market', *Applied Economics*, **32**, 1353–63.

Springer Science and Business Media for article: Luigi Buzzacchi, Stefan Szymanski and Tommaso M. Valletti (2003), 'Equality of Opportunity and Equality of Outcome: Open Leagues, Closed Leagues and Competitive Balance', *Journal of Industry, Competition and Trade*, **3** (3), September, 167–86.

Every effort has been made to trace all the copyright holders but if any have been inadvertently overlooked the publishers will be pleased to make the necessary arrangement at the first opportunity.

In addition the publishers wish to thank the Library at the University of Warwick, UK, and the Library of Indiana University at Bloomington, USA, for their assistance in obtaining these articles.

Part I
Competitive Balance and League Structure

[1]

The future of League football: a critique of the report of the Chester Committee of Enquiry

N. JENNETT[1] and P.J. SLOANE[2]

[1] North Staffordshire Polytechnic, UK
[2] University of Aberdeen, Scotland, UK

Professional football in England has been in decline for many years when measured in terms of paying spectators. In response to the growing financial problems of member clubs the Football League invited Sir Norman Chester, Chairman of an earlier investigation in 1968, to analyse the game's problems and recommend solutions including a possible restructuring of the League. The recommendations of the Chester Committee of Enquiry are evaluated from the perspective of the economist, drawing attention to the objectives of football clubs, the structure of costs, the nature of competition and the demand for the product. It is concluded that the recommendations, though in certain respects supportable, are in others flawed by failure to appreciate the economic features of the industry.

Introduction

In recent years the problems facing the football industry have become increasingly serious. Attendances at Football League games have declined from a peak of 41.3 million in 1948–49 to 18.4 million in 1983–84. Further, while in the past increases in admission charges have more than compensated for the reduction in the number of spectators, in recent seasons real incomes of clubs have fallen. This has put the future of a growing number of clubs in doubt and major rescue operations have had to be mounted to save, among others, Bristol City, Wolverhampton Wanderers, Hull City, Charlton Athletic and Derby County. An analysis of the balance sheets of the individual League clubs by Financial Intelligence and Research (1982) found that the League as a whole had operating losses of over £6 million in 1981/82, though this was largely offset by £5.9 million in donations and grants. At that time League clubs had net liabilities of some £25 million and only in 18 clubs were current assets in excess of current liabilities.

* This is an amended and non-technical version of a paper published by the *Journal of Industrial Affairs* which appears here for a wider, non-specialist readership with the permission of the Editor.

Leisure Studies 4 (1985) 39–56
© 1985 E. & F.N. Spon Ltd.   0261–4367/85 $03.00 + .12

N. Jennett and P. J. Sloane

However, the economic problems of the Football League have a long history. In 1964 the then Secretary of the League, Alan Hardaker, produced his own blue print for survival, *Pattern of Football*, which recommended fundamental changes in the structure of the League. In 1966, following representations made by the Football League and the Football Association about the deteriorating financial position of the professional game and the need for additional funds for its improvement and administration, the Secretary of State for Education and Science set up a Committee of Investigation:

to enquire into the state of Association Football at all levels, including the organisation, management, finance and administration, and the means by which the game may be developed for the public good.

When the resulting 'Chester Report' (Department of Education and Science, 1968) appeared, its proposals included reforms both of the structure of the League competition and of the transfer system, but these proposals were rejected by the League clubs. The instability of the existing retain and transfer system was a particular cause of concern and in 1971 the relevant ministers referred to the Commission on Industrial Relations the question of industrial relations between professional footballers and their employers, and the promotion of any necessary or desirable improvement in them (Commission on Industrial Relations, 1974). When in April 1978 the retain and transfer system was finally substituted by freedom of contract subject to a transfer fee negotiated between the clubs, or, in the event of failure to agree, determined by an independent tribunal, the resulting escalation of players' salaries in a relatively labour-intensive industry added to the economic problems facing the clubs as a consequence of declining attendances.

It was in response to these problems that the Football League produced a further plan, *Fight for Survival* in 1980, followed in 1981 by Management Committee proposals which suggested, amongst other things, replacing the third and fourth divisions of the Football League by three geographically based Leagues of 18 teams.

Finally, following a crisis meeting of the Chairmen of the 92 Football League clubs held in February 1982, the suggestion emerged that a further Committee of Investigation along the lines of the one set up in 1966 should be formed and the chairman of the previous enquiry, Sir Norman Chester, was asked to act in a similar capacity. The second Chester Committee's terms of reference were:

to review the structure of the League's championship and cup competitions and to make recommendations as to future viability.

When the Committee reported (Football League, 1983), however, the League clubs quickly rejected the majority of its proposals.

The Chester analysis of the state of the Football League

The basic premiss underlying the Chester analysis is that the football industry is suffering considerable problems of lack of liquidity and increasing current indebtedness resulting from the sharp increase in costs suffered by many clubs since the 1970s and declining real revenues in the current recession. This raises two issues of principle relating to the size and composition of the League and the extent, purpose and basis of the distribution of sponsorship and other income. The Report emphasizes the need to take a long-term perspective and to view its proposals as a whole rather than as a series of disconnected points. In this spirit we examine both revenues and costs.

Revenues

As the Report correctly points out, attendance figures are not 'an accurate indicator of the financial fortunes of clubs' (para. 190). They are, however, an important determinant of club revenues, and so the Report considers some explanations of the declining attendances at Football League games. These explanations are analysed here with some factors not considered by the Chester Committee.

The Committee examined three possible explanations of the trend in League attendances for much of the post-war period (para. 27):

(a) Changes in the structure and habits of society.
(b) The economic recession.
(c) Other factors emerging from market research.

Under the first of these headings the Committee considered such factors as shifts in population from urban areas and changing leisure habits. The Report is particularly concerned to draw attention to the relationship between the changing incomes of consumers and football attendances. It points out that between 1961 and 1981, real after-tax income per head in Britain increased by some 50%. Over the same period there was significant growth of car ownership and expansion of television. Both of these changes appear to be associated with the growth of incomes. If football watching was similarly related to rising incomes, the result would have been growing League attendances. However, economists, notably Bird (1982), have found evidence of a negative relationship between income growth and watching football: as real incomes have increased, spectators have turned increasingly to other leisure pursuits.

This effect is reinforced by changes in the distribution of population. As the Report points out, the composition of the Football League has changed relatively little for over 50 years. For the most part football clubs are located in urban industrial centres which, although growing at the time of the clubs' establishment, have suffered significant loss of population in recent years. The Report indicates that the populations of the principal cities of the Metropolitan Counties fell by 8.4% from 1961 to 1971, and by a further 10% from 1971 to 1981. Over the same period smaller towns and rural areas have tended to enjoy growing populations.

The effects of these population changes might be interpreted in two ways, although both imply a reduction in attendances. On the one hand, migration from inner cities (where football grounds tend to be located) to the suburbs implies an increased price in real terms (that is allowing for inflation) of attending football as travelling distances and costs increase. However, the changed distribution of population might simply be a reflection of long-run growth of real incomes. As real incomes have increased households have been able to bear the higher travel-to-work costs necessitated by removal to suburban and out of town locations. If de-population of the cities is a result of income growth and if football spectating tends to fall as incomes rise then there is likely to be a relationship between population change and declining football attendances.

However, an explanation based on the propensity of football supporters to switch to other leisure activities as their incomes grow fails to explain why League attendances have fallen during the recession since 1979. In discussing this issue, the Report seems to be implying an opposite relationship between changes in incomes and spectating at football matches. The Committee draws attention to the growth of unemployment in areas in which League clubs are concentrated, suggesting that the associated reductions in incomes in these areas will cause falling attendances.

Leisure and entertainment spending generally increased in real terms in the 1970s, with entertainment spending falling off in the post-1979 recession period. There are at least two possible explanations of why football attendances moved against the trend of real leisure spending up to 1979 but with it thereafter. One is that attendance charges have increased relative to other prices in recent years. It appears to have been the Chester Committee's impression that this has been the case. Unfortunately, there is little reliable information on admission prices, particularly since minimum League admission charges were discontinued in 1981. However, the Committee agreed (para. 85) that over the past 15 years charges may have increased at up to twice the rate of the general Retail Prices Index.

An alternative explanation might be that a period of income growth has, in effect, introduced football supporters to a range of new leisure habits, and such a brief period of falling incomes does not lead to a switch back to football spectating. Individuals may be *committed* to a new pattern of leisure spending (for example, hire purchase payments on new cars, foreign holidays, sports' club membership) so that temporary reductions in income reduce the resources they have available for watching football.

Neither of these explanations is particularly comforting for the football industry. They suggest that an economic upturn can, at best, provide temporary relief. The appropriate response would appear to be to change the nature of the product offered by football clubs, for example, by providing more comfortable stadiums, easier access to parking facilities and so on, to increase the appeal of football at a time of growing incomes (the effect of new stadiums on sports attendances in the United States is discussed by Noll, 1974). The success of the major North American team sports in attracting growing attendences as real incomes have risen indicates that spectator sports need not necessarily be regarded as inferior leisure activities. For example Markham and Teplitz (1981) report that 'spectator sports as a whole benefitted greatly as a result of increased leisure spending. Between 1960 and 1978 personal expenditures for spectator sports rose sixfold.'

Under the heading 'Other Factors', the Committee speculated on the role of issues such as hooliganism and the poor 'image' presented in the media of the professional game. It has not proved easy to assess these factors adequately in research work. A study of Scottish football attendances by Cairns (1983b) notes the possible influence of crowd violence, but omits this as an explanatory variable in the model. Bird (1982) finds no evidence for attributing declining attendances to hooliganism, the number of goals scored in the League or the influence of television.

Two other important determinants of attendances were, however, neglected by the Committee in their deliberations. The first is the role of 'uncertainty of outcome' in determining spectator interests in sports events, and the second the changes in real admission prices.

Uncertainty of outcome

The influence of uncertainty of outcome on demand is unique in being applicable only to the special circumstances of sports events. It has been recognized in the literature as being the crucial determinant of quality in sporting contests. Quality involves not only the skills of the competitors but also the extent to which these skills are balanced and the importance (in the context of the championship or tournament) of the result of the contest. In the Football League, the closer is overall competition, the larger are attendances expected to be. Uncertainty of outcome is discussed more fully elsewhere, for example Cairns (1983a), but in principle two dimensions can be isolated. The first is the extent to which a single team or two or more teams dominate a series of championships, where 'over-domination' may kill overall spectators' interest – 'long run' uncertainty of outcome. Alternatively, 'short run' uncertainty of outcome concerns the closeness of competition in particular annual championship races. The closer the competition throughout the season and the longer the championship in doubt, the larger the attendances.

Theory suggests, then, that there would be advantages to the Football League from promoting more balanced playing strengths among clubs. This might be achieved in a number of ways, for example by inhibiting, through a device like the old 'retain and transfer' system, the ability of wealthy clubs to attract even more talented players, or by attempting to equalize the revenues available to all clubs within the League. The neglect of this point was a serious omission in the Chester analysis, particularly in view of some of the recommendations made by the Committee, examined in section 3.

Admission prices

The increase in real admission charges to football identified by the Committee (para. 85) and discussed above will have contributed to declining attendances. Correctly, the Committee concentrated on the gate receipts generated from attendances, rather than on attendance figures alone. However, one interesting issue not considered was the question of why clubs have apparently failed to maximize these revenues. League clubs are committed to a fixed number of League championship games each season. Given this commitment, if the addition to total costs of an extra spectator is assumed to be negligible, then a football club which was seeking to maximize its profits would attempt to charge admission prices which maximized its gate revenue. However, the evidence of Bird (1982) suggests that – recent increases notwithstanding – clubs charge prices which are too low to do this.

Therefore, the first response to the current crisis in clubs' revenues might be to increase attendance prices. This will undoubtedly reduce attendances but, if Bird is correct, a given percentage increase in prices will cause a smaller percentage fall in admissions, and so total *revenues* will rise. The extent to which clubs are unwilling to do this indicates a concern with attendances other than as a source of revenue. In other words, club managements are concerned with 'other objectives' (in this case large crowds), if necessary at the expense of commercial considerations.

The Chester Committee draws attention to a lack of commercial awareness among clubs in a number of other areas. There has been a rather slow development of a potentially important source of revenues from sponsorship. The Report itself points to little or no market research by clubs, poor promotion and marketing and a general lack of responsiveness to consumer demands. Again, this situation contrasts markedly with that in the United States where, for example, the National Football League signed a 5-year television contract in 1982 for $2000 million. Advertising of the product is also regarded as a normal part of business activity by US team sports. In 1979, the 26 major baseball clubs spent no less than $22 million on sales publicity and promotion.

The pertinent question is: why have British clubs been apparently reluctant to exploit new sources of revenue? In part the explanation may be the longstanding view in Britain (see Mason, 1980) that sport and a commercial orientation are incompatible. In professional football, however, a more plausible explanation concerns the nature of the objectives of clubs and their managements. In so far as clubs are not primarily motivated by the desire to make profits, their responsiveness to changing market conditions may involve costs in terms of their other objectives — be these conservatism and a desire to retain the present League organization or a wish to retain maximum discretion in the hands of Boards of Directors*. If club behaviour can indeed be best explained in terms of these kinds of non-profit objectives by Directors, then Chester's exhortation to greater commercial awareness may well fall on deaf ears. Here again, the contrast with the United States is instructive. Baseball franchises are often traded for what can be very large fees ($18 million for the Boston Red Sox, $21.5 million for the New York Mets and so on). Indeed, in January 1979 the median length of ownership of a baseball franchise was only 8 years in the American League and 14.5 years in the National League (Markham and Teplitz, 1981). Threat of take-over and possible geographical removal of a franchise is an important component of the imposition of the disciplines of the market on clubs and their managements.

These issues of property rights and ownership are of crucial importance, and it is a major weakness that these are not fully explored in the Report.

Costs and expenses

Rising expenditures are the second element of the problem relating to club finances identified by the Chester Committee. There have recently been a number of areas of growth in expenditures. One issue examined by the Report was recent trends in the player transfer market. As the Committee concedes, it is extremely difficult to assess the effect on the League clubs as a whole of the boom in transfer fees in 1979–80 and the subsequent decline in real terms to early 1970s levels. However, in a study undertaken on behalf of the Football League by Arthur Anderson and Co. (1982) it is suggested that 'it is not necessarily the transfer fee which is of concern to the clubs but the increase in wage costs, signing-on fees etc. that such transfers bring with them. Very often in order to attract a player, clubs offer a substantially higher wage to him which has an adverse effect on the existing wage structure. Currently, however, there is little activity in the transfer market so that the poorer clubs in financial difficulties will be unable to sell a player to make ends meet.' In a further study, undertaken by the FA Secretary, of 80 of the 92 League clubs accounts for 1978/79, it was found that there was a total loss on transfers to the Football League as a whole of about £2 million (mainly to Scottish clubs). The Committee's only recommendation on this issue is that fees should be paid more quickly by clubs (as a means of keeping their size in check).

A second area of recent high expenditure has been on ground safety and improvement following the 1975 Safety of Sports Grounds Act. It is argued that for many clubs these represent 'once and for all' payments, although they have burdened some clubs with high interest charges.

The most interesting item of growing expenditure, however, concerns playing costs and wages. The Committee approached this issue by asking whether player salaries might be considered 'too high' (para. 17). The conclusion was that there was no answer to the question! In general economists might possibly agree, but can provide a useful framework within which to analyse the issue.

Economists examining players' salaries in professional team sports in the United States have shown a remarkable degree of agreement. Although *average* salaries in major league baseball are in the region of £100 000 or more, studies (notably Scully, 1974 and Medoff, 1976) have almost invariably concluded that professional clubs 'exploit' their players. Exploitation in this sense refers to paying players less than the value of the extra attendances they generate as a result of their performances. The studies referred to above indicate that players have frequently been paid less than this value.

The Chester Committee's reflections on players' pay determination are also of much interest:

In theory at least a club is willing to pay what it thinks the services of the player are worth in team performance and revenue earning power. If it pays more than this it is being charitable or financially improvident (para. 17).

The main problem with this argument is that it fails to distinguish between the concepts 'team performance' and 'revenue-earning power'. It has been one of the major propositions of the British literature that 'exploitation' in the North American sense is unlikely among professional footballers because of the non-profit orientation of clubs. In other words, because clubs are prepared to sacrifice profits for playing success they may be prepared to pay players a salary in

The future of League football　　　　47

excess of their revenue-earning power. Clubs will attempt to equate additional spending on playing staff with the 'value' (a combination of additional revenues plus the valuation of playing success) of player performances. It is not clear whether the Chester Committee would regard this as 'charitable' or 'improvident' or both.

Although the Report draws no conclusions on whether salaries are 'too high', the implication of its analysis is clear. Total wage bills rose between 1979–80 and 1980–81 by 45% against an increase in general prices of 20%. This followed a decade in which the total salary bill increased only in line with price inflation. But experience in 1979–80 involved two other features. First, the number of registered Football League players fell; second, the increase of over 45% in players' average salaries occurred at a time of falling real gate receipts. This reduction in real revenues was most marked in Division Four, yet it was here that the increase in the total wage bill was largest! The result was that, over 1980–81 and 1981–82, players' earnings exceeded gross match receipts in both the Third and Fourth Divisions.

The Committee makes no concrete recommendations to deal with the problem of growing costs and expenses, but simply comments that a close working relationship between Manager and Directors is desirable,

always bearing in mind that the Chairman and his fellow Directors are accountable to the shareholders for the financial health of the club. We consider that Directors should direct in all matters of finance and general policy (para. 121).

While it is difficult to dissent from these sentiments, in many respects this is indicative of the fundamental weakness of the Report – the question of what the Committee perceives to be the objectives of clubs and their Directors. Shareholders are obviously not motivated by the desire for profits. This places Directors in a relationship with shareholders unlike that which operates in most other enterprises. The relationship between football club boards and shareholders is also complicated by two other factors. First, of the 91 Football League clubs with limited liability (Nottingham Forest being the exception), 34 are in a position where Directors hold over 50% of voting shares. Second, as Financial Intelligence and Research (1982) reports

One of the most anomalous aspects of . . . the financial status of English League Football Clubs . . . (proves to be) . . . the extent to which the Articles of Association of many clubs permit the Directors total control over the issuing of new shares . . . It is extraordinary to find in many cases that Directors by a simple whim and resolution, have been able to issue new voting shares at par to one or two of their own number without any apparent regard to the dilution effect which such issues have on the voting strength of persons outside the board.

Directors of football clubs apparently can retain – and have retained – control in their own hands, while voting shares – when these become available – often trade at prices greatly in excess of their par values. Thus, not only are Directors neglecting a potentially highly attractive means of raising long-term capital, but they are also effectively nullifying a major mechanism for the efficient allocation of resources in a market economy – the constraints placed on a firm's Directors by the possible threat of take-over. In these circumstances, Directors need only act so as to avoid liquidation; to expect them to act as if they were functioning under market constraints without the incentives to do so must be unrealistic. The neglect of this vital point is a major weakness in the Chester analysis.

The virtues of wider share ownership appear to be considerable in the case of football clubs. The ability of a large number of supporters to participate in the decision-making process would make clubs more responsive to consumer needs. And the apparent willingness of large numbers of supporters to respond to share issues by clubs could raise substantial amounts of additional capital required to alleviate short-run financial problems or to finance new capital projects such as ground improvements. A good example of the advantages of this strategy comes from the experience of Tottenham Hotspur – the first football club to have its shares traded on the London Stock Exchange. Spurs' offer of 3.8 million £1 shares was oversubscribed some 4.5 times and raised around £3.3 million for the club to pay debts and undertake ground improvements. It is regrettable that the Chester Committee did not explore in some detail this potentially major source of new funds.

The Chester prescription

The proposals

The Report's main recommendations can be summarized as follows:

(a) *The marketing of League football*

The Report suggests that clubs adopt a new customer orientation. To this end, the League should commission and finance, from sponsorship revenues, market research and other marketing activities, including advertising.

(b) *League structure*

The Committee unanimously rejected any proposals to increase the size of the Football League and wished where possible to see reductions through 'natural wastage'.

With one dissenter, the Committee recommended that the size of the

First Division be reduced to 20 teams. The majority recommendation was that the Second Division should comprise 24 clubs, and that the Third Division should be enlarged, comprising four sections of 12 clubs each. These four sections were to compete in two half-season series, playing a total of 44 section matches over the season as a whole. At the season's close, promotion 'play-offs' would involve the top two clubs from each section in each half-season series. Hence, between 8 and 16 clubs would be involved in the 'play-off' for promotion to Division Two. Bottom clubs would compete in a similar relegation 'play-off'. The minority view recommended that the Second and Third Divisions should each comprise 22 clubs. The clubs which are currently in the Football League but which would be excluded from it in this proposal (primarily from the present Division Four) would join selected members of the Alliance League in an Intermediate League with its own Management Committee, but they would have the right to compete for the Milk Cup and to receive a share of payments made by the Pools Promoters' Association for the use of copyright fixture lists, but not to any other levy payments.

Both these schemes envisaged an automatic link between the Football League and the Alliance Premier Division. The Committee presented this as a separate recommendation should the reorganization schemes be rejected by the League clubs (as indeed they later were).

(c) *Financial arrangements*

i. The Committee recommended a major change in the distribution of League revenues between clubs. The practice of sharing part of the gate receipts between home and visiting clubs should end, but there should be an equal division of receipts between the home and the visiting teams in FA and Milk Cup ties. The practice of sharing equally revenues from television rights between all League clubs should also be discontinued.

ii. The Committee recommended the removal of the current limit of one paid Director on club boards and some relaxation of dividend controls.

iii. The League should take a greater interest in the accounting practices of clubs and improve its access to information on the financial state of clubs.

(d) *The constitution of the League*

Current League rules specifying a 75% majority of those entitled to vote to implement changes in League organization should be replaced by a 60% majority.

An evaluation

The remaining part of this section gives an evaluation of the rationale for, and implications of, some of these proposals.

The Committee's recommendations for the improvement of the marketing of professional football appear to be wholly sensible. For the most part they are probably uncontroversial, although it is unlikely that the same could be said of the analysis from which the proposals flow. In fact the Committee makes – with some force – a case for consumer choice.

League clubs are commercial enterprises: their financial success depends on meeting the needs of their customers (para. 66).

The Committee discussed briefly the role that sponsorship might play in generating revenues for the professional game. Given the Committee's decision to interpret their terms of reference widely, and to include 'any matters which bear on the finances of clubs' (para. 2) it is unfortunate that the issue of sponsorship was not considered in greater detail, for there *may* be a case for collective action on this issue also. The League imposes few controls on the ability of its constituent clubs to secure sponsorship arrangements. One result is that relatively wealthy and successful clubs may be able to consolidate their dominance with the aid of sponsors' resources. There is a clear risk of a breakdown of competitive balance or 'uncertainty of outcome' in this situation, and that may justify some kind of redistribution by the League from more to less favoured clubs. Admittedly, the implications of this proposal are out of line with the tenor of much of the remainder of the Report (particularly recommendations on financial arrangements), but this is a crucial issue and is considered below in detail.

For all their disagreements over the appropriate nature of League organization, the Chester Committee appeared to be unanimous in the view that the present League structure is not sustainable. The Committee hints that:

changes in the social, economic and sporting life of a country cannot be ignored and may require adjustments in long established arrangements. Any organisation which cannot adapt itself to such changes . . . sooner or later will find even more drastic changes necessary (para. 136).

The Report begins by broaching the major question of whether or not it could be argued that the League is 'too big'. Implicitly, at least, it appears to be the view of the Chairman that this is the case. The justification for this view is that the fixed sums of money which the League has available from sponsorship, television rights, copyright fees from the Pools Promoters' Association and so on for distribution to its constituent clubs are being too widely spread. In other words current arrangements involve an excessive degree of financing of the

The future of League football 51

poorer clubs by the wealthier ones, and this has two potentially damaging consequences:

i. It diverts funds which could be used to improve spectator facilities to subsidizing clubs which are providing a product consumers clearly do not value at its cost of production. (In 1981–82 and 1980–81 in aggregate, clubs in both the Third and Fourth Divisions paid their players more than they received as gross match receipts.) In view of the arguments examined in section 2 – particularly those referring to the importance to League football of following the American example of moving 'up market' – the case for a reduction in *inter*-division subsidies appears to be strong.

ii. The second major factor explaining the Chairman's desire to concentrate more resources in the hands of the League's larger clubs is his concern to avoid the emergence of a 'super-league' or breakaway group of First Division clubs. As the Report notes:

. . . some of the top clubs though not anxious to break away from the Football League are concerned that their special interests are in danger of being subordinated to the claims of the clubs in the lower divisions (para. 159).

To the extent that the objective of the League is further to concentrate resources in the hands of larger clubs, a reduction in inter-division transfers of income would appear to be a sensible policy – particularly in comparison with the option discussed later in the Report and examined further below.

These factors basically provide the rationale for the minority proposal on League structure outlined above. The second important element of the minority proposal (the automatic link, through promotion and relegation, from the Intermediate League to the smaller Football League) also appears to have many merits. Over a long period, it would enable the best-supported teams to graduate to the Football League, without suffering from the vagaries of the League's current procedures for election and re-election.

In contrast to the logic of the minority proposal, the majority proposal raises more questions than it answers. A League of 92 clubs is envisaged. Does this imply that the proponents of the majority scheme reject the notion that there is 'too much' inter-division subsidization (a somewhat strange position considering their views on the sharing of gate receipts)?

This proposal purports to generate extra revenue by, in effect, promoting short-run uncertainty of outcome through increasing the number of significant games in a season as far as the lower division clubs are concerned. While this would appear to have some merits, difficulties remain. What of the case where a club completes the first half of the season in a promotion position, but slumps to a relegation position in the second half? Logically, would these clubs have to be excluded from both sets of play-offs? In this case contenders for promotion from the first half of the season would merely have to avoid the danger of relegation in the season's second period. There would be a reduced incentive to win the League for a second time and, under these circumstances, spectator interest might well be expected to wane, thus depressing attendances. Finally, it should be recognized that for most clubs, the majority scheme will mean a reduced number of matches. In a labour-intensive industry with players on fixed contracts, additional games will add *relatively* little to clubs' total costs. Under these circumstances, there might well be a case for increasing – not reducing – the number of games played by Third and Fourth Division clubs.

In many respects, the discussion of the League's financial arrangements proves to be of greatest interest to those concerned with the economics of professional football. The most significant issue is the Committee's proposal for altering – mostly to the detriment of the poorer clubs and those with the smallest population bases on which to draw – the distribution of League revenues.

The Report examines what the Committee regards as the piecemeal development of revenue redistribution among League clubs. There are basically three elements to this: (i) the levy, (ii) pooled payments from sponsorship arrangements and television rights, (iii) the division of gate receipts between the two competing clubs in League games.

The Committee notes the considerable disquiet among the League's larger members at the degree of inter-division transfers of income implicit in (i) and (ii), going so far as to state:

This is the issue which if not settled amicably in the near future could split the League (para. 211).

In analysing the rationale for these transfers, the Committee comes closest to accepting a purely market-orientated view. The Report clearly rejects the view that the pool payments either could or *should* operate to keep the poorer clubs 'financially viable', arguing:

. . . some clubs . . . are no longer in localities which can sustain a traditional League club . . . Social forces, including the movement of population . . . have removed the basic support on which their original viability depended. *In cases of this kind the infusion of extra money may be challenged as a failure to face the facts* (para. 215, our emphasis).

Furthermore, the Committee appears at this stage to recognize the non-commercial objectives of clubs, arguing (para. 216) that the dominating requirement of playing success leads to a propensity to push up club overdrafts.

In view of this apparent market orientation and the argument that over-subsidization may prevent any wealthy club moving up-market in order to increase the appeal of football at a time of economic recovery, then – bearing in mind one important caveat expressed below – the Committee appears to have made a strong case for reducing inter-division transfers of income. Ironically, however, the actual proposals made by the Committee are inexplicable in these terms!

The Report proposed that the current arrangements for sharing gate receipts between competing teams in League games be replaced by an arrangement in which home teams retain all of the gate receipts. The removal of the pooled element of receipts in FA and Milk Cup ties was also recommended, as were extra payments for clubs whose games were frequently televised. Otherwise the levy system remains intact. In other words, having criticised the extent of inter-division income redistribution, the Committee has proposed a scheme which leaves inter-division transfers largely unaltered but reduces the extent of intra-division redistributions of revenue. This not only fails to meet the Committee's objective, but is actually harmful, for again the Report has ignored the role of uncertainty of outcome as a determinant of attendances at League games. It is clear that where clubs are prepared to sacrifice profits to playing performance, then those clubs in areas of large population and which have significant drawing power may be able to use their resources to acquire ever-superior playing talent, consolidating their position of dominance and killing overall spectator interest in the League. In effect, domination by one or a few clubs may have undesirable effects on the League as a whole, and this may justify collective action to safeguard competitive balance. One obvious method might be to redistribute resources from wealthy and well-supported clubs to those with lesser drawing power.

In these terms, a strong case could be made for a scheme which, having defined an optimal League size, then (with due allowance for incentives for efficiency) divides revenues more or less equally between all the competing clubs. However, in view of the Chester Committee's disagreement over the optimal size for the League and an acceptance of the Committee's point that over-subsidization of small clubs may inhibit the ability of larger clubs to improve spectator facilities, this is probably unrealistic. But if this challenges the case for inter-division redistributions, the argument for intra-division redistribution to promote uncertainty of outcome remains. So, even accepting the Committee's logic the decision to retain the levy but end gate receipt sharing is inexplicable.

In fact the Report justifies its recommendation in other terms – that retention of gate receipts will reward attractive play and enable clubs to experiment with admission charges. The first point could, in principle, have been verified with the information available to the Committee, but no evidence is presented. Evidence from Scotland, however, suggests that the populations of club locations was the determining factor in whether or not clubs gained from retaining gate receipts, not League performance. The same may well be true in England and Wales. On the second issue it is currently simply a matter of assertion as to whether the retention of, say, 60%, 70% or 80% of gate receipts would affect the incentive to innovate. An arrangement based on a fixed sum per spectator, however, does have the advantage of giving clubs the incentive to maximize *revenues* – which is close to the profit maximizing position.

The case for many of the changes outlined above was, according to the Committee, that general managerial efficiency would be improved. Two of the other changes in financial arrangements proposed by the Committee will also contribute to this: first, the relaxation of dividend controls and removal of the restriction to one paid Director on club boards; second, the recommendation of standardized accounting practices and financial targets for clubs. A study of clubs' accounting practices by Arthur Anderson & Co. (1982) found that these were chaotic. The problem arises from the different accounting presentation used by each club, from the lack of disclosure of sources of finance and valuation of players and from the different accounting years of the various clubs. This is particularly serious in an industry in which the welfare of individual clubs is related to the welfare of others.

It has been a theme of this analysis that a number of the problems apparently facing football have resulted from the game's ability to avoid many of the disciplines of the market system. It has been argued both here and by Sloane (1980) that in large part this stems from relatively weak property rights in the ownership of football clubs. Because of dividend controls, limitations on share transfers and so on, it would be very difficult for owners to make profits out of football. This must reduce owners' incentives to ensure that managers and directors make financially prudent decisions. In this sense, some of the Chester proposals may have been a step in the right direction in introducing new incentives towards a more explicitly commercial orientation. Developments like this will not be universally welcomed (for example, see Gratton and Lisewski, 1981) but it is at least arguable that the alternative is the continuing decline of the professional game.

Conclusions

The 1983 Chester Report was published on 28 March. Less than one month later (26 April) the majority of the Report's proposals were rejected in an extraordinary general meeting of the League Clubs' Chairmen. These decisions had been widely anticipated and the Chairmen were severely criticized in the Press.

The response of the clubs to the Report was unfortunate in particular because they have not adopted an alternative coherent strategy. The outcome, however, was probably no surprise to the Committee itself. This explains its request that the Report be viewed as a whole, rather than as a series of disconnected points (para. 16) and its recommendation that the League's ultra-conservative voting rule (requiring a three-quarters majority to adopt changes) be replaced by a constitution based on a majority of two-thirds. These were sensible points to make, although in large part the Committee's inability to recommend unanimous proposals on League size or structure seriously limit the extent to which the Report can be viewed as a coherent whole. None the less it is ironic that the one major proposal which the League clubs decided to adopt 'in isolation' at their Annual Meeting in June 1983 is one of the least appropriate made by the Committee – the recommendation to adopt retention of all gate receipts by home clubs.

It seems to be no great exaggeration to describe the state of the football industry as one of crisis. The analysis and prescription of the Chester Committee was certainly not flawless – its major weaknesses being a failure to recognize the role of uncertainty of outcome as a determinant of demand for sports fixtures and the implications for the Report's recommendations of the non-profit maximizing objectives of club managements. Nevertheless, as a contribution to debate, at least, it deserved the fuller attention of the League than has apparently been the case.

It is in recognition of the importance of this debate, for the future of football as a professional spectator sport, and as a contribution to it, that this paper is offered. Recognition of the need to improve the attractiveness of the product would seem to imply a smaller number of major clubs, but a more even revenue-earning capacity among them. Improved efficiency would also seem to demand greater openness in the distribution of share-ownership and responsiveness to the requirements of an increasingly competitive leisure market. The strengthening of property rights in club ownership and therefore greater exposure to the disciplines of the market may be necessary to provide the incentives to the club directors to respond quickly to the challenges of the current state of crisis in football. Hence, more fundamental changes than have so far been contemplated by the clubs themselves seem to be a *sine qua non* for a thriving football industry.

56   *N. Jennett and P. J. Sloane*

References

Arthur Anderson & Co. (1982) *The Finance and Taxation of Football Clubs*, Football Association and Football League, London.

Bird, P. (1982) The demand for league football, *Applied Economics* **14**, 637–49.

Cairns, J. (1983a) Economic analysis of league sports – a critical review of the literature, *University of Aberdeen, Department of Political Economy Discussion Paper 83–01.*

Cairns, J. (1983b) The demand for Scottish football 1971–80, *University of Aberdeen, Department of Political Economy Discussion Paper 83–05.*

Commission on Industrial Relations (1974) *Professional Football Report No. 87*, HMSO, London.

Department of Education and Science (1968) *Report of the Committee on Football* (Chairman D.N. Chester), HMSO, London.

Financial Intelligence and Research (1982) *English League Football Clubs – Financial Status and Performance*, FIR, London.

Football League (1983) *Report of the Committee of Enquiry into Structure and Finance* (Chairman Sir N. Chester), Lytham St. Annes.

Gratton, C. and Lisewski, B. (1981) The economics of sport in Britain: a case of market failure?, *British Review of Economic Issues* **2**, 63–75.

Markham, J.W. and Teplitz, P.V. (1981) *Baseball Economics and Public Policy*, Lexington Books, D.C. Heath and Co., Lexington, Mass.

Mason, T. (1980) *Association Football and English Society 1863–1915*, The Harvester Press, Brighton.

Medoff, M. (1976) On monopsonistic exploitation in professional baseball, *Quarterly Review of Economics and Business* **16**, 113–21.

Noll, R.G. (ed.) (1974) *Government and the Sports Business*, The Brookings Institution, Washington.

Scully, G. (1974) Pay and performance in major league baseball, *American Economic Review* **64**, 915–30.

Sloane, P.J. (1971) The economics of professional football: the football club as a utility maximiser, *Scottish Journal of Political Economy* **17**, 121–46.

Sloane, P.J. (1980) *Sport in the Market?*, Institute of Economic Affairs, London.

[2]

Applied Economics, 1987, **19**, 259–275

Evaluating changes in league structure: the reorganization of the Scottish Football League

JOHN A. CAIRNS

Department of Political Economy, University of Aberdeen, Edward Wright Building, Dunbar Street, Old Aberdeen, AB9 2TY, UK

This article investigates the relationship between league structure and the demand for professional team sport using data from the Scottish Football League (SFL) 1971 to 1980. The SFL was restructured in 1975 and thus provides an excellent opportunity for the empirical analysis of the influence of league structure. The general channels by which league structure affects demand are explored. Estimates are made of the impact on individual clubs by predicting what attendances would have been in the absence of the league reorganization. Finally, the distribution of attendances across clubs is examined for evidence of the influence of league structure.

I. INTRODUCTION

League structure has received very limited analysis in the extensive team sports literature.[1] The determinants of demand have been studied for a number of sports in a number of countries but no study has enquired directly into the influence that league structure has on demand.[2]

The Scottish Football League (SFL) started in 1890 with one division of ten clubs. A second division was created in 1893, and the two division structure continued until 1975. The number of clubs in each division has varied from 10 to 20. From 1955 up until 1975 there were 18 clubs in the top division. Since 1975 the SFL has comprised a Premier Division with 10 members, and a First and Second Division, each with 14 members. These changes were principally an attempt to make the product more attractive. Aggregate League Championship and League Cup attendances had fallen from 6.4 million in 1956–7 to 4.5 million by 1971–2. Attendances appeared to be continuing to decline, and it was hoped that a new structure would reverse or at least staunch the loss of spectators.

An evaluation of the impact of the reorganization is of considerable interest, both at the academic level as a contribution to the economics of professional team sports and in terms of its

---

[1]See, for example, Gross (1979) and Rivett (1975).
[2]For a detailed review of the literature see Cairns *et al.* (1986). Studies of the demand for football include Hart *et al.*(1975), Gartner and Pommerehne (1978), Bird (1982) and Jennett (1984).

policy relevance. In Scotland the new structure has been the subject of continual dispute and remains a live issue, while the English Football League, which has faced years of declining attendances and has recently had its weak economic situation exacerbated by major crowd control and crowd safety problems, is actively addressing the issue of league structure.

II. LEAGUE STRUCTURE AND DEMAND

There are a number of ways in which alternative league structures might influence demand. The *level* of attendances depends, to a large extent, on the overall attractiveness of the contests on offer, one element of which is the uncertainty of outcome. The structure of the league influences the degree of inequality in the distribution of team quality and via this channel affects the uncertainty of outcome. The structure also affects the importance of different matches; through its impact on the number and frequency of contests and by changing the valuation of success in individual matches.

The league structure decision also influences the *distribution* of attendances, when it leads to changes in the average market size of the participant clubs in each league. The distribution between leagues and the effective distribution between clubs (if gate-sharing is practised) will both change.

Uncertainty of outcome

The introduction of smaller divisions should increase uncertainty of outcome by increasing team homogeneity with respect to skill. Uncertainty of outcome takes a number of forms; uncertainty with respect to the outcome of individual matches, with respect to the outcome of the championship and the absence of long-run domination of the championship by a particular club.

It is likely that the new structure reduces the number of games where the outcome is far from uncertain. This is difficult to demonstrate conclusively since economists have not yet modelled successfully the expectations of potential spectators.

Seasonal uncertainty refers to the outcome of the championship. It is suggested that demand will be higher the closer is the contest: the more teams that might win and the longer such close competition lasts. The annual coefficient of variation of end-of-season points totals was estimated to see whether or not uncertainty of *seasonal* outcome increased following the reorganization.[3] The annual value based on all clubs in the top division appears to be similar 1971–5 and 1975–80; that is, there was no increase in uncertainty of outcome (see Table 1). Moreover, when the coefficient of variation is estimated for the top six clubs in each season, uncertainty appears to have decreased (albeit slightly) rather than increased.

There is more variation in the annual figures after reorganization. After 1975 some seasons have been closer and others have been less close than under the old system. An explanation might be that, while teams are of generally more uniform standard (thus giving closer outcomes),

[3] An approach suggested by Rottenberg (1956).

Table 1. *Coefficients of variation for end-of-season outcomes, 1971 to 1980*

Season		Coefficients of variation	
		League	Top six clubs
1971–2		0.3010	0.1653
1972–3		0.3100	0.1539
1973–4		0.2807	0.1349
1974–5		0.3031	0.1379
1975–6		0.3229	0.1882
1976–7		0.2977	0.1840
1977–8		0.3145	0.2206
1978–9		0.2684	0.1143
1979–80		0.2512	0.1299
1971–5	average	0.2986	0.1480
1975–80	average	0.2909	0.1674

if one or two sides are particularly strong in any one year their dominance is amplified by playing their nearest competitors four times rather than twice.

Under the old system Celtic enjoyed a period of unparalleled domination (they won the championship every year from 1965–6 to 1973–4). A comparison of the ten seasons prior to the reorganization with the ten since suggests long-run domination has been reduced.[4]

Relative importance of different matches

Number and frequency of matches. The league structure adopted will influence the number of games played by each club since typically each club meets every other club a specified number of times. Since 1975 the SFL programme involves one more home match for each team in the top division. While total seasonal attendance for a club is related to the number of matches played, it is unlikely that such a change has a readily discernible effect. But if the programme was, say, reduced to 30 matches or increased to 42 per club there would surely be a marked impact on attendance.[5]

A change in the number of league matches might alter the mean frequency of matches. For example, relatively long league programmes, particularly when the disruptive influence of weather is recognized, can cause the frequency of matches towards the end of the season to be quite high. When home matches rise above, say, one per fortnight, average attendance might

---

[4]Before, Celtic won 9 times and Rangers once. After, Celtic won 4 times, Aberdeen 3 times, Rangers twice and Dundee United once. The picture is less clear if a longer time period is considered, such as the 20 years prior to reorganization.
[5]Siegfried and Eisenberg (1980) report that additional matches raise the total and reduce average attendances.

fall.[6] This has implications not just for the number of league fixtures and their scheduling but also for the numbers of non-league matches that are permitted or encouraged.

Valuation of success in individual matches. After the 1975 reorganization of the SFL an increased proportion of matches 'counted' in the sense of being title challenges, relegation battles or relevant to entry to European competitions. A large league can have a considerable number of middle-of-the-table games in which little is genuinely at stake. Such matches are characterized by relatively low attendances not owing to lack of uncertainty as considered above, but rather because of the potential attenders' relatively low valuation of success.

Two main factors are relevant when determining whether a club is in contention for the league championship: points won relative to other leading clubs and the number of matches played.[7] Championship contention is largely relevant to the second half of the season. Otherwise, performance variables are adequate to capture leading and trailing clubs. Any definition is unavoidably arbitrary. As an example, consider a club as in contention if first or ith ($i \neq 1$) and an 80 % success rate in the remaining matches would be good enough to beat the current leader if they only enjoyed a 50 % success rate (and half the club's programme has been completed). This implies being not more than 3 points adrift with 5 matches to play; not more than 6 points adrift with 10 matches to play and not more than 9 points behind with 15 games remaining.

Using this definition, the proportion of matches where the home side is in contention for the championship doubles after the reorganization. The figures are presented in Table 2. The extensive disruption of the competition caused by the severe winter has imparted an upward bias to the measure for the 1978–9 season.[8]

Table 2. *Percentage of matches where home team is in contention for the League Championship*

1971–2	1972–3	1973–4	1974–5		1971–5
5.23	10.46	6.54	2.83		6.94
1975–6	1976–7	1977–8	1978–9	1979–80	1975–80*
16.11	11.11	11.67	27.78	16.56	13.75

*excluding 1978–9.

Definitions of being in contention for relegation are also arbitrary. For example, let a club be in contention for relegation if relegation is not absolutely inevitable and it is the last third of the season and a one-third success rate in the matches that remain will put the club down if rival clubs enjoy a two-third success rate. If this definition is adopted over the period 1971–4 the

[6] To explore this type of behaviour, the number of home games in the past two weeks (*NOG*) was used as an explanatory variable. It was significant for Aberdeen but not for Dundee United or Partick Thistle (see Appendix A).

[7] Jennett (1984) starts from similar premises. However, his measure uses information unavailable to potential attenders and no role is played by notions of expected relative performance of one club compared to the others.

[8] A situation is created where some clubs have many more games left to play compared with others. The anticipated points total of these clubs with 'games in hand' will be artificially lower than for those with 'points in the bag'.

home club was in contention for relegation in 9.37% of matches, as compared with 9.63% for the period 1975–8.[9]

Market size

The average market size of clubs will be larger in the Premier League than in the old First Division if city size and team strength are correlated. However, this need not be the case since the identity of the clubs in the Premier League is determined by playing success and not directly by market size.

There is no unique method for determining the size of a club's market.[10] This paper uses the number of males aged between 10 and 64 years resident in the local authority of the club. Mid-year population estimates are available for each authority but local government was reorganized in the 1970s. Estimates are presented using three years: 1973 (the last year with the 'old' boundaries), 1974 (the first year with the 'new' boundaries) and 1980. Table 3 shows that average market size increased substantially after the reorganization. While this qualitative conclusion is highly reliable, the quantitative message of Table 3 must be treated more cautiously because a club's market area is not always well defined by local administrative boundaries and when there is more than one club in the same area, sharing assumptions must be made.

Table 3. *Average market size for First Division clubs 1971–5 and Premier League clubs 1975–80*

	1971–5		1975–80	
	Males 10–64	Index no.	Males 10–64	Index no.
Pre-local government reorganization areas (1973)	39 000	100.0	57 200	146.7
Post-local government reorganization areas (1974)	53 000	100.0	69 900	131.9
Post-local government reorganization areas (1980)	50 900	100.0	65 800	129.3

Source: R. G. Scotland Report Part 2, 1973, 1974, 1980, HMSO.

III. IMPACT ON INDIVIDUAL CLUBS

To establish whether or not the introduction of the Premier League improved the attractiveness of the product and as a result increased demand requires a model which explains the level of

[9]Note that this definition ignores matches where relegation is certain. These have increased – the bottom club finished on average 3.7 points behind the bottom non-relegated club 1971–4, and 15.0 points behind 1975–8.
[10]US studies, such as Demmert (1973), use the total population of the relevant Standard Metropolitan Statistical Area. Jennett (1984) uses total population within the appropriate local government district and Hart et al. (1975) use total male population of the urban parliamentary constituencies surrounding the club's ground.

demand both before and after the reorganization. The ways in which the structure of demand has altered with the introduction of the smaller league are of particular interest.

Considerations of space preclude a detailed discussion of the determinants of demand.[11] The recent performance of the home club is likely to be an important factor since it is a guide to the likelihood of success. The current league position (*LGPO*) and the points scored in the previous three home games (*POINTS*) are assumed to capture this influence. In the last section it was stressed that whether or not the team was in contention for the league championship (*CONTEN*) would influence the consumer's perception of the attractiveness of a particular contest.

The identity of the opposition matters in that certain matches are of special interest, possibly for reasons of tradition or geographical proximity. Example of such games are those against Celtic or Rangers (*BIG*) or local rivals (*DERBY*). Spectators may be influenced by the current ranking of the opposition (*LGPOV*). The higher the ranking, the greater will be the expected quality of the visiting side.

The timing of the match affects the relative attractiveness of different matches. The impact of the day of the week (and in the SFL the time of day) is captured by including a dummy variable (*WKDY*) which distinguishes weekday evening from Saturday afternoon matches. The impact of the time of year is analysed by including variables which take account of climatological factors, such as maximum temperature, rainfall and sunshine recorded on the day of the match, and by a variable representing the stage of the season (*STIME*).

Minimum adult and juvenile prices deflated by a retail price index were included, as was a measure of contention for relegation. Neither variable had a significant role to play in explaining variations in attendances. Suitable local income statistics were unavailable and as a crude alternative the monthly unemployment rate for the travel-to-work area in which the home club was located was included. The remaining variables are those to test for slope and intercept shifts associated with the introduction of the Premier League, such as changes in the time trend or in the numbers attracted by matches involving particular teams.

The demand functions, estimated using individual match attendances at the home league games over the four years prior to and the five years after reorganization, reveal changes in structure associated with the introduction of the Premier League. No fewer than five distinct effects can be observed. The demand functions for the three clubs, Aberdeen, Dundee United and Partick Thistle, are reproduced in Appendix A.

The information contained in these estimated demand functions can be used to quantify the impact of the league reorganization on these three clubs. The example of adult attendances at the home matches of Aberdeen FC (Table A1) can serve to illustrate the approach followed, in that all five effects are present.

Time trend. The coefficients of *TIME* and *PTIME* imply a quite marked downward time trend prior to reorganization which disappears after the introduction of the Premier League. It is possible to estimate the averted loss of spectators. Assume a 32-week (64 time unit)[12] season and let b_1 be the decline in attendance per unit time. Then, over a season of 18 evenly spaced

---

[11]See Cairns (1983) for a fuller discussion of data problems, omitted variables etc.
[12]Even numbers represent Saturdays, and the odd values can be used for mid-week games.

home matches the 'loss' of spectators would be:

$$18(32b_1)$$

Over the period 1975–80 there would be five such seasons. However, the time trend goes on working in the close season and thus to get the true 1975–80 loss of spectators had the time trend not been eliminated this must be taken into account by adding:

$$18(104b_1) + 2(18)104b_1 + 3(18)104b_1 + 4(18)104b_1$$

Therefore, the averted decline in adult attendances 1975–80 was

$$21\ 600b_1 \text{ or } 356\ 400$$

since b_1 is none other than the coefficient of *PTIME*.

Premier League dummy. The large negative coefficient of *PREMIER* can be multiplied by the number of home league matches (90) to give a loss of 524 295 spectators. This is *prima facie* evidence of a marked deleterious impact. However, this must be considered in association with the responsiveness to recent performance effect.

Recent performance. Prior to reorganization the recent performance of the home club (points won in the previous three home matches) had no significant impact. After reorganization recent performance (coefficient of *PPOINTS*) has a statistically and quantitatively significant impact. Taken with the negative intercept shift this positive slope dummy indicates a rotation of the attendance–performance relation such that recent performance becomes an important determinant of demand. The magnitude of this effect will depend on how well a team performs. The average number of points won in home league games after reorganization was calculated (1.39 for Aberdeen), and multiplied by three to give an average recent performance figure. This was multiplied by the coefficient of *PPOINTS* to give an increased demand due to the new responsiveness of attendances to performance.

'Big' matches. Certain matches have a tradition of being of particular spectator interest and since clubs in the Premier League meet each other twice at home and twice away, these 'big' matches occur more frequently. Attendances at such games are still above average but not as high as before the reorganization (the coefficient of *PBIG*). The coefficients of *BIG* and *PBIG* can be used to estimate the overall impact of making these 'big' games more frequent.

League position. A club who is nth in the Premier League might arguably have been nth in the old 18 club First Division. However, the average league position of visiting clubs should rise by about four places when a 10-club league is substituted for an 18-club one. This implies an increase of 63 108 adult attendances (90 times 4 times the coefficient of *LGPOV*).

If the five effects are combined, the estimated gain in adult spectators 1975–80 associated with the introduction of the Premier League is 188 876. The impact of the Premier League on Aberdeen's juvenile attendances and on Dundee United and Partick Thistle can be calculated by the use of the appropriate estimated demand function and an application of the same principles. These estimates are reported in Table 4. The rough magnitudes are relevant rather than the specific, spuriously precise values presented. The calculations are at best only as good as the estimated demand functions upon which they are based. For example, would the downward time trend apparent for Aberdeen adults have actually continued at the same rate up until 1980 had the league not been reconstructed?

Table 4. *Impact of league reorganization*

	Aberdeen			Dundee United		Partick Thistle		
	Adults[a]	Juveniles[b]	Juveniles[c]	Adults[d]	Juveniles[d]	Adults[e]	Adults[f]	Juveniles[g]
PTIME	356 400	—	77 544	—	—	—	152 004	—
PREMIER	−524 295	113 787	—	−205 812	—	−353 304	−542 419	−47 354
PBIG	23 334	3825	3507	61 567	15 521	54 004	57 082	28 999
POINTS	270 329	—	—	159 775	—	219 563	203 012	—
LGPOV	63 108	28 980	27 288	62 748	19 548	46 598	45 302	10 253
Total	188 876	146 592	108 339	78 278	35 069	−33 139	−85 019	−8102

a Based on Table A1.
b Based on Equation 2 Table A2.
c Based on Equation 1 Table A2.
d Based on Table A3.
e Based on Equation 2 Table A4.
f Based on Equation 1 Table A4.
g Based on Equation 3 Table A4.

The case of Partick Thistle is complicated by their failure to qualify for the Premier League in 1975–6. They, however, did have a successful season in which they gained promotion. Thus the net effect of this season was downward, but not markedly, and while it is attributable to the reorganization, it has not been included in Table 4.

The evidence presented in Table 4 can be restated in a per match form (see Table 5). It suggests that, in terms of home League Championship attendances, Aberdeen and Dundee United were gainers from reorganization, and that Partick Thistle lost. Real admission prices were higher in the period 1975–80 than 1971–5, and gate-sharing did exist. Thus the apparent 'losses' of Partick Thistle are possible overestimates of the deleterious impact upon them of the league reorganization.

Table 5. *Estimated per match 'increase' after reorganization*

	Aberdeen	Dundee United	Partick Thistle
Lower	3302[a,c]	1259	− 1293[f,g]
Upper	3727[a,b]	1259	− 573[e,g]

Notes as for Table 4.

The teams which gained were those that achieved a measure of sporting success 1975–80 (each only finished outside the top four once), while the loser, Partick Thistle, never finished higher than fifth. One plausible interpretation is that the introduction of the Premier League has changed the nature of the league competition to one in which the potential rewards for success and penalties for failures are more marked than in the past. For evidence, it is possible to cite the rotation of the attendance–performance relationship that occurred in the case of the adult attenders of all three clubs and the doubling of the proportion of matches where the home team was in contention for the championship.

The impact of being in contention has been omitted from Tables 4 and 5 since it is not clear for *individual* clubs the extent to which the increased *CONTEN* games are due to the change in league structure as opposed to simply improved performance by the club. Thus the estimates of increased attendances in Table 5 are possibly underestimates.

IV. THE DISTRIBUTION OF ATTENDANCES BETWEEN CLUBS

The distribution of attendances both between and within leagues is related to the structure of league adopted. The reduction in the size of the top division increased the average market size by around 30 % by eliminating a number of clubs located in relatively small population centres. Therefore we would expect to find a shift in favour of the 'top' clubs. *Intra*-league distribution might also be expected to have changed if the smaller divisions result in reduced skill differences between competing teams.

Table 6 presents an analysis of the distribution of total home League Championship and League Cup attendances for all members of the SFL. Atkinson's equally distributed equivalent

Table 6. *Distribution of League and League Cup attendances:*
1971–80

Season	Equally distributed equivalent measure		
	$E = 0.5$	$E = 1.5$	$E = 2.0$
1971–2	0.30	0.69	0.72
1972–3	0.29	0.60	0.69
1973–4	0.26	0.57	0.65
1974–5	0.31	0.63	0.71
1975–6	0.35	0.68	0.76
1976–7	0.32	0.64	0.72
1977–8	0.33	0.63	0.71
1978–9	0.34	0.66	0.73
1979–80	0.32	0.63	0.71

measure has been used in preference to other measures such as the Gini coefficient. It permits differing value judgements regarding the welfare significance of inequality.[13] The higher the value of the index, the greater the inequality. The ranking of seasonal attendance distributions in terms of inequality appears to be invariant over a range of E judgements. Comparing 1971–5 with 1975–80, inequality has risen slightly. Table 7 shows a clearer increase in inequality when only Championship matches are considered.[14]

Table 7. *Distribution of League attendances*

	Season	Equally distributed equivalent measure		
		$E = 0.5$	$E = 1.5$	$E = 2.0$
All SFL clubs	1971–2	0.25	0.59	0.68
	1972–3	0.24	0.57	0.67
	1978–9	0.30	0.64	0.71
	1979–80	0.29	0.63	0.70
Eleven best-supported clubs	1971–2	0.07	0.24	0.30
	1972–3	0.10	0.26	0.33
	1978–9	0.09	0.20	0.26
	1979–80	0.10	0.27	0.35
Ten best-supported clubs in each season	1971–2	0.07	0.19	0.23
	1972–3	0.08	0.20	0.25
	1978–9	0.05	0.13	0.17
	1979–80	0.05	0.14	0.17

[13]Atkinson (1970).
[14]The restricted years analysed are a product of data availablity rather than a judgement that those examined are of primary importance.

To examine the distribution of attendances between the top clubs these top clubs must first be identified. One approach involves a subjective evaluation of the footballing skills of the various clubs, possibly supplemented with evidence on playing success, international appearances by team members etc. An alternative approach based on attendances is followed here. Eleven clubs had an aggregate attendace in excess of one million and more than one-fifth higher than the next best supported club over the period 1971–80. The index of inequality for these clubs shows no unambiguous change (Table 7). But the reorganization introduced a smaller top league, and increased relative divisional mobility, and arguably the present choice of definition has compounded these factors. Since the smaller league is of primary interest and the increased mobility is to a certain extent incidental, the index for the ten best supported club in *each* season was calculated. It indicates reduced inequality.[15]

V. EVALUATION OF THE REORGANIZATION

It is not easy to judge the success or failure of the 1975 reorganization of the SFL. Notwithstanding the empirical problems involved in isolating the impact of the change in league structure, the primary difficulty is the identification of an appropriate evaluative perspective. One possibility is to ask whether it has represented an improvement from the viewpoint of the SFL. The concerns and the objectives of the League must be identified. The SFL handbook states explicitly that the objective of the League is to provide competitions for and to guard the interests of the member clubs.[16]

However, the interests of the member clubs are far from identical. The 38 members differ widely in terms of size of market, playing skills, capacity and quality of stadia etc. One common feature is that they are nearly all fairly long-lived institutions. Of the current 38 only 3 are less than 60 years old and most (three quarters) were formed in the nineteenth century. This implies a strong individual club interest in survival.

The League secures its own future and that of individual clubs through the rules by which it regulates both the product and the labour market. The main forms of product market regulation include the suppression of competition, the maintenance of the 'integrity of the product' and revenue-sharing to improve the product. The various labour market rules which give clubs an element of monopsonistic advantage can be interpreted as means of lowering labour costs or reducing the inequality in the distribution of skills.

Every club enjoys the same constitutional power: one vote per club. Since any change in the rules requires a two-thirds majority all clubs wield considerable, and in principle equal, influence; an influence which is dependent on securing the support of a number of like-minded clubs and which is independent of wealth or sporting success. Full control of the business of the League is vested in the League Management Committee (LMC), except for business controlled by the General Meeting (such as changes of the rules). There is considerable scope for the LMC to be representative of the majority view.[17]

[15]Despite two traditionally 'top ten' sides spending some seasons in the First Division.
[16]Scottish Football League (1980).
[17]The clubs in each division elect 3 members with rotation of members whereby each year the third of the representatives who have been in office longest must retire, as must those reaching 70 and those who represent a club which changes its division. There are in addition 3 office-bearers who require 50% support in order to secure election.

But the LMC's views are not a reliable guide to the views of the membership as a whole, as was shown by the March 1982 meeting where the LMC proposal for reorganization failed to command even a simple majority. In general, it is not possible to evaluate a change from the perspective of the SFL. Unanimity would attach to any policy whose sole effect was to increase attendances. But most policies will have a number of effects and are likely to have a differential impact across the League membership. The variety of underlying interests ensures that there will usually be both gainers and losers and thus differences of opinion concerning any new development.

While the survival of the 1975 structure for eleven seasons perhaps suggests that the reorganization has been a success, its continued existence may derive from the inability of any new proposal to generate a coalition yielding the two-thirds majority necessary for change.

The evidence presented in Section III does support the view that the new set-up has changed the nature of the product, in particular, the increased responsiveness of attendances to recent performance and the elimination of downward time trends. The widely-felt need for such a change would appear to have provided the motivation for reorganization. Thus it can be claimed that the introduction of the Premier League has been a success, while not denying that it might not command majority, positive approval.

An interesting (if not entirely unexpected) effect has been on the distribution of attendances. As shown in Section IV, League-wide inequality has widened in favour of the top third, while inequality narrowed within this group. A case can be made that this is desirable, based largely on the view that what is important is the health of these top clubs. Such a view is highly contentious.

VI. CONCLUSIONS

This paper presents some clear evidence on the impact of league structure upon the demand for football. Manipulation of the league structure can change the nature of the product. In the SFL case, it has been associated with significant gains and losses for individual clubs and distinct changes in the distribution of attendances. The analysis restricted attention to the impact on attendances. A more comprehensive study would have to examine the impact of league structure upon revenue.

The costs of participation are also influenced by league structure. One minor aspect is the costs of travel for the clubs. A more important dimension is illustrated by the case of the introduction of a 'super-league' (such as the Premier League). The costs that it is necessary to incur to compete effectively (in sporting terms) will be related to the costs confronting the other clubs making up the top flight. For example, in order to attract and retain players of the appropriate calibre it is necessary to offer remuneration and terms of employment that are not markedly inferior to those of your competitors. This generates specific problems by raising the long-term costs of participation without the guarantee of permanently raised revenue flows.

The evidence produced by this study is of relevance to the English Football League, which has experienced a marked decline in attendance.[18] English football appears to be out of line with

---

[18]First Division attendances have tended to decline steadily from a post-war peak of 17.9m, although there was a partial recovery after the 1966 World Cup. They fell every year from 1976–7 (13.6m) to 1983–4 (8.7m). The significance of the small rise in 1984–5 is as yet unclear.

European practice, where 16 or 18 club top divisions are the norm, and only France with 20 clubs approaches the extremes of the English Football League. A recent Committee of Enquiry advocated a reduction of the First Division by two clubs.[19] The chairman (although not the committee) favoured a shift from the existing four divisions of 92 clubs to a league of three divisions with 64 members, the primary motivation being that the available 'cake' could then be shared among fewer clubs. These proposals and the report as a whole failed to recognize the potential impact of league structure on demand.

Further research is needed in order to generalize about the impact of league structure. One interesting topic that cannot be investigated by considering only one country is the role played by the size and distribution of markets in determining league structure. Also, it is necessary to move beyond an examination of demand to consider the function of league structure decisions in terms of forestalling the emergence of rival organizations.[20]

APPENDIX A: ESTIMATED DEMAND FUNCTIONS

Table A1. *Aberdeen FC adult attendances: 1971–80*

CNST	16 626.8	LGPOV	−175.3
	(9.70)**		(−3.11)**
BIG	10 707.4	LGPO	−431.7
	(10.19)**		(−3.16)**
PBIG	−4187.0	CONTEN	1884.6
	(−3.35)**		(3.23)**
TIME	−17.8	NOG	−506.2
	(−5.75)**		(−1.76)
PTIME	16.5	STIME	−49.6
	(3.92)**		(−3.93)**
PREMIER	−5825.5	RAIN	−18.6
	(−2.42)*		(−1.74)
POINTS	−255.8	SUN	12.8
	(−1.01)		(1.68)
PPOINTS	720.3	$\bar{R}^2$	0.74
	(2.24)*	F	27.2**

Number of observations = 128; equation estimated by OLS; *t*-statistics in parentheses; D–W statistics not reported owing to uneven spacing of observations; *5 % significance; **1 % significance; for variable definitions see Appendix B.

---

[19] The Football League (1983). They suggested that a reduction of four matches in the league programme would improve the quality of the national team and noted that international success might boost League demand.
[20] The events of the past season in both Scotland and England, which occurred too recently for inclusion in this paper, provide considerable material for such an analysis.

Table A3. Dundee United FC attendances: 1971–80

	(1) AATT	(2) JATT
CNST	5681.0	2039.2
	(6.08)**	(10.36)**
BIG	6728.1	1744.8
	(15.30)**	(13.49)**
CONTEN	1291.0	219.2
	(2.68)**	(1.56)
DERBY	5724.0	1926.8
	(6.69)**	(7.75)**
WKDY	-420.5	-279.6
	(-0.99)	(-2.26)*
LGPOV	-174.3	-54.3
	(-4.07)**	(-4.83)**
PREMIER	-2286.8	
	(-2.33)*	
POINTS	-73.7	62.5
	(-0.40)	(1.90)
PPOINTS	455.2	
	(1.95)	
STIME	-15.43	-3.70
	(-1.85)	(-1.48)
RAIN		-2.46
		(-1.58)
R̄²	0.73	0.72
F	43.9**	47.1**

Notes as for Table A1, except number of observations = 141.

Table A2. Aberdeen FC juvenile attendances: 1971–80

	(1)	(2)
CNST	5266.6	5036.1
	(10.18)**	(9.37)**
BIG	3546.7	3460.3
	(10.18)**	(9.60)**
PBIG	-1598.0	-1538.9
	(-3.86)**	(-3.56)**
TIME	-4.25	-2.08
	(-4.81)**	(-3.44)**
PTIME	3.59	
	(5.06)**	
PREMIER		1264.3
		(4.00)**
POINTS	102.5	109.5
	(1.92)	(1.98)
LGPOV	-75.8	-80.5
	(-4.03)**	(-4.14)**
LGPO	-286.5	-337.7
	(-6.66)**	(-7.84)**
CONTEN	633.8	776.6
	(3.26)**	(3.90)**
NOG	-203.4	-163.4
	(-2.08)*	(-1.62)
STIME	-11.1	-12.0
	(-2.74)**	(-2.87)**
RAIN	-7.50	-8.04
	(-2.13)*	(-2.20)*
DAMAX	3.97	3.98
	(1.95)	(1.88)
R̄²	0.76	0.74
F	34.3**	31.3**

Notes as for Table A1.

Table A4. *Partick Thistle FC attendances: 1972–5 and 1976–80*

	(1) *AATT*	(2) *AATT*	(3) *JATT*
CNST	10 890.4	9991.6	1706.8
	(5.73)**	(5.74)**	(5.07)**
BIG	13 399.4	13 429.7	2101.9
	(16.20)**	(16.09)**	(10.51)**
PBIG	−3132.1	−3339.6	761.5
	(−3.16)**	(−3.35)**	(3.21)**
PREMIER	−7533.6	−4907.0	−657.7
	(−4.04)**	(−4.00)**	(−2.72)**
LGPO	−250.7	−259.8	−52.5
	(−2.48)*	(−2.57)*	(−2.40)*
LGPOV	−157.3	−161.8	−35.6
	(−3.63)**	(−3.69)**	(−3.40)**
POINTS	−507.3	−602.4	
	(−2.01)*	(−2.40)*	
PPOINTS	778.9	842.4	
	(2.80)**	(3.04)**	
TIME	−5.05		0.93
	(−1.62)		(2.52)*
PTIME	7.23		
	(2.02)*		
WKDY	−1897.4	−1805.8	−607.6
	(−4.28)**	(−4.08)**	(−5.83)**
CONTEN	1527.9	1700.4	
	(2.02)*	(2.27)*	
RAIN	−19.2	−19.1	−3.40
	(−2.73)**	(−2.74)**	(−2.03)*
$\bar{R}^2$	0.89	0.88	0.87
F	65.8**	76.9**	82.2**

Notes as for Table A1, except number of observations = 101.

APPENDIX B: VARIABLE DEFINITIONS

AATT : the number of persons attending a match who have paid at least the adult minimum admission price.

BIG : a dummy variable taking the value 1 where the opposition is Rangers or Celtic and 0 otherwise.

CONTEN : a dummy variable taking the value 1 when the home team is in contention for the League Championship and 0 otherwise. A team is described as being in contention whenever in the second half of the season a success rate of less than 80% in the remaining matches will secure victory over rivals enjoying a 50% success rate.

DAMAX : maximum temperature in tenths of a degree Centigrade recorded on the day of the match.

DERBY : a dummy variable taking the value 1 when Dundee United FC play Dundee FC and 0 otherwise.

JATT : the number of juveniles and OAPs paying the juvenile minimum admission price.

LGPO : the league position of the home club prior to match.

LGPOV : the league position of the visiting club prior to match.

NOG : the number of home games played by the home club in the past two weeks.

POINTS : points scored by the home team in previous three home matches.

PREMIER : a dummy variable taking the value 1 for matches played August 1975 onwards and 0 otherwise.

P (variable name) : a dummy variable the product of *PREMIER* and the variable name.

RAIN : tenths of millimetres of rain falling between 0900 hours and 2100 hours on the day of the match.

STIME : a time trend taking the value 1 at the start of each season and increasing by two per week.

SUN : tenths of hours of sunshine on the day of match.

TIME : a time trend taking the value 1 for the opening league match of the 1971–2 season and increasing at the rate of 2 per week thereafter. For mid-week matches the index is assumed to be the previous Saturday value plus 1.

WKDY : a dummy variable taking the value of 1 for non-holiday weekdays and zero otherwise.

ACKNOWLEDGEMENTS

Thanks are due to Dr K. Hartley and Professor P. J. Sloane for commenting on earlier drafts and to the Nuffield Foundation for financial support.

REFERENCES

Atkinson, A. B. (1970) On the measurement of inequality, *Journal of Economic Theory*, **2**, 244–63.

Bird, P. J. W. N. (1982) The demand for league football, *Applied Economics*, **14**, 637–49.

Cairns, J. A. (1983) *The demand for Scottish football, 1971–80*, Discussion Paper No. 83-05, Department of Political Economy, University of Aberdeen.

Cairns, J. A., Jennett, N. and Sloane, P. J. (1986) The economics of professional team sports: a survey of theory and evidence, *Journal of Economic Studies*, **13**, 3–80.

Demmert, H. G. (1973) *The Economics of Professional Team Sports*, D. C. Heath and Co., Lexington, Massachusetts.

The Football League (1983) *Report of the Committee of Enquiry into Structure and Finance*, (Chairman: Sir Norman Chester) Lytham St. Annes.

Gartner, M. and Pommerehne, W. W. (1978) Der Fussballzuschauer – ein homo oeconomicus?, *Jahrbuch für Sozial Wissenschaft*, **29**, 88–107.

Gross, E. (1979) Sports leagues: a model for a theory of organizational stratification, *International Review of Sports Sociology*, **14**, 103–12.

Hart, R. A., Hutton, J. and Sharot, T. (1975) A statistical analysis of Association football attendances, *Journal of the Royal Statistical Society*, (Series C), **24**, 17–27.

Jennett, N. (1984) Attendances, uncertainty of outcome and policy in Scottish League football, *Scottish Journal of Political Economy*, **31**, 176–98.

Rivett, P. (1975) The structure of league football, *Operational Research Quarterly*, **26**, 801–12.

Rottenberg, S. (1956) The baseball player's labour market, *Journal of Political Economy*, **64**, 242–58.

Scottish Football League (1980) *Handbook 1980–81*, Glasgow.

Siegfried, J. J. and Eisenberg, J. D. (1980) The demand for minor league baseball, *Atlantic Economic Journal*, **8**, 59–69.

[3]

The Americanization of European football

Thomas Hoehn and Stefan Szymanski

LECG Limited and Imperial College Management School; Imperial College Management
School

1. INTRODUCTION

> Le football est le seul facteur de mondialisation qui échappe à la tutelle américaine. Si
> le monde de l'image est dominé par Hollywood et celui de l'argent par Wall Street, la
> planète foot est très peu nord-américaine.[1] (Vallet, 1998)

European football as we know it may soon be a thing of the past. Six years after the
completion of the Single Market programme, one of the major remaining segmentations
of national markets in Europe is under threat. National championships organized under
the auspices of national football associations and European cup competitions organized
by UEFA, the federation of national football associations, are being challenged by
private interests that seek to break up the old order. Over the summer of 1998 Media
Partners, Milan, were actively courting the top European football clubs. They tried to
persuade them of the attractions of a European Superleague and the viability of their
proposals to set up a new league by the year 2000. In the event, a compromise was
reached by the dozen clubs that had been openly toying with the idea of joining a
Superleague outside the established structure (see *Financial Times*, 15 October 1998). As
of the 1999/2000 season, the UEFA Champions League will be vastly expanded and
offer more matches at the European level than ever. For the leading countries, the

We thank Kai A. Konrad, Carmen Matutes, Paul Seabright and Panel members for helpful comments. We also acknowledge
with thanks the helpful assistance of Chantelle Bramley, Alan Castle, Martin Schimke and Anna Smith.

[1] 'Soccer is the only contributor to globalization that has escaped American hegemony. The world of cinema may be
dominated by Hollywood and that of money by Wall Street, but soccer is scarcely North American.'

qualifying opportunities will be enhanced, allowing several clubs to participate, not just the domestic league champions and the runners-up, as at present.

The fundamental question is whether this compromise represents an equilibrium or whether tensions in the present system of open multiple league structures will continue to drive clubs towards a true European Superleague, possibly with a hermetic structure. European competition authorities have become increasingly interested in the commercial organization of sport, and of football in particular (Wachtmeister, 1998). The European Commission has queried the arrangements between governing bodies and external marketing organizations, broadcasters or sponsors several times over the last year. Formula One, sponsorship agreements of the Danish tennis federation, and the allocation of tickets to the 1998 Football World Cup are just three examples of cases where the Commission has launched major investigations or made high-profile interventions (Ratliff, 1998).

This paper develops a framework to analyse the role of European competition policy in sports. We start with the basic model of a hermetic league that represents essentially the structure of American sport leagues. We then consider the current European structure of multiple leagues, where the top clubs participate in both domestic and international competition. We can then assess how international competition affects the competitive balance between clubs at the domestic level. The comparison between US-style hermetic and European systems offers an insight into the advantages of controversial redistributive measures that are typical in team sports.

In American sports, each league governs its own competition but has no jurisdiction over rival leagues. From time to time, new leagues may be created to compete with existing leagues, but there is no mobility within American leagues – no promotion and demotion. In contrast, the essentially European character of football organization is its unitary structure within a hierarchy of governing bodies and leagues. Governing bodies license all forms of football and in addition administer their own competitions (e.g., the FA Cup or the UEFA Cup). Clubs compete simultaneously at many levels and are subject to rules of promotion and demotion that permit mobility within the hierarchy.

The American model may represent a natural equilibrium for European football. Most researchers have argued that leagues that are more balanced, in the sense that competition results in a more even distribution of winning records, will be more attractive to consumers (El-Hodiri and Quirk, 1971; Jennett, 1984; Peel and Thomas, 1988). We show how the interlocking nature of European competition has created an unbalanced system and that a stand-alone Superleague is likely to sustain a more balanced competition.

This paper addresses the following three policy issues. First, should the European Commission attempt to protect the existing fragmented structure of European football – with its traditions and its strict hierarchy of national leagues controlled by self-regulated governing bodies – when a transnational league system appears the most plausible market solution? Secondly, if a dominant European Superleague were to emerge, should UEFA control the governing body or would it be in the public interest to maintain a separate organization entrusted with the commercial administration of the sport? Thirdly, what stance should the Commission take towards redistributive measures of the Superleague that may enhance the competitive balance between the participating teams, but may also act as a co-ordination mechanism for extracting monopoly rents?

The paper is structured as follows. The recent commercialization of and the main policy interventions in European football are reviewed in section 2. Section 3 compares the current structure with American sports leagues. Section 4 analyses competitive balance under American and European conditions to illustrate the fundamental policy issues. In section 5, we consider in detail the policy issues raised above.

2. RECENT TRENDS IN EUROPEAN FOOTBALL

2.1. Increased commercialization

UEFA, the European governing body of football, estimated that the 1996 Champions League, the premier club competition in Europe, attracted 3.5 billion viewers in Italy, France, Germany, the UK, Spain and the Netherlands, including an audience of 60 million for the final. Association football was invented in English public schools in the early nineteenth century and had spread around the world by the end of the century (see, e.g., Walvin, 1994). Football clubs have existed since the 1850s and most of the major European clubs are around 100 years old. As a legal entity, a club is usually an association of members who pay an annual subscription and are entitled to vote on policy at an annual general meeting (AGM). A club's day-to-day business is run by a club committee appointed at the AGM, whose members must accept financial liability in raising funds or borrowing for club activities. As football attracted spectators and footballers became paid professionals, the clubs evolved into businesses as well as sporting organizations. To facilitate the raising of capital and avoid the difficulties associated with unlimited liability, English clubs started to incorporate as limited liability companies in the late nineteenth century. By the 1920s, almost all the professional clubs in England had converted to limited liability status.[2]

In other parts of Europe, the legal structures have been more varied. Some clubs have been run as members' clubs, with ownership spread out among a large number of supporters and with limited financial powers. Typical of this have been the German clubs, which have maintained the traditional legal structure of a *Verein* (social private club). This is explicitly recognized in law as a non-profit-making entity and combines the football club with other sporting activities (Galli, 1998). Alternatively, clubs have been owned by industrial enterprises (e.g., PSV Eindhoven) or controlled by wealthy industrialists (e.g., AC Milan by Silvio Berlusconi). Other examples of such close relationships include Fiat and Juventus, Peugeot and Sochaux, Bayer and Bayer Leverkusen, and Volvo and Gothenburg. In Spain, the dire state of management and the

---

[2] All professional clubs in England are therefore subject to the commercial law and the statutes of the UK Companies Act.

excessive degree of indebtedness of Spanish clubs led to legislation in 1990 that reformed the legal nature of football clubs.[3] Most clubs are still associations whose members are mostly fans (for example, Barcelona has 104 000 members).[4] In France, clubs are able to choose from a variety of legal structures which include a 'corporation with a sporting objective', a 'mixed economy company' and an association (club) (see, e.g., Bourg and Gouguet, 1998). These differing legal structures effectively restrict the ability of owners and directors in terms of their objectives, and are often viewed as important restraints on the commercialization of the game.

It is only in the last decade or so that European football has become a commercially significant operation. For example, in 1986 the combined annual turnover of the 22 First Division clubs in England was £50 million. Since then football has enjoyed an economic boom that has turned it into a significant business. Increasingly, football has been 'gentrified' – transformed from an essentially working-class pastime sold at commodity prices into a middle-class entertainment. The quality of stadium accommodation has improved, clubs have developed their merchandising arms, and the value of broadcasting rights has increased dramatically. A rough indication of the economic magnitude of the clubs is given in Table 1. Revenues vary even among the top teams in each league. If the more lowly ranked clubs were included in this table, the disparities would become much more pronounced.

Clubs have increasingly looked to the financial markets to supply investment capital. In the mid-1990s, football clubs in the UK discovered the stock market as a source of finance and today there are 23 clubs listed on either the London Stock Exchange or the AIM (twenty in England and three in Scotland). In the summer of 1998, the Italian club Lazio Rome floated on the Milan Stock Exchange and Ajax of the Netherlands floated on the Amsterdam Stock Exchange. A number of other major European clubs, such as Juventus, AC Milan, Borussia Dortmund, Atlético Madrid and Marseille, are said to be seeking a listing or considering share issues. Flotation has in many cases involved a significant organizational restructuring. In 1997 the members of Borussia Dortmund voted to transform the mutually owned club into a shareholding company.[5] In other countries, the transformation has required a change in the law. Italian clubs have been able to adopt limited liability status like their British counterparts following the enactment of a series of laws relating to the treatment of sporting enterprises (see Lazio Offering Circular, 1998).

Television has played a significant role in the commercialization of European football. In the 1960s, broadcasting rights for league matches generated a few million US dollars of income for the game. By the 1990s, the development of pay-TV, satellite, cable and pay-per-view increased the revenue generation into the hundreds of millions. In 1997 the

---

[3] In Spain, football clubs can form SAD, a special case of the more usual Sociedad Anónima (SA).

[4] 'Barca' is an interesting example because the club seems as much a political symbol of Catalan nationalism as a sporting entity.

[5] This change will also require the assent of the league authorities, but this is expected to be granted.

Table 1. Football club finances

Club	Year	Total revenue (£m)	Wages/ revenue (%)	Wage bill (£m)	Profit
England					
Manchester United	1997	87.9	26	22.6	27.6
Newcastle	1997	41.1	43	17.5	8.3
Liverpool	1997	39.2	38	15.0	7.6
Tottenham	1997	27.9	43	12.1	7.6
Arsenal	1997	27.2	56	15.3	−1.6
Chelsea	1997	23.7	63	14.9	−0.4
Aston Villa	1997	22.1	46	10.1	−3.9
Leeds	1997	21.8	57	12.3	−9.7
Everton	1997	18.9	58	10.9	−2.9
Germany					
Bayern München	n/a	57.0	23	13.1	5.2
Borussia Dortmund	n/a	44.7	31	13.8	0.2
Italy					
Juventus	1997	51.9	56	29.1	0.7
AC Milan	1997	46.3	74	34.3	−9.6
Inter Milan	1997	38.1	47	17.9	−7.6
Roma	1997	26.3	52	13.7	0.2
Parma	1997	27.9	55	15.3	−9.0
Lazio	1997	27.3	56	15.3	0.1
Fiorentina	1997	25.8	69	17.8	−3.7
France					
Paris Saint-Germain	1996	28.4	43	12.1	2.5
Bordeaux	1996	14.5	42	6.1	0.2
Spain					
Barcelona	1996	41.3	42	17.5	n/a

Sources: Deloitte & Touche (1998a,b); SID Sport Informationsdienst.

annual value of league TV contracts in the UK, France, Italy, Spain and Germany combined was in the region of $1 billion (see Table 2). In 1996 FIFA sold the world commercial rights (excluding the USA) for the 2002 and 2006 World Cups to the Sporis/Kirch group for $2.5 billion.

However, the significance of TV income should not be overstated. For example, Manchester United currently generates about 15% of its revenue from TV contracts, far less than from selling tickets to matches or from merchandising, catering and conferences.[6] In the case of Bayern München, the top-rated German football club, merchandising is said to be worth 50% of its total revenues of DM165 million (see Sport Informationsdienst). The excitement surrounding TV contracts has as much to do with the remaining potential for enhancing this source of income as with their current value.

---

[6] A similar story emerges for the top Italian clubs (see Deloitte & Touche, 1998b).

Table 2. Annual revenues from domestic TV rights to domestic league games (£m)

	Free-to-air TV	Pay- TV/PPV	Total
England	18[a]	168[b]	186
Germany	52	27	79
France[c]	31	75	106
Spain[c]	–	130	130
Italy[d]	32	38	70

[a] £73 million paid by the BBC over four years for Saturday evening highlights.
[b] £670 million paid by BSkyB over four years for 60 live matches per season.
[c] *Source:* Bourg and Gouguet (1998).
[d] *Source:* Deloitte & Touche (1998b).

Perhaps even more fundamental to the long-term structure of European football has been the developing trend towards ownership of clubs by media companies. In Italy, Silvio Berlusconi added AC Milan to his media empire in 1986. In the mid-1990s, Canal Plus bought Paris Saint-Germain. In September 1998 the UK satellite broadcaster BSkyB made a bid of £625 million for Manchester United Football Club. Other UK broadcasters are considering similar investments for top clubs such as Newcastle and Arsenal. The media companies are likely to provide the strongest backing for a Superleague. Indeed, Berlusconi was attempting to create a Superleague in 1988. The proposals that emerged in the summer of 1998 were simply the latest in a long line of attempted breakaways.

The commercialization of football has gone hand in hand with an increased involvement of the law in the business of sport. In particular, the current labour market arrangements of clubs have been significantly affected by the Bosman judgment of the European court, while recent competition law cases in Germany, the Netherlands and the UK have challenged the legality of selling broadcasting rights collectively through the leagues.

2.2. Policy interventions

The trends described above raise major questions of public policy. In the near future, the new Champions League proposals agreed by UEFA in the autumn of 1998 will need to be cleared with the Competition Directorate of the European Commission, DG IV. So far, football has faced limited intervention from antitrust authorities largely because of the relative economic insignificance of sports. This has changed in the 1990s. A number of major cases dealing with the sale of broadcasting rights and the promotion of football have been investigated by national and European competition authorities (Temple Lang, 1997; Ratliff, 1998). In various official pronouncements, the Commission has made it clear that it now wants to treat sport like other businesses for the application of European competition law. Before this more recent development, the increased commercialization of sport and, in particular, the emergence of the professional athlete in individual (tennis) and team (football) sports led to a number of employment issues coming to the fore at the national level.

In the past, the governing bodies of football in Europe maintained a number of labour market restrictions. The effect of these restrictions was in general to hold down the wages paid to players and, so the clubs claimed, to redistribute income to weaker teams in the leagues. The main labour market restriction has been the payment of transfer fees. Most European countries operated a version of the 'retain and transfer' system. At the end of each season, a club would assign a player to the 'retained' list, which would make him unavailable for transfer to any other club; alternatively, they would place him on the 'transfer' list, setting a price that they would be prepared to accept in exchange for permitting the player to move to another club. If no club was willing to pay the fee, then the player could not move, even if the current club had no use for his services. This system, and its variants, was finally outlawed by the Bosman judgment of the European Court of Justice in 1995 (Court of Justice of the European Communities, Case C-415/93).

The Bosman case challenged two elements of the player transfer regime: first, the right of clubs to demand a transfer fee for players out of contract; and secondly, the right of UEFA to impose limits on the number of 'foreign' players appearing for a team in any competition. These restrictions were held in contravention of Article 48 of the Treaty of Rome, which guarantees freedom of movement of labour within the European Union. The ruling did not outlaw the payment of transfer fees for players within contract, which even before Bosman accounted for the majority of actual transfers. The Bosman ruling provides clubs with incentives to write longer-term contracts with players in order to protect any investment they may make in a player. Three-year contracts were the norm before Bosman. Contracts as long as five or even ten years are becoming increasingly common now. UEFA and the national associations have consulted with the Commission and a new system is being introduced that will entitle clubs to receive transfer fees for players under the age of 24 in recognition of a club's investment in a player's development. However, this ruling might still run foul of European competition law.

In the aftermath of the Bosman ruling, many clubs and football officials argued that the ruling would weaken the poorer clubs while strengthening the big city clubs.[7] In the Bosman ruling, Advocate-General Lenz made it clear that football clubs may be entitled to enter into restrictive arrangements if they promote competitive balance. Thus agreements necessary 'to ensure by means of specific measures that a certain balance is preserved between the clubs' were lawful (Bosman, 734). However, the specific restrictions dealt with by the courts were deemed neither strictly necessary for competitive balance nor in proportion to that legitimate aim. This is a view that has been emphasized by the Commission. It is too early to detect any long-term shifts caused by the Bosman decision, but there has not as yet been a significant run of bankruptcies.

---

[7] Mike Bateson, then chairman of Torquay United, a minor English club, expressed a common viewpoint: 'I am damned if I'm going to put my money into a youth system just to let the bigger clubs snaffle up the product. The fat cats may get fatter, but the scrawny ones down this end will die of starvation. A lot more players are going to be out of work.'

On the product market, the application of competition law, both national and European, has focused on the way football and other sports are marketed. In Germany, the Bundeskartellamt (German Cartel Office) successfully challenged the centralized sale of broadcasting rights of the domestic games in two UEFA competitions, the UEFA Cup and the Cup Winners' Cup. Its decision in 1994 to block an amendment of the rulebook of the German Football Association (DFB) which would have transferred rights away from clubs was taken on appeal to the Supreme Court, which upheld its initial decision in the court's ruling of December 1997 (BGH, Beschluss v. 11.12.97–KVR 7/96). In its decision, the German Supreme Court argued, among other things, that the German football clubs are entities that are subject to the provision of the antitrust legislation. Without the amended rule granting the DFB exclusive rights to the domestic games in the two UEFA competitions, the German clubs would continue to sell these rights on an individual club basis, as is the case in other European countries. The DFB, the court argues, adds nothing in terms of the organization of the game or the broadcast itself. The only purpose of the amended rule is to increase the revenues from a centralized sale. Thus, the court argued that the challenged rule restricted competition without any compensating benefits to the consumer or the sport itself.

In the Netherlands, Feyenoord attempted to negotiate its own TV contract following the collective sale of rights by the Dutch Football Association (KNVB) to a pay-TV channel called Sport 7. Feyenoord's case was upheld in court and the Dutch Minister for Economic Affairs wrote to KNVB stating that collective selling of rights was in breach of competition law. The competition authority has also challenged the collective sale of highlights, arguing that even these could be sold on a club-by-club basis. In the UK, the Office of Fair Trading has brought a case in the Restrictive Practices Courts challenging the collective sale of Premier League rights.

Both the Dutch and UK cases are analogous to the German case, but go further. Both the KNVB and the FA Premier League are arguably involved in the organization of their league championships and cannot be dismissed as not adding but simply appropriating value in the same way as DFB in the case of UEFA broadcasting rights. The extent of interdependence between clubs has led some US observers to argue that clubs cannot properly be thought of as economic competitors at all. The economic unit can be thought of as a league itself, and any restraints imposed by a league organization on member clubs are not vertical restraints, but simply internal organizational devices. Accordingly, there is no more relevance to the antitrust authorities in an agreement made between member clubs than there is in the internal allocation of responsibilities between subsidiaries of a large corporation. Examples of syndicated leagues, in which competition between teams is co-ordinated and financed centrally are not unknown in team sports and this method of organization bears some relation to the organization of individualistic sports such as tennis, golf and even Formula One, where centralized selling of broadcasting rights may be deemed acceptable. On the other hand, football clubs in Europe are genuinely independent entities, responsible for their own financial policies. Furthermore, in Europe, where teams are often located in close proximity to each other and compete to attract both players and fans, the restrictions implicit in collective selling can go beyond the mere co-ordination required to produce an attractive product and can lead to cartelization and rent extraction. When clubs are viewed as producers of substitutable brand identities, rather than merely complementary producers of a competitive match, market restrictions require much closer scrutiny.

These challenges to the existing organization of the marketing of football in Europe are having an effect on the behaviour of clubs. The potential freedom of clubs to sell rights to their home games individually is partially responsible for the investor interest of media companies in football clubs. At the moment, the European Commission is holding back intervening in the affairs of the Premier League. However, with the reform of the Champions League, the competition watchdogs in Brussels will no doubt get involved in a major way. In the words of Commissioner Van Miert (1997):

> Special features of the sporting world place restrictions on the production and organization of sporting events which would be inadmissible in other sectors of the economy ... if the spectator is to enjoy an interesting and high-quality event, the outcome of the competition must be uncertain. For this reason there must be a balance of strength between the opponents ... since the interests of the various clubs are intertwined, the market is intrinsically unstable whenever there is a financial imbalance between the clubs. This imbalance must therefore be corrected ... I have always argued for solutions based on a solidarity fund between clubs (a percentage of earnings should be shared) ... the league would then function as a body responsible for the redistribution of income ... the question which still has to be solved in this connection is how far the establishment of such a fund would enable joint sales of broadcasting rights to qualify for exemption.

The implication here is that the Commission may be willing to look favourably on collective selling if it is a means for redistributing income and effectively promotes competitive balance.

3. AMERICA VERSUS EUROPE

There are two main differences between the structure and organization of sporting leagues in the USA and Europe. First, the US leagues are generally 'hermetic'. New teams are seldom admitted to a league, and there is no annual promotion and relegation between junior leagues and senior leagues. Expansion franchises are admitted on agreement between existing league members and the entry fee is divided among them. They are also closed, in the sense that member teams do not compete simultaneously in different competitions; nor, with occasional exceptions, do teams release players to compete for national team competitions (one exception being the 1996 Olympic basketball team). US leagues approximate quite closely a joint venture. In the extreme, some leagues, such as the current US soccer league, are syndicated: ownership is pooled and players can be allocated centrally to different teams to maintain competitive balance.

Clubs easily perceive their joint interests. They can expect to be competing together in more or less the same format from year to year. In Europe this sense of solidarity is undermined by the fact that the composition of each league division changes from year to year and that the set of competitors differs in different competitions. While the US system sounds far less competitive from the point of view of the clubs, more competition emerges at the level of the league. Since the Second World War, for example, there have been four attempts by new leagues to enter the American Football market. Three of these failed and one was absorbed by the NFL. Arguably, the threat of entry imposes some competitive pressure on the activities of the leagues. Entry is also made feasible by the much lower density of top clubs. Thus with only 30 Major League Baseball franchises for the whole country, many cities lack a major team. By contrast, in European football most major cities can boast at least one major team, and sometimes more than one.

Secondly, US league authorities have tried to maintain a competitive balance between the clubs through intervention in the labour market or redistribution of club revenues. The main intervention in the player market has been the 'rookie draft' system. When players finish college or high school and enter professional sports, the clubs within the league take turns to pick players, with the first pick being awarded to the team that finished last in the previous season's competition, the second pick to the second last team, and so on. Poorly performing teams can acquire the best young talent and therefore improve their standing in the following year. The system also limits the ability of players to market themselves, and a number of legal challenges have led to some amendments of the system. Player contracts are typically longer in US sports than in European football. For example, in baseball five- or six-year contracts are common, compared to a more typical three-year contract in Europe. Other restrictions imposed by US leagues include salary caps on the overall wage bill of clubs. These were introduced through a process of collective bargaining in the NBA in 1984 and the NFL in 1994.

The main vehicle for redistribution in US leagues has been the sharing of national broadcast revenues. The Sports Broadcasting Act of 1962 exempted collective selling of national broadcasting rights by the members of leagues from antitrust scrutiny,[8] in direct recognition of the redistributive function of such revenues. Typically, these are shared equally among the clubs. Broadcast income is typically a much greater share of total income in the USA, averaging 32% of income in baseball, 34% in basketball and 63% in American Football (Sheehan, 1996). By contrast, for most European clubs, television income has been negligible up until the 1990s. In Europe, broadcasting agreements typically include a performance-related element and a fixed share. For example, the Premier League contract shares half of the contract value equally among the teams, 25% on the basis of league performance and 25% on the basis of the number of games televised.

---

[8] This is one of the main kinds of antitrust exemption granted to sports in the USA. The others are the baseball exemption granted by the Supreme Court in the 1920s, and the expiation for collective bargaining agreements between player unions and league authorities representing the clubs.

In Italy, income from free-to-air broadcasts is shared equally and pay-TV income (including pay-per-view) is distributed on the basis of performance. In Germany, clubs receive a fixed share plus a fixed amount for every home game and a lesser amount for every away game broadcast. In the USA, the club itself retains local broadcasting income.

Some US leagues also redistribute gate income. In the NFL, 40% of net gate receipts go to the visiting team, leading some US critics to describe the NFL as 'socialist'. In baseball, revenue sharing is less pronounced (20% to the visiting team in the American League, 10% to the visiting team in the National League), and in basketball there is no gate sharing. Gate sharing arrangements have been limited in European football. In England, an agreement used to set minimum admission prices, and on this basis awarded up to a 20% share of gate income to the visiting team, but this agreement was abolished in 1983. Since the creation of the Premier League in 1992, all gate receipts have been retained by the home team. In the FA and League Cups, the home and away clubs receive 45% each of the gate, while 10% is divided equally among all entrants of the competition (except in the semi-finals and the final of the FA Cup, where the clubs receive less and the FA receives a share). In Italy, there is no league gate sharing except for the top Italian clubs, which get a small percentage (less than 5%) of the ticket

Table 3. Differences in structure of US and European sports leagues

	US sports	Football in Europe
League system	Closed, no promotion or relegation Teams compete in single league competition	Open, annual promotion and relegation Teams may compete simultaneously in many competitions
League functions	Collective sale of TV rights Centralized marketing	Collective sale of TV rights
Competition between clubs	Limited substitution by consumers	Significant potential for substitution
Competition between leagues	Numerous cases of entry by rival leagues	All leagues contained within the established hierarchy
Player market	Rookie draft Salary caps (NFL, NBA) Collective bargaining	Active transfer market
Revenue sharing	Equal division of national broadcasting income Gate sharing (NFL 40%, baseball average 15%, NBA 0%)	Sharing of television income Little or no sharing of league gate revenues Some sharing of gate from cup competitions
Competition policy	Antitrust exemption for baseball Sports Broadcasting Act exempts national TV deals from antitrust	Centralized sale of TV rights under attack Selected interventions (ticket allocation FIFA)

revenues at away matches. In cup competitions, the same rule applies in Italy as elsewhere in Europe, with both teams sharing the net receipts. In Germany, 6% of league gate revenues is paid to the DFB and the rest is kept by the home team, while in cup competitions a 10% share goes to the DFB and the clubs split the remainder 50:50.

In Europe-wide competitions, teams have kept their gate receipts while paying a small share to UEFA (except in finals, where the authorities have taken a larger share and the remainder has been split between the teams). In the Cup Winners' Cup and UEFA Cup, UEFA has left it to the national associations to determine how broadcasting contracts should be negotiated.

Table 3 summarizes the main differences described in this section.

4. CONTESTS IN HERMETIC AND OPEN LEAGUES

The comparison between league structures in the USA and Europe suggests a fundamentally different approach to the organization of league competitions. These differences revolve around the mechanism through which competitive balance between clubs is promoted by the leagues and their stand-alone nature, in contrast to the open multi-league structure of European football.

4.1. Some fundamentals

Teams involved in league competitions effectively operate as collections of talent. A description of league structures is based on two fundamental hypotheses:

- For each team, increased wage expenditure leads to better performance on the pitch.
- For each team, improved performance on the pitch leads to increased revenues.

Each of these relationships is a consequence of the operation of markets. Teams consisting of better players generally perform better than their rivals. In the market for players, clubs must pay the going rate to attract stars. The talent and ability of individual players is by comparison with most labour markets readily apparent, and hence sellers can demand what they are worth and buyers can expect to achieve a given level of performance given what they spend. The outcome of league competition is not entirely predictable and chance plays a significant role in the outcome of competition. However, the dominant factor in explaining performance is wage expenditure. Improved performance on the pitch generates increased revenue because at the margin fans are attracted by success, and advertising, television and sponsorship income tends to be highly sensitive to success.

The validity of these hypotheses can be confirmed using accounting data from English football. Figure 1, taken from Szymanski and Kuypers (1999), illustrates the relationship between wage expenditure and league position for a sample of 39 clubs between 1978 and 1996. Figure 2 illustrates the relationship between league position and revenue. The financial data are taken from the published company accounts and wages refer to the

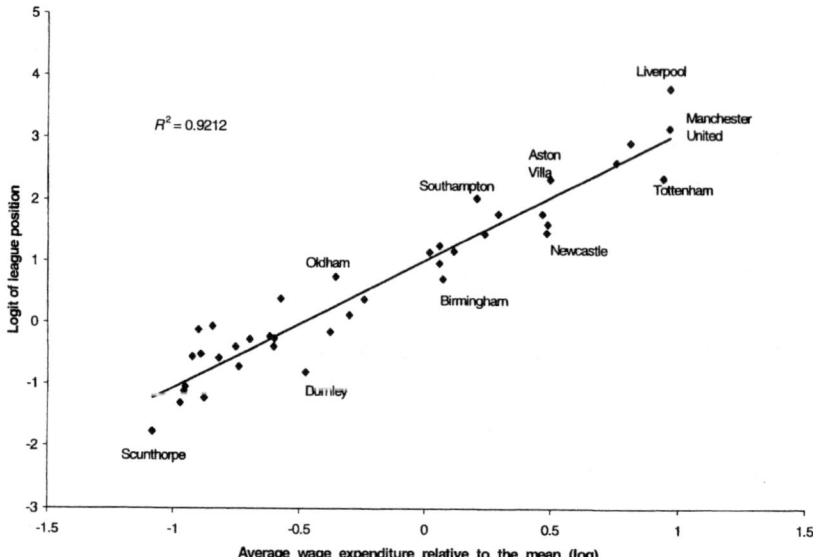

Figure 1. Wage expenditure and league position, 39 clubs, 1978–96

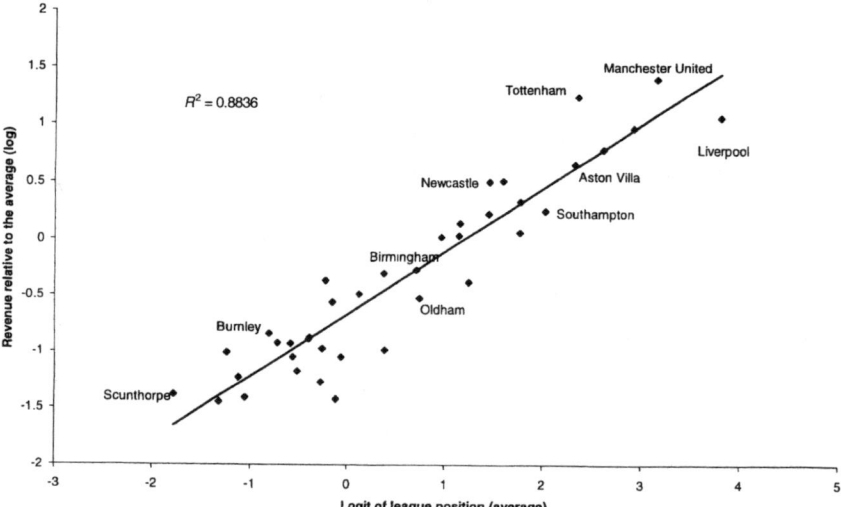

Figure 2. League position and revenue, 39 clubs, 1978–96

total wage bill of the club. For each club, performance was measured as an average of league position. Wage expenditure was measured as a ratio of wage spending in one year to the average of all other clubs in that year (what matters for league performance is not absolute expenditure on players, but spending relative to your rivals). For the graph, relative wage spending was averaged over all years in the sample. The same transformations were made to club revenue data. What is striking is the power of these relationships, illustrated by the R^2 of these simple regressions. Szymanski and Smith (1997) adopted a more sophisticated approach to the estimation of these relationships, but confirmed the relationships found here.

4.2. Contests in a hermetic league

We now analyse more formally some of the policy dilemmas, borrowing from the literature on contests and tournaments, similar to that used in the US team sports literature.[9]

We consider first a closed American-style league. For simplicity, suppose there are just two clubs that hire playing talent and compete against each other in matches. Success on the pitch depends on outspending your rival. On-the-pitch success is measured by win percentage (the percentage of matches won in a season) as is conventional in the US literature (see, e.g., El-Hodiri and Quirk, 1971; Fort and Quirk, 1995). We adopt a special case of a contest success function that has been introduced and axiomatized in other areas of economics to describe the win percentage w_{12} of team 1 when playing team 2, as a function of the relative quantity of playing talent (t) on each side:[10]

$$w_{12} = \frac{t_1}{t_1 + t_2} \tag{1}$$

We assume that team revenues depend on three factors: success on the field, drawing power and attractiveness of the league competition. Success is expressed in win per cent. Drawing power depends on a team's location, history, reputation and so on. Well-supported teams, such as Manchester United, Bayern München and Barcelona, have higher revenues than their domestic rivals given the same league position. An important factor for the attractiveness of the league may be how balanced competition is. More balance, measured by the success of the teams participating in the league, may enhance overall demand for matches (either in the form of attendance at games or in terms of broadcasting). To capture these three sources of revenues, we specify a revenue function,

---

[9] Contests of different kinds have been widely modelled in the economics literature. Examples include rent seeking in the public sector (e.g., Tullock, 1980), rivalry in R & D (e.g., Loury, 1979), competition for market share (e.g., Monahan, 1987) and labour markets (e.g., Lazear and Rosen, 1981). A useful review of the mathematical properties of these models is provided by Nti (1997).

[10] In line with Atkinson *et al.* (1988), we assume that a team's playing talent can be approximated by a perfectly divisible aggregation over the different specializations within the team.

which depends on the success of the team, its drawing power and the balance of competition.

$$R_1 = \mu_1[\phi w_{12} + (1 - \phi)w_{12}w_{21}] \tag{2}$$

In this function μ_i represents the drawing power of team i, and ϕ represents the balance in the revenue function between the demand for 'own team winning' and the demand for a competitive balance. When $\phi = 1$ revenues depend only on win percentage, while when $\phi = 0$ revenues depend only on the degree of competitive balance. We assume that there is a competitive market for talent, which can be bought at a constant marginal cost per unit. Profit π_1 of team 1 is therefore the difference between revenue R_1 and expenditure t_1 for talent.

As a benchmark, we assume that each club maximizes its own profits. This is the view that has generally been adopted in the US literature (e.g., Noll, 1985; Quirk and Fort 1992). In the European literature (e.g., Sloane, 1971) it has been conventional to assume that clubs are 'utility maximizers', where utility may incorporate factors such as success on the pitch, popularity of the club and profit considerations.

The equilibrium of simultaneous choice of expenditure for talent for $\phi = 1$ is well known from the contest literature. If both teams have the same drawing power, each wins with probability $1/2$ and each spends $1/4$ of the total revenue on talent expenditure. If the contest becomes less even – for example, because one team's drawing power is higher than that of the other team – this team chooses higher expenditure, wins with a higher probability and has a higher payoff than the other team in the equilibrium. Intuitively, as the drawing power of team 1 relative to team 2 increases, its marginal revenue of talent increases for all levels of talent, so that team 1 invests more than team 2, achieving a higher win percentage and profit. Team 2 anticipates this increase in team 1's investment and actually decreases its own investment. Thus when winning matters, the investments of teams in playing talent are strategic substitutes in the terminology of Bulow *et al.* (1985).

Suppose now that there is a demand for competitive balance: $\phi < 1$. Let team 1 have a greater drawing power than team 2. Revenues for each team are enhanced when the other team is more evenly matched. This introduces an element of strategic complementarity between the teams. In other words, each team has an incentive to match its opponent's investment in talent, in order to generate the maximum feasible profit in the market. Furthermore, in the absence of any outside competitive pressure, each team will recognize its complementarity and seek to reduce its investment in talent. Simulations show that, as ϕ falls, both teams reduce their investment in talent, but the team with greater drawing power does so proportionately more, so that competitive balance improves.

We now consider the effect of revenue sharing. Suppose a percentage α of each club's income is retained, with the remainder being shared out among its rivals. This might be thought of as a situation where the visiting team at each match receives a fixed share of the gate revenue. Team 1's revenue becomes $\alpha R_1 + (1 - \alpha)R_2$, and analogously for team

2. While revenue sharing is generally justified by league authorities in terms of enhancing competitive balance, revenue sharing is also a mechanism for internalizing the effects of competition. Reduced competition may be desirable from the point of view of team-owners, but not desirable from the point of view of consumers. Suppose teams had equal drawing power ($\mu_1 = \mu_2$) so the league starts out in competitive balance. Revenue sharing will not alter competitive balance, but reduce investment in players. This reflects a wider point: any agreement to share out the prizes in a contest undermines the incentives for contestants to try and win. Fort and Quirk (1995) argue that

> gate sharing has no effect on competitive balance in a league. Instead, an increase in α (more liberal gate sharing) has the effect of lowering player salaries ... looking into the effect of gate sharing on league-wide profits, the answer is unambiguous in the case where there is no local TV. Gate sharing has no effect on competitive balance, and hence no effect on league-wide revenues. Further, gate sharing leads to lower talent costs; league wide profits go up with more gate sharing.

In fact, gate sharing will affect competitive balance, but in general the effect will be adverse. Consider an unbalanced league where only own team winning matters. When there is no revenue sharing, each team competes to attract talent. When revenue is shared, both teams want to invest in such a way as to maximize total returns of both clubs. Since the bigger club has the greater marginal income from success, it makes sense to engineer a reduction in competitive balance. Even if competitive balance matters, if some extra value is attached to own team winning, sharing will always lead to a reduction in competitive balance. This is illustrated by the simulation results in Table 4.

The finding is in contrast to conventional explanations, but may depend on the particular sharing rule. To see the problem with gate sharing, consider its effect on the incentive to win matches. Under gate sharing, teams playing away from home want their opponents to win (so long as own team winning increases home team revenues). Gate sharing thus appears like a tax on winning. Redistribution mechanisms that tax clubs on a lump-sum basis will avoid these kinds of disincentive effect, and if lump-sum taxes are then redistributed on the basis of performance, they may tend to improve competitive balance by equalizing opportunities to generate revenues. It is possible that collectively negotiated broadcasting contracts could satisfy these requirements. However, if collective

Table 4. Win percentage, investment in talent and profits as the revenue sharing grows

α	w_{12}	l_1	l_2	π_1	π_2
1.0	0.551	0.17	0.14	0.43	0.21
0.9	0.556	0.13	0.11	0.44	0.26
0.8	0.563	0.10	0.08	0.45	0.32
0.7	0.572	0.07	0.05	0.46	0.37
0.6	0.584	0.03	0.02	0.47	0.42

Note: Assumptions: $\mu_1 = 1.5$, $\mu_2 = 1$, $c = 1$, $\phi = 0.5$.

selling is used as a mechanism for cartelizing the market, any benefits for competitive balance may be outweighed by the dead-weight loss from higher prices and restricted output.

Given the theoretical prediction that revenue sharing will adversely affect competitive balance and investment incentives, it is perhaps surprising that the NFL in the USA manages to maintain both a relatively balanced competition and a high level of playing investment. One explanation might have to do with the objectives of owners. If owners were interested in maximizing success on the pitch rather than profits, then all redistributed income would go into player investment and the disincentive effects of revenue sharing would disappear.

Another explanation for the competitiveness of US team sports such as the NFL might be the array of alternative restrictive devices, particularly in the player market, outlined in section 3. Those mechanisms resemble a system of handicapping, which is a frequently used method for inducing more effort in asymmetric contests. Handicapping, while potentially limiting the incentive to invest, does not create the same kinds of incentive to collude. One factor that has facilitated the creation of widely accepted handicapping systems is the unionization of team sports in the USA. Thus mechanisms such as salary caps have been negotiated through the unions, which have in return secured agreements on *minimum* as well as maximum wages. It is perhaps ironic that in Europe the significantly lower level of unionization and the relatively low influence of player unions have prevented the development of potentially beneficial handicapping systems.

4.3. Competitive balance and income redistribution in multiple open leagues

In European football, the top clubs usually compete simultaneously in one of the three UEFA competitions while also competing in the domestic league. UEFA competitions have always been a significant potential source of income. For example, appearance in the 1996/7 UEFA Champions League was worth around £4 million per club in broadcast revenues alone, compared to an average Premier League income of £17 million in that year. In the autumn of 1998, Media Partners, the promoters of the breakaway Superleague, were suggesting that the top European clubs could be paid

Table 5. The dominance of the top clubs

	Italy	Germany	Spain	England
Period	1988–96	1988–98[a]	1988–97	1991–7
Number of places in top division	18	18	20	20
Number of clubs appearing in top division	35	35	38	31
Number of European competition places	56	64	55	32
Number of clubs in European competition	14	23	16	13
Share of top 7 clubs (%)	80	73	75	81
Share of top 3 clubs (%)	43	39	47	48

[a] Excluding 1997.

£20 million per year for their broadcast rights. Appearances in European competitions are not evenly distributed among the clubs.

Table 5 shows the number of clubs that appeared in the top division in four countries over a ten-year period, and the proportion of European appearances of the biggest clubs (the data only run from 1991 for England, since in the previous five years English clubs were banned from European competition). In each case, the three biggest teams account for between 40 and 50% of all competition places won (the teams were AC Milan, Inter Milan, Juventus, Bayern München, Borussia Dortmund, Werder Bremen, Real Madrid, Barcelona, Atlético Madrid, Manchester United, Liverpool and Arsenal). The seven largest teams (roughly 20% of all top division participants in each country) accounted for roughly 80% of all European places. Taking into account that the bigger teams tend to survive more rounds in the competition, then their share of all European matches played is even greater.

For simplicity, let there be two national leagues each composed of two teams, and one team from each league also competes in an inter-league competition. This situation is represented schematically in Figure 3.

Revenue in the Euroleague (the inter-league competition) depends on own team winning and competitive balance in the same way as it did in the hermetic context. For simplicity, we suppose that teams have the same potential drawing power, but the relative value of the Euroleague can vary. Clearly the value of European competition relative to domestic competition has grown significantly in recent years. Even though the drawing power of clubs is equal, the existence of an elite international competition automatically creates domestic competitive imbalance. We label clubs 1 and 3 the teams that compete in both domestic league and inter-league competition, while clubs 2 and 4

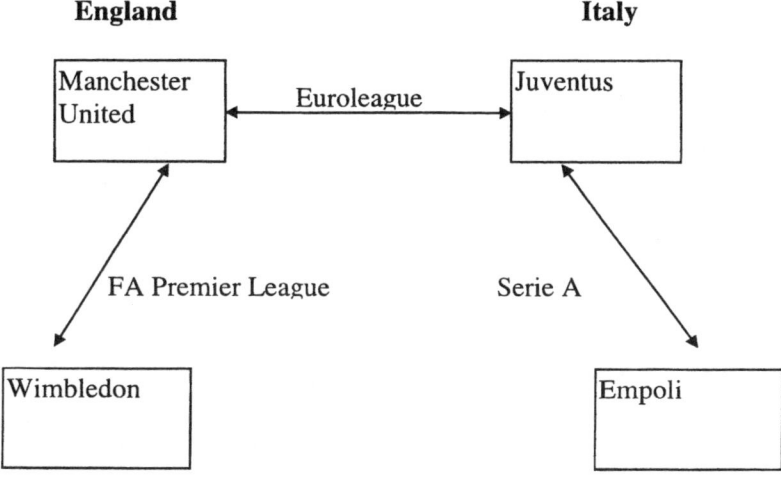

Figure 3. Schematic representation of European soccer leagues

compete in the domestic competition only. Thus clubs 2 and 4 have revenues as in equation (2) for playing clubs 1 and 3, respectively, whereas clubs 1 and 3 have revenues as in equation (2) from playing clubs 2 and 4, respectively, plus the additional revenue $\vartheta[w_{13} - (1 - \phi)(w_{13})^2]$ and $\vartheta[w_{13} - (1 - \phi)(w_{31})^2]$ of playing against each other. The parameter ϑ denotes the relative importance of the inter-league competition in terms of revenue generation. The main proposition of this paper – namely that a European Superleague will become like an American sports league, with its members not competing in other competitions – can be shown by considering the effect of the parameter ϑ. As ϑ grows, the investment of the Euroleague teams in talent also grows. While this maintains competitive balance in the Euroleague, the smaller teams in national competition are left behind and domestic competition becomes more unbalanced. The more competitive balance is valued, the faster the value of domestic competition is eroded. This is illustrated in Table 6.

Here the two countries are assumed to be symmetric. Hence, the outcome for team 3 is the same as for team 1, and the outcome for team 4 is the same as for team 2. As the value of the Euroleague increases, the investment of the competing teams grows. Given that team 2 (the purely domestic team) is always a strategic substitute for team 1 unless competitive balance is the only source of income ($\phi = 0$), then the increased investment of team 1 will lead to falling investment on the part of team 2. Thus competitive balance in the domestic league falls. As long as the two Euroleague teams have equal revenue-generating capacities, competition remains balanced. While total revenue in the domestic league falls, team 2 is more adversely affected than team 1. As a result, team 2's profitability is driven towards zero. Assuming that clubs have some fixed costs (which are not modelled here), then purely domestic teams will incur financial losses. Furthermore, we have not modelled here the additional costs, both fixed and variable, of the Euroleague teams competing in their domestic leagues, but if these costs are substantial, they may cause participation in the domestic league to be unprofitable. From this we conclude that single-league competition for the top clubs is the most plausible equilibrium for European football.

Could revenue sharing help to preserve the participation of the top teams in the domestic leagues? Our discussion in the previous section suggests that this is unlikely. International competition is like having a larger revenue base. When domestic teams share revenues, they are likely to want to concentrate talent in the stronger club for the

Table 6. Win percentage, investment in talent and profits as the Euroleague grows

ϑ	w_{12}	l_1	l_2	π_1	π_2	R_{12}	R_{21}
1	0.60	0.22	0.144	0.58	0.17	0.42	0.32
2	0.68	0.32	0.148	0.88	0.12	0.45	0.27
3	0.75	0.42	0.141	1.17	0.08	0.47	0.22
4	0.81	0.53	0.125	1.45	0.05	0.48	0.17
5	0.86	0.64	0.102	1.72	0.03	0.49	0.13

Note: Assumptions: $\phi = 0.5$, $c = 1$.

Table 7. Win percentage, investment in talent and profits with increasing revenue sharing in a multiple league structure

α	w_{12}	l_1	l_2	π_1	π_2	$R_{12}+R_{21}$
1.0	0.60	0.22	0.14	0.58	0.17	0.739
0.9	0.61	0.19	0.12	0.60	0.20	0.737
0.8	0.63	0.17	0.10	0.61	0.23	0.734
0.7	0.64	0.14	0.08	0.63	0.26	0.730
0.6	0.66	0.11	0.06	0.64	0.29	0.725

Note: Assumptions: $\vartheta = 1$, $\phi = 0.5$, $\epsilon = 1$.

same reasons as in the hermetic context. This will, if anything, lead to a less balanced domestic competition. We illustrate this in Table 7 with simulations of a contest in which there is domestic revenue sharing (we assume that teams will not share Euroleague revenues with their domestic rivals).

Domestic revenue sharing works in the same way as it did in the hermetic league model where one team had more power, although the reason is slightly different. Revenue sharing reduces the incentive of each team to invest in talent, but the effect on the Euroleague team is mitigated by its incentive to preserve its revenues from that competition. This means that the purely national team reduces its investment by more than the team playing internationally as well, and hence competitive balance deteriorates in the domestic leagues. While this serves to reduce the revenues in the domestic league, profits increase because the lower investment effect dominates.[11]

4.4. Extensions

Our analysis in this section suggests that the interlocking system of leagues that currently operates in Europe is untenable because of the increasing dominance of competition in a Euroleague. Members of a Euroleague invest more in playing talent than the remainder of clubs, causing domestic leagues to become increasingly unbalanced. The most natural solution for this problem is for the Euroleague members to cease playing in the national leagues, thus making those competitions more balanced. The forces driving this change may be even greater than our analysis suggests. First, if there are fixed costs associated with operating in a league, then as domestic competition becomes unbalanced, the smaller club will be driven into losses and will want to quit the domestic competition altogether. Secondly, there are additional costs, both variable and fixed, for the Euroleague teams involved in participating in two leagues simultaneously. Under the current plans, Euroleague clubs will be playing two matches a week. Most players will be unable to play in both fixtures, and hence teams will need larger squads. While in our

[11] It might be argued that this result is an artefact of the effect that there is no specific demand to watch high levels of talent in its own right. This effect might be added by making revenue a function of total talent as well. While this would tend to diminish the effects somewhat, it would not change our qualitative results unless the 'own team winning' effect disappeared altogether.

analysis revenues increase marginally for the Euroleague clubs as they dominate the domestic competition, we believe that this effect is likely to be more than offset by the cost of participating in two leagues.

In the new equilibrium, the relationship between a European Superleague and the domestic leagues would be analogous to that between the major and minor leagues in American baseball or that between the NFL and college football. This leads naturally to a set of policy questions, including the desirability of encouraging this transformation, the role of the football authorities, particularly UEFA, in promoting rival competitions, and the scope for redistribution mechanisms and 'solidarity' between the clubs.

5. CONCLUSIONS AND POLICY IMPLICATIONS

The proposals for a European Superleague presented by Mediaset in the summer of 1998 have served to focus minds. At once UEFA and the national associations have been forced to reconsider the existing structure of competition and make significant concessions to the top clubs in the form of a revamped Champions League, with many more matches being played between European clubs. In due course, the Competition Directorate of the Commission in Brussels will be asked to approve the new arrangements proposed by UEFA. This comes at a time when Brussels is in the process of formulating its general policy on sport. This will mean making a number of policy decisions with far-reaching consequences.

Some commentators have argued that the revamped Champions League is the culmination of developments and already represents a European Superleague. This argument seems fundamentally to miss the point. The attraction of a Superleague for the top clubs lies in their ability to increase income by playing significantly more games against their larger European rivals. The new Champions League achieves this, but the leading clubs will be required to participate simultaneously in an extended mid-week European competition while competing with equal vigour in the domestic league at weekends. This solution seems out of touch with reality. The oldest league rule in football is that teams should field their strongest team in league matches.[12] It would be physically impossible for the best eleven players in a squad to play a domestic season of around 34 matches combined with a similar number of mid-week matches over a 40-week season. In practice, players would have to be rested, and clubs would have to allocate priority to different competitions (as in fact they tend to do already). The domestic competition will come to be seen as the 'reserve' tournament for the top clubs, downgrading national leagues to the status of second-team competitions. A proper European Superleague will have to break this historic link with domestic league competitions and become truly pan-European in structure.

---

[12] This rule appeared in the original rules of the Football League in 1888 and according to Inglis (1988) is the only rule not to have been amended.

5.1. Welfare implications

Assessing the welfare implications of changes in the structure of football (and sports in general) is notoriously difficult. The appropriate measure of welfare is the sum of firm profits and consumer surplus, just like in any other industry. However, measuring both profits and consumer surplus is difficult. Few clubs report profits in their accounts. If clubs are not profit maximizers, then it is the 'utility' generated for the owners of the club that should be measured, and this is even more problematic. As far as consumers are concerned, it may be useful to differentiate committed fans from less committed 'armchair supporters'. This distinction is implicit in the revenue function of our contest analysis, where the committed fan might be thought of as caring only about his or her own team winning, while the armchair fan cares mainly about a well-balanced contest (although in practice there is probably a complete spectrum of preference). Committed fans are rather like long-term investors, or *noyaux durs*. They spend both time and money on supporting their club in the expectation of long-term sporting success. By contrast, the armchair fan wants to be entertained and considers only the immediate return on consuming a match. Each type of fan's welfare may be affected quite differently by club policies.

5.1.1. Towards a US-style Superleague. Moving from the current European system to a more American structure should be beneficial for clubs. The big clubs will be able to focus on the competition that generates the greatest proportion of their income. Smaller clubs in the top domestic league would lose by no longer competing against Superleague teams that may bring with them large groups of supporters, but this loss is likely to be offset by the improvement in competitive balance in the domestic competition. In the long term, it may be more profitable to be a leading club in a second-rank competition than a no-hoper in the top competition.

For consumers, the effect on the *noyaux durs* will be analogous to that on the clubs, since these supporters are, properly speaking, stakeholders in the club. Armchair fans gain unambiguously because there will be a greater supply of well-balanced contests. However, this happy story depends in part on the long-term relationship between the Superleague and the domestic leagues. In particular, will there be promotion and relegation, or will the Superleague become truly hermetic like the American leagues? Closure benefits the incumbents and represents a welfare loss for the outsiders, who lose the option that they might one day reach the Superleague.

In practice, this distinction may not be as stark as it first appears. Even if the league were closed, the Superleague would almost certainly permit the creation of expansion franchises. This would mean less frequent entry than occurs under the current system, and would restrict entry to those clubs large enough to benefit the entire league and provide balanced competition. The sale of expansion franchises is a mechanism by which the externality created by the quality of entrant teams is internalized. The shift to a franchise system would enhance the welfare of the incumbent teams and maximize the attractiveness of the Superleague, while diminishing the welfare of the excluded outsiders. The other potential effect of 'closure' is to reduce incentives. This effect has been widely commented on in the press (incumbents will not try so hard because there is no threat of demotion), but seems fairly implausible when one considers the highly competitive nature of closed US leagues. One reason that this may not be a real problem is that, even if a league is closed, there will always be the threat of entry by rival leagues if competition in the Superleague is not effective.

5.1.2. Promotion and demotion. If promotion and demotion are preserved as of right, then the likely impact on the competitive balance of the Superleague will be adverse compared to a system where entry is restricted on the basis of available resources. It will always be the case, even in a league system based on a large number of matches, that relatively weak teams will occasionally be promoted. Such teams seldom fare well in a higher division and are usually demoted in the following season, having provided a relatively low standard of competition. However, even if it is true, it is not clear that this effect will reduce welfare. While consumers may value competitive balance, there is also the possibility that they enjoy unbalanced 'David and Goliath' contests that will occasionally produce surprise results.

Perhaps more worrying from a welfare point of view is the possibility that the very largest clubs may be demoted. The effect of such demotions is clearly adverse for the supporters, who in themselves are a significant fraction of consumers, but such demotions also tend to affect adversely interest in the competition as a whole. Moreover, once demoted, such clubs are usually promoted back up with ease in the following season, thus diminishing the uncertainty associated with the outcome of the junior championship. Despite the increased welfare associated with fans of lesser clubs being able to see their team compete against a major, this effect seems unlikely to offset the adverse effects.

It seems clear that the proposals of Media Partners for a hermetic Superleague were aimed specifically at preventing this outcome, rather than limiting the access of the smaller clubs. It might therefore appear that an ideal compromise would allow permanent membership for big clubs while preserving promotion and demotion for weaker clubs. Unfortunately, as well as the fundamental problem of defining the 'big' and the 'small', such a system would be widely viewed as unfair, and this would in our view significantly undermine the attractiveness of the competition. Level playing fields matter.

It seems, therefore, that there is a straight choice between promotions and demotions as opposed to some kind of a franchise system. A franchise system, so long as it provided clear rules for the access of clubs, would be a better system because it enables teams to internalize the effects of unbalanced competition. This would also be fairer than the current system, which discriminates against moderate-strength clubs in strong leagues in favour of weak clubs in even weaker leagues.

5.2. Policy issues

We believe that a European Superleague in soccer that resembles the Major League Baseball or the National Football League in the USA is the market equilibrium. However, the competition authorities or even the member states have significant powers to block such an outcome or to limit its viability. For example, if Brussels were to accept the collective broadcasting arrangements of the current system, while indicating that if the Superleague members tried to break away entirely they would not be permitted to enter into such arrangements, that would have the effect of supporting the current system. We do not believe this is in the best interests of the clubs or the consumers (committed or otherwise), mainly because of the likely increase in unbalanced competition as the Superleaguers increasingly dominate domestic competitions.

There are policy dilemmas in endorsing the shift towards a hermetic Superleague. The most prominent are issues concerning (1) access, (2) redistributive measures and (3) the scope for inter-league competition and the role of UEFA.

5.2.1. Access to the Superleague. While there might be some political benefits in a European Superleague, promoting the notion of a European identity, the impact on member states would vary widely. Core countries such as Italy, Spain, England and Germany would be very well represented in any Superleague competition, given the strength of their top clubs. Some major European footballing nations such as France (World Cup holders, after all) might be less well represented, given the relative weakness of their clubs and the tendency for their top players to play overseas. Some smaller nations might be well represented because of the disproportionate strength of their clubs (e.g., the Netherlands with Ajax, PSV and Feyenoord). Other smaller nations with strong footballing traditions (e.g., Norway) might tend to suffer little representation, again because their top players play overseas.

A Superleague will offer only restricted access to the weaker clubs, as has always been the case with the European competitions. In the traditional cup structure of European competitions, weaker clubs that were strong in weak leagues (e.g., top clubs from Iceland) gained access to European competition through the qualifying rounds. Such access might be justified on regional policy grounds, even if the system discriminated against second-rank clubs in strong leagues. The access of these weaker teams will decline in the absence of intervention (and we believe that such intervention would be unworkable and largely ineffective).

This suggests a regional policy dilemma. Even if a Superleague remained open to promotion and relegation, some nations or regions (e.g., Wales) might never be represented in a Superleague. In our view, this is not a problem that can be solved by enforced maintenance of the status quo. Since weaker clubs do not enjoy much success in the top European competitions as it is, there is little to be gained by preserving unbalanced competition. We believe that policy-makers should focus more on entry conditions and redistribution of income.

5.2.2. Redistribution. Our analysis suggests that the competition authorities should approach redistribution mechanisms in dominant sports leagues with a healthy degree of scepticism. Redistribution among the clubs is essentially a way of softening the effects of competition. Rather than promoting competitive balance, certain mechanisms may reduce the incentive to compete and worsen competitive balance. The trick is to design forms of redistribution that avoid or limit the adverse effects on competition. Alternative mechanisms for balancing competition are those that have been widely used in the USA such as the rookie draft and salary caps. If these mechanisms are not used simply to raise profitability, they will tend to increase the competitive balance of the league and can allow consumers to enjoy the same quality of competition at a lower cost. Any kind of restriction will create an incentive for avoidance and the effectiveness of any scheme will depend on the ability of authorities to enforce it. However, a closed Superleague may create a better chance to do this than the existing system. It is hard to imagine how a rookie draft system would operate in a system of open leagues with promotion and relegation, since the whole system is predicated on a recognized career progression from minor to major leagues. A closed Superleague would overcome this problem. Salary caps are also more likely to be implementable among a closed set of Superleague teams with more or less equal resources. Such a system could be consistent with EU laws on the freedom of movement of labour as well as the articles on competition as long as the system were perceived to provide a clear benefit to the players (as it does in the USA). A natural corollary of a European Superleague would be a European Players' Union that might negotiate on salary issues and other relevant issues such as health and safety.

There seems to be greater potential for redistribution among the leagues. This may happen anyway as the big clubs move to buy up the smaller clubs and use them as farm teams. A system such as this seems to have operated for some years in Spanish soccer without any obvious adverse effects on the quality of competition among the top clubs, and a similar observation can be made about competition in the USA. However, there is also a case for a system of redistribution from the senior leagues to the junior leagues. Again, such a system might be difficult to implement within the existing structure where the beneficiaries are potential future competitors of the top clubs, but might be more acceptable within a closed Superleague.

5.2.3. The scope for inter-league competition and the role of UEFA. The continuing role of UEFA is problematic. As the organizer of the Champions League, UEFA is likely to continue to be the promoter of the dominant European competition while acting as regulator of all competitions. As the Superleague evolves, it will increasingly face a conflict of interest between its promotion of its main product and the interests of the national leagues that it regulates.

One problem is the co-ordination of the fixture list for the expanded Champions League. Currently UEFA decides when fixtures in its own competitions are played and determines the permissible 'windows' for broadcasting matches within Europe. UEFA has an incentive to ensure that its own fixtures make use of the most attractive slots, and as a result of expansion will remove some available slots for the national leagues. Through its regulation of broadcasting windows, it also restricts the ability of leagues and clubs to generate broadcasting income. While this restriction has traditionally been imposed with a view to promoting lower-level national competitions, there is also a potential conflict of interest with UEFA's promotion of its own league. Thus while it may be revenue maximizing to create a Superleague, if UEFA is perceived to be co-ordinating the commercial development of football through its power as the governing body, it is likely to face investigation for abuse of its dominant position.

UEFA can defend itself against such charges by demonstrating that its actions promote the sport as a whole rather than the interests of the elite clubs. But this becomes a difficult line to hold if the top clubs are hermetically sealed in a dominant league. UEFA might use a significant proportion of the income to fund the development of the game, but in this case the clubs might feel they could do better by going it alone and keeping all the money for themselves. So UEFA appears to be caught in a catch-22 situation: as a promoter, it is liable to find itself either subject to an antitrust suit or deserted by its teams. In this situation it may be that UEFA has to choose between its roles as regulator and promoter. It would appear that there is growing scope for UEFA to exercise its regulatory functions.

5.3. Prospects for a true Superleague

Our final comments concern the prospects for a Superleague. A long-term solution must be both commercially viable and DG IV compatible. Our analysis suggests that the revamped UEFA Champions League has several major flaws. So what do we think would be a viable structure for a true European Superleague?

The structure outlined in Table 8 is purely hypothetical in its composition of teams and regional organization. We are not central planners and do not claim to know what is best for the European public. Nevertheless, the desirable features that could represent an equilibrium structure for European football can be spelled out. Top clubs are attracted by the possibility of repeated encounters with the top clubs and stars from rival leagues. In this way, the top clubs can enhance the level of opposition and therefore enhance their own revenue-generating potential. Many of the top clubs would also like to abandon fixtures against much weaker clubs that tend to be found at the foot of the domestic leagues, since these matches generate less income while involving significant injury risks for top players. However, the problem for clubs wanting to create a Superleague is that, while they want more regular competition with top international rivals, they also want to preserve valuable domestic rivalries. For example, in Germany, Bayern München might want to play Juventus, Inter Milan, Barcelona, Real Madrid, Ajax, Arsenal and Manchester United more often, but they do not want to surrender regular fixtures against Kaiserslautern, Borussia Dortmund, Borussia Mönchengladbach, FC Köln, Bayer Leverkusen, Hamburg, Werder Bremen or Eintracht Frankfurt (and possibly others). The same argument would apply *mutatis mutandis* in every country. Thus

Table 8. Possible structure and organization of a European Football Conference

South West League 4 countries, 15 clubs			Northern League 7 countries, 15 clubs		
Paris Saint-Germain	Fra	8717	Ajax	Ned	7858
AS Monaco	Fra	5764	Feyenoord	Ned	6208
Girondins Bordeaux	Fra	4917	PSV Eindhoven	Ned	4833
FC Nantes	Fra	3875	Manchester United	Eng	6617
Olympique Marseille	Fra	1500	Aston Villa	Eng	4375
FC Barcelona	Esp	7381	Arsenal	Eng	4167
Real Madrid	Esp	5951	Liverpool	Eng	3875
Atlético Madrid	Esp	4000	Newcastle United	Eng	3500
Deportivo La Coruna	Esp	3833	Chelsea	Eng	3264
Real Zaragoza	Esp	3333	Rosenborg BK	Nor	5458
FC Porto	Por	6538	Brondby IF	Den	5250
Benfica	Por	6458	Celtic	Sco	3250
Sporting CP Lisbon	Por	5667	Glasgow Rangers	Sco	2167
Club Brugge	Bel	4750	AIK Solna Stockholm	Swe	3167
Anderlecht	Bel	3858	MyPa-47	Fin	1000
Average UEFA ranking coeff.		**5103**	**Average UEFA ranking coeff.**		**4333**
Competitive imbalance		34%	Competitive imbalance		39%
Eastern League 14 countries, 15 clubs			Central League 3 countries, 15 clubs		
Spartak Moscow	Rus	7158	Juventus	Ita	8265
Lokomotive Moscow	Rus	3000	Lazio Roma	Ita	7193
Slavia Praha	Cze	5483	AC Parma	Ita	7139
Panathinaikos	Gre	5350	Inter Milan	Ita	6735
Galatasaray	Tur	3833	AC Milan	Ita	6303
Steaua Bucuresti	Rum	4833	Fiorentina	Ita	1375
Ferencvaros	Hun	4083	Napoli	Ita	1167
Dinamo Kiev	Ukr	3375	Borussia Dortmund	Ger	7716
Rapid Wien	Aut	3417	Bayern München	Ger	6825
Dinamo Tbilisi	Geo	3000	Bayer Leverkusen	Ger	4600
Croatia Zagreb	Cro	3000	Werder Bremen	Ger	3217
Slovan Bratislava	Svk	2750	1.FC Kaiserslautern	Ger	3000
Legia Warsaw	Pol	2250	Eintracht Frankfurt	Ger	2750
Dinamo Minsk	Bls	2500	Hamburger SV	Ger	1167
Lokomotiv Sofia	Bul	1000	Grasshopper Club	Sui	3167
Average UEFA ranking coeff.		**3669**	**Average UEFA ranking coeff.**		**4708**
Competitive imbalance		40%	Competitive imbalance		53%

a breakaway has to enrol a large number of clubs from the start in order to achieve critical mass.

To accommodate both national and international rivalries would require a league with at least 60 teams. This would not be feasible under a conventional football system where all play all twice, home and away. A hierarchical system would not be attractive either, given that one of the reasons for putting together a Superleague is to play more often with other top European teams, not avoid them. An alternative to this might be a

US conference system where teams are organized in sub-groups. Each season a club plays all the members of its own conference and in addition a limited number of teams from outside the conference, chosen on the basis of historic performance (to maintain a rough competitive balance). Such a system based around, say, four regional conferences of 15–20 teams might enable clubs to preserve domestic competition while enhancing international competition. If each conference contained 15 teams, then each team would play 28 matches against teams from its own league and in addition would play 6 teams from each of the other conferences (once only) over the course of the regular season, bringing the total number of games to 46. The selection of opponents would be based on past performance, so as to create a more balanced set of matches and to give the weaker teams a better chance in the championship. At the end of the regular season, a play-off system would involve, let's say, the top two teams in each league, with three rounds leading to the final and the status of European football champion.

We have constructed a hypothetical Superleague, primarily to illustrate the way in which a competition might operate. The conference members are listed in Table 8. The composition of a Superleague would be subject to negotiation, but we have adopted some simple rules of thumb. For the larger footballing nations, such as England, Germany, Italy, France and Spain, five, six or seven clubs have been selected firstly on the basis of their respective UEFA rankings. For another category of countries, two or three clubs have been selected. Smaller countries have one club to represent them. The decision as to how to group the teams has been made primarily on the basis of geography. In addition, countries have been grouped together where regional or historic rivalries are strong or the style of football is similar. A special league has been created to accommodate the countries of eastern Europe, with one team for each country except Russia. This is for two reasons. Income differentials between these clubs are less than with other European clubs. Second, the attractiveness of matches with eastern clubs is generally lower for the top European clubs, and including them as part of other leagues would undermine the league's attractiveness in the short term. In the longer term, however, eastern European clubs can be expected to benefit from inclusion in the European Superleague and be able to develop strong teams of their own.

Table 8 also lists the 1998 UEFA rankings for each team. This allows the calculation of two indicators: the average ranking points of the teams assembled in the league; and the inequality of teams in terms of their respective UEFA ranking points. In our example, the South-Western League scores highest in terms of average UEFA rankings, combining the top clubs from France, Spain, Portugal and Belgium. The Eastern League scores lowest in term of average rankings, but is quite evenly balanced.

Participation in domestic league competitions would not be permitted for teams playing in this European Superleague because a combined fixture list would be impossible to manage for even the largest teams and there would be a negative effect on competitive balance modelled above in section 4. This does not mean that Superleague clubs could not compete in domestic cup competitions, which are played in a different format. Promotion opportunities and threats of relegation are other possible features that could be incorporated in a European Superleague, but perhaps only with difficulty.

Supporting measures to maintain the attractiveness of domestic competitions could be introduced along the lines of the rookie draft in the USA. For example, clubs participating in the European Superleague could agree among themselves a rule whereby no player under the age of twenty would be played in conference matches. This would give clubs involved in the domestic league competition *de facto* exclusivity for competitive matches involving emerging stars of the game. This may sound like a significant restriction on the free movement of players in the European Union and likely to fall foul of the Bosman ruling. But this is not necessarily the case. First, it is arguable that in the wider market for players, the hiring restraint of 60 clubs is not a major distortion. Secondly, the wider benefits to European football are potentially substantial. Domestic league competitions would be more attractive than without such a restriction. Intense interest would be focused on the performance of those players who will become eligible to play in the European Superleague, creating an additional spectator interest in domestic league games. And thirdly, there is the income redistribution effect between leagues benefiting clubs that have on their books a promising young player under long-term contract, from which they can release him at the age of twenty for an appropriate consideration.

REFERENCES

Atkinson S., L. Stanley and J. Tschirhart (1988). 'Revenue sharing as an incentive in an agency problem: an example from the National Football League', *Rand Journal of Economics*.

Bourg, J.-F. and J.-J. Gouguet (1998). *Analyse Economique du Sport*, Presses Universitaires de France.

Bulow, J., J. Geanokoplos and P. Klemperer (1985). 'Multimarket oligopoly, strategic substitutes and complements', *Journal of Political Economy*.

Burguet, R., R. Caminal and C. Matutes (1998). 'Golden cages for showy birds: optimal switching costs in the labor market', IAE, mimeo.

Deloitte & Touche (1998a). *Annual Review of Football Finance 1997*.

Deloitte & Touche (1998b). *Financial Review of Serie A*.

El-Hodiri, M. and J. Quirk (1971). 'An economic analysis of a professional sports league', *Journal of Political Economy*.

Fort, R. and J. Quirk (1995). 'Cross subsidization, incentives and outcomes in professional team sports leagues', *Journal of Economic Literature*.

Galli, A. (1998). 'Rechtsformgestaltung und Lizenzierungspraxis im Berufsfussball: Die Situation in England, Italien und Spanien vor dem Hintergrund der Regelungen in Deutschland', *Sport und Recht*.

Inglis, S. (1988). *English League Football and the Men Who Made It*, Willow Books, London.

Jennett, N. (1984). 'Attendances, uncertainty of outcome and policy in the Scottish football league', *Scottish Journal of Political Economy*.

Lazear, E. and S. Rosen (1981). 'Rank-order tournaments as optimum labor contracts', *Journal of Political Economy*.

Loury, G. (1979). 'Market structure and innovation', *Quarterly Journal of Economics*.

Monahan, G. (1987). 'The structure of equilibria in market share attraction models', *Management Science*.

Noll, R. (1985). *The Economic Viability of Professional Baseball*, Report to the Major League Baseball Players' Association.

Nti, K. (1997). 'Comparative statics of contests and rent-seeking games', *International Economic Review*.

Peel, D. and D. Thomas (1988). 'Outcome uncertainty and the demand for football: an analysis of match attendances in the English football league', *Scottish Journal of Political Economy*.

Quirk, J. and R. Fort (1992). *Pay Dirt: The Business of Professional Team Sports*, Princeton University Press, Princeton, NJ.

Ratliff, J. (1998). 'EC competition law and sport', paper presented at the British Association for Sport and the Law, London, October.

Sheehan, R. (1996). *Keeping Score: The Economics of Big-Time Sports*, Diamond Communications, South Bend, IN.

Sloane, P.J. (1971). 'The economics of professional football: the football club as a utility maximizer', *Scottish Journal of Political Economy*.

Szymanski, S. and T. Kuypers (1999). *Winners and Losers: The Business Strategy of Football*, Penguin, Harmondsworth.

Szymanski, S. and R. Smith (1997). 'The English football industry: profit, performance and industrial structure', *International Review of Applied Economics*.

Temple Lang, J. (1997). 'Media, multimedia and European Community antitrust law', paper presented at the Fordham Corporate Law Institute, October.

Tullock, G. (1980). 'Efficient rent seeking', in J.M. Buchanan, R.D. Tollison and G. Tullock (eds.), *Toward a Theory of the Rent Seeking Society*, Texas A & M University Press, Austin, TX.

Vallet, O. (1998). 'Le football entre religion et politique', in P. Boniface (ed.), *Géopolitique du Football*, Editions Complexe.

Van Miert, K. (1997). Speech to the European Sport Forum, 27th November, http://europa.eu.int:80/en/comm/dg10/sport/nl/b news5.html.

Wachtmeister, A.M. (1998). 'Broadcasting of sport events and competition law', Competition Policy Newsletter DG IV, no. 2.

Walvin, J. (1994). *The People's Game*, Mainstream, Edinburgh.

[4]

The Economic Journal, 111 (February), F69–F84. © Royal Economic Society 2001. Published by Blackwell Publishers, 108 Cowley Road, Oxford OX4 1JF, UK and 350 Main Street, Malden, MA 02148, USA.

INCOME INEQUALITY, COMPETITIVE BALANCE AND THE ATTRACTIVENESS OF TEAM SPORTS: SOME EVIDENCE AND A NATURAL EXPERIMENT FROM ENGLISH SOCCER*

Stefan Szymanski

This paper examines the relationship between financial inequality, competitive balance and attendance at English professional league soccer. It shows that while financial inequality among the clubs has increased, competitive balance has remained relatively stable and match attendance appears unrelated to competitive balance. A clearer test of the relationship is suggested by comparison with FA Cup matches. Because income inequality is primarily driven by inter- rather than intra-divisional inequality, the FA Cup has been a much more unbalanced competition than the divisional championships. Attendance at FA Cup matches relative to the corresponding league matches has fallen over the last twenty years.

It is widely accepted that a degree of competitive balance is an essential feature of attractive team sports.[1] Sporting competition is a process that establishes a hierarchy among the participants – winners and losers. Competitive balance refers to the rational expectations of fans about who will be the winners. In a perfectly balanced contest, each participant starts with an equal chance of winning, so that the outcome will be completely uncertain. If there is no competitive balance then the exact outcome can be predicted with probability one. Without at least a degree of competitive balance, fans will lose interest in a competition. However, it is less clear that every decline in competitive balance will lead to a falling off of fan interest.

This is not merely a matter of academic concern. In the recent Premier League Broadcasting case, heard in the UK Restrictive Practices Court, the court decided that selling broadcast rights collectively (and preventing clubs from selling any broadcast rights individually) was in the public interest, in part because the collective sale promoted financial equality, which in turn promoted competitive balance/uncertainty of outcome. Similar views underlie the US Sports Broadcasting Act of 1961 (which exempts the collective sale of broadcast rights on national TV from antitrust prosecution), and the comments of the Advocate General of the European Court of Justice in the Bosman case.

Thus the received opinion contains two logical steps: (i) increasing income

---

* I would like to thank Syariza Kamsan for valuable research assistance. I also thank Steve Ross, Chris Walters, seminar participants at Edinburgh University, Salford University, London Economics and two anonymous referees for valuable comments.

[1] This may be a peculiarly modern phenomenon reflecting ethical sensitivities – the Romans, for instance, appear to have enjoyed the unbalanced contest between lions and Christians.

inequality tends to reduce competitive balance and (ii) competitive imbalance tends to reduce fan interest.[2]

This paper does two things. First it develops a simple theoretical model of league competition to show that increasing competitive balance is not always desirable. Fan interest depends on several factors, and while competitive balance is one, an equally important consideration is the success of each of the teams that fans support. If fan support is unequally distributed between teams (e.g. for demographic reasons) then a utilitarian welfare function is likely to suggest that imbalance in favour of more strongly supported teams is optimal. For example, it is currently said that 50% of committed football fans in England support Manchester United – if this is so it is difficult to argue that aggregate welfare is not enhanced by the relative success of this team.

The second contribution of this paper is to suggest a natural experiment to test for the relationship between income inequality, competitive balance and fan interest. Testing for the existence of the hypothesised relationships is fraught with difficulties because of the many factors that affect fan interest from season to season. While it may be possible to test whether or not the competitive balance of a match affects interest (e.g. attendance) it is more difficult to test for the competitive balance of an entire competition. Yet in terms of the theory, it is presumably the competitive balance of a competition which is most important in the long run.

English soccer provides a natural experiment that overcomes these problems. Because teams compete simultaneously in both league (Football League and Premier League) competition and cup (FA Cup) competition, we can compare the trend in support for each of these competitions. In the league competitions teams are segregated into divisions, while in the Cup competition teams from different divisions can be drawn against each other. Over recent years income inequality has grown, most noticeably between rather than within the divisions. This implies that the FA Cup has become a much more unbalanced competition relative to the league division championships. We can thus ask whether attendance at FA Cup matches has declined relative to league matches. We do this by creating a matched sample of same-division matches played in the league and the Cup (these constitute around half of all matches in most seasons). The matching controls for many of the possible differences between matches (e.g. team strength, local interest, demographic and economic factors). What remains can be attributed to the intrinsic imbalance of the FA Cup relative to league championships.

---

[2] '... An important element in the maintenance of the quality of the Premier League competition is competitive balance, that is to say the unpredictability of the outcome of a high proportion of the matches played within the competition and thus uncertainty about which club will win the championship ... we accept that an increase in financial inequality will tend to result in a reduction of competitive balance' *RPC Court Judgment, Premier League.*

'[A] professional league can flourish only if there is no too glaring imbalance between the clubs taking part. If the league is clearly dominated by one team, the necessary tension is absent and the interest of the spectators will probably lapse within a foreseeable period ... it is of fundamental importance to share income out between the clubs in a reasonable manner ...' *Advocate-General Lenz, Bosman.*

The results do indeed show a relative decline in attendance at same-division matches. The rest of this paper is set out as follows. The next section develops a simple theoretical analysis of league structure and competitive balance. The following section develops the natural experiment and discusses some robustness issues. The final section draws some conclusions.

1. Competitive Balance in Theory

The relationship between income distribution, competitive balance and the attractiveness of sporting competition has received a limited amount of attention in the theoretical literature. This literature has been primarily been concerned with the proposition that income redistribution will lead to greater equality of outcomes. Quirk and Fort (1992) and Vrooman (1995) analysed this question and concluded that competitive balance would be unaffected by redistributive mechanisms such as gate sharing. Under gate sharing, the visiting team receives a fixed percentage of the home team gate (e.g. in the US NFL 40% of gate income is allocated to the visitors). The basis of their argument is as follows. If teams earn more from home matches when they are expected to win (i.e. winning teams attract more support) and the visiting team share the gate revenue, then the visiting team would prefer to be less successful compared to the case where they do not share in the gate receipts. This will lead both teams to invest less in winning (i.e. to invest less in playing talent) compared to the case where there is no gate sharing, but in their models this effect impacts equally on both teams so that competitive balance is unaffected.

Szymanski (1998) argues that gate sharing may even have the perverse effect of reducing competitive balance. In a model where there is constant marginal cost of talent but revenue is a strictly convex function of playing success (measured by win percentage), gate sharing will diminish the investment incentives of small market teams by more than that of large market teams. Intuitively, small teams stand to gain more from the success of the big teams than the big teams stand to gain from the success of the small teams. Hence small teams reduce investment in talent by more than the big teams. However, that paper also shows that the impact of redistribution on competitive balance depends critically on the objectives of the teams and on the type of redistribution scheme. The standard models of team sports in the United States assume clubs are profit maximisers, while researchers in Europe (e.g. Sloane (1971)) have presented evidence that, at least traditionally, clubs have been 'win maximisers' (or some variant of this). Win maximisation implies all surplus income is reinvested in talent. Under these circumstances, income redistribution from large to small clubs will tend to improve competitive balance.

Even if clubs are profit maximisers, schemes that raise income independently of playing success (e.g. collective selling of TV income), and then redistribute that income on the basis of playing success, will tend to improve competitive balance. This is because what matters for competitive balance is the investment decision of the teams, which in turn depends on the access of teams to the income pool *ex ante*, rather than the *ex post* share-out. Income raised through lump sum taxes will not distort incentives while redistribution on the basis of performance will give equal incentives to all. Teams with a small drawing power are no longer deterred from investing in talent because of the limits imposed by their local market.

TV income is an interesting case, not least because of the interest expressed by competition authorities in the desirability of centralised collective selling. In theory, collective selling and the distribution of TV income purely on merit (e.g. on the basis of league ranking) will enhance competitive balance by giving small market teams equal access to the TV market. A club with a small local market can finance a successful team if TV income is the dominant source of finance. In practice collective TV revenues tend to be distributed equally (as in the US NFL) or only partly on the basis of merit. In the English Premier League only 25% is distributed on the basis of league ranking, while 50% is allocated as an equal share and the remaining 25% is awarded on the basis of the number of TV appearances.

However, these researchers have also questioned the value of competitive balance. If some teams draw on larger (or more devoted) fan bases, then the success of these teams will yield greater total utility than the success of teams with small fan bases. The important theoretical issue is whether unfettered competition or a regulated market will deliver the socially optimal outcome. A simple model may help to illustrate this point. Suppose that there is a sports competition consisting of two teams, one of which enjoys a larger domestic market than the other, in the sense that it will generate a higher level of fan utility for a given level of playing success. Fan utility depends on playing success, which in turn depends on the proportion of playing talent hired by each team. Hence the fan utility for each team can be written as follows:

$$U_1 = \mu_1 w_1 = \frac{\mu_1 t_1}{t_1 + t_2}, \qquad U_2 = \mu_2 w_2 = \frac{\mu_2 t_2}{t_1 + t_2} \qquad (1)$$

where $\mu_1 > \mu_2$ reflects the intensity of support, w is the win percentage of each team and t is the quantity of playing talent hired by each team. Total utility will depend not only on the utility of committed team fans, but also on spectators with no particular loyalty to a team. These supporters might be labelled 'uncommitted', or, more pejoratively, 'couch potatoes', watching matches on TV and motivated only by an attractive spectacle. The utility of these spectators is thus dependent on competitive balance.[3] We adopt here a simple cardinal representation of total utility:

$$U = U_1 + U_2 + \theta w_1 w_2 \qquad (2)$$

where θ represents the weight of couch potatoes relative to committed team fans in total utility. Maximising total utility with respect to the win percentage yields following social optimum:

[3] Most fans are likely to value the total quality of the playing talent involved in a match as well as competitive balance. The addition of total playing talent as an argument in the social welfare function will not affect the qualitative results.

$$w_1^* = \frac{1}{2} + \frac{\mu_1 - \mu_2}{2\theta}. \tag{3}$$

As θ becomes very large, only competitive balance matters. However, depending on the difference between the intensity of support for each team, as θ diminishes the social optimum implies higher degrees of inequality. Unless the two teams are equally well supported, there will exist a critical value of θ which implies that total utility would be maximised even if the more popular team never lost. The model implies a trade-off between the interests of the committed and uncommitted fans. The optimal balance depends on the relative weights placed on each of these populations.

It is clear from this that if redistribution of income led to an equal distribution of resources the outcome would be an equally balanced contest. This would be socially optimal only if either the intensity of support for each team were equal or the weight attached to utility of the uncommitted fans dominated completely. Perfect balance is not generally desirable.

To model the outcome of a competitive market some assumptions are required about the objectives of clubs and the form of their objective functions. Here it will be assumed that clubs are profit maximisers, in line with the US literature, and an increasingly plausible assumption in English soccer now that the largest clubs are quoted on the stock market. It is assumed that the clubs are able to appropriate a fraction of the utility of fans through the sale of tickets and related products, while they can hire playing talent in the market at a constant marginal cost. Thus

$$\pi_i = \phi_i \mu_i w_i - c t_i \tag{4}$$

where ϕ is the fraction of winning utility that the clubs can appropriate. It is also assumed that clubs are unable to appropriate any of the utility derived by the uncommitted fans. This may be somewhat extreme, but in general one might expect that it is relatively difficult to generate income from this group. It is easy to show that profit maximisation implies the ratio of talent at each club will equal the ratio of intensity of support (μ_1/μ_2). Comparing this with the socially optimal level of talent at each club implied by (3), it is clear that the socially optimal level of competitive balance would arise only by chance. If $\mu_1 = \mu_2$ the market outcome is socially optimal. However if $\mu_1 > \mu_2$ then the social optimum would only be achieved for a particular value of θ. This critical value is increasing in μ_1. In other words, the greater the weight attached to the utility of uncommitted fans the stronger the intensity of support for team 1 would have to be to achieve the social optimum. If intensity of support for team 1 is too large, the contest will be less balanced than the social optimum, if it is too small the contest will be more balanced than is socially optimal.

A simple model such as this captures some basic ideas about the relationship between inequality in the distribution of resources, competitive balance and social optimality. The basic insight is that while perfect competitive balance is not desirable, the market equilibrium is unlikely to achieve the social optimum. In particular, intensely supported teams are likely to create excessively unbalanced competitions. This might be taken as grounds for limited redistribution. Whether members of a league or the league authorities themselves will be able to impose such redistribution depends largely on their ability to appropriate the surplus of uncommitted fans – otherwise they have no incentive to act and no basis for an agreement. In such cases, intervention by an independent regulator committed to the best interest of the sport will be desirable, at least in theory.

2. Competitive Balance: A Natural Experiment

2.1. *The Trend in English League Soccer*

Before developing the natural experiment it is useful to review the data from the league alone to indicate the difficulty in analysing competitive balance. This paper deals with competitive balance in a sense which has not generally been examined in the earlier literature. Kuypers (1997)[4] defines competitive balance in three senses: the balance of attractiveness of a match, the closeness of a championship race and the absence of long run domination. Most previous studies have concentrated on competitive balance in the first two senses. Thus Jennett (1984), Peel and Thomas (1988), Cairns (1988), Jones and Ferguson (1988) and Kuypers (1997) concentrate on the match uncertainty. They hypothesise that uncertain matches will attract greater support and focus on finding suitable proxies for match uncertainty. Demmert (1973), Noll (1974), Whitney (1988) and Kuypers concentrate on the closeness of specific championship races and examine whether this increases attendance at matches. In the present study the focus of interest is the balance of the entire championship over a period of time. In league competition this can be measured by the variance of team winning (win percentage) over time or the dominance of high ranks by particular teams. For Cup competition, since the teams also participate in hierarchical leagues, competitive balance can be analysed by looking at the success of teams from different divisions.

The growing financial inequality in English is widely remarked upon. However, most of this growth in inequality is inter- rather than intra-divisional, as is shown in Fig. 1. This graph shows the coefficient of variation of income for a sample of 39 clubs over the 22-year period 1976/7 to 1997/8. This makes it difficult to test for the impact of growing inequality in league soccer, since there are no inter-divisional matches. Moreover, it is not evident that there has been any significant increase in intra-divisional competitive balance either within or between seasons. Table 1 illustrates the absence of any significant trend in dominance over time, measured by the number of teams accounting for the top positions over different time periods (three and seven years). While there is some slight evidence of increasing dominance in the Premier League over the last three years in the sample, there is no clear trend.

It is useful to consider the mobility of teams between the divisions. In any

---

[4] Kuypers (1997) and Szymanski and Kuypers (1999) provide a useful survey; for an earlier survey see Cairns *et al.* (1986).

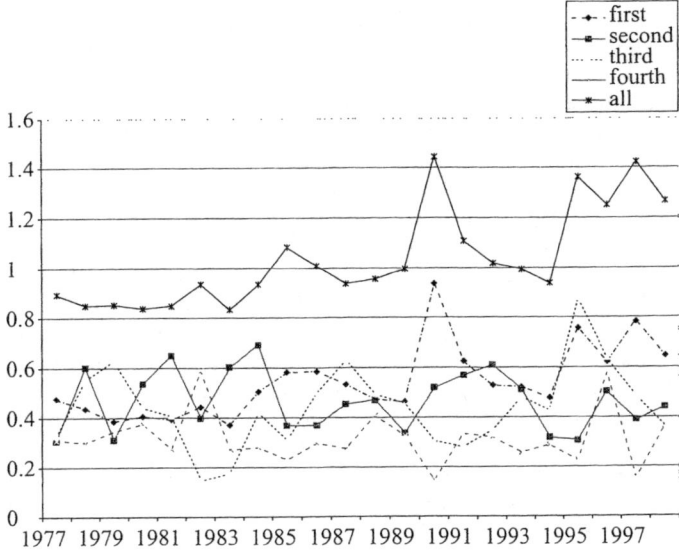

Fig. 1. *Coefficient of Variation of Sales by Division 1977–1998*

Table 1
Number of Teams in Each of the Top N Positions by 3 and 7 Year Intervals
(1978–98)

(a) *Three Year Intervals*

Number of teams in top 3				Number of teams in top 5				Number of teams in top 10			
		division				division				division	
Period	1	2	3	4	Period	1	2	3	4	Period	1	2	3	4
1	6	9	9	6	1	9	12	15	11	1	13	18	18	16
2	6	8	9	9	2	9	11	12	13	2	13	15	19	22
3	6	9	7	8	3	8	13	11	13	3	11	20	16	22
4	6	9	8	8	4	8	14	14	12	4	12	18	18	21
5	8	7	9	7	5	10	11	13	11	5	15	19	20	21
6	6	7	6	8	6	10	11	12	11	6	15	18	19	19
7	4	8	9	8	7	7	13	13	13	7	13	19	18	22

(b) *Seven Year Intervals*

Number of teams in top 3				Number of teams in top 5				Number of teams in top 10			
Period	1	2	3	4	Period	1	2	3	4	Period	1	2	3	4
1	8	17	15	17	1	10	17	22	23	1	12	19	25	31
2	7	14	17	19	2	9	17	20	28	2	11	21	23	34
3	8	12	16	20	3	11	17	19	27	3	15	17	25	31

one year there are 92 league clubs, and over the seasons 1976/7 to 1997/8 there have been 99 teams participating in the four divisions, given that there have been a small number of demotions to the lower semi-professional divisions. Of these 99 teams, only 5 have never been relegated or promoted over the period, indicating that there is a fairly high degree of mobility between the divisions.[5] Furthermore, over the period more teams have ranged between three divisions (43) than have moved only between two (32), while 12 teams managed to visit all four divisions over the space of 22 years.

Dominance within seasons is considered in Fig. 2. This shows the standard deviation of win percentage over time. This measure is the mostly widely used indicator of competitive balance in the US literature and although there are a greater proportion of drawn games in soccer, win percentage is still a reliable indicator of success. It is closely correlated with the more usual measures of success such as league position (correlation coefficient 0.91) and points scored (0.95). Perhaps surprisingly, the charts show that there is no clear trend in win percentage, suggesting that divisional championships have not tended to become more one sided over time. Fig. 2 also illustrates the change in attendance at league matches over the 22 seasons, that may be taken as an indicator of fan interest. There have been two very distinct phases – a secular decline in attendance until 1985 and a consistent increase thereafter. This is in itself puzzling given that most pundits have generally dated the recovery of

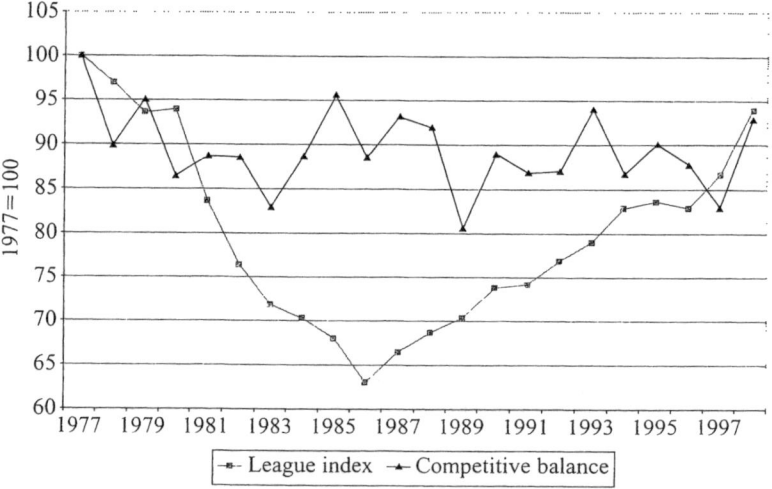

Fig. 2. *Competitive Balance and League Attendance Trends 1977–1998*

---

[5] Four of these teams have remained in the top division (Arsenal, Coventry, Everton and Liverpool) while one has remained in the lowest division (Rochdale).

interest in English football at 1990 (when England reached the semi-final of the World Cup) or even 1992 (the foundation of the Premier League). There were still problems in English football in the late 1980s (high levels of crowd violence, poor facilities at stadiums and high levels of policing. Worst of all was the Hillsborough stadium disaster of 1989 in which 95 fans were crushed to death).

One explanation may be derived from the model outlined in Section 1. The trend growth in financial inequality started from a point in the early post-war period when income was quite evenly distributed and clubs were restricted by a maximum wage rule that limited team expenditure. Thus until 1961 teams with large potential supporter bases were constrained to hire teams of roughly equal ability to those with small potential supporter bases. In terms of the model, the constrained equilibrium meant that the success of the larger teams was below the optimal level. Once the maximum wage was abolished clubs could utilise their greater resources to achieve a higher rate of success and this may have led both to less competitive balance and greater interest in the league football.

2.2. *The Natural Experiment*

The idea of a natural experiment is to identify two sets of data in which competitive balance differed significantly but all other relevant factors are the same. In US team sports where clubs compete only in a single tournament, such natural experiments are not available, but this is not true of soccer. Traditionally teams participate in two main competitions during the season, a league competition and a cup, or knock-out competition. The oldest such competition in the world is the FA Cup in which all 92 league clubs compete annually. The FA Cup is in fact open to all registered football clubs in England, and amateur teams compete in preliminary rounds. However, the first round of the Cup consists mainly of the teams in the two lowest divisions. The teams in the top two divisions do not enter the competition until the third round which consists of 64 teams.

In each round of the competition the matches are determined by a random draw. In many cases the opposing teams are from different divisions, but on average one third of matches from the third round onwards are contests between teams from the same division, and an even greater proportion of matches in rounds 1 and 2 are same-division matches. This is the basis for a natural experiment. Using a sample of about one thousand same-division FA Cup matches over the last 22 years we can compare attendance with attendance at the equivalent league fixture played in the same season (this includes equivalence in the sense that the same team has home advantage). As was pointed out in the previous section, the main source of the growth in inequality between league teams has been the growth of inter-divisional income inequality. If income inequality leads to a less balanced contest, we should expect to see a lower degree of fan interest in a Cup fixture, which forms part of a more unequal championship than the corresponding league fixture. The test is therefore not a test of the attractiveness of a fixture in its own right, say as a function of the quality of the teams or the history of competition between the two teams, rather it is a test of the relative attractiveness of the championships in which the two teams are participating. In fact it is a very low powered test. It excludes from consideration matches between teams from different divisions which might be thought to be particularly unbalanced and therefore to attract fewer spectators. These contests are excluded because there are no equivalent league fixtures with which they can be compared.

Of course, the natural experiment cannot control for every possible source of difference between the two fixtures. Match attendance can be affected by the current form of the two teams, the day of the week on which a match is played (weekend matches tend to have higher attendance) and the point of the season at which the match is played (end of season matches tend to have higher attendance). These factors can be controlled for through a regression analysis, although one might expect that in a matched sample as large as one thousand these factors would not exert systematic effect.

While the data make clear that income inequality between the divisions has grown over recent years, it is not so easy to establish that competitive balance has in fact declined. The standard deviation of win percentage or other indicators of success make little sense in this context. One way to compare is to look at the survival of teams from different divisions. There is surprisingly little evidence of a trend toward domination by the larger clubs, perhaps because even in 1977 the large clubs dominated the FA Cup. Thus in that season 78% of all appearances in the FA Cup from the third round on were from teams in the first and second division. Given that 64 teams enter the third round of which 44 are from the top two divisions, the theoretical maximum share of the top two divisions is 84% (106 out of 126 appearances) while the theoretical minimum is 44% (56 appearances). Over the period the share of the top two divisions never fell below 72%, within 12% of the theoretical maximum (see Fig. 3). The top division clubs dominate the final rounds of the competition. There were only three cases of a club from outside the top division appearing in the final in the 22 years from 1977 to 1998, and only 15 cases out of a possible 88 of such a team playing in a semi-final. The lowest number of top division clubs to survive to the fourth round in any year during this period was 10, while on average 14 survived. Since the Premier League was reduced to 20 teams in 1996 at least 15 teams have survived the third round in each year.

There is some evidence of increasing dominance. The proportion of cases where a team from a lower division wins a match has declined. Between 1977 and 1987 on average just over 11 of the 63 matches played per season (from round 3 on) resulted in a win for the lower division team. From 1988 to 1998 the average fell to just under 10. The incidence of 'giantkilling', defined as a team beating an opponent placed at least two divisions higher, has also fallen. Such events are in any case rare, there having been only 67 cases in the 22 seasons covered by the data, an average of 3 per season. Between 1977 and 1987 there were 42 cases, an average of over four per season, while between 1988 and 1998 there were only 25 cases, an average of only just over 2 per

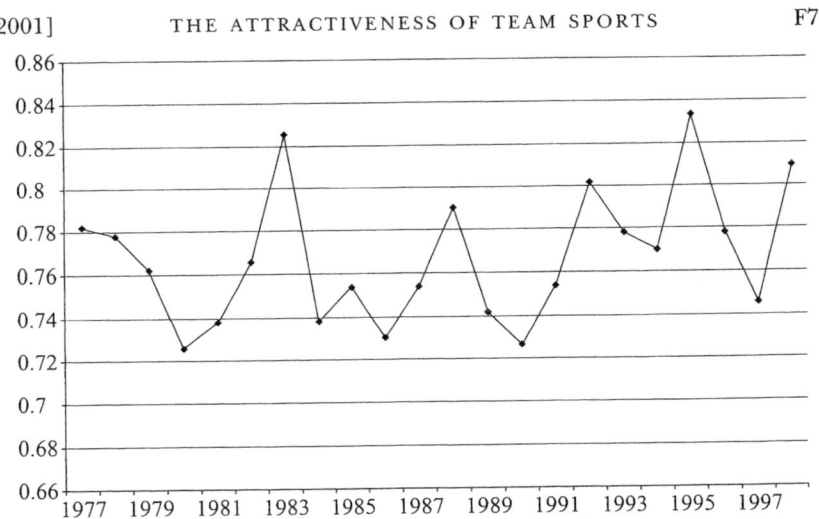

Fig. 3. *Share of Division 1 & 2 Teams in all FA Cup Matches Played from the Third Round Onwards*

season. This evidence seems to suggest that an already unbalanced contest has become yet more unbalanced.

The natural experiment suggested here is that if the competitive balance of a championship taken as a whole affects the attractiveness of individual matches, we should see a relative decline in attendance at matches in a championship whose balance is deteriorating faster. Since the inequality of income has grown faster as between participants in the FA Cup competition and participants in divisional championships, we should expect to see a relative decline in attendance at FA Cup matches. This does indeed appear to be the case, based on the sample of 997 same division matches played between 1977 and 1998.[6]

Fig. 4 shows a graph of the ratio of average attendance at FA Cup and league matches over time. FA Cup matches are traditionally better supported than league matches, and between 1977 and 1987 the average FA Cup fixture would attract an audience 43% larger than the equivalent league match. This difference declined to 25% in the second half of the data period, and declined almost continuously until 1998 in which year FA Cup matches attracted a slightly smaller audience on average. Thus even with this very low powered test, there appears to be have been a significant decline in the relative attractiveness of the FA Cup during a period when inter-divisional income inequality was

[6] The database includes replays of drawn matches. The inclusion of these games might be thought to bias the average FA Cup gate downwards since replays tend to be scheduled at times other than the weekend, making it more difficult for fans to attend. On the other hand, a replay may be a good indicator of an exciting match, since the previous draw already indicates a degree of competitive balance. In any case, a separate analysis of decisive matches only did not indicate any systematic difference in the underlying trend.

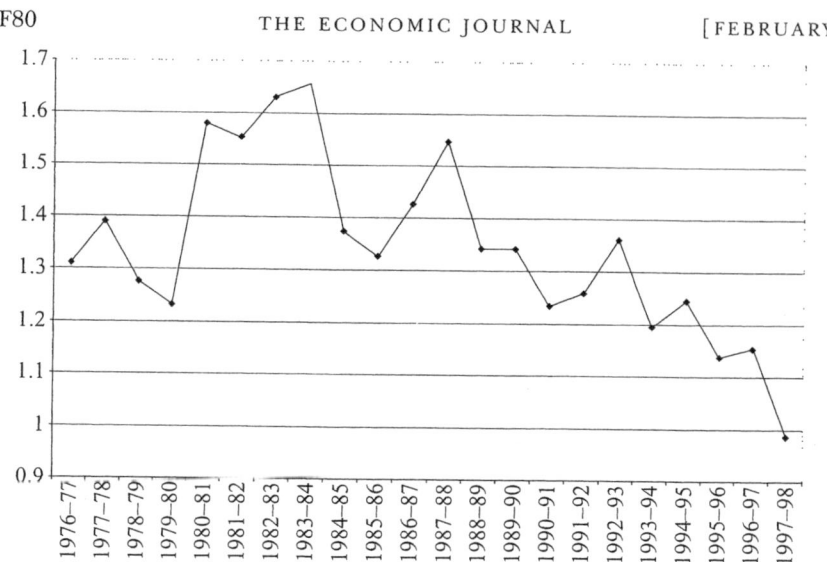

Fig. 4. *FA/League Attendance Ratio*

growing and there appears to have been some deterioration in the competitive balance of the FA Cup.

The database was compiled using matches from the first two rounds of the Cup, involving the lower divisions, as well as the later rounds. This ensures that the sample contains a large number of Cup matches between teams in the lower divisions. It might be suspected that the effect shown here was related primarily to the Premier League, where much of the media interest has been focused. It might also be suspected that the results were due to the fact that many top division cup matches tended to be played to capacity stadia, and that the falling ratio was an artefact of this constraint during a period when interest in football was growing. To deal with this issue and other potential factors that might influence attendance a regression approach was adopted.

The matched sample for the seasons 1982/3 to 1997/8 was used to analyse any trend in attendance at FA Cup matches relative to league matches. The results are reported in Table 2. Column 1 reports an OLS equation for the full data set. Column 2 reports a Tobit equation for the full sample, with upper censoring to account for the fact that about 10% of matches appear to have been played at capacity. The capacity figure was approximated as 95% of the figure reported in the Rothmans Football Yearbook. This Rothmans figure is likely to be an overstatement because capacity is limited for some matches by the requirement to have adequate segregation of fans, leaving many seats deliberately unoccupied.[7] Column 3 reports an OLS equation for the sample omitting top division teams, which account for 92% of sell-outs in the data.

---

[7] Capacity data is problematic. The Rothmans figure is also misleading for the 1990s when there was significant stadium rebuilding, often during the season. However, no other capacity figures are available.

Table 2
Attendance Regressions 1982/3–1997/8 Seasons

	OLS whole sample	Tobit whole sample	OLS excluding first division
Constant	28,323	27,774	12,867
	(23.095)	(38.317)	(13.814)
2nd division	−11,442	−11,181	
	(−19.592)	(−18.416)	
3rd division	−17,525	−17,012	−6,452.5
	(−35.905)	(−41.573)	(−15.001)
4th division	−20,043	−19,373	−8,402
	(−40.134)	(−48.418)	(−19.973)
Sum of team league positions	−262.38	−174.58	−138.34
	(−12.73)	(−12.812)	(−7.852)
Match played on Sunday	1,690.8	1,609.4	913.31
	(1.712)	(1.949)	(1.104)
Season month	129.73	−201.89	253.44
	(1.301)	(−3.149)	(3.397)
Replay	−1,145.1	−1,080.2	458.53
	(−1.812)	(−2.536)	(0.758)
FA Cup match 1983–86	3,617.5	3,519.9	1,998.8
	(4.322)	(6.706)	(2.815)
FA Cup match 1987–90	3,456.3	3,283.3	1,989.3
	(4.255)	(7.408)	(3.777)
FA Cup match 1991–94	912.61	926.63	543.19
	(1.410)	(1.803)	(1.302)
FA Cup match 1995–98	−138.29	−179.21	279.83
	(−0.166)	(−0.35)	(0.449)
Observations	1,286	1,286	772
R^2	0.637		0.479
Log L	−13,856	−12,713	−7,766

Heteroscedastic consistent t-statistics in parentheses. Time dummies included but not reported. Tobit coefficients are marginal effects.

The models were estimated with heteroscedastic consistent errors. In the case of the Tobit estimation a multiplicative model of heteroscedasticity was adopted (see Greene (1993)). In both the OLS and Tobit models there was evidence of non-normality using Pagan Vella tests. This is known to be a particular problem in the Tobit model since it renders the estimator inconsistent. However, the consonance of the Tobit and OLS results provides a little comfort.

The regressions account for the day of the week the game was played, the sum of league positions, the month and whether the match was an FA Cup replay as well as divisional and time dummies. Sunday matches tended to attract a higher attendance than Saturday matches, possibly because broadcast matches are usually scheduled for a Sunday and broadcasters select the most attractive games.

Most FA Cup replays are in midweek, and as a result these two variables tended to pick up the same effect. If anything, the replay variable worked better. The sum of league positions variable (positions at the date the game was played) picks up the quality of the teams on show. If competitive balance mattered for attendance at individual matches, one might have expected that the absolute difference in league positions would be significant – but in fact it was not.

The FA Cup effects are represented as dummies for successive four year periods. The estimates suggest that between 1982/3 and 1989/90 an FA Cup match would attract about 3,000 more spectators than an league match. The OLS figure is somewhat higher, the figure for the lower three divisions is somewhat lower. For the seasons 1990/1 to 1993/4 FA Cup matches still attracted more bodies on average, but the size of this effect (between 500 and 1,000 people) is not statistically significant at the conventional 5% level.[8] The dummy variables for the last four-year period (1995–8) are all much smaller (two indicate a negative impact of FA Cup matches on attendance) and are all statistically insignificant. Thus the regression analysis appears to support the evidence of Fig. 4 – in the 1980s FA Cup matches would attract significantly higher attendance than equivalent league matches – in the 1990s this effect has disappeared, and FA Cup matches attract attendances that are no higher on average than equivalent League matches. The 'magic of the Cup' seems to be fading.

Before concluding there are two possible flaws in the natural experiment that should be considered. If other factors had altered the relative attractiveness of attending matches in league and Cup competitions then the trend in the ratio might be attributed to these factors rather than competitive balance. Firstly, if the price of tickets for Cup matches relative to league matches had risen, this might have caused the relative decline in attendance. Price data are not available for the entire period, but the annual Football Trust Digest of Football Statistics provides an analysis of FA Cup and League gate receipts between 1984/5 and 1994/5. The ratio of prices derived from these data shows no overall trend, during a period when the relative decline of FA Cup attendance was pronounced. A more serious question is raised by the increasing tendency to sell season tickets. This means that for an increasing proportion of fans the marginal cost of attendance at league matches is effectively zero. This could account for the relative decline of interest in the FA Cup. However, the fact that clubs can sell an increasing proportion of seats for league matches in advance suggests that the attractiveness of the league competition has increased. If interest in the FA Cup had grown at the same rate, we might observe FA Cup season tickets being sold or simply higher prices for FA Cup matches. The fact that we do not suggests that the relative attractiveness of the Cup has indeed declined.

A second weakness of the experiment might be that the structure of the competitions themselves had changed enhancing the relative attractiveness of the League. Since 1986/7 a system of playoffs for some promotion places was introduced into the lower three divisions. The effect of this was to give more teams at any given time an interest in the possibility of promotion, and to involve every team a longer fraction of the season in contention. This has

---

[8] In the Tobit model the marginal effect is significant at the 10% level.

almost certainly stimulated interest in league competition in the lower divisions. To see if this effect was driving the relative decline of FA Cup attendance, those matched pairs which involved league matches played from March onwards (at which point progressively more teams are ruled out of contention) were omitted from the sample. However, for the remaining matches the relative decline of FA Cup attendance appeared just as pronounced as for the full sample.

3. Conclusions

This paper has attempted to draw out the relationship between the unequal distribution of resources, competitive balance and the interest of the fans. The resurgence of interest in English league football, in particular the Premier League, has occurred at a time when the distribution of income has become much more unequal. Many commentators have bemoaned this fact, worrying that it will lead to a decline of interest in soccer. So far, there is only weak evidence that the concentration of income has been associated with a decline in competitive balance, and no evidence at all that it has reduced interest in league football. It may be that the polarisation of recent years has been an adjustment away from an excessively egalitarian distribution toward an unequal distribution that more accurately reflects the interest of the fans. It may also be the case that competitive balance is only sensitive to very large changes in the income distribution, and hence growth in inequality may only have caused small changes in competitive balance.

There are many factors that influence attendance, and isolating the effect of competitive balance using only a short time series is unlikely to reveal capture all the dynamics of the underlying relationship. However, by comparing same-division fixtures that occur in both the FA Cup and the league we can conduct a natural experiment on the effect of growing inequality. The only important difference between the matched pairs is the competition in which they are played. Other sources of difference such as home advantage, the quality of the teams, form over recent seasons and so on are filtered out by the matching. Since inter-divisional inequality has grown much faster than intra-divisional equality, the FA Cup is a competition where the resources of the participants have become more unevenly distributed (compared to the league) over time. The data show, just as one might have predicted, that this relative increase in inequality has led to a relative decline in attendance. In the 1970s it was not unusual for attendance at an FA Cup match to be 50% higher than the attendance at the equivalent league fixture. By 1998 the average attendance at FA Cup matches was lower than at the matched fixture. Thus the natural experiment appears to confirm the standard hypothesis about the impact of income inequality and competitive balance on the attractiveness of sporting competition.

Imperial College London

F84   THE ECONOMIC JOURNAL   [FEBRUARY 2001]

References

Cairns, J. A. (1988). 'Outcome uncertainty and the demand for football', University of Aberdeen Department of Economics Discussion paper 88-02.

Cairns, J. A., Jennett, N. and Sloane, P. J. (1986). 'The economics of professional team sports: a survey of theory and evidence'. *Journal of Economic Studies*, vol. 13, pp. 3–80.

Court of Justice of the European Communities (1995). Case C-415/93 (The Bosman Judgment).

Demmert, H. (1973). *The Economics of Professional Team Sports*, Massachusetts: Lexington Books.

Greene, W. (1993). *Econometric Analysis*. Second Edition. Basingstoke: Macmillan.

Fort, R. and Quirk, J. (1995). 'Cross-subsidisation, incentives and outcomes in professional team sports leagues'. *Journal of Economic Literature*, vol. 33, September, pp. 1265–99.

Jennett, N. (1984). 'Attendance, uncertainty of outcome and policy in Scottish league football'. *Scottish Journal of Political Economy*, vol. 31, pp. 176–98.

Jones, J. C. H. and Ferguson, D. G. (1988). 'Location and survival in the national hockey league'. *The Journal of Industrial Economics*, vol. 36, no. 4, pp. 443–57.

Kuypers, T. (1997). Unpublished PhD Thesis. University College London.

Noll, R. (ed) (1974). 'Government and the sports business'. Brookings Papers.

Peel, D. and Thomas, D. (1988). 'Outcome uncertainty and the demand for football'. *Scottish Journal of Political Economy*, vol. 35, pp. 242–9.

Restrictive Practices Court (1999). 'In the Matter of an Agreement between the Football Association Premier League Limited and the Football Association Limited and the Football League Limited and their Respective Member Clubs and in the Matter of an Agreement relating to the supply of services facilitating the broadcasting on television of Premier League football matches and the supply of services consisting in the broadcasting on television of such matches.' (28th July).

Quirk, J. and Fort, R. (1992). Pay Dirt: The Business of Professional Team Sports, New Jersey: Princeton University Press.

Sloane, P. J. (1971). 'The economics of professional football: the football club as a utility maximizer'. *Scottish Journal of Political Economy*, vol. 17, no. 2, pp. 121–46.

Szymanski, S. (1998). 'Hermetic leagues, open leagues and the impact of revenue sharing on competitive balance', paper submitted as evidence to the Restrictive Practices Court in the Premier League/Sky/BBC case.

Szymanski, S. and Kuypers, T. (1999). *Winners and Losers: The Business Strategy of Football*, Penguin Books.

Vrooman, J. (1995). 'A general theory of professional sports leagues'. *Southern Economic Journal*, vol. 61, no. 4, pp. 971–90.

Whitney, J. (1988). 'Winning games versus winning championships: the economics of fan interest and team performance'. *Economic Inquiry*, vol. 26, October, pp. 703–24.

[5]

The Economics of Promotion and Relegation in Sports Leagues

The Case of English Football

ROGER G. NOLL
Stanford University

In most of the world's professional sports leagues, the worst teams in better leagues are demoted while the best teams in weaker leagues are promoted. This article examines the economics of promotion and relegation, using data from English football (soccer). The crucial findings are as follows: players earn higher wages under promotion and relegation, promotion and relegation has a net positive effect on attendance, and the effect of promotion and relegation on competitive balance is ambiguous. The unbalancing effect arises because the system places some teams in leagues in which they have no realistic chance to afford a winning team, thereby causing teams to spend less on players during their (brief) stay in a higher league than they spent while trying to be promoted from as lesser league. The article concludes with an analysis of how promotion and relegation might be implemented in North America.

Unlike in the United States, most of the world's major professional sports leagues are not composed of a permanent roster of teams. Instead, major leagues promote and demote teams at the end of the season. The primary criterion for promotion and relegation is on-field success: The best teams in the highest ranking minor league are promoted to the major league, and the worst teams in the latter are reassigned to the former.[1] In larger countries, several lower leagues are organized hierarchically and the same promotion and relegation system applies down the line. In English football (soccer), for example, the hierarchy involves seven levels of leagues, and the bottom two levels are further divided into hierarchical divisions.

The primary difference between a system of leagues with fixed membership and a promotion/relegation system is that the latter permits a form of entry that is not feasible under the former. In leagues of fixed membership, entry occurs through expansion of a league or the formation of a new, competitive league. In the United

AUTHOR'S NOTE: *An earlier version of this article was presented at the annual meetings of the American Economic Association in January 2001.*

JOURNAL OF SPORTS ECONOMICS, Vol. 3 No. 2, May 2002   169–203

States, expansion has been the primary means of entry into major leagues, although at some time during the 20th century the four most popular team sports experienced successful entry in that at least some of teams in a new league merged into the established league.[2] Entry and exit of leagues are substantially more common for minor league sports.

To prospective entrants, expansion and league entry have disadvantages. Expansion requires super-majority approval from established teams and entails paying a substantial entrance fee. Entry by an entire league requires that the incumbent league has left several viable franchise locations unexploited and that several entrants—not just one—are willing to suffer significant financial losses in the early years while the new league becomes established.

Promotion and relegation do not rule out these forms of entry, but this system makes other forms of entry feasible. First, an entrepreneur can buy a minor league team, hire high-quality players and coaches, and earn promotion to a higher league. Second, an entrepreneur can form a new team, enter into the bottom league, and then gain promotion to higher levels. In both cases, after a few years of successful play a team can be promoted all the way to the major league, although in the case of de novo entry in England this strategy requires at least eight promotions and therefore takes at least a decade.

These forms of entry require no approval by, and no payment of expansion franchises to, existing major league teams.[3] The main disadvantages of this form of entry are that teams must start at the bottom rather than immediately enter at the league level that they seek and then must dominate lower leagues to gain promotion, which implies that they may have to field teams that are too good (and too expensive) for the leagues in which they play.

The purpose of this article is to explore how promotion and relegation affect the economics of a sports team and league. Two questions are theoretical: Under what conditions will leagues with promotion and relegation experience more entry? and How does promotion and relegation alter the business strategy of established teams and leagues? The other questions are empirical: Does promotion and relegation produce measurable effects on entry and operations? To answer the second set of questions, this article examines the history of English football.

To my knowledge, these issues have been addressed only in simultaneous research by Stefan Szymanski and his coauthors and the references therein (see Hall, Szymanski, & Zimbalist, 2002 [this issue] and the references therein). Ross and Szymanski (2000) present a theoretical model that predicts that promotion and relegation increase the incentive of teams to invest in team quality to the benefit of fans, and argue that U.S. leagues should be required to adopt promotion and relegation through antitrust action against these leagues for their practices regarding team territorial rights, expansion, relocation, and stadium financing. The economic arguments of Hall et al. (2002) have many similarities with those advanced in this article; however, this article takes a somewhat different approach and addresses some different questions.

THEORETICAL ISSUES

Entry in team sports has two distinct components. One is entry of a team into a specific location, and the other is a net increase in the number of teams that play in a league. Although the second type of entry requires the first, the first does not require the second. That is, a team can enter a particular location by changing the place it plays its home matches (relocation), or a new team can enter one location while an old team in another location exits the industry. For example, baseball's announced contraction plans may be combined with plans to enter lucrative new areas through expansion rather than relocation of its weakest franchises. Note that both relocation and promotion/relegation require entry and exit in different local markets. Alternatively, entry can cause a net increase in the number of teams (expansion, new leagues).

Promotion and relegation are a substitute for either relocation or expansion. In the first case, a higher league enters a new city (the home of the promoted team) while simultaneously exiting the home of the demoted team, whereas the lower league does the opposite. In the second case, a higher league promotes more teams than it demotes. If every league in the hierarchy follows this practice, the effect is net entry for the sport through the creation of new teams at the bottom of the hierarchy of leagues. Likewise, leagues can demote more teams than they promote as a means of contraction.

Team Strategies

The strategic decisions of a team are first whether to enter or exit the industry and then, conditional on entering (or not exiting), the level in the hierarchy of leagues to seek. The tactical decisions include picking the optimal team quality—that is, acquiring players and coaches of appropriate skill—to achieve the target league. Although the sequence of decisions is first to make the entry/exit decision, then the decision about league level, and finally a sequence of annual team quality decisions, logically each earlier decision is based on expectations about the financial consequences of later decisions, so it makes sense to discuss decisions about league attainment and team quality before examining the entry decision.

Team quality. The effects of promotion and relegation on team quality depend on how movement between leagues affects team profits. In principle, promotion and relegation can affect profits in two ways: A team's revenues and costs may differ in different leagues, and the presence of relegation and promotion may affect the interest of fans (and hence revenues).

Conceivably, good and bad teams could benefit from the promotion and relegation system. For the best teams, the reason is clear: Promotion is an additional reward for winning, and so conceivably can increase fan interest in games, assuming that fans prefer that their home team compete at a higher level. For the worst teams, the prospect of relegation also conceivably could increase interest because more is at stake in late-season games and because fans expect that in the next season the average quality of opponents may be lower. Whether these effects are present, of course, is an empirical matter, but if they are then sports that make use of promotion and relegation will earn higher revenues.

The other effect of promotion and relegation on team profits has to do with whether a team actually is better or worse off financially by being promoted to a higher league. To understand why promotion may not be profitable requires delving into the standard economic theory of a sports league. A sports team operates in two types of markets: a local market for selling tickets and concessions and a national or even international market for selling broadcast and licensing rights. In both cases, the demand for a team's products depends on its absolute quality, the quality of its opponents, and the team's tradition (or playing history). In addition, especially for local products, demand depends on exogenous demographic attributes of the city in which the team plays home games. In general, teams in more populous, wealthier markets will generate more revenue, holding constant the quality of the team and its opponents and the number and quality of its local competitors. All else being equal, a team in a better market will have a higher marginal revenue product of increments to team quality, so that teams that play in the best locations generally have a higher optimal quality than teams in worse locations.

Ignoring the possibility that the existence of the promotion and relegation system increases demand and taking as exogenous the number of teams in each league, the optimal distribution of teams among a hierarchy of leagues is for the best league to contain the teams that face the most intensive demand for the sport and for each league in the hierarchy to contain the teams with the best markets among those remaining after higher leagues have been filled. A promotion and relegation system forces a departure from the optimal allocation of teams at least half the time (and most likely virtually all of the time), given the unavoidable uncertainty associated with won-lost records during a league season as well as the requirement to relegate some teams even if the composition of the league is optimal. Thus, promotion/relegation inevitably has costs in terms of sportwide profitability.

Promotion and relegation reduce total revenues in a sport in the following way. When a team in a better market is demoted while a team in a worse market is promoted, all teams except the promoted team are likely to suffer financially. The demoted team will have an optimal relative quality in the lower league that is stronger than the team that was promoted, and so its demotion will reduce the expected won-loss record and hence the revenues of every team in the lower league. Likewise, the promoted team will have a lower optimal relative quality in the higher league than the team that was demoted. Hence, every other team in the higher league must play one home game with a team that has lower average quality than the team it replaced, causing each to have lower revenues. In both leagues, therefore, promotion/relegation reduces outcome uncertainty (competitive balance) and thereby reduces the demand for the other teams.

Although promotion/relegation inevitably creates a cost, this cost could be small. That is, if the differences in local market demand are small among a large number of teams, the revenue loss from distributing teams suboptimally is likely to be small and may be offset by the demand-enhancing effects of promotion and relegation as described above. Indeed, the most plausible explanation for the widespread adoption of promotion/relegation systems, given that they are certain to cause a suboptimal distribution of teams among leagues, is that the demand-enhancing effect is present and that differences in market conditions are small among lower echelon teams in a stronger league and higher echelon teams in a weaker league.

Although theory does not yield a robust qualitative prediction about the effect of promotion on a team's profits, a team in a lower league may have an incentive to seek promotion to a higher league than the one to which it would be assigned if the sport maximized joint profits. Whether such an incentive exists depends on two factors. One factor is the possibility that a promotion and relegation system causes an increase in the demand for games involving teams that are candidates to change leagues, as discussed above. The other factor is the effect of promotion on team-specific revenues and costs.

In general, promotion into a league that is too strong for the market in which the team is located will have two economic effects. On the plus side, because the team's opponents are better and the higher league receives more attention from the press (basically, free advertising), the demand for the team's products should increase. On the negative side, the optimal quality of the team will be higher in absolute terms but lower in relation to other teams in its league. Promotion increases the marginal revenue product of quality and so causes the team to spend more on players if it joins a higher league. But a team from a market that, under an optimal assignment of teams to leagues, would be assigned to the lower league will have a higher optimal relative quality in the lower league than its optimal relative quality in the better league. Thus, a team that should be in a lower league from the perspective of sportwide profit maximization expects to finish higher in the standings in the lower league but spend more money for players in the better league.

Whether promotion is profitable to a team, then, depends on the net effect of all of these factors. Specifically, are the benefits of promotion (more revenues from playing better opponents, more exposure, and the possible demand-enhancing effects of the prospect of promotion in the year in which promotion is earned and of demotion later when the team returns to its optimal league) greater or less than the costs (higher salaries and a lower finish in the better league)? As a practical matter, this question is empirical, not theoretical, but the answer almost certainly is in the affirmative, for teams never refuse to be promoted.

The last important effect of promotion/relegation is on the overall quality of play. This effect is apparent from a simplified model of a sports league, as initially developed by El Hodiri and Quirk (1974). Assume that teams face revenues, R, and costs that are a function of quality, q, that the revenue function, $R(q)$, displays diminishing returns to quality, that is, that $R'(q) > 0$ and $R''(q) < 0$, and that the cost function is simply the amount of quality times its unit cost, or wq.[4] Finally, assume that teams maximize net revenues.[5]

In a league of fixed membership, the team solves this problem separately each year, which can be written as

$$Max_q \{R(q) - wq\} \tag{1}$$

and which yields the familiar first-order condition that marginal revenue equals marginal cost:

$$R' - w = 0. \tag{2}$$

Note that this equation implies competitive imbalance among teams that operate in markets with different demand intensity.[6] Suppose that at average team quality, q^*, Team 1 has more intense demand for team quality than Team 2. In this case, net revenues will increase if a unit of player quality is transferred from Team 2 to Team 1. To obtain equilibrium in Equation 2, the better teams need to acquire more quality than teams in weaker markets to drive the marginal revenue product of quality to its unit cost in every market.

In a promotion/relegation system, this year's decision about team quality affects the league in which the team plays next year. Assume that the team has a probability p of being promoted and a probability r of being relegated, with $p' > 0$ and $r' < 0$, and that q^*, q^p, and q^r represent, respectively, expected optimal team quality if the team stays in the same league, is promoted, or is relegated. Then, letting i represent the rate of time preference, the team's profit maximization problem for this period must take into account these contingencies and becomes

$$Max \; R(q) - wq + (1 - i) \tag{3}$$
$$\left\{ p \left[R^p \left(q^p \right) - wq^p \right] + r \left[R^r \left(q^r \right) - wq^r \right] + (1 - p - r)[R(q^*) - wq^*] \right\}.$$

The first-order condition for this problem is

$$(R' - w) + (1 - i)(p'[R^p(q^p) - wq^p] + r'[R^r(q^r) - wq^r] - (p' + r')[R(q^*) - wq^*] = 0. \tag{4}$$

This equation contains the difference between marginal revenue and marginal cost this season (as above) plus the financial consequences of promotion and relegation. If playing in higher leagues is more profitable then the second term is positive, which means that the quality level that solves Equations 1 and 2 is too small to solve Equations 3 and 4. Thus, holding constant market conditions and team locations, teams seek higher quality under promotion and relegation than they would seek in leagues of fixed size if teams are more profitable in higher leagues.[7] In the top league, teams at the top of the standings face a very low value of r and $p = 0$, so the prospect of promotion and relegation has virtually no weight in Equation 4. Hence, the equilibrium spread in team quality in the top league is lower than it would be in a league of the same teams with fixed membership. In other words, the effect of promotion and relegation is to increase competitive balance in the top league among the teams that are members; however, because the teams in the top league may not be the optimal allocation of teams to that league, this effect could be offset by the presence of teams in weak markets that have low optimal relative quality in the top league.

The extent to which promotion/relegation improves the overall quality of play depends on the supply of inputs for all teams in the market. The assumption that the supply of inputs is not perfectly inelastic is unexceptional for all inputs except players. For players, supply elasticity has two elements. One component is related to whether children decide to devote themselves to developing their athletic skills and then, as teens, to launch a career in sports. Presumably this elasticity is tiny, especially in the short run. The other element is the nationwide supply of existing players to professional teams. Because soccer is the primary sport in much of the world (most of Europe, Latin America, and Africa), even for a soccer power like England the supply of professional soccer talent is likely to be reasonably elastic, although not perfectly so if players prefer to play in their home country. Hence, the preceding simple model yields two important conclusions:

1. Holding the demand for soccer constant across countries and team locations within those countries, a nation with promotion/relegation will have stronger teams than a nation with leagues of fixed size. For example, the primary soccer league in the United States, Major League Soccer (MLS), always will be weaker than the top European leagues even if soccer becomes as popular in the United States as it is in Europe because MLS does not practice promotion and relegation.
2. The adoption of a promotion/relegation system will increase the wages of players as long as the world supply of professional soccer players is not perfectly elastic. This effect is not due solely to the possibility that promotion/relegation may increase demand but is a consequence of the fact that expenditures on players today are an investment in that they are a cost of gaining entry into a better league (or of avoiding demotion to a lower league), which causes this year's players to have greater value than they would without promotion and relegation.

Entry and exit. The preceding model has implications with respect to the simultaneous entry of one city and exit of another in a league. Recall that promotion/relegation generates more of this form of entry and exit than does voluntary relocation in a league of fixed size. A team moves from one location to another while staying in the same league because it believes that the new location is sufficiently more

176   JOURNAL OF SPORTS ECONOMICS / May 2002

profitable that it will offset the costs of relocating. Because the cost of quality is the same in all locations, the source of profit differentials is differences in the intensity of demand. Hence, team relocation in closed leagues tends to be from weaker to stronger markets. By contrast, in a promotion/relegation system, a new city is added to a higher league because the team in that city does well on the field and perceives its profits to be enhanced by joining a better league, whereas the new city in the lower league is added coercively—the entrant has been forced to exit a more profitable league because of its poor on-field performance. In at least some cases, the demoted team would not want to relocate to the city of the team that replaced it through promotion/relegation.

Another form of entry into a league, whether from de novo creation of a new team or a permanent change in the league assignment of an existing team, arises when the entering team operates in a more lucrative local market than the worst existing team. Exogenous changes in the geographic distribution of people and wealth affect team revenue functions and so alter the set of optimal locations for teams in a league. In a world of perfect information, incumbent teams in a league would be able to identify these locations, and teams could relocate as soon as demographic shifts changed the list of optimal team locations. But if local market responsiveness in areas without a team is uncertain, local entrepreneurs plausibly can detect a favorable shift in local demand before teams that are located elsewhere. Under these conditions, an old team is likely to start to improve or a new team is likely to be formed in a growing local market before another existing team detects that the area is more profitable than its current location.

The preceding argument provides an unobvious economic explanation for a phenomenon that, among sports aficionados, is regarded as a cultural difference between North America and the rest of the world: In other nations, major league teams virtually never relocate. The absence of team movements is attributed to the deep roots that a team has in its local community and, as a result, the unacceptability of relocation to its fans—even in the United States, fans have deeply resented some relocations (e.g., the Brooklyn Dodgers and Cleveland Browns). In any case, this observation, if true, can be interpreted as an assertion that in most of the world relocation costs are higher relative to the costs of forming a new team than they are in the United States. De novo entry can be cheaper under promotion/relegation for two reasons: Expansion fees are avoided and information costs associated with assessing new markets may be lower for residents of an emerging market. Hence, the absence of team relocation is a plausible consequence of a system of promotion and relegation.

League strategies. The principal strategic decision of a league is to determine its size. The decision to expand is a response to growing demand, which makes an increasing number of locations viable franchise sites. But expansion is not usually in the interests of the most successful teams. Expansion entails increasing the number of teams in smaller markets that have no serious chance of winning a championship. Hence, on average, expansion reduces the average revenue of teams because it reduces the average market potential of teams and hence the average quality and consequentiality of matches. Moreover, expansion requires adding competitors in national markets like broadcasting and licensing or, if national rights are pooled by the league, sharing the revenues from these rights among more partners. Thus, if expansion teams have, on average, weaker demand than incumbents, expansion reduces the national revenue of incumbents.

For the most part, leagues expand not because doing so is in the best interests of incumbents but because they are forced to do so. One purpose of expansion is to inhibit entry by competitive leagues. Another purpose is to satisfy demands from political officials in return for their support for favorable policies regarding sports, such as favorable tax treatments, antitrust exemptions, and stadium subsidies.[8]

New leagues are formed to take advantage of two sources of excess demand for professional sports. First, monopoly leagues usually do not place multiple teams in areas in which demand is sufficient to support more than one or two teams and, by setting monopoly prices, undersupply demand for products in national markets, such as television broadcasts. Second, monopoly leagues typically do not place teams in all financially viable franchise locations.

In leagues of fixed size, both types of excess demand arise for three reasons. First, teams either have exclusive territorial rights or, collectively, teams in areas that could support entrants can veto territory-invading expansion or relocation if either requires a supermajority vote of incumbent teams. Second, incumbent leagues set a monopoly price for an expansion team that exceeds that which is justified by the revenue potential of some otherwise viable locations. Third, relocation costs and imperfect information prevent efficient team relocation and league identification of all financially attractive expansion sites. In deciding on expansion, then, leagues seek to balance the benefits to incumbents of expansion and a lower probability of successful entry by competitive leagues against the cost of adding to the number of teams in weak markets or increasing competition in strong markets. Inevitably, this calculation leads a monopoly league to be smaller than the number of teams that would exist under competition or the absence of league-created entry barriers.

The promotion/relegation system reduces pressures to expand by providing a mechanism whereby teams in markets that have become stronger due to demographic shifts can enter an established league. Promotion/relegation has two benefits to incumbents: The system creates a barrier to entry by new leagues into unoccupied attractive markets (a team in a lower league is already there and likely to seek promotion itself if the market warrants it) and it provides a mechanism for limiting the total number of teams in the league that play in weak markets. Whereas this system denies incumbents the opportunity to charge expansion fees, it compensates them by not forcing them to play more games against weak teams and to share national markets with more teams. But regardless of whether promotion/relegation is more or less profitable for the best teams than expansion, the one unambiguous prediction is that leagues using this system ought to be less inclined to expand.

The last effect of a decision to adopt promotion/relegation pertains to its effects on player costs. Abstracting from the demand-enhancing effects of the system, leagues have a good reason to adopt fixed membership—doing so reduces equilibrium quality and, if player supply is not perfectly elastic, player wages. Yet all major European soccer powers use promotion/relegation, which seems to be at odds with the assumption that leagues maximize profits.

Two explanations for this phenomenon are consistent with the standard economic model of a for-profit sports league.

First, until very recently, the world market for soccer players was monopsonized. Players were signed to their first contracts while still in their midteens, sometimes by an amateur or semiprofessional team that was owned and operated by the professional team in their home neighborhood. Subsequently, if a player switched teams after a contract expired, the new team was forced to pay compensation—a transfer fee—to the old team. For strong professional players, transfer fees typically ran in the millions of dollars, which was an order of magnitude more than the players' salaries. These fees applied to international transfers as well as movements within the same country and were enforced by the international governing body of soccer, the Federation Internationale de Football Associations (FIFA). Thus, secure monopsonization of the player market ensured that at least some of the demand-enhancing effect of promotion/relegation would be passed on to teams.

This explanation for promotion/relegation may have disappeared. In December 1995, the European Court held that the transfer fee system violated the single-market principle by inhibiting free movement of labor (see Jeanrenaud & Késenne, 1999). As a result, European players can move freely within Europe after their contracts expire. The industry is seeking special legislation from the European Union to allow the monopsony in the player market to be reinstated, but if this fails then the transfer fee rules throughout the world are very likely to disappear, causing the market for the best players to become competitive.

A second explanation for the dominance of promotion/relegation arises from the fact that an extremely lucrative part of professional soccer is international matches, especially between the best teams in the top leagues. In Europe, the top teams in national Division 1 leagues qualify for the Champions League in the following season, which involves playing several very lucrative matches. Leagues want their best teams to be competitive in the Champions League to make participation in these matches more profitable. Hence, it makes sense to adopt a system that, all else equal, produces stronger teams. Thus, adoption of promotion/relegation is much like an arms race: Conceivably, all teams and top leagues would be better off without it, but once one nation adopts the system, the others have a financial incentive to follow.

THE ENGLISH NATIONWIDE FOOTBALL LEAGUE

England is widely regarded as having one of the most successful sports leagues in the world—the English Premier League. For the league as a whole, average revenues per team in 1999-2000 exceeded $50 million, and average accounting profits per team were about $5 million (for data sources, see the appendix). At present, 10 members of the Premier League and 7 members of Division 1 are publicly traded corporations. Together, these 17 teams had a market capitalization in 2000 of more than $3 billion, or about $200 million each. The market cap of the most successful team, Manchester United, hovers around $1 billion, making it among the two or three most valuable sports franchises in the world. Thus, the English Premier League is roughly comparable to Major League Baseball (MLB), the National Basketball Association (NBA), and probably behind only the National Football League (NFL) in profits per team and average franchise value, while its best teams are comparable to the best in any league, including the NFL.

The basic institutional structure of English football has been stable for several decades. As in all countries, the overall governing body for English soccer is FIFA, located in Switzerland. FIFA determines the eligibility of teams and players for international competitions, such as the World Cup, and insists that internationally sanctioned teams must play only other sanctioned teams or else they and their players lose eligibility for international competition. Because international competition is very important to players and teams, this sanctioning power enables FIFA to regulate the business activities of soccer.

Below FIFA is the Union of European Football Associations (UEFA), which sets rules for European Football that are not dictated by FIFA, organizes international competitions within Europe, and supervises national football organizations. The Football Association (FA) represents all of the British Isles in UEFA, including Ireland as well as England, Northern Ireland, Scotland, and Wales. Each of these political jurisdictions has its own top (Division 1) league, its own hierarchy of minor leagues, and its own national team for competing in the World Cup, the Olympics, and other international championships. The FA sanctions and governs all professional and amateur football leagues and teams in the British Isles.

The Premier League stands at the top of the hierarchy of English leagues. Below it three other leagues collectively are called the Nationwide Football League and individually were called Divisions 2, 3, and 4 until 1992 but since have been called Divisions 1, 2, and 3. Historically, all four leagues collectively were called the Nationwide Football League until 1983, when the leagues began to sell their names to corporate sponsors. The leagues were known as the Canon League Divisions 1 through 4 from 1983-1986, the Today League in 1986-1987, and the Barclays League from 1987-1992, when the Premier League decided to withdraw from the Nationwide Football League. In the 1992-1993 season, the lower leagues became Divisions 1, 2, and 3 and retained the name Barclays League, whereas the top league became the English Football Association Premier League. In 1993, the top league sold its name to Carling and has been known as the Carling Premier League since. Meanwhile, Divisions 1 through 3 were the Endsleigh League from 1993 to 1996 but have been just the Nationwide Football League since then. To avoid confusion, the names of leagues herein will be simply Premier and Division 1, 2, and 3 for all historical periods.

Beneath these leagues are a large number of lesser clubs and leagues. The highest ranking of the remaining leagues is the Nationwide Conference. Several teams in the Conference have played in the Nationwide Football League and even the Premier League in the past. Although teams in the Conference and below must not be fully professional they can pay players, and many aspire to membership in the top four leagues and so employ several players who are sufficiently talented that they could play for a team in one of the top four professional leagues. Below the Nationwide Conference are three leagues of roughly equal stature: the Unibond League, the Dr. Martens League, and the Ryman Football League. Unibond has two divisions (premier and first), Dr. Martens has three (premier and coequal eastern and western divisions), and Rymans has four (premier, first, second, and third divisions). Finally, below these leagues are 22 "nonleague" leagues, several of which are further divided into hierarchical divisions. As one proceeds down the list, rules about paying players become increasingly restrictive.

At each stage of the hierarchy, leagues engage in promotion and relegation. In addition to promotion and relegation between adjacent pairs of the four top leagues, since 1987 Division 3 usually has exchanged one team per year with the Nationwide Conference while the latter drops three teams each year and accepts one team each from the premier divisions of Unibond, Dr. Martens, and Ryman. These leagues, in turn, exchange teams with the leagues below them, and the lowest ranking divisions in these three leagues exchange teams with the top regional "nonleague" leagues.

Entry

The purpose of this section is to examine entry and exit in the top four English leagues to see if this history supports the theoretical arguments about the effect of promotion and relegation on entry into a major league and to determine the extent to which promotion and relegation cause instability in league membership through entry and exit. To summarize, the core predictions of the theory of a sports league are that the system of promotion and relegation reduces the rate of expansion and the entry of new major leagues but provides opportunities for new teams to enter or for teams in more rapidly growing markets to improve their quality and earn promotion while teams in declining markets gradually descend the hierarchy of leagues.

Unfortunately, the effect of promotion and relegation on the entry of new leagues is not observable because of the institutional rules of football. In England, as elsewhere, entry of top-ranking leagues is essentially impossible in the present environment. One of FIFA's rules is that if a national team or any professional and amateur team wants to compete internationally, whether in major championships or just friendly (exhibition) matches, it must have a national governing body that enforces FIFA rules, grants franchises to leagues and teams, and certifies the eligibility of players. Another FIFA policy is that each country should have only one major league, usually called Division 1, although in England it has been called the Premier League since 1992. In the United States, MLS is the designated Division 1 league. Thus, entry of competing major leagues is precluded because FIFA and the English soccer authority are unlikely to sanction one. Nevertheless, FIFA and its subsidiary bodies (including the FA and the U.S. Soccer Federation) do allow entry of competing minor leagues. In England, monopoly leagues occupy the first five levels of the hierarchy, but the lower levels have competitive leagues.

An important aspect of the history of English football is that neither leagues nor the FA recognizes territorial rights. Teams can form anywhere, can move their home venues, and can be promoted into a league with a nearby local competitor. The only limitations are league rules regarding the suitability of a playing site in terms of the size and quality of the field and stadium. Because territorial rights are not enforced, large cities have many teams. From 1990-1991 to 2001-2002, 18 of the 36 teams that have played in the Premier League come from multiteam markets. London alone is home to 10 teams that played in the Premier League during this period, and Liverpool, Manchester, Nottingham, and Sheffield have had 2 Premier League members each. By contrast, the much larger United States has only four multiteam markets in the major leagues (and none in MLS): New York in all four major sports (baseball, basketball, football, and hockey), Los Angeles in three sports, San Francisco in two sports, and Chicago in one sport. Only New York has three teams in one sport (hockey). The absence of territorial rights reduces the "big market, small market" demand disparity; however, this check is limited because the most successful teams enjoy some immunity to competition due to the fan attachments that they have accumulated during their histories.

Early in the history of English football the primary mechanism for entry was the creation of new leagues to increase the number of levels in the hierarchy, but expansion of existing leagues also was important. The Premier League was organized in 1888 as a league of 12 teams, and in 1891 it expanded to 14. In 1892, Division 1 entered with 16 teams, and promotion and relegation began at the end of its first season. In 1893 and 1894, 2 Division 1 teams were promoted to the Premier League while only 1 team was relegated, thereby expanding the Premier League to 15 and then 16 teams. In 1893 and 1894, Division 1 added 1 team to retain its size of 16. In 1898, both leagues expanded to 18. The Premier League did so by promoting 2 teams while relegating none, whereas Division 1 simply expanded by 4. In 1905, both leagues expanded to 20 in the same fashion. World War I interrupted play from 1915 to 1919, but when play resumed both leagues expanded to 22 teams, a gain of 4 per league. This expansion was the last for the upper echelon of English football, for the combined size of these two leagues has remained at 44 teams ever since.

Division 2 was created in 1920 with 22 teams, and then in 1921 expanded to two leagues, a northern branch of 20 teams and a southern branch of 22. Both leagues were included in the promotion/relegation system as the league champion in each branch was promoted while the 2 worst teams in Division 1 were demoted. Two years later, the northern branch expanded to 22 teams. Thus, in 1923, the top four English football leagues included 88 teams, compared to 92 today. In essence, the size of top professional football in England has remained roughly the same for more than three fourths of a century.

Except for 1931-1932, when the north branch of Division 2 had 21 teams after one of its members folded, all leagues remained at these sizes until after World War II. Play again was suspended during the war, from three games into the season in 1939 to the fall of 1946. When play resumed, all four leagues reentered with exactly the same size and composition. The last expansion was in 1950, when the two branches of Division 2 expanded to 24 teams each and the Nationwide Football League reached its current size of 92 members.

Of the 92 positions in the top four English leagues that were created between 1888 and 1950, 70 slots arose from entry of new leagues and 22 represent expansion of existing leagues. For more than 50 years thereafter, no net entry has occurred, either from new leagues at this level of quality or expansion of existing leagues. The economic growth of the past 50 years, the arrival of television with its new major source of revenues, the creation of lucrative international competitions for professional teams, and the boom in sports since the mid-1970s have substantially increased the demand for English football and the revenues of the teams. But this growth in demand has not led to growth in the number of teams in the top four professional leagues. By contrast, the number of teams in the four major professional sports in the United States has more than doubled in this period. Nine new leagues have entered, six of which have survived by being merged into the established league, and all four leagues have added expansion teams every few years since the 1960s. Thus, for more than half a century, the behavior of the top four leagues in England and the four American major leagues is consistent with the theoretical prediction that a system of promotion and relegation reduces the propensity of new leagues to enter and old leagues to expand.

Two major changes since 1950 have diminished effective quality-adjusted supply. The first was the restructuring of Division 2 in 1958, when Division 3 was created by demoting half the teams in the two branches of Division 2. The second was the contraction of the Premier League from 22 to 20 teams. The Premier League shrunk from 22 teams in 1986-1987 to 21 in 1987-1988 to 20 in 1988-1989, but then in 1991-1992 it temporarily returned to 22. Then, after it withdrew from the Nationwide Football League, the Premier League shrunk back to 20 in 1995-1996, where it remains today. These changes were undertaken by promoting and demoting different numbers of teams.

The main benefit of promotion and relegation is that it enables entry of teams into high-quality leagues; however, extensive entry is not guaranteed. Instead, the same small core group of teams could simply rotate membership in the leagues, with neither entry nor exit among this group. The following review of the history of promotion and relegation practices in England shows that a core group of teams tends to dominate the Premier League but that the system of promotion and relegation has produced considerable instability in about one third of Premier League membership and in the membership of lower leagues.

The effect of the promotion/relegation system has varied greatly during the history of English football because the number of teams promoted each year has changed many times. The standard practice from 1893 through 1970 was to demote 2 Premier League teams and to promote 2 Division 1 teams each year. Since the 1970s, the standard practice has been to promote and demote 3 teams. Likewise, the number of teams demoted from Division 1 and promoted from Division 2 initially was 1, but when two Division 2 leagues were created, Division 1 promoted the winner of both Division 2 leagues. After Division 2 placed half its teams in Division 3, promotion and relegation between Divisions 1 and 2 involved 3 teams from each league. When Division 2 north and south became Divisions 2 and 3, these leagues immediately began to promote and relegate 4 teams each year.

Another important changing feature of English football is the mechanism for relegating teams out of Division 3. From the formation of the Premier League in 1888 through the 2001-2002 season, 127 different teams have played in at least one of the four top leagues. Of these, two losses from the roster of teams were due to mergers, so 94 of the 127-member teams are now in one of the four leagues. Thus, the number of teams that have entered and exited the four-league structure is 33 during 103 seasons, or fewer than 1 new team every 3 years.

In its first 45 years (through 1932), the number of teams that left the four-league structure was 18, or 1 team every 2.5 years. Then, between 1932 and 1950, no teams left the four leagues. Thus, the four Nationwide Football League divisions were a closed league between 1932 and 1950, which is also the last year in which the Nationwide League expanded.

Beginning with the 1950-1951 season, formal promotion and relegation occasionally took place but not on a regular basis. Division 3 does not automatically relegate and promote a team every year. Instead, the members of the Nationwide Football League decide whether to demote a team and promote another at the end of the season, based on on-field and financial performance and the suitability of a team's venue. In some cases the demoted team is not the team that finished at the bottom of Division 3.

The first postwar relegation from Division 3 occurred in 1951, when New Brighton was relegated. The next demotion took place in 1960, with the loss of Gateshead. During the 1961-1962 season, Accrington Stanley withdrew from the league after 33 games (of a scheduled 46). Thus, between 1950 and 1970, 3 teams left the Nationwide League, or 1 every 7 years, which is a much slower rate of turnover than occurred between 1888 and 1932.

184   JOURNAL OF SPORTS ECONOMICS / May 2002

Relegation from Division 3 became more common in the 1970s. Bradford Park Avenue, which had once been a member of the Premier League, was removed from Division 3 in 1970, and additional teams were removed in 1972 and 1977. After another hiatus, 1 team per year was removed from 1987 until 1990, then none in 1991. In 1992, 2 teams voluntarily withdrew from Division 3, followed by 1 relegation in 1993. After the Premier League declared its independence from the other leagues and decided to contract, relegation from Division 3 ceased during the ensuing adjustment period, but annual relegation began again in 1997. Thus, between 1951 and 2001, 18 teams were promoted to Division 3 from the Nationwide Football Conference, of which 15 took slots made available by relegation and 3 replaced a squad that withdrew. Twelve promotions have occurred since 1987, or about 4 every 5 years, which is the fastest turnover rate by simultaneous entry and exit since the 1920s and early 1930s.

The effect of entry in the postwar era on the upper two leagues has not been very substantial. Including the 4 expansion teams of 1950, 22 teams have been promoted to Division 3 since 1950 (including Colchester United twice, for a total of 23 promotions). Among these, only Wimbledon, which was promoted to Division 3 in 1977, has ascended to the Premier League. Five of the 21 have been promoted to Division 1. Among the 1950 expansion teams, 3 (Gillingham, Scunthorpe, and Shrewsbury) played several years in Division 1, whereas Colchester United has divided its time roughly equally between Divisions 2 and 3 (with 2 years, 1990-1992, in the Conference). Peterborough United (1960) and Oxford United (1962) also have ascended to Division 1. No team that has been promoted from the Conference after 1977 has played in Division 1.

Nine of the 21 teams that have entered since 1950 have been relegated back to the Conference. Barnet, Hereford United, Maidstone United, Scarborough, and Workington were relegated from Division 3 and never returned, whereas Colchester United, Darlington, Halifax Town, and Lincoln City were relegated and then promoted back. These 9 and 7 other teams that have been promoted to Division 3 have either stayed there or peaked at Division 2, although 5 of these have entered since 1997 and so have not had much time to ascend the hierarchy.

In half a century, promotion and relegation between Division 3 and the Nationwide Conference has brought 19 teams into the Nationwide Football League. The net effect of the promotion/relegation system has been to change the identities of 13 of the 92 members of the top four leagues because 3 teams quit Division 3 voluntarily and 3 more were relegated and then promoted back. Ten of these 13 additions thus far involve switches in the composition of only the bottom two leagues.

The teams that have been promoted to Division 3 from the Conference are not recent entrants into football. Of the 92 teams in the top four leagues in 2001-2002, 71 were formed in the 19th century. The youngest teams are Colchester United (formed in 1937), Peterborough United (formed in 1934), and Wigan Athletic (formed in 1932), although several have undergone reorganizations or mergers since they were founded. Wimbledon, which has the most recent rise from entry into Division 3 in 1977 to Premier League membership in 1992, was founded in 1889 as an amateur squad and then began its climb up the hierarchy when it became professional in 1964, rising to Division 3 in 13 years and the Premier League in 15 more.

The most recent entrant to Division 3, Rushden and Diamonds, reveals the more typical pattern of team improvement. Rushden Town was formed in 1889 and Irthlingborough Diamonds was formed in 1947. In 1992, the teams merged under a new leader, Max Griggs of the R. Griggs Group that manufactures Dr. Martens footware and sponsors a minor league that feeds the Nationwide Conference. The team then began its ascent up the hierarchy, reaching Division 3 in 9 years.[9]

The remarkable aspect of the nature and effects of entry into the Nationwide Football League is that it implies relatively little change in the optimal composition of the four top professional leagues for a half century and virtually no change in the optimal composition of the top two leagues. Examination of the histories of the older teams, however, reveals substantial change in the composition of the four leagues among the 70 teams that have belonged to the Nationwide Football League continuously since the end of the war.

The history of the Premier League reveals two core facts. First, a few teams have rarely spent any significant time out of the Premier League and account for most of its championships. Second, there is considerable turnover in Premier League membership among teams that are not frequent challengers for the Premier League championship.

Premier League championships have been relatively concentrated. A total of 61 teams played in the Premier League between 1888-1889 and 2000-2001, and 23 have won the championship. Whereas only about one third of the teams that played in the Premier League and one sixth of all Nationwide Football League members have won a championship, the number of different champions exceeds the current membership of the league (20) and its peak membership (22).

Because of war interruptions, the Premier League crowned 102 champions in the 113 years between 1888-1889 and 2000-2001. Eight teams—Liverpool (18), Manchester United (14), Arsenal (11), Everton (9), Aston Villa (7), Sunderland (6), Newcastle United (4), and Sheffield Wednesday (4)—account for more than 70% of these championships. Moreover, all of these teams have been in either the Premier League or Division 1 for nearly every season in the 20th century. Everton has spent 99 of its 103 seasons in the Premier League, having last played in Division 1 in 1953-1954, and Arsenal has played in the Premier League every year since 1919. Manchester United has missed 2 Premier League seasons since 1936.

The original 12 members of the Premier League have proven to be very durable participants at the top level of English football. Five were members of the Premier League in 2001-2002: Aston Villa, Blackburn Rovers, Bolton Wanderers, Derby County, and Everton. Four were in Division 1 in 2001-2002: Burnley, Preston North

186   JOURNAL OF SPORTS ECONOMICS / May 2002

End, West Bromwich Albion, and Wolverhampton Wanderers. Two original members played in Divison 2 (Notts County and Stoke City), and 1 (Accrington) was disbanded in 1893 after 5 years in the Premier League.

Table 1 lists all members of the Premier League during its history. The 8 most frequent members were members of the Premier League or Division 1 in the 19th century. Of the 20 Premier League members in 2001-2002, 9 rank among the top 10 teams in total appearances in the league and 16 rank among the top 25. The 2001-2002 team with the fewest Premier League years is Fulham at 13, and the 2001-2002 member with the fewest number of years in the four top leagues is Ipswich Town with 57. Finally, of the 61 teams that have played at least once in the Premier League, only one no longer exists (Accrington). Three others are no longer in any of the top four leagues but play in lower leagues: Bradford Park Avenue (Unibond Divison 1), Darwen (First North Western Train League Division 2), and Glossop North End (First North Western Train League Division 1).

Table 2 shows the composition of the Premier League since the 1990-1991 season. A total of 36 teams have played in the Premier League during these 12 years, when the league varied in size between 20 and 22 teams. As is summarized in Table 3, the teams that played in the Premier League fall into three basic categories: a core of more or less permanent members, a group that is referred to as yo-yo teams because they move up and down with regularity, and a group of teams that only occasionally make the Premier League (and then for only 1 or 2 years).

In the first group are 9 teams that played in the league all 12 seasons since 1990 and 5 more that played between 9 and 11 seasons. Thus, of the 20 current slots in the Premier League, 13 slots (on average) are occupied by 14 teams that constitute the core membership. Another 12 teams spent between 4 and 8 years in the Premier League during this period, and these constitute the yo-yo group. Finally, 10 more teams spent 3 or fewer years in the Premier League. These teams tended to be very inconsistent in their play, as 8 of the 10 also played in Division 2 during the decade compared to only 1 of the yo-yo group. Indeed, 2 of these 8 (Fulham and Notts County) played in all four leagues in 12 years.

The top 10 teams in the 1990s have had a very long run. During the past 25 years, 5 of these teams (Arsenal, Everton, Liverpool, Manchester United, and Tottenham Hotspur) have played every season in the Premier League. Among the other 5, Aston Villa spent 1986-1987 in Division 1, Chelsea and Leeds spent several years in Division 1 in the 1980s, Southampton had a similar spell in the 1970s, and Coventry City was relegated to Division 1 in 2001 for the first time since 1966-1967.

The histories of the group of recent occasional Premier League teams reveals the most interesting aspect of entry and exit in the promotion/relegation system, which is the inconsistency of many of the teams.

The Bolton Wanderers were an original member of the Premier League in 1888 and were a fixture into the 1960s. With the exception of a brief visit to the Premier League in the late 1970s, the team then sank into the lower divisions, and as late as

TABLE 1:   English Premier League Composition, 1888-2002

| Team | Number of Years | | Team | Number of Years | |
	Premier League	Football League		Premier League	Football League
Everton[a]	99	103	Blackpool	27	95
Aston Villa[a]	91	103	Ipswich Town[a]	26	57
Liverpool[a]	87	98	Portsmouth	26	75
Arsenal[a]	85	98	Bury	22	97
Manchester United[a]	77	99	Charlton Athletic[a]	21	74
Sunderland[a]	74	101	Norwich City	20	75
Manchester City	73	99	Queen's Park Rangers	20	75
Newcastle United[a]	72	98	Luton Town	16	78
Chelsea[a]	67	86	Cardiff City	15	75
Tottenham Hotspur[a]	67	83	Wimbledon	14	26
West Bromwich Albion	68	103	Fulham[a]	13	84
Sheffield Wednesday	66	99	Bradford City	12	88
Derby County[a]	64	103	Crystal Palace	12	75
Bolton Wanderers[a]	63	103	Grimsby Town	12	98
Blackburn Rovers[a]	62	103	Oldham Athletic	12	84
Sheffield United	59	99	Bristol City	9	90
Wolverhampton Wanderers	59	103	Watford	7	75
Nottingham Forest	56	99	Accrington[b]	5	5
Middlesbrough[a]	53	92	Brentford	5	75
Stoke City	52	85	Brighton/Hove Albion	4	75
Burnley	51	103	Bradford Park Avenue[c]	3	51
Birmingham City	50	99	Oxford United	3	40
Leeds United[a]	48	75	Darwen[c]	2	8
West Ham United[a]	47	76	Millwall	2	75
Preston North End	46	103	Swansea City	2	75
Leicester City[a]	45	97	Barnsley	1	93
Coventry City	34	76	Carlisle United	1	67
Southampton[a]	32	75	Glossop North End[c]	1	17
Huddersfield Town	30	81	Leyton Orient	1	86
Notts County	30	103	Northampton Town	1	75
			Swindon Town	1	75

a. Premier League members from 2001-2002.
b. Disbanded.
c. Now play in lower classification leagues.

1987-1988 was playing in Division 3. The team then revived, climbing back to regain Premier League membership in 1995-1996. Bolton is now a yo-yo team, spending 3 of the past 7 years in the Premier League and 4 in Division 1.

Notts County is another original member of the Premier League that spent most of its time in either the Premier League or Division 1 before World War II but after-

TABLE 2:   League Composition in British Football From 1990-1991 to 2001-2002

Team	Teams With Premier League Status											
	1990	1991	1992	1993	1994	1995	1996	1997	1998	1999	2000	2001
Arsenal	P	P	P	P	P	P	P	P	P	P	P	P
Aston Villa	P	P	P	P	P	P	P	P	P	P	P	P
Barnsley	1	1	1	1	1	1	1	P	1	1	1	1
Blackburn Rovers	1	1	P	P	P	P	P	P	P	1	1	P
Bolton Wanderers	2	2	2	1	1	P	1	P	1	1	1	P
Bradford City	2	2	2	2	2	2	1	1	1	P	P	1
Charlton Athletic	1	1	1	1	1	1	1	1	P	1	P	P
Chelsea	P	P	P	P	P	P	P	P	P	P	P	P
Coventry City	P	P	P	P	P	P	P	P	P	P	P	1
Crystal Palace	P	P	P	1	P	1	1	P	1	1	1	1
Derby County	P	1	1	1	1	1	P	P	P	P	P	P
Everton	P	P	P	P	P	P	P	P	P	P	P	P
Fulham	2	2	2	2	3	3	3	2	2	1	1	P
Ipswich Town	1	1	P	P	P	1	1	1	1	1	P	P
Leeds United	P	P	P	P	P	P	P	P	P	P	P	P
Leicester City	1	1	1	1	P	1	P	P	P	P	P	P
Liverpool	P	P	P	P	P	P	P	P	P	P	P	P
Luton Town	P	P	1	1	1	1	2	2	2	2	2	3
Manchester City	P	P	P	P	P	P	1	1	2	1	P	1
Manchester United	P	P	P	P	P	P	P	P	P	P	P	P
Middlesbrough	1	1	P	1	1	P	P	1	P	P	P	P
Newcastle United	1	1	1	P	P	P	P	P	P	P	P	P
Norwich City	P	P	P	P	P	1	1	1	1	1	1	1
Nottingham Forest	P	P	P	1	P	P	P	1	P	1	1	1
Notts County	1	P	1	1	1	2	2	3	2	2	2	2
Oldham Athletic	1	P	P	P	1	1	1	2	2	2	2	2
Queen's Park Rangers	P	P	P	P	P	P	1	1	1	1	1	2
Sheffield United	P	P	P	P	1	1	1	1	1	1	1	1
Sheffield Wednesday	1	P	P	P	P	P	P	P	P	P	1	1
Southampton	P	P	P	P	P	P	P	P	P	P	P	P
Sunderland	P	1	1	1	1	1	P	1	1	P	P	P
Swindon Town	1	1	1	P	1	2	1	1	1	1	2	2
Tottenham Hotspur	P	P	P	P	P	P	P	P	P	P	P	P
Watford	1	1	1	1	1	1	2	1	1	P	1	1
West Ham United	1	P	1	P	P	P	P	P	P	P	P	P
Wimbledon	P	P	P	P	P	P	P	P	P	P	1	1

NOTE: P = Premier League, 1 = Division 1, 2 = Division 2, and 3 = Division 3.

TABLE 3:   Concentration in Premier League Membership, 1991-2002

Number of Years in Premier League	Number of Teams	Team Name
12	9	Arsenal, Aston Villa, Chelsea, Everton, Leeds United, Liverpool, Manchester United, Southampton, and Tottenham Hotspur
11	1	Coventry City
10	2	Wimbledon and West Ham United
9	2	Newcastle United and Sheffield Wednesday
8	1	Blackburn Rovers
7	5	Derby County, Leicester City, Manchester City, Middlesbrough, and Nottingham Forest
6	1	Queen's Park Rangers
5	4	Crystal Palace, Ipswich Town, Norwich City, and Sunderland
4	1	Sheffield United
3	3	Bolton Wanderers, Charlton Athletic, and Oldham Athletic
2	2	Bradford City and Luton Town
1	5	Barnsley, Fulham, Notts County, Swindon Town, and Watford

ward sank all the way to Division 3. Since then it has ascended to the Premier League twice, once in the early 1980s and again in the early 1990s; however, between 1992 and 1998 it fell all the way back to Division 3, then climbed back to Division 2.

Watford spent most of the 1950s, 1960s, and 1970s in Division 2, then in the late 1970s began to improve until, in the mid-1980s, it played in the Premier League. Demoted to Division 1 in 1988, the team sank to Division 2 in 1997; however, after being purchased by pop star Elton John, the team climbed back for a 1-year stay in the Premier League in 1999-2000.

Table 4 summarizes the league memberships for the past 11 years of the teams that did not play in the Premier League during the 1990s. During this period, the three lower divisions contained between 72 and 74 teams. A total of 90 teams played in one of these divisions during the period, and 63 of these did not play in the Premier League. Only 4 of these 63 teams played in the same league for all 11 years: Portsmouth and Wolverhampton in Division 1, AFC Bournemouth in Division 2, and Rochdale in Division 3. Fifteen teams played in all three leagues, and 4 more played in Divisions 2 and 3 plus the lower minor leagues. The remaining 40 teams played in two leagues (possibly including the Nationwide Conference). By contrast, of the 36 teams that played in the Premier League during this period, 9 played every season in the Premier League and 17 others played only in the Premier League and Division 1. Eight teams played in three leagues and 2 played in four. Thus, the teams that make the Premier League tend to be more consistent in quality than the teams that either never or only rarely make the Premier League.

190 JOURNAL OF SPORTS ECONOMICS / May 2002

TABLE 4: League Composition in British Football, 1991-2002

Team	Other Football League Teams										
	1991	*1992*	*1993*	*1994*	*1995*	*1996*	*1997*	*1998*	*1999*	*2000*	*2001*
AFC Bournemouth	2	2	2	2	2	2	2	2	2	2	2
Aldershot	3	a	a	a	a	a	a	a	a	a	a
Barnet	3	3	2	3	3	3	3	3	3	3	a
Birmingham City	2	1	1	2	1	1	1	1	1	1	1
Blackpool	3	2	2	2	2	2	2	2	2	3	2
Brentford	2	1	2	2	2	2	2	3	2	2	2
Brighton/Hove Albion	1	2	2	2	2	3	3	3	3	3	2
Bristol City	1	1	1	1	2	2	2	1	2	2	2
Bristol Rovers	1	1	2	2	2	2	2	2	2	2	3
Burnley	3	2	2	1	2	2	2	2	2	1	1
Bury	2	3	3	3	3	2	1	1	2	2	2
Cambridge United	1	1	2	2	3	3	3	3	2	2	2
Cardiff City	3	3	2	2	3	3	3	3	2	3	2
Carlisle United	3	3	3	3	2	3	2	3	3	3	3
Cheltenham Town	a	a	a	a	a	a	a	a	3	3	3
Chester City	2	2	3	2	3	3	3	3	3	a	a
Chesterfield	3	3	3	3	2	2	2	2	2	3	2
Colchester United	a	3	3	3	3	3	3	2	2	2	2
Crewe Alexandra	3	3	3	2	2	2	1	1	1	1	1
Darlington	2	3	3	3	3	3	3	3	3	3	3
Doncaster Rovers	3	3	3	3	3	3	3	a	a	a	a
Exeter City	2	2	2	3	3	3	3	3	3	3	3
Gillingham	3	3	3	3	3	2	2	2	2	1	1
Grimsby Town	1	1	1	1	1	1	2	1	1	1	1
Halifax Town	3	3	a	a	a	a	a	3	3	3	3
Hartlepool United	2	2	2	3	3	3	3	3	3	3	3
Hereford United	3	3	3	3	3	3	a	a	a	a	a
Huddersfield Town	2	2	2	2	1	1	1	1	1	1	2
Hull City	2	2	2	2	2	3	3	3	3	3	3
Kidderminster Harriers	a	a	a	a	a	a	a	a	a	3	3
Leyton Orient	2	2	2	2	3	3	3	3	3	3	3
Lincoln City	3	3	3	3	3	3	3	2	3	3	3
Macclesfield Town	a	a	a	a	a	a	3	2	3	3	3
Maidstone United	3	a	a	a	a	a	a	a	a	a	a
Mansfield Town	3	2	3	3	3	3	3	3	3	3	3
Millwall	1	1	1	1	1	2	2	2	2	2	1
Northampton Town	3	3	3	3	3	3	2	2	3	2	2
Oxford United	1	1	1	2	2	1	1	1	2	2	3
Peterborough United	2	1	1	2	2	2	3	3	3	2	2
Plymouth Argyle	1	2	2	2	3	2	2	3	3	3	3
Portsmouth	1	1	1	1	1	1	1	1	1	1	1
Port Vale	1	2	2	1	1	1	1	1	1	2	2
Preston North End	2	2	3	3	3	2	2	2	2	1	1
Reading	2	2	2	1	1	1	1	2	2	2	2
Rochdale	3	3	3	3	3	3	3	3	3	3	3

TABLE 4:   Continued

Team	Other Football League Teams										
	1991	1992	1993	1994	1995	1996	1997	1998	1999	2000	2001
Rotherham United	3	2	2	2	2	2	3	3	3	2	1
Rushden & Diamonds	a	a	a	a	a	a	a	a	a	a	3
Scarborough	3	3	3	3	3	3	3	3	a	a	a
Scunthorpe United	3	3	3	3	3	3	3	3	2	3	3
Shrewsbury Town	2	3	3	2	2	2	3	3	3	3	3
Southend United	1	1	1	1	1	1	2	3	3	3	3
Stockport County	2	2	2	2	2	2	1	1	1	1	1
Stoke City	2	2	1	1	1	1	1	2	2	2	2
Swansea City	2	2	2	2	2	3	3	3	3	2	3
Torquay United	2	3	3	3	3	3	3	3	3	3	3
Tranmere Rovers	1	1	1	1	1	1	1	1	1	1	2
Walsall	3	3	3	3	2	2	2	2	1	2	1
West Bromwich Albion	2	2	1	1	1	1	1	1	1	1	1
Wigan Athletic	2	2	3	3	3	3	2	2	2	2	2
Wolverhampton Wanderers	1	1	1	1	1	1	1	1	1	1	1
Wrexham	3	3	2	2	2	2	2	2	2	2	2
Wycombe Wanderers	a	a	3	2	2	2	2	2	2	2	2
York City	3	3	2	2	2	2	2	2	3	3	3

NOTE: 1 = Division 1, 2 = Division 2, and 3 = Division 3. Since the 1992-1993 season, the professional soccer leagues in England have been named the Premier League and Divisions 1, 2, and 3. During the 1992 season and before, the same leagues were named Divisions 1, 2, 3, and 4. To avoid confusion, the new league names have been applied to 1992.
a. Not a member of the Nationwide Football League.

The implication of the preceding observation is that turnover within the three divisions is extensive. Except for Premier League members, teams cannot conveniently be divided into a large majority that have a stable league assignment and a minority that are on the margins between two leagues and so alternate back and forth. The dramatic rise and fall of about one fourth of the teams in a decade, and the slower but real turnover that takes place among the teams that do not stay in the Premier League for long runs, show that during the course of a decade the promotion and relegation system has a substantial effect on the composition of all of the leagues. A surprisingly large fraction of teams in the lower leagues occasionally have runs that last several years in which they ascend to Division 1, and maybe even the Premier League for a few years, before falling back to Divisions 2 and 3. The next section examines recent history to determine the financial consequences of these runs.

TABLE 5:   Revenue Rankings of Promoted Teams: 1997-1998 and 1998-1999

	1997-1998		*1998-1999*	
League	*Promoted Team*	*Revenue Rank*	*Promoted Team*	*Revenue Rank*
Division 1	Bradford City	6	Charlton Athletic	14
	Sunderland	1	Middlesbrough	2
	Watford	10	Nottingham Forrest	5
Division 2	Fulham	2	Bristol City	2
	Manchester City	1	Grimsby Town	9
	Walsall	6	Watford	4
Division 3	Brentford	17	Colchester City	19
	Cambridge United	4	Leicester City	7
	Cardiff City	2	Macclesfield Town	NA[a]
	Scunthorpe United	8	Notts County	3

NOTE: NA = not applicable.
a. Macclesfield Town did not make its financial reports public in 1998-1999; however, since entering Division 3 in 1997, it has not been among the leaders in revenues in years when its revenues were reported.

INCENTIVES UNDER PROMOTION/RELEGATION

The preceding section documents the extensive turnover in league memberships, especially for Divisions 1, 2, and 3. Recall that the economic theory of a sports league points to an inefficiency of turnover: An assignment of teams among the leagues may not be a good match with relative local market demands. The promotions of 1997-1998 and 1998-1999 illustrate the problem. Table 5 shows that many of the teams that were promoted in these years were not among their league's leaders in revenues. Had promotion been based on revenues rather than on-field performance, fewer than half of these teams would have been promoted.

Because the allocation of teams among leagues does not maximize total revenues, the financial performance of the leagues exhibits several interesting patterns. As shown in Table 6, each league shows very large revenue disparities among teams in the league. In the Premier League, Manchester United has far more revenues than any other team, so revenues for the next best team are also shown. In all leagues, revenue disparities are larger than for major leagues in the United States.

As shown in Table 6, in every league a few teams have lower revenues than the revenues earned by the strongest teams in lower leagues. Indeed, in 2 of the 5 years, the revenue of the best team in Division 2 either surpassed or came within £1 million of the worst Premier League team, and in every year the best teams in Division 3 had roughly the same revenue as the worst team in Division 1. Table 7 shows the details of this relationship for the Premier League and Division 1. During the past 5 years, on average 3 Division 1 teams have captured more revenues than the weakest

TABLE 6: Revenue Inequality in English Soccer: 1994-1995 to 1998-1999 (in thousands of pounds)

	1994-1995	1995-1996	1996-1997	1997-1998	1998-1999
Premier League					
Highest revenue	60,622	53,316	87,939	87,875	110,920
Next best	24,723	28,970	41,134	49,177	59,092
Lowest revenue	5,189	5,874	9,238	12,520	13,448
Ratio from highest to lowest	11.68	9.08	9.52	7.02	8.25
Ratio from next best to lowest	3.99	4.93	4.45	3.93	4.39
Division 1					
Highest revenue	7,565	10,450	12,727	18,825	24,078
Lowest revenue	1,697	2,173	2,152	2,111	2,271
Ratio	4.46	4.81	5.91	8.92	10.60
Division 2					
Highest revenue	6,942	4,441	5,061	4,533	12,731
Lowest revenue	827	941	799	1,127	1,243
Ratio	8.39	4.72	6.33	4.02	10.24
Division 3					
Highest revenue	1,860	2,876	2,847	1,886	2,043
Lowest revenue	541	528	722	717	702
Ratio	3.44	5.45	3.94	2.63	2.91

TABLE 7: Revenue Overlap Between Premier League and Division 1: 1997-1998 and 1998-1999 (in thousands of pounds)

			Number of Teams in Gap	
Year	Highest Revenue in Division 1	Lowest Revenue in Premier League	Division 1	Premier League
1994-1995	7,565	5,189	3	4
1995-1996	10,450	5,874	5	6
1996-1997	12,727	9,238	2	4
1997-1998	18,825	12,520	4	5
1998-1999	24,078	13,448	1	9

team in the Premier League, and on average 5.6 Premier League teams have had lower revenues than the Division 1 team with the highest revenues. In these cases, teams in the lower division draw better than other teams that finish ahead of them in the standings in the same division in 1 year and in the next year when these teams are promoted.

The substantial overlap in team revenues among the leagues reflects two factors. First, in every year a fairly large number of teams play in lower leagues than their market demand justifies. Second, the revenue data are consistent with the hypothesis that the promotion/relegation system has a positive benefit for at least some teams in that revenues are enhanced by the prospect of promotion. A more formal econometric model is necessary to disentangle these effects completely but quite a bit can be discerned from the raw data.

The financial data provide clear evidence that league assignment affects revenues and so creates a powerful incentive to seek promotion. Table 8 contains revenues, attendance, wages, and net transfer fees for teams in years around their promotion and/or relegation between the Premier League and Division 1. The table segregates the teams into four groups according to how many times they were promoted and relegated. In every case both revenues and attendance increase when a team is promoted, with the average increase nearly £5 million. Attendance at home league matches is probably a better indicator of the revenue effect of league status than is revenues, for the latter reflects many other revenue sources, such as participation in tournaments and international matches and the "parachute" policy of giving some of the television revenues of the Premier League to teams that have been demoted in the previous 2 seasons. Hence, revenues can vary from year to year for extraneous reasons. On average, a promotion to the Premier League was accompanied by an increase in home attendance of about 6,000 per game. Of course, revenues and attendance in both leagues were growing during this period but not by nearly this amount.

Interestingly, demotion is not always accompanied by a drop in revenues and attendance. For the 5 teams that were permanently demoted from the Premier League, revenues increased slightly for 3 and fell by a large amount for 2, causing an average net revenue loss for all 5 of more than £400,000 per team. For teams that spent 1 year in the Premier League, revenues declined for 2 out of 3 and for the group as a whole by about £500,000 per team. For the three demotions among the 2 teams that changed leagues four or more times in consecutive years, two were associated with revenue declines and the average net loss was about £700,000. In all cases but one, demotion was accompanied by a drop in attendance, typically by a few thousand per game. Thus, demotion usually causes teams to be worse off financially; however, the drop in revenues and attendance is less than the gains from promotion, so that teams end up better off in the demotion year than they would have been had they not played in the Premier League in the previous season. These facts confirm that promotion has a hysteresis effect: The benefits of promotion persist after a team is demoted and average more than £4 million in the first year after relegation.

The meaning of the data on transfer fees and wages is not as clear as it is for revenues and attendance. Wages include all employees, not just players, and in particular the salaries of management. Hence, movements in wage data do not necessarily reveal the trend in total player salaries. Transfer fees reveal the attempt of teams to

TABLE 8: Effects of Promotion and Relegation in Premier League, 1992-1999 (in thousands of pounds)

	Teams That Were Promoted Once and Stayed Through 1999 (wages and attendance unavailable)	
	Blackburn Rovers (1992)	Newcastle United (1993)
Revenues[a]		
Before	2,067	8,743
After	6,305	17,004
Net transfer fees[b]		
Before	(6,840)	(6,248)
After	(395)	1,366

	Teams That Were Demoted Once and Stayed Through 1999[c]				
	Manchester City (1996)	Notts County (1992)	Oldham Athletic (1994)	Queens Park Rangers (1996)	Sheffield United (1994)
Revenues					
Before	12,698	2,764	5,764	7,173	5,431
After	12,727	2,906	4,023	7,497	4,325
Net transfer fees					
Before	(2,588)	428	9	700	(46)
After	(1,754)	1,477	3,479	(3,556)	2,404
Wages					
Before	6,426	NA	3,088	5,010	3,146
After	7,200	NA	2,739	6,659	3,145
Attendance[d]					
Before	27,869	NA	12,563	15,683	19,462
After	26,753	NA	8,444	12,544	14,462

	Teams That Moved Twice: Promoted Then Relegated in Consecutive Years		
	Barnsley (1997-1999)	Sunderland (1996-1998)	Swindon Town (1993-1995)
Revenues			
Year 1	3,658	7,166	3,373
Year 2	12,694	13,415	5,415
Year 3	7,640	18,825	4,772
Net transfer fees			
Year 1	273	(1,812)	455
Year 2	(5,656)	(842)	(660)
Year 3	(512)	(2,018)	1,834
Wages			
Year 1	2,613	4,451	NA
Year 2	4,172	5,703	2,711
Year 3	7,077	8,161	3,393

(continued)

196   JOURNAL OF SPORTS ECONOMICS / May 2002

TABLE 8:   Continued

	Teams That Moved Twice: Promoted Then Relegated in Consecutive Years		
	Barnsley (1997-1999)	Sunderland (1996-1998)	Swindon Town (1993-1995)
Attendance			
Year 1	11,356	17,482	10,715
Year 2	18,449	20,865	15,274
Year 3	16,269	33,492	9,744

	Teams That Changed Leagues in 4 or 5 Consecutive Years				
	Year 1 (P)	Year 2 (P)	Year 3 (R)	Year 4 (P)	Year 5 (R)
Leicester City (1993-1997)					
Revenues	6,233	9,697	9,272	17,320	—
Transfer fees	(2,267)	1,418	(980)	(4,709)	—
Wages	3,132	4,421	5,449	8,914	—
Attendance	16,005	19,572	16,530	20,184	
Bolton Wanderers (1994-1999)					
Revenues	5,488	6,742	7,653	15,711	12,604
Transfer fees	(851)	553	(1,587)	623	1,323
Wages	2,682	3,312	6,159	9,625	10,039
Attendance	13,029	18,822	15,826	24,352	18,240

NOTE: NA = not applicable, P = promotion, and R = relegation.
a. Revenues are from all sources except sales of player rights (transfer fees).
b. Transfer fees are recorded as the difference between sales and purchases, and numbers in parentheses represent net purchases.
c. Norwich City is also in this category but insufficient data are available to include it.
d. Attendance is average per league match.

improve their team (a positive number) or to sell quality players (a negative number); however, these numbers also are affected by extraneous events, such as injuries, retirements, and unevenness through the years in the number of players who seek employment with another team after their contracts expire. In some cases, teams seriously seek to improve themselves to stay in or return to the Premier League, as reflected in large expenditures on player transfers and higher wage bills.

Notwithstanding the caveats, the data indicate that teams do not all pursue the same strategies in response to promotion and relegation. In some cases, teams take advantage of their promotion to sell the players that made promotion possible and consequently stay briefly in the Premier League. In other cases, teams on the cusp between Division 1 and the Premier League put forth great effort to gain and keep promotion.

The Bolton Wanderers exemplify the first strategy. In the years before their two promotions in the 1990s, they had substantial net expenditures on transfer fees and then had net sales of players during the years they were in the Premier League. They also were net sellers of players when they were demoted in 1999.

The Wolverhampton Wanderers have a similar history to Bolton but with a different outcome. Wolverhampton is 1 of 3 teams that played in Division 1 throughout the 1990s and is always among the leaders in attendance. In the past 5 years, Wolverhampton's rank in revenues among Division 1 teams has averaged 2.4. Twice it has had the highest ranking, and in all years its revenues have surpassed the revenues of the lowest ranking Premier League teams. Nevertheless, Wolverhampton has not been promoted to the Premier League, finishing 3rd, 20th, 4th, 7th, 9th, and 12th (average 8.9) during the past 5 years.[10] Wolverhampton's stable membership in Division 1 has three possible explanations: luck (the difference between Wolverhampton and Bolton, with similar team quality, may be due to randomness in which teams are promoted), management that does a slightly better job of calibrating team quality (if promotion, on balance, is unprofitable), or management that does a slightly worse job of controlling team quality (if occasional promotion is profitable).

Manchester City apparently pursued the opposite strategy of Bolton and Wolverhampton. The team was a large net purchaser of player contracts in both its final year in the Premier League and its 1st year in Division 1, but to no avail as it slipped all the way to Division 2 two years after its demotion; however, the team did climb back to the Premier League for the 2000-2001 season but was then relegated in 2001. Likewise, Sunderland tried first to stay in and then to return to the Premier League by being a substantial net purchaser of player contracts and eventually succeeded for the 1999-2000 season, climbing to finish 7th in the Premier League in 2000-2001.

Leicester City seems to have pursued both strategies. In 1993-1994, the team spent heavily on net transfer fees and improved enough to ascend to the Premier League. But in 1994-1995, the team had a net gain of £1.4 million in player sales (more than enough to offset the higher salary bill it paid that year) and was demoted back to Division 1. After demotion, the team once again spent a substantial amount on transfer fees and was promoted. But the second time the team spent still more on salaries and transfer fees and succeeded in sticking in the Premier League, where it remains 6 years later.

The propensity of some teams to weaken themselves after promotion is to be expected from the fact that some promoted teams are not among the revenue leaders of the league from which they were promoted. The yo-yo teams plausibly operate in markets that cannot sustain competitive teams in the Premier League, so when they are promoted they do not make a serious attempt to stay. In this case, the motivation for promotion is not to obtain a permanent place in the higher league but to take advantage of the hysteresis effect in attendance. For teams in lower leagues that have higher revenues than some teams in higher leagues, the incentives are likely to

198   JOURNAL OF SPORTS ECONOMICS / May 2002

be different. Their best assignment is likely to be in the higher league, and so they are more likely to make the expenditures that are necessary to increase their chance of staying in the higher league. The puzzling case is Wolverhampton, which always does better financially than several Premier League teams yet seems to have found a permanent home in Division 1.

IMPLICATIONS

The financial and playing field experiences of the four leading British football leagues are generally consistent with the predictions of the theoretical model that can be tested using the financial data that are available. Promotion/relegation clearly has led to turnover in league membership among the four leading leagues; however, promotion and relegation between Division 3 and the National Conference has led to very little successful entry into the top echelon of teams. Apparently the combined size of the four leading leagues is sufficiently large that almost all viable franchise locations—especially for the top two leagues—were occupied early in the 20th century. Nevertheless, turnover between the Premier League and lower leagues is substantial in the time frame of a decade. Teams that play in rapidly growing markets or that switch from poor to strong management can rapidly ascend from Division 3 to the top leagues.

The financial information indicates that promotion is financially attractive as well as desired by fans. Both revenues and attendance at league matches tend to increase substantially when teams are promoted. Moreover, the reward from promotion seems to endure for a while after a team is demoted, giving teams that are marginal for a higher league a financial incentive to field teams that bounce back and forth between a higher and lower league.

Of course, this article is only a beginning. The next step is to estimate econometric models of team performance, revenues, attendance, wages, transfer fees, and other financial variables to provide more precise estimates of the effects described above and to determine whether the noisy indicators of player costs can sustain tests of the effects of promotion and relegation on team strategies regarding players.

Applications to North America

Drawing conclusions about United States and Canadian sports from the experience of English football is hazardous and, as a practical matter, probably irrelevant because North American leagues are not likely to experiment with so dramatic a change in format as the introduction of promotion and relegation. Nevertheless, the English football system seems to be a very attractive solution to the perpetual problem of leagues with substantial disparities in on-field success and revenue among their teams.

Promotion and relegation have three significant advantages and one significant disadvantage. On the plus side, this system allows the top league to be smaller, have higher average revenues, and be more balanced competitively, although the latter effect is muted by the yo-yo teams that seek only occasional, brief promotion to profit from the hysteresis effect on revenues. On the negative side, teams that are relegated do worse financially than they would if they finished in the bottom group of teams in the higher league. This disadvantage may be offset by the advantages but the issue cannot be resolved without running an experiment.

A promotion/relegation system can be implemented in two ways: by constructing a lower league from the existing minor league system or by dividing the existing major league. Sports with independent minor league teams are the most likely candidates for the first method.

Changing relations with minor leagues is not likely to be viewed favorably in baseball. The vast majority of minor league baseball teams, and all in the top two classifications, operate as farm teams for major league franchises. This structure enables major league teams to monopsonize the market for players who have any serious chance of becoming major leaguers through the amateur draft. Farm teams are expensive—MLB teams spend around $12 million per year on scouting amateurs and providing players to minor league affiliates—but this cost is more than offset by the salary suppression that arises from the fact that players must have 3 years of major league experience before they qualify for salary arbitration and 6 years before they become unrestricted free agents. In addition, baseball has some attractive open markets that are valuable as potential expansion sites, most notably Northern Virginia and Northern New Jersey, which would be lost if minor league teams in those areas could qualify for promotion to the majors. Thus, baseball does not appear to be a good candidate for rearranging its minor league structure to accommodate promotion and relegation.

Football has three significant minor leagues: Arena Football (indoors), the Canadian Football League (CFL), and the World League of American Football (in Europe). The NFL owns Arena Football and the World League, but the CFL is independent. Because of the difference in format, Arena Football is inappropriate for a promotion/relegation system with the NFL; however, both the CFL and World League are good candidates.

The advantages to the NFL of adopting a promotion/relegation system are that it provides a mechanism for expanding into Canadian and European markets that are already proven and it enables the NFL to sell World League franchises at a substantial premium. Likewise, the CFL, which tried unsuccessfully to enter the United States in the mid-1990s, probably would jump at the chance to become a Division 1 to the NFL's Premier status. The NFL almost certainly would insist that neither the CFL nor an independent World League place teams in the territories of existing NFL franchises, and in return would promise not to expand or to relocate teams to the areas occupied by teams in these leagues.

The disadvantage of this plan to the NFL is that it would lose the high expansion fees that await it in U.S. cities that are likely to be a viable home for an NFL team. Most notably, Los Angeles almost certainly would become an expansion target of

200   JOURNAL OF SPORTS ECONOMICS / May 2002

the CFL if teams in that league could be promoted to the NFL. Whereas the NFL has few open markets that are as attractive as Los Angeles, the experiences of the Jacksonville and Carolina expansion teams and the relocation of the Houston Oilers to Nashville indicate that NFL teams can be financially viable in a large number of cities. As a result, the NFL has more plausible expansion cities remaining in the United States than any other sport; however, the loss of these expansion fees, due in part to the fact that expansion cannot be much faster than two teams every several years, would be partially offset by the enhanced value of World League franchises.

Both basketball and hockey provide interesting (if still not very plausible) possibilities. Both sports have independent minor leagues, but in both sports these leagues have disadvantages as candidates for promotion and relegation. Farm relationships with teams and the major leagues are common in hockey. Basketball's best minor league, the Continental Basketball Association, failed during the 2000-2001 season. Favoring a promotion and relegation system are the fact that basketball and hockey have expanded about as far as is plausible and have several franchises that play in weak markets and/or field persistently weak teams, so they have little to lose by experimenting with promotion/relegation.

The second approach to implementing a promotion/relegation system is to divide the existing major leagues to create a significantly smaller top league. The basic idea would be to shrink the top "major-major" league to something between 16 and 20 teams. Perhaps in tandem with expansion or promotion of some minor league teams, the remaining major league teams would be placed in a "minor-major" league with a comparable number of teams. All teams in both leagues would be treated as a "major league" in that all would participate in league governance, would have the same relationship with minor leagues, and would participate in the market for major league players. As the Premier League did when it shrunk to 20 teams and Division 2 did when it reorganized from two coequal leagues to the present Divisions 2 and 3, leagues would implement this system by demoting the major league teams with the weakest records in the season before the plan was implemented. To make the system more palatable to owners, players, and fans of demoted teams, the system could promote the 4 best teams in the lower league at the end of each season.

In 2001, baseball announced a plan to disband at least 2 and maybe more franchises as its solution to revenue disparities in the sport. This action seems to have been motivated primarily by the desire to stop sharing local revenues with low-revenue teams. Moving to a hierarchy of leagues with promotion and relegation achieves the same objective without eliminating teams. A structure of two 8-team leagues at both the major-major and minor-major level, each with two divisions, would enable baseball to return to a better balanced schedule: 16 games against each opponent in the same division, 12 games against each team in the other division of the same league, and 8 games against each team in the other league, for a total of 160 games. The League Championship series would be against the division winners of the higher leagues, followed by the World Series.

The loss of the first round of the playoffs could be replaced by a tournament resembling the FA cup in England, in which teams in both major-major and minor-major leagues play in a single-elimination tournament with matches based on a random draw rather than seeding. This tournament could be scheduled by creating a 1-week hiatus in the regular season schedule during the summer, before the All-Star game. To create an incentive to win, revenues from the broadcast rights to these games could be divided unequally so that teams and players receive a significant financial bonus for winning each game.

Basketball and hockey also might benefit from splitting into a two-league hierarchy. Both sports have several franchises that are financially weak and persistently doormats in the league standings, and that have few remaining opportunities for expansion or relocation. Thus, these sports also seem to have relatively little to lose by dividing into a hierarchy of two leagues and implementing promotion and relegation.

As in baseball, a smaller league would enable basketball to create a second championship, patterned after the National Collegiate Athletic Association (NCAA) basketball tournament (but without seeding) as a series of single-elimination games during a week in the middle of the season. Both the draw for matches and the location of the games (which would be the home team) would be determined randomly to give a small advantage to some weaker teams. As with baseball and NCAA basketball, the television proceeds for the tournament could be allocated on the basis of games won rather than shared equally, to create an incentive to take the tournament seriously.

Because the worst NFL teams remain financially strong and because the opportunity for a second type of championship is less attractive, shrinking the size of the major-major league is not attractive in football. The better model for the NFL probably is to create promotion/relegation deals with the two existing leagues.

In summary, promising avenues for implementing a system of promotion and relegation are available in all four sports. The main problem is that all require a substantial reorganization of the existing structure of the major league. Reforms of such major proportions, no matter how attractive, are not likely to be implemented because doing so would require supermajority support from the existing set of major league teams. In all sports, finding any reform that commands overwhelming support is very difficult, so there is little immediate prospect that these reforms would even be considered, let alone adopted. Nevertheless, contemplating their likely effects is an interesting and instructive exercise, particularly in light of the hand-wringing by owners in each sport concerning their financial plight.

APPENDIX

The data reported in this article come from several sources.

The playing histories for the Nationwide Football League are from a Web site that contains the historical records of all of the major European leagues, www.soccer-links.com/ info/. The histories of the Nationwide Football League teams, as well as standings for all English leagues (including those below the top four), can be found in Glenda Rollin and Jack Rollin's *Rothmans Football Yearbook 2000-2001* (1969/2000). Another useful source of information is the Rec.Sport.Soccer Statistics Foundation, especially the data compilations on historical performance information by Ross (1996) and Pietarinen (2001).

Financial information comes from an annual compilation of the financial statements of nearly all British football clubs that is edited by Gerry Boon, the *Annual Review of Football Finance* (1996/2000). English law requires financial disclosure for all corporations, and the publisher Deloitte and Touche compile these data annually. The major problems with the financial data are that some teams provide too little information to permit meaningful comparisons of some elements of all financial reports and that some teams release their reports too late for inclusion in the volume. About a dozen of the 92 teams fall into one of these categories each year. Deloitte and Touche attempts to reconcile reports that use different accounting systems, but these attempts are limited by data availability. The series on wages is of dubious value because it lumps together players, coaches, and all other personnel. Likewise, the data on transfer fees were of limited usefulness until recently, when the British government imposed a uniform system of accounts on sports teams. As is the case for sports teams in the United States, the data on profits were not very useful because of differences among the teams in practices regarding administrative costs and related businesses.

NOTES

1. Secondary criteria are a team's stadium quality, revenue potential, and adherence to league rules. In some cases relegated teams are not those with the worst records, and teams are denied promotion because of operational shortcomings.

2. New U.S. leagues that managed to have at least one team enter an established major league were the American League and the Federal League in baseball, the Basketball Association of America, the first American Basketball League (1947-1949) and the American Basketball Association in basketball, the All-American Football Conference and the American Football League in football, and the World Hockey Association in hockey. Only one entrant, the Basketball Association of America (BAA), has managed to supplant the incumbent as the dominant league. In the late 1940s, the BAA merged with the incumbent National Basketball League and the first American Basketball League to form the National Basketball Association. Most of the teams in the merged entity were from the BAA. See Noll (1991) for a history of this era.

3. Entry into the lowest league requires approval, but low leagues do not charge high entry fees.

4. The underlying assumption is that teams are price-takers in inputs to team quality, which implies that each team operates in a competitive market for players, coaches, executives, and stadiums. The model developed by Ross and Szymanski (2000) assumes that leagues also face a perfectly elastic supply of quality so that all of the effects of promotion and relegation on demand cause increased quality rather than higher wages. The rapid escalation in soccer player salaries during the past few years as reve-

nues of top teams have grown suggests that, in fact, much of the increased demand for quality leads to wage increases.

5. Although industry leaders and some scholars dispute the profit-maximization assumption, this debate is not important for our purposes. Because many soccer teams are organized as publicly traded corporations, the profit-maximization assumption seems unexceptional. But even if owners have more complex motives, these can be captured by the standard model by assuming that the revenue function, $R(q)$, has two components: funds received, F, and the willingness to pay of ownership to have a victorious team, V. If both F and V are functions of team success, and expected success is a function of team quality, the profit-maximization problem remains maximizing $R(q) - wq = F(q) + V(q) - wq$, and the conclusions in the main text remain valid.

6. If Team 1 enjoys more intense demand than Team 2 and if the teams have competitive balance (i.e., if $q_1 = q_2$), then $R'_1 > R'_1$ so that both cannot satisfy Equation 2.

7. This result is the same as the result in Ross and Szymanski (2000). The latter assumes an explicit form for the revenue function and derives the magnitude of the incentive effect on team quality under promotion and relegation.

8. For example, to obtain an antitrust exemption for their merger, the National Football League and American Football League granted an expansion franchise to New Orleans, the home of Senator Russell Long, who sponsored the legislation.

9. The history of the team cheerily is told on its Web site, www.thediamonds.com.

10. In 1994-1995 and 1996-1997, Wolverhampton qualified for the playoffs for promotion but lost.

REFERENCES

Boon, G. (Ed.). (2000). *Annual review of football finances*. London: Deloitte and Touche. (Original work published 1996)

El Hodiri, M., & Quirk, J. P. (1974). An economic theory of a sports league. In R. G. Noll (Ed.), *Government and the sports business* (pp. 33-80). Washington, DC: Brookings Institution.

Hall, S., Szymanski, S., & Zimbalist, A. (2002). Testing causality between team performance and payroll: The cases of Major League Baseball and English soccer. *Journal of Sports Economics, 3*(2), 149-168.

Jeanrenaud, C., & Késanne, S. (Eds.). (1999). *Competition policy in professional sports: Europe after the Bosman case*. Brussells, Germany: Standaard Editions.

Noll, R. G. (1991). Professional basketball: Economic and business perspectives. In P. D. Staudohar & J. A. Mangan (Eds.), *The business of professional sports* (pp. 18-47). Urbana: University of Illinois Press.

Pietarinen, H. (2001). *England—First level all-time tables*. Retrieved from Rec.Sport.Soccer Statistics Foundation

Rollin, G., & Rollin, J. (Eds.). (2000). *Rothman's football yearbook 2000-2001*. London: Headline Book. (Original work published 1969)

Ross, J. M. (1996). *English club divisional movements 1888-1996*. Retrieved from Rec.Sport.Soccer Statistics Foundation

Ross, S. A., & Szymanski, S. (2000). *Open competition in sports leagues*. Retrieved from http://papers.ssrn.com/paper.taf?abstract_id=243756

Roger G. Noll is a Morris M. Doyle Professor of Public Policy in the Department of Economics at Stanford University.

[6]

 Journal of Industry, Competition and Trade, 3:3, 167–186, 2003
© 2003 Kluwer Academic Publishers. Manufactured in The Netherlands.

Equality of Opportunity and Equality of Outcome: Open Leagues, Closed Leagues and Competitive Balance[*]

LUIGI BUZZACCHI   luigi.buzzacchi@polito.it
Politecnico di Torino

STEFAN SZYMANSKI   szy@ic.ac.uk
Imperial College London

TOMMASO M. VALLETTI[†]   t.valletti@ic.ac.uk
The Business School, Imperial College London, 53 Prince's Gate, Exhibition Road, London SW7 2PG, UK

Abstract. This paper compares conventional static measures of competitive balance with measures that take account of the mobility of teams into the upper ranks of professional leagues, which we call dynamic competitive balance. We use this measure to compare the open soccer leagues that permit entry by the process of promotion and relegation, to the closed leagues of North America where there is no automatic right of entry. We also identify the theoretical distribution of entrants to the top k ranks assuming that all teams have equal probabilities of winning. We find that the open leagues (OL) we study are less balanced, dynamically, than closed leagues (CL), and also that OL lie much further away from the theoretical distribution than CL.

Keywords: sports leagues, competitive balance

1. Introduction

> "All schemes used in the United States punish excellence in one way or another. The European football approach punishes failure by promoting excellent minor league teams to the majors and demoting (relegating) poor performing major league teams back down to the minors. The revenue loss from a potential demotion to a lower class of play is severe punishment for low quality—severe enough that salary treaties, league sharing arrangements, and unified player drafts are so far thought to be unnecessary, even though star salaries are enormous. It is an interesting economic question as to which system achieves better results."
>
> Rosen and Sanderson (2001)

Since Superbowl I in 1967 the NFL has expanded from a league of 16 teams to one of 32. During this period 17 different franchises have won the Superbowl. In Serie A, the top division of Italian soccer, 48 different teams have participated since 1967, but there have

---

*   We thank the Editor and an anonymous referee for helpful comments.
†   Corresponding author.

been only 11 different winners.[1] Serie A has had more teams not because it is a larger league—in most seasons only 18 teams compete for the championship title. However, the institution of promotion and relegation permits new teams to enter the league each year. Nonetheless, despite having more competitors, fewer teams seem to have a chance of winning—less than quarter of the teams in Serie A over the period have one, compared to half of the current NFL franchises. Moreover, a similar story emerges if any of the North American leagues are compared to the national soccer leagues of Europe.[2] In other words, soccer leagues tend to be much less balanced than the major leagues. However, this is not true when measured in the way that has been conventionally adopted in the sports literature. This paper proposes a way of measuring competitive balance that permits comparison between the North American closed leagues (CL) and the open leagues (OL) of Europe.

This enables us to address some important policy issues. It is a long-standing proposition in sports economics that "better" means "more balanced" results (*e.g.* Rottenberg, 1956). Competitive balance refers to the expectations of fans about who will be the winner. In a perfectly balanced contest fans believe all outcomes are equally possible so there is complete outcome uncertainty. In a perfectly unbalanced contest the winner is known *ex ante* with probability 1. It seems reasonable to suppose that without at least some degree of competitive balance, fans will loose interest in a competition. A stronger proposition would be that, all else equal, a more balanced contest is a more interesting one. This proposition is widely accepted (see Szymanski, 2003 for a survey of the evidence). Most importantly, it has frequently been accepted by the courts as a justification for restrictive agreements concerning the sharing of revenues or restraints in the player market (*e.g.* salary caps and roster limits).

Measuring the extent to which a competition is balanced, therefore, is a critical issue. However, this is no simple issue. The measure widely cited in the existing literature (see, *e.g.* Quirk and Fort, 1992) is the standard deviation of winning percentages in a season. According to this measure, the greater the variance in outcomes in a season, the less balanced is the contest. The principal weakness of this measure is that it takes no account of the identity of the teams across seasons. Applying this measure to North American and European leagues produces the seemingly perverse result that European leagues are if anything slightly more balanced than North American leagues. This is an artifact of the European system of promotion and relegation, by which the worst performing teams in a league in each season are demoted to the immediately junior league—so that no team can afford to give up once it is out of contention for the title.

The novel measure of competitive balance that we develop in this paper permits a comparison to be made between different sports leagues across time, in particular taking the account of the promotion and relegation system. This measure focuses on the identity of teams, and the frequency with which they approach the possibility of winning the title.

---

1 In fact, going back to 1945 only 12 different teams have won Serie A.
2 Soccer is by far the dominant team sport in Europe. Sports such as Rugby, cricket, basketball and ice hockey trail a long way behind in terms of popularity.

What we show is that the North American major leagues (we consider Major League Baseball, the National Football League and the National Hockey League) are much more balanced than the dominant soccer leagues of Europe (we compare the top divisions of the English, Italian and Belgian leagues) in the sense that a greater proportion of teams in the league are likely to experience any given level of success within a given period of time. However, the North American leagues are more or less closed to entry by new teams, whereas European leagues have a system of promotion and relegation which gives many more teams access to the highest level of play (the top division). In other words, we find equality of outcomes in the closed North American leagues while in Europe, we find equality of opportunity within a system that is dominated by a small number of teams.

Previous studies of competitive balance have measured either "match uncertainty" or "seasonal uncertainty", and both of these measures can be compared across leagues. Match uncertainty refers simply to expectations about a particular game, and this can be measured, for example, by studying pre-match betting odds.[3] However, interest in a league competition goes beyond uncertainty about a particular match and many fans are attracted by uncertainty about the overall outcome of the championship. Seasonal uncertainty, the closeness of an overall championship race, can be measured in a number of ways, *e.g.* the number of games behind the leader that the following k teams are as the season ends, the date at which at the championship outcome becomes known with certainty, or more generally, the standard deviation of success (*e.g.* win percentage) among the teams.

These measures tell us something about competitive balance in a "static" sense—the balance of a particular match or season, but for many fans there is also interest in competitive balance in a "dynamic" sense: do particular teams dominate the championship over time? This paper proposes a natural basis for comparing dynamic competitive balance among leagues and a theoretical benchmark.[4] The natural basis is to consider the cumulative frequency of teams entering the top k ranks of a league (ranked by some measure such as win percentage). By analogy we can think of dynamic competitive balance like the spread of an epidemic—the more balanced a league the more rapidly teams enter the ranks of the top k.

This raises an important additional consideration. In a "closed" league of, say, 20 teams, the top k can only ever be drawn from that 20 teams.[5] The more teams, the greater the potential for entry into the top k, just as the absolute number of people succumbing to a disease must be increasing in the total population. Leagues in North America are typically closed in the sense used above (although there can be some new entry from the sale of additional franchises and league mergers). By contrast, in most other countries leagues are "open" in the sense that at the end of each season the worst performing

---

3 A review of these studies is provided by Szymanski and Kuypers (1999).

4 Humphreys (2002) and Koop (2002) have proposed alternative methods for evaluating the evolution of competitive balance over time, but in both the cases the method is not naturally adapted to inter league comparisons.

5 Abstracting, for the moment from franchise expansion.

teams are demoted to the immediately junior league and replaced by the best performing teams from that league. The European Commission (1998) has gone so far as to suggest that "the system of promotion and relegation is one of the key features of the European model of sport". Given this hierarchical structure it is apparent that the population of potential entrants into the major league is, over time, much larger (and possibly unlimited) compared to a closed league.

One central concern of this paper is whether this "equality of opportunity" translates into equality of outcome, as measured by competitive balance. Our theoretical benchmark approaches this issue by asking how many teams would be expected to enter the top k ranks in a league system where resources were so distributed that each match played were perfectly balanced. In other words, if success were purely random (because all sources of systematic variation, such as resource inequality, had been removed) how much mobility would there be in a given league structure? Calculating this benchmark for a CL with a fixed number of teams is relatively straightforward, but as we show the case of an OL is more complex. However, by deriving these values we can compare actual with theoretical mobility and derive a kind of Gini coefficient, measuring the closeness of league outcomes to a perfectly balanced ideal. It turns out that North American leagues are far closer to the theoretical ideal than their European counterparts, a phenomenon that can be accounted for by the much greater extent of resource equalization measures in North America, *e.g.* gate revenue sharing, collective merchandising, draft rules, salary caps and so on.

The paper is set out as follows. In Section 2, we survey the literature comparing North American leagues and European soccer leagues. In Section 3, we compare measures of static and dynamic competitive balance for North American major league sports and the dominant national sports leagues in Europe for soccer. In Section 4, we derive our theoretical benchmark for CL and OLs. In Section 5, we consider the difference in mobility comparing theoretical and actual measures. Section 6 concludes.

2. North American and European sports leagues

As the quote at the beginning of this paper indicates, there are substantial differences in the organizational framework of North American and European sports leagues and many of these are illustrated in Table 1.[6] First, in North America, there are four significant team sports competing for market share compared to a single dominant team sport in Europe-soccer. However, in North America, there is a single league that dominates competition in each sport, whereas in Europe the national league of each country is normally dominant in its own territory, with limited penetration elsewhere (in some ways the regional conferences of the NCAA bear some resemblance to this). Four leagues currently dominate Europe due to their large populations, wealth and traditional obsession with

---

6   Adapted from Hoehn and Szymanski (1999) who review the differences between North American and European soccer.

Table 1. Differences in structure of U.S. and European sports leagues.

	U.S. Sports	Football in Europe
League system	Closed, no promotion or relegation	Open, annual promotion and relegation
	Teams compete in single league competition	Teams may compete simultaneously in many competitions
League functions	Collective sale of TV rights Centralized marketing	Collective sale of TV rights
Competition between clubs	Limited substitution by consumers	Significant potential for substitution
Competition between leagues	Numerous cases of entry by rival leagues	All leagues contained within the established hierarchy
Player market	Rookie draft Salary caps (NFL, NBA) Collective bargaining	Active transfer market
Revenue sharing	Equal division of national broadcast income	Sharing of television income
	Gate sharing (NFL 40%, Baseball average 15%, NBA 0%)	Little or no sharing of league gate revenues
		Some sharing of gate from cup competitions
Competition policy	Antitrust exemption for baseball	Centralized sale of TV rights under attack
	Sports Broadcasting Act exempts national TV deals from antitrust	Selected interventions (ticket allocation FIFA)

soccer: England, Germany, Italy and Spain. Another significant difference is that North American teams and players typically play in only one league or competition in any one season. In Europe however, teams can compete in two national competitions (the league and the knock-out Cup[7]), an international league or cup competition for European clubs, while in addition the players can be selected to represent the national team[8]—and national representative competition is in most cases even more popular than club competition.

Economic arrangements in North American and European team sports also differ significantly. On the revenue side there is a much lower incidence of revenue sharing in Europe. On the expenditure side there are almost no restrictions in the player market and trading for cash is the accepted norm (more than 10% of players move team each season) compared to the U.S. where rules and custom inhibit player mobility.

The principal difference that this paper focuses on is the existence of promotion and relegation. In Europe leagues are typically organized in an ascending hierarchy by a governing body vested with responsibility for the development of sport as a whole. At the end of each season the worst performing teams in each division are demoted to the

---

7 Playoff are not widely used. A league competition followed by playoffs can be thought of as an integrated League and Cup competition.
8 Clubs are obliged as part of their obligations to their national federation to release their players and receive no compensation. Secession from the federations is seldom considered an option. In France, for example, the national federation has a statutory monopoly over the organization of league competition.

immediately junior division and replaced by the best performing teams in the junior division. Hence, it is in principle possible for team to rise from the lowest to the highest level of competition, and vice versa. The existence of this system in Europe and not in North America is essentially an accident of history (see Ross and Szymanski, 2001 for a description of the historical underpinnings), and while the discussion in this paper focuses primarily on soccer, this system has been adopted in even in sports imported into Europe from North America, such as basketball.

A further difference between North American leagues and European leagues has been the subject of some controversy, and this is the widely held belief in Europe that North American clubs are run by profit maximizers whereas European clubs embrace purely sporting objectives, such as win maximization subject to a budget constraint (the locus classicus is Sloane (1971)), and many of the implications of these assumptions for league rules have been analyzed by Kesenne (see, *e.g.* Kesenne, 2000). However, it is also clear that until recently there was limited financial return to be gained from team sports in Europe, a situation which has been transformed dramatically in the 1990s—and some authors see a shift toward more commercially oriented policies and the increasing pursuit of profit (see, *e.g.* Andreff and Staudohar, 2000).

While it is clear that there are many differences, the comparative study of North American and European leagues is still at an early stage.[9] In two recent papers, Noll (2002) and Ross and Szymanski (2002) consider what impact the promotion and relegation system would have on North American leagues if introduced there, but further research is required to understand the consequences of institutional differences. By focusing on competitive balance, this paper aims to provide a starting point for a theoretical analysis of the properties of these institutions.

3. Static and dynamic competitive balance

Most measures of competitive balance in the literature are essentially static—they analyze the equality of winning opportunities for individual matches or for a championship season taken as a whole.[10] For example, Quirk and Fort (1995) hypothesize that if seasonal win percentages become less dispersed then a league has become more competitively balanced. They review some allegedly balance-enhancing reforms in the North American professional leagues (*e.g.* the introduction of the salary cap in the NBA in 1984, the NFL rookie draft introduced in 1936 and the beginning of free agency in baseball in 1976). In general, they find no significant change in the standard deviation after the reforms and therefore conclude that there is no evidence that competitive balance was in fact enhanced.

---

9 Hall et al. (2002) attempt a limited comparison of the economics of Major League Baseball and English soccer.

10 An exception is Szymanski (2001) who compares the competitive balance of two different competitions.

Table 2. Actual standard deviation of win percentages divided by idealized standard deviation.

Decade	MLB (1950–99)	NFL (1950–99)	NHL (1949–98)	England (1949–98)	Italy (1949–98)	Belgium (1953–2000)
1950s	2.23	1.48	2.04	1.15	1.33	1.26
1960s	2.05	1.63	1.93	1.33	1.50	1.45
1970s	1.88	1.60	2.61	1.44	1.47	1.54
1980s	1.66	1.46	2.08	1.48	1.34	1.67
1990s	1.68	1.51	1.83	1.40	1.61	1.67

Note: Ties (draws) are treated as half a win. European leagues refer to the top division of the national soccer league.

Horowitz (1997) uses an entropy index to measure changes in competitive balance over time in Major League Baseball (and finds that there is underlying trend toward increasing balance over the period 1903–1995). Applying the concept of entropy to a CL seems natural enough, but it is less clear how one might extend this to a league with promotion and relegation. Quirk and Fort (1992) look at balance over time by adopting another measure based on seasonal variance. If a given league were perfectly balanced the winning probability for each team in each match would be 0.5, which would also be the expected value of the seasonal win percentage. The standard deviation of this win percentage would then be $0.5/\sqrt{m}$ where m is the number of matches played. This can be used as an ''idealized'' measure of the standard deviation for a particular league. Expressing the actual standard deviation as a ratio of the idealized standard deviation thus provides a basis for comparing the degree of competitive balance of different leagues.

In this paper, we have chosen to compare three North American leagues (Major League Baseball (MLB), The National Football League (NFL) and the National Hockey League (NHL)) to three national soccer leagues in Europe (Italy, England and Belgium). In terms of revenues and broadcast audiences the first two in each region are somewhat larger than third, but within both regions the basic league structures are comparable. Above all, the North American leagues are all closed and the European soccer leagues all open. In Table 2 we compute the ratio of actual to idealized standard deviation for North American major league sports and European soccer leagues. As Quirk and Fort have noted, the data for the North American leagues indicate a trend toward competitive balance over time in baseball, but no trend in the NFL or NHL. On this measure the NFL has tended to be the most balanced of the North American leagues and the NHL the least balanced. As has been noted in the work of Kipker (2000), the European soccer leagues seem by comparison to be more balanced (although the European trend is toward less balance). Thus, in the 1950s each of the three European leagues had lower standard deviations than any of the North American leagues, and in the case of England the actual standard deviation was only 15% higher than the idealized standard deviation. However, by the 1990s the gap had narrowed considerably, and for instance, the NFL seemed more balanced than either Italian of Belgian top divisions.

The principal weakness of a static measure of competitive balance such as this is that it takes no account of the identity of the successful teams.[11] So for example, according to the data the NFL was less balanced than the top soccer division in England, but in between 1990 and 1999 6 different teams won the Superbowl whereas in England only 5 different teams won the League Championship. Moreover, in England one team won the title on 5 occasions (Manchester United), whereas the biggest winner in the U.S. won only 3 times (Dallas).[12] To consider the dynamics more fully we have looked at the number of different teams winning the league title and the number of teams entering the top ranks.[13]

We conjecture that fans care about balance in the sense that they want a reasonable prospect that the identity of the winners will change from time to time (although they may also care about the variance of success among the teams within the season). "Turbulence" at the top increases the interest of fans of a greater number of teams. If, say, each team experiences diminishing returns to success in terms of fan interest, then a league that is more balanced in this dynamic sense will be more successful. This point has been made elsewhere, see *e.g.* Ross and Lucke (1997) and Szymanski (2001) who finds some empirical support for the conjecture. In this paper, our aim is to compare dynamic competitive balance across open and closed league. To do this, we have looked at the number of entrants into the ranks, first over the full 50 years of data, then over 40 years, 30 years, 20 years and 10 years. The data is reported in Tables 3 and 4.

Table 3 shows the number of different teams with the highest win percentage in each season. The North American leagues have developed the post season play-off season over the period in question in order to involve more teams in the championship race for longer. The play-off system introduces more randomness in outcomes and therefore adds to uncertainty even if the teams are not well balanced competitively. Since we are interested in competitive balance rather than uncertainty itself in this paper we have restricted ourselves to considering win percentages during the regular season only (see note to Table 3).

For the North American leagues the NFL had the greatest number of teams entering the top rank for 4 out of the 5 periods considered, although in the last decade the performance

---

11 This fact may also produce uninformative information within a given period. For instance the standard deviation of winning percentages tends to put too much weight among weaker teams. To give an example, imagine 10 teams competing in a league in a given year. In the first scenario, there is a team much stronger than everybody else that wins every single match, while the remaining teams have identical strength and win 50% of the matches. In the second scenario, there are 5 slightly stronger teams and 5 slightly weaker teams, where a team has 50% chance of winning a match among "equals", while a stronger team has 80% probability of winning against a weaker team. Despite it would be natural to describe as more balanced the second scenario, the normalized standard deviation of win percentages would yield the same numerical value in both cases.

12 Rolling the data two years further forward would highlight the point even more clearly: only 4 winning teams in England, one of which won 7 of the 10 titles, while in the NFL there were 7 different winners.

13 League rank is the standard measure of performance in Europe. For North American leagues we have ranked teams according to their regular season win percentage.

Table 3. Teams that had the highest winning percentage or were winners of the league championship.

Period	MLB	NFL	NHL	England	Italy	Belgium
50–99	16	20	13	16	12	10
60–99	16	18	13	13	12	8
70–99	14	14	12	9	10	8
80–99	12	9	10	7	7	7
90–99	6	7	7	5	4	4

Note: North American teams selected on the basis of regular season win percentage. European teams selected on the basis on actual championship wins. Traditionally, 2 points were awarded for win, 1 for a draw (tie). Tied winning percentages were then decided on goal difference. However, from the 1980s onward leagues introduced the award of 3 point for a win and 1 for a draw. In the data, the champions always had the highest win percentage, but in 9 out of the 150 championships considered the champions were tied in win percentage with the team ranked second (on goal difference). In 1995, Blackburn Rovers won the English championship on the basis of the new points system but would have tied on the old points system (which is the same as our measure of win percentage) and had an inferior goal difference to the team ranked second.

of all 3 leagues looks remarkably similar on this measure (notwithstanding the recent dominance of the New York Yankees in baseball).

For any of the 5 ranges considered, both the Italian and Belgian leagues had less variation in the number of teams appearing in this rank than any of the North American leagues. Only when the last 40 or 50 years are considered did the English league have as many teams entering the top rank, and for both of these ranges the NFL had more teams achieving the highest win percentage. Thus, despite the greater opportunity through promotion and relegation for teams to reach the highest rank, there seems to be relatively less turnover at the very top in open European leagues than in the closed North American leagues. On average over the last 30 years there have been 50% more teams achieving the highest rank in North America compared Europe.[14]

The story told by Table 4 is slightly different. Looking at the last 10 years, a very large fraction of all teams in the each of the North American leagues managed a top 5 finish in term of win percentage. Forty-six per cent more teams in the CLs achieved this feat on average than in the open European leagues. However, as we go back further the number of teams entering the top ranks does not increase significantly for the North American case, but does in the European case. Clearly, once all the members of a closed league have entered the top 5, the population of entrants can only increase through franchise expansion. In an OL, however, there need be no limit to the increase in the population. Thus, in the case of England there were only 16 teams entering the top 5 ranks over the last decade, but 34 teams entered over the entire 50 year period, more than for any league in the sample (during this period the top division was restricted to 22 or fewer members in each season). Over this lengthy period the number of teams entering the top 5 in North America and Europe is almost identical. Thus, openness in Europe seems to give roughly

---

14   In writing this paper we have looked at some of the descriptive statistics for other European leagues such as Germany, Portugal, Scotland and Spain. In all cases, a similar pattern emerges to that described here.

Table 4. Teams that entered the top 5 ranks.

Period	MLB	NFL	NHL	England	Italy	Belgium*
51–00	28	31	21	34	19	32
61–00	28	30	21	27	18	28
71–00	28	29	21	24	18	24
81–00	28	28	21	22	14	21
91–00	23	26	18	16	12	18

*1953–2000 only.
Note: all teams selected on the basis of regular season win percentage.

similar opportunities over a very long period time, even if there are fewer opportunities over relatively short timespans. Whether this is enough to make an open European league as competitively balanced as a closed North American league in the eyes of the fans must be doubtful at least.

In order to set this picture in a proper perspective, we now consider the theoretical probability of teams entering the top k of ranks for open and closed leagues, under the hypothesis that in each season each contestant in a division has an equal probability of winning each match.

4. Entry in the top k ranks

4.1. Closed leagues

We consider first the case of n teams that are grouped together and compete in a CL with no system of promotion and relegation. Under the hypothesis that the outcome of the championship in a given year is purely random, each team has the same probability $1/n$ of being ranked 1st, 2nd, . . . , n-th. The probability that a team is ranked in the top k places in a generic year is then $w(k) = k/n$. After T years, the probability that a given team has been placed at least once in the top k places is $w(k, T) = 1 - (1 - w(k))^T = 1 - [(n - k)/n]^T$. Finally, the expected number of teams that has won one of the top k positions in the first T years is:

$$y^{CL}(k, T) = nw(k, T) = n - \frac{(n - k)^T}{n^{T-1}} \qquad (1)$$

Equation (1) represents our benchmark for a CL. In particular, the expected number of teams that has won the title at least once after T years is simply $y^{CL}(1, T) = [n^T - (n - 1)^T]/n^{T-1}$, increasing at a decreasing rate over time, from 1 when $T = 1$, to n when T tends to infinity.

4.2. Open leagues

We now consider the typical European way of organizing a team contest. There are L leagues ordered from the top division to the lowest one: league 1 is the "premier" league that awards the championships while league L is the lowest league. League l consists of n_l teams, $l = 1, \ldots, L$. In a generic period, a team in league l can either remain in the same league, or go to an "adjacent" league. We denote respectively by $p(l)$ and by $r(l)$ the total number of promotions to the league above and the total number of teams relegated to the league below league l.[15] If the outcome of each league is random, the probability that a team is in division l at time t is:

$$d(l,t) = d(l,t-1)\frac{n_l - r(l) - p(l)}{n_l} + d(l-1,t-1)\frac{r(l-1)}{n_{l-1}}$$
$$+ d(l+1,t-1)\frac{p(l+1)}{n_{l+1}} \tag{2}$$

where $l = 1, \ldots, L$ and $r(L) = p(1) = 0$, $d(0, t) = d(L+1, t) = 0$.[16] It can be verified that

$$\sum_{l=1}^{L} d(l,t) = \sum_{l=1}^{L} d(l,t-1) = 1$$

since a team starts at $t = 0$ in some league with probability 1, *i.e.* $d(l, 0)$ is 1 for only one value of l and 0 otherwise. In order to take into account the initial distribution of teams, we denote with a subscript l the league where a team starts at the beginning, $d_l(j, 0) = 1$ if $j = l$ and 0 if $j \neq l$.

The probability that a team is ranked in one of the top k places of the premier division in a generic year t is given by the joint probability $d_l(1, t)k/n_1$. We are now in a position to calculate the probability that, after T years, a team that started in league l in the initial period $t = 0$ has been placed at least once in the top k places of the top division. This probability depends on initial conditions and corresponds to the complement to 1 of the probability that such team has never been placed in the top k positions, *i.e.* the team was either in a lower division or in the top one but never "picked" one of the top placements:

$$w_l(k,T) = 1 - \prod_{t=0}^{T}\left[\sum_{l=2}^{L} d_l(l,t) + \frac{n_1 - k}{n_1}d_l(1,t)\right]$$
$$= 1 - \prod_{t=0}^{T}\left[1 - \frac{d_l(1,t)k}{n_1}\right] \tag{3}$$

The expected number of teams that has been placed in the top k positions after T years is:

$$y^{OL}(k,T) = \sum_{l=1}^{L} n_l w_l(k,T) \tag{4}$$

15 In principle, both $p()$ and $r()$ should depend on t; however, we can drop the dependency from time under the hypothesis of random ranking as long as the number of teams in a given league is constant over time. In practice, the number of promotions and relegations can change between periods and this feature can be easily accommodated in our framework.

16 To ensure that the number of teams in a given league is constant overtime, we assume $p(l) = r(l-1)$.

Equations (2), (3) and (4) represent the benchmark for an OL and it is the counterpart to Equation (1). Once it is known the number of teams in each league, as well as the number of teams promoted and relegated to adjacent leagues and the initial conditions, it is immediate to obtain the value of the expected number of teams observed in the top positions after T years. For instance, if a total number n of teams is split equally among L leagues, the teams are ordered in a way such that $d_1(1, 0) = 1$ for the first group of n/L teams, $d_2(2, 0) = 1$ for the second bunch of n/L teams and so on, and if 1 team is promoted and 1 team is relegated in any period, the expected number of teams that has won the premier league at least once after T years is given by[17]

$$y^{OL}(1, T) = \left(\frac{n}{L}\right) \sum_{l=1}^{L} \left(1 - \prod_{t=0}^{T} [1 - d_l(1, t)L/n]\right)$$

$$d_l(1, t) = [d_l(1, t-1)(n/L - 1) + d_l(2, t-1)]L/n$$

$$d_l(l, t) = [d_l(l, t-1)(n/L - 2) + d_l(l-1, t-1) + d_l(l+1, t-1)]L/n$$

$$l = 2, 3, \ldots, L - 1$$

$$d_l(L, t) = [d_l(L, t-1)(n/L - 1) + d_l(L-1, t-1)]L/n$$

5. Mobility in theory and in practice

In the previous sections, we have looked at the actual number of entrants into top ranks and derived the theoretical distributions of teams appearing in top positions in closed and open leagues under the assumption of equal winning probabilities. In this section, we compare the difference between the actual and theoretical distributions.

We apply the theory of the previous section to the precise structure of each league. Table 5 shows the number of teams that would have been expected to achieve the highest seasonal win percentage (if all teams had equal win probabilities) over the same periods considered in Table 3. Table 6 shows the theoretical prediction of entrants into the top 5 of win percentages (if all teams had equal win probabilities), analogous to the actual data of Table 4.[18]

In general, there are two conflicting effects that produce differences in the theoretical predictions for the closed North American and open European leagues. First, in recent decades the expansion of North American leagues to around 30 teams has increased the

---

17 With a simple spreadsheet it is immediate to confirm that with the same total number of teams $y^{OL}(1, T) < y^{CL}(1, T)$ for any $T > 1$. The difference between the two expected numbers of winning teams becomes smaller as T grows, or if "turbulence" is increased by increasing the number of teams promoted/relegated in any period.

18 Numbers in Tables 4 and 5 are rounded. They were obtained taking into account entry and exit of teams, as well as variations in the number of promotions and relegations over time. For instance, in England the third division was split in 1959 into a 3rd and a 4th division. Our calculations do take into account all such institutional features and are available on request.

Table 5. Theoretical number of teams with highest seasonal winning percentage under equal playing strength.

Period	MLB	NFL	NHL	England	Italy	Belgium
51–00	22	23	18	37	40	39
61–00	21	21	18	32	33	31
71–00	18	19	17	26	26	24
81–00	14	15	14	18	18	17
91–00	9	9	9	9	9	9

number of potential winners relative to the European leagues where the size of the top division varies in size between 16 and 22 teams. The second effect is that promotion and relegation gives more teams an opportunity to enter the major league. With equal winning probabilities it can be seen that these two effects would have canceled each other out over the last decade and the CL would have produced as many winners as the open leagues. Over time however, the promotion and relegation effects increasingly dominates the expansion effect and over a 50 year period the open leagues should have produced around twice as many winners as the closed leagues.

In all cases, the actual number of winners in each cell of Table 3 is smaller than the theoretical prediction, but the shortfall is much more pronounced for the open leagues.

Table 6 illustrates a sharper contrast between the OL and CLs. Even in a relatively short period of time the promotion effect dominates the expansion effect so that under equal win probabilities the OLs could have been expected to see more entrants into the top 5 ranks. This contrasts with Table 4 where it was shown that in reality the situation was the reverse—more teams entered the top 5 ranks in the CLs compared to the OLs. Even within a 10 year period most teams in a CL should enter the top 5 ranks—so over a longer period of time the theoretical number of entrants does not increase by much. However, for open leagues the theoretically possible number of entrants increases rapidly, so that over 50 years the number of entrants under equal win probabilities is around one hundred. Once again, the gap between theory and reality is much greater for the open leagues.

To illustrate the size of the gap Figures 1 and 2 show the relationship between theoretical and actual entry to the top for NFL while Figures 3 and 4 offer the same comparison for Serie A, the top soccer division of Italy. In each figure, the broken lines represent the theoretical number of entrants for each of the 5 time ranges, while the solid lines illustrate the actual rate of entry. The figures also provide some perspective on the

Table 6. Theoretical number of teams with top 5 seasonal winning percentage under equal playing strength.

Period	MLB	NFL	NHL	England	Italy	Belgium
51–00	28	29	25	82	104	100
61–00	28	29	25	78	94	84
71–00	28	29	25	70	78	67
81–00	28	29	25	57	58	48
91–00	25	25	24	32	33	28

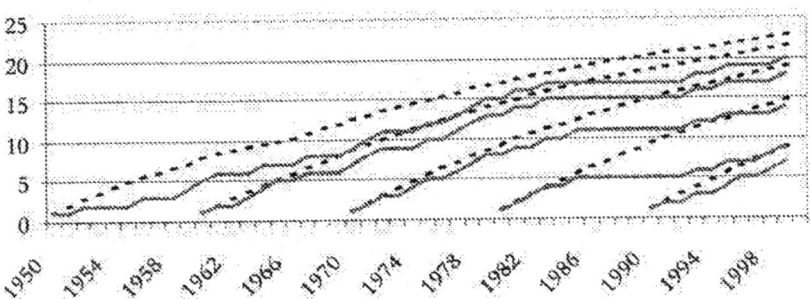

Figure 1. Entry to the highest rank in the NFL.

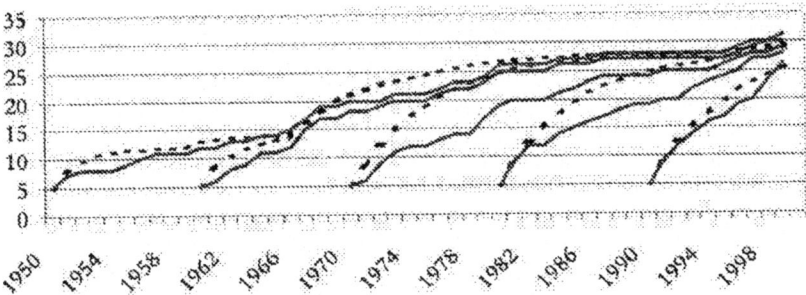

Figure 2. Entry to the top 5 ranks in the NFL.

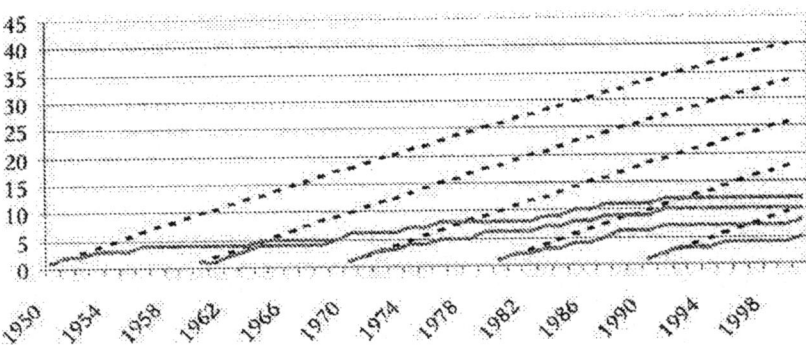

Figure 3. Entry to the highest rank in Italy.

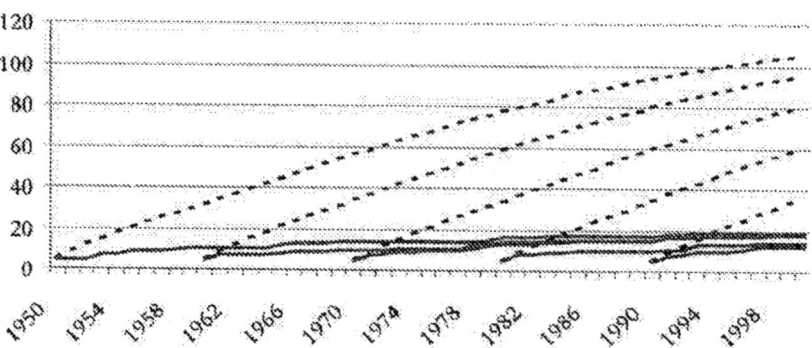

Figure 4. Entry to the top 5 ranks in Italy.

expected and actual entry on a year by year basis. Figures 1 and 2 show that actual entry is quite close to theoretical entry assuming equal playing strengths, suggesting that in dynamic terms the NFL is a fairly balanced competition (particularly looking at entry into the top 5 win percentages). On the other hand, Figures 3 and 4 demonstrate a large gap between theoretical and actual entry in Italy. Actual entry increases only very slowly, both for into the group of champions and into the top 5, and there is no evidence of convergence towards the theoretical limit. This suggests that equality of opportunity in open leagues in Europe has not translated into any equality of outcomes.

While these charts paint a very clear picture, it is desirable to quantify the differences between the OL and CLs in some way. We propose a Gini-type index that relates theoretical to actual entry. Thus, we calculate an index G where

$$G(T^*) = \frac{\sum_{T=1}^{T^*} y^L(k,T) - \sum_{T=1}^{T^*} y_a^L(k,T)}{\sum_{T=1}^{T^*} y^L(k,T)} \tag{5}$$

where T^* is the range of years considered and $y^L(k,T)$ and $y_a^L(k,T)$ are respectively the theoretical and the actual number of teams appearing in rank k or higher in a given league $L = \{CL, OL\}$ over a period of T years. Thus a value of G close to zero indicates a perfectly balanced league while a value of G close to unity indicates a perfectly unbalanced league.[19] Table 7 reports the G-index for the highest seasonal win percentage across the leagues.

For every period considered the G-index for the closed leagues is lower than the G-index for the OLs, suggesting that the closed leagues were closer to the theoretical distribution under equal winning probabilities. In fact, the G-index for the CLs never rose above 0.5, while for the OLs value is either above or close to 0.5 for almost all periods.

---

19 This indicator depends on the starting year; moreover the longer the time series the less informative is the more recent data.

Table 7. G-index for teams with highest seasonal winning percentage.

Period	MLB	NFL	NHL	England	Italy	Belgium
51–00	0.34	0.19	0.42	0.44	0.66	0.70
61–00	0.30	0.15	0.36	0.44	0.55	0.70
71–00	0.30	0.21	0.40	0.54	0.48	0.62
81–00	0.05	0.39	0.39	0.57	0.44	0.51
91–00	0.19	0.24	0.12	0.24	0.38	0.54

Table 8. G-index for teams with top 5 seasonal winning percentage.

Period	MLB	NFL	NHL	England	Italy	Belgium
51–00	0.16	0.04	0.18	0.54	0.78	0.64
61–00	0.18	0.08	0.20	0.60	0.77	0.59
71–00	0.17	0.17	0.23	0.58	0.70	0.59
81–00	0.09	0.15	0.17	0.53	0.67	0.53
91–00	0.11	0.07	0.14	0.35	0.51	0.37

Looking at the individual leagues, there is some indication that baseball has become more balanced over the last 20 years while there is no obvious trend in the NFL or NHL. For the open leagues Belgium was generally furthest away from the theoretical distribution under equal win probabilities, but for the individual leagues there was no clear trend over time.

As far as the top 5 are concerned, the G-index scores for the CLs are all very similar and close to 0. Comparing Tables 7 and 8 this suggests that the CLs have been more successful at creating contenders rather than sharing out the most successful slot. However, since the ultimate Championship winners have been determined by play-offs that are more random than the regular season, this is probably not a problem. By contrast, the G-index for the OL suggest that entry into the top 5 has been more or less as difficult as into the top rank, and without a system of play-offs this suggests both little mobility at the top and considerably less competitive balance than in the closed leagues.

6. Conclusions and policy implications

This paper has proposed a measure of competitive balance that is dynamic, taking into account the turnover of teams at the top over time, rather than conventional measures that tend to emphasize *within-* but not *between-*season competitive balance. We have shown that by a conventional measure the open soccer leagues of Europe are, if anything, more balanced than the North American closed leagues. However, by the dynamic measure of competitive balance the OLs appear significantly less balanced than the closed leagues. We believe that the dynamic measure presents a better picture of competitive balance than the static measure.

One reason for believing that this is a better picture is that we have calculated the theoretical distribution of winning teams under the null hypothesis of equal winning probabilities for the teams, and shown that the open leagues deviate far more from the theoretical distribution than the OLs. The hypothesis that the Europe's open leagues are competitively balanced is far harder to support than the hypothesis that North America's CLs are balanced.

It is important to ask why the European pattern should be so different from the North American one. In general, successful teams draw more support, so that the greater concentration of success in Europe suggests more concentrated support. For example, clubs from Milan (AC and Inter) and Turin (Juventus) have dominated the championship with relatively few other population centers. For example, Rome (population 3.5 m) can boast only four championship titles since the start of the Serie A in 1929, compared to Turin's 28 (population 1.5 m).[20] However, it is by no means clear that fans of Roma and Lazio are less interested or less willing to pay for success than their more successful northern rivals. Moreover, while in many countries the most successful teams have been located in the largest cities (most notably in the case of Spain with Real Madrid and Barcelona) in many other countries this is not clear. In England, for example, league competition has for the last 30 years been dominated by teams from Liverpool (3rd largest population,[21] 13 titles) and Manchester (7th largest, 7 titles) while London based teams have won only 4 titles and Birmingham (2nd largest) have won only a single title.

If concentration is not a product of population endowments, it may be a product of hysteresis. Dynasties are not unknown in North American sports, most notably the Yankees in baseball.[22] But dynasties are usually seen as a significant source of competitive imbalance needing to be counteracted with redistributive measures either in the labour market (*e.g.* salary caps, roster limits) or in the product market (revenue sharing).[23] Such measures are much less widely adopted in Europe. Labor markets operate almost entirely free of any constraints while revenue sharing is rare and limited in extent. But if competitive balance promotes interest in the sport why wouldn't European leagues take on the kind of extensive redistribution seen in North America?

Two possible answers suggest themselves. One is that competitive balance in the sense described here does not matter to the fans. There certainly does not appear to be less interest in European soccer than in North American sports. But as long as the contest within each season is close (*e.g.* measured by standard deviation of win percent) then fans may be indifferent to dominance by a small number of teams over many seasons. This suggests one way in which the study of competitive balance should develop, *i.e.* to focus on the number of teams that need to be in contention to make the contest interesting.

---

20   Tommasi (2000).
21   Source: www.citypopulation.de, Thomas Brinkhoff.
22   See Levi et al. (2000) for a discussion of baseball's competitive balance problem.
23   These measures are reviewed in detail in Szymanski (2003).

A second possible explanation is that the promotion and relegation system itself mitigates against welfare enhancing redistribution schemes. Szymanski and Valletti (2003) compare the incentive to redistribute income in closed and open league systems (*i.e.* with promotion and relegation). They argue that the cost of revenue sharing to large drawing teams is the foregone income from current success, while the benefit is their share in a more valuable (because more balanced) contest. In a closed league every team is guaranteed to participate in that contest, while in an open league any team might be relegated in the future. Thus a strong team has a weaker incentive to share its revenues in an open system.[24] From a policy point of view, perhaps the most interesting topics for further debate are (a) whether the alternative sources of interest in European soccer compensate fans for the relative lack of competitive balance and (b) returning to the Rosen and Sanderson quotation at the beginning of the paper, whether the choice of balance enhancing measures are hindered by the promotion and relegation system itself.

Annex

In this annex, we propose an indicator alternative to the G-index. As a first step, we calculate—as with the G-index—$y^L(k, T)$, *i.e.* the theoretical number of teams appearing in rank k over a period of T years. This number takes into account all the precise details of a certain league that may have changed over time. Then, we calculate $n(k, T)$, *i.e.* the equivalent dimension of a closed league with a constant structure that would have generated then same number of teams appearing in rank k over the same period. In the third step, we consider the actual number $y^L_a(k, T)$ and then construct $n_e(k, T)$, *i.e.* the theoretical dimension of a closed league with a constant structure that would have generated the same number. Finally, our indicator is given by the ratio $n_e(k, T)/n(k, T)$. Results are reported in Table A1. A league is balanced the closer is the E-index to 1, *i.e.* to the equivalent theoretical benchmark. Notice that this exercise allows to construct an indicator that is homogeneous both for open and for closed leagues. This indicator gives a snapshot of competitive balance at the end of a given period, without concentrating on how a particular configuration is reached over time—contrary to the G-index. Results illustrate once again the sharp contrast between open and closed leagues.

---

24   A third reason, suggested by a referee, is that the wider range of competitions on offer in Europe may offset the lack of dynamic competitive balance. For example, in one season the top teams compete in a domestic league, a domestic (knock-out) Cup competition, the European Champions' League, and in addition the top players are selected to play for their national team in international competition. There is certainly a greater array of competition in Europe, but this does not explain why the fans would not find a more balanced league competition more interesting or why the league authorities would not choose to try to make it so. Moreover, Szymanski (2001) provides evidence that lack of competitive balance in the English FA Cup is leading to declining interest in that competition.

Table A1. *E*-index for teams with highest seasonal winning percentage.

Period	MLB	NFL	NHL	England	Italy	Belgium
51–00	0.65	0.83	0.67	0.21	0.12	0.11
61–00	0.67	0.75	0.65	0.15	0.12	0.09
71–00	0.61	0.58	0.58	0.10	0.12	0.13
81–00	0.62	0.36	0.49	0.07	0.11	0.15
91–00	0.29	0.41	0.36	0.13	0.09	0.13

Table A2. *E*-index for teams with top 5 seasonal winning percentage.

Period	MLB	NFL	NHL	England	Italy	Belgium
51–00	1.00	1.06	0.84	0.39	0.16	0.29
61–00	1.00	1.02	0.84	0.31	0.16	0.29
71–00	1.00	0.99	0.89	0.29	0.18	0.31
81–00	1.01	0.97	0.83	0.28	0.18	0.37
91–00	0.91	1.06	0.70	0.34	0.23	0.51

References

Andreff, W. and Staudohar, P., "The evolving model of european sports finance," Journal of Sports Economics, vol. 1 no. 3, pp. 257–276, 2000.

European Commission, The European Model of Sport. Consultation paper of DGX, Brussels, 1998.

Fort, R. and Quirk, J., "Cross subsidization, incentives and outcomes in professional team sports leagues," Journal of Economic Literature, vol. XXXIII no. 3, pp. 1265–1299, 1995.

Hall, S., Szymanski, S., and Zimbalist, A., "Testing causality between team performance and payroll: the case of major league baseball and english soccer," Journal of Sports Economics, vol. 3 no. 2, pp. 149–168, 2002.

Hoehn, T. and Szymanski, S., "The Americanization of European football," Economic Policy, vol. 28, pp. 205–240, 1999.

Horowitz, I. "The increasing competitive balance in major league baseball," Review of Industrial Organization, vol. 12, pp. 373–387, 1997.

Humphreys, B., "Alternative measures of competitive balance in sports leagues," Journal of Sports Economics, vol. 3 no. 2, pp. 133–148, 2002.

Kesenne, S., "Revenue sharing and competitive balance in professional team sports," Journal of Sports Economics, vol. 1 no. 1, pp. 56–65, 2000.

Kipker, I., "Determinanten der zuschauernachfrage im professionellen teamsport: Wie wichtig ist die sportliche ausgeglichenheit?" Unpublished chapter of Ph.D. dissertation, 2000.

Koop, G., "Modelling the evolution of distributions: an application to Major League Baseball," University of Glasgow Discussion Paper, 2002.

Levi, R., Mitchell, G., Volcker, P., and Will, G., The report of the independent members of the commissioner's blue ribbon panel on baseball economics. Major League Baseball, NY, 2000.

Noll, R., "The economics of promotion and relegation in sports leagues; the case of English football," Journal of Sports Economics, vol. 3 no. 2, pp. 169–203, 2002.

Quirk, J. and Fort, R., Pay Dirt: The Business of Professional Team Sports. Princeton University Press: New Jersey, 1992.

Rosen, S. and Sanderson, A., "Labour markets in professional sports," Economic Journal, vol. 111 no. 469, pp. F47–F68, 2001.

Ross, S. and Lucke, R., "Why highly paid athletes deserve more antitrust protection than unionized factory workers," Antitrust Bulletin, vol. 42 no. 3, pp. 641–679, 1997.

Ross, S. and Szymanski, S., "Promotion and relegation," World Economics, vol. 2 no. 2, pp. 179–190, 2001.

Ross, S. and Szymanski, S. "Open competition in league sports," Wisconsin Law Review, vol. 2002 no. 3, pp. 625–656, 2002.

Rottenberg, S., "The baseball players' labor market," Journal of Political Economy, vol. 64, pp. 242–258, 1956.

Sloane, P.J., "The economics of professional football: the football club as a utility maximizer," Scottish Journal of Political Economy, vol. 17 no. 2, pp. 121–146, 1971.

Szymanski, S., "Income inequality, competitive balance and the attractiveness of team sports: Some evidence and a natural experiment from English soccer," Economic Journal, vol. 111 no. 469, pp. F69–F84, 2001.

Szymanski, S., "The economic design of sporting contests," Journal of Economic Literature, forthcoming, 2003.

Szymanski, S. and Kuypers, T., Winners and losers: the business strategy of football. Penguin Book: London, 1999.

Szymanski, S. and Valletti, T., "Promotion and relegation in sporting contests," Imperial College Business School Discussion paper, 2003.

Tommasi, R., Storia della Serie A. Edizioni Marchesi Grafiche, Rome, 2000.

[7]

Scottish Journal of Political Economy, Vol. 51, No. 3, August 2004
© Scottish Economic Society 2004, Published by Blackwell Publishing, 9600 Garsington Road, Oxford OX4 2DQ, UK and 350 Main Street, Malden, MA 02148, USA

REVENUE DIVERGENCE AND COMPETITIVE BALANCE IN A DIVISIONAL SPORTS LEAGUE

Stephen Dobson* and John Goddard**

ABSTRACT

The North American model of resource allocation in professional sports leagues is adapted for English (association) football. Comparisons are drawn between the equilibrium allocations of playing talent under objective functions of profit maximisation and win percent maximisation subject to a financial constraint. Empirical revenue functions are reported for 1926–1999. These indicate a shift in the composition of demand favouring big-city teams and an increase in the sensitivity of revenue to performance. An analysis of match results in the FA Cup suggests an increase in competitive imbalance between teams at different levels of the league's divisional hierarchy, as the theory suggests.

I INTRODUCTION

In the North American (NA) literature on resource allocation in professional team sports leagues, relative market sizes are the final arbiter of the allocation of playing talent between teams, and therefore of competitive balance (Rottenberg, 1956; El Hodiri and Quirk, 1971; Fort and Quirk, 1995; Vrooman, 1995). Although the standard NA model is demand-driven, the empirical NA literature tends to concentrate on the link between the supply side of the players' labour market and competitive balance. For example, Scully (1989), Fort and Quirk (1995), Vrooman (1995) and Eckard (1998) present empirical tests of the invariance proposition: that the efficient allocation of playing talent does not depend on players' contractual status, and is therefore unaffected by the introduction of free agency. In a recent review of this literature, Eckard (2001) finds that "(t)aken together, the results are consistent with the invariance proposition, namely, balance did not change" (p.430).

The present article focuses primarily on demand-side determinants of competitive balance. Specifically, it seeks to demonstrate and draw connections between two empirical propositions concerning professional (association)

*University of Otago, New Zealand
**University of Wales Swansea

360   STEPHEN DOBSON AND JOHN GODDARD

football (or soccer) in England and Wales:[1] first, between the 1920s and 1990s there was increasing divergence in the base levels of spectator demand enjoyed by teams with distinct identifying characteristics; and second, over the same period there was increasing competitive imbalance within the league as a whole. According to the standard model, the second proposition should follow from the first. Since long-term change in the composition of demand has been a major influence on the historical development of English football, the latter should provide a vehicle for empirical scrutiny of the theory, from a perspective that differs from that of most of the NA literature.

The key distinguishing features of the NA and European models for the organisation of professional team sports have been the subject of some discussion in the recent literature (Hoehn and Szymanski, 1999; Fort, 2000). In the present context, the following five features appear to be most relevant: (i) English football's hierarchical divisional structure[2] ensures that membership at the highest level is open to any non-league team with sufficient talent to achieve promotion; (ii) win percent, revenue or utility maximisation subject to a financial constraint is widely assumed to describe the motivations of most English football team owners more appropriately than profit maximisation; (iii) full free agency rights for players over the age of 24 were only established relatively recently, following the European Court of Justice's 1995 Bosman ruling; (iv) relaxation of the regulations restricting the employment of foreign players, also due to the Bosman ruling, implies the market for playing talent has recently become international rather than national; and (v) geographical distances between team home towns are small, making segmentation between spectator catchment areas low and travel to home and away fixtures a practical proposition for many fans.

The content and structure of the paper are as follows. Section II discusses the adaptation of the standard NA model of resource allocation into a form suitable for the analysis of English football. Particular attention is paid to the implications for competitive balance of a team objective function of win percent maximisation subject to a financial constraint, rather than profit maximisation. Consideration is also given to the effect of the shape of the revenue function on the comparison between outcomes under these two objective functions. Section III presents estimated revenue functions for English football teams, and draws inferences about the phenomenon of revenue divergence. Section IV discusses the measurement of competitive balance between teams operating at different levels of a hierarchical, divisional league structure. A statistical analysis of win

---

[1] Although the 92-strong membership of the Premier League and Football League currently includes three Welsh teams, for convenience this paper refers to English football from this point onward.

[2] League competition in English professional football is currently organised into four divisions: the Premier League (PL) comprising 20 teams; and Football League (FL) comprising three divisions (FLD1–FLD3) of 24 teams each. Three or four teams per season are promoted and relegated between adjacent FL divisions, and between FLD1 and PL. A four-division structure, with total membership close to the current complement of 92 teams, has operated since the 1921–2 season. Before the 1992–3 season, all teams were members of the FL and the divisions were numbered 1 to 4.

probabilities in cup ties (in which teams from different divisions meet head-on) is used to identify long-term trends in competitive balance. Section V summarises and concludes.

II   REVENUE AND COMPETITIVE BALANCE: THEORETICAL CONSIDERATIONS

Section II discusses the adaptation of the standard NA model of resource allocation in professional team sports to English football. Previously, the properties of a model of this type under an objective function of win percent maximisation subject to a zero profit (break-even) constraint have been examined by Késenne (1996), who finds that the distribution of playing talent between teams may be more unequal than in the case of profit maximisation. In other contributions based on frameworks similar to the NA model, Hoehn and Szymanski (1999) consider the effect of the participation of the most successful football teams in European competition on competitive balance in domestic leagues, and Késenne (2000) discusses the implications for competitive balance of the introduction of a NA-style salary cap.

At a general level, the institutional, historical and economic characteristics of English football differ from those of the leading NA professional sports in respect of (at least) five major characteristics, as follows.

(i) Membership of the top professional sports leagues in NA is determined by the award of franchises. In contrast English football's Premier League (PL) and Football League (FL) teams compete within a hierarchical divisional structure. At the end of each season, several teams are promoted and relegated between divisions, so divisional membership is determined by competitive prowess. From casual inspection of team revenues data, it is clear that revenue is primarily dependent on each team's position within the league as a whole, rather than within its own division. Therefore the use of the win ratio as an argument of the revenue function, standard practice in the NA literature, is inappropriate; but it is reasonable to replace the win ratio with team i's normalised league position $L_i = (n+1 - \text{pos}_i)/n$, where pos_i is team i's actual league position (1 = top of PL; n = bottom of FL). With the total supply of talent assumed fixed L_i is monotonic in talent, and from this point onward L_i is interpreted directly as a talent measure.[3]

(ii) Most NA major league sports teams are highly profitable. This is partly due to the restrictions the franchise system imposes on supply, as well as the restraining influence on wage expenditure of salary caps in football and basketball (Quirk and Fort, 1999). A profit maximisation (PM) objective function has been adopted uncontroversially in most of the NA literature. In English football in contrast, the intense competitive pressure generated by the league's divisional

---

[3] L_i is discrete, while talent is normally assumed to be continuous. When n is large, however, the distinction becomes negligible.

structure has certainly contributed to the chronic loss-making propensities of most PL and FL teams. Following Sloane (1971), most researchers have argued that win percent, revenue or utility maximisation subject to a financial constraint is a more suitable objective function than PM.

(iii) Full free agency rights for English footballers over the age of 24 were established by the European Court of Justice's (ECJ) 1995 Bosman ruling. Prior to 1995, progress toward free agency was incremental. Before 1963 a player's current team exercised complete discretion as to whether he could move to another team, irrespective of its decision whether or not to extend his present employment contract. In 1963 this discretion became contingent on renewal of the contract. In 1978 an out-of-contract player became entitled to move irrespective of his employer's wishes. His new employer, however, would still be liable to pay compensation in the form of a transfer fee. In 1995 out-of-contract players (over age 24) became entitled to move with no liability for compensation. Before 1978 teams motivated primarily by winning rather than profit probably had little incentive, and could not be forced, to allow their best players to move. Since 1978 and especially since 1995, mobility (at the behest of players) has increased considerably, with flows of talent naturally reflecting differences between teams' ability-to-pay. A closer relationship between demand shifts and competitive balance might therefore be expected post-1978 than pre-1978.

(iv) Because few (if any) other countries operate professional leagues in the same sports on a comparable scale, product and labour markets in NA (especially at the top level) are effectively closed. In England, a regulation restricting to three the number of non-British players PL and FL teams could field remained in force until 1995, when the ECJ adjudged the application of this provision to EU nationals to be contrary to European employment law. Consequently, post-1995 many more foreign players have been employed, especially in the PL.[4] An open labour market may suggest a need for the relaxation of the standard model's assumption that the total supply of talent is fixed. The standard closed labour market assumption is however a reasonable description of reality for most of the period under scrutiny, and this assumption is retained in the present article. Open labour market models are discussed elsewhere by Hoehn and Szymanski (1999) and Dobson and Goddard (2001).

(v) The standard model assumes each team's spectator demand is proportional to its home-town population: a reasonable assumption in NA where catchment areas are predominantly local (due to large distances between towns), and all but the largest cities have at most

[4] According to data published in *Rothmans Football Yearbook*, in 2001 29.1% of players employed by PL teams were born outside the UK or Ireland. For the FL the corresponding figure was 13.4%. In 1986, the equivalent figures were 5.0% (for the old division 1) and 2.0% (divisions 2 to 4).

one team in each major league sport. In English football neither of these conditions pertains. Geographical segmentation between catchment areas is less than in NA because distances are shorter. Wherever they reside, regular travel to home and away fixtures is a practical proposition for many sports fans; and with extensive television coverage of all leading teams available nationally, home-town population is a highly imperfect indicator of each team's popularity. In the model developed below, a set of time-varying individual effects is used to capture all relevant demographic, historical and socio-economic influences, including for example variations in disposable incomes, on each team's base level of spectator demand.

The rest of section II describes an adapted version of the NA model suitable for English football. The basic framework is similar to the one used in a recent paper by Fort and Quirk (2004), who show that under the most general assumptions concerning the properties of the revenue and cost functions, the comparison between competitive balance under assumptions of PM on the one hand, and win percent maximisation subject to a financial constraint (WM from this point onward) on the other, is indeterminate. The present discussion seeks to extend this insight, by drawing a number of specific comparisons between outcomes under PM and WM objective functions, for cases where restrictions are imposed on the revenue and cost functions. It also provides a theoretical basis for the empirical revenue function estimations that are reported in section III.

In the two-team model, team i's revenue function in terms of its talent, measured by its normalised league position L_i, is $R_i(L_i) = A_i\rho(L_i)$. A_i is an individual effect reflecting team i's market size and any other (unspecified) determinants of revenue; $A_1 > A_2$ is assumed. The function $\rho(L_i)$ is assumed to be concave, or $\rho''(L_i) < 0$.[5]

Team i's cost function is $C_i(L_i) = pL_i + F_i$, where p is the cost of an additional unit of talent. Under PM F_i is interpreted as team i's fixed costs; in the PM case, however, F_i does not influence the equilibrium allocation of playing talent. Under WM F_i can be interpreted as the sum of team i's fixed costs and minimum required profit (or maximum tolerable loss). A break-even financial constraint has been widely assumed in the European literature based on WM (Fort and Quirk, 2004). The present formulation affords more flexibility, and depending on the relative magnitudes of team i's fixed costs and the loss (if any) its owner is prepared to tolerate, F_i can be positive, zero or negative.

Team i's profit function (incorporating the financial constraint in the WM case) is $\Pi_i(L_i) = R_i(L_i) - C_i(L_i) = A_i\rho(L_i) - pL_i - F_i$. It is useful to define the marginal revenue (per incremental unit of talent employed) and average revenue (per unit of talent employed) functions, $MR_i(L_i) = A_i\rho'(L_i)$ and $AR_i(L_i) =$

---

[5] $R_i(L_i)$ is slightly more restrictive than the revenue function used by Fort and Quirk (2004), because any differences between teams derive from the individual effects only, while the function $\rho(L_i)$ is the same for all teams. Fort and Quirk impose no such restrictions on their counterpart of $R_i(L_i)$. As well as league position, the empirical revenue functions reported in section III of this paper include a term allowing for the closeness of intra-divisional competition, in an attempt to incorporate one version of the uncertainty of outcome hypothesis.

$A_i \bar{\rho}(L_i)$, where $\rho'(L_i) = \partial \rho(L_i)/\partial L_i$ and $\bar{\rho}(L_i) = \rho(L_i)/L_i$. The elasticity of revenue with respect to talent is:

$$\varepsilon(L_i) = [\partial R_i(L_i)/\partial L_i][L_i/R_i(L_i)] = MR_i(L_i)/AR_i(L_i) = \rho'(L_i)/\bar{\rho}(L_i).$$

In this formulation, $\varepsilon(L_i)$ depends on L_i but not on A_i. The direction of the relationship between L_i and $\varepsilon(L_i)$, indicated by the sign of $\varepsilon' = \partial \varepsilon(L_i)/\partial L_i$, plays an important part in the comparisons between the PM and WM equilibria that follow. Each of the three possibilities $\varepsilon' > 0$, $\varepsilon' = 0$ and $\varepsilon' < 0$ is considered below.

Under PM, p adjusts to p^* such that $MR_1(L_1^*) = MR_2(L_2^*) = p^*$. $A_1 > A_2$ ensures $L_1^* > L_2^*$. A convenient measure of competitive balance under PM is L_1^*/L_2^*, analogous to the 'ratio of win ratios' measure widely used in the NA literature. If $L_1^*/L_2^* = 1$ both teams are of equal strength. The extent to which L_1^*/L_2^* exceeds unity measures the extent of team 1's dominance over team 2.

In the PM models of Fort and Quirk (1995) and Vrooman (1995), competition becomes more unbalanced if the difference between population sizes increases; in the present case the equivalent condition is an increase in the difference between A_1 and A_2. This result follows because each team's competitive strength is proportional to its relative market size at the PM equilibrium. Competition also becomes more unbalanced if the elasticity of revenue with respect to win ratio increases; here the equivalent condition is an increase in $\varepsilon(L_i)$. If this elasticity increases, it is efficient for the big-city team to employ more talent and the small-town team less, because the former's revenue gain exceeds the latter's loss.

Under WM, p adjusts to p^+ such that: $\Pi_1(L_1^+) = \Pi_2(L_2^+) = 0$ or $AR_1(L_1^+) - F_1/L_1^+ = AR_2(L_2^+) - F_2/L_2^+ = p^+$. Fort and Quirk (2004) show that depending on the precise nature of the revenue and cost assumptions, competition may be more balanced, equally balanced or less balanced under WM than it is under PM. However, by imposing certain restrictions on the revenue and cost functions, specific comparisons can be drawn in a number of particular cases, as follows.

Case 1: $F_1 = F_2 = 0$ (zero fixed costs). The WM equilibrium condition reduces to $AR_1(L_1^+) = AR_2(L_2^+)$. If $\varepsilon(L_i)$ is constant in L_i or $\varepsilon' = 0$, competition is equally balanced under WM and PM. It can also be shown that if $\varepsilon(L_i)$ is increasing in L_i or $\varepsilon' > 0$, competition is more balanced under WM than under PM; and if $\varepsilon(L_i)$ is decreasing in L_i or $\varepsilon' < 0$, competition is less balanced under WM than under PM.[6]

Case 2: $F_1 = F_2 = F \neq 0$ (non-zero fixed costs are the same for both teams). The WM equilibrium condition simplifies to $AR_1(L_1^+) - F/L_1^+ = AR_2(L_2^+) - F/L_2^+$. If $F > 0$ and $\varepsilon' \leq 0$, competition is less balanced under WM than under PM. If $F < 0$ and $\varepsilon' > 0$, competition is more balanced under WM than under PM. In other cases, the comparison between WM and PM is indeterminate.

Case 3: $F_1 \neq F_2$ (non-zero fixed costs differ between teams). If $F_1 < F_2$, $F_2 > 0$ and $\varepsilon' \leq 0$, competition is less balanced under WM than under PM. If $F_1 > F_2$,

---

[6] At the PM equilibrium, $MR_1(L_1^*) = MR_2(L_2^*)$ implies $\varepsilon(L_1^*)AR_1(L_1^*) = \varepsilon(L_2^*)AR_2(L_2^*)$. If $\varepsilon' > 0$ and $\varepsilon(L_1^*) > \varepsilon(L_2^*)$, $AR_1(L_1^*) < AR_2(L_2^*)$. This implies $L_1^+ < L_1^*$ (and $L_2^+ > L_2^*$) is required for $AR_1(L_1^+) = AR_2(L_2^+)$. Similarly, if $\varepsilon' = 0$ and $\varepsilon(L_1^*) = \varepsilon(L_2^*)$, $AR_1(L_1^*) = AR_2(L_2^*)$ and $L_1^+ = L_1^*$ is required. If $\varepsilon' < 0$ and $\varepsilon(L_1^*) < \varepsilon(L_2^*)$, $AR_1(L_1^*) > AR_2(L_2^*)$ and $L_1^+ > L_1^*$ is required.

$F_1 > 0$ and $\varepsilon' > 0$, competition is more balanced under WM than under PM. In other cases, the comparison between WM and PM is indeterminate.[7]

The estimated revenue functions reported in section III provide empirical evidence concerning the shape of the revenue function for PL and FL member teams, and a specific test to distinguish between the cases $\varepsilon' > 0$, $\varepsilon' = 0$ and $\varepsilon' < 0$. The outcome of this test will also permit a narrowing of the range of empirically relevant comparisons between competitive balance under the PM and WM objective functions.

III   EMPIRICAL REVENUE FUNCTIONS FOR ENGLISH FOOTBALL

Section III reports empirical counterparts of the theoretical revenue functions developed in section II. The data comprises annual gate revenues for all PL and FL football teams between the 1926–7 and 1998–9 seasons inclusive, obtained from the FL's archives and Football Trust (various issues). For most of this period, gate revenue was by far the most important component of total revenue. Recently, however, the share of gate revenue in total revenue has fallen, and the rate of decline has been faster in the PL than in the FL. For recent years gate revenue data will therefore tend to yield a conservative estimate of the overall extent of revenue divergence.[8]

To describe the main changes in the distribution of revenue between teams with broadly similar demographic, geographic and historical characteristics, Dobson and Goddard (1998) classify the PL and FL member teams into five groups. G1 (Group 1) contains four major London teams that tend to attract significant levels of support from all parts of London and beyond, and ten major teams from five other cities with populations larger than 500,000: Birmingham, Liverpool, Leeds, Manchester and Sheffield. G2 contains teams from northern and midlands cities with populations in the range 250,000–500,000. G3 contains teams from southern towns other than London, and the minor London teams not included in G1. The two remaining groups contain teams from smaller northern and midlands towns, sub-divided into pre-1922 (G4) and post-1922 (G5) league entrants.[9]

Between the 1920s and 1990s there were marked contrasts in fortunes between groups, in terms of both performance and revenue indicators,

---

[7] In the case $F_1 = F_2 = F$, if $F > 0$ and $\varepsilon' \le 0$, $AR_1(L_1^*) - F/L_1^* > AR_2(L_2^*) - F/L_2^*$, because $AR_1(L_1^*) \ge AR_2(L_2^*)$ and $L_1^* > L_2^*$. Therefore $L_1^+ > L_1^*$ is required to satisfy the WM equilibrium condition. If $F < 0$ and $\varepsilon' > 0$, $AR_1(L_1^*) - F/L_1^* < AR_2(L_2^*) - F/L_2^*$, because $AR_1(L_1^*) < AR_2(L_2^*)$ and $L_1^* > L_2^*$. Therefore $L_1^+ < L_1^*$ is required. In the case $F_1 \ne F_2$, if $F_1 < F_2$, $F_2 > 0$ and $\varepsilon' \le 0$, $AR_1(L_1^*) - F_1/L_1^* > AR_2(L_2^*) - F_2/L_2^*$. Therefore $L_1^+ > L_1^*$ is required. If $F_1 > F_2$, $F_1 > 0$ and $\varepsilon' > 0$, $AR_1(L_1^*) - F_1/L_1^* < AR_2(L_2^*) - F_2/L_2^*$. Therefore $L_1^+ < L_1^*$ is required.

[8] While total revenue (from all sources) would be preferable in many respects to gate revenue, the former is only obtainable from company accounts, and many teams have not filed accounts regularly. Advantages of the gate revenue data set include comprehensiveness and consistency: there are no missing observations, and all data are compiled on an identical basis in accordance with league regulations.

[9] The classification criteria and the composition of the groups are detailed in Dobson and Goddard (1998). Populations are from the 1961 census, the closest to the mid-point of the observation period. The group classifications are based on exogenous characteristics of the teams, and not on their performance or revenue over the period under scrutiny.

366 STEPHEN DOBSON AND JOHN GODDARD

Table 1

Estimation results: revenue function

Season end-year = t:	1926	1936	1949	1959	1969	1979	1989	1999
(a) League performance score (%) by group:								
G1	26.9	25.5	25.1	25.7	26.3	25.0	24.1	25.9
G2	19.0	19.6	17.7	16.0	16.4	16.4	17.8	17.3
G3	18.4	22.4	24.1	27.0	30.7	35.1	36.2	30.0
G4	21.3	21.4	20.7	18.6	15.9	13.0	12.3	17.2
G5	14.4	11.1	12.4	12.8	10.7	10.5	9.6	9.7
(b) % share of gate revenue by group:								
G1	32.8	34.9	29.0	31.7	40.2	39.3	39.9	43.5
G2	18.6	17.9	21.3	17.6	19.2	16.5	18.3	20.8
G3	21.6	23.8	24.2	25.9	24.8	27.6	27.4	19.6
G4	16.9	15.9	16.3	15.3	9.4	10.2	8.7	12.5
G5	10.1	7.4	9.1	9.5	6.4	6.5	5.7	3.5
(c) Group mean values of $\exp(\hat{\alpha}_{i,t})$:								
G1 ($g = 1$)	.0189	.0209	.0233	.0285	.0347	.0399	.0406	.0349
G2 ($g = 2$)	.0125	.0157	.0178	.0206	.0219	.0231	.0221	.0208
G3 ($g = 3$)	.0119	.0124	.0135	.0153	.0170	.0166	.0142	.0098
G4 ($g = 4$)	.0094	.0117	.0128	.0139	.0142	.0137	.0125	.0126
G5 ($g = 5$)	.0059	.0067	.0073	.0088	.0099	.0106	.0083	.0047
(d) Cross-sectional standard deviation of $\exp(\hat{\alpha}_{i,t})$:								
$s[\exp(\hat{\alpha}_{i,t})]$	.0051	.0059	.0067	.0079	.0095	.0114	.0126	.0130
(e) Other estimated parameters:								
$\hat{\beta}_t$		.6075	.5831	.5340	.6386	.8821	1.0801	.9178	.8373
$\hat{\delta}_t$		.0778	.0864	.0808	.0975	.1294	.1560	.1456	.1362
$\hat{\phi}_t$		−.2109[a]	−.0756[a]	−.0115	.0668	.1094[a]	.1164[a]	.0877[a]	.0233
(f) Elasticity of revenue w.r.t. league position for the median team ($L_{i,t} = 0.5$):								
$\hat{\varepsilon}_t(0.5)$	.4996	.4633	.4220	.5034	.7026	.8638	.7160	.6485

Notes:
League performance scores (panel (a)) are calculated by expressing the sum of $L_{i,t}$ over all teams in Group g as a percentage of the sum of $L_{i,t}$ over all teams. In panel (e), all reported $\hat{\beta}_t$ and $\hat{\delta}_t$ are significantly different from zero at the 1% level. For $\hat{\phi}_t$, [a] denotes significantly different from zero at the 1% level.

described in detail by Dobson and Goddard (1998). Summary data are shown in Panels (a) and (b) of Table 1. For the purposes of the present discussion, the most important feature is a long-term shift in the composition of demand favouring the big-city teams at the expense of their small-town counterparts. Over the period as a whole this is reflected in an increase in G1's revenue share of more than ten percentage points, while G1's performance was virtually unchanged.

Economists, sociologists and social historians have all attempted to explain this shift in the composition of demand (Dunning *et al.*, 1988; Walvin,

1994; Russell, 1997). The geographical bond between teams and their spectators certainly appears to have been stronger in the first half of the 20th century than subsequently. Prior to the late-1950s financial and logistical constraints militated against regular long-distance travel to sports fixtures for most spectators. Thereafter rising affluence, combined with improvements in public and private transport enabled big-city teams, in particular, to begin to draw support at a national rather than purely local or regional level, and to drain support from small-town teams. Demographic change also tended to weaken links between communities and their local teams. Suburbanisation implied population shifts away from urban districts where most stadia were located. Meanwhile the expanding reach of televised football focused public attention on a handful of star players of the most glamorous teams, also favouring the latter at the expense of their less widely exposed small-town counterparts.

The effects of such developments are incorporated into the empirical revenue functions reported below by permitting variation over time and between groups in the revenue function parameters. In the empirical revenue functions, $R_{i,t}$ and $L_{i,t}$ are equivalent to R_i (revenue) and L_i (normalised league position as a measure of talent) as defined in section II; and $r_{i,t} = R_{i,t}/\Sigma_i R_{i,t}$ is team i's normalised revenue (actual revenue as a proportion of total league revenue). In view of the importance attached to the uncertainty of outcome hypothesis in the sports economics literature (Humphreys, 2002), the following measure of the closeness of competition within each division in each season is also included as a revenue function covariate: $v_{i,t}$ = the coefficient of variation (standard deviation divided by mean) of the points totals of all teams in team i's division in season t's final divisional table. The empirical revenue function specification is as follows:

$$\ln(r_{i,t}) = \alpha_{i,t} + \beta_t \ln(L_{i,t}) + \delta_t [\ln(L_{i,t})]^2 + \phi_t \ln(v_{i,t}) + u_{i,t}$$

where $u_{i,t}$ is a random disturbance term, and $\alpha_{i,t}$, β_t, δ_t and ϕ_t are time-varying revenue function parameters. For estimation, some restrictions on these parameters are required: each is assumed to be polynomial in t.[10] In this formulation, the elasticity of revenue with respect to league position, the equivalent of $\varepsilon(L_i)$ in section II, is $\beta_t + 2\delta_t \ln(L_{i,t})$. This elasticity is increasing in $L_{i,t}$ if $\delta_t > 0$, constant if $\delta_t = 0$, and decreasing if $\delta_t < 0$.

---

[10] The polynomial functional forms are:

$$\alpha_{i,t} = a_{i,0} + \sum_{m=1}^{M_1} a_{i,m} t^m; \; \beta_t = b_0 + \sum_{m=1}^{M_2} b_m t^m; \; \delta_t = d_0 + \sum_{m=1}^{M_2} d_m t^m; \; \phi_t = f_0 + \sum_{m=1}^{M_3} f_m t^m$$

$\alpha_{i,t}$ are time-varying home team individual effects, allowing for variation between teams and over time in base levels of spectator demand. β_t, δ_t and ϕ_t are also subject to polynomial trends, which are assumed not to vary between teams. F-tests indicated that $M_1 = 3$, $M_2 = 9$ and $M_3 = 2$ provide an adequate representation of the polynomial trends; higher-order terms beyond these values tested insignificant. t varies from 1 (1925–6 season) to 67 (1998–9 season); there is no break in t for the seven-year period when football was suspended during the Second World War. Teams with fewer than ten time series observations are excluded from the estimations.

The revenue function estimation results are reported in Table 1. Panel (c) reports the group mean values of $\exp(\hat{\alpha}_{i,t})$ (the empirical counterparts of the individual effects A_i) for selected seasons. These provide an indication of shifts between the five groups in the composition of aggregate spectator demand for the league as a whole, after controlling for team performance. The increase in the G1 teams' mean value of $\exp(\hat{\alpha}_{i,t})$ over the entire period is unsurprising in view of the increase in G1's revenue share described above, although the upward trend in G1's mean $\exp(\hat{\alpha}_{i,t})$ was reversed during the 1990s. The cross-sectional standard deviation (across all teams) of $\exp(\hat{\alpha}_{i,t})$, denoted $s[\exp(\hat{\alpha}_{i,t})]$, provides a convenient summary measure of divergence between teams in base levels of spectator demand. Panel (d) shows that this measure has increased steadily over time.

Panel (e) of Table 1 shows the estimated values of β_t, δ_t and ϕ_t. All values of $\hat{\beta}_t$ and $\hat{\delta}_t$ are positive and significant at the 1% level, and appear to be well defined. Both of these parameters increased sharply in absolute terms between the 1950s and the 1970s, though more recently there has been a downward drift. The variation over time in the elasticity of revenue with respect to league position is similar. For the league's median team with $L_{i,t} = 0.5$, the values of the estimated elasticity, $\hat{\varepsilon}_t(0.5) = \hat{\beta}_t + 2\hat{\delta}_t \ln(0.5)$, are reported in panel (f). In terms of the discussion in section II, the positive sign of $\hat{\delta}_t$ provides empirical support for the case $\varepsilon' > 0$: the empirical revenue function is more elastic (with respect to league position) for teams near the top of the league than for those near the bottom. For the median team, this elasticity is estimated to have varied within the range 0.40 to 0.90. Figures 1 and 2 plot the movement in the series $s[\exp(\hat{\alpha}_{i,t})]$ and $\hat{\varepsilon}_t(0.5)$ for the entire 1926–1999 period.

In contrast to the results for β_t and δ_t, the estimates of ϕ_t are not signed consistently, and do not appear to be well defined. In accordance with the uncertainty of outcome hypothesis, negatively signed values of $\hat{\phi}_t$ are obtained for 1926, 1936 and 1949; of these the first two are significant at the 1% level. The remaining values of $\hat{\phi}_t$ are positively signed, and those for 1969, 1979 and 1989 are significant. Overall the empirical results do not appear to support the hypothesis that spectator demand (as reflected in the revenue function) increases if competition at divisional level becomes closer.

Section III concludes by revisiting briefly the comparisons between competitive balance at the PM and WM equilibria that were drawn in section II. The estimation results suggest the range of empirically relevant comparisons can be limited to the case $\varepsilon' > 0$. Accordingly these can be re-stated as follows. If $F_1 = F_2 = 0$, competition is more balanced under WM than under PM. If $F_1 = F_2 = F < 0$, competition is more balanced under WM than under PM; if $F_1 = F_2 = F > 0$ the comparison between PM and WM is indeterminate. If $F_1 > F_2$ and $F_1 > 0$, competition is more balanced under WM than under PM. Finally, if $F_1 > F_2$ and $F_1 < 0$ or if $F_1 < F_2$, the comparison between WM and PM is indeterminate. In those cases for which specific conclusions can be drawn WM appears to produce closer competitive balance than PM; but this comparison can not be generalised over all possible cases.

IV Measuring Competitive Balance Using FA Cup Match Results Data

In the empirical NA team sports literature, it is standard practice to measure competitive balance using the cross-sectional variance or standard deviation of the win ratios of member teams (Fort and Quirk, 1995; Eckard, 1998, 2001; Humphreys, 2002). This procedure is unsuitable for English football, however, because of its divisional competitive structure. Intra-divisional variation in win ratios may say something about competitive balance across the league as a whole: greater imbalance might be discernible within divisions to some extent. Yet such measures are unlikely to provide a powerful measure. Most of the action is inter- rather than intra-divisional, but inter-division variation is not considered.

However, all PL and FL member teams take part in a competition that does allow direct comparisons between the playing strengths of teams from different divisions. The FA Cup (Football Association Challenge Cup) is a sudden-death knock-out tournament involving both league and non-league teams. For spectators, a major attraction is the cup's propensity to produce shock results, such as the elimination of a PL team by an opponent from the lower reaches of the FL or from non-league.[11]

Recently, Szymanski (2001) has used FA Cup match attendance data in an effort to identify trends in competitive balance in English football since the 1970s. Analysing cup attendances in matches where a corresponding league fixture (between the same teams in the same season) took place, Szymanski finds that cup attendances declined relative to league attendances. In the demand for sports literature, one version of the uncertainty of outcome hypothesis is that attendances depend on the level of competitive balance between all teams in the competition concerned. Accordingly Szymanski interprets declining cup attendances as signifying increasing inter-divisional competitive imbalance between league teams. League attendances are less affected, because rising competitive imbalance is mainly an inter- rather than an intra-divisional phenomenon. Here, competitive balance is measured directly using match results data, rather than indirectly via a hypothesised relationship with attendance.

In section IV, inferences about changes in competitive balance are drawn directly from a statistical investigation of trends in win probabilities in cup matches conditional on league position. Koning (2000) and Dobson and Goddard (2001) use ordered probit regression to model league match results in football. Adapting this approach, the model describing the result of the cup match between home team i and away team j played in season t, denoted $y_{i,j,t}$, is:

$$\text{Home win} \Rightarrow y_{i,j,t} = 1 \quad \text{if} \quad \mu_2 < y^*_{i,j,t} + \varepsilon_{i,j,t}$$
$$\text{Draw} \Rightarrow y_{i,j,t} = 0.5 \quad \text{if} \quad \mu_1 < y^*_{i,j,t} + \varepsilon_{i,j,t} \leq \mu_2$$
$$\text{Away win} \Rightarrow y_{i,j,t} = 0 \quad \text{if} \quad y^*_{i,j,t} + \varepsilon_{i,j,t} \leq \mu_1$$

---

[11] The FA Cup is English football's principal knock-out cup competition, open to all PL and FL teams as well as non-league teams. The latter take part in a preliminary qualifying tournament. FLD2 and FLD3 teams enter in Round 1. Survivors are joined by PL and FLD1 teams in Round 3. Further rounds reduce the 64 Round 3 contestants to two finalists in Round 8. From Round 1 onwards, a random draw determines who plays whom and who has home advantage; there are no seedings.

STEPHEN DOBSON AND JOHN GODDARD

where $y^*_{i,j,t} = \gamma_{0,t} + \gamma_{1,t} L_{i,t} + \gamma_{2,t} L_{j,t}$; $\varepsilon_{i,j,t}$ is a standard normal disturbance term; $\gamma_{k,t}$ ($k = 0, 1, 2$) are time-varying parameters ($\gamma_{1,t} < 0$ and $\gamma_{2,t} > 0$ are expected) which follow a polynomial functional form;[12] and μ_1 and μ_2 are additional cut-off parameters.

The data comprises FA Cup matches played between the 1921–2 and 2001–2 seasons inclusive (except 1945–6 when the FA Cup was staged but the league was suspended) that were either first matches or (first) replays involving two league member teams, between Round 1 and the quarter-finals (currently Round 6) inclusive. Second and subsequent replays, semi-finals and finals are excluded because these matches are usually played at neutral venues. Match results are recorded after 90 or 120 minutes' play; results of penalty shoot-outs are not recorded.[13]

Since the rules concerning match duration differ between first matches and replays, the parameters of the ordered probit model also differ, and separate estimations are required. The estimated home win, draw and away win probabilities are $h^{(z)}(L_{i,t}, L_{j,t}) = 1 - \Phi(\hat{\mu}_2 - \hat{y}^*_{i,j,t})$, $d^{(z)}(L_{i,t}, L_{j,t}) = \Phi(\hat{\mu}_2 - \hat{y}^*_{i,j,t}) - \Phi(\hat{\mu}_1 - \hat{y}^*_{i,j,t})$ and $a^{(z)}(L_{i,t}, L_{j,t}) = \Phi(\hat{\mu}_1 - \hat{y}^*_{i,j,t})$ respectively, where Φ is the standard normal distribution function; $z = 1$ denotes a first match; and $z = 2$ denotes a replay. Let $E(y_{i,j,t})$ represent the expected outcome for team i after the first match or after the (first) replay if the first match is drawn, calculated as a probability-weighted average of scores of 1 if team i wins the tie; 0.5 if the tie is level; and 0 if team i loses:

$$E(y_{i,j,t}) = h^{(1)}(L_{i,t}, L_{j,t}) + d^{(1)}(L_{i,t}, L_{j,t})\{a^{(2)}(L_{j,t}, L_{i,t}) + 0.5d^{(2)}(L_{j,t}, L_{i,t})\}$$

If team i initially plays away to team j, the expected outcome for team i is $1 - E(y_{j,i,t})$. Team i's expected outcome, conditional on league positions but unconditional on which team initially plays at home, is $w_t(L_{i,t}, L_{j,t}) = 0.5\{1 + E(y_{i,j,t}) - E(y_{j,i,t})\}$. Variations over time in $w_t(\bar{L}_i, \bar{L}_j)$ for constant values of $\bar{L}_i$ and $\bar{L}_j$ provide an indication of trends in competitive balance. An alternative summary measure is $s(w_t)$, the cross-sectional standard deviation (across i) of $w_t(L_{i,t}, 0.5)$: the expected outcomes (as defined above) of all teams against the league's median team.

---

[12] The polynomial functional form is: $\gamma_{k,t} = g_{k,0} + \sum_{m=1}^{M_4} g_{k,m} t^m$. In this expression $g_{0,0}$ is redundant and is set to zero. Ordered probit regression is used to obtain estimates of the parameters μ_1, μ_2, $g_{k,m}$, and therefore $\gamma_{k,t}$. Chi-square tests for the joint significance of the additional coefficients introduced by increasing M_4, based on the omitted variables version of Weiss's (1997) Lagrange Multiplier (LM) test, indicate that $M_4 = 3$ provides an adequate representation of the trend in $\gamma_{k,t}$.

[13] If the first match of an FA Cup tie produces a winner after 90 minutes' play, this result settles the tie. If the first match is level after 90 minutes, a replay is staged at the home of the team initially drawn away. If the replay produces a winner after 90 minutes, this settles the tie. If the replay is level after 90 minutes, 30 minutes' extra time is played. Until 1993–4, if the replay was still level after 120 minutes, further replays were staged until a winner emerged. Since 1993–4, penalty shoot-outs have settled ties level after 120 minutes of the (first) replay (210 minutes in total). The introduction of penalty shoot-outs in the 1993–4 season should not affect the parameters, since this change only affects what happens *after* 210 minutes' play.

Table 2

Estimation results: competitive balance

Season end-year = t:	1926	1936	1949	1959	1969	1979	1989	1999
(a) Proportion of home wins, draws and away wins, cup matches, 10 seasons up to and including t:								
Home wins	n/a	0.530	0.531	0.464	0.485	0.500	0.487	0.453
Draws	n/a	0.218	0.199	0.244	0.245	0.268	0.250	0.259
Away wins	n/a	0.252	0.270	0.293	0.271	0.232	0.263	0.288
(b) Ordered probit estimation results, first matches: $\hat{\mu}_1 = -0.881$; $\hat{\mu}_2 = -0.089$; obs. = 5438								
$\hat{\gamma}_{0,t}$	−0.013	−0.112	−0.146	−0.172	−0.167	−0.145	−0.119	−0.101
$\hat{\gamma}_{1,t}$	1.160	1.314	1.335	1.301	1.246	1.242	1.363	1.682
$\hat{\gamma}_{2,t}$	−1.141	−1.417	−1.458	−1.407	−1.314	−1.302	−1.498	−2.024
(c) Ordered probit estimation results, replays: $\hat{\mu}_1 = -0.916$; $\hat{\mu}_2 = -0.545$; obs. = 1498								
$\hat{\gamma}_{0,t}$	−0.021	−0.183	−0.242	−0.289	−0.290	−0.265	−0.234	−0.217
$\hat{\gamma}_{1,t}$	1.303	1.042	1.022	1.136	1.338	1.515	1.554	1.342
$\hat{\gamma}_{2,t}$	−1.352	−1.230	−1.210	−1.255	−1.380	−1.567	−1.798	−2.055
(d) Selected win probabilities conditional on (re-scaled) league position:								
$w_t(0.75,0.25)$	0.747	0.781	0.787	0.784	0.779	0.783	0.809	0.862
$w_t(0.9,0.1)$	0.853	0.892	0.897	0.895	0.888	0.891	0.915	0.957
(e) Cross-sectional standard deviation of win probabilities against median team:								
$s(w_t)$	0.1504	0.1712	0.1733	0.1719	0.1686	0.1715	0.1883	0.2261

The estimation results are reported in Table 2. Panel (b) reports the estimates of $\gamma_{k,t}$ for the first matches of cup ties for selected seasons. Panel (c) reports the equivalent estimates for replays. In both cases, the decrease over time in the numerical value of $\hat{\gamma}_{0,t}$ controls for a decline in the importance of home advantage, apparent in the summary data reported in panel (a). Meanwhile $\hat{\gamma}_{1,t}$ and $\hat{\gamma}_{2,t}$ both tend to increase in absolute value.[14] Cup results have therefore become increasingly correlated with league positions. By the end of the period, any given difference in league positions counted for more than it had in earlier times, suggesting increasing competitive imbalance between teams at different levels of the league hierarchy.

Panels (d) and (e) of Table 2 report further summary measures of the trend in competitive balance. Panel (d) reports the trends in $w_t(0.75,0.25)$ and $w_t(0.9,0.1)$: the probabilities of success (after a maximum of 210 minutes) for teams positioned at the 10th and 25th percentile of the league hierarchy, against teams positioned at the 75th and 90th percentiles respectively, conditional on league

---

[14] There is some ambiguity in the results for $\hat{\gamma}_{1,t}$ in the replays estimation, which is based on fewer observations than the estimation for first matches. In this case there is a form of selection bias against teams from the lower reaches of the FL, relatively few of which survive to contest a replay having been drawn away in the first match.

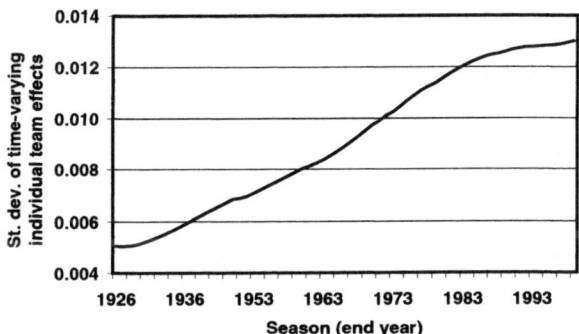

Figure 1. Standard deviation of time-varying individual team effects, $s[\exp(\hat{\alpha}_{i,t})]$.

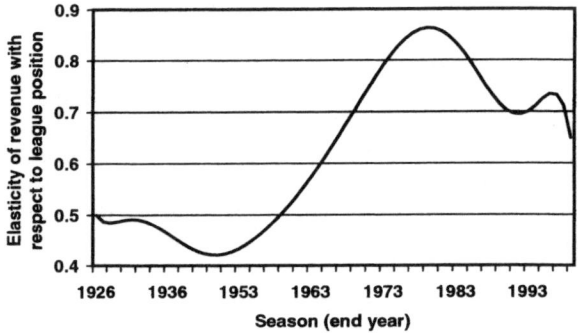

Figure 2. Elasticity of revenue with respect to league position for the median team, $\hat{\varepsilon}_t(0.5)$.

positions but unconditional on home advantage. These data show that the probability of a shock result declined considerably over the period.

For selected seasons, panel (e) of Table 2 reports $s(w_t)$ as defined above. The full series is plotted in Figure 3. According to the theoretical models described in section II, the trend in $s(w_t)$ shown in Figure 3 should be linked to trends in $s[\exp(\hat{\alpha}_{i,t})]$ and $\hat{\varepsilon}_t(0.5)$ shown in Figures 1 and 2. Clearly the long-term trend in all three series is upward, so to this extent the empirical findings are consistent with the theory. There are some inconsistencies, however, in the timing of the principal movements in $s(w_t)$ on the one hand, and $s[\exp(\hat{\alpha}_{i,t})]$ and $\hat{\varepsilon}_t(0.5)$ on the other, which rule out the successful estimation of an econometric relationship (in cointegration form) between these series.

This failure is perhaps unsurprising in view of the following: first, the link between the series is established indirectly from the reduced form of a (highly stylised) theoretical model, and not directly through any behavioural relation; second, the link is likely to have been influenced by various changes on the

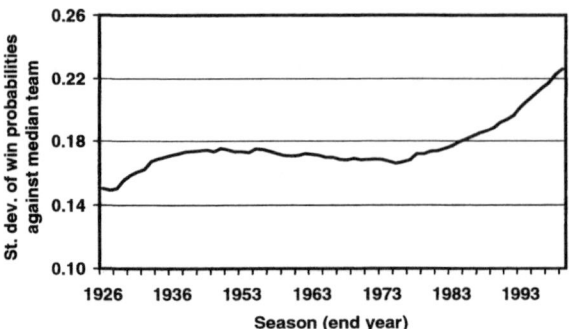

Figure 3. Standard deviation of win probabilities against the median team, $s(w_t)$.

supply side that are not modelled explicitly in the present analysis; and third, the choice of any specific measures of revenue divergence and competitive balance is to some extent arbitrary. Accordingly, instead of seeking to establish an econometric relationship between $s[\exp(\hat{\alpha}_{i,t})]$, $\hat{\varepsilon}_t(0.5)$ and $s(w_t)$, the rest of section IV attempts a less formal interpretation of Figures 1 to 3.

The increase in $s(w_t)$ in the 1920s and 1930s may only be partially attributable to parallel changes in the parameters of the revenue function: although $s[\exp(\hat{\alpha}_{i,t})]$ increased over this period, $\hat{\varepsilon}_t(0.5)$ declined. The growth of a more professional ethos in football during the inter-war period provides an alternative, non-demand side interpretation of the tendency for competitive imbalance to increase. The modern-day football manager's job specification, including responsibility for all aspects of team affairs and the acquisition and disposal of players, first began to evolve between the wars (Walvin, 1994). As the style of management of the leading teams (in particular) moved onto a more professional footing, it is unsurprising to find the emergence of a larger competitive gap between these teams and the rest.

The second significant increase in competitive balance beginning in the late-1970s was both preceded and accompanied by pronounced increases in $s[\exp(\hat{\alpha}_{i,t})]$ and $\hat{\varepsilon}_t(0.5)$. The peculiarities of pre-1978 contractual arrangements (see section II) may explain why these demand shifts did not feed through immediately into rising competitive imbalance during the 1960s and most of the 1970s. Before 1978 a lack of player mobility may have helped keep the lid on the damaging consequences for competitive balance of the shifting composition of spectator demand.[15] After 1978, when out-of-contract players secured the right to initiate a transfer and restraints on player mobility were eased, competitive imbalance started to rise. During the 1990s, the rate of growth in $s(w_t)$ accelerated while growth in $s[\exp(\hat{\alpha}_{i,t})]$ slowed, and $\hat{\varepsilon}_t(0.5)$ dropped back to

[15] Eckard (2001) argues along similar lines that a lack of player mobility prevented the NA major league baseball players' labour market from functioning in accordance with the standard resource allocation model prior to the 1976 introduction of free agency.

1960s levels. Post-1995 adjustments to the distribution of playing talent following Bosman, especially due to the relaxation of restrictions on the employment of foreign talent, might be partly responsible for this further rise in competitive imbalance. However, as noted above it is also likely that the gate revenue data understates the full extent of revenue divergence in the 1990s. Therefore further change in the composition of demand, not fully reflected in $s(w_t)$, may also have contributed to rising competitive imbalance during this period.

V Conclusion

The theoretical model of resource allocation in professional sports leagues widely used in North America suggests that competitive balance is demand-driven. Ultimately, the allocation of playing talent between teams is dependent on each team's relative market size. This article has considered the adaptation of theoretical models developed in North America to English (association) football. Empirical football team revenue functions have been reported, estimated using annual data from the 1920s to the 1990s. A direct measure of competitive balance between teams at all levels of the league's divisional hierarchy, based on a statistical analysis of match results cup competition, has been developed.

The theoretical model predicts that under profit maximising assumptions, competition will become more unbalanced, either if there is divergence between teams' base levels of spectator demand, or if the elasticity of team revenue with respect to league position increases. Empirically, both of these conditions have been met. Big-city teams experienced an increase in their base levels of demand relative to their small-town counterparts, and there was divergence in revenue shares. For the league's median team, the estimated elasticity of revenue increased over the period as a whole.

In general, the comparison between competitive balance at the equilibria associated with profit maximisation (PM) on the one hand, and win percent maximisation subject to a financial constraint (WM) on the other, is indeterminate. Depending on the precise nature of the revenue functions and cost assumptions, competition may be more balanced, equally balanced or less balanced under WM than under PM. However, a finding that the empirical revenue function is more elastic (with respect to league position) for teams near the top of the league than for teams near the bottom reduces the range of empirically relevant comparisons. If the sum of fixed costs and the profit constraint is zero for both teams, competition is more balanced under WM than under PM. If the sum of fixed costs and the profit constraint is non-zero for one or both teams, either competition is either more balanced under WM than under PM or the comparison remains indeterminate.

The statistical analysis of FA Cup match results indicates that there has indeed been an increase in competitive imbalance between teams operating at different levels of the league's hierarchy, as the theoretical model predicts. Competitive imbalance appears to have increased in the late-1920s and 1930s. It has been suggested that this may be partly due to the emergence of a more professional ethos in football during this period, as well as demand-side shifts. A further significant increase in competitive imbalance has been underway since the late-1970s and especially during the 1990s. This was preceded by changes in the composition of demand whose initial impact on competitive balance may have been dampened by a lack of mobility in the players' transfer market. Contractual changes implemented in 1963, 1978 and 1995 have eased restrictions on player mobility. Consequently the most talented players have gravitated increasingly towards the highest-paying teams, and inter-divisional competitive imbalance has risen accordingly.

REFERENCES

DOBSON, S. M. and GODDARD, J. A. (1998) Performance, revenue and cross subsidisation in the English Football League, 1927–94. *Economic History Review*, **51**, pp. 763–85.
DOBSON, S. M. and GODDARD, J. A. (2001). *The Economics of Football*. Cambridge: Cambridge University Press.
DUNNING, E., MURPHY, P. and WILLIAMS, J. (1988). *The Roots of Football Hooliganism: An Historical and Sociological Study*. London and New York: Routledge and Kegan Paul.
ECKARD, E. W. (1998). The NCAA cartel and competitive balance in college football. *Review of Economic Organization*, **13**, pp. 347–69.
ECKARD, E. W. (2001). Free agency, competitive balance, and diminishing returns to pennant competition. *Economic Inquiry*, **39**, pp. 430–43.
EL-HODIRI, M. and QUIRK, J. (1971). An economic model of a professional sports league. *Journal of Political Economy*, **79**, pp. 1302–19.
FOOTBALL TRUST (various) *Digest of Football Statistics*. Leicester: University of Leicester.
FORT, R. (2000). European and North American sports differences (?). *Scottish Journal of Political Economy*, **47**, pp. 431–55.
FORT, R. and QUIRK, J. (1995). Cross-subsidization, incentives, and outcomes in professional team sports leagues. *Journal of Economic Literature*, **33**, pp. 1265–99.
FORT, R. and QUIRK, J. (2004). Owner objectives and competitive balance. *Journal of Sports Economics*, **5**, 20–32.
HOEHN, T. and SZYMANSKI, S. (1999). The Americanization of European football. *Economic Policy*, pp. 205–40.
HUMPHREYS, B. (2002). Alternative measures of competitive balance. *Journal of Sports Economics*, **3**, pp. 133–48.
KÉSENNE, S. (1996). League management in professional team sports with win maximising clubs. *European Journal for Sport Management*, **2**, pp. 14–22.
KÉSENNE, S. (2000). The impact of salary caps in professional team sports. *Scottish Journal of Political Economy*, **47**, pp. 422–30.
KONING, R. H. (2000). Balance in competition in Dutch soccer. *The Statistician*, **49**, pp. 419–31.
QUIRK, J. and FORT, R. (1999). *Hard Ball: The Abuse of Power in Pro Team Sports*. Princeton: Princeton University Press.
ROTTENBERG, S. (1956). The baseball player's labor-market. *Journal of Political Economy*, **64**, pp. 242–58.
RUSSELL, D. (1997). *Football and the English: A Social History of Association Football in England, 1863-1995*. Preston: Carnegie.
SCULLY, G. (1989). *The Business of Major League Baseball*. Chicago: University of Chicago Press.
SLOANE, P. (1971). The economics of professional football: the football club as utility maximiser. *Scottish Journal of Political Economy*, **17**, pp. 121–46.
SZYMANSKI, S. (2001). Income inequality, competitive imbalance and the attractiveness of team sports: some evidence and a natural experiment from English soccer. *Economic Journal*, **111**, pp. F59–84.

376 STEPHEN DOBSON AND JOHN GODDARD

VROOMAN, J. (1995). A general theory of professional sports leagues. *Southern Economic Journal*, **61**, pp. 971–90.

WALVIN, J. (1994). *The People's Game: The History of Football Revisited.* Edinburgh: Mainstream.

WEISS, A. A. (1997). Specification tests in ordered logit and probit models. *Econometric Reviews*, **16**, pp. 361–91.

Date of receipt of final manuscript: September 2003

Part II
Industrial Performance

[8]

SCOTTISH JOURNAL

OF

POLITICAL ECONOMY

June 1971

THE ECONOMICS OF PROFESSIONAL FOOTBALL: THE FOOTBALL CLUB AS A UTILITY MAXIMISER*

PETER J. SLOANE

I

INTRODUCTION

The paucity of the literature devoted to the subject would seem to indicate a certain reluctance on the part of economists to consider the case of professional sporting activity produced as a service to the community. Whilst several North American contributions on the economics of sport exist, including Rottenberg (1956), Neale (1964) and Jones (1969), there appears to have been no attempt to apply economic theory to the particular case of British professional football, save for the author's own recent contribution (1969) and not surprisingly the lack of a sound theoretical framework is evident in two relatively recent reports covering economic aspects of football (P.E.P. 1966 and Department of Education and Science 1968). Both these reports included recommendations for the reform of the economic organisation of the Football League. The terms of reference of the Committee on Football, for instance, were ' to enquire into the state of Association Football at all levels, including the organisation, management, finance and adminis-

* I am grateful to H. W. Richardson, D. Greenwood, B. Chiplin and Professors L. C. Hunter and D. S. Lees, for reading through an early draft of this paper and for contributing a number of useful suggestions. Needless to say, any errors or omissions remain my own. This article forms part of a wider study on the economics of professional football. The employment features of the sport are discussed in the author's 1969 paper ' The Labour Market in Professional Football '.

tration and the means by which the game may be developed for the public good; and to make recommendations '.

Among the recommendations were suggested alterations in the size and structure of the league and in the retain and transfer system, both of which have a crucial bearing on the degree of competition and financial viability of the industry. It is argued that a clear theoretical framework with respect to the objectives of football clubs and the nature of competition under which they operate is a necessary pre-requisite for policy recommendations. This paper attempts to provide such a framework; firstly, by outlining the economic and organisational characteristics of the professional game and secondly, by considering possible objectives of football club behaviour, selecting the one which would appear most appropriate and scrutinising the predictions which follow from such assumptions. Finally, the structure and organisation of the league are examined in the light of this analysis.

I I

ECONOMIC AND ORGANISATIONAL CHARACTERISTICS OF PROFESSIONAL FOOTBALL

The analysis in this paper is limited to the case of the English Football League, though most of the features discussed apply equally to other national leagues. The member clubs of the Football League have an annual turnover in excess of £10 million and total attendances at league games currently approximate around a figure of 30 million. Ancillary activities such as football pools, equipment and literature further enhance the economic importance of football. A major football club can compare with a small to medium-sized firm both in terms of turnover and profits. The P.E.P. report found that in the 1964-65 season, for instance, the total income of the twenty-two first division clubs amounted to £4,269,000, or an average income approaching £200,000 per club. In recent seasons several clubs have reported profits in excess of £100,000. Yet the fact remains that a majority of league clubs operate at a loss and only remain solvent through income derived from non-footballing activities[1] (i.e. pools, social clubs, donations and more recently sponsorship by industrial firms). This financial instability is masked by the fact that clubs frequently pay out large sums to obtain the signature of star players and transfer fees for top class players in English football have

---

[1] Though Football League attendances rose in the 1966-7 and 1967-8 seasons, they had previously fallen from a peak of 41·2 million in 1948-49 to 32·5 million by 1959-60 (a fall of approximately 20 per cent.), and declined further to a trough of just over 27 million in 1965-66. In fact until recently it might have appeared that football was an inferior good. With increased affluence and car ownership other leisure pursuits became obtainable and were substituted for football, whilst television provided the opportunity of viewing a game without being physically present at the stadium. The resurgence of interest in 1966-7 was in no small part stimulated by the staging of the 1966 World Cup competition in England and by the success of the England team in winning the trophy.

escalated towards £200,000. Despite such apparent extravagance the dependence of football clubs on external sources of income was demonstrated in the P.E.P. report which revealed that in the 1964-65 season, for instance, 29 per cent. of the third division and 28 per cent. of the fourth division clubs' income was derived from supporters' clubs and development associations and notwithstanding this fact many of them made a loss over the year. Furthermore, reliance on external sources of income is no less typical in the case of the larger clubs.

The Football League comprises 92 member clubs, divided 22 in each of the first and second divisions and 24 in each of the third and fourth divisions and this provides a total of 42 league games per season in the first and second divisions and 46 games in the third and fourth divisions. In addition there is a Football League cup competition organised on a knock-out basis by the Football League and an F.A. Cup competition organised by the Football Association, which is also responsible for International games against other countries. Several clubs compete in various European competitions, qualification for which depends upon performance in the above domestic club competitions during the previous season. Since such international competitions attract large attendances this increases the financial importance of being successful in home tournaments and also adds to spectator interest.

Professional football is governed by a dual authority and this has given rise to periodic disputes. The Football Association is the national governing body of the game and its rules are binding on all leagues and clubs. Because the vast majority of clubs are amateur it is able to pay only limited attention to the professional game. This vacuum is filled by the Football League which directly caters for the interests of the various league clubs. Policy decisions of the Football League are determined largely by the clubs themselves at their Annual General Meeting. The Football League is, however, under the direct jurisdiction of the Football Association. It is the responsibility of the Football Association to approve the rules of the league and to deal with disciplinary cases arising from league games. Despite its concern for the overall well-being of the game the Football Association is to a large degree, however, dependent on the league clubs, since the largest part of its annual income arises from their activities and players.

The nature of the product decrees that the governing body in football must have considerable powers of control over the individual league clubs. As pointed out by Rottenberg (1956), Neale (1964) and Jones (1969), it is an unique feature of professional sporting activity that in order to produce a saleable output clubs must combine together to produce a game. Therefore, competition is characterised by mutual interdependence, such that a club can only survive provided other clubs remain viable entities, and as Jones (1969) points out, ' the actions of each club must be constrained by the operational necessity of maintaining the league '. Thus in the football service industry in contrast to manufacturing industry, the stimulation for combination

derives from natural mutual advantages rather than from the mutual disadvantages of cut-throat competition.

Recognition of mutual interdependence is clearly reflected in the financial
arrangements of the league. In addition to the sharing of gate receipts (and
the contributions received from supporters' organisations, etc.), clubs have
two further major sources of income. Firstly, a club may obtain a transfer fee
for the sale of a registered player to another club. Unless a fee is agreed
upon, a player on a club's retained list according to the rules of the league is
not freely mobile. The transfer fee is one means of protecting the poorer
club, since such a payment serves to *lessen* the hardship derived from the
loss of a star player and thus to maintain greater equality between clubs.
Secondly, income is distributed to league clubs by both the F.A. and the
Football League. A pool is collected by the league from a levy on net
receipts of League, League Cup and European Cup competitions and also
from T.V. and broadcasting income, which is then divided equally between
all league clubs. In addition fees obtained from the Pools Promoters' Association for the reproduction of fixture lists are used to offset expenses such as
the Provident Fund and the Players' Personal Accident Fund together with
referees' and linesmen's fees, besides the league's own administrative
expenses, all of which would otherwise be a burden on the clubs themselves.
The Football Association also distributes a pool equally amongst the 92
league clubs as entrants of the F.A. Cup competition from a levy on gate
receipts in that competition. The importance of this disbursement of income
by the ruling bodies stems from its redistribution of wealth, since the large
clubs contribute more and the smaller clubs less than they receive back,
thereby helping to maintain equality of competition. The importance of this
redistribution is indicated in the Chester Report which estimates that in
the 1966-67 season such payments amounted to more than £11,000 per club.
Yet, if competition becomes more unequal, the interests of the game as a
whole might require a larger proportion of gate receipts being redistributed
in this manner, though possibly between a smaller number of clubs.

The paradox of competition in football is that whilst a club's objective is
to finish the season in a higher league position than any of its rivals it has
also a vested interest in the continuing success of its rivals in the league, for
the more successful the rival in terms of league position and popularity,
the larger will be the total attendance resulting from the common product.
A qualification is that a match between two lowly teams fighting to escape
relegation will often attract a larger attendance than a match between two
middle-of-the-table teams. Uncertainty as well as the quality of the football
creates interest. Rottenberg (1956) argues with some validity that the closer
the competition, the larger attendances over the season, but Football League
attendance figures do not *altogether* substantiate this view. The uncertainty
of outcome of the league title race may be partly replaced by the uncertainty
of the length of a team's winning run. However, the long run domination

of the league over several seasons by one or two clubs may diminish interest and lower attendances, particularly of other clubs.[2]

Competition between clubs is limited to some extent because the market is regional. Where a club is the sole league member in an area it can be said to possess a local monopoly, since distance confers protection, and attendances will be a direct function of the football interest and population potential of the area. Where more than one club is situated in a particular city there exists a spatial duopoly or oligopoly situation, but in this case competition is normally minimised by arranging home fixtures to avoid clashes (a form of market sharing).

An individual club requires the survival of a number of clubs of reasonable standard (and consequent ability to attract large attendances) but not necessarily the survival of any one club. Indeed, in the case of multi-club cities it might be regarded as advantageous were all but one club to go out of existence, leaving a local monopoly. But local rivalry stimulates demand and empirical evidence suggests teams in multi-club cities are at least as well supported per head of population as local monopoly clubs (viz. the Manchester, Liverpool and larger London clubs). On the other hand, there is no doubt that local competition is harmful to those clubs competing with teams in a higher division than themselves, but the solution implied in this case is merely the extinction of the smaller club.

Competition in the Football League is structured by organisation into four divisions, and a system of promotion and relegation between them. Vertical mobility is a stimulus to improve performance since relegation to a lower division may, amongst other things, lead to financial loss. It is significant that both the Chester and P.E.P. reports have recommended that competition should be enhanced by raising the number of clubs which are to be promoted and relegated, thereby increasing the degree of uncertainty. In theory, the Football League is not a closed shop. The bottom four teams of the fourth division must seek re-election at the end of the season by the votes of member clubs, and non-league clubs may apply for election, so that there is some freedom of entry. In the event, existing members are usually re-elected by tacit agreement or practice, though occasionally non-league teams with outstanding qualifications have gained entry (e.g. Cambridge United in 1970).[3]

Football League clubs also face external competition from other leagues in the same area, from other sports and from other leisure pursuits. There are a number of regional leagues of a lower standard than the Football

---

[2] This is clearly shown by the case of the Scottish League which is dominated by two clubs (Rangers and Celtic). This domination is so strong that the attendances of these two clubs together on any given Saturday will almost certainly be greater than the combined attendances at all other league grounds. The fact that attendances of these two clubs have not declined reflects the fierceness of competition between them.

[3] In several European countries there exists a pyramid of leagues and the top teams of the 'feeder' leagues gain automatic entry. Recently it has been suggested that the top teams in the Northern Premier and Southern Leagues should gain automatic entry at the expense of the bottom teams in the Fourth Division.

126   PETER J. SLOANE

League, which employ mainly part-time professional or amateur players and attract smaller attendances. The impact of such leagues on Football League attendances is, however, marginal. Competition from other sports is also limited to some extent by the seasonal character of many of them and by deliberate minimisation of clashes through careful arrangement of fixtures. Other leisure pursuits have provided an increasing challenge to football. The private car whilst facilitating transport to games also enables a wider range of activities to be undertaken. There is a whole series of pastimes with high cross elasticities of demand in relation to football. Television ownership is of particular importance not only as a close substitute (comparing favourably in adverse weather conditions) but also because football itself may be televised. Recently this form of competition has been closely regulated by the ruling bodies of the game, since live television revenue may not offset the resultant loss in gate receipts.[4] There has, however, been a greater readiness to allow films of games to be shown at times which do not clash with fixtures. Indeed both television and the press provide a large amount of free advertising for football. Manufacturing industry, by contrast, is faced with considerable costs for comparable periods of television time (or advertising space) devoted to product promotion, whilst football advertising occurs even on non-commercial channels.

III

MARKET STRUCTURE AND INTER-CLUB RELATIONS

Two major economic questions arise from the foregoing analysis:
(a) Can cross-subsidisation, a policy generally repugnant to economists, be justified in the football case?
(b) What is the nature of competition and its effect on efficiency? (Is the market structure of the Football League one of monopoly or oligopoly?)
These two questions are in fact inter-related since they both stem from mutual inter-dependence.

(a) Cross-subsidisation

Economists have generally been critical of cross-subsidisation as an economic policy, particularly in the case of the nationalised industries where it is most apparent. William G. Shepherd (1964) has defined cross-subsidisation as 'the covering of financial losses on individual services and production units (according to allocable costs and revenues) by profits accruing elsewhere in the same enterprise'. Cross-subsidisation, therefore, occurs where

---

[4] In 1968 the B.B.C. made an offer worth almost £3 million over a three year period, which involved, in addition to present arrangements, the live screening of one league match each Thursday, a day on which league clubs normally do not have fixtures. This was rejected on the grounds that it might still tend to reduce attendances at Saturday and other weekday fixtures.

ECONOMICS OF PROFESSIONAL FOOTBALL   127

part of a service is known to be unremunerative (i.e. where marginal revenue is known to be less than marginal cost). The football case is rather unusual because it is not an individual enterprise which subsidises unremunerative services, but separate enterprises which subsidise unremunerative ones. This occurs through the redistribution of gate receipts effected by the Football League. Such cross-subsidisation in general may also result simply from a failure to indulge in price discrimination. In the football case this is not totally correct since only minimum prices are fixed by the Football League, the product is not homogeneous and one type of price discrimination is achieved by charging different prices for different parts of the ground.

Criticisms of such a policy of cross-subsidisation have rested upon the argument that it results in a distortion of the price mechanism and a mis-allocation of resources. If some services are run at a loss, other services must of necessity earn super-normal profits (unless the enterprise itself is to be subsidised). Therefore, demand will be artificially stimulated in the under-priced sector with excessive utilisation of production and investment resources according to normal market criteria, whilst demand in the over-priced sector will be artificially restricted via contraction in total demand and substitution of other services. However, as Shepherd suggests, we must remember that this argument is based on a perfectly competitive static model, whilst in the real world the theory of the second best may apply. Further, in the football case cross-subsidisation involves a transfer of money resources after they have been earned. Thus, misallocation of resources would result only indirectly through under-investment in the richer sector. Without such cross-subsidisation many of the poorer clubs would be forced out of the league. This, under normal market criteria, would merely reflect consumer tastes. But in the football case there will be a feed-back effect with results which will be harmful to the subsidising clubs in the long-run, since they will be faced with poorer quality teams at the least or more likely a smaller number of teams, both of which would result in a fall in total revenue over the season. Therefore, one cannot regard the poorer clubs simply in relation to themselves. The nature of the industry may imply that it is impossible for all clubs to be profitable at any one time. In order to maximise uncertainty there is every justification for cross-subsidisation in football. This will not necessarily reduce total demand in the subsidising sector (more likely the reverse). The main danger is that such an equalisation of resources may lower the capability of the richer clubs and consequently their performance at international level.

(b) *Market Structure*

The overall importance of group interests and the extent of the league organisation's control of member clubs has led Neale (1964) to argue that from the standpoint of economic theory the league is in fact the 'firm' in the case of professional sports. He suggests not only is there a joint product, but a stream of utilities is produced including what he terms a 'league standing effect' which derives from the industry as a whole. This leads him to conclude that the 'firm' (the league) is a natural monopoly.

However, at least as far as the Football League is concerned, one must reject Neale's 'firm' hypothesis despite the fact that this body is registered as a limited liability company. True, as he suggests, the league organisation is the equivalent of a trade association; and this leads him to argue that the league is the decision-making unit (whilst the clubs take the profits). But, in fact, the Football League merely sets the rules within which clubs are free to operate as they see best. Most economic as opposed to organisational decisions emanate from the individual clubs (e.g. how many players to employ, how much capital expenditure to make on ground improvements or whether or not to close down). Though price and output (in the case of the Football League minimum admission charges and number of league games) are regulated by the league organisation, the latter merely reflects the common interest of the individual clubs, and this is a far from abnormal cartel arrangement. In theory, one tends to distinguish between a cartel and a firm, because the interests of member firms in the former frequently diverge. The fact that clubs together produce a joint product is neither a necessary nor a sufficient condition for analysing the industry as though the league was a firm.

The suggestion that the league is the firm and the clubs its constituent parts seems to over-emphasise mutual interdependence and to hide the conflicts that frequently do arise as between, for instance, larger and smaller clubs. It must be remembered also that clubs engage in competitions other than those run by the league organisation and which are a very important source of revenue (e.g. the F.A. Cup and the various European competitions). Neale's definition makes their inclusion in the analysis rather difficult.

It follows from Neale's (1964) analysis that the market structure is, therefore, one of monopoly. Because of mutual interdependence monopoly might be regarded as unprofitable with respect to sporting activity. But Neale rejects this view on the grounds that receipts depend upon competition between the teams (i.e. football matches), not upon business competition among the clubs (i.e. price/quality competitiveness). A higher degree of economic collusion (e.g. redistribution of resources) will lead to more sporting competition (closely matched teams) and consequently greater profits. Economic and sporting competition are inversely related. Whilst one would reject the view of the football industry as a pure monopoly for the reasons outlined above, Neale's analysis does point to the need to distinguish clearly between the two types of competition. It is sporting competition that maximises uncertainty, and, therefore, revenue. Economic competition is in fact limited by the nature of the joint product, the spatial distribution of teams and the temporal distribution of matches. Variations in the quality of the product are possible and competition could be enhanced by the charging of lower prices by a particular club. Generally speaking, however, this type of competition is discouraged by the Football League, so that economic competition internal to the league is limited, but external competition occurs between the Football League and other forms of entertainment.

Rottenberg (1956) implicitly assumes an oligopolistic market structure when he refers to the baseball league as ' a collusive combination '. Jones (1969) does so explicitly suggesting that the goal of the league is to maximise joint profits of its member clubs. He suggests, however, that this will conflict with the (assumed) goal of clubs, which is to maximise their individual profits, so that a qualified joint profit maximisation position will be achieved which is compatible with the survival of the league. Group equilibrium occurs when

> ' clubs are earning profits that are sufficient to keep them within the league and so preserve the viability of that organisation '.

But Jones fails to realise that in terms of viability it is the *distribution* of profits that is crucial and this does not necessarily imply joint profit *maximisation*. Nor is this consistent with a situation in which many clubs make long-run losses which are not offset by a redistribution of income. Jones admits clubs will only accept joint profit maximisation if no club has the incentive for winning continually, but even on the profit maximisation hypothesis this incentive exists since lucrative international competitions require member clubs to be consistent winners.

One needs, however, to examine how closely football corresponds to the industrial oligopolistic structure. The form of competition in professional football differs from the typical oligopolistic market case, since football clubs do not need to pay regard to the conjectural variations of their competitors' behaviour with respect to price/output policy (the collusive organisation of the league ensuring that this is the case even for neighbouring clubs). Jones stresses another factor, however, suggesting that

> 'Although most of the conditions for stable collusion are present—small numbers and a formal organisation making policing easier, markets are spatially separated, there is no unilateral price policy, and there is group control over new innovations and entrants—the factor that distinguishes the professional sporting leagues from other oligopolistic coteries is mutual dependence.'

However, one might argue that this is a difference of degree rather than kind. Almarin Phillips (1960 and 1961) and O. E. Williamson (1965) have suggested that even in the industrial oligopolistic case one needs a theory of inter-firm organisation on the grounds that firms are members of groups and assumptions about the motivations of the individual group members are not sufficient to explain group behaviour. As Phillips (1960) suggests

> ' Under conditions of mutual interdependence . . . the problem of an optimal adjustment on the part of the individual concern is a far more complicated process than the operating of appropriate marginal functions because the firm must adjust to a group situation.'

130   P E T E R   J.   S L O A N E

Whilst the objective of the group in the industrial market will be to resolve the indeterminacy which accompanies oligopoly, in the football case it will be to preserve the equality of competing teams. Division of labour between firms arises because each has an individual entity and goals concerning output, profits and price in the industrial case and playing success in the football case. Such sub-goals may result in conflict among the firms. As one generalisation, Phillips (1960) suggests that the more assymetrical the distribution of power within the industry the less formal need be the inter-firm organisation. In football, however, we again see another case of the inversion of the normal rules, since the more assymetrical the distribution of power the greater the need for the central body to redistribute resources. Phillips (1961) suggests some important policy implications. In such cases excessive rivalry which destabilises the market is a possibility, so that there may be sound economic reasons for exempting such collusive organisations from monopoly and restrictive practices legislation or there is the possibility that some form of government regulation may improve performance. Phillips suggests that industries exhibiting excess rivalry historically

> ' do not exhibit self-correcting tendencies until conditions arise which, from an anti-trust standpoint mean less, not more, rivalry. The establishment of workable competition occurs mainly through some combination of a reduced number of firms, the rise of leadership power and more formal interfirm organisation '.

The structural inter-dependence of football, though different from that of the industrial case, is likely to be extreme. This is the justification for the restrictive activities or arrangements of the Football League such as the retain and transfer system, cross subsidisation, minimisation of fixture clashes and minimum price-fixing.

I V

THE OBJECTIVES OF THE FOOTBALL CLUB

The previous consideration of the economics of professional football leads to the view that there are certain features which distinguish the football club from the normal business enterprise. Even in the theory of the firm, given the lack of empirical data, there is by no means unanimity as to which assumption of firm behaviour is most likely to provide valid predictions. Therefore, we must examine closely those features of the theory of the firm which are appropriate and those which are inappropriate for analysing football club behaviour.

A major stimulus to the re-examination of received knowledge was the pioneer work of Berle and Means (1932) who emphasised the divorce between ownership and control, which in turn meant that under certain circumstances management may seek and have the ability to choose between alternative goals. In other words the firm may be multi-goal orientated and managers capable of discretionary behaviour. As Kaysen (1957) has suggested

'No longer the agent of proprietorship seeking to maximise return on investment management sees itself as responsible to stockholders, employees, customers, the general public, and, perhaps most important, the firm itself as an institution.'

On the one hand shareholders are interested in long-run profits. On the other hand management will be more concerned with the firm's market position, sales revenue or size (particularly where salary is directly related to market share, sales, or assets, rather than profits).

The ability to indulge in such non-profit goals rests on imperfectly competitive conditions and/or imperfect knowledge. Once the existence of monopoly or uncertainty is allowed the organisational attributes of the firm can no longer be ignored and alternative theories may be entertained. Suggestions have included sales maximisation (Baumol, 1959), growth maximisation (Marris, 1964), security maximisation (Rothschild, 1947), satisficing behaviour (Simon, 1959) and utility maximisation (Williamson, 1963), all of which to varying degrees require a minimum profits constraint. Of these growth has a limited meaning in the football context (e.g. growth by acquisition is not possible). Satisficing would seem to beg the question, since as Marris (1964) has suggested it presupposes some other objective which for one reason or another is unattainable. If we accept rising aspiration levels it approaches a maximising solution, whilst operationally in any event its predictions with respect to price/output decisions based on changing demand and supply conditions will be identical to a profit maximising model unless surplus profits are available over and above required profits.

Before we examine four possible maximising assumptions—profits, security, sales and utility—in relation to football, it is necessary to examine how far there is a divorce between ownership and control in the football club and whether this differs from the normal case. Since Football League clubs are with one exception (Nottingham Forest) private limited liability companies, ownership is in the hands of the shareholders, and their representatives on the board of directors often, though not always, have a very considerable say in the day to day running of the club, probably more so than the average (non-managing) director of a business firm. The manager (particularly as in the vast majority of cases he is an ex-player) is likely to be more concerned with successful team performances than with the financial stability of his club. It is interesting to note that Football Association rules prohibit the payment of fees to directors and consequently exclude paid managers from a seat on the board. The major way, however, in which the divorce between ownership and control will differ from the conventional case is that in the normal business enterprise profits must be sufficient to give the shareholders a market rate of return on their capital, whilst it is unlikely that football club shareholders are primarily interested in financial gain since income from this source is severely limited by an F.A. rule which specifies that the maximum dividend payable in respect of any year shall be $7\frac{1}{2}$ per cent. (or 5 per cent. free of income tax) and many clubs in fact pay

132   PETER J. SLOANE

no dividends.[5] Though football shares are marketable because of the psychic income effect (obtained from the ability to participate in the club) and capital gains might be made, shares change hands infrequently and discussions at shareholders' meetings tend to centre on football rather than financial performance, unless of course the financial situation is so serious that remedial action has to be taken. Thus, where conflicts arise they will result from the fact that insufficient finance is forthcoming to maintain playing performance at an acceptable level rather than from a clash over objectives. If the bank manager is not amenable to an overdraft, the directors (or the supporters' club) will have to provide such finance, and this they may be prepared to do only on condition that they are given greater control in the running of the club both financially and sportswise. This may not be acceptable to the manager in particular.

We are now in a position to examine our four assumptions of club behaviour.

1) **Profit maximisation.** As suggested earlier it is only recently that economists have begun to examine the economic problems of professional sports. It is somewhat surprising therefore that such contributions should have analysed clubs using the assumption of profit maximisation which to some extent is in the process of being discarded or at least modified in the theory of the firm. This is particularly so in view of the fact that the use of this traditional assumption is even less likely to provide valid predictions than in the case of the business enterprise, since some clubs make heavy losses which occur even in the *long-run,* so that they cannot be explained away as the result of loss minimising behaviour, otherwise such clubs would leave the industry. Such clubs manage to stay in existence only through donations from directors, supporters' clubs, social clubs and pools. It is in fact estimated that the 92 league clubs are losing about £1 million per annum from the game and whilst 12 or so clubs make combined profits of about £½ million the rest have overdrafts of between £1 million and £2 million. The second division as a whole in fact pays more money out in wages alone (about £2 million) than is taken at the gate. This situation has led the league to examine the possibility of setting up a holding company, thereby combining the profits and losses of all clubs. Since the league as a whole runs at a loss this would retain income lost to the game through the payment of corporation tax by a few profitable clubs. The predictions of profit maximising behaviour are scrutinised below.

2) **Security.** It can be argued that long-run survival is the major objective at least of those clubs in the lower reaches of the third and fourth divisions of the Football League which year after year run at a loss, largely because poor playing performances mean poor gates. If this is the case, decisions will aim at maximising the security level of the organisation, and we observe that such clubs do transfer their better players to the richer clubs, which

_____

[5] No such rule applies in the case of the Scottish League and the Chester Committee recommended the maximum be raised to 15 per cent. in the case of Football League Clubs whose shares are freely transferable.

solves their short-run problem of financial insolvency but minimises their long-run probability of playing success. The security motive must, therefore, be built into our model.

3) Sales Maximisation. Maximisation of attendances might be regarded as a primary objective since part of the satisfaction derived from football as a form of entertainment undoubtedly arises from the congregation of vast crowds which provide a particular element of supporter participation and atmosphere. Thus, when a club suffers from declining gates it will often be prepared to spend large sums of money on new players, perhaps without much prospect of obtaining a market return on the capital investment. The maximisation of total attendances would be of paramount importance if empty terraces detract sufficiently from the atmosphere of the game. That clubs do *not* attempt to maximise sales *revenue*, as suggested by Baumol (1957) in the case of the business firm, is supported by the evidence that, in the case of important games for which there is a large demand tickets may be offered on the black market at many times their face value. (The supply of tickets is of course completely fixed by the capacity of the ground.) Likewise at least in the case of league games, identical prices are charged regardless of the quality of the opposition, whilst a differential pricing policy could increase total revenue (and profits). (The clubs are only constrained by the league rules with respect to *minimum* admission charges.) On the other hand clubs may fear a loss of goodwill to the detriment of their long-run position if prices were raised for important league games, so that they could be said to be attempting to maximise *long-run* sales revenue. More recently, however, clubs have shown some awareness that product demand is directly related to the importance of the game and prices have been increased for European Cup and other competitive games. There are grounds, therefore, for including the size of attendance as part of the general preference function.

4) Utility Maximisation. This seems intuitively to be the most appealing in the football case since we may regard football as a consumption activity. Production and consumption occur simultaneously and football is largely a leisure pursuit. Directors are usually successful businessmen in a different field. A major drawback to the general introduction of the utility maximisation assumption in the theory of the firm is that it may be rationalised so that it is consistent with almost any type of behaviour and therefore tends to lack operational significance. As indicated by Marris (1964) businessmen can choose from a wide range of policies. However, as he himself notes *en passant*, football is an exception in which we have established criteria by which competence is to be judged—the performance of the team on the field of play. This follows despite any dichotomy between ownership and control, from the common objective on the part of all members of the football club— including the employees. In sociological terms the football club differs from the business enterprise, because it is not a pluralistic system of divergent interests but at least approaches a unitary system. As Fox (1966) suggests in relation to the latter,

134 PETER J. SLOANE

' The vision is closest to the professional football team, for here combined with the team structure and its associated loyalties, one finds a substantial measure of management prerogative at the top in the persons · of the manager, trainer, and board members. Team spirit and undivided management authority co-exist to the benefit of all.'

The football club resembles a unitary system precisely because it is not primarily a profit-maximising enterprise. It is quite apparent that directors and shareholders invest money in football clubs not because of expectations of pecuniary income but for such psychological reasons as the urge for power, the desire for prestige, the propensity to group identification and the related feeling of group loyalty (see Gordon, 1945).[6] Football clubs are essentially based on tradition, which derives from their position in the social structure of their particular localities. The gathering together of partizan supporters breeds a club (or brand) loyalty, which *per se* yields utility, so that supporters as well as directors are prepared to donate money without regard to financial gain.[7] One would therefore tend to agree broadly with the assertion of the P.E.P. Report (1966) that the objective of the football club is

' to provide entertainment in the form of a football match. The objective is not to maximise profits, but to achieve playing success whilst remaining solvent '.

[6] That people are prepared to invest in football clubs without regard to financial rates of return is illustrated by the experience of Aston Villa, which in March 1969 had a successful offer for sale of a minimum of 20,000 ordinary shares of £5 each at £5 per share in order to help the club out of its financial difficulties. Despite the fact that substantial losses had been made in four of the previous five years and that it was not possible to forecast a profit or loss for the current financial year, and in any event it was unlikely that a dividend would be paid, the issue was over-subscribed.
   Herbert A. Simon, ' Decision-making in Economics ', *American Economic Review*, 1959, points out that even in the case of the business firm ' the entrepreneur may obtain all kinds of psychic incomes from the firm quite apart from monetary rewards. If he is to maximise his utility, he will sometimes balance a loss of profits against an increase of psychic income.'
   This effect will be much stronger in football since the product gives satisfaction not only to the consumers but also to those engaged in the productive process. Rottenberg, although questioning in his analysis of the baseball labour market whether it is sensible to assume that clubs are profit maximisers in view of the fact that their owners may be interested in providing opportunities of sport *per se*, thereby obtaining a large psychic income, nevertheless goes on to conduct his analysis in terms of profit maximisation on the grounds that people will be unwilling to invest large sums of capital with a high risk of loss merely for the pure joy of association with the game. But this contradicts experience, so far as British football is concerned. Since rich businessmen *are* often willing to pour vast sums of money into clubs psychic income may be very large.
   [7] A certain glamour attaches to the name of long standing members of the league and pride in past performances is much in evidence. Such traditions cannot be ignored in an economic analysis since they have marked economic effects, e.g. on attendances at games. Furthermore, a football club provides external social benefits, serving as a source of advertisement for a town in terms of prestige, and the matches themselves create additional consumer sales and increased use of local transport facilities. It has even been suggested that industrial output may vary directly with the performances of the local team through a positive or negative morale effect. The existence of such externalities has led to suggestions that local authorities should support ailing teams and also explains why some firms are prepared to support local clubs.

The fact that the football club is closest to the unitary system helps us to deal with what would be an awkward question. Namely, whose utility is in fact being maximised? This problem does not arise in the case of the conventional business firm, since it is clear that it is management who exercise control and ensure their own utility is maximised subject to certain outside constraints, such as satisfying shareholders. In the case of the football club the position is not so straight-forward since the manager is not really responsible for many ' business ' activities, which fall to some extent on the Board of Directors, and the question of control is not a simple one. However, we must remember that the directors and to a certain degree the manager himself are consumers as well as the spectators, so that it may be argued that playing success is the *objective* of all the relevant participants in the club—directors, shareholders, managers and supporters' clubs. However, divergent interests and, therefore, conflict may arise over *financial constraints,* which are likely to receive greater attention from the directors than from either the manager or supporters' club. The directors must in one way or another maintain the financial viability of the club, and may not, therefore, be prepared to pay out large sums on the transfer market when playing performance may warrant such action. It should be noted, on the other hand, that behaviour might well be affected by the very fact of continued losses and the willingness of supporters to subsidise the club. For instance, the supporters' club may threaten to withdraw funds unless the club enters the transfer market. Though the directors may not feel this to be a wise course of action with respect to the club's own finance such action might be taken because it is thought this will ensure (or preserve) the willingness of consumers to continue subsidising the club. Whilst it could be argued that this is consistent with profit maximising behaviour which embraces all sources of income for the club, such subsidisation can only be *explained* by utility maximisation, otherwise the club would cease to exist if subsidisation were required in the long run. Alternatively, let us suppose that a club was successful results-wise but failed to attract satisfactory attendances, perhaps because success resulted from tightly defensive football, introduced by the manager, which yielded few goals.[8] Would the directors be satisfied in this case? Clearly if maximisation of playing success were the sole criterion the answer would be in the affirmative and this might explain the recent (international) trend towards defensive football.[9] If, on the other hand, attendances were felt to be of predominant importance, the directors might recommend the manager to adopt a more attractive attacking style of play, even at the risk of poorer results. Whether attendances would in fact increase were adverse results to follow is, however, highly debatable. Where there is con-

---

[8] Though, of course, the rate of goalscoring is an important factor in determining the quality of the entertainment, in the case of those supporters closely tied to a particular club paramount importance seems to be attached to victory on the field. Therefore, defensive football may reduce attendances by decreasing the number of ' floating spectators ' rather than influencing the ' hard-core ' supporter.

[9] The win-at-any-cost attitude might also explain the tendency to violence and unsporting behaviour on the field of play.

PETER J. SLOANE

flict between these objectives utility maximisation is taken to imply first of all maximisation of playing success.

Making use of Marris's (1964) formulation we may write

$$U = u(C^{\bullet}, V)$$

where U = utility function
$C^{\bullet}$ = satisfaction
V = security

Therefore, it is suggested that clubs aim to maximise utility subject to financial viability, or a minimum security constraint, which we may take to include subsidy income. These two variables will have to be traded off. Probably the manager's psychological preference system will rank $C^{\bullet}$ relatively more highly than that of the directors who are not only more aware of V but may actually devote their own resources towards its achievement. Marris includes the fear of take-over by another company in V. In football the equivalent fear is loss of position by the directors and managers. This formulation may be made more explicit by adapting Williamson's (1963) utility maximisation model. The football club will then be operated so as to maximise:

$$U = u(P, A, X, \pi_R - \pi_0 - T)$$

subject to $\pi_R \geq \pi_0 + T$

where P = playing success
A = average attendance
X = health of the league
π_R = recorded profits
π_0 = minimum after-tax profits
T = taxes

Both π_0 and π_R may in fact be negative in which case $T = 0$. This is possible because the club has external sources of finance F_X. If we assume π_0 is the amount of profits (positive or negative) required to keep the club in existence the constraint then becomes

$$\pi_{e_R} + F_X \geq \pi_0 + T$$

$\pi_R - \pi_0 - T$ is retained in the utility function because this not only maintains the viability of the club, but also helps to ensure P max. X indicates the importance of mutual interdependence which is a function in part of the distribution of income. Utility is derived from the health of the league because it is better to win a keenly fought competition than to win easily. Where these variables conflict it is assumed that P takes paramount importance.

It might be argued that P, A, and π will all be highly correlated, in which case the utility maximising and profit maximising models would yield similar predictions. But, that the assumption of utility maximisation yields quite different predictions than that of profit maximisation on which previous analyses have been based, can be illustrated by reference to Rottenberg's (1956) analysis of the baseball labour market. Firstly, he argues

' It should not be thought that wealthy teams will invariably want to assemble winning combinations of players . . . A team will seek to maximise the difference between its revenues and its costs. If this quantity is maximised, for any given club, by assembling a team of players who are of lower quality than those of another club in its league, it will pay the former to run behind.'[10]

Utility maximisation suggests that clubs would never adopt ' running behind ' as a deliberate policy but always strive to maximise their playing success with the proviso, of course, that there will exist constraints on the amounts clubs can raise for new players which ultimately reflect drawing potential (in the absence of rich benefactors). Likewise, a policy of sales maximisation would also rule out ' running behind '.

Secondly, Rottenberg points out that should a competitive advantage lie with particular areas (say, because football interest among the population is not constant) then differences in revenue will occur. Further, he suggests that a vicious (or virtuous) circle will come into play.

'A self-generating process begins to operate to increase the magnitude of the differences. If the revenues of Team A are larger than those of Team B . . . despite the equality of market size Team A is in a position to contract the better players by offering a higher price: Team A then wins more games than B, and its relative attendances and revenues increase. Now it is in a still better position to outbid B for players.'

The vicious circle implicity assumes that the purchase of star players automatically results in improved performances. This may not necessarily follow since football is increasingly a team game relying on the constructive combination of individual talents. That the risk premium of transfer dealings is high is shown by the number of clubs which have failed to escape relegation or to gain honours after large expenditure on players. Nonetheless concentration of resources does threaten to remove the uncertainty which provides an essential part of the game's attraction.

Rottenberg argues, however, that this self-generating process will begin to rectify itself. Briefly, the argument runs that after a point the law of

---

[10] Profit maximisation might imply a low level of performance, since the cost of obtaining additional players on the transfer market in order to improve performance might be prohibitive.

As a corollary to the above Rottenberg also suggests that a rational club will seek to maximise the rent it derives from each player, so that, for example, it will be indifferent between buying a player whom it estimates to be worth £100,000 and would cost only £80,000 and a player worth £50,000 to the club who would cost £30,000. Under conditions of utility maximisation the preference would lie with the more skilled (and, therefore, more valuable) player, for although the rent derived from the services of each player is the same absolutely, greater satisfaction would be obtained from the play of the more highly skilled performer. In practice one player bought at a cost of £100,000 is likely to be worth more than five players, each costing £20,000, since the latter being in all probability no improvement on existing players will not signficantly increase attendances, whilst the former might do so. Consequently it is harder to justify the fees paid for players at the lower end of the scale than it is the very high fees paid for star performers.

diminishing returns will set in as some clubs become bigger; that is the purchase of additional players will eventually increase total product at a decreasing rate. This will operate together with diseconomies of scale in the long run; for if one regards the size of a team as a function of the number of players under contract weighted by ability and assumes that there is an inelastic supply of high grade talent in the industry as a whole, diseconomies of scale will set in when one team becomes so superior to the others that interest begins to wane and attendances fall. At such a point it will become more profitable for the successful team to sell some of its star players to poorer clubs, because if clubs are profit maximisers they will prefer winning by close margins rather than by large ones (on the supposition that this will increase attendances, thereby increasing revenue). The result is, therefore, that star players will be distributed more or less equally between teams.[11]

It is quite apparent, even accepting that closeness of competition determines the size of attendance, that the whole of Rottenberg's (1956) argument rests upon his assumption that teams (or clubs) are profit maximisers. However, if one assumes that clubs are utility maximisers, this result may not follow and star players will not necessarily be more or less equally distributed between teams. Teams may attempt to maximise their playing success and retain star players irrespective of their size in relation to other clubs, particularly in view of the fact that even if a club is very successful in its own national league it may have to face a sterner challenge in international competitions (such as the European Cup Competition). Further, only those clubs with large bank balances or assets are likely to be able to afford the signature of a star player. Finally, Rottenberg's analysis wrongly assumes that players will always be willing to move from a successful to a less successful club, and even if a cash differential is provided, this is not necessarily the case. The assumption of utility maximisation suggests there is no theoretical reason why the process of increasing concentration should be halted, unless long-run group interests (the viability of the league) predominate over short-run individual interests (the playing success of individual clubs). Certainly, whilst one or two other clubs threaten to challenge for honours, the successful club is unlikely to transfer its star players, a policy which in any event would be highly unpopular with supporters. It is highly probable that the degree of concentration will be greater than that which maximises joint (and perhaps individual) profits. Increased concentration may *eventually* be halted, but this would seem to require collective action on the part of the league as a whole, rather than resulting simply from the fact that each club is striving to serve its own ends. Fundamentally, however, the question is an empirical one.

In the case of the Football League there have been indications of increasing concentration on gate receipts accounted for by the largest clubs.

---

[11] This is part of Rottenberg's argument that a free market could be successfully operated in baseball, since no collusion is required to bring about this result. The question of a free market is discussed further in 'The Labour Market in Professional Football ', op. cit.

In 1966-67 the Chester Report notes that the two Manchester and two Liverpool clubs attracted a quarter of all first division attendances to their games and this total was greater than that of the entire 24 clubs of the fourth division. Leading clubs in large population centres have tended to become richer as they are able to rely on larger gates, so that in the event of deterioration in playing performances they are able, because of the size of their resources, to obtain new players in the transfer market. In this way there has been an increasing tendency for star players to be concentrated in a smaller number of clubs, though the process has not yet gone as far as the situation reached in some other countries, including Scotland, where success seems to revolve around one, two or three clubs, with rare exceptions. The Chester Report suggests that

> ' the broad pattern of the top clubs getting more profitable and the lower clubs getting deeper into debt seems to be formidably and remorselessly established '.

What are the implications of increasing concentration? Firstly to the extent that smaller clubs are forced out of the league through their inability to match the performances of larger clubs and ensuing low gates the Football League might operate with a small number of clubs. Consumer welfare would be diminished to the extent that top class football would be provided in a small number of population centres and smaller size would not guarantee competitive equality between clubs, so that one or two teams might still remain dominant. Consumer welfare might be increased on the other hand if smaller size led to a higher average level of performance. However, historically the Football League has tended to grow rather than diminish in size and clubs forced out of the league through financial necessity have been replaced by non-league professional clubs which provide annually a large number of applications for league status. If increasing concentration occurred and yet the league remained the same size, general interest would begin to wane as one or two clubs monopolised the winning of the league title with the result that total attendances would fall, even if the successful clubs maintained their own gates. In this respect if teams were to become more and more unequally matched it might even be found necessary to handicap teams in some way in order to revive interest by strengthening the degree of competition (c.f. horse-racing). Since any attempt to tamper with the rules of the game would receive fierce opposition from all sides the only other solution would be to intensify the present arrangements for the redistribution of income. For instance, an extreme possibility would be for all income from gates to be pooled and divided equally between all clubs. Since this would not be in the direct interest of the larger clubs this would require the Football League taking upon itself a far greater degree of control over the individual member clubs than presently exists. This is not likely to be an acceptable proposition, since apart from the opposition of the larger clubs, it might lead to a lower level of performance from such clubs and an inability to compete on an international basis. A less extreme form of redistribution would be the imposition of a tax on transfer payments paid out in the form of a subsidy to the poorer clubs. Since the Football League already makes a levy of 10 per cent. in respect of such payments this would be relatively easy to implement, though it might be rather more difficult to establish the exact criteria for the allocation of this revenue. One measure that has been taken and has a similar effect to income redistribution is the loaning of players to clubs in a lower division for varying periods of time. This not only redistributes playing talent but also provides young players with league experience sooner than might have been anticipated. The question of redistribution is however related to the size of the league. Should very uneconomic clubs be maintained at the expense of the richer clubs? This question is examined in the ensuing section.

V

The Size and Structure of the League

In recent years much discussion has centred on the question of whether or not the Football League should be reduced in scale, generally through possessing a smaller number of clubs in each division. In addition it is suggested that smaller clubs should consider merging with other clubs located nearby. This has derived from an awareness of the growing financial problems of clubs in the lower divisions, many of which have accumulated large deficits and are struggling for survival. Whilst first division clubs have been able to maintain average attendances in excess of 30,000 there has been a fall off in support in the lower divisions. In fact there is evidence that a substitution effect has taken place. The growth of car ownership has meant a growing number of supporters are not tied to their local club but are prepared to travel 20 miles or so to see a first division match in preference to a local fourth division encounter. In fact in 1964 the League Management Committee itself suggested a structure of five divisions of twenty clubs, with the proviso that the two lowest divisions should be regionalised, but this failed to get the necessary voting majority. The P.E.P. Report also concluded that the first and second divisions should be reduced in stages to sixteen clubs each and the third and fourth divisions be replaced by regional divisions as applied before the 1958-59 season. The Chester Committee found three major disadvantages in the existing pattern of football.

(1) The fixture list for top clubs was overburdened, this being particularly apparent in severe weather conditions when a large number of games are postponed.

(2) Competition slackens for a number of clubs as the season progresses and the likelihood of either promotion or relegation diminishes.

(3) The fourth division as a whole is increasingly making heavy losses on its footballing operations.

The Committee concluded that the first division should be reduced from 22 to 18 clubs, that the size of the remaining four divisions should be either 18, 20 and two divisions of 22, or alternatively four divisions of 20 clubs, and that the lowest two divisions should be regionalised on a North-South basis as was formerly the case. Further, in order to increase competition, promotion and relegation should both involve four clubs in each division per season save for the regional divisions which would each have only two clubs promoted to the third division. Of these proposals only the P.E.P. Report suggests an actual reduction in the total number of league clubs despite the apparent acceptance of the fact that English league football is conducted on too extensive a basis given the current financial resources available to clubs and the cost of maintaining league football on its present scale. However, all these proposals lack any suggestion of economic guidelines by which to judge the size of the league. Further, we must remember that the question of size cannot be separated from the vicious circle caused by increased concentration of resources. We require criteria according to which we can define and measure the optimum size of league and also the size which would maximise profits or utility.

If clubs are utility maximisers non-economic factors may be very important, i.e. a league structure of unwieldy size might be preferred because the omission of clubs with a long tradition (though they be uneconomic to run) is felt to involve a great loss of consumer welfare. In this event the optimal size tends to be the *status quo* and it is perhaps more illuminating to carry out the analysis on more traditional lines. A further problem follows from the fact that clubs engage in other competitions besides that of the league, and some market research is probably required to ascertain the whereabouts of the consumers' satiation level of demand for football. Due to the emergence of new competitions the number of matches per club[12] has increased over recent years without a *prima facie* decline in average attendance for those clubs involved. Yet it is doubtful if the number of games could be increased much further without this effect being felt.

Let us suppose that the objective of clubs is to maximise some measure of output. To maximise the total output of games would require a very large league; to maximise total attendances would probably require a somewhat smaller league, since it would be *possible* to arrange a larger number of fixtures than would satiate demand: whilst to maximise total revenue would also seem to require a large league. Though it might be argued in this case that, if the league is a monopoly facing a downward sloping demand curve, it would pay to raise prices by restricting output somewhat, dimensions of time and space limit this result. In order to measure optimum size one must consider the costs of producing a given output. In the case

---

[12] This increase in matches has largely been facilitated by the almost universal adoption of floodlighting by clubs, which enables games to take place in the evenings, and Saturday afternoon games to have later kick-off times, thereby increasing the level of demand by enabling a greater number to attend matches.

142   P E T E R   J.   S L O A N E

of football fixed costs (e.g. the upkeep and modernisation of stadia)[13] are
likely to be quite high. Under the present system of players' contracts quite
a large proportion of the players' salaries will also be a fixed cost in the
short-run, only that part of the salary in the form of bonuses being a variable
cost. Although an increase in matches probably presupposes an increased
pool of first team players, it seems reasonable to suppose that the average
cost curve of the football club is downward sloping, whether one measures
output in terms of matches, attendances or receipts. If this is the case, the
limit to size must lie on the demand side or result from the fact that it is
only feasible to play so many matches in one season. Finally, in view of
the nature of competition optimal size might be considered as that which
maximises total revenue subject to all clubs being more or less viable, thus
allowing for the essential interdependency of clubs. In other words, not only
the size of revenue, but its distribution is important. This might suggest a
relatively small-sized league, since a large number of clubs may not be able
to compete on even terms, as is illustrated by the case of the Scottish League.
But this is also a function of the level of demand and the supply of skilled
players.

A relatively painless way of effecting such a reduction in size or alternatively of changing the composition of the Football League whilst maintaining
its present size is the encouragement of amalgamation of existing league
clubs. It has been suggested that some clubs in close proximity might merge
(e.g. in Sheffield, Nottingham and Bristol, which each possess two league
teams). Such mergers would allow a more intensive use of facilities, since
one stadium would be required instead of two and this would be allied to
the concentration of crowd support into one club.[14] Also the sale of the
obsolete stadium in a congested area would realise a large sum of money.
The Chester Report has come out in favour of such combinations on the
grounds that it would allow for better recreational facilities. Furthermore, it
appears that the structure of the league has not adequately responded to
population and economic changes. If, for instance, clubs such as Rochdale
and Oldham or Bolton and Bury were to amalgamate this would allow clubs
from growing population areas, such as the new towns, to gain entry to the
league. In the above case the clubs concerned are already faced with fierce
competition from the more glamorous Manchester clubs so that the football
spectating facilities of the area would only be diminished marginally. Similarly, if clubs in the same city were to amalgamate the loss of welfare would

---

[13] There will also be an optimal size of stadium. A certain average level of
capacity must be taken up for clubs to break even (an attendance of around 30,000
being the break-even point for first division clubs). The club must decide what level
of excess capacity is acceptable. The smaller the degree of excess capacity the lower
the break-even point, but the greater the loss of revenue from big games when
demand exceeds availability of places. A similar decision must also be made with
respect to seating capacity, for whilst this increases average revenue, it generally
diminishes the overall capacity of the ground.

[14] In fact it is unlikely that total attendances would be the sum of the attendances
of the formerly independent clubs, since a proportion of supporters would previously
have watched both teams' matches.

not be so severe, particularly where one of the teams was struggling in a lower division, whilst in cities such as Bristol amalgamation might enable the support of one team in a higher division than either of its existing teams.[15] However, a note of caution is required before recommending a wholesale reduction in the number of clubs within an area. It has been found in the case of the cinema that given equal population densities an inter-regional difference of 10 per cent. in the number of cinemas relatively to population was associated with a difference in the same direction of more than 8 per cent. of the number of admissions per head (Spraos, 1962). In other words, a substantial amount of the demand for cinema seats was supply induced. Would then a reduced concentration of clubs within an area mean a general loss of spectators to the game? We have observed that local rivalry stimulates demand. Nevertheless there is reason to believe that this effect would be less marked in the football case. Firstly, quality differences are more marked in the case of football clubs—different cinemas can show the same films, whilst fourth division clubs cannot present first division football—and the continued concentration of crowd support towards the larger clubs would tend to diminish the loss. Secondly, one function of the existence of several cinemas within a town is to allow a choice of films, whilst in football fixture clashes are generally avoided. ' Choice ' would be reduced by amalgamation where the existence of two clubs allows spectators to watch a game each Saturday. But on balance it would seem that the loss of choice would be less in the football case.

Whilst an argument can be made out in favour of changing the composition of the league, albeit gradually, one would not recommend a reduction in league size on purely economic grounds, unless there existed a strong direct relationship between league size and concentration, since the greater the number of games, other things being equal, the larger total receipts.[16] The suggested ' super league ' of sixteen clubs would involve a loss of twelve league games per club over the season which would reduce clubs' income considerably whilst raising their average fixed costs. This is unlikely to be offset by increased average attendances which would result from the fact that a higher percentage of clubs would be engaged in championship or relegation struggles. Though alternative competitions may be inaugurated to offset the loss of matches, they are not likely to be as attractive to spectators as league matches. It is difficult also to accept the argument that such a league would lead to a higher overall level of performance since it is hard to envisage in what way this league would differ from the existing first

---

[15] It is also suggested that even if clubs were to retain their own identity, costs could be considerably lowered were they to share the same ground, as frequently is the case in multi-club cities on the continent, thereby spreading fixed costs over a larger number of games.

[16] It might be thought that the increased quantity supplied on the market would require a lower price in order to sell the larger number of matches (or attendance per match would fall with prices fixed). However, this is not necessarily the case since we are not dealing with a homogeneous commodity and the time period involved and the satiation level of demand for football must be specified.

144 PETER J. SLOANE

division. If promotion and relegation were to be abolished this would tend to work in the opposite direction, whilst also diminishing uncertainty and interest. There is little advantage to be obtained by clubs in lower divisions through a reduction in their numbers. The solution to their problems would seem to rest on reduced costs by the employment of more part-time professional and amateur players or a reduction in staff through the abandonment of a reserve team and a reversion to regionalisation in the case of the third and fourth divisions, thereby reducing travelling costs.

Unfortunately since the size of the Football League has remained static since the war we have no means of testing the strength of the relationship between size and concentration so that the argument for reduced size falls back to the question of fatigue effects, which have, it is claimed, tended to affect adversely performances of teams in European competitions, since the first division of the Football League possesses a larger number of clubs than any equivalent league in Europe. Greater success in such competitions would not only increase the incomes of clubs engaged in them but through such a demonstration of prowess might tend also to boost general attendances at league games (as followed success in the 1966 World Cup Competition). Since, however, reduced size is likely on balance to reduce income, alternative measures of eliminating fatigue resulting from an over-accumulation of fixtures may have more appeal to clubs. One measure which has already taken place is an extension to the length of the playing season, but such a diminution in the length of the summer break may also make players jaded (as well as spectators). A further possibility is for the more successful clubs to follow the growing tendency to build up a first team pool of fifteen or sixteen players, thereby giving greater opportunity of resting individual players. As these are far less costly alternatives there seem few economic grounds on which to advocate wholesale reductions in the size of the league.

ECONOMICS OF PROFESSIONAL FOOTBALL   145

VI

CONCLUSION

To summarise, therefore, the football club is seen to differ from the normal business enterprise. The profit goal would appear to exert a smaller influence on behaviour in the former case and the use of the profit maximising assumption has led to predicted results which do not appear to hold in practice. In particular the nature of competition is diametrically opposed to that of business competition and this in turn has implications for the structure of the industry. Two wider implications might be drawn from this study. Firstly, the assumption of utility maximisation might provide more valid predictions than profit maximisation in professional sports generally and in other forms of entertainment. Secondly, in the case of such activities there would appear to be some justification for restriction of competition in one form or another in order to maintain the degree of *sporting* competition and, therefore, the financial stability of the game. Economic analysis certainly does find an application in this field, but it is, indeed, dangerous to infer that the *normal* economic prescriptions are always or even mainly applicable to such cases.

University of Nottingham

146 PETER J. SLOANE

REFERENCES

BAUMOL, W. (1959). *Business Behaviour, Value and Growth.* New York, 1959.
BERLE, A. A. and MEANS, G. (1932). *The Modern Corporation and Private Property.* New York, 1932.
DEPARTMENT OF EDUCATION AND SCIENCE (1968). *Report of the Committee on Football* (under D. N. Chester). H.M.S.O., 1968. (Generally referred to as the Chester Report.)
FOX, A. (1966). *Industrial Sociology and Industrial Relations.* Royal Commission on Trade Unions and Employers' Association Research Paper 3, H.M.S.O., 1966.
GORDON, R. A. (1945). *Business Leadership in the Large Corporation.* Washington D.C., 1945.
JONES, J. C. H. (1969). The Economics of the National Hockey League. *Canadian Journal of Economics,* February, 1969.
KAYSEN, C. (1957). The Social Significance of the Modern Corporation. *American Economic Review,* May, 1957.
MARRIS, R. (1964). *The Economic Theory of 'Managerial' Capitalism.* London, 1964.
NEALE, W. C. (1964). The Peculiar Economics of Professional Sports: A Contribution to the Theory of the Firm in Sporting Competition and in Market Competition. *Quarterly Journal of Economics, February,* 1964.
POLITICAL AND ECONOMIC PLANNING (1966). English Professional Football. *Planning,* vol. XXXII, No. 496, June. 1966.
PHILLIPS, Almarin (1960). A Theory of Inter-firm Organisation. *Quarterly Journal of Economics,* November, 1960.
PHILLIPS, Almarin (1961). Policy Implications of the Theory of Inter-firm Organisation. *American Economic Association, Papers and Proceedings, 1961.*
ROTHSCHILD, K. W. (1947). Price Theory and Oligopoly. *Economic Journal,* 1947.
ROTTENBERG, S. (1956). The Baseball Players' Labour Market. *Journal of Political Economy,* June, 1956.
SHEPHERD, W. G. (1964). Cross-subsidising and Allocation in Public Firms. *Oxford Economic Papers.* 1964.
SIMON, H. A. (1959). Decision-making in Economics. *American Economic Review,* June, 1959.
SLOANE, P. J. (1969). The Labour Market in Professional Football. *British Journal of Industrial Relations,* July, 1969.
SPRAOS, JOHN (1962). *The Decline of the Cinema; An Economist's Report.* London, 1962.
WILLIAMSON, O. E. (1963). Managerial Discretion and Business Behaviour. *American Economic Review,* Vol. 53, 1963.
WILLIAMSON, O. E. A Dynamic Theory of Inter-firm Behaviour. *Quarterly Journal of Economics,* 1965.

The English Football Industry: profit, performance and industrial structure

STEFAN SZYMANSKI & RON SMITH

ABSTRACT *The English (Association) Football League is a long established industrial cartel selling a highly popular product with only imperfect substitutes. Despite that, the majority of its member clubs lose money and the industry has faced successive financial crises over the last decade. This paper develops an empirical model of the financial performance of English League clubs using a high quality dataset of 48 clubs over the period 1974–89. The underlying model explains how rents are competed away through the maximising behaviour of club owners subject to production constraints. This model is parameterised by a system of equations which describe the behaviour of a maximising owner subject to demand and production constraints. The model is then used to examine the coordination failure which lies at the heart of the English Football League's decline and to assess the prospects for the Premier League.*

1. Introduction

The idea of an industry, a set of competing specialist firms within a well-defined market, is little more than a metaphor in most of the economy, but in the area of professional team sports it represents a very precise description. This paper analyses the structure of the English Football industry. Despite what is generally perceived to be a very high and price inelastic demand for the services of professional football teams the clubs themselves seldom make money. In many other industries we see firms engaging in tacitly collusive behaviour in order to mitigate the impact of competition; in football we do not see such behaviour, at least in aggregate. In this paper we present a theoretical model of the behaviour of football club owners which rationalises the observed intensity of competition. We then fit that model to data for 48 English Football League Clubs over the period 1974–89. Thus we model the period before the changes during the 1990s, which we discuss below.

There is a large literature on the economics of professional team sports, which is surveyed in Cairns *et al.* (1986). Most of this literature has been concerned with one of two issues, first estimating the demand for professional team sports, and secondly trying to identify the objective function of professional clubs. However, few papers have attempted to marry the analysis of supply and demand conditions

Stefan Szymanski, Imperial College Management School, 53 Prince's Gate, Exhibition Road, London SW7 2PG, UK.
Ron Smith, Birkbeck College, London University, 7/15 Gresse Street, London W1P 2LL, UK.

0269-2171/97/010135-19 © 1997 Journals Oxford Ltd

in order to derive an equilibrium model of team performance. We attempt to develop such a model using accounting data as well as League performance data. The analysis highlights a coordination failure which encourages club owners to neglect the infrastructure of League Football whilst concentrating on short-term playing performance. Given that in most cases English clubs are neither the recipients of open-ended financial backing from industrialists nor receive significant support for the upkeep of stadia from municipal authorities, as is common in other countries, most clubs live on the brink of financial failure. Whilst these problems have been pointed out by previous research (see for example the Chester Reports of 1968 and 1983 (commissioned by the Football League); Jennett & Sloane, 1985; Arnold & Beneviste, 1987; and most recently the Taylor Report, 1989) there have been no previous attempts to model the economic problem systematically and confront it with the data.[1] The data set combines information on League performance and attendance with accounting data on revenue, wage and transfer expenditure.[2] The sample means are given in Tables 1a and 1b.

The broad structure of the model, which is set out in detail in Section 2, is as follow. Football skills are bought on a competitive market for players, with the quality adjusted wage being determined as a Nash equilibrium between the clubs. The amount of skill a club purchases determines its position in the League. This corresponds to the production function of the industry which we estimate. Position in the League determines the revenue a club earns from gate receipts, television rights, sponsorship, etc., and this corresponds to the demand function of the industry which we also estimate. Combining the estimated demand and production functions with the budget constraint we derive the empirical trade-off that the club faces between profit and position in the league. This has a negative slope which indicates that increased spending on players is not self-financing through higher performance and revenue. The objective function of the owner of the club depends on both profits and position (see for example, Sloane, 1971). Maximisation of the objective function, subject to the profit-position constraint, determines the optimal level of wages and thus the club's profits and position in the League. Whereas each individual club faces a negative trade-off between profit and position, between clubs profits and position are positively related. This is because clubs differ in their endowment, their inherent capability and revenue generating potential, and these differences in endowment generate the observed distribution of profit and position.

The estimates of the model are presented in Section 3, Section 4 deals with some econometric issues and Section 5 looks at some alternative specifications. Section 6 discusses some of the implications of the industrial structure and in particular how the interaction of non-profit objectives with the lack of an effective market for corporate control inhibits restructuring of the industry. This is discussed in the light of the changes introduced in the 1990s.

2. A Model of the English Football League

The English Football League contained 92 clubs divided into four divisions.[3] We will consider a particular club, i, which can be characterised by the quality of its performance, Q_i, a function of its position in the League. Most managers and owners seem to regard this as the most significant indicator of the performance of a club. Whilst success in Cup competitions such as the FA Cup is highly prized,

Table 1a. Average annual performance by club, 1974–89

	League position	Turnover	Gate receipts	Wage spend	Net transfer spend	Pre-tax profits	Number of major cup games
Liverpool	2	3592	3208	1630	617	172	14
Everton	7	2943	2263	1486	416	25	10
Arsenal	7	921	2206	1493	307	205	10
Manchester United	8	4653	4340	1700	493	− 17	10
Tottenham Hotspur	11	3337	2868	1695	501	20	10
Aston Villa	14	2368	1593	1049	285	59	10
Coventry	14	1416	1050	963	− 152	− 33	8
Southampton	15	1470	1113	817	312	− 110	9
West Ham	16	2144	1980	1135	276	38	9
Leeds	18	1649	1604	1039	251	− 379	8
West Bromwich Albion	19	1560	1191	919	− 53	19	8
Newcastle	20	1810	1810	950	60	− 64	7
Luton	21	1546	1392	845	30	− 18	8
Leicester	21	1343	976	758	− 73	− 11	7
Chelsea	22	2530	1964	920	− 82	− 182	7
Birmingham	23	1167	947	886	− 68	− 96	7
Sheffield Wednesday	33	1271	1009	734	35	65	7
Oldham	35	638	368	412	− 93	− 28	6
Blackburn Rovers	35	586	421	465	− 85	7	6
Sheffield United	39	894	758	512	0	− 258	6
Bolton	42	803	510	566	41	− 317	5
Shrewsbury	44	353	251	315	− 31	− 55	5
Hull City	46	482	293	401	− 17	− 81	5
Bristol Rovers	47	523	394	310	− 64	− 126	5
Carlisle	49	436	308	342	− 48	− 13	5
Burnley	49	652	506	607	− 312	− 96	6
Plymouth	50	1026	411	425	− 38	18	5
Barnsley	50	445	387	391	− 2	− 82	5
Preston	54	565	331	395	− 101	− 34	4
Gillingham	55	494	473	336	− 4	− 153	4
Walsall	55	375	246	310	− 11	− 4	5
Huddersfield	56	519	380	438	− 91	24	5
Swindon	57	614	422	394	2	− 50	6
Rotherham	58	422	239	318	− 3	− 156	5
Cambridge	59	468	181	294	− 8	− 14	4
Wrexham	60	543	266	342	− 32	− 42	5
Reading	62	606	367	372	− 19	− 1	4
Brentford	63	592	351	343	17	− 32	4
Bury	66	325	184	301	− 57	− 19	4
Southend	66	436	245	258	− 43	− 70	4
Port Vale	67	425	186	322	9	9	4
Mansfield	68	352	216	317	− 59	− 67	4
Colchester	68	399	200	244	− 18	− 63	4
Lincoln	68	427	264	258	− 24	− 40	3
Peterborough	70	338	203	289	− 4	− 55	5
Northampton	77	317	181	255	− 47	− 38	3
Scunthorpe	81	348	201	259	− 13	− 67	4
Rochdale	86	205	152	171	− 24	− 126	3

Table 1b. Summary statistics by year (1985 Prices £000)

Year	Position	Turnover	Gate receipts	Wage bill	Net transfer spend	Pre-tax profits	Average weekly League gate (000)
1974	44	872	729	500	− 31	− 90	14.5
1975	43	796	665	480	0	− 87	15.1
1976	43	876	739	467	4	1	14.5
1977	41	912	751	454	20	31	15.1
1978	42	1075	862	508	53	33	15.0
1979	42	1059	834	564	103	− 41	14.1
1980	44	1062	815	621	80	9	13.7
1981	43	1075	804	657	61	− 114	12.4
1982	43	1064	779	686	104	− 274	11.6
1983	42	1090	817	641	30	− 54	10.8
1984	43	1206	924	639	25	9	10.9
1985	43	1265	965	684	21	− 17	10.8
1986	43	1169	913	700	55	− 123	10.2
1987	42	1314	1007	718	71	− 9	10.6
1988	43	1378	1053	782	23	6	10.6
1989	44	1562	1147	892	42	− 52	11.0

Net transfers means total expenditure minus total income from transfers. A negative figure means a net income for the club.

League position represents the outcome of sustained effort over an eight-month period, in which each club plays every other club in its division twice, without the random element introduced by the draw in a knock-out competition. In the empirical applications, in order to obtain linearity of the estimated relationships we used the negative of the log-odds (logit) of position: so quality is measured[4] as − log(position/93 − position).

In our model, clubs purchase players in a competitive labour market. In reality, prior to 1963 the clubs had an effective monopoly over the players on their own books, since a transfer required the consent of both clubs involved. Whilst a market for players existed in the sense that transfers did occur, the market was limited and likened to slavery (Sloane, 1969). Until 1977 the 'retain and transfer' system imposed some restrictions on the freedom of players to move between clubs but the market for players became much more active in the late 1960s and early 1970s. In 1977, the Professional Footballers' Association succeeded in establishing freedom of contract, and players are now almost completely free to accept the best contract on offer.[5] Each year several hundred players move clubs, although only a small fraction are transferred for the large sums advertised in the newspapers. The market leads clubs to bid against each other competitively in order to secure the services of the best players. The effort and performance of players is easily observed and monitored, thus skill is readily identifiable.[6]

One important piece of evidence which we believe supports our assertion that the market is competitive is the fact that the performance and the wage bill of a club are very highly correlated. This suggests that the payment to teams is closely related to output. Figure 1 plots the average value of our measure of quality over

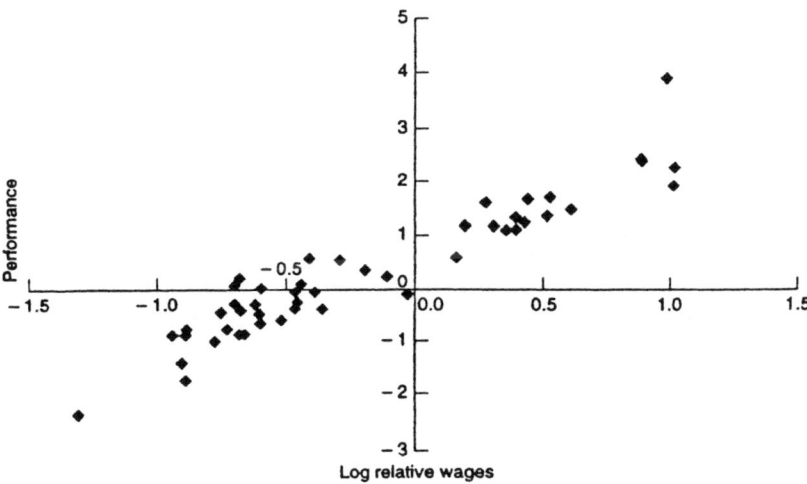

Fig. 1. Wages and performance: averages 1974–89.

1974–89 against the average of the logarithm of the wages paid by the club relative to average wages in the year over all clubs. The transformation seems to have induced linearity, the relationship is positive and fairly close.[7] The most noticeable outlier is Liverpool, the highest performing club, which spends considerably less on wages than one would expect from the average relationship.[8]

Whilst there have been some papers on the operation of the English soccer labour market (e.g. Ruddock, 1979; Carmichael & Thomas, 1992) we know of no studies which have tested for the existence of a competitive labour market along the lines of US studies of the baseball labour market. This literature is surveyed in Cairns *et al.* (1986). These studies use data on individual salary levels and estimated marginal revenue product, which should be equal in a competitive market. They find that the system of labour contracts which prevailed prior to 1976 (which resembled English soccer's 'retain and transfer' system) was associated with salaries well below estimated marginal revenue product, but after 1976 when freedom of contract was established salaries rose considerably and were closer, if not identical to marginal revenue product. Separate tests for racial discrimination tended to suggest that major league baseball was not a perfectly competitive labour market. Replication of this type of work is not easy for soccer, or most team sports, since disentangling the contribution of the individual from the rest of the team is problematic, whilst in baseball the contribution of the individual in terms of hitting and pitching is much easier to identify. However, if the baseball literature is relevant at all, it does suggest that freedom of contract enables one to treat labour markets as approximately competitive, as we do here.

In our model the wage bill of the club is $W = wL$, where w is the quality adjusted wage rate and L the quantity of playing skills the club employs. There is a limited supply of playing skills and the labour market clears when total expenditure of all clubs is equal to the total wage bill corresponding to this supply, giving a wage rate of

$$w_t = \frac{\sum_{i=1}^{N} W_{it}}{\sum_{i=1}^{N} L_{it}} \qquad (1)$$

Thus, the expenditure of each club depends on the proportion of the total playing skill they demand and the total expenditure by all clubs. This formulation assumes the existence of a Nash equilibrium in wages, i.e. each club bids for players in such a way as to maximise its objective function (discussed below), assuming that all other clubs do likewise. Thus, the share of the available playing skill that a club commands is equal to its share of the total wage-bill of all clubs

$$\frac{L_{it}}{\sum_{i=1}^{N} L_{it}} = \frac{w_t L_{it}}{w_t \sum_{i=1}^{N} L_{it}} = \frac{W_{it}}{\sum_{i=1}^{N} W_{it}} \qquad (2)$$

We will characterise the technology of the club by two equations, corresponding to a production function and a demand function, the parameters of which will, in general, differ between clubs. The production function describes how performance is produced by the quality adjusted inputs of skilled players, purchased on a competitive market, relative to the inputs of other teams. Clubs differ in their inherent performance potential as a result of such factors as history and intrinsic management differences.[9] Relative inputs are measured by relative wages. In the empirical implementation we allow for variations in total expenditure on wages by all clubs, but treating this as fixed for the moment, we can write the production function in terms of a clubs' expenditure on wages

$$Q_{it} = c_i + dW_{it} \qquad (3)$$

Each club faces a budget constraint. which generates profits as a function of the set of decision variables that we model

$$P_{it} = p_{it}G_{it} + O_{it} - T_{it} - N_{it} - W_{it} \qquad (4)$$

where upper case P refers to profit and lower case p refers to ticket price, G to gate attendance, O is other income sources, such as TV and sponsorship (discussed further in Section 6), T is transfers and N is non-wage expenditure. Each club faces a demand function from fans which specifies how Gate attendances, for a given quality of team, depend on ticket prices

$$G_{it} = f(p_{it}, Q_{it}) \qquad (5)$$

In order to estimate these demand functions we assume that they are separable and linear in prices and quality. They differ between clubs because of the size of their catchment area, local population density, traditions, etc.[10] Each club is assumed to charge a price which maximises net gate revenue, so that price can be substituted out to give a reduced form function in which gate revenue depends on perform-ance.[11] If, in addition, we assume that other revenue, from TV etc, also depends on performance, then total revenue becomes a function of the club specific intercept, the performance of the team. which depends on its quality, and chance, captured by a stochastic error term. This ignores general shifts in attendance and revenue which affect all clubs, for example the weather and the general decline in attendances but we shall return to these secular trends in Section 6.[12] The systematic component of the revenue equation (conditional on gate prices) is thus

$$R_{it} = a_i + bQ_{it} \tag{6}$$

We shall assume that non-wage expenditures, N, and net transfers T are linked to wage costs

$$N_{it} + T_{it} = \tau W_{it} \tag{7}$$

As will be seen below, empirically this works quite well. Proper treatment of transfers raises inter-temporal aspects which are a matter for further research.[13] Clubs acquire playing skill in one of two ways. Though recruitment and training programmes directed at the young people in their locality they develop their own talent. Secondly they purchase already developed talent through the transfer market. Overall this is a market. for human capital. Some of this human capital is firm specific, paid for by the club, and so the club requires compensation when a player leaves to join another club. We can think of each club's investment programme generating a team with value (wage-cost) W^A. The optimisation, described below generates a desired wage-bill W^*. Transfers are determined as

$$T = v(W^* - W^A) \tag{8}$$

a linear function of wages as we assumed above. Clubs with a high desired wage bill, will buy players (i.e. $T > 0$) and clubs with a low desired wage bill will sell players ($T < 0$). This is broadly consistent with the data. Clubs lower down the League, whose training and recruitment may be very good, earn significant income by selling players to clubs at the top of the League whose demand for playing skills is so great that it exceeds their ability to generate them by their own local investment.

Profits are the difference between revenue and total expenditure, thus at any moment in time

$$P_i = R_i - (1 + \tau)W_i \tag{9}$$

Thus the profit–quality trade-off the owner faces is

$$P_i = \pi_i + \phi Q_i \tag{10}$$

where

$$\pi_i = (a_i d + (1 + \tau)c_i)/d$$

and

$$\phi = b - (1 + \tau)/d$$

In this simple model profits are just a linear function of expenditure. If they were a positive function, then the owner faces no conflict, he can have both more profits and more quality by spending more. We shall assume that this is not the case (the estimates below confirm this) and that the owner faces a trade-off, summarised by (10). All clubs face the same price, given by the slope, but differ in their endowment, determined by the intercept. Intercepts differ, because clubs differ in their inherent revenue potential and in their efficiency in converting player inputs into performance. In the empirical applications, this intercept will also be shifted over time by the total revenue and the total expenditure on wages of all clubs, and we shall assume an intertemporal objective function with quadratic costs of adjustment, leading to a partial adjustment model.

We assume that the owner cares about both quality and profits so that the owner's objective function can be written as

$$W = P_i - (\alpha/2) \; P_i^2 + \beta \; Q_i - (\gamma/2) \; Q_i^2 \tag{11}$$

The correct way to identify the objectives of a football club has always been a matter of some controversy. Since it is the owners who make all the key financial decisions we have focused on owners. Sloane (1971) discusses this issue in some detail and argues that the objective of the football club is essentially to achieve playing success whilst remaining solvent. One reason why profit maximisation on its own is not a very plausible objective to assume is that unlike most large corporations whose ownership is embodied in shares which are actively traded on a stock market, there is a very limited market for corporate control. Normally the market for corporate control imposes a constraint on those who control a company to maximise profits. The absence of a market in football club ownership is in striking contrast to the Football, Baseball and Hockey franchises of North America. English clubs are usually tightly controlled by a small number of Board directors (see for example, Jennett & Sloane, 1985, p. 47). However, whilst most football clubs repeatedly report financial losses, being subsidised by their owners; these owners must place some limit on the extent of the subsidy. Our assumption is consistent with the idea that owners have some limit in mind, but that this differs between club. Welfare is maximised by quality of

$$Q_i^* = (\beta + \phi(1 + \alpha\pi_i))/(\gamma + \alpha\phi^2) \tag{12}$$

and the team will make profits (losses) of

$$P_i^* = (\pi_i\gamma + \phi(1 + \phi\beta))/(\gamma + \alpha\phi^2) \tag{13}$$

The team is more likely to make a profit if the owner puts less weight on quality relative to profits or if the team has a higher inherent endowment.

Although each individual owner faces a negative trade-off between performance and profits, over teams we will observe a positive association. As the break-even performance increases, an owner would choose higher levels of both profits and performance (assuming they are both normal goods) tracing out the equivalent of an income expansion locus. This is shown in Fig. 2. The more similar are the tastes of different owners, then the closer will be the cross-section relation between profits and performance. Figure 3 plots the observed relationship over the sample between average performance and average profit margin (logarithm of the expenditure/cost ratio). As the theory suggests, the relationship is significantly positive although there is a considerable scatter, which would be consistent with preferences between performance and profits differing between owners.

3. Empirical Results

This section presents basic estimates for simple versions of the revenue, performance and total cost functions. Extended versions are considered in the next two sections, but the basic estimates are robust to these extensions.

Above, we assumed that adjustment of revenue to quality and of quality to position was instantaneous, for empirical implementation, we allow for partial adjustment, because both success and failure generate considerable persistence. The data were transformed to produce linearity and the transformed variables will

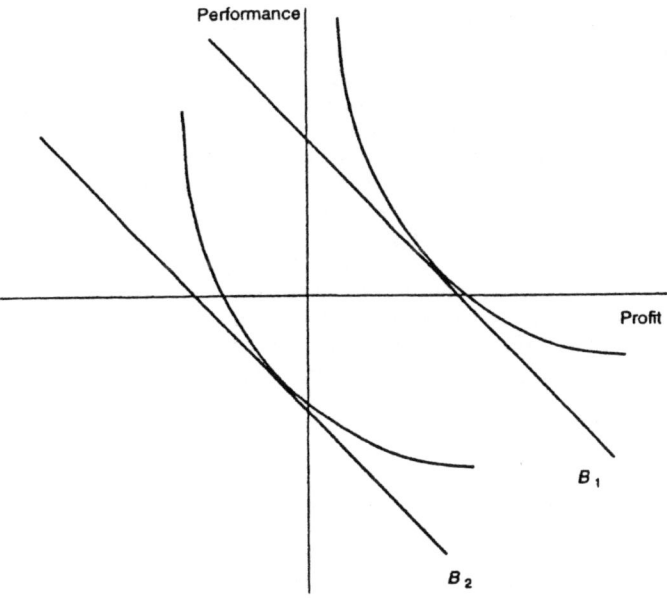

Fig. 2. The profit–performance trade-off for differently endowed clubs.

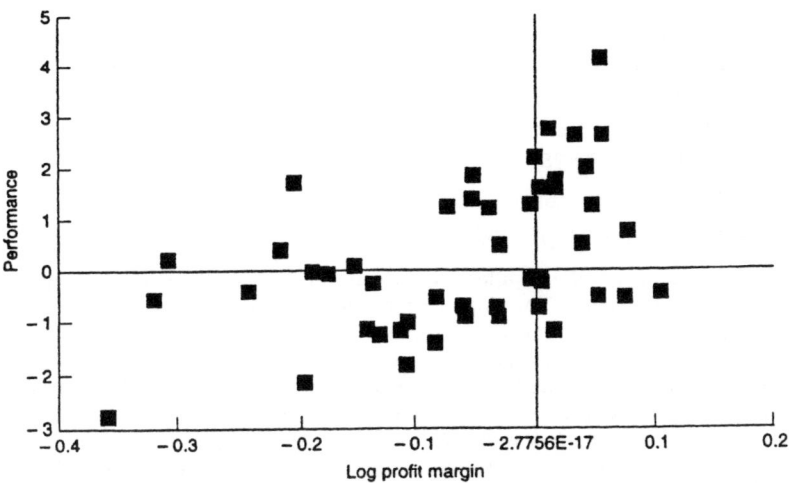

Fig. 3. Profits and performance. Averages 1974–89.

be denoted by lower case letters. As was explained in the last section, quality was measured by the negative of the log-odds of position in the league, N which can run from 1 (top) to 92 (bottom). Thus, in our empirical applications $q = -\ln\{N/(93 - N)\}$. Labour input, w, was measured as the deviation of the logarithms of expenditure on wages by the club from its mean for that year over all clubs. Revenue, r, was measured by the deviation of the logarithm of revenue from its mean over all clubs.[14] These transformations induce a broadly linear relation between profit margin log(revenue/costs) and performance (the logit of position), as can be seen from Fig. 3. They also imply a relationship between the absolute level of profits and position that fits the pattern observed. Clubs high in the League make profits, clubs in the middle make large absolute losses and clubs at the bottom of the League make small absolute losses.

The estimated model for the revenue function is

$$(r_{it} - \bar{r}_t) = \lambda a_i + \lambda b q_{it} + (1 - \lambda)(r_{it-1} - \bar{r}_{t-1}) + \varepsilon_{it} \tag{14}$$

and for the production function is

$$q_{it} = \mu c_i + \mu d(w_{it} - \bar{w}_t) + (1 - \mu)q_{i,t-1} + \varepsilon_{i,t-1} \tag{15}$$

Both functions were estimated by OLS allowing for club specific intercepts on pooled data (for the 48 clubs over 15 years (1974 was used for lags): 720 observations). Wu–Hausman tests (using lagged revenue, performance and wages as instruments) indicated that both performance and wages could be treated as exogenous ($t = 0.56$ and 1.75 respectively).

The estimate of the revenue function is

$$(r_{it} - \bar{r}_t) = \lambda a_i + 0.134q_{it} + 0.466 (r_{it-1} - \bar{r}_{t-1}) \quad R^2 = 0.94$$
$$\phantom{(r_{it} - \bar{r}_t) = \lambda a_i +} (0.012) \quad\;\; (0.031)$$

and for the production function is

$$q_{it} = \mu c_i + 1.076 (w_{it} - \bar{w}_t) + 0.427q_{it-1} \qquad\qquad R^2 = 0.85$$
$$\phantom{q_{it} = \mu c_i +} (0.120) \qquad\qquad (0.057)$$

Standard errors are given in parentheses. Clearly there is substantial persistence, both in performance and revenue. The implied estimates of the long run revenue and performance parameters (with standard errors in parentheses) are

$$b = 0.252 \qquad d = 1.894$$
$$(0.019) \qquad\;\; (0.178)$$

In the logarithmic formulation, the profit margin of the club can be written

$$(R/C) = ac(1 + \tau)^{-1} Q^{(b - 1/d)}$$

where a and c are the (antilogarithms) of the intercepts in the revenue and performance functions. The slope of the budget constraint is $b - 1/d = -0.28$, which is negative as assumed.

The 48 club specific intercepts in the performance function are of some interest. When transformed, they indicate the notional position the club would have had in the League had it spent the average amount on wages. If we imagine notional Divisions divided at average positions 22, 44 and 68; our sample of 48 clubs would be divided into 14 First. 7 Second, 21 Third, and 6 Fourth Division Clubs on the basis of their average position over the 16 years. If we examine the intercepts, the notional average position they would have had, were they to spend average amounts on wages, we find only 1 First (Liverpool), 31 Second, 16 Third and no Fourth Division clubs. On the basis of the intercepts, all but five clubs would have average positions between 25 and 55. The two below 25 are Liverpool and Shrewsbury; the three above 55 are Scunthorpe, Rochdale and Burnley.

When estimated by OLS on the whole panel, the relation between the logarithms of total costs and wages is given by

$$c_{it} = 0.272 + 1.038w_{it} \qquad\qquad R^2 = 0.833$$
$$(0.099)\ (0.017)$$

The hypothesis that total costs are proportional to wages, over all clubs, would just be rejected at the 5% level, $t = 2.27$, but would be accepted if the significance level is adjusted to take account of sample size in the way explained below. If club specific intercepts are included, the result is

$$c_{it} = \alpha_i + 0.922w_{it} \qquad\qquad R^2 = 0.88$$
$$(0.020)$$

which suggests that the club-specific intercepts in the total cost function are positively correlated with the level of wages a club chooses.

4. Econometric Issues

The results above are based on the assumption that the slopes are constant across clubs. If the slopes are not the same, then pooled estimators of dynamic models can give very misleading estimates, Pesaran & Smith (1995) discuss the issues. In dynamic heterogeneous models the appropriate estimator is the Swamy (1971) Random Coefficient Model (RCM), which estimates the weighted average of the 48 individual time-series regressions for each club. In fact the RCM estimates of the long-run coefficients are almost identical to the panel estimates in this case: $d = 1.86$ (0.465) and $b = 0.28$ (0.048).

In testing for coefficient equality in large samples, it is inappropriate to keep the size of the test or significance level constant at the conventional 5% level. As the sample increases one would wish to use the extra information to reduce both type one and type two errors rather than just type two as would be implied by using a constant size. A consistent way of doing this is provided by the Posterior Odds Criterion,[15] see Klein & Brown (1984). The F statistics for coefficient equality (i.e. testing 48 separate regressions against the fixed effect pooled model) are 1.748 for the revenue equation and 1.586 for the performance equation; both with 94 and 576 degrees of freedom. The null would be rejected at the 1% level for the first and accepted for the second. However, if one uses the Posterior Odds Criterion, which allows for the effect of sample size on model selection, the pooled model is clearly chosen in both cases. Lagged exogenous variables were not significant either with the fixed effect or Swamy estimator.

The fixed effect estimator is inconsistent (N going to infinity fixed T) when lagged dependent variables are included. But the bias declines quite rapidly with T and the fact that the fixed effect and RCM estimates are so similar confirms that this is not a problem. Neither random-effect nor cross-section estimators would be appropriate in this case, since the effects are almost certainly correlated with the regressors: for instance the intercept in the quality equation will determine the optimal expenditure on wages which is the regressor in that equation.

Table 2. Demand equation. Dependent variable: log gate attendances (A)

Year effects	Excluded		Included	
	Coeff.	t-statistic	Coeff.	t-statistic
Price	− 0.38	− 8.05	− 0.19	− 2.01
Q	0.20	13.46	0.20	14.86
$A(-1)$	0.50	13.24	0.45	11.84
$D2$	0.10	2.19	0.09	1.96
$D3$	0.18	2.86	0.15	2.48
$D4$	0.41	4.96	0.38	4.88
$P1$	0.27	3.50	0.30	4.20
$P2$	0.30	4.97	0.33	5.83
$P3$	0.01	0.17	0.03	0.79
$R1$	− 0.37	− 4.58	− 0.40	− 5.29
$R2$	− 0.11	− 1.98	− 0.13	− 2.43
$R3$	− 0.11	− 2.62	− 0.11	− 2.95
CUP	0.01	2.55	0.01	3.61
R^2	0.95		0.96	

5. Further Issues

In this section, we present estimates of the demand function (Table 2) for attendance and an extended revenue function (Table 3) which allows for a number of other influences. The estimates above assume a homogenous competition, in fact League competitions are divided into four Divisions.[16] Each year some clubs in each division get relegated to the division below, and some clubs of the lower divisions get promoted to the division above, the number involved has varied over the sample. Thus, the division a club belongs to is a non-linear function of lagged position. If revenue depended on which division the club played in rather than position as such, this non-linearity would bias the results. To test for the effect of being in a particular division, three Division dummy variables, $D2$, $D3$ and $D4$, were added for being in divisions 2, 3 and 4 respectively. To test for the effect of promotion or relegation the changes in the Division dummies were also added: $P1$, $P2$, $P3$ and $R1$, $R2$, $R3$, where the former take a value of 1 if the club was promoted to the relevant division and 0 otherwise, and the latter take a value of 1 if the club was relegated from the relevant division and zero otherwise.

Revenue also depends on performance in Cup competitions since this generates extra games as well as (more speculatively) increased support for the club as a whole. We collected data on the number of rounds played in each year by each club in each of the FA Cup, The League Cup (variously known as the Milk Cup, the Rumbelows Cup and now the Coca-Cola Cup), and the various European club competitions, the European Cup, The UEFA Cup and the European Cup Winners' Cup. The variable CUP is the total number of games played in any of these cups. When entered separately, their effects were not significantly different, either in the demand function or the revenue function.

The demand function explains the logarithm of average annual gate attendance by the logarithm of price (gate revenue per person, deflated by the RPI). Our data on gate attendances refer to League games whilst gate revenue covers all games played. In order to adjust for this in our price series we define this as gate revenue divided by average gate times the number of league games plus half the number of cup games all divided by the RPI.[17] Gate revenue was not available for all clubs, so that for this exercise our sample was reduced to 659 observations. Also included were performance, lagged attendance, the divisional, promotion and relegation dummies and the number of Cup games played. Club specific intercepts were included and the equation was estimated with and without year specific intercepts. In our study we have not attempted to capture the effect of uncertainty of outcome, which has been shown to affect demand (see for example Peel & Thomas, 1988) since our data are annual rather than match by match. The club specific intercepts capture effects such as local population size, age and gender structure and wealth, which will influence demand for football. Given the severe difficulties in defining these variables properly,[18] we do not believe that using club specific intercepts is in practice likely to involve much loss of accuracy.

The implied long run price elasticity from the equation without time dummies for each year is − 0.76 but this falls to − 0.34 when time dummies are allowed (with a *t*-statistic of − 2.05). This suggests that the price elasticity picks up the effect of the secular decline in the demand for football unless time dummies are included. The finding that demand is price inelastic is in line with earlier studies looking at the demand for football over the longer term.[19] If we suppose that football clubs are local monopolists this implies that there is considerable scope to increase profits through higher prices. However, we believe there is reason to be sceptical about this conclusion. There are (at least) three possible approaches to interpreting these estimates.

(i)   Misspecification induced by aggregating gate attendances. Suppose clubs set prices in such a way as to ensure that the ground is full for every game, taking into account the different attractiveness of each fixture. This would be consistent with a high elasticity of demand being rationally exploited by a price discriminating monopolist but would not show up in our estimates.

(ii) Misspecification of the production function: if attendances are an input into the performance of a team. then this consideration will feed through the objective function of the owner into the price setting decision, making it rational to charge low prices even though a pure profit maximiser might set higher prices.

(iii) Owners may not be monopolists at all. Even if other clubs are not good substitutes for the local product, then other leisure activities may be. If clubs are competing against these activities then their capacity to set higher prices may be limited.

It should be noted that the crucial parameter in our argument, the slope of the profit position trade-off does not depend on this elasticity. All the promotion and relegation dummies are significant except for promotion from the Fourth to the Third Division. They suggest that there is a one-off boost to revenue on promotion to the first and second divisions, which disappears in subsequent years, and also that there is a one-off dip in revenues after relegation from the first, second or third divisions which also disappears in later years. These seem to be picking factors such as supporter morale. Promotion generates an enthusiasm which is not sustained in later years, whilst relegation creates an initial despair and loss of support which is partly recaptured once the initial depression has worn off.

Table 3. Revenue equation

Variable	Coefficient	Absolute t-statistic
Q	0.11	7.76
$R(-1)$	0.46	14
$D2$	0.00	0.03
$D3$	0.02	0.41
$D4$	0.09	1.24
$P1$	0.21	2.82
$P2$	0.25	4.10
$P3$	0.06	1.47
$R1$	-0.42	-5.39
$R2$	-0.06	-1.14
$R3$	-0.08	-2.05
CUP	0.03	9.25
$R^2 = 0.95$		

The significant positive values of the lower division dummies, do not indicate that members of the lower divisions get larger attendances than first division clubs, but that they get more than would be expected from extrapolating the relationships between attendance and performance, price, etc of a first division club. This might reflect the possibility that first division clubs are capacity constrained.

As might be expected, cup performances increase gate attendances significantly, although it is perhaps surprising that the restriction that all cups increase attendances equiproportionately is accepted by the data. For the European club championships there are only a very small number of observations in our sample, but it is striking that the League Cup is apparently as popular as the FA Cup, since this competition was often criticised as being superfluous and uninteresting.

The revenue function was re-estimated including the additional variables (except relative price which was not significant in any case) and the results are given in Table 3. The long-run effect of performance on revenue is 0.21 (0.03) which is not significantly different from the earlier estimates without the additional variables. The divisional dummies are now insignificant. This means that for a given position in the League, being in a particular division exerts no additional effect on revenue, the positive relative effects of being in a lower division on attendance being offset by the negative effects on other revenues. By contrast the promotion dummies are significant for the first and second divisions and the relegation dummy is significant for the first and third divisions.

6. Market Structure

Conditional on the club-specific intercepts and aggregate wages and revenues, the model described above explains the main features of the market: only the top clubs make profits and there is a high degree of concentration. The top five clubs in terms of average League position account for some 20% of all income over our sample period. Were club owners profit maximisers, the loss makers would be likely to exit, raising the profitability of those remaining and bringing the industry back toward an equilibrium where firms generate non-negative profits. But given the owners' objective functions this does not happen, and given the lack of a market in corporate control they are not constrained by threat of take-over. Jennett & Sloane (1985) also argue that the wider shareholding, which would be associated with a market for corporate control, would provide a source of capital for the improvement of facilities.

This leads one to ask if the observed market structure is efficient either in terms of the general interest or in terms of the joint interest of the owners. Football has aspects of a quasi-public good in that it provides entertainment to a fairly wide public of fans. This public good is produced as a joint product, with a private good, the personal interests of the club owner. The interests of the owner may differ from the general interest, particularly in relation to the setting of ticket prices. Clubs are generally thought of as local monopolists and therefore pricing is likely to involve a dead-weight loss. Perhaps more interesting than this fairly standard economic problem is the issue of whether the manner of competition between club owners promotes either the joint interests of the owners or the broader general interest.

Competition between clubs on ticket prices is not likely to be a general phenomenon. Competition takes place for position in the League, and the medium for this competition is the market for playing talents.[20] Clearly the Nash equilibrium will not be the joint profit maximising one, since increased competition is a negative sum game. Competing for position itself is a zero sum game, but an owner who wishes to improve position, spends money on players. But spending on players puts upward pressure on the quality adjusted wage rate, increases the rent extracted by players and puts downward pressure on profits. The removal of what was effectively an indenture system in the early 1960s has provoked a spiral in players' wages which can be seen in Table 1b.[21] The clubs themselves are well aware of this phenomenon but the scope for outright collusion is (now) limited by the law while the possibility of sustaining tacit collusion is limited by the improbability of credible punishment strategies.[22]

A consequence of this 'excessive' competition for players is that clubs have fewer resources available for the purchase of other inputs required to produce services consumed jointly with attendance at a football match: a safe, comfortable environment, refreshments and so on. During the 1980s a series of tragic accidents in football stadia highlighted the problem: English grounds were antiquated and dangerous, attractive to few other than hooligans, while the clubs had neither the means not the will to change matters. Given that competition for players was also competing away all economic profit, the clubs had no incentive to improve the football environment since any extra profits generated would pass immediately to the players. Thus, not only was the structure of competition against the joint interest of the owners, but it also acted against the general interest.[23]

This story characterises English football up to 1989, the end of the period covered by our data set. Since then, however, two critical developments have helped to transform the picture. First, the implementation of the Taylor Report commissioned by the government after the Hillsborough disaster has obliged clubs to invest in all-seater stadia which has had the side-effect of modernising the facilities to make them more attractive to spectators. By obliging clubs to do something collectively, which it would not have been individually rational to do (for standard prisoner's dilemma reasons) the government has helped to push the clubs towards an alternative to the low quality equilibrium in which they were caught.[24]

Secondly, increasing competition among the television companies has increased the available funds for football clubs. In particular, competition from satellite broadcasting upset the pre-existing terrestrial 'duopsony', and brought about a tenfold increase in broadcast revenues. The most notable effect of this change was to cause the leading clubs to break away from the rest of the Football League to form the Premier League and so keep almost all the broadcast revenues for themselves. However, the Premier League has so far been little different from the old First Division. In the short term the extra funding has helped to pay for the rebuilding programme for the larger clubs. In the long term it has created a powerful vested interest, not in the performance of individual clubs but in the attractiveness of football as a whole. This may act as a focus for coordination between clubs in the future.

Both of these developments have had the effect of providing a focus on the interests of the entire sport and so have helped to deal with the prisoner's dilemma element in the owner's problem. Fortuitously, these developments seem to have coincided with a more general increase of interest in football. The post-war trough in League attendances occurred in the season 1985/6. Since then there has been a steady increase in attendances despite rising real ticket prices. This may be connected with increased effectiveness of policing at Football grounds leading to a lower incidence of hooliganism.[25] Overall, the future of English football seems brighter than at any other time since the late 1940s.

7. Conclusions

Over the period covered by our data, English League Football is an interesting example of a mature industry with a set of very characteristic problems. Like many old industries it had to deal with declining demand and competition from more technologically advanced leisure products. Most firms made losses, its plant was antiquated and grossly under-utilised and heavy investment was required both to meet government mandated safety standards and to improve the quality of the product sufficiently to compete on modern markets. Firms in this industry have little control over their main input cost, players, which are traded on a competitive market. Of course, many mature industries are very profitable.

The interesting question is why market forces so often fail to restructure such industries. In this case, and perhaps others, the answer seems to lie in the failure of the market for corporate control. Obstacles to take-over and acquisition allow current owners to follow non-profit objectives, allow small groups to veto changes which might be in the general interest and inhibit the internalisation of the externalities inherent in adjustment. Only when external forces impose a coordinated strategy on the competing firms is there any prospect of change. In the case of English Football, the Taylor Report and the TV companies have provided a focus for coordination.

Our model has a number of potential applications. It can be used to derive the required expenditure to raise a club from a low position to the top of the League. It is also possible to analyse the effect of the new League structure in England and Wales, which combines a Premier League of top clubs (organised by the FA) and a rump of Football League clubs. Finally, the model can be used to analyse the impact of other reforms which may be proposed for the organisation of English football in the future, and to understand their chances of success by understanding the likely impact on the distribution of profits throughout the industry.

Notes

We are grateful to Sean Wilkins for excellent research assistance in collecting the data and to two anonymous referees for constructive comments. The paper was written while the second author was visiting the Centre for Economic Forecasting, London Business School.

1. In fact the organisational structure of studying English League football is relatively easy to study since all clubs are independent limited companies whose annual accounts are lodged at Companies House. To the best of our knowledge most economic research on football emanates from the UK, although there are some exceptions such as Gartner & Pommerehne (1978), Janssens & Kesenne (1987).
2. We obtained all the accounting lodged at Companies House for the 92 clubs in the English League (in 1990). Since the accounts of some clubs were incomplete or did not break down the data in sufficient detail we focused on the 48 with complete records for the period 1974–89. To check the representativeness of our sample we calculated its average position in each sample year. The highest was 41st and the lowest 44th (against a population average of 46th). Whilst there is some bias toward the top of the League, we do not believe this is significant.
3. Until 1992, these were the First, Second, Third and Fourth divisions. Since the start of the 1992/93 season, they are the Premier, First, Second and Third. The old first division left the Football League, to form the Premier Division, organised by the Football Association, mainly in order to avoid having to share TV revenue with lower division clubs.
4. One advantage of this functional form is that it imposes reflecting barriers at positions 1 and 92. This is an approximation at the lower barrier since there have been a small number of exits over our sample period. Treating the ranking as a continuous variable also introduces a small approximation.
5. After our estimation period the European Court judgment on the Bosman case further changed the position.
6. This means that the 'agency' problem common to many markets for highly skilled labour is not as pressing in the market for football players. An alternative view of the market for players is provided by Carmichael & Thomas (1992) who present a bargaining model of transfers. In their approach the transfer price of each player is the outcome of a bargain between each club, the price being determined by the threat points and bargaining strength of each side. Where buyers and sellers have market power, transfers will not reflect the value of the individual's contribution to the team. Unfortunately measuring these individual contributions is problematic in football (unlike, for example, baseball, see Cairns et al., 1986) and the two approaches are difficult to distinguish empirically.
7. In particular, the fit is much better than comparable regressions of measures of corporate performance on payments to top executives, e.g. Smith & Szymanski (1995).
8. Another outlier of the same sort is Nottingham Forest whose accounts are only available from 1982 onwards and so are not included in the data set. These cases, which involve non-appropriable sources of competitive advantage, are discussed in more detail in dell'Osso & Szymanski (1991).
9. Strictly, this is an ownership rather than management difference, since managers can be hired on a competitive market and their wages will be included in the total payment for skill. The intercept captures a separate club specific effect partly associated with the tendency of the owners to interfere. For instance, Brian Clough, probably the ablest English manager of his generation was sacked by Brighton and Leeds partly because the owners could not get on with him.
10. Hart et al. (1975), Smart & Goddard (1991), Cairns (1987), Bird (1982), Jennett (1984), Walker (1986) and Peel & Thomas (1988), present estimates of football demand functions. Other studies have included variables such as population within a local catchment area, seats as a proportion of ground capacity and local unemployment rates. In our analysis these effects are picked up by year and club-specific intercepts.
11. This follows conveniently from our separability assumption as well as the fact that we ignore possible feedback effects from attendances to performance quality. Were such mechanisms allowed then there could be a trade-off between ticket prices and performance. Whilst our estimates reported below lead us to believe that any such effects are likely to be small in practice, we discuss their possible impact in Section 5.

12. For empirical implementation we shall proxy these by average revenue over all clubs, which will be added to the equation.
13. See also Carmichael & Thomas (1992).
14. Using deviations from year means is equivalent to including year specific intercepts, given that q also has mean zero.
15. This chooses the model which has the higher value of a criterion which is calculated as the maximised Log-Likelihood less the number of parameters times half the log of the sample size.
16. Up to 1987, the first two divisions had 22 clubs each, while the third and fourth divisions had 24. In 1988, the numbers were 21, 23, 24, 24; in 1989, 20 in the first, 24 in the other three.
17. This approximation is flawed in four possible ways. First, it assumes that half of all cup games are played at home, whilst the actual proportion depends on the draw. However, over time this should not induce any systematic bias in the estimates. Secondly it ignores replays which will lead to slight overestimate of prices. Thirdly it assumes that gate attendances at cup games equal attendances at League games on average. Whilst attendances at particular cup fixtures may be much larger than average, we do not believe that this bias will be very great on average (one Arsenal fan told us that the largest gates of the season are for games against the other leading clubs: Manchester United, Liverpool, Tottenham, regardless of whether they are cup or league matches). Fourthly the estimate does not allow for the possibility that clubs raise prices for cup games. In fact the brisk business of ticket touts at popular games suggest that clubs are not varying their prices by enough to account for the differing attractiveness of different games.
18. For example, it is hard to choose the precise catchment area for a club and this is certainly not likely to be stable over time given factors such as increased car ownership. Wealth effects are likely to be important, but it is again hard to define the wealth of a potential catchment area precisely.
19. Bird (1982) estimates a price elasticity of − 0.2 using data for 1948–80. A recent study by Dobson & Goddard (1996) using data for 1925 to 1992 estimates an elasticity of − 0.015. Our much higher estimate probably arises from the fact that the period covered by our data set was one of rapidly increasing real prices and, generally, falling attendances. Earlier periods had relatively stable prices and attendances (see for example Dobson & Goddard, 1996, Figs 1, 2 and 3).
20. The most famous recent example is Jack Walker, the owner of Blackburn Rovers, who raised the club from the bottom of the (old) second division to Premier League Champions by spending about £50m over a five year period. However it must be admitted that attempts by sugar daddies to pull off similar feats at other clubs have often failed.
21. The average annual increase over the period was nearly 4% in real terms, which is a very high rate to sustain over such an extended period.
22. Tacit collusion would involve an unwritten agreement not to pay too much to players combined with the threat of some sort of punishment for clubs which cheated on the arrangement. The punishment would need to raise the costs of the cheater's strategy: it is not clear how this could work in practice.
23. More critical fans often blame the quality of the management that runs a club for failure to innovate, but a zero profit industry is unlikely to attract the most talented (commercial) managers.
24. The government has also helped to fund these changes, but most of the burden is borne by the clubs.
25. In and around the grounds at least.

References

Arnold, A. J. & Beneviste, I. (1987) Wealth and poverty in the English football league, *Accounting and Business Research*, 17, pp. 195–203.
Bird, P. J. (1982) The demand for league football, *Applied Economics*, 14, pp. 637–649.
Cairns, J. A. (1987) Evaluating changes in league structure: the reorganisation of the Scottish Football League, *Applied Economics*, 19, pp. 259–275.
Cairns, J., Jennett, N. & Sloane, P. J. (1986) The economics of professional team sports: a survey of theory and evidence, *Journal of Economic Studies*, 13, pp. 1–80.
Carmichael, F. & Thomas, D. (1992) Bargaining in the transfer market: theory and evidence, mimeo, University of Aberystwyth.
dell'Osso, F. & Szymanski, S. (1991) Who are the champions? An analysis of football architecture, *Business Strategy Review*, Summer 1991, pp. 113–130.
Dobson, S. M. & Goddard, J. A. (1996) The demand for professional league football in England and Wales, 1925–1992, *Journal of the Royal Statistical Society*, forthcoming.

Gartner, M. & Pommerehne, W. (1978) Der Fussballzuschauer—ein Homo Oeconomicus? *Jarhbuch fur Sozial Wissenschaft*, 29, pp. 88–107.

Hart, R. A., Hutton, J. & Sharot, T. (1975) A statistical analysis of association football attendances, *Applied Statistics*, 24, pp. 17–27.

Janssens, P. & Kesenne, S. (1987) Belgian soccer attendances, *Tijdschrift voor Economie en Management*, 32, pp. 305–315.

Jennett, N. (1984) Attendance, uncertainty of outcome and policy in Scottish League Football, *Scottish Journal of Political Economy*, 31, pp. 176–198.

Jennett, N. & Sloane, P. J. (1985) The future of League football: a critique of the report of the Chester Committee of Enquiry, *Leisure Studies*, 4, pp. 39–56.

Klein, R. W. & Brown, S. J. (1984) Model selection when there is 'minimal' prior information, *Econometrica*, 52, pp. 1291–1312.

Peel, D. & Thomas, D. (1988) Outcome uncertainty and the demand for football, *Scottish Journal of Political Economy*, 35, pp. 242–249.

Pesaran, M. H. & Smith, R. (1995) Estimating long-run relationships from dynamic heterogenous panels, *Journal of Econometrics*, 68, pp. 79–113.

Ruddock, L. (1979) The market for professional footballers: an economic analysis, *Economics*, 15, pp. 70–72.

Sloane, P. J. (1969) The labour market in professional football, *British Journal of Industrial Relations*, 7, pp. 181–199.

Sloane, P. J. (1971) The economics of professional football: the football club as a utility maximiser, *Scottish Journal of Political Economy*, 8, pp. 121–146.

Smart, R. A. & Goddard, J. A. (1991) The determinants of standing and seated football attendances: evidence from three Scottish League clubs, *Quarterly Economic Commentary*, 16, pp. 61–64.

Smith, R. & Szymanski, S. (1995) Executive pay and performance, the empirical importance of the participation constraint, *International Journal of the Economics of Business*, 2, pp. 485–495.

Swamy, P. A. V. (1971) *Statistical Inference in Random Coefficient Regression Models* (Berlin, Springer-Verlag).

Taylor, Rt Hon Lord Justice (1989) *The Hillsborough Stadium Disaster* (HMSO) Cm962.

Walker, B. (1986) The demand for professional League Football and the success of football league teams: some city size effects, *Urban Studies*, 23, pp. 209–220.

[10]

Applied Economics, 1998, **30**, 1641–1651

Performance and revenue in professional league football: evidence from Granger causality tests

S.M. DOBSON and J.A. GODDARD*

*Department of Economics, University of Hull, UK and *School of Accounting, Banking and Economics, University of Wales, Bangor, UK*

Using a dataset comprising annual performance (measured by final league position) and gate revenue for 77 Football League clubs which maintained unbroken league membership between 1946 and 1994, the relationship between performance and revenue is investigated using cointegration and causality tests. A cointegrating relationship between performance and revenue is established in only 10 cases out of 77, although it is argued that some caution is required in interpreting these results, due to the low power of the relevant tests in relatively small samples. In Granger causality tests, more evidence is found of causality running from lagged revenue to current performance than of causality in the opposite direction, while the dependence of performance on revenue seems to be greater for the smaller clubs than for the larger. These results lend empirical support to the popular view that, unless checked by mechanisms for revenue redistribution within the league, the natural tendency is for success to become concentrated increasingly among a small group of elite, wealthy clubs.

I. INTRODUCTION

Recent changes in both the financial structure and the organization of professional league football in England and Wales have fuelled popular discussion about the extent to which a relative increase in the financial power of a small group of elite clubs at the top end of the league structure creates a tendency for playing success also to be concentrated increasingly among the same group of clubs.

Such developments include the withdrawal in 1992 of the former division 1 clubs from the Football League to form a break-away Premier League, which since 1992 has been considerably more effective than was the Football League previously in exploiting commercial opportunities in areas such as sponsorship, merchandizing and the sale of television rights. Also significant has been the relaxation of a number of regulations which previously restricted mobility in the players' transfer market, especially at international level. The abolition of the 'three players rule' (which prevented clubs from fielding more than three overseas players at any one time) and the European Court of Justice ruling in the Bosman case (which prevents a club holding

the registration of an out-of-contract player from receiving a fee if the player moves to another club in a different EU country) have created greater flexibility in the football labour market, arguably making it easier for the clubs with the most resources to secure the best players simply by paying them more than the rest can afford. However, while the complaint that the odds of success seem to be loaded in favour of the wealthiest clubs may have achieved new impetus as a result of recent developments, there is no doubt that the same complaint has a history as long as that of professional league competition itself.

As pointed out by Davies *et al.* (1995) in a study of rugby league performance and attendance, these considerations are to some extent counter to the approach which has been adopted in most previous econometric studies of the demand for professional team sports. Typically in this literature, a single equation is estimated in which the dependent variable, attendance, is explained by independent variables which, as well as various team performance measures, may include factors such as admission price, income and population. The individual observations are either match attendances (see Peel and Thomas, 1996; Wilson and Sim, 1995;

Baimbridge *et al.*, 1996 for recent examples; and Cairns, 1990 for a survey of the earlier literature) or season-by-season average or aggregate attendances (Bird, 1982; Burkitt and Cameron, 1992; Dobson and Goddard, 1995, 1996; Simmons, 1996; Szymanski and Smith, 1997). Implicit in the specification of the empirical model is a presumption that the direction of causality runs from performance to attendance (a successful team will attract more spectators) but not the other way round (a team with large attendances has the resources to attract better players and thereby generate better performance). Davies *et al.* (1995) argue that if reverse causality (from attendance to performance) is present, then at best the dynamics in most previous econometric models have been specified incorrectly, and at worst, misleading policy recommendations may have arisen in some cases. Granger causality tests (Granger, 1969) provide a suitable framework within which such patterns of causality can be investigated, as well as allowing the dynamics of performance and attendance time series to be modelled with considerable flexibility and without needing to impose any prior assumptions (e.g. about lag length and structure) before estimation takes place.

This paper follows the approach developed by Davies *et al.* (1995), using an England and Wales Football League (and Premier League) dataset on season-by-season team performance and gate revenues, which encompasses the period between the 1946–7 and 1993–4 seasons (inclusive). Because the two papers adopt similar methodologies, we now comment in some detail on the two main improvements which we believe this paper offers *vis-a-vis* the Davies *et al.* study.

The first improvement comes by testing for Granger causality between gate revenue and performance (rather than attendance and performance). The use of revenue data offers two advantages over attendance. First, if it is access to financial resources which allows clubs to attract better players so as to improve performance, then revenue is a more appropriate measure of financial strength than attendance. Secondly, if successful performance generates more demand, clubs may respond either by allowing attendances to increase, or by raising admission prices. An attendance series captures the former response but not the latter,

whereas a revenue series captures both. Where a club is already operating close to its ground's physical capacity, it is likely to respond to excess ticket demand by raising prices.[1] All of these points suggest that it is more appropriate to test for Granger causality between performance and revenue, rather than attendance. A limitation which remains is that total revenue (from all sources) would be preferable in many respects to gate revenue. However, the former could only be obtained from club company accounts, which are not available over a sufficient time period to permit an analysis of the type implemented here. In any event, it seems likely that revenues from sources such as merchandizing, sponsorship and television are closely correlated with gate revenues for most clubs.

Our second improvement derives from the fact that our dataset is both comprehensive, and more extensive in its duration than that of Davies *et al.* Although we have performance and revenue data for all 103 clubs which competed in the Football League between 1946 and 1994, we have restricted the Granger causality analysis to the 77 clubs which maintained Football (or Premier) League membership continuously during this period. Nevertheless, a cross section of 77 clubs allows us to derive some very much more general conclusions than were possible in the earlier study (which used data on just five major rugby league clubs). Indeed, we do not even attempt to draw conclusions about the dynamic structure of the performance–revenue relationship which are specific to individual clubs in the manner attempted by Davies *et al.* Instead, we search for patterns of Granger causality which appear common across all 77 clubs taken as a whole, or across five groups of clubs with similar characteristics which are used to classify the sample of 77.[2]

The five group definitions are based on three criteria which are distinct from performance or revenue: local population, date of initial entry into the league, and broad geographical location (even though, as shown below, these characteristics are highly correlated with both performance and revenue indicators). Broad group definitions are as follows: Group 1 (G1) comprises major clubs from the largest cities (with populations greater than half million in the 1961 Census) which entered the League before its early-1920s expansion;[3] G2 comprises clubs from other large

[1] Recently, the coincidence of reductions in many ground capacities (resulting from the replacement of standing by seated accommodation) with an increase in spectator demand for attendance has elicited precisely this response from many leading clubs.
[2] We take the view that it is unrealistic to search for strong conclusions about differences between clubs in the dynamic structure of the performance–revenue relationship from the significance or otherwise of individual lagged variable coefficients obtained from estimations using 30 (Davies *et al.*) or even 48 (in the present study) time series observations. This is simply because the relevant tests lack power in such small samples. Like Davies *et al.*, we prefer to carry out separate estimations for individual clubs, and therefore do not wish to pool our data cross-sectionally. However, by compiling the results of the individual tests at an aggregate level, we are able to address the problem of low power, at least in an informal manner. So although we do not consider the result of any individual significance test to be conclusive, if a coefficient is significant in say 30 cases out of 77, this certainly indicates a stronger overall effect than if the proportion is 15 out of 77.
[3] In the 1920–21 season, Football League membership increased from 44 clubs to 66 with the incorporation of 22 former Southern League clubs into a new division 3 (south). In 1921–22, a 20 club (subsequently expanded to 22) division 3 (north) was created, increasing total membership to 86. The combined membership of the Premier League and Football League stands currently at 92, after further small adjustments in size in 1923–24 and 1950–51.

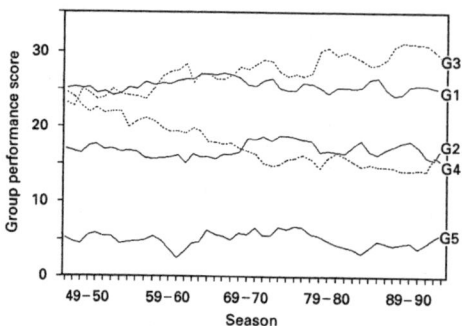

Fig. 1. *Group performance (% total score), 1946–47 to 1993–94*

Fig. 2. *Group revenue (% share), 1946–47 to 1993–94*

(around $\frac{1}{4}$ to $\frac{1}{2}$ million) population centres in the Midlands and the North, which entered before the 1920s; G3 comprises all clubs from London, the South of England and South Wales not in G1 (most of which entered during or after the early-1920s expansion); G4 and G5 comprise clubs from the smaller towns in the Midlands and the North which entered before and after the early-1920s expansion respectively. The membership of the five groups is identified in the left hand column of Table 1.

Figures 1 and 2 show performance and gate revenue share measures for the clubs in each of the five groups between the 1946–7 and 1993–4 seasons. For each club, we measure performance in season t, p_t, on a scale of 1 to 92, where $p_t = 92$ indicates the club finished 1st in division 1 (or the Premier League), $p_t = 2$ indicates 2nd, and so on. Each club's revenue measure, r_t, is its percentage share of aggregate league gate revenue. The performance data were obtained from various issues of *Rothmans Football Yearbook*, and the revenue data from the Football League's archives and (for recent seasons) *Digest of Football Statistics*. Figure 1 shows the total performance score for clubs in each of the five groups, expressed as a percentage of the total performance score for all league clubs (including clubs not in the sample). Similarly, Fig. 2 shows the percentage shares of aggregate league gate revenue for clubs in each of the five groups. The levels of the plots in Figs 1 and 2 are influenced by the numbers of clubs in each group (so the more numerous G3 clubs 'outperform' the G1 clubs in Fig. 1). However, our main interest is in the movements of the plots rather than their levels.

The main features of Figs 1 and 2 are as follows. G1 clubs have enjoyed an increase of around 15 percentage points in their revenue share, even though their performance has remained approximately static. G2 clubs have held steady in terms of both indicators. The performance of G3 clubs has improved steadily while their revenue share has been rough-

ly constant. This primarily reflects a catching up process for a number of relatively strong southern clubs, which entered the League relatively late (many in the early-1920s), and which as a group have been consolidating and improving their average position throughout most of the time since. The improved revenue share of G1 and performance of G3 are both mainly at the expense of clubs in G4, which have experienced a marked decline in both indicators. The fortunes of the nine surviving G5 clubs have held reasonably steady, although a pattern of decline would be more evident if G5 were expanded to include other clubs with similar characteristics which have not maintained a continuous League presence.

II. EMPIRICAL TECHNIQUES

In this section, bivariate tests of Granger causality between performance and revenue are carried out for the 77 clubs which enjoyed continuous membership of the Football (or Premier) League between the 1946–7 and 1993–4 seasons inclusive. Multivariate tests (which might include other variables impacting on performance and/or revenue, such as demographic or economic variables at local level) are not considered, since we lack suitable time series data. For each club, the evolution of p_t and r_t (see Section 1) can be represented in its most general form as a vector autoregression (VAR) as follows:

$$\begin{pmatrix} p_t \\ r_t \end{pmatrix} = \begin{pmatrix} c_1 \\ c_2 \end{pmatrix} + \begin{pmatrix} d_1 t \\ d_2 t \end{pmatrix} + \begin{pmatrix} \phi_{11}^{(1)} & \phi_{12}^{(1)} \\ \phi_{21}^{(1)} & \phi_{22}^{(1)} \end{pmatrix} \begin{pmatrix} p_{t-1} \\ r_{t-1} \end{pmatrix} + \cdots$$

$$+ \begin{pmatrix} \phi_{11}^{(m)} & \phi_{12}^{(m)} \\ \phi_{21}^{(m)} & \phi_{22}^{(m)} \end{pmatrix} \begin{pmatrix} p_{t-m} \\ r_{t-m} \end{pmatrix} + \begin{pmatrix} u_{1t} \\ u_{2t} \end{pmatrix} \qquad (1)$$

S. M. Dobson and J. A. Goddard

where u_{it} $(i = 1, 2)$ are random error terms, c_i, d_i and $\phi_{ij}^{(k)}$ $(i, j = 1, 2;\ k = 1 \ldots m)$ are constants and t represents a deterministic time trend. The time trend is included to allow for the long term trends in performance and revenue share identified in Section I among the clubs in some of the groups. However, for some sets of values of the parameters $\phi_{ij}^{(k)}$, the trend becomes redundant and we can set $d_i = 0$ (see below).

Before any tests of the relationship between p_t and r_t can be carried out, two issues concerning Equation 1 need to be addressed. The first is the choice of the number of lagged terms, m, to include on the right hand side of the VAR to capture the dynamics of the process generating p_t and r_t. The second is the question whether the series p_t and r_t are stationary, in which case Equation 1 represents a suitable formulation of the data generating process for purposes of estimation and hypothesis testing, or whether p_t and r_t are nonstationary, in which case it is more appropriate to work with a transformed version of Equation 1, expressed in either difference or error correction form.[4]

The lag length can be determined by comparing estimations of Equation 1 with $m = m_0$ against $m = m_0 - 1$, with $m = m_0 - 1$ against $m = m_0 - 2$, and so on. Additional lagged terms are deleted successively until a point is reached at which further deletions significantly reduce the quality of the fitted model. The likelihood ratio test statistic for the joint significance of the coefficients on the mth lagged terms, $\phi_{ij}^{(m)}$, whose distribution under the null is $\chi^2(4)$, is:

$$\lambda = (T - m)\{\ln|\hat{\Omega}_{m-1}| - \ln|\hat{\Omega}_m|\}$$

where T is the total number of time series observations; $\hat{\Omega}_m$ is the (2×2) residual covariance matrix obtained by estimating Equation 1 as a system of two seemingly unrelated regressions with m lags, estimated using the observations for $t = m + 1 \ldots T (\hat{\Omega}_m = \{\hat{\omega}_{ij}\}, \hat{\omega}_{ij} = \Sigma \hat{u}_{it}\hat{u}_{jt}/(T - m)$ for $i, j = 1, 2)$; and $\hat{\Omega}_{m-1}$ is the covariance matrix from the VAR with $m - 1$ lags also estimated using the observations for $t = m + 1 \ldots T$. Carrying out this procedure for each of

the 77 clubs individually, $H_0: m = 3$ was rejected in favour of $H_1: m = 4$ in 7 cases; $m = 2$ was rejected in favour of $m = 3$ in 4 cases; $m = 1$ was rejected in favour of $m = 2$ in 16 cases; and $m = 0$ was rejected in favour of $m = 1$ in all 77 cases.[5] As it seems desirable to adopt the same specification for all clubs to facilitate comparisons between clubs of subsequent test results, these findings suggest that $m = 2$ is the appropriate lag length for the VAR.[6]

Intuitively, the stationarity or nonstationarity of p_t and r_t hinges on the question whether, for each club, there exist 'equilibrium' levels of performance and revenue share towards which the club has a tendency to revert in the long run, even though it may depart from them (perhaps by a large distance) in the short term; or whether it is possible for a club, as a result of a few seasons of exceptional success or failure, to affect a permanent change to its expected position in the future, without any automatic tendency to gravitate back towards its former status.[7] Technically, the stationarity or nonstationarity of p_t and r_t is important because if these series are nonstationary, likelihood ratio (and other) tests of $H_0: \phi_{12}^{(k)} = 0$ for $k = 1 \ldots m$ (which if accepted implies lagged revenue does not appear in the performance equation) and $H_0: \phi_{21}^{(k)} = 0$ (lagged performance does not appear in the revenue equation) do not follow the standard asymptotic distributions, and will therefore give rise to misleading inferences if applied indiscriminately (Hamilton, 1994). This is the case even though the same difficulty does not arise with the tests for lag structure reported above. In order to establish whether adjustment to the model specification is needed before estimation, it is convenient to reparameterize Equation 1 (with $m = 2$) as follows:

$$\begin{pmatrix} \Delta p_t \\ \Delta r_t \end{pmatrix} = \begin{pmatrix} c_1 \\ c_2 \end{pmatrix} + \begin{pmatrix} d_1 t \\ d_2 t \end{pmatrix} + \begin{pmatrix} \xi_{11} & \xi_{12} \\ \xi_{21} & \xi_{22} \end{pmatrix} \begin{pmatrix} \Delta p_{t-1} \\ \Delta r_{t-1} \end{pmatrix}$$

$$+ \begin{pmatrix} \pi_{11} & \pi_{12} \\ \pi_{21} & \pi_{22} \end{pmatrix} \begin{pmatrix} p_{t-1} \\ r_{t-1} \end{pmatrix} + \begin{pmatrix} u_{1t} \\ u_{2t} \end{pmatrix} \qquad (2)$$

---

[4] An issue which we do not pursue in this paper is that the data generating process for p_t is in fact rather more complex than is captured by standard assumptions concerning u_{1t} in Equation 1. For example, p_t is bounded above at 92 and below at 1; this imposes constraints on the distribution of u_{1t} for clubs at or near the top or bottom of the league. Promotion and relegation also imposes constraints on the direction of movement in p_t between certain values in successive seasons. Without attempting any justification, we assume that the impact of these constraints on the tests which follow is sufficiently small to be ignored.

[5] Testing using the bivariate version of Akaike's Information Criterion, which recommends the lag length which minimises $AIC = \ln|\Omega_m| + (2k^*/T)$, where k^* is the total number of parameters in the VAR with m lags, produces a very similar distribution of results, although with a slight tendency towards the recommendation of less parsimonious specifications than the likelihood ratio test for a few clubs. The equivalent rejection rates using AIC were 14 ($m = 3$ in favour of $m = 4$); 8 ($m = 2$ in favour of $m = 3$); 22 ($m = 1$ in favour of $m = 2$); and all 77 ($m = 0$ in favour of $m = 1$).

[6] Seven rejections of $H_0: m = 3$ against $H_1: m = 4$ gives a rejection rate of 0.091, which does not test as significantly different from 0.05 at the 5% level. Therefore, the 7 rejections can plausibly be considered as Type I errors, suggesting that a lag length of $m = 4$ is not necessary. On the same criterion, the 16 rejections of $H_0: m = 1$ against $H_1: m = 2$ are too numerous to be attributable to Type I error, so we conclude $m = 2$ is the appropriate lag length.

[7] Anecdotal evidence can support either view. For example, evidence of stationarity can be found in the case histories of 'big' clubs which have hit hard times and subsequently recovered (e.g. Sheffield Wednesday in the 1970s, Wolverhampton in the 1980s) and 'small' clubs which have temporarily prospered before returning to relative obscurity (e.g. Northampton in the 1960s, Swansea in the late-1970s and early-1980s). On the other hand, the continued success of Wimbledon, which entered the League in 1977 and spent several years in the lower divisions attracting small attendances before a meteoric mid-1980s ascent to division 1 status, argues persuasively in favour of a nonstationarity assumption.

Performance and revenue in league football   1645

where $\xi_{ii} = -\phi_{ii}^{(2)}$, $\xi_{ij} = -\phi_{ij}^{(2)}$, $\pi_{ii} = \phi_{ii}^{(1)} + \phi_{ii}^{(2)} - 1$, $\pi_{ij} = \phi_{ij}^{(1)} + \phi_{ij}^{(2)}$, and $\Delta p_t = p_t - p_{t-1}$ etc.

Johansen (1988, 1991) has shown that the stationarity or nonstationarity of p_t and r_t, and consequently the choice of specification for purposes of estimation and inference, depends upon whether the parameters $\phi_{ij}^{(k)}$ are such that it is possible to impose restrictions on the rank of the matrix $\Pi(=\{\pi_{ij}\})$ in Equation 2. There are three cases. First, if rank(Π) = 2 (so no restrictions are possible), the VAR does not contain a unit root. p_t and r_t are stationary, although they may contain a deterministic time trend. The following (the same as Equation 1 with $m = 2$) then represents the most appropriate specification:

$$\begin{pmatrix} p_t \\ r_t \end{pmatrix} = \begin{pmatrix} c_1 \\ c_2 \end{pmatrix} + \begin{pmatrix} d_1 t \\ d_2 t \end{pmatrix} + \begin{pmatrix} \phi_{11}^{(1)} & \phi_{12}^{(1)} \\ \phi_{21}^{(1)} & \phi_{22}^{(1)} \end{pmatrix} \begin{pmatrix} p_{t-1} \\ r_{t-1} \end{pmatrix}$$
$$+ \begin{pmatrix} \phi_{11}^{(2)} & \phi_{12}^{(2)} \\ \phi_{21}^{(2)} & \phi_{22}^{(2)} \end{pmatrix} \begin{pmatrix} p_{t-2} \\ r_{t-2} \end{pmatrix} + \begin{pmatrix} u_{1t} \\ u_{2t} \end{pmatrix} \quad (3)$$

The relevant hypotheses for the causality tests are $H_0: \phi_{12}^{(1)} = \phi_{12}^{(2)} = 0$ (lagged revenue does not affect current performance) and $H_0: \phi_{21}^{(1)} = \phi_{21}^{(2)} = 0$ (lagged performance does not affect current revenue). These can be tested using the likelihood ratio statistic $\lambda = (T-2)\{\ln|\hat{\Omega}_R| - \ln|\hat{\Omega}_U|\}$ where $\hat{\Omega}_R$ and $\hat{\Omega}_U$ are the restricted and unrestricted residual covariance matrices obtained by estimating Equation 3 as a system of two seemingly unrelated regressions. Under each null, λ follows an asymptotic $\chi^2(2)$ distribution.

Secondly, if rank(Π) = 1, this implies that the VAR does contain a unit root. p_t and r_t are nonstationary, but it is possible to find a linear combination of the two series, $z_t = p_t - \beta r_t$, which is stationary. In other words, p_t and r_t are cointegrated. The condition rank(Π) = 1 implies a (2×1) vector $\alpha = \{\alpha_i\}$ can be found such that

$$\begin{pmatrix} \alpha_1 \\ \alpha_2 \end{pmatrix} (1 - \beta) = \begin{pmatrix} \pi_{11} & \pi_{12} \\ \pi_{21} & \pi_{22} \end{pmatrix}$$

The VAR can be written in error correction form as follows:

$$\begin{pmatrix} \Delta p_t \\ \Delta r_t \end{pmatrix} = \begin{pmatrix} c_1 \\ c_2 \end{pmatrix} + \begin{pmatrix} \xi_{11} & \xi_{12} \\ \xi_{21} & \xi_{22} \end{pmatrix} \begin{pmatrix} \Delta p_{t-1} \\ \Delta r_{t-1} \end{pmatrix} + \begin{pmatrix} \alpha_1 \\ \alpha_2 \end{pmatrix} z_{t-1} + \begin{pmatrix} u_{1t} \\ u_{2t} \end{pmatrix}$$
$$(4)$$

As p_t and r_t are nonstationary, any time trend is captured by the constant terms c_i, so we can set $d_i = 0$. All series in Equation 4 are stationary, so the same likelihood ratio procedure can be used to test $H_0: \xi_{12} = \alpha_1 = 0$ (lagged revenue does not appear in the performance equation) and $H_0: \xi_{21} = \alpha_2 = 0$ (lagged performance does not appear in the revenue equation). This formulation also allows us to distinguish inter-relationships between the series affecting the short run dynamics (by testing $\xi_{12} = 0$ and $\xi_{21} = 0$) from those affecting the long run relationship through the error correction term (by testing $\alpha_1 = 0$ and $\alpha_2 = 0$).

Thirdly, if rank(Π) = 0 (i.e. $\pi_{ij} = 0$ for $i, j = 1, 2$), the VAR does contain a unit root. In this case it is not possible to find a stationary linear combination of p_t and r_t, and the data generating process should be expressed in pure difference form as follows:

$$\begin{pmatrix} \Delta p_t \\ \Delta r_t \end{pmatrix} = \begin{pmatrix} c_1 \\ c_2 \end{pmatrix} + \begin{pmatrix} \xi_{11} & \xi_{12} \\ \xi_{21} & \xi_{22} \end{pmatrix} \begin{pmatrix} \Delta p_{t-1} \\ \Delta r_{t-1} \end{pmatrix} + \begin{pmatrix} u_{1t} \\ u_{2t} \end{pmatrix} \quad (5)$$

As before, the presence of a unit root implies the deterministic trend is redundant. Although there is no long run, equilibrium relationship between p_t and r_t, the specification does allow for short run effects. Likelihood ratio tests of H_0: $\xi_{12} = 0$ and H_0: $\xi_{21} = 0$ can be used to establish whether there is causality from revenue to performance, or from performance to revenue, respectively.

Johansen (1988, 1991) also provides a framework to determine which of the three specifications discussed above should be adopted. For a VAR with two equations, this is a two-step procedure as follows:

(1) Test H_0: rank(Π) = 0 against H_1: rank(Π) $\geqslant$ 1. If H_0 is accepted, the VAR is diagnosed as nonstationary with no cointegrating relationship, so Equation 5 is adopted. If H_0 is rejected, proceed to step 2. Two alternative tests of H_0, based on the maximal eigenvalue statistic and the trace statistic, are available.

(2) Test H_0: rank(Π) $\leqslant$ 1 against H_1: rank(Π) = 2. If H_0 is accepted and provided $\hat{\beta} > 0$, the VAR is diagnosed as nonstationary with a satisfactory cointegrating relationship (in accordance with expectations of a positive relationship between performance and revenue) so Equation 4 is adopted. If H_0 is accepted and $\hat{\beta} < 0$, the VAR is diagnosed as nonstationary with no satisfactory cointegrating relationship, so Equation 5 is adopted. If H_0 is rejected the VAR is diagnosed as stationary, so Equation 3 is adopted.

III. RESULTS

Table 1 shows the diagnoses of the status of the VARs for each of the 77 clubs obtained by following the procedure described in the previous paragraph. Columns 1 and 2 show the results of the tests for H_0: rank(Π) = 0 using the maximal eigenvalue statistic and the trace statistic respectively (step 1), and column 3 shows the test for H_0: rank(Π) $\leqslant$ 1 (step 2). Since the maximal eigenvalue statistic and the trace statistic can give contradictory results, two sets of overall diagnoses for the VAR (stationary; nonstationary and cointegrated; nonstationary and not cointegrated) are possible at each significance level. These are reported (at the 5% and 10% levels) in columns 4 to 7. As the results from the two procedures are generally similar, the commentary will refer only to the tests based on the maximal eigenvalue statistic.

S. M. Dobson and J. A. Goddard

Table 1. *Cointegration tests*

	H_0: rank(Π) $= 0$		H_0: rank(Π) $\leqslant 1$	Diagnosis 5% level		10% level	
	ME	Trace		ME	Trace	ME	Trace
GROUP 1							
Arsenal	23.38**	27.62**	4.24**	s	s	s	s
Aston Villa	11.65	18.65**	6.99**	n	s	n	s
Birmingham	9.59	14.60***	5.01**	n	n	n	s
Chelsea	19.56**	24.13**	4.58**	n	n	n	n
Everton	12.58***	19.79**	7.20**	n	s	s	s
Leeds	11.34	13.45***	2.11	n	n	n	c
Liverpool	6.53	7.51	0.98	n	n	n	n
Manchester Utd	14.16**	22.81**	8.14**	s	s	s	s
Manchester City	14.09**	15.21***	1.12	n	n	n	n
Sheffield Utd	12.03	17.18**	5.15**	n	n	n	n
Sheffield Wed	5.91	8.43	2.52	n	n	n	n
Tottenham	17.70**	22.65**	4.96**	s	s	s	s
West Bromwich	15.47**	16.19**	0.72	c	c	c	c
West Ham	5.56	7.57	2.01	n	n	n	n
GROUP 2							
Bradford	8.62	13.66***	5.04**	n	n	n	s
Coventry	6.61	8.52	1.91	n	n	n	n
Derby	14.87**	18.74**	3.87**	s	s	s	s
Hull	10.90	19.40**	8.51**	n	s	n	s
Leicester	9.94	16.41**	6.47**	n	s	n	s
Newcastle	16.82**	29.99**	13.17**	s	s	s	s
Nottm Forest	10.26	15.89**	5.64**	n	s	n	s
Notts County	10.65	14.91***	4.26**	n	n	n	s
Port Vale	10.04	14.17***	4.13**	n	n	n	s
Stoke	13.83***	21.51**	7.68**	n	s	s	s
Sunderland	13.16***	22.13**	8.97**	n	s	s	s
Wolverhampton	24.72**	29.80**	5.08**	s	s	s	s
GROUP 3							
Bournemouth	12.72***	19.01**	6.30**	n	s	s	s
Brentford	6.04	9.78	3.74***	n	n	n	n
Brighton	11.21	14.40***	3.19***	n	n	n	s
Bristol City	10.42	15.51**	5.09**	n	s	n	s
Bristol Rovs	16.20**	18.75**	2.55	c	c	c	c
Cardiff	12.73***	15.20***	2.47	n	n	c	c
Charlton	12.57***	19.64**	7.06**	n	s	s	s
Crystal Palace	15.21**	16.48**	1.27	c	c	c	c
Exeter	9.46	11.23	1.77	n	n	n	n
Fulham	22.33**	24.70**	2.38	c	c	c	c
Ipswich	9.05	13.02	3.97**	n	n	n	n
Leyton Orient	6.74	11.09	4.35**	n	n	n	n
Luton	19.13**	23.82**	4.68**	s	s	s	s
Millwall	9.13	11.73	2.60	n	n	n	n
Northampton	13.28***	17.72**	4.44**	n	s	s	s
Norwich	15.63**	20.10**	4.47**	s	s	s	s
Plymouth	11.86	15.89**	4.03**	n	s	n	s
Portsmouth	9.37	10.78	1.41	n	n	n	n
QPR	11.81	16.31**	4.50**	n	n	n	n
Reading	6.96	9.30	2.34	n	n	n	n
Southampton	10.97	14.02***	3.05***	n	n	n	s
Southend	11.84	17.24**	5.40**	n	s	n	s
Swindon	13.90***	15.74**	1.84	n	c	c	c
Torquay	37.42**	39.78**	2.36	c	c	c	c
Watford	13.42***	16.66**	3.24***	n	c	s	s

continued overleaf

Table 1. (*continued*)

| | H_0: rank(Π) = 0 | | H_0: rank(Π) $\leqslant$ 1 | Diagnosis | | | |
| | | | | 5% level | | 10% level | |
	ME	Trace		ME	Trace	ME	Trace
GROUP 4							
Barnsley	17.44**	21.77**	4.32**	s	s	s	s
Blackburn	6.81	9.41	2.60	n	n	n	n
Blackpool	10.49	10.58	0.09	n	n	n	n
Bolton	15.78**	18.55**	2.77***	c	c	s	s
Burnley	13.93***	14.46**	0.53	n	n	c	c
Bury	12.16***	13.11	0.95	n	n	c	n
Crewe	9.64	14.91***	5.27**	n	n	n	s
Doncaster	9.62	12.53	2.91***	n	n	n	n
Grimsby	25.69**	28.10**	2.41	c	c	c	c
Huddersfield	10.86	15.41***	4.56**	n	n	n	s
Middlesbrough	23.09**	25.50**	2.41	c	c	c	c
Oldham	17.83**	28.20**	10.38**	s	s	s	s
Preston	8.15	10.19	2.04	n	n	n	n
Rotherham	14.16**	15.69**	1.53	c	c	c	c
Stockport	12.94***	16.60**	3.66***	n	c	s	s
GROUP 5							
Carlisle	11.90	16.70**	4.80**	n	s	n	s
Chester	11.15	14.36***	3.21***	n	n	n	n
Chesterfield	16.13**	19.40**	3.27***	c	c	s	s
Hartlepool	20.26**	23.86**	3.59***	n	n	n	n
Mansfield	14.06***	18.36**	4.30**	n	s	s	s
Rochdale	29.26**	36.29**	7.09**	s	s	s	s
Swansea	21.91**	31.46**	4.55**	s	s	s	s
Tranmere	15.06**	20.89**	5.84**	s	s	s	s
Walsall	8.26	12.54	4.29**	n	n	n	n
Wrexham	13.11***	18.58**	5.47**	n	s	s	s
York	17.68**	27.34**	9.66**	s	s	s	s
Overall summary (number of diagnoses)							
		stationary (3)		14	30	26	42
		cointegration (4)		10	13	12	12
		non-stationary (5)		53	34	39	23

Note: Columns 1 to 3 show the results of tests on rank (Π) in (2). Columns 4 to 7 show the diagnoses produced by the tests, using the maximal eigenvalue and trace statistics, at the 5% and 10% significance levels.
ME = Maximal Eigenvalue Statistic; Trace = Trace Statistic.
** = Significant at 5% level; *** = Significant at 10% level.
s = Stationary diagnosis; c = nonstationary/cointegration diagnosis; *n = nonstationary/no cointegration diagnosis.

At the 5% level, in 53 of the 77 cases, the VAR is diagnosed as nonstationary with no cointegrating relationship. Performance and revenue are diagnosed as non-stationary but cointegrated in 10 cases, and in a further 14 cases the VAR is diagnosed as stationary. Only one of the ten cases for which cointegration is diagnosed occurs among the 26 clubs in G1 and G2, whereas there are nine diagnoses of cointegration among the 51 smaller clubs in G3, G4 and G5. A link between performance and revenue therefore seems to be more evident for the smaller clubs than for the larger.

Although the overall proportions of diagnoses of cointegration and stationarity are relatively small, both require the rejection of H_0: rank (Π) = 0 (see Section II) and cointegra-

tion also requires the acceptance of H_0: rank(Π) $\leqslant$ 1. In view of the relatively low power of most unit root and cointegration tests in small samples (see e.g. Maddala, 1992 for general discussion and Kremers *et al.*, 1992 for a Monte Carlo analysis) the evidence against cointegration (or stationarity) is less persuasive than would be apparent from a superficial reading of these results. Twenty-four rejections of H_0: rank(Π) = 0 out of 77 is considerably more than could plausibly be attributed to Type I error at the 5% level, and there must also be a certain (unknown) proportion of Type II errors among the 53 acceptances.

In view of the results shown in Table 1, it seems difficult to argue on empirical grounds that a common specification for

Table 2. *Granger causality tests*

Equation	3		4			5					Preferred specification (model)	Preferred specification p to r	r to p
Direction of causality →	p to r	r to p		p to r	r to p		r to p		p to r	r to p			
Test statistic	λ_1	λ_2	λ_3	λ_4	λ_5	λ_6	λ_7	λ_8	λ_9	λ_{10}			
GROUP 1													
Arsenal	2.55	4.39	0.29	2.07	2.29	9.53**	11.02**	16.39**	0.22	5.36**	(3) (5)		
Aston Villa	3.85	6.96**	1.65	5.36**	6.47**	0.73	3.45***	6.67**	1.11	3.22***	(5) (5)		
Birmingham	5.31***	5.32**	2.72***	6.35**	7.92**	0.82	0.07	0.84	1.57	0.77	(5) (5)	yes	yes
Chelsea	12.15*	4.47	16.48*	14.77**	22.43*	7.78*	9.50*	13.43*	7.65*	3.93**	(5) (5)	yes	yes
Everton	2.01	3.11	0.02	2.91**	3.44	0.10	2.79***	3.97	0.53	1.18	(5) (5)		
Leeds	2.41	7.17**	0.19	4.30**	4.65***	0.03	11.29*	12.62*	0.35	1.33	(5) (5)		
Liverpool	0.92	5.09***	0.29	0.15	0.35	0.17	6.39*	6.54**	0.20	0.15	(5) (5)		
Manchester Utd	0.29	1.59	2.32	5.13**	5.38***	0.31	14.15*	14.73*	0.25	0.58	(3) (3)		
Manchester City	0.98	1.21	2.98***	1.54	3.14	1.20	14.08*	14.10*	1.60	0.02	(5) (5)		
Sheffield Utd	9.99*	1.52	10.58*	10.38*	17.74**	3.29***	4.74**	5.95***	7.36*	1.21	(5) (5)	yes	yes
Sheffield Wed	1.22	9.85*	2.25	0.06	2.25	4.20**	2.67	11.09*	2.19	8.41*	(5) (5)	yes	yes
Tottenham	0.29	3.69	0.96	2.26	2.36	0.74	17.61*	17.66*	0.10	0.05	(3) (3)		
West Bromwich	2.38	1.64	0.85	14.10*	15.64**	1.88	2.13	2.82	1.54	0.68	(4) (4)		
West Ham	0.10	0.04	0.26	0.70	0.77	0.02	5.38**	3.24	0.07	0.02	(5) (5)		
GROUP 2													
Bradford	2.06	9.30*	2.03	5.19**	5.26***	3.55***	0.11	2.12	0.07	4.98**	(5) (5)		yes
Coventry	0.30	5.84***	0.36	3.51**	4.15	1.55	0.41	8.54**	0.64	2.18	(5) (5)		yes
Derby	5.19***	8.30**	4.46**	3.12***	5.33***	0.23	14.66*	14.99*	2.21	1.21	(3) (3)	yes	yes
Hull	2.27	2.06	0.37	6.60**	6.80**	0.00	8.94*	0.93	0.20	0.61	(5) (5)		
Leicester	3.47	7.13**	3.19***	1.10	3.39	8.40*	9.35*	1.08	2.28	3.78***	(5) (5)	yes	yes
Newcastle	2.47	7.56**	0.05	0.07	0.10	0.46	13.57*	0.26	0.03	5.32**	(5) (5)		
Nottm Forest	0.76	0.07	0.56	4.27**	4.31	0.04	0.42	5.39***	0.05	0.01	(5) (5)		
Notts County	1.18	4.96***	0.02	5.18**	5.33***	0.12	0.11	10.65*	0.14	0.16	(5) (5)		
Port Vale	0.42	9.92*	0.06	0.05	0.08	6.18**	8.37*	18.47*	0.03	7.08*	(5) (5)		yes
Stoke	3.38	5.66***	0.60	3.05**	3.77	0.03	3.07***	5.21***	0.72	1.05	(5) (5)		
Sunderland	6.59**	2.02	1.33	8.21**	9.68*	0.33	0.47	2.59	1.47	0.10	(5) (5)		
Wolverhampton	0.78	4.78***	0.42	2.15	2.47	0.04	5.54**	0.41	0.32	1.38	(3) (3)		
GROUP 3													
Bournemouth	3.72	5.48***	2.75***	11.68**	13.19**	6.90*	2.58	14.58*	1.51	4.79**	(5) (5)		yes
Brentford	8.39**	0.41	1.98	5.84**	8.66**	0.01	3.11***	3.69	2.81***	0.13	(5) (5)		
Brighton	4.84***	7.97**	0.03	5.40**	6.76**	0.08	12.32*	5.09***	1.36	3.45***	(3) (3)		yes
Bristol City	0.39	7.19**	0.23	10.39*	10.85*	9.76*	3.05***	15.87*	0.46	7.60*	(5) (5)	yes	yes
Bristol Rovs	0.82	3.70	0.03	4.14**	4.41	0.63	15.96*	9.55*	0.27	2.51	(4) (4)		
Cardiff	0.71	7.50**	0.71	3.16**	3.52	2.04	1.58	13.13*	0.37	3.63***	(5) (5)		
Charlton	4.03	4.51	1.28	2.36	4.67**	1.13	1.48	18.89*	2.31	0.64	(4) (4)		
Crystal Palace	3.43	6.92**	0.19	14.68*	15.20*	6.34**	6.21*	0.43	0.52	2.33	(4) (4)	yes	
Exeter	1.21	5.98***	0.03	4.83**	6.24**	5.93**	8.38*	0.27	1.41	6.25**	(4) (4)		yes
Fulham	2.66	5.74***	2.61	0.24	2.91	2.49	14.66*	15.44*	2.67	0.33	(4) (4)		
Ipswich	3.35	2.47	0.32	7.51*	8.04**	0.64	2.05	4.12	0.52	0.11	(4) (4)	yes	
Leyton Orient	4.25	0.41	1.50	1.16	2.56	0.01	0.81	0.57	1.40	0.12	(5) (5)		
Luton	6.61**	1.16	2.08	9.39*	11.07*	0.41	0.10	6.91**	1.68	0.31	(3) (3)	yes	yes
Millwall	0.09	0.30	0.00	8.68**	8.69**	0.51	0.95	13.05*	0.01	0.13	(5) (5)		yes
Northampton	1.68	8.56**	1.08	0.31	1.13	0.04	8.17*	3.72	0.82	5.02**	(5) (5)		yes

continued overleaf

Club	1	2	3	4	5	6	7	8	9	10	r	11	12/13
Norwich	1.62	1.30	1.64	5.44**	6.02**	0.42	0.42	8.58***	0.59	0.97	(3)		
Plymouth	6.91**	4.61***	0.65	14.66*	16.80*	0.55	11.63*	4.93***	2.14	2.95***	(5)		
Portsmouth	0.08	3.32	0.55	1.94	2.25	0.00	2.59	2.44	0.31	0.57	(5)		
QPR	1.65	0.09	0.14	7.25*	8.04**	0.00	0.22	11.39*	0.79	0.04	(5)		
Reading	3.33	1.29	6.52**	7.35*	9.60	1.85	9.66*	5.35***	2.25	1.21	(5)		
Southampton	0.65	2.54	0.08	1.32	1.81	0.00	3.18***	12.26*	0.49	0.51	(5)		
Southend	1.20	5.25***	2.89***	0.09	3.06	3.05***	1.80	23.84*	2.97***	6.18**	(5)	yes	
Swindon	1.04	10.04**	0.02	4.25**	4.91***	4.62**	0.36	17.68*	0.66	7.26**	(4)	yes	
Torquay	3.69	12.28*	5.41**	6.35**	7.04**	0.03	24.35*	2.46	0.69	2.42	(4)		yes
Watford	2.57	11.47**	0.39	0.14	0.97	0.94	5.12**	1.65	0.83	6.18**	(5)	yes	
GROUP 4													
Barnsley	1.06	15.11**	0.29	5.84**	5.85**	6.10**	3.11**	5.97**	0.01	9.94*	(3)	yes	
Blackburn	2.19	5.90***	0.09	0.05	0.21	0.04	3.49***	12.60*	0.16	0.23	(5)		
Blackpool	2.10	1.76	0.30	0.11	0.34	1.03	8.49*	1.38	0.23	0.09	(5)		
Bolton	0.79	6.09***	0.00	1.67	1.70	0.81	2.16	7.87**	0.03	2.77***	(4)	yes	
Burnley	2.86	2.46	1.85	8.63**	10.31*	2.33	0.02	6.58**	1.68	2.42	(5)		
Bury	3.65	2.26	1.60	4.60**	4.77***	0.70	11.13*	7.37**	0.18	0.26	(5)		
Crewe	3.64	6.07**	0.31	4.53**	6.53**	2.27	7.64*	15.77*	2.00	4.62**	(5)	yes	
Doncaster	3.76	18.83**	0.06	3.20**	3.32	3.27***	8.27*	14.63*	0.12	15.56**	(4)	yes	
Grimsby	4.80***	13.22*	1.71	2.21	7.37**	3.33***	5.13**	2.16	5.16**	12.55**	(4)		yes
Huddersfield	6.95***	2.74	0.09	13.04*	13.35*	2.39	0.38	13.19*	0.31	2.08	(5)		
Middlesbrough	2.62	3.38	0.50	10.32*	11.13*	0.71	0.36	1.39	0.81	1.29	(4)		yes
Oldham	1.63	3.99	1.83	4.80**	6.35**	5.67**	0.25	3.16	1.55	5.73**	(3)		
Preston	7.57**	3.22	0.01	2.86**	3.35	1.44	12.31*	10.87*	0.49	0.29	(5)		
Rotherham	1.13	0.04	0.09	3.03***	4.60	0.94	0.98	7.98**	1.56	0.40	(4)	yes	
Stockport	0.68	8.71**	2.44	0.63	2.45	2.85***	1.61	8.62**	1.82	6.26**	(5)	yes	
GROUP 5													
Carlisle	10.71**	0.30	5.92**	7.73**	13.45*	0.01	0.11	7.62**	5.71**	0.00	(5)		yes
Chester	7.27**	0.49	6.92**	16.79*	18.31*	2.02	6.49**	26.77*	1.52	0.43	(5)	yes	
Chesterfield	0.47	0.99	0.27	0.02	0.40	0.01	4.38**	11.29*	0.38	0.97	(4)		
Hartlepool	0.07	2.37	0.58	5.92**	6.12**	0.00	11.82*	0.11	0.20	0.25	(5)		
Mansfield	6.86**	7.92***	7.10*	12.39*	12.91*	0.07	16.62*	6.92**	0.52	3.59***	(5)	yes	
Rochdale	1.62	5.70***	0.21	3.35**	5.61**	0.55	10.26*	12.07*	2.26	5.94**	(3)		
Swansea	3.05	3.00	1.92	0.17	1.97	0.04	7.17*	20.21*	1.30	1.45	(3)		
Tranmere	3.87	5.06***	0.61	2.71**	2.71	0.02	6.73*	16.20*	0.00	0.99	(3)		
Walsall	3.58	0.46	4.27**	11.96*	13.17*	1.11	6.26**	7.72**	1.21	0.32	(5)		
Wrexham	3.24	7.32**	6.40**	2.24	6.93**	2.39	2.47	8.43**	4.69**	5.96**	(4)	yes	yes
York	0.47	7.22**	3.10**	8.05**	8.69**	7.43*	0.55	7.90**	0.64	7.35*	(3)	yes	

Overall summary Number of cases significant at:

1% level	3	4	21	17	6	29	31	2	8
5% level	11	10	41	34	13	39	46	5	22
10% level	15	16	51	44	19	47	53	7	29

Notes: Columns 1 to 10 show the results of Granger causality tests based on Equations 3, 4 and 5, for lagged performance in the revenue equation (p to r) and lagged revenue in the performance equation (r to p).

Column 11 shows the preferred specification (out of Equations 3, 4 and 5), diagnosed by the cointegration tests using the maximal eigenvalue statistic and a 5% significance level, as reported in Table 1.

Columns 12 and 13 identify cases in which Granger causality is diagnosed in the preferred specification at the 5% significance level (using λ_5 and λ_8 in cases where Equation 4 is the preferred specification).

λ_i are likelihood ratio statistics (distributed $\chi^2(r)$ where r = number of restrictions) for the following null hypotheses:

λ_1: $\phi_{12}^{(1)} = \phi_{12}^{(2)} = 0$ in Equation 3 λ_2: $\phi_{21}^{(1)} = \phi_{21}^{(2)} = 0$ in Equation 3 λ_3: $\zeta_{12} = 0$ in Equation 3 λ_4: $\alpha = 0$ in Equation 4

λ_5: $\zeta_{12} = \alpha_1 = 0$ in Equation 4 λ_6: $\zeta_{21} = 0$ in Equation 4 λ_7: $\alpha_2 = 0$ in Equation 4 λ_8: $\zeta_{21} = \alpha_2 = 0$ in Equation 4

λ_9: $\zeta_{12} = 0$ in Equation 5 λ_{10}: $\zeta_{21} = 0$ in Equation 5

*significant at 1% level   **significant at 5% level   ***significant at 10% level

*significant at 1% level   **significant at 5% level   ***significant at 10% level

S. M. Dobson and J. A. Goddard

the VAR (Equations 3, 4 or 5) should be used in the Granger causality tests for all clubs. On the other hand, lacking any strong theoretical argument as to why the VAR should be nonstationary or cointegrated for some clubs and stationary for others, the use of different specifications for different clubs also seems questionable. Basing the Granger causality tests solely on the specification diagnosed individually for each club is likely to imply specification error in a large number of cases, due to Type I and II error as discussed above.

Our approach is to remain agnostic on the issue of model specification. In columns 1 to 10 of Table 2, we report three complete sets of Granger causality tests, using Equations 3, 4 and 5 respectively as a common specification for all 77 clubs. For Equation 4, the tests for Granger causality affecting the short run dynamics, the error correction term, and both together, are shown separately. Column 11 shows the 'preferred' specification (Equations 3, 4 or 5) diagnosed using the maximal eigenvalue statistic at the 5% significance level (as in Table 1). Columns 12 and 13 identify cases in which the tests for Granger causality are positive in the preferred specification (again, testing at the 5% level). If similar patterns are evident in the three original sets of results, and in those compiled using the preferred specifications, this should allow us to draw inferences about the patterns of Granger causality, without needing to commit ourselves either to a common VAR specification for all 77 clubs, or to different specifications for individual clubs or groups of clubs.

Comparing the results of the Granger causality tests shown in Table 2, it is apparent that the null of no Granger causality is rejected more frequently using the error correction specification Equation 4 than with either Equations 3 or 5. This is because with Equation 4, the null implies the deletion from one of the equations of the entire error correction term, which is a more severe restriction than those tested under Equations 3 and 5. Nevertheless, drawing comparisons between the results within each set of tests, a consistent pattern does emerge. The number of cases in which a relationship is detected between lagged revenue and current performance is almost always greater (and usually much greater) than the number in which a relationship is detected between lagged performance and current revenue. The same pattern is evident when the results from the preferred specifications for each club are compared, where there are only ten diagnoses of Granger causality from lagged performance to current revenue, but 24 diagnoses from lagged revenue to current performance.

Comparing the 'preferred specification' results between the five groups of clubs, the number of diagnoses of Granger causality from revenue to performance appears to be proportionately smaller among the 'big city' clubs of G1 than among the other four groups. Using the maximal eigenvalue statistic and a 5% significance level, in G1 there are only two rejections of the no Granger causality null out of 14, a proportion of 14.3%. For G2, G3, G4 and G5

combined, there are 22 rejections out of 63, or 34.9%. In recent years, this might reflect the lesser dependence of the larger clubs on gate receipts, given their greater potential to attract television revenues, sponsorship and other sources of income; however, it is not entirely clear whether this sort of explanation would suffice for the post-war period as a whole. Other than this, there appears to be little evidence of marked differences among the other four groups of clubs in the pattern of acceptances and rejections of the null in the various formulations of the Granger causality tests.

IV. CONCLUSIONS

The following general conclusions can be drawn from the analysis. First, after classifying clubs according to characteristics other than performance and revenue, it is clear that different types of club have had markedly different experiences as regards both performance and revenue since the 1940s. Specifically, the major clubs from the largest cities have enjoyed a large increase in their percentage share of revenue which is not explained by a corresponding improvement in performance. Southern clubs (other than the major London clubs) have enjoyed a steady improvement in performance but no corresponding trend in market share. Correspondingly, the relative position of the older clubs from smaller towns in the Midlands and North has deteriorated in terms of both performance and revenue.

This evidence of heterogeneity among clubs may in part explain the diversity in the results obtained when the 77 club-specific VARs are tested for stationarity, nonstationarity and cointegration, and for Granger causality between performance and revenue. However, a recurrent argument of this paper has been that the lack of power of the relevant tests (even with time series comprising 48 annual observations) could quite easily account for the differences in test results between clubs. In view of this, for purposes of presentation and interpretation of the results, we prefer to look for patterns in results aggregated across clubs, rather than attempt to draw strong inferences from individual results.

Despite these caveats, several conclusions do emerge from the empirical analysis. Most importantly, there is strong evidence that the influence of lagged revenue on current performance is greater than the influence of lagged performance on current revenue. This complements a similar finding by Davies *et al.* (1995) concerning performance and attendance, based on a much smaller rugby league dataset. Somewhat ironically, our results also suggest that the link between lagged revenue and current performance may be weaker for the wealthiest clubs than for the rest; i.e. the clubs which draw the largest attendances and charge the highest admission prices are also those whose future success depends least on their current gate revenues.

Limited evidence is found to support the notion that our performance and/or revenue measures are stationary, or if not, that a long run cointegrating relationship exists between them. Evidence of cointegration appears stronger for the smaller clubs (G3, G4 and G5) than for those from the largest cities or other major provincial centres (G1 and G2). However, although the sample proportions of stationary or cointegration diagnoses are too high to be attributable purely to Type I error, we are unable to reject null hypotheses of non-stationarity without cointegration for a majority of clubs in all groups.

Observers who prefer sporting competition to be meritocratic may be disappointed in (but perhaps unsurprised by) these results, which lend empirical support to the popular notion that the chances of success are loaded in favour of the wealthiest clubs. Although we have examined only the relationship between league gate revenues and performance, it seems plausible to suggest that a continuation of the current tendency for the leading clubs (in particular) to augment receipts from ticket sales with additional revenue from other sources can be expected to lead to a further concentration of playing success among a small group of elite clubs in the future. A possible policy implication for the football authorities is that to preserve some degree of competitive balance within the league, there will be a continued and perhaps enhanced need for revenue redistribution between clubs, through mechanisms such as the transfer system (the future of which looks uncertain, however, in the light of the 1995 Bosman ruling) or the pooling of television and sponsorship proceeds.

REFERENCES

Baimbridge, M., Cameron, S. and Dawson, P. (1996) Satellite television and the demand for football, *Scottish Journal of Political Economy*, **43**(3), 317–33.

Bird, P. (1982) The demand for league football, *Applied Economics*, **14**(6), 637–49.

Burkitt, B. and Cameron, S. (1992) Impact of league reconstruction on team sport attendances: the case of rugby league, *Applied Economics*, **24**(2), 265–71.

Cairns, J. A. (1990) The demand for professional team sports, *British Review of Economic Issues*, **12**(28), 1–20.

Davies, B., Downward, P. and Jackson, I. (1995) The demand for rugby league: evidence from causality tests, *Applied Economics*, **27**(10), 1003–07.

Digest of Football Statistics, various issues, The Football Trust, Leicester.

Dobson, S. and Goddard, J. (1995) The demand for professional league football in England and Wales, 1925–92, *Journal of the Royal Statistical Society Series D, The Statistician*, **44**(2), 259–77.

Dobson, S. and Goddard, J. (1996) The demand for football in the regions of England and Wales, *Regional Studies*, **30**(5), 443–53.

Granger, C. W. J. (1969) Investigating causal relations by econometric models and cross-spectral methods, *Econometrica*, **37**(1), 24–36.

Hamilton, J. (1994) *Time Series Analysis*, Princeton, New Jersey.

Johansen, S. (1988) Statistical analysis of cointegration vectors, *Journal of Economic Dynamics and Control*, **12**(2/3), 231–54.

Johansen, S. (1991) Estimation and hypothesis testing of cointegration vectors in Gaussian vector autoregression models, *Econometrica*, **59**(6), 1551–80.

Kremers, J. J. M., Ericsson, N. R. and Dolado, J. J. (1992) The power of cointegration tests, *Oxford Bulletin of Economics and Statistics*, **54**(3), 325–48.

Maddala, G. S. (1992) *Introduction to Econometrics*, 2nd edn, Macmillan, New York.

Peel, D. and Thomas, D. (1996) Attendance demand: an investigation of repeat fixtures, *Applied Economics Letters*, **3**(6), 391–94.

Rothmans Football Yearbook, various issues, Headline, London.

Simmons, R. (1996) The demand for English league football: a club level analysis, *Applied Economics*, **28**(2), 139–55.

Szymanski, S. and Smith, R. (1997) The English football industry: performance, profit and industrial structure, *International Review of Applied Economics*, **11**(2), 135–54.

Wilson, P. R. D. and Sim, B. (1995) The demand for semi-pro football in Malaysia 1989–91: a panel data approach, *Applied Economics*, **27**(1), 131–38.

[11]

Economic History Review, LI, 4(1998), pp. 763–785

Performance, revenue, and cross subsidization in the Football League, 1927-1994[1]

By STEPHEN DOBSON and JOHN GODDARD

T his article examines the factors influencing both the generation and the distribution of revenues in elite professional football in England and Wales during the period 1927-94. It does so at a time of extraordinary financial dynamism, when the economic importance of professional football in England and Wales has never been greater. Annual rates of growth of turnover exceeding 20 per cent in several years during the 1990s have resulted in an aggregate turnover figure of £387 million being achieved in 1993-4 (the final season covered by this study), and exceeded substantially thereafter. Several football clubs are already listed on the stock market or the alternative investments market, and at the time of writing a number of others are preparing to join them. Football has contributed to significant growth in the turnover of associated sectors including sports and leisurewear, and subscription television. With developments such as the introduction of pay-per-view television now imminent, the prospects for continued growth appear to be great, although difficult to quantify. It is against this highly buoyant financial background that we attempt a timely historical review of the evolution of certain key features of the economic structure of professional football.

The total revenue generated by any professional sporting league competition depends upon the amounts of money being obtained through gate revenues and from other sources such as television fees, sponsorship, income from merchandising, plus the income obtained from sales of players to clubs outside the league (for example, overseas). Some of this revenue is generated directly by the clubs themselves and some is raised by the relevant sporting authorities operating on behalf of the individual clubs (for instance, by selling television rights or by negotiating sponsorship deals for the league as a whole). This revenue, together with any monies raised from other sources (perhaps through capital markets, or donations from wealthy benefactors) is available to spend on players' salaries, other costs (including stadium maintenance and development), and purchases of players from outside the league.

The distribution of the total revenue among the clubs then depends on two factors: first, on the performance of individual clubs, which

[1] We are grateful to Michael Turner and to anonymous referees for comments on an earlier draft of this article. We also thank Lorna Parnell for allowing us access to the Football League's archives. The usual disclaimer applies.

determines the extent to which clubs can attract paying spectators and income from the other sources indicated above; and secondly, on mechanisms that have evolved or have been developed which serve to redistribute revenues among member clubs. In different sports, the latter may include rules governing player transfers (where a fee may be payable when a player moves from one club to another), explicit arrangements for sharing gate receipts, and rules governing the allocation of television and sponsorship monies raised through deals other than those which apply specifically to individual clubs.

As well as using data already in the public domain,[2] we draw on two unpublished datasets which we have compiled. The first consists of data on the gate revenues from all Football League matches from the mid-1920s onwards, collected from the archives of the Football League. The 1926-7 season, the first for which these records are available, is the starting date for our data analysis. The second source comprises financial data for a sample of 47 clubs for which we were able to obtain a continuous set of company accounts for the period 1973-94.

The article is structured as follows. Section I provides a brief overview of the literature on the economic analysis of sporting league competition. A major concern of this literature has been to explain why mechanisms restricting labour mobility and providing for revenue redistribution are a pervasive feature of professional sporting leagues in most countries. This discussion provides a framework for our analysis of professional football in England and Wales in the next two sections. Section II describes changes in the distribution of playing success among clubs within the league, and considers the extent to which these changes are reflected in trends in attendances and gate revenues. Then, in section III we consider the extent to which these developments have been strengthened or qualified by the operation of the various mechanisms for reallocating revenues or restricting the free movement of resources within the industry. Finally, section IV offers some conclusions.

I

Of fundamental importance in the economic analysis of professional team sports is the notion that sporting leagues are distinguished from other industries by the nature of their product. Teams must cooperate with each other in order to produce individual matches and a viable league (or cup) competition, and the 'industry' is characterized by joint production of a common product.[3] The overall importance of the collective interest has led subsequent writers to argue that, from the standpoint of economic theory, the league as a whole should be considered as the most relevant decision-making unit or 'firm'.[4]

---

[2] The main sources are *Digest of football statistics*, *Rothmans football yearbook*, and Tabner, *Through the turnstiles*.

[3] This idea was articulated by Rottenberg, 'Baseball player's labor market'.

[4] See, e.g., Neale, 'Peculiar economics'.

THE FOOTBALL LEAGUE, 1927-1994 765

This view has been qualified by Sloane, who argues (with reference to football in the UK) that while the authorities set the rules, individual teams are free to operate as they think best within these constraints, making their own decisions as to how many players to employ, or whether to stay in business. To argue that the league is the firm and the teams its constituent parts overemphasizes mutual interdependence.[5] Nevertheless, it remains clear that professional sporting leagues are not competitive industries which teams can enter and leave at will. They are cartels, with entry and exit rigidly controlled. It follows from this that we should expect to find, within a sporting league, specific rules about who plays whom, when and where, how divisional titles are determined, and how revenues are to be distributed.[6]

While joint production is a key feature of sporting leagues, much previous economic analysis focuses on the notion of competitive balance. It is suggested that league revenues are larger (and spectator interest better sustained) if the results of individual matches and the league competition as a whole are uncertain. The uncertainty of outcome hypothesis is used to justify restricting free economic competition between individual teams in a number of areas. It provides a major explanation for the rules concerning pooling of revenues and limitations on the mobility of players,[7] which are pervasive in many sporting leagues, and whose economic rationale, according to this interpretation, is to maintain the playing strengths (or survival) of sufficient clubs to maintain a vigorous level of competition throughout the league as a whole.

In the United States in particular, the sporting authorities have manipulated off-field competition in the belief that this will yield greater joint profits than single team profit maximization.[8] Player contracts in sports including baseball, football, and basketball have for many years contained a 'reserve clause', which tied a player to the team owning the contract for the length of the player's career or until the contract was sold. In baseball, player-initiated transfers without the consent of the club holding the contract were prohibited. Several US sports have rules governing the signing of new players from minor leagues. Under the draft clause in baseball, the acquisition of new players is regulated by giving clubs first choice of players in inverse relation to their position in the previous year's league table.[9] While the reserve clause has all but disappeared (players are now free agents in most US sports), the sporting authorities have devised other ways of maintaining competitive balance. In basketball for instance, the 'salary cap' prevents teams from bidding freely to

[5] Sloane, 'Economics of professional football'.
[6] Gramlich, 'Natural experiment'.
[7] Sloane, *Sport in the market*.
[8] Rules relating to player mobility and arrangements for the sharing of gate receipts have also featured prominently in a number of UK sports other than football. At various times, labour market restrictions and revenue-sharing schemes have operated in rugby league, cricket, and speedway.
[9] Sloane, 'Restricting competition'.

lure players, ensuring instead that clubs compete with each other on equal terms.[10]

According to the uncertainty of outcome hypothesis, revenue-sharing arrangements help to ensure that sufficient clubs have the financial resources to attract and retain the most talented players, so that competitive balance is not damaged by an excessive concentration of talent among a few clubs. In US sports apart from basketball, match gate receipts are shared between the home and away teams, with the home team typically retaining around 80 per cent.[11] Television revenues are also pooled; the most egalitarian arrangement is in football, where most of the revenue comes from the television contract, whose proceeds are shared equally among all teams.[12]

Thus, the joint nature of the product produced by sporting leagues, and the desire to maintain competitive balance, have resulted in sporting authorities devising mechanisms which try to influence the distribution of revenue and playing talent. While the nature of these arrangements may vary between sports, between countries, and over time, the structure of most sporting leagues includes provisions for some forms of explicit or implicit cross subsidization, and some restraints on off-field economic competition between league members.[13]

II

The English Football League first achieved membership of a magnitude comparable to the combined strength of the present Premiership and Endsleigh League competitions (92 teams) shortly after the First World War. In the 1920-1 season, 22 teams from the Southern League were added to the existing membership of 44 teams (competing in two divisions) to form the new Division 3 (South), and the following season (1921-2) a new Division 3 (North) was created comprising 20 teams (22 from 1923-4). Between 1919-20 and 1923-4 the league therefore doubled in size from 44 to 88 teams. From 1921-2, 69 teams maintained continuous league membership up to the 1993-4 season, and 77 were in continuous membership from the end of the Second World War until 1993-4.

There have been five important structural changes since the early 1920s. The first comprised a further increase in membership from 88 to 92 teams from the 1950-1 season. This was followed by the reorganization of the lower two divisions into Divisions 3 and 4, with membership determined on merit (by promotion and relegation) rather than by geographical location. Next came an increase in mobility within the league, with three (rather than two) teams promoted and relegated between Divisions 1 and 2 and Divisions 2 and 3 each season from 1973-4

---

[10] Gramlich, 'Natural experiment'.

[11] Vrooman, 'General theory'.

[12] Gramlich, 'Natural experiment'.

[13] In principle, economists tend to be critical of cross subsidization if it results in distortion of the price mechanism and misallocation of resources. For a fuller discussion of cross subsidization and its relevance to sporting leagues, see Arnold and Benveniste, 'Cross-subsidisation'.

© *Economic History Society 1998*

onwards (and a play-off system introduced in 1986-7 to determine one of the promotion places for each division). The fourth change included several adjustments to the size of the divisions during the late 1980s and early 1990s, with automatic promotion and relegation between Division 4 and the top non-league competition also implemented in a number of seasons during this period. Finally, there was the withdrawal from the Football League of Division 1 teams to form a breakaway Premier League (since renamed the Premiership) in 1992-3, a development which has not affected the basic competitive structure of professional league football, but which has had profound organizational and financial implications.

Table 1. *Aggregate league attendance, gate receipts, and admission prices, 1927-1994*

	League attendance (millions)		Gate revenues (£'000)		Real gate revenues (1927 = 100)	Average admission price (£)	Real average admission price (1927 = 100)
	total	coefficient of variation	total	coefficient of variation			
1927	23.4	0.65	1 373	0.69	100	0.06	100
1932	21.8	0.66	1 263	0.73	110	0.06	118
1937	26.4	0.63	1 575	0.72	133	0.06	118
1947	35.4	0.61	2 933	0.70	183	0.08	121
1952	39.0	0.57	4 135	0.65	197	0.11	118
1957	32.7	0.57	4 311	0.67	171	0.13	122
1962	28.0	0.63	4 981	0.76	175	0.18	146
1967	28.9	0.73	6 931	0.90	205	0.24	166
1972	28.7	0.77	10 814	0.95	238	0.38	194
1973	25.4	0.85	11 823	1.00	241	0.46	222
1974	25.0	0.79	13 174	0.97	239	0.53	223
1975	25.6	0.81	15 180	0.98	228	0.59	209
1976	24.9	0.83	18 822	0.97	231	0.76	217
1977	26.0	0.82	22 220	0.97	234	0.85	210
1978	25.4	0.84	26 651	1.00	257	1.05	236
1979	24.5	0.83	28 960	0.95	254	1.18	243
1980	24.6	0.79	36 911	0.95	272	1.50	258
1981	21.9	0.82	40 239	1.02	264	1.84	281
1982	20.0	0.84	40 523	1.04	239	2.03	279
1983	18.8	0.82	42 096	1.03	236	2.24	294
1984	18.3	0.84	44 760	1.06	239	2.44	304
1985	17.8	0.92	49 276	1.17	249	2.77	327
1986	16.5	0.94	48 901	1.15	236	2.97	334
1987	17.4	0.89	55 844	1.08	259	3.21	348
1988	18.0	0.81	63 906	1.00	287	3.56	373
1989	18.5	0.77	72 885	0.98	304	3.95	384
1990	19.5	0.77	87 219	0.97	337	4.48	405
1991	19.5	0.81	103 691	1.04	369	5.32	442
1992	20.4	0.83	127 329	1.09	435	6.25	499
1993	20.6	0.77	146 238	1.10	485	7.09	549
1994	21.7	0.82	163 655	1.10	534	7.55	576

Notes: In order to keep the table to a manageable size, figures are given for every fifth year only, up to the early 1970s. Years are end-years of football seasons; i.e. 1927 is the 1926-7 season, and so on.
Gate revenues and admission prices are deflated using the retail price index.
Sources: Tabner, *Through the turnstiles*; *Digest of football statistics* (various issues); *Rothmans Football Yearbook* (various issues); Football League archives.

Table 1 highlights some of the main trends in attendance, admission prices, and gate revenues between the 1926-7 and 1993-4 seasons. During the interwar period attendances mirrored the fortunes of the national economy fairly closely. After the First World War attendances experienced a short boom followed by a period of decline, and then recovery from the 1932-3 season onwards. It has been suggested by Bird that football became an inferior good after 1945;[14] but there is no evidence for this in the interwar period. Jones argues that football was a normal good (attendances increased as incomes rose) because working-class earnings had yet to rise to levels at which alternative leisure pursuits became affordable.[15] Real gate revenues rose gently before 1939, mainly because the effect of a falling price level outweighed the effect of declining attendances on the real revenue indices up to 1931-2. Average admission prices were almost constant (in absolute terms) throughout the interwar years at 6 pence ($14\frac{1}{2}$d.) per spectator. Throughout the interwar period and beyond, Football League regulations existed to inhibit price competition between clubs, preventing them from admitting spectators for less than a minimum admission price, which remained unchanged at 5p (12d.) until after the Second World War.[16]

In the late 1940s attendances surged, reaching an all-time high of just above 41 million in 1948-9. From then until the mid-1980s the trend was consistently downward, although with short interludes, most notably following England's World Cup victory in 1966. The downward trend accelerated in the early 1980s, partly because of economic recession (which affected many traditional footballing towns especially badly[17]) and partly because of the problem of hooliganism.[18] The reversal in favour of a sustained upward trend in attendances from the 1986-7 season onwards was initially as unexpected as it was welcome.[19] At first it may have been attributable to the near disappearance of football hooliganism, whose incidence went into rapid decline following the 1985 Heysel disaster (sparked by a hooligan incident), and especially after the 1989 Hillsborough disaster (among whose causes there was no hooligan element). It has been sustained by factors such as the physical reconstruction after 1989 of many formerly dilapidated football stadiums; and, in the mid-1990s, football's skilful exploitation of selective aspects of its

---

[14] Bird, 'Demand for league football'.

[15] Jones, 'Economic aspects'.

[16] The rules dictating a minimum admission price remained in force until the mid-1970s, by which time it had reached 40p (see Bird, 'Demand for league football').

[17] e.g. the Lancashire towns of Blackburn, Bolton, Burnley, and Preston, all of whose clubs were among the 12 founder members which competed in the first Football League competition in 1888-9. The coefficients of variation for the attendance series indicate that the relative variation across clubs in attendance tends to be inversely related to the overall level of attendance. Therefore, the smaller clubs suffer proportionately more than the larger when aggregate attendances are falling, and benefit proportionately more when attendances are rising. A similar pattern is evident in the coefficients of variation for the gate revenue series, although in this case there is also a more pronounced trend towards greater inequality between clubs over the long term.

[18] Dunning, Murphy, and Williams, *Roots of football hooliganism*.

[19] When attendances were declining most rapidly in the early 1980s, a report in the *Economist* (9 May 1981) had spoken of 'a coming crisis in football similar to the secondary banking and property blitz in the City of London in 1974-5'.

own 'heritage'[20] to reposition itself as a fashionable and increasingly upmarket leisure activity for spectators.

After 1945, gate revenues in real terms tended to mirror attendances until around the mid-1960s, as admission prices increased roughly in line with inflation. Thereafter, admission prices (and revenues) began to outpace inflation, partly in response to cost pressures induced by the abolition of the maximum wage in 1961 (see below). Between the early 1970s and the mid-1980s, revenues remained roughly constant in real terms, with reduced attendances being offset by increased admission prices. Although the real price increases may have contributed towards the fall in attendances, factors such as hooliganism, changing patterns of work and leisure, and declining standards of on-field entertainment are more commonly cited as explanatory factors. This suggests that the increase in admission prices should be interpreted primarily as a (largely successful) attempt to insulate revenues from the effects of declining attendances caused by non-price factors.[21] Since 1986-7 revenues have increased much more sharply than is explained by the upward trend in attendances, because admission prices have risen at a rate which is unprecedented historically. The fact that these price increases have coincided with rising attendances provides testimony to the strength of the recovery in professional football's popularity.

Table 2. *Percentage shares of aggregate attendance and gate revenue by division, 1927-1994*

	Attendance				Gate revenue			
	D1	*D2*	*D3S/D3*	*D3N/D4*	*D1*	*D2*	*D3S/D3*	*D3N/D4*
1927-33	45.0	28.0	16.4	10.6	47.1	28.0	15.8	9.0
1934-9	44.4	28.9	16.2	10.5	47.1	28.8	15.4	8.7
1947-52	42.3	28.9	17.2	11.6	44.5	29.4	16.1	10.0
1953-8	43.3	26.5	17.6	12.7	46.4	26.7	16.5	10.5
1959-64	43.9	25.8	18.3	12.0	47.9	26.2	16.2	9.6
1965-70	48.6	25.2	15.2	10.9	55.0	23.7	12.9	8.4
1971-6	51.2	24.8	15.3	8.7	57.5	23.6	12.4	6.5
1977-82	51.6	24.4	15.0	9.0	57.9	23.9	11.9	6.2
1983-8	50.7	25.6	14.9	8.8	58.5	23.7	11.7	6.0
1989-94	45.4	31.0	15.1	8.5	55.1	28.1	11.2	5.7

Note: Years are end-years of football seasons.
Sources: as tab. 1

Table 2 summarizes the changes which have taken place since the mid-1920s in the distribution of aggregate attendance and gate revenue between clubs in the four divisions of the Football League. For Division 1 clubs, the main change during this period was a marked increase in

[20] Examples include the popular success of Hornby's book *Fever pitch*, an autobiography of 1970s suburban adolescence as an Arsenal supporter; and the extensive use of 1966 World Cup imagery in the marketing and promotion of the 1996 European Championship competition.

[21] Two recent econometric studies have obtained an estimated price elasticity of demand of around 1. See Dobson and Goddard, 'Demand for professional league football'; Simmons, 'Demand for English league football'.

© Economic History Society 1998

770   STEPHEN DOBSON AND JOHN GODDARD

market share of about 8 per cent (measured in terms of attendance) or 10 per cent (in terms of gate revenue), which took place between the mid-1960s and mid-1970s. It is interesting to note that clubs in the top division have recently experienced a decline in their attendance share, which has created a corresponding, although smaller, downturn in revenue share. The fall in attendance share is mainly attributable to lower capacity constraints, both during and after the reconstruction of most stadiums in line with the requirements of the Taylor report on Hillsborough.

Table 3. *Performance scores and percentage shares of aggregate attendance and gate revenue by group, 1927-1994*

	Group 1	Group 2	Group 3	Group 4	Group 5
(i) Performance					
1927-33	26.4	19.5	21.3	20.8	12.0
1934-9	25.5	19.4	22.5	21.2	11.4
1947-52	24.9	18.1	23.6	21.1	12.2
1953-8	25.0	16.8	24.9	20.1	13.2
1959-64	26.1	16.2	28.5	18.0	11.1
1965-70	26.4	16.5	30.4	16.2	10.4
1971-6	25.2	18.4	31.8	13.5	11.2
1977-82	25.0	17.0	33.4	14.0	10.7
1983-8	25.2	17.0	34.3	13.1	10.4
1989-94	24.9	16.9	35.9	13.7	8.6
(ii) Attendance					
1927-33	32.3	18.4	23.2	16.2	9.9
1934-9	32.0	17.8	24.6	16.0	9.7
1947-52	28.5	19.2	25.1	16.8	10.4
1953-8	28.3	17.9	26.0	16.2	11.6
1959-64	31.0	17.0	27.2	14.6	10.2
1965-70	33.3	19.1	26.3	12.2	9.1
1971-6	35.5	18.3	27.7	11.2	7.3
1977-82	36.1	17.0	27.6	11.4	7.8
1983-8	37.3	17.4	28.3	9.8	7.2
1989-94	35.9	18.2	27.4	11.8	6.7
(iii) Gate revenue					
1927-33	33.3	19.2	23.0	16.2	8.4
1934-9	33.3	18.6	24.0	15.9	8.1
1947-52	29.0	20.9	24.1	17.0	9.0
1953-8	29.9	18.9	25.2	16.2	9.8
1959-64	33.7	17.9	26.2	13.9	8.3
1965-70	38.1	20.2	24.2	10.5	7.0
1971-6	40.3	18.8	25.9	9.5	5.5
1977-82	40.3	17.7	26.5	9.5	6.1
1983-8	42.9	16.8	27.5	7.6	5.3
1989-94	43.1	17.1	25.7	9.5	4.6

Note: Years are end-years of football seasons.
Sources: as tab. 1

The data in table 2 are driven to some extent by changes in the composition of the four divisions. In order to measure more effectively the main changes in the distribution of performance, attendance, and revenue between clubs of similar characteristics, table 3 classifies the clubs into five groups, using three objective criteria in an attempt to achieve homogeneity within groups. The three criteria are: town popu-

THE FOOTBALL LEAGUE, 1927-1994   771

lation as shown in the 1961 census; date of initial entry into the league; and geographical location (for which there are two broad categories: south and midlands/north). Group 1 clubs are 'major' clubs from towns with populations larger than 500,000, all of which entered the league before its expansion in the early 1920s. Group 2 comprises clubs from towns with populations in the range 250,000-500,000 in the midlands/north (i.e. all English regions from the east midlands and west midlands northwards).[22] Group 3 includes all other clubs from towns in the south (i.e. the south east, south west, and East Anglia regions, plus south Wales) with populations below 500,000, as well as the smaller London clubs not included in Group 1; most of these clubs (except Bristol City, Luton, Fulham, and Leyton Orient) joined the league during or after its early 1920s expansion. Group 4 includes all clubs from smaller towns in the midlands/north which entered the league before 1920, and Group 5 contains clubs from the same regions which entered during or after the early 1920s expansion.[23]

Table 3 shows the percentage shares of each of the five groups in aggregate attendance and revenue, and an aggregate performance score calculated by awarding 92 points to the club which finished first in Division 1, 91 points to the club which finished second, and so on. Unsurprisingly, in view of their high base levels of support, the Group 1 clubs' attendance share is consistently several percentage points higher than their performance score. However, more striking is an increase of about 8 percentage points in these clubs' attendance share (and 10 points in revenue share) between the late 1950s and the early 1970s, during which period their performance (as a group) was virtually unchanged; these increases have been sustained since the early 1970s. Therefore,

---

[22] A 'major' club is one which (in the authors' judgement) draws significant support from all parts of its town and surrounding districts. Two London clubs (Fulham and Leyton Orient) which satisfy the other criteria for Group 1 membership are excluded because their support is judged to be more localized than this definition allows. West Bromwich Albion is considered to be located within Birmingham, and therefore qualifies for Group 1 membership. Group 2 contains two clubs (Derby and Sunderland) which fall marginally short of the population requirement but which were nevertheless deemed worthy of membership of a group consisting of long-established clubs from major provincial centres.

[23] The full list of clubs by group is as follows:

Group 1: Arsenal, Chelsea, Tottenham, West Ham, Aston Villa, Birmingham, West Bromwich Albion, Leeds, Sheffield United, Sheffield Wednesday, Everton, Liverpool, Manchester City, Manchester United.

Group 2: Derby, Leicester, Notts County, Nottingham Forest, Coventry, Port Vale, Stoke, Wolverhampton, Bradford City, Bradford PA, Hull, Newcastle, Sunderland.

Group 3: Bristol City, Bristol Rovers, Cardiff, Newport, Swansea, Barnet, Brentford, Charlton, Crystal Palace, Fulham, Leyton Orient, Millwall, QPR, Thames, Watford, Wimbledon, Brighton, Luton, Oxford, Portsmouth, Reading, Southampton, Southend, Bournemouth, Plymouth, Ipswich, Norwich, Aldershot, Colchester, Gillingham, Maidstone, Exeter, Swindon, Torquay, Cambridge, Peterborough, Aberdare, Merthyr.

Group 4: Blackburn, Blackpool, Bolton, Oldham, Preston, Stockport, Gateshead, Middlesbrough, Huddersfield, Barnsley, Doncaster, Grimsby, Rotherham, Burnley, Bury, Crewe, Chesterfield, Lincoln, Walsall.

Group 5: Wrexham, Shrewsbury, Hereford, Northampton, Mansfield, Halifax, Rochdale, Scarborough, Scunthorpe, York, Accrington, Chester, Nelson, New Brighton, Southport, Stalybridge, Tranmere, Wigan, Ashington, Barrow, Carlisle, Darlington, Durham, Hartlepool, Workington.

during the 1960s in particular, there was a significant shift in the composition of total football attendances in favour of the Group 1 clubs, which increased their revenues even faster by raising their admission prices by more than other clubs.

Table 4.   *Gate revenue and total revenue for sample of 47 clubs, classified by group, 1974-1994*

| | Total revenue (£'000), average per club | | | | | Gate revenue as % of total revenue, average per club | | | | |
| | Group | | | | | Group | | | | |
	1	*2*	*3*	*4*	*5*	*1*	*2*	*3*	*4*	*5*
1974	431	410	183	151	102	84.9	73.5	62.6	59.8	59.0
1975	523	433	205	181	118	81.0	72.0	63.1	57.7	63.4
1976	701	610	272	224	143	82.8	63.9	65.5	63.7	62.3
1977	965	678	344	268	149	83.7	56.1	55.8	61.0	65.8
1978	1,202	696	426	292	203	82.4	60.3	48.5	64.1	59.8
1979	1,378	836	587	368	208	78.5	49.4	49.0	65.0	63.0
1980	1,712	942	732	505	294	74.3	53.1	50.0	51.6	51.4
1981	1,783	1,159	843	482	276	74.6	46.6	50.4	56.8	51.3
1982	1,957	1,082	851	537	292	73.3	46.1	48.0	50.6	48.7
1983	2,009	1,196	866	530	334	76.4	47.8	50.5	56.9	45.1
1984	2,569	1,220	894	566	317	72.1	54.9	49.6	50.9	49.9
1985	3,174	1,232	932	567	382	69.4	59.8	50.2	46.6	49.6
1986	2,986	1,340	827	504	345	72.9	56.5	57.2	49.6	51.6
1987	3,241	1,548	1,029	639	374	75.3	67.8	56.4	50.5	59.9
1988	3,632	2,048	1,266	759	478	75.5	55.4	52.1	56.6	47.6
1989	4,495	2,387	1,488	992	522	70.9	57.0	49.6	49.5	50.0
1990	5,786	2,685	1,725	1,294	559	62.6	59.2	53.0	51.2	51.3
1991	7,602	2,619	2,176	1,358	603	59.7	63.4	46.1	49.3	55.3
1992	8,615	3,436	2,385	1,692	721	64.0	56.4	49.2	50.0	43.6
1993	10,873	4,257	3,457	2,254	718	62.2	55.7	36.1	46.6	45.9
1994	12,928	4,829	4,055	2,631	803	61.2	55.0	35.0	45.7	45.1

Note: Clubs included:
Group 1:   Arsenal, Aston Villa, Everton, Liverpool, Manchester United, Sheffield United, Sheffield Wednesday, West Bromwich Albion
Group 2:   Coventry, Derby, Hull, Leicester, Newcastle, Port Vale, Stoke
Group 3:   Bristol Rovers, Exeter, Norwich, Plymouth, Portsmouth, Reading, Southampton, Southend, Swansea, Swindon, Torquay
Group 4:   Barnsley, Blackburn, Bolton, Burnley, Bury, Huddersfield, Lincoln, Oldham, Preston, Rotherham, Walsall
Group 5:   Carlisle, Darlington, Halifax, Mansfield, Northampton, Rochdale, Scunthorpe, Shrewsbury, Wrexham, York
Years are end-years of football seasons.
Source: Company accounts

Since the 1920s, the major provincial clubs in Group 2 have experienced a gentle decline in performance and revenue share and a relatively static share of attendance. For the southern clubs in Group 3, a progressive improvement in performance has been rewarded by only very modest increases in attendance and revenue share. Even when successful, these clubs have therefore found it difficult to widen their appeal significantly. The smaller clubs from the midlands/north (Groups 4 and 5) have suffered the biggest decline in performance, attendance, and revenue share. In particular, the revenue share of clubs in Group 4 has been even more markedly affected than their attendance share by their deteriorating performance. The fortunes of the northern clubs admitted in 1921 (most of Group 5) have been in stark contrast to their southern counterparts in Group 3, with long-term reductions in their attendance, revenue, and performance indices, and with none establishing themselves as regular competitors in the top two divisions by the end of the period.

The revenue data in tables 1, 2, and 3 refer only to gate revenues from league fixtures. Evidence on aggregate revenues from all sources is more difficult to obtain on a consistent basis; however, table 4 provides some evidence, from our sample of 47 clubs for which company accounts were available continuously over the period 1973-4 to 1993-4 (the clubs have been allocated to the same groups as described above). Table 4 demonstrates that throughout the period, smaller clubs have been more dependent than larger clubs on income sources other than gate revenues.[24] It also highlights the growth in importance of non-gate revenue sources for clubs at all levels over the same period.

III

In this section we consider the extent to which the trends identified in section II have been strengthened or qualified by the operation of implicit or explicit mechanisms for the redistribution of resources among professional football clubs. These mechanisms are discussed under two headings: the labour market (including the transfer system); and revenues from television, pooling of gate receipts, and sponsorship.

The maximum wage and the retain-and-transfer system were key features of the labour market in professional football from the late nineteenth century onwards. Both were designed to prevent the clubs with the greatest resources from securing all the most talented players simply by outbidding other clubs for their services, an outcome which might be expected in a fully flexible football labour market.[25] Both survived in their original form until the early 1960s, when the maximum wage was abolished and the retain-and-transfer system overhauled.

In 1922 the maximum wage was reduced from £9 to £8 per week

---

[24] Walvin attributes the lesser reliance of the smaller clubs on gate revenues to necessity, born of the escalating costs of running a club following the abolition of the maximum wage (see section III). 'Clubs of all shapes and sizes resorted to ever more elaborate schemes for raising money, simply to pay the weekly bills ... without spending any money on much needed improvements in the stadiums. In this they were greatly helped by their supporters clubs, by local sponsors and the like. In the lower reaches of the game, clubs were glad to receive free kit, free footballs; anything that might help defray the soaring costs of running the clubs.' (Walvin, *People's game*, p. 177).

[25] 'The maximum wage was an integral part of the Football League. It was felt that it enabled an equality of opportunity for all the clubs to hold their best players ... it enabled clubs like Huddersfield, Blackpool, Bolton, Preston and Blackburn who weren't in highly populated industrial areas to do extremely well. ... The retain-and-transfer system was effectively there to protect those clubs that had developed their talent from having them poached, compensating them for the loss of that talent if those players left.' Michael Gliksten, quoted in Taylor and Ward, *Kicking and screaming*, p. 152. On the other hand, it is widely accepted that clubs also resorted to illegal practices in order to attract and retain players. For example, in the mid-1950s Liverpool was reputed to have guaranteed each of the 15 men in its first team squad £15,000 over a four-year period. Tom Finney of Preston North End and England took 12 years to earn the same amount (see PEP Report, 'English professional football').

(£6 during the summer). Average weekly earnings of male employees in engineering were £2.65 in 1924.[26] Immediately after the Second World War, the maximum wage was raised to £12 (£10 in the summer). This settlement represented a narrowing of differentials; average weekly earnings for male manual employees in 1947 were £6.60. By the time the maximum was raised to £20 (£17 in the summer) in 1958, the gap had narrowed further, with average weekly earnings then having reached £12.83.[27] Under intense pressure from the players' union (the Professional Footballers Association), the maximum wage was abolished in 1961, and since then wages have risen exponentially. Table 5 shows data on expenditure on wages and salaries for the sample of 47 clubs with company accounts. The figures include the remuneration of all employees (not just players), but it is certain that players' wages account for a very substantial part of the overall growth. Among all the clubs included, total expenditure on wages and salaries rose from £6.7 million in 1973-4 to £113.4 million in 1993-4, which represents an increase of 196 per cent in real terms. The largest real increase (276 per cent) is recorded by clubs in Group 1.

By restraining both growth in players' salaries overall and divergences between the remuneration of players operating at the top and bottom ends of the league, the maximum wage undoubtedly played a significant role in maintaining a degree of uniformity in the financial structure of professional football at all levels, which has been eroded progressively during the period since its abolition.[28] Towards the end of its lifetime, the ultimate beneficiaries of the maximum wage were probably the paying spectators, who as late as 1959-60 were being charged an average admission price only 23 per cent higher in real terms than in 1925-6 (despite the very much larger rise in real disposable incomes which had occurred over the same period). In 1959-60, the average admission price per spectator at Arsenal, at 19p the most expensive in the league, was less than twice that at Rochdale, at 10p the cheapest. It is no coincidence that the pressure for abolition mounted progressively as the postwar economic recovery continued at full pace, and the magnitude of the spectators' implicit consumer surplus grew with rising affluence. As soon as the wage restraint was lifted and salaries started to escalate, especially at the top end of the league, admission prices followed suit, and presumably much of the surplus began to shift from the spectators to the players.[29] By 1993-4, the gap between the highest average admission

---

[26] See *British labour statistics*.

[27] Not all footballers were paid the maximum. In 1958, when a player earning the maximum would have been paid around £1,000 per year, average earnings varied between £894 for Division 1 players and £770 for those in Division 4 (see PEP Report, 'English professional football').

[28] Increasing inequality between clubs in expenditure on salaries is evidenced by the progressive rise in the overall coefficient of variation between 1974 and 1994 (see table 5). Any trends in the amount of variation between the clubs within each of the five groups are less easily discernible.

[29] 'The wages . . . (the senior British clubs) . . . paid their players had the effect of inflating wages throughout the game. The freeing of wages produced a dramatic increase in the costs of professional football. These added costs led inevitably to regular, increased admission prices.' (Walvin, *People's game*, p. 177).

THE FOOTBALL LEAGUE, 1927-1994   775

Table 5. *Nominal and real expenditure on salaries for sample of 47 clubs, classified by group, 1974-1994*

	Gp 1	Gp 2	Gp 3	Gp 4	Gp 5	All
No. of clubs	8	7	11	11	10	47
(i) Nominal (average per club, £ million)						
1974	264	198	117	107	70	142
1975	297	218	137	116	84	160
1976	341	275	153	139	93	187
1977	420	303	171	163	108	218
1978	501	345	203	192	131	257
1979	611	430	263	242	156	319
1980	804	503	354	329	209	416
1981	958	569	455	390	251	499
1982	1,101	613	525	436	272	562
1983	1,124	618	456	403	272	542
1984	1,215	665	498	406	257	572
1985	1,436	648	512	411	285	617
1986	1,528	744	555	416	319	666
1987	1,646	807	562	469	332	712
1988	1,794	954	638	554	371	805
1989	2,079	1,280	736	611	432	951
1990	2,695	1,498	995	710	519	1,191
1991	3,495	1,875	1,222	966	599	1,514
1992	4,417	2,118	1,546	1,307	592	1,861
1993	4,878	2,365	1,808	1,472	618	2,082
1994	5,697	2,704	2,095	1,721	694	2,413
(ii) Real, 1974 = 100						
1974	100	100	100	100	100	100
1975	95	94	99	92	102	96
1976	87	94	88	88	90	89
1977	93	90	85	89	91	90
1978	99	91	90	93	98	94
1979	111	105	108	108	107	108
1980	125	104	124	91	123	114
1981	129	102	138	129	128	125
1982	132	99	142	129	124	126
1983	127	94	116	112	116	114
1984	131	96	121	108	105	115
1985	148	89	118	104	111	118
1986	149	97	122	100	118	121
1987	155	102	119	109	118	125
1988	162	115	130	124	127	136
1989	177	146	141	128	139	151
1990	213	158	177	138	155	175
1991	251	180	197	171	163	203
1992	305	195	240	222	155	239
1993	327	212	272	243	157	260
1994	376	238	310	279	173	296

Notes: Clubs included are as in tab. 4. Salary expenditure is deflated using the retail price index. Years are end-years of football seasons.
For nominal expenditure, coefficients of variation calculated at five-yearly intervals are as follows: for 1974: Group 1, 0.31, Group 2, 0.40, Group 3, 0.43, Group 4, 0.49, Group 5, 0.29, All, 0.61; for 1979: Group 1, 0.45, Group 2, 0.27, Group 3, 0.41, Group 4, 0.40, Group 5, 0.36, All, 0.62; for 1984, Group 1, 0.38, Group 2, 0.41, Group 3, 0.51, Group 4, 0.24, Group 5, 0.30, All, 0.70; for 1989, Group 1, 0.46, Group 2, 0.50, Group 3, 0.52, Group 4, 0.23, Group 5, 0.26, All, 0.79; for 1994, Group 1, 0.39, Group 2, 0.48, Group 3, 0.60, Group 4, 0.97, Group 5, 0.21, All, 0.89
Source: Company accounts

charge (again Arsenal, at £13.20) and the lowest (Scarborough at £2.47) had increased to a ratio of more than five, mirroring the increasing divergence in salary expenditures between Group 1 clubs and the others shown in table 5.

The second major labour market reform of the early 1960s was concluded with the 1963 High Court ruling in favour of the player George Eastham in a historic case against Newcastle United. Prior to 1963, all player contracts were renewable annually at the club's discretion, and clubs were entitled to retain a player's registration even if the contract was not being renewed. In theory and sometimes in practice, this enabled a club to prevent an out-of-contract player from earning a living.[30] The 1963 High Court ruling adjudged this system an unreasonable restraint of trade. From then on, the club holding the registration had to offer a new contract at least as remunerative and of the same duration as the expired contact (which could be for one or two years) in order to retain the player's registration; if such a contract was not forthcoming, the player became a free agent. However, transfers were still at the discretion of the selling club, which retained absolute power to frustrate a player's desire for a move so long as it was prepared to continue to remunerate at the same level as before.

This system lasted until 1977, when players were awarded the right to decide on a move at the expiry of their contracts. However, the out-of-contract player was still not completely free, since if the former club was offering a new contract at least as remunerative as the expired contract, it could demand a fee, to be settled by FA tribunal (with the decision binding on all parties) in cases where the clubs could not agree. The 1977 system has survived intact until the present for players moving between clubs within the UK. However, for changes of club which involve moves across national borders within the European Union, the 1995 European Court of Justice ruling in the Jean Marc Bosman case established the principle of complete freedom of movement for out-of-contract players, with no transfer fee payable to the former club.

Although we do not have comprehensive data on transfer expenditure prior to the 1970s, it seems certain that the labour market reforms of the early 1960s tended to encourage increased levels of expenditure in the transfer market since they created the opportunity for the richer clubs to attract players by offering more generous packages of remuneration.[31] On the other hand, both the 1977 reform and (especially) the more recent Bosman ruling, by limiting the value to his present club of the

---

[30] 'When a player was signed on by a club, he lost his right to transfer his services to any other club. The club owned him. When you combine this with a maximum wage, it means that the player not only binds himself to a club for his playing life, but is also subjected to this absurdly small payment, and it was a medieval serf system.' Sir Philip Goodhart, quoted in Taylor and Ward, *Kicking and screaming*, p. 158. 'A few days after my seventeenth birthday I became a bondsman, a serf, a slave. And, more than willingly.' (Guthrie and Caldwell, *Soccer rebel*, p. 13.)

[31] The first six-figure transfer fee was paid shortly after the 1966 World Cup, when Alan Ball moved from Blackpool to Everton for £110,000. In the next three years there were 10 further moves involving fees of at least £100,000.

player whose contract is drawing towards its conclusion, would be expected to have the opposite effect.

In fact, as table 6 shows, there was no clear trend in aggregate transfer expenditure within the league throughout the 1970s and 1980s in real terms, or relative to gate revenues.[32] Table 6 certainly lends no credence to the common complaint (voiced regularly during the past 30 years) that the transfer market is periodically out of control. Nevertheless, there is considerable year-on-year variability in aggregate expenditure, although in part this reflects the relatively small number of transactions which make up the total. The one apparently unsustainable burst of activity, when some of the characteristics of a boom-bust cycle were apparent, peaked during the 1979-80 season, following the first £1 million transfer (Trevor Francis from Birmingham to Nottingham Forest) in February 1979. Recently, total expenditure has shown a more sustained upward trend both in real terms and relative to gate receipts. However, if increasing television revenues are also taken into account, a ratio of transfer expenditure to gate revenues of between 50 per cent and 65 per cent in most seasons since 1987-8 looks quite consistent with the slightly lower values usually recorded before then.

The role of the transfer market as a mechanism for redistributing monies between clubs at different levels of the League is demonstrated by the fact that Division 1/Premiership clubs recorded a net surplus in their dealings with other league clubs in only two of the 22 seasons included in table 6. Although there is again considerable year-on-year variability, it seems clear that the importance of the transfer market in channelling funds from the top clubs to the rest has grown. For example, for the 11 seasons from 1972-3 to 1982-3 inclusive, the average value of the net deficit as a percentage of gate revenues for Division 1 clubs was 4.6 per cent; for the next 11 seasons up to 1993-4, this had increased to 7.3 per cent. This was reflected in corresponding increases of the transfer surpluses of the lower division clubs, which have amounted to more than 30 per cent of gate revenues in some seasons.

Televised transmission of football in Britain began in 1938 with the broadcast of England v. Scotland and the FA Cup final, but regular coverage of Football League matches did not start until the launch of the BBC's recorded highlights programme 'Match of the day' in 1964. From then until the late 1970s, the BBC and ITV operated an effective cartel which was successful in containing the fees paid by the television companies. The proceeds were distributed evenly among all league clubs, with the amount received by each increasing modestly from £1,300 in 1967-8 to £5,800 in 1978-9. The first attempted breach in the BBC/ITV stranglehold occurred in 1978 when the ITV company London Weekend Television attempted to reach an arrangement for exclusive rights to cover

---

[32] Table 5 does not include expenditure on players brought into the league from non-league clubs (which represents a relatively small sum) or from overseas (which, during the period covered by table 5, was also relatively small although not insignificant, including as it did several transfers of top international players). Very recently expenditure on overseas players has grown substantially, and now constitutes a highly important part of total transfer expenditure.

Table 6. *Transfer expenditure within the Football League, 1973-1994*

(i) Gross expenditure

	Total (£ million)					Real (1973 = 100)					% league gate revenues
	D1	D2	D3	D4	Total	D1	D2	D3	D4	Total	
1973	3.2	1.8	0.7	0.2	5.8	100	100	100	100	100	49.1
1974	3.7	2.0	0.9	0.3	6.9	106	104	117	136	108	52.4
1975	4.2	1.8	0.8	0.2	7.0	102	102	77	92	93	46.1
1976	2.2	0.5	0.5	0.2	3.5	43	18	50	63	37	18.6
1977	4.7	1.5	0.6	0.2	6.9	78	46	45	56	64	31.1
1978	7.6	2.6	1.1	0.4	11.6	112	68	82	90	95	43.5
1979	9.1	4.8	2.5	0.8	17.2	124	117	168	185	129	59.4
1980	18.3	9.3	3.7	1.5	32.8	214	196	206	290	210	88.9
1981	11.9	6.3	2.7	0.3	21.2	121	115	130	53	118	52.7
1982	18.0	2.6	1.3	0.5	22.3	163	42	56	76	111	55.0
1983	6.3	2.3	1.5	0.1	10.2	53	36	62	17	48	24.2
1984	8.4	2.7	1.5	0.4	12.9	68	40	57	50	58	28.8
1985	9.5	3.3	1.1	0.3	14.2	73	46	41	44	60	28.8
1986	10.9	2.8	1.4	0.4	15.6	80	37	49	50	63	31.9
1987	16.4	3.9	1.8	0.7	22.8	117	50	61	85	89	40.8
1988	23.0	9.5	3.2	1.0	36.8	157	117	105	113	138	57.6
1989	25.3	15.9	3.4	1.6	46.2	162	183	106	164	162	63.4
1990	26.6	19.4	5.8	3.3	55.1	159	208	167	318	180	63.2
1991	26.4	13.5	4.9	1.2	46.0	143	131	129	102	137	44.4
1992	46.4	24.4	2.7	1.4	74.8	241	228	67	115	213	58.7
1993	50.8	19.1	2.8	0.5	73.2	256	173	67	42	202	50.1
1994	66.9	20.4	3.2	1.3	91.8	332	182	77	102	250	56.1

(ii) Net expenditure

	Total (£ million)				% league gate revenues			
	D1	D2	D3	D4	D1	D2	D3	D4
1973	0.4	−0.1	−0.3	−0.1	5.7	−3.7	−18.0	−9.2
1974	0.2	0.3	−0.2	−0.3	2.4	9.1	−14.5	−30.9
1975	0.6	−0.2	−0.3	−0.1	7.9	−5.1	−15.7	−13.5
1976	0.7	−0.7	0.0	−0.0	6.9	−15.1	−1.6	−4.4
1977	0.5	0.0	−0.3	−0.2	4.1	−0.6	−9.5	−19.0
1978	1.8	−1.1	−0.5	−0.2	11.3	−16.6	−19.4	−11.4
1979	0.2	−0.6	0.3	0.2	1.2	−9.0	8.3	7.6
1980	0.6	0.6	−0.7	−0.5	3.0	6.7	−15.2	−21.2
1981	−0.9	0.5	0.6	−0.2	−3.9	5.3	10.7	−7.4
1982	2.4	−1.9	−0.3	−0.3	10.1	−20.2	−7.5	−9.3
1983	0.4	−0.4	0.5	−0.5	1.9	−3.4	8.7	−24.1
1984	2.2	−1.3	−0.5	−0.4	9.0	−9.9	−8.8	−16.2
1985	2.2	−1.2	−0.9	−0.1	6.9	−11.8	−16.1	−3.8
1986	1.2	−0.7	−0.3	−0.2	3.9	−7.6	−5.3	−6.5
1987	4.1	−2.4	−1.4	−0.4	12.3	−19.4	−24.5	−8.7
1988	5.5	−2.6	−1.5	−1.3	15.8	−15.2	−19.4	−30.1
1989	0.8	1.2	−1.3	−0.7	2.1	5.7	−13.9	−14.2
1990	−3.5	0.8	1.5	1.1	−8.2	2.9	15.9	18.9
1991	7.4	−5.1	−0.3	−2.0	13.3	−16.7	−2.7	−30.9
1992	3.6	3.7	−5.3	−2.0	4.7	11.7	−39.7	−29.1
1993	6.0	−2.0	−3.2	−0.8	7.0	−5.4	−17.9	−12.4
1994	13.0	−6.0	−5.9	−1.1	13.3	−14.0	−37.4	−15.6

Notes: Transfer expenditure is deflated using the retail price index.
Years are end-years of football seasons.
Source: Digest of football statistics, various issues

and distribute televised football around the ITV network. Complaints to the Office of Fair Trading prevented the arrangement from going ahead, but in the subsequently renegotiated contract, the amount received by each club rose to £23,900 from 1979-80 onwards. Regular live coverage of league fixtures, shared between the BBC and ITV, took place for the first time in the 1983-4 and 1984-5 seasons, at an annual cost of £2.6 million for 10 matches. It was suspended during 1985-6 following the breakdown of negotiations between the Football League and the television companies. Tensions between the larger and smaller clubs about the distribution of revenues, and the parlous financial state of football resulting from the continuing decline in gate revenues meant that the companies probably retained the upper hand in negotiations at this time. The two-year contract settled in 1986 providing 14 matches at an annual cost of £3.1 million was still modest by later standards.

The emergence of the two satellite broadcasters British Satellite Broadcasting (BSB) and Sky triggered a radical shift in the structure of the negotiations, the impact of which was evident for the first time in 1988 when ITV secured exclusive rights to show 18 matches per season between 1988-9 and 1991-2 at a much increased annual fee of £11 million. The BBC and BSB collaborated to purchase joint rights to show FA Cup and England matches. The distribution of the rewards among the clubs also changed significantly, amid threats from the elite clubs to break from the League and enter separate negotiations with the television companies. Roughly £8.25 million of the £11 million paid by ITV in 1988-9 went to the Division 1 clubs, with around £3.5 million (42.4 per cent of £8.25 million) received by Arsenal, Everton, Liverpool, Manchester United, and Tottenham, the five clubs targeted for the majority of ITC's coverage.[33]

As the close of the ITV contract approached, it became clear that the next negotiation would be shaped both by the desire of the newly merged satellite operator BSkyB[34] to secure an increased share of the coverage, and by the disparate ambitions of the clubs seeking to maximize their own individual shares of the proceeds. Strategically, BSkyB correctly identified football as a necessary (and probably sufficient) ingredient which would allow satellite to achieve a viable level of market penetration prior to the extension of subscription charges from films to sports and other areas.[35] Meanwhile, the continued manoeuvre among the clubs culminated in the announcement early in 1991 that Division 1 would break completely from the Football League to form the new Premier League (Premiership), under the auspices of the Football Association, from 1992-3.

---

[33] Goldberg and Wragg, 'It's not a knockout'. See also Baimbridge, Cameron, and Dawson, 'Satellite television'.

[34] BSkyB was formed as a result of the effective takeover of the ailing BSB by Sky in November 1990.

[35] The successful sports subscription service of the French station Canal Plus was seen as a prototype in this respect.

In negotiations documented extensively by Fynn and Guest,[36] BSkyB was narrowly successful in prising the contract for live Premiership coverage from ITV, at a cost of £304 million spread over five years. The proceeds were shared exclusively among the Premiership clubs, but the distribution within this group, which depended partly on television appearances and partly on final league position, was more equitable than under the previous ITV contract.[37] The BBC/BSkyB collaboration for the FA Cup and internationals continued at a cost of £75 million over four years, with the BBC also permitted to screen evening highlights of Saturday Premiership matches. ITV subsequently secured rights to live Sunday coverage of selected Football League fixtures, for fees which varied by region but which amounted to more in total than had been paid to the former Division 2, 3, and 4 clubs under the previous ITV contract (although their share expressed as a proportion of the total television monies was much reduced).

If one of the recurrent themes shaping the negotiations of successive recent television contracts has been the desire of the top clubs to claim an increasing share of the available revenue, a similar trend has also led to the erosion or abandonment of the two main explicit mechanisms for revenue sharing among league clubs, which had operated unchanged from the 1920s through to the early 1980s. The first of these schemes required 20 per cent of the notional receipts from every match to be paid to the visiting club. Notional receipts were based on minimum admission charges, with certain deductions permitted (e.g. for costs of policing and stewarding). This arrangement was abolished in 1983, since when clubs have retained all the proceeds from their home fixtures. The second revenue-sharing scheme saw 4 per cent of all notional receipts paid into a pool, the proceeds from which were distributed evenly among all 92 clubs. The 4 per cent levy was reduced to 3 per cent in 1986, and the redistributive impact of the scheme was further reduced in 1992-3 by the creation of the Premiership, whose members did not contribute to the pool. The 3 per cent levy and arrangements for equal distribution of the proceeds are still effective within the Football League.

The erosion of the explicit schemes for redistribution of receipts from league fixtures has coincided with, and to some extent been compensated by, an increase in the number of cup competitions, which operate with different revenue-sharing arrangements. A second knock-out cup tournament contested by all league clubs, the League Cup, was first introduced in 1960.[38] A separate cup competition for teams from the lower two divisions has operated successfully (under the names of successive sponsors) since 1984-5, while an attempt to establish a third tournament open to all league clubs eventually foundered after the 1991-2 season,

---

[36] Fynn and Guest, *Out of time.*

[37] In 1993-4, for example, of an estimated total payout of £34.9 million to the Premiership clubs from the BSkyB/BBC contracts, the five highest earners were Manchester United, Blackburn, Newcastle, Leeds, and Arsenal, with a combined payout of £10.8 million (30.9% of the total).

[38] For the first few years of the League Cup competition, some of the major clubs refused to participate.

suggesting that saturation point had been reached. Cup competitions create an element of cross subsidy from the richer clubs to the poorer at several levels: first, a club from a lower division may be able to attract an abnormally large attendance by being drawn to play a top club; secondly, the rules for pooling receipts, both between the two clubs contesting each tie, and among all the clubs taking part in the competition, allow for a greater element of redistribution than is the case for league fixtures; and thirdly, all clubs share in the proceeds of sponsorship agreements, whose details for league and cup competitions up to 1993-4 are shown in table 7.

Table 7. *Competition sponsorship, 1983-1994 (£'000)*

	Premiership	Football League	League Cup	Other cups	Total
1983			395		395
1984		1,000	570		1,570
1985		1,100	690	30	1,820
1986		424	518	48	990
1987		800	563	58	1,421
1988		1,300	575	68	1,943
1989		1,500	595	178	2,273
1990		1,750	650	188	2,588
1991		2,200	1,000	283	3,483
1992		2,300	1,050	450	3,800
1993		1,000	1,100	209	2,309
1994	3,000	1,000	1,150	207	5,357

Note: Years are end-years of football seasons.
Source: *Digest of football statistics*, 1993-4

The overall impact of the various pooling mechanisms on club finances is difficult to trace over time, but it seems clear that the creation of the Premiership has eroded the extent of cross subsidy between the top clubs and the rest. Including pooled gate receipts for both league and cup fixtures, as well as proceeds from competition sponsorship (but not television fees), the net contribution of the Division 1 (Premier League in 1992-3) clubs fell from £1.145 million in 1991-2 to £457,000 in 1992-3. Despite an increase in the net contribution of the Division 2 (Division 1) clubs from £670,000 to £1.49 million, the net proceeds of the Division 3 and 4 (2 and 3) clubs fell from £1.212 million to £607,000.[39]

However, although the size of the cross subsidy is somewhat reduced, the shift is relatively small in comparison with the implicit cross subsidy created by the transfer market; as table 6 shows, the net transfer proceeds of the clubs in the two lower divisions were £7.3 million and £4 million in the same two seasons. The reduction in cross subsidy is also small relative to the overall increase in gate revenues, from which the lower division clubs have benefited as much as the Premiership clubs in relative terms. In 1991-2 these were £20.2 million for the clubs in the two lowest divisions; in 1992-3 the figure was £24.5 million. Section IV further

[39] *Digest of football statistics.*

considers the likely implications for the future of cross subsidy within professional football.

IV

This article has examined the factors influencing the generation and the distribution of financial resources in the football industry since the 1920s. Membership of the league has altered relatively little, but there have been some marked shifts in the distribution of playing success, attendances, and gate revenues. In terms of playing success, the main change has been a steady and sustained improvement in the fortunes of southern clubs, most of which entered the league in the early 1920s, and whose upward mobility has been mainly at the expense of clubs from smaller towns in the north and midlands. In terms of shares in gate revenues and (to a lesser extent) attendances, there was a marked shift in favour of the major clubs from the largest cities between the late 1950s and early 1970s; this share has remained steady (at its increased level) since the 1970s.

The joint nature of production in league competition and the need for competitive balance in order to maintain uncertainty of outcome are factors cited widely in the economics of sports literature as providing an economic rationale for rules restricting free, atomistic economic competition between individual clubs. Various restrictions of this kind have operated throughout the history of professional football, and some still do today. This article has examined the effects of contractual regulations restricting player mobility in the transfer market, and arrangements for the pooling of gate and television revenues, on the distribution of aggregate revenues between clubs. Both have created an element of cross subsidy (explicit or implicit), which has undoubtedly been crucial in ensuring the survival of many of the smaller clubs, especially during the 1970s and early 1980s when attendances were declining and football finances were at their most parlous.

Both the history of professional football and comparisons with other sports (in the UK and elsewhere) tend to suggest that mechanisms providing explicit or implicit types of cross subsidy are a pervasive feature of sporting league competition. Nevertheless, in recent years football has witnessed a tendency towards the erosion (at least in relative terms) of the importance of several of the redistributive mechanisms that have been described in this article. This trend may well be hastened by factors such as the Bosman ruling and the imminent introduction of pay-per-view television. The Bosman ruling seems likely to limit the effectiveness of the transfer market as a means for redistributing revenues within the league. At the time of writing, there are clear indications that increased player mobility across European borders, combined with the relaxation of the 'three player ruling', which limited the number of overseas players who could be fielded at any one time, is leading to a significant increase in the net flow of transfer monies from the Premiership to other European countries, and a corresponding reduction in the net flow to the (non-

Premiership) Football League clubs.[40] Discussions are currently in progress to bring transfer regulations at both national and international (i.e. beyond EU boundaries) levels into line with the Bosman ruling. The possibility of televising football through pay-per-view subscription services will enhance significantly the revenue-earning potential of the major clubs. These seem certain to exploit the bargaining power conferred by ultimate ownership of the property rights in televised transmissions, mainly to their individual (rather than to the collective) advantage.

Despite these tendencies, we are more sanguine than some commentators about the ability of professional football at all levels to survive within the present league structure, for several reasons. It is sometimes suggested that excessive concentration of financial power among a few clubs will damage the viability of the league as a whole by creating competitive imbalance, as the more powerful clubs outbid the rest for the services of the most talented players. We are not convinced by this argument. Our own historical data show that the share in aggregate league gate revenues of 14 'major' clubs from the largest cities increased by about 10 per cent between the late 1950s and the early 1970s, without any attendant change in playing success. This illustrates the point that changes in the league's financial structure do not necessarily have a direct impact on competitive balance. If a footballer's talent derives primarily from nature rather than nurture, the availability of footballers at all levels of ability (ignoring flows to and from overseas) will be much the same irrespective of the professional game's financial structure. The insurmountable fact that only 11 players can be fielded at any one time limits the incentive for any one club simply to accumulate players, and similarly discourages players who may not expect regular first team selection from joining major clubs which are already heavily staffed.[41]

Although it is clear that the distribution of total revenues within football has become more unequal, the absolute magnitude of the revenues has increased dramatically in recent years, to the benefit of clubs at all levels. Ultimately, of course, the viability of the smaller clubs depends on their absolute rather than their relative financial strength.[42] The increased stridency of the demands of 'major' clubs to retain more of the revenues they themselves generate may simply reflect the fact that at a time when football finances are buoyant, cross subsidy is not needed to the same extent as at certain times in the past to ensure the financial viability of clubs at all levels within the league.[43] In analysing the relationship between

---

[40] Touche Ross, *Survey of football club accounts.*

[41] Recent moves to allow clubs to nominate a larger number of substitutes, and for some clubs to field second choice teams in certain fixtures (e.g. in the League Cup) do not affect this observation in any fundamental way.

[42] Increasing relative divergence in the revenue-earning capabilities of clubs at different levels is mirrored by similar divergence in the remuneration of players. However, here as well, the attractiveness to lower division players of football as a profession depends on their remuneration in absolute terms (or relative to other available sources of employment) and not relative to players at the top of the earnings scale.

[43] We recognize that this view is not necessarily shared by all boards of directors, especially those outside the Premiership.

the financial structure of the league as a whole and the attitudes of individual clubs, it is evidently difficult completely to disentangle cause and effect. For example, the current fashion favouring stock market flotation seems likely to encourage a more individualistic, profit motivated attitude on the part of the management of the clubs concerned. But on the other hand, flotation is only possible or desirable against an optimistic financial background, which suggests a climate in which clubs can afford to pursue self-interested objectives without serious detriment to the greater good.

Whether or not there is a need for cross subsidy within football at present, many of the sport's most fundamental economic characteristics (jointness of production, and a product much of whose popular appeal lies in uncertainty of outcome, as well as historical continuity and tradition) have not changed substantially.[44] History suggests that whenever cross subsidy is required to ensure the survival of a desired number of clubs, mechanisms of one sort or another evolve to satisfy this need.

University of Hull
University of Wales, Bangor

---

[44] This point may require some qualification in the light of the growing importance of competition at European level. The recent evolution of the European Cup into the Champions League is believed by some to herald moves towards a larger European league competition with weekly fixtures, perhaps running in parallel with existing domestic league structures. Although this kind of development could have highly significant implications for many of the economic features of professional football which we have described in this article, at the time of writing its precise timing, structure, and impact remain largely matters for speculation.

Footnote references
Arnold, T., and Benveniste, I., 'Cross-subsidisation and competition policy in English professional football', *J. Ind. Aff.*, 15 (1988), pp. 2-14.
Baimbridge, M., Cameron, S., and Dawson, P., 'Satellite television and the demand for football: a whole new ball game', *Scot. J. Pol. Econ.*, 43 (1996), pp. 317-33.
Bird, P., 'The demand for league football', *App. Econ.*, 14 (1982), pp. 637-49.
Digest of football statistics (Leicester, various issues).
Dobson, S.M. and Goddard, J.A., 'The demand for professional league football in England and Wales, 1925-92', *J.R.S.S.*, ser. D, 44 (1995), pp. 259-77.
Dunning, E., Murphy, P., and Williams, J., *The roots of football hooliganism: an historical and sociological study* (1988).
Fynn, A. and Guest, L., *Out of time: why football isn't working* (1994).
Goldberg, A. and Wragg, S., 'It's not a knockout: English football and globalisation', in J. Williams and S. Wragg, eds., *British football and social change: getting into Europe* (Leicester, 1991).
Gramlich, E.M., 'A natural experiment in styles of capitalism: professional sports', *Qu. Rev. Econ. Finance*, 34 (1994), pp. 121-30.
Guthrie, J. and Caldwell, D., *Soccer rebel: the evolution of the professional footballer* (1976).
Hornby, N., *Fever pitch* (1992).
Jones, S.G., 'The economic aspects of association football in England, 1918-39', *Brit. J. Sports Hist.*, 1 (1984), pp. 286-99.
Neale, W.C., 'The peculiar economics of professional sports', *Qu. J. Econ.*, 78 (1964), pp. 1-14.
PEP Report, 'English professional football', *Planning*, 32 (1966), no. 496.
Rothmans football yearbook (various issues).
Rottenberg, S., 'The baseball player's labor market', *J. Pol. Econ.*, 64 (1956), pp. 242-58.
Simmons, R., 'The demand for English league football: a club level analysis', *App. Econ.*, 28 (1996), pp. 139-55.
Sloane, P., 'The economics of professional football: the football club as a utility maximiser', *Scot. J. Pol. Econ.*, 17 (1971), pp. 121-46.
Sloane, P., 'Restricting competition in professional team sports', *Bull. Econ. Res.*, 28 (1976), pp. 3-22.

Sloane, P., *Sport in the market* (1980).
Tabner, B., *Through the turnstiles* (Harefield, 1992).
Taylor, R. and Ward, A., *Kicking and screaming: an oral history of football in England* (1995).
Touche Ross, *Survey of football club accounts* (Manchester, 1996).
Vrooman, J., 'A general theory of professional sports leagues', *South. Econ. J.*, 61 (1995), pp. 971-90.
Walvin, J., *The people's game: the history of football revisited* (Edinburgh, 1994).

Official publications
Department of Labour and Productivity, *British labour statistics, historical abstract 1886-1968* (1971).

[12]

Revenue Convergence in the English Soccer League

STEPHEN DOBSON
The Queen's University of Belfast

JOHN GODDARD
University of Wales Swansea

CARLYN RAMLOGAN
The Queen's University of Belfast

Tests of the convergence hypothesis using annual gate revenue data for English professional soccer clubs for the period 1926 to 1997 are reported. The distribution of gate revenues among clubs is found to have widened markedly, and there is no evidence of convergence for the period as a whole. However, a sequence of tests for 5-yearly subperiods shows evidence of convergence during long subperiods: specifically, up to the late 1950s and between the mid-1970s and late 1980s. These features of the data inform an analysis of the social, economic, and historical development of English professional soccer.

Describing the pattern and modeling the process by which a group of economic units increase or decrease in size (according to some measure) over time, both in absolute terms and relative to one another, is an important endeavor in a number of fields of empirical economic enquiry. In industrial economics, for example, empirical tests of Gibrat's law or the law of proportionate effect (LPE) show whether the smaller firms in an industry grow faster than the larger firms or whether there is no relationship or a positive relationship between firm size and growth. Gibrat (1931) showed that if individual firm growth rates are independent of firm size, then concentration will increase progressively as certain firms become large fortuitously and establish a dominant market share.[1] In international economics and macroeconomics, considerable effort has been devoted recently to investigating whether the per capita incomes of different countries or regions tend to converge over time. In this case, the notion of convergence derives from the neoclassical tradition (Solow, 1956) and owes much of its popularity to the work of Baumol (1986) and Barro (1991).[2]

For many years, economists studying professional team sports have been aware of the link between the distribution of revenue among the members of sports

JOURNAL OF SPORTS ECONOMICS, Vol. 2 No. 3, August 2001   257–274
© 2001 Sage Publications

leagues and the degree of competitive balance. There is a collective interest in maintaining reasonable equality in playing strength so that the outcomes of individual matches and the league competition as a whole are sufficiently uncertain to sustain spectator interest (Fort & Quirk, 1995; Hoehn & Szymanski, 1999; Jennett, 1984; Neale, 1964; Peel & Thomas, 1988; Quirk & El-Hodiri, 1971; Rottenberg, 1956; Vrooman, 1995). If economic disparities between league members become too large, competitive balance and uncertainty of outcome may be jeopardized.

Conversely, if a sports league competition has demonstrated its competitive viability by surviving in a similar form over a long period, then an inverse relationship between the size and growth of league members measured in revenue terms, or convergence in revenues (in the technical sense of the term), might be expected. Using the empirical methodologies of the LPE and convergence literatures, this article tests for evidence of convergence between the annual gate revenues of the clubs that competed in the English Football League and Premier League during the 1926 through 1997 seasons (inclusive).[3]

It is worth commenting a little further on the relationship between tests of the convergence hypothesis based on revenue data and other tests for changes in competitive balance over time that have been used in the economics-of-team-sports literature. Using North American data, Bennett and Fizel (1995), Fort and Quirk (1995), Vrooman (1995), and Eckard (1998) all tested empirically for changes in competitive balance by examining trends in the cross-sectional variance or standard deviation of the win ratios of member teams of professional or college leagues in several sports, including baseball, basketball, and (American) football. A trend in the variance of win ratios is a meaningful indicator of changes in competitive balance in hermetic leagues with no promotion and relegation, where membership only changes occasionally due to reallocation of franchises. But the same measure is less informative if applied to a league with a hierarchical divisional structure, where divisional membership changes constantly due to promotion and relegation. In this case, league match results or win ratios provide little or no direct evidence about changes in competitive balance across the league as a whole. The use of revenue-based convergence measures, in contrast, provides a suitable yardstick for drawing comparisons between the fortunes of teams at all levels within the league's divisional structure, even though the standard of comparison is economic or financial rather than competitive in the sporting sense of the term. Nevertheless, it seems highly likely that a trend toward economic convergence or divergence would have implications for trends in competitive balance in sporting terms, even though the present article does not test for the latter directly.

Because of the limited availability of firm-level data with an adequate time dimension and because the population of firms in most industries tends to be highly variable over time due to entry, exit, and merger, most empirical firm-level studies of the LPE are based on data sets with a large cross-sectional dimension in which growth is measured over a relatively short period. The present gate revenue data set is somewhat unique in offering the luxury of an observation period spanning more than 70 years at firm level. Of course, the cooperative, mutually dependent, and zero-sum nature of relationships between the member clubs of any sports league makes this something of a special case, relative to nonsports industries. Nevertheless, the extensive duration of the data set (itself a product of sports being a special case) allows the possibility of identifying separate periods of structural stability (when convergence prevails) and structural change (when convergence breaks down) within the complete observation period, in a way that is not normally possible in industry studies of the LPE based on far shorter observation periods.

The rest of the article is structured as follows. The next section describes the empirical methodology used to test the LPE and measure convergence and presents the results of the convergence tests. The following section then interprets the results in the context of the economic development of the English soccer industry. The final section provides a summary and conclusions.

TESTING THE CONVERGENCE HYPOTHESIS

Empirical tests of the LPE are characteristically based on a cross sectional regression of the form

$$y_{it} - y_{it-T} = \beta_0 + \beta_1 y_{it-T} + \sum_{j=1}^{J} \gamma_j x_{ji} + u_{it},$$

where y_{it} represents the logarithmic size of firm i at time t. u_{it} is a disturbance term with $E(u_{it}) = 0$ and $\mathrm{var}(u_{it}) = \sigma_u^2$, where $E(.)$ and $\mathrm{var}(.)$ are across i. x_{ji} represents the values of J covariates for firm i, which for simplicity are assumed to be time invariant. β_0, β_1, and γ_j are parameters. This specification can be estimated with or without covariates. If there are no covariates, $\gamma_j = 0$ for $j = 1 \ldots J$.

If $\beta_1 > 0$, larger firms grow faster than smaller firms. If $\beta_1 = 0$, there is no relationship between firm size and growth and the LPE holds. In both cases where $\beta_1 \geq 0$, $\mathrm{var}(y_{it})$ is increasing with respect to t and does not converge toward any finite value. If $\beta_1 < 0$, smaller firms grow faster than larger firms. In this case, by defining μ_i as the value to which the log size of firm i is mean reverting in the long term σ_y^2 and as the value to which $\mathrm{var}(y_{it})$ is convergent in the long term, it can be shown

$$\mu_i = -\left(\beta_0 + \sum_{j=1}^{J} \gamma_j x_{ji} \right) / \beta_1; \qquad \sigma_y^2 = \left(\sum_{j=1}^{J} \gamma_j^2 \sigma_j^2 + \sigma_u^2 \right) / \{1 - (\beta_1 + 1)^2\}$$

where $\sigma_j^2 = \mathrm{var}(x_{ji})$ (and x_{ji} are assumed to be uncorrelated). In the short term, the dispersion of firm sizes is increasing over time if $\mathrm{var}(y_{it}) < \sigma_y^2$ and is decreasing if $\mathrm{var}(y_{it}) > \sigma_y^2$. If the estimated value of β_1 is significantly below zero, this constitutes evidence against the LPE.

In the terminology of the convergence literature, there is evidence of unconditional beta convergence if the estimated value of β_1 is significantly smaller than zero when the model is estimated with no covariates ($\gamma_j = 0$), and there is evidence of conditional beta convergence if the estimated value of β_1 is significantly smaller than zero when the model is estimated with covariates ($\gamma_j \neq 0$). There is evidence of sigma convergence if var(y_{it}) is decreasing over time. As shown above, unconditional beta convergence is a necessary but not a sufficient condition for sigma convergence. In the technical sense of the term, beta convergence does not necessarily imply that the cross-sectional standard deviation of firm sizes tends to decline over time.

The gate revenue data used in the convergence tests were obtained from the Football League's archives and *Digest of Football Statistics* (Football Trust, 1995, 1996, 1997). In total, 109 clubs competed in the Football League (and Premier League) between the 1926 and 1997 seasons. The league first achieved a membership comparable to the present complement of Premier League and Football League clubs between 1920 and 1922. The main subsequent changes have been an increase in membership from 88 to 92 teams during the 1951 season; the reorganization of the two lower divisions into Divisions 3 and 4, with membership determined by promotion and relegation (rather than geographical location) since the 1958 season; and greater mobility within the league with three (rather than two) teams promoted and relegated between Divisions 1 and 2 and Divisions 2 and 3 each season since the 1974 season (play-offs were introduced in 1987 to determine one promotion place for each division, and promotion and relegation between Division 4 and the top nonleague competition was also implemented on several occasions during the 1980s and 1990s); and the withdrawal from the Football League of Division 1 teams to form the Premier League in the 1993 season, a development that has not affected fundamentally the league's competitive structure but which has had profound organizational and financial implications.

Key features of the data set are summarized in Table 1 and Figures 1 and 2. Table 1 shows annual league attendance in aggregate and by division for selected interwar seasons and at five-season intervals for the postwar period. Table 1 also shows trends in annual aggregate gate revenues (nominal and real) and average admission prices. To show the main changes in the distribution of revenue and attendance among clubs with broadly similar characteristics, in Figures 1 and 2 the classification system of Dobson and Goddard (1998) is adopted (see note on Figure 1). This produces five groups of similar clubs, based on population, geographical location, and date of initial entry into the league.[4] Figures 1 and 2 show the percentage distribution of aggregate attendance and gate revenue among the five groups.

The sigma convergence results are shown in the final column of Table 1, which reports the standard deviation of the logarithms of the gate revenues of all clubs at five-season intervals. There is little discernible trend in the standard deviation through most of the 1920s and 1930s. The postwar boom in attendance was accompanied by a slight narrowing of the dispersion of revenues between clubs. From the late 1950s onward, however, the standard deviation increased markedly before leveling off during the mid-1970s. There was then little further change until the late

TABLE 1: Attendance, Revenue, Admission Prices, and Dispersion of Revenue

Season	Attendance					Revenue		Admission Price		SD log revenue, $S(y_{it})$
	Aggregate Millions	Division 1	Division 2	Division 3 South and Division 3	Division 3 North and Division 4	Aggregate Millions (£)	Real	Average (£)	Real	
1926	23.0	10.4	6.1	3.9	2.6	1.4	100.0	0.06	100.0	0.690
1931	21.1	9.5	6.1	3.2	2.3	1.2	107.9	0.06	118.4	0.744
1934	22.5	10.4	5.8	3.8	2.5	1.3	119.7	0.06	122.9	0.731
1936	24.7	11.4	6.9	4.0	2.4	1.5	126.6	0.06	118.3	0.781
1939	27.0	11.5	8.6	4.0	2.9	1.6	128.9	0.06	110.0	0.734
1947	35.4	14.9	11.0	5.6	3.9	2.9	184.6	0.08	120.3	0.757
1952	39.0	16.1	11.1	6.9	4.9	4.1	189.0	0.11	111.8	0.680
1957	32.7	13.8	8.7	5.6	4.6	4.3	166.9	0.13	117.8	0.659
1962	28.0	12.0	7.5	5.2	3.3	5.0	171.2	0.18	141.0	0.755
1967	28.9	14.2	7.3	4.4	3.0	6.9	202.5	0.24	161.7	0.851
1972	28.7	14.5	6.8	4.7	2.7	10.8	229.5	0.38	184.5	0.963
1977	26.0	13.6	6.2	4.1	2.1	22.2	222.2	0.85	196.9	1.043
1982	20.0	10.4	4.8	2.8	2.0	40.5	230.2	2.03	265.4	0.994
1987	17.4	9.1	4.2	2.4	1.7	55.8	253.0	3.21	335.7	0.988
1992	20.4	10.0	5.8	3.0	1.6	127.5	424.9	6.25	480.7	1.038
1997	22.8	10.8	6.9	3.2	1.9	244.8	713.9	10.74	722.0	1.146

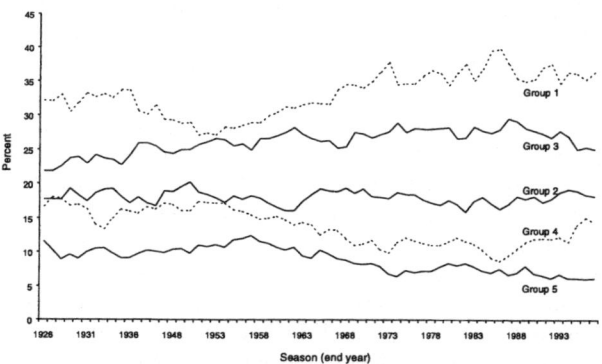

Figure 1:   Percentage Share of Aggregate Attendance

NOTE: Group 1 = Arsenal, Aston Villa, Birmingham, Chelsea, Everton, Leeds, Liverpool, Manchester City, Manchester United, Sheffield United, Sheffield Wednesday, Tottenham, West Bromwich, and West Ham; Group 2 = Bradford City, Bradford Park Avenue, Coventry, Derby, Hull, Leicester, Newcastle, Notts County, Nottingham Forest, Port Vale, Stoke, Sunderland, and Wolverhampton; Group 3 = Aberdare, Aldershot, Barnet, Bournemouth, Brentford, Brighton, Bristol City, Bristol Rovers, Cambridge, Cardiff, Charlton, Colchester, Crystal Palace, Exeter, Fulham, Gillingham, Ipswich, Leyton Orient, Luton, Maidstone, Merthyr, Millwall, Newport, Norwich, Oxford, Peterborough, Portsmouth, Plymouth, Queens Park Rangers, Reading, Southampton, Southend, Swansea, Swindon, Thames, Torquay, Watford, and Wimbledon; Group 4 = Barnsley, Blackburn, Blackpool, Bolton, Burnley, Bury, Chesterfield, Crewe, Doncaster, Gateshead, Grimsby, Huddersfield, Lincoln, Middlesbrough, Oldham, Preston, Rotherham, Stockport, Walsall; and Group 5 = Accrington, Ashington, Barrow, Carlisle, Chester, Darlington, Durham, Halifax, Hartlepool, Hereford, Mansfield, Nelson, New Brighton, Northampton, Rochdale, Scarborough, Scunthorpe, Shrewsbury, Southport, Stalybridge, Tranmere, Wigan, Workington, Wrexham, and York.

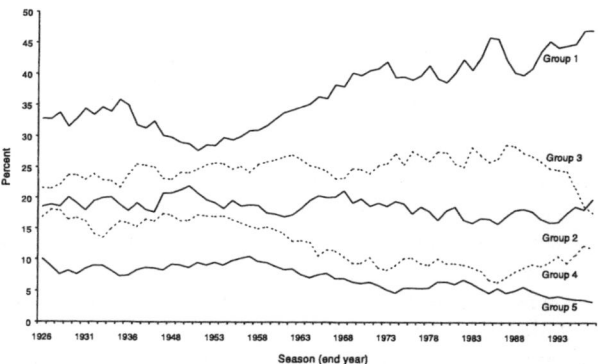

Figure 2:   Percentage Share of Aggregate Revenue

NOTE: See Figure 1 for the definitions of Groups 1 through 5.

1980s, which saw a slight narrowing of the dispersion. During the 1990s, however, the standard deviation increased steadily, reaching its highest value ever in 1997. For the period covered by Table 1 as a whole, there is clearly no evidence of sigma convergence in the gate revenue data. Instead, the dispersion of aggregate gate revenue among clubs has widened considerably. As suggested above, however, much of the increase in the standard deviation has taken place over relatively short subperiods: specifically, between the late 1950s and mid-1970s and again more recently during the 1990s. The rise in inequality during these subperiods is clearly visible in Figure 2 in particular.

The unconditional and conditional convergence estimation results are reported in Table 2. In all estimations, growth in revenues is measured over five-season intervals, starting with the interval 1926 to 1931 and finishing with 1992 to 1997. Because of the interruption caused by the Second World War, estimations for the 1930s are reported for two overlapping five-season periods: 1931 to 1936 and 1934 to 1939. For the interwar period, there is only weak evidence of unconditional beta convergence. The estimates of β_1 for 1926 to 1931 and 1931 to 1936 are negative but not significantly different from zero, although the estimate for 1934 to 1939 is negative and significant at the 10% level.

For the conditional beta convergence estimates, the following additional covariates are included in the estimations:

x_{1i} = log of population recorded in the 1961 census for the local authority district in which club i's ground is situated.[5]

x_{2i} = number of other clubs situated within a 30-mile radius of club i's ground that competed in the league at any time between the 1926 and 1997 seasons.[6]

x_{3i} = the number of years between club i's first season as a league member and the 1997 season.

All three prewar conditional beta estimates are negative, significant, and considerably larger in absolute terms than the corresponding unconditional estimates. The explanation for the discrepancy seems to lie in the estimates of the other coefficients in the conditional model. The estimates of γ_1, γ_2, and γ_3 are all significantly different from zero for 1926 to 1931, and γ_1 and γ_2 are also significant for 1931 to 1936. For the interwar period, therefore, the unconditional model appears to be misspecified, resulting in biased estimates of β_1. According to the conditional model, there was beta convergence in revenues during the 1920s and 1930s.

For the postwar period, both the unconditional and conditional estimates of β are negative and significant for 1947 to 1952 and 1952 to 1957, suggesting that beta convergence in revenues was maintained during this period. For the next four 5-year periods, however, none of the unconditional estimates of β are significant. Two of the four conditional estimates are significant at the 10% level only. The significant estimates (1962 to 1967 and 1967 to 1972) are smaller in absolute terms than any of the estimates for the periods up to 1957 and between 1977 and 1992. In

TABLE 2:   Unconditional and Conditional Convergence Estimation Results

Period	Unconditional Convergence Estimate			Conditional Convergence Estimate						
	β_0	β_1	R^2	β_0	β_1	γ_1	γ_2	γ_3	R^2	n
1926 to 1931	0.275	−0.042	0.006	−2.334[b]	−0.178[b]	0.102[a]	0.621[b]	−0.022[a]	0.174	84
	(0.49)	(−0.71)		(−2.00)	(−2.34)	(3.04)	(2.08)	(−3.28)		
1931 to 1936	0.567	−0.049	0.008	−2.083	−0.214[a]	0.093[b]	0.670[b]	0.002	0.130	85
	(1.04)	(−0.84)		(−1.63)	(−2.72)	(2.37)	(2.07)	(0.22)		
1934 to 1939	0.987[b]	−0.086[c]	0.040	0.188	−0.161[b]	0.054	0.187	−0.002	0.074	87
	(2.30)	(−1.88)		(0.18)	(−2.26)	(1.58)	(0.67)	(−0.25)		
1947 to 1952	1.985[a]	−0.159[a]	0.180	0.853	−0.232[a]	0.038	0.313	−0.001	0.218	87
	(5.28)	(−4.32)		(1.05)	(−4.31)	(1.40)	(1.45)	(−0.17)		
1952 to 1957	1.284[a]	−0.118[a]	0.080	0.131	−0.204[a]	0.023	0.411[b]	−0.007	0.138	92
	(2.90)	(−2.80)		(0.20)	(−3.45)	(0.82)	(2.36)	(−1.13)		
1957 to 1962	−0.216	0.027	0.002	0.305	0.023	0.064[c]	−0.289	−0.002	0.066	90
	(−0.33)	(0.44)		(0.34)	(0.27)	(1.68)	(−1.17)	(−0.19)		
1962 to 1967	0.578	−0.032	0.003	−0.799	−0.133[c]	0.064	0.377	−0.004	0.057	91
	(0.87)	(−0.51)		(−0.78)	(−1.71)	(1.40)	(1.60)	(−0.37)		
1967 to 1972	0.547	−0.017	0.001	−0.921	−0.134[c]	0.149[a]	0.237	−0.024[b]	0.110	91
	(0.84)	(−0.28)		(−0.92)	(−1.85)	(3.12)	(1.03)	(−2.31)		
1972 to 1977	0.682	−0.003	0.000	−0.550	−0.060	0.024	0.367[c]	−0.005	0.037	91
	(1.17)	(−0.07)		(−0.60)	(−0.90)	(0.47)	(1.78)	(−0.48)		
1977 to 1982	2.463[a]	−0.157[a]	0.081	1.301	−0.230[a]	0.058	0.298	−0.002	0.122	90
	(3.65)	(−2.79)		(1.31)	(−3.29)	(1.05)	(1.38)	(−0.15)		
1982 to 1987	2.381[a]	−0.165[a]	0.086	2.988[a]	−0.165[b]	0.081	−0.373	0.000	0.166	92
	(3.33)	(−2.91)		(3.22)	(−2.40)	(1.55)	(−1.97)	(0.03)		
1987 to 1992	2.200[a]	−0.108[b]	0.042	0.469	−0.203[a]	0.108[b]	0.374[b]	−0.008	0.144	90
	(3.08)	(−1.96)		(0.50)	(−3.26)	(2.19)	(2.24)	(−0.72)		
1992 to 1997	0.036	0.033	0.004	−0.217	−0.016	−0.010	0.213[c]	0.014	0.076	90
	(0.05)	(0.62)		(−0.27)	(−0.24)	(−0.19)	(1.83)	(1.31)		

NOTE: Numbers in parentheses are t statistics. The empirical models are as follows:

Unconditional convergence is $y_{it} - y_{it-T} = \beta_0 + \beta_1 y_{it-T} + u_{it}$ and

conditional convergence is $y_{it} - y_{it-T} = \beta_0 + \beta_1 y_{it-T} + \gamma_1 x_{1i} + \gamma_2 x_{2i} + \gamma_3 x_{3i} + u_{it}$

where y_{it} = log gate revenue of club i in year t; x_{1i} = log of population recorded in the 1961 census for the local authority district in which club i's ground is situated; x_{2i} = number of other clubs situated within a 30-mile radius of club i's ground that competed in the league at any time between the 1926 and 1997 seasons; x_{3i} = the number of years between club i's first season as a league member and the 1997 season.
a. Significantly different from zero, two-tailed test, at the 1% level.
b. Significantly different from zero, two-tailed test, at the 5% level.
c. Significantly different from zero, two-tailed test, at the 10% level.

other words, beta convergence weakened or disappeared completely between the late 1950s and the late 1970s. In the next three estimations (1977 to 1982, 1982 to 1987, and 1987 to 1992), beta convergence is reestablished, with negative and significant unconditional and conditional estimates reported in all of these cases. The 1992 to 1997 estimated (conditional) β, however, is negative but insignificant.

The Economics of Association Football II

The estimates of γ_1, the coefficient on log population in the conditional estimations, are positive in all but 1 case and significantly greater than zero at the 10% level in 5 out of 13 cases. This suggests that when there is beta convergence, the average values toward which individual clubs' revenues are mean reverting are related to the local population base. Although two of the five significant estimates of γ_1 are for the first two 5-year estimations, significant estimates are also obtained for much later periods. Despite the progressive increase over time in the geographical mobility of spectators, there is no strong evidence that the relationship between population was any weaker, say, in the 1990s than in the 1930s. By the 1980s and 1990s, the size of the population living in the club's near locality was less important in determining directly the number of spectators able to attend home matches as it had been earlier. Nevertheless, that the teams with the largest national followings were invariably those from the largest cities may explain the persistence over time of the relationship between log population and revenue (see also Figure 2).

Unsurprisingly, the duration of the club's league membership appears to exert a stronger influence on average revenue toward the start of the period, with the two largest estimates of γ_2 obtained for 1926 to 1931 and 1931 to 1936. It seems reasonable to expect that age would exert a stronger influence in the 1930s, when the difference between clubs that were 10 and 30 years old might be more important than in the 1970s, when the difference between clubs that were 50 and 70 years old might be largely irrelevant. Finally, negative estimates of γ_3 are obtained for 10 of the 13 five-year periods reported in Table 2, but only two of the estimates are significant. This suggests that the extent of local competition exerted a weaker influence on clubs' average revenues than the size of the local population base.

REVENUE CONVERGENCE AND THE ECONOMIC DEVELOPMENT OF PROFESSIONAL SOCCER

In a period during which revenues show evidence of beta convergence and the standard deviation of revenues shows no tendency to change systematically, professional soccer's economic structure exhibits characteristics of equilibrium: There is no tendency for the distribution of revenues among clubs to change systematically over time. Conversely, a period during which beta convergence breaks down or during which the standard deviation of revenues tends to increase over time can be characterized as one of transition between an old and a new structural order.

The results reported in the previous section suggest that between the early 1920s and the late 1990s, the economic structure of the English professional soccer industry has passed through two distinct equilibrium phases and two transitional periods. The first and highly durable equilibrium phase lasted from the early 1920s until the late 1950s. The 1960s were a period of transition toward a second and less durable equilibrium, which had materialized by the mid-1970s. This second equilibrium phase lasted from the mid-1970s until the end of the 1980s. Subsequently, the 1990s have been another transitional period, during which the industry has undergone further radical transformation toward another equilibrium whose ultimate nature is not yet fully defined. In this section, key features of the economic development of the English professional soccer industry since the 1920s are interpreted within this chronological framework. The discussion is organized into subsections covering the pre- and post-1958 periods.

1922 to 1958

The results of the convergence tests suggest that there was relative stability in the economic structure of professional soccer during the period between the expansion of the league in the early 1920s and the end of the 1950s. Despite significant fluctuations in aggregate attendance and gate revenues (see Table 1), the distribution across clubs of differing characteristics remained quite stable (see Figures 1 and 2). During the interwar period, trends in attendance and revenue mirrored the fortunes of the national economy closely, with a short postwar boom followed by a period of decline from the 1922 season and then a gradual recovery from 1932 onward. Following the Second World War, attendance surged briefly, achieving an all-time high in the 1949 season. The dispersion of both attendance and revenue seems to have narrowed slightly when attendance was at its peak in the late 1940s. The boom was relatively short lived, however, and was followed by a sustained decline in attendance that continued until the 1986 season.

The strength of the geographical bond between clubs and their spectators was a major factor contributing toward the relatively stable and egalitarian distribution of revenues within the league. To some extent, clubs were shielded from the full economic consequences of fluctuations in their fortunes on the field of play by an element of spatial monopoly conferred by their spectators' lack of geographical mobility. Specific evidence on the geographical composition of soccer crowds is rather sparse, but it seems certain that the proportion of home supporters drawn from each club's immediate vicinity was much greater than in later periods.[7] Soccer's egalitarian economic structure was buttressed by direct restraints on price and wage competition throughout this period. A minimum admission price of one shilling (£0.05) applied throughout the interwar period. Subject to periodic increases, a minimum remained in force until the 1970s (Bird, 1982), although its importance declined over time as clubs chose increasingly to exceed the minimum. Its objective was to prevent clubs from using direct price competition as a means of attracting spectators at the expense of other clubs in the same geographical catchment area.

Prior to the reforms of the early 1960s (see below), both the maximum wage and various restrictions on player mobility sustained by the retain-and-transfer system limited the extent of economic competition in soccer's labor market. Here, the main objective was similar and complementary to that of the minimum admission price: to prevent the clubs with the greatest financial strength from outbidding other clubs for the services of the most talented players (Dobson & Goddard, 1998; Russell, 1997; Walvin, 1994). The stability of soccer's financial structure between the early

1920s and late 1950s is reflected in the fact that the proportionate increases in the minimum and average admission price and in the maximum wage were all very similar. Clubs seem to have responded to fluctuations in attendance and revenue primarily by adjusting the number of players employed on professional terms. For example, Fishwick (1989) quoted official statistics that show that during the post–Second World War boom, the total number of professionals increased from 5,000 in 1939 to 7,000 by the end of the 1940s, roughly 4,000 of whom were registered with league clubs. By 1983, the number of professionals registered with league clubs had fallen to just more than 1,500 (Russell, 1997).

Walvin (1994) and Russell (1997) both emphasized the significance of radio coverage in stimulating interest and helping to establish soccer as the national sport, following the broadcast of the first radio commentary by the British Broadcasting Corporation in January 1927. A complementary development, which also widened interest, was the introduction of the Football Pools by Littlewoods and Vernons. Annual pool's revenues reached £30 million by the mid-1930s, a figure approximately 20 times as large as the aggregate annual league gate revenues during the same period. An eventual consequence of the growth of national media coverage was the emergence of teams with national followings and, as a corollary, the diminution of the bonds between the smaller clubs and the spectators living in their immediate vicinities (see below).

Despite the longevity and stability of the economic structure within which professional soccer had functioned since the early 1920s, by the end of the 1950s there were signs that a number of pressures were beginning to build, which would lead eventually to far-reaching changes. Some of these, including rising incomes, changing patterns of leisure activity, and geographical shifts of population, were socioeconomic and demographic. Within soccer itself, symptoms of change included a downward trend in attendance that had been underway since the end of the 1940s, an increase in the incidence of crowd disorderliness since the mid-1950s, and mounting player unrest manifested in increasingly assertive demands for improved remuneration and terms of employment. The value of $s(y_{it})$ begins to increase systematically from 1958, which seems the most convenient single date at which to locate the passing of the old structural order.[8]

1958 Onward

The results of the convergence tests reported in the previous section suggest that the period since the end of the 1950s may usefully be divided into three subperiods: a transitional phase (1958 to 1974) when beta convergence broke down and the gap between the rich and poor members of the league widened, a new equilibrium phase (1974 to 1989) when beta convergence was reestablished and the gap between rich and poor remained roughly constant, and another transitional phase (from 1989 onward) when convergence again broke down and inequality widened further.

Between the peak season of 1949 and the nadir that was finally reached in 1986, aggregate attendance declined by 61%. For the period as a whole, the rate of decline was proportionately greater in the lower divisions than in the top division. However, it is apparent from the divisional attendance shares (Table 1) and from the trends in the group shares (Figures 1 and 2) that the most significant changes in the distributions of attendance and gate revenue among clubs took place between the late 1950s and the early 1970s. Thereafter, the decline in attendance (and its adverse effect on revenues) affected clubs at all levels within the league to a similar extent. Naturally, these features of the data are reflected closely in the empirical beta and sigma convergence results.

In explaining the sustained postwar decline in soccer's popularity as a spectator sport, social historians have emphasized the growth of the "affluent society," with the emergence of more home-oriented and privatized patterns of leisure activity and with the range of options extended in particular by television and the car. Many women became less willing to acquiesce in a home-based or child-minding function, and men's leisure was centered on the pub, club, or soccer terrace (Dunning, Murphy, & Williams, 1988; Walvin, 1994). The increase in incidents of crowd misconduct both inside and outside soccer stadiums can also be attributed at least in part to broader social changes. But whatever the causes, there is little doubt that the inconvenience, fears, and discomforts caused by hooliganism and the countermeasures taken by clubs and the police prompted many spectators to switch from the terraces to the living room and TV set in pursuit of their soccer entertainment.

Although the first televised soccer transmissions date back as far as 1938, it was not until the early 1950s, when sufficient households gained access to TV sets that television's potential to transform matches into national events began to be realized. League highlights were first transmitted sporadically from 1955 and regularly from 1964 onward. Live coverage of league matches began in 1983. Until the late 1970s, the British Broadcasting Corporation and Independent Television operated an effective cartel that succeeded in containing the fees, which were distributed equally between all league clubs. During the 1980s, the leading clubs were successful both in obtaining a succession of higher fees and in securing a greater share for themselves.[9] Although the direct impact of television on soccer's aggregate finances remained relatively small, its indirect impact in arousing national interest in the top teams and their star players cannot be overemphasized.

From the late 1950s onward, rising affluence combined with improvements in both public and private transport, including the spread of car ownership and the construction of the motorway network, led to important changes in the geographical composition of demand. With long-distance travel now a practical proposition for many spectators, the top clubs began to drain support from their smaller counterparts. That the most fashionable clubs tend to be located within the largest metropolitan districts may explain why the direct relationship between population and mean attendance, identified in the conditional convergence estimates in Table 2, does not appear to weaken during the observation period. For this reason, the estimates may mask that the fashionable clubs' spectators were drawn increasingly from beyond the clubs' immediate vicinities. The apparent erosion over time of the link between the extent of local competition and mean attendance could also be explained by the diminishing geographical segmentation of the clubs' individual markets.

The abolition of the maximum wage in 1961 and the reform of the retain-and-transfer system that followed in 1963 had a key influence on soccer's newly emerging economic structure.[10] Ultimately, the spectators paid the bill for the reversal of the erosion of differentials between players' and other wages that had occurred between the 1920s and 1950s. Although attendance fell by 11% between 1961 and 1978, in real terms gate revenue increased by 47% and average admission prices by 65%.[11] The most dramatic and visible effect of the contractual changes was in increasing differentials between a relatively small number of star players and the rest. A few players became instant celebrities, drawing unprecedented earnings from sponsorship and endorsements, as well as from soccer. Again, television played its part in generating recognition and publicity.

As the economy entered recession, the first part of the 1980s saw acceleration in the downward trend in attendance. The clubs' capacity to shield themselves from the financial consequences of falling attendance by charging increased admission prices for an essentially unchanged product seemed to have reached its limit at this time. In real terms, gate revenues for the four seasons from 1982 to 1985 were approximately 5% lower than for seasons 1978 to 1981. Many of the disappearing spectators were still watching their soccer on television, but television revenues provided scant financial compensation to the clubs. Against this rapidly deteriorating background, the economic viability of professional soccer as a whole began to look distinctly fragile.

The seriousness of the hooliganism phenomenon was emphasized in the most tragic circumstances, by the deaths of 38 spectators as a result of a hooligan-related incident in Brussels at a Liverpool-Juventus match in May 1985. This happened only a few days after a wooden grandstand caught fire during a match at Bradford, resulting in 55 deaths. After 96 spectators were crushed to death against a section of perimeter fencing at Hillsborough, Sheffield in April 1989, the pressure for change finally became irresistible.

In terms of the convergence model, the impact of the many changes that have been implemented since the end of the 1980s is reflected in the virtual disappearance of beta convergence and a further increase in the standard deviation of revenues. Much of what has taken place during the 1990s has been discussed extensively elsewhere, and here only a brief and highly schematic description is attempted. Developments in four areas, however, seem especially relevant in the context of the preceding historical account.

First, mainly as a consequence of the growth of satellite, cable, and digital television, soccer's dual status as both spectator sport and television spectacle has become more realistically reflected in the balance between the revenues it derives from both sources. Television also played a central role in the restructuring of soccer's organizational arrangements and the creation of the Premier League in 1992 (Conn, 1997; Flynn & Guest, 1994). At the time of writing, the full extent of the market for televised soccer delivered through subscription or pay-per-view services is still uncertain. Although the momentum may now be slowing, the explosive growth in television revenue over recent years has probably not yet run its full course.

Second, further liberalization of the rules governing soccer's labor market, especially the removal of restrictions on the use of overseas players and the arrival of freedom of contract following the landmark 1995 European Court of Justice ruling in the Jean Marc Bosman case (*Union Royale Belge des Sociétés de Football Association v. Bosman*, 1995), have led to even greater disparities between the earning potential of the top players and the rest. In the United Kingdom, it is widely perceived that the influx of talented overseas players has also led to marked improvements in playing standards.

Third, improved facilities and surveillance technologies and, perhaps, a new public mood of revulsion following the worst excesses of the 1970s and 1980s have contributed to the marginalization of the hooliganism phenomenon at club level, although sadly the same cannot be said for matches involving the England national side. At club level, Russell (1997) was surely correct to draw the obvious connection with the reversal in the downward trend in attendance from the 1987 season onward and, more generally, with soccer's rehabilitation as the most popular and fashionable national sport.

Fourth and finally, the reconstruction or conversion of all major stadiums to provide all-seated accommodation has been instrumental in strengthening soccer's appeal as a middle-class spectator sport. During the 1990s, clubs have been able to raise admission prices substantially and achieve increases in attendance, for what is demonstrably a better product in terms of the facilities on offer. Whether watching in person or on television, it is clear that much of the increased middle-class interest is focused on the leading clubs, reinforcing trends that have been underway over a much longer period. The resulting increase in inequality in the distribution of revenues, however, has taken place against a background of rising rather than falling demand at all levels, which has done much to offset the most adverse financial consequences for the league's less affluent member clubs.

CONCLUSION

This article has investigated the existence and extent of convergence in the revenues of English professional soccer clubs over time, using a revenue data set that extends from the 1920s to the 1990s. The investigation draws on empirical techniques borrowed from the industrial economics literature on the LPE and the macroeconomics literature on convergence in per capita gross domestic product. For the 70-year observation period as a whole, there is no evidence to reject the LPE, so there is no evidence of convergence between soccer clubs in revenues. For long subperiods within the 70-year period, however, the LPE cannot be rejected and the convergence hypothesis appears valid.

In periods when revenues show evidence of convergence, the economic structure of the professional soccer industry exhibits characteristics of equilibrium. Periods when convergence breaks down, on the other hand, can be characterized as transitional between an old and a new structural order. On these criteria, English soccer appears to have passed through two distinct equilibrium phases between the early 1920s and the end of the 20th century and through two periods of transition, the second of which was still in progress at the end of the 20th century.

The first equilibrium phase lasted from the early 1920s until the late 1950s. On the demand side, the market was highly segmented geographically, with clubs drawing spectators predominantly from their own localities. The maximum wage and minimum admission price also exerted a powerful leveling effect between the richer and poorer clubs. By the end of the 1950s, however, the existing structural order was under strain. Social and demographic changes, new patterns of leisure activity, the growth of home and car ownership, the spread of television, and the revival of the hooliganism phenomenon all affected both demand and costs in ways that, during the 1960s in particular, led to a transition toward a new but less durable equilibrium structure.

The second equilibrium phase began during the mid-1970s and lasted until the end of the 1980s. But in comparison with the phase that ran between the 1920s and 1950s, it was a much more turbulent period. By the end of the 1980s, soccer was engulfed in an atmosphere of crisis that, at the time, seemed serious enough to threaten the very survival of the sport at the professional level. Soccer's somewhat unexpected rehabilitation during the 1990s as the most popular and fashionable national sport coincided with a further sharp rise in economic inequality between clubs.

Testing for changes in competitive balance in sporting terms has been an important objective in some of the recent U.S. literature on the empirical economics of team sports. It has been argued that in the present case, there are no direct counterparts of the tests that have typically been applied in North America. This is due to the hierarchical divisional structures and fluctuating divisional memberships that prevail in soccer, both in England and elsewhere throughout Europe. Consequently, this study has focused on economic (rather than sporting) convergence and divergence, measured in revenue terms. It seems highly likely, however, that trends in economic and sporting inequality are closely interlinked. Empirical quantification of the nature of this link over the long term would appear to offer an interesting future challenge for sports economists and historians.

NOTES

1. The results of empirical studies have been mixed. Some early studies found no relationship or a positive relationship between size and growth (Mansfield, 1962; Singh & Whittington, 1975). Others identify an inverse relationship and therefore reject the law of proportionate effect (Dunne & Hughes, 1994; Evans, 1987; Hall, 1987; Hart & Prais, 1956). Sutton (1997) reviewed the theoretical and empirical literature.

2. de la Fuente (1997) and Temple (1999) provided recent reviews of the convergence literature.

3. For convenience, seasons are identified by their end year: So, 1925 to 1926 is the 1926 season and so on. 1926 is the first season for which complete records of gate revenues are available, and 1997 is the last for which this data were available at the time of writing. Although total revenues (from all sources) would be preferable in many respects to gate revenues, the former are only obtainable from club company accounts, and most clubs have not filed accounts systematically until recently. Most previous firm-level studies of the law of proportionate effect use assets or equity firm size measures. The present use of revenue is dictated not only by availability of data but also by the financial structure of the typical soccer club. Apart from a stadium and (in many cases) a training ground, most clubs possess few assets, with purchases and sales of players normally regarded as current (rather than capital) items for accounting purposes. Nevertheless, the use of data on gate revenue rather than total revenue data is a limitation of the present analysis, especially in respect to recent seasons when the proportion of gate revenue to total revenue has been in decline.

4. Group 1 contains the four London clubs that, throughout their histories, have attracted support most extensively throughout London and beyond (Arsenal, Chelsea, Tottenham, and West Ham). Group 1 also includes clubs from other major cities with populations larger than 500,000 in the 1961 census (Birmingham, Liverpool, Leeds, Manchester, and Sheffield). Group 2 contains clubs from cities with populations in the range 250,000 to 500,000 located in the midlands and north of England. Group 3 contains clubs from southern towns other than London and the smaller London clubs with more localized support that are not included in Group 1. Most Group 3 clubs entered the league during or after its early 1920s expansion. The remaining groups contain clubs from smaller towns in the midlands and north, broken down into pre-1922 (Group 4) and post-1922 (Group 5) league entrants. This subdivision of clubs is used for the construction of Figures 1 and 2 only and does not affect the convergence estimations reported below, all of which are based on the complete population of clubs.

5. The 1961 Population Census is used as it is the nearest to the midpoint of the observation period. A referee has pointed out that x_{1i} is not predetermined for the pre-1961 estimations and that changes in population between 1926 and 1961 could partly account for differences between clubs. Clearly, it would be preferable to use a shifting population measure applicable to the base period for each estimation; however, regular and sweeping changes to the geographical boundaries over which the census data are compiled preclude this option. The use of 1921 census data would offer the benefit of making x_{1i} predetermined throughout but at the cost of rendering the population measure less meaningful for estimations pertaining to later periods. In any case, the variation in town populations over time is considerably smaller than the cross-sectional variation between towns. Every census captures the feature that Birmingham is a much larger town than Brighton, which in turn is much larger than Bury, and essentially this is all that is required of the cross-sectional population variable.

6. The use of a 30-mile radius in the definition of x_{2i} is arbitrary. Estimations with the definition of x_{2i} based on a 20-mile and a 50-mile radius produced very similar results.

7. Although both financial and time constraints militated against regular travel to away matches in the 1930s and 1940s, occasional big games (especially Football Association Cup ties) were capable of attracting several thousand traveling spectators (Dunning, Murphy, & Williams, 1988). Fishwick (1989) suggested that location within a city could have implications for a club's propensity to attract support. Although Sheffield United's central location was an advantage before the First World War, by the 1930s slum clearances and the construction of new suburban estates helped Sheffield Wednesday, located 2 to 3 miles north of the city center, establish itself as the better supported team.

8. Symbolically, 1958 was also the year of the Munich air crash. The widespread sympathy that this disaster aroused may subsequently have helped to establish Manchester United as the first club with a fully national rather than predominantly local or regional following. More generally, the declining geographical segmentation of the leading clubs' spectator catchment areas is an important feature of the post-1958 period.

9. This process culminated in 1988 when Independent Television paid £11 million per season for exclusive broadcasting rights for the next four seasons, with just five clubs (Arsenal, Everton, Liverpool, Manchester United, and Tottenham) receiving 32% of the total fee. Even as a result of the 1988 agreement, television revenues were quite small relative to aggregate gate revenues (which increased from £72.9 million to £127.3 million over the same four seasons). Some of the smaller clubs' share of the television fee, however, could represent the difference between solvency and bankruptcy.

10. Between 1963 and 1978, players were entitled to move at the expiry of their contracts if their present club did not offer new terms at least as remunerative as before. From 1978, out-of-contract players could insist on a move even if a new contract was offered, with the transfer fee imposed by a tribunal if the two clubs could not agree.

11. Dobson and Goddard (1995), Simmons (1996), and Szymanski and Smith (1997) all reported relatively low price-elasticity estimates, based on time series attendance data.

REFERENCES

Barro, R. J. (1991). Economic growth in a cross section of countries. *Quarterly Journal of Economics, 104*, 407-444.

Baumol, W. J. (1986). Productivity growth, convergence and welfare: What the long-run data show. *American Economic Review, 76*, 1072-1085.

Bennett, R. W., & Fizel, J. L. (1995). Telecast deregulation and competitive balance. *American Journal of Economics and Sociology, 54*, 183-199.

Bird, P. (1982). The demand for league football. *Applied Economics, 14*, 637-649.

Conn, D. (1997). *The football business: Fair game in the '90s?* Edinburgh, Scotland: Mainstream.

de la Fuente, A. (1997). The empirics of growth and convergence: A selective review. *Journal of Economic Dynamics and Control, 21*, 23-73.

Dobson, S., & Goddard, J. (1995). The demand for professional league football in England and Wales 1925-92. *Journal of the Royal Statistical Society Series D, 44*, 259-277.

Dobson, S., & Goddard, J. (1998). Performance, revenue and cross-subsidisation in the Football League, 1927-94. *Economic History Review, 51*, 763-785.

Dunne, P., & Hughes, A. (1994). Age, size, growth and survival: UK companies in the late 1980s. *Journal of Industrial Economics, 35*, 567-581.

Dunning, E., Murphy, P., & Williams, J. (1988). *The roots of football hooliganism: An historical and sociological study.* London: Routledge Kegan Paul.

Eckard, E. W. (1998). The NCAA cartel and competitive balance in college football. *Review of Economic Organization, 13*, 347-369.

Evans, D. S. (1987). Tests of alternative theories of firm growth. *Journal of Political Economy, 95*, 657-674.

Fishwick, N. (1989). *English football and society, 1910-1950.* Manchester, UK: Manchester University Press.

Flynn, A., & Guest, L. (1994). *Out of time: Why football isn't working.* London: Simon & Schuster.

Football Trust. (1995). *Digest of football statistics.* Leicester, UK: University of Leicester.

Football Trust. (1996). *Digest of football statistics.* Leicester, UK: University of Leicester.

Football Trust. (1997). *Digest of football statistics.* Leicester, UK: University of Leicester.

Fort, R., & Quirk, J. (1995). Cross-subsidization, incentives, and outcomes in professional team sports leagues. *Journal of Economic Literature, 33*, 1265-1299.

Gibrat, R. (1931). *Les inégalités economiques* [Economic inequalities]. Paris: Librairie du Recueil Sirey.

Hall, B. (1987). The relationship between firm size and firm growth in the US manufacturing sector. *Journal of Industrial Economics, 35*, 583-606.

Hart, P. E., & Prais, S. J. (1956). The analysis of business concentration: A statistical approach. *Journal of the Royal Statistical Society Series A, 119*, 150-191.

Hoehn, T., & Szymanski, S. (1999). The Americanization of European football. *Economic Policy, 28*, 205-240.

Jennett, N. (1984). Attendances, uncertainty of outcome and policy in Scottish league football. *Scottish Journal of Political Economy, 31*, 176-198.

Mansfield, E. (1962). Entry, Gibrat's Law, innovation and the growth of firms. *American Economic Review, 52*, 1023-1051.

Neale, W. C. (1964). The peculiar economics of professional sports. *Quarterly Journal of Economics, 78*, 1-14.

Peel, D. A., & Thomas, D. (1988). Outcome uncertainty and the demand for football. *Scottish Journal of Political Economy, 35*, 242-249.

Quirk, J., & El-Hodiri, M. (1971). An economic model of a professional sports league. *Journal of Political Economy, 79*, 1302-1319.

Rottenberg, S. (1956). The baseball player's labor market. *Journal of Political Economy, 64*, 242-258.

Russell, D. (1997) *Football and the English: A social history of association football in England 1863-1995*. Preston, UK: Carnegie.

Simmons, R. (1996). The demand for English league football: A club level analysis. *Applied Economics, 28*, 139-155.

Singh, A., & Whittington, G. (1975). The size and growth of firms. *Review of Economic Studies, 42*, 15-26.

Solow, R. M. (1956). A contribution to the theory of economic growth. *Quarterly Journal of Economics, 70*, 65-94.

Sutton, J. (1997). Gibrat's legacy. *Journal of Economic Literature, 35*, 40-59.

Szymanski, S., & Smith, R. (1997). The English football industry: Profit, performance and industrial structure. *International Review of Applied Economics, 11*, 135-153.

Temple, J. (1999). The new growth evidence. *Journal of Economic Literature, 37*, 112-156.

Union Royale Belge des Sociétés de Football Association v. Bosman, Case C415/93 (European Court of Justice, 1995).

Vrooman, J. (1995). A general theory of professional sports leagues. *Southern Economic Journal, 64*, 971-990.

Walvin, J. (1994). *The people's game: The history of football revisited*. Edinburgh, Scotland: Mainstream.

Stephen Dobson is a senior lecturer in economics at the School of Management and Economics at The Queen's University of Belfast in the United Kingdom.

John Goddard is a senior lecturer in economics in the Department of Economics at the University of Wales in Swansea, United Kingdom.

Carlyn Ramlogan is a research fellow in the Department of Agricultural and Food Economics at The Queen's University of Belfast in the United Kingdom.

[13]

Testing Causality Between Team Performance and Payroll

The Cases of Major League Baseball and English Soccer

STEPHEN HALL
STEFAN SZYMANSKI
Imperial College

ANDREW S. ZIMBALIST
Smith College

The link between team payroll and competitive balance plays a central role in the theory of team sports but is seldom investigated empirically. This paper uses data on team payrolls in Major League Baseball between 1980 and 2000 to examine the link and implements Granger causality tests to establish whether the relationship runs from payroll to performance or vice versa. While there is no evidence that causality runs from payroll to performance over the entire sample period, the data shows that the cross section correlation between payroll and performance increased significantly in the 1990s. As a comparison, the paper examines the relationship between pay and performance in English soccer, and it is shown that Granger causality from higher payrolls to better performance cannot be rejected. We argue that this difference may be a consequence of the open market for player talent that obtains in soccer compared to the significant restrictions on trade that exist in Major League Baseball.

The Commissioner's Blue Ribbon Panel on baseball economics was established "to consider whether revenue disparities among clubs are seriously damaging competitive balance, and, if so, to recommend structural reforms to ameliorate the problem" (Levin, Mitchell, Volcker & Will, 2000). The Panel's report published in July 2000 concluded, inter alia, that "large and growing disparities exist" and that revenue sharing and the payroll tax "have produced neither the intended moderating of payroll disparities nor improved competitive balance" (p. 1). In this article, we examine player payrolls and their effect on outcomes, notably the winning records

AUTHORS' NOTE: *We wish to thank Roger Noll, Shreya Jain, and Bhavani Harimohan for their comments and research assistance.*

JOURNAL OF SPORTS ECONOMICS, Vol. 3 No. 2, May 2002   149–168
© 2002 Sage Publications

of the teams. There are two aspects to our approach. First, we explore whether there is in fact a large variation in payrolls among the teams that is correlated with winning. Clearly, a (positive) correlation between payrolls and playing success is a sine qua non for establishing that revenue disparities play any role in determining competitive balance. Moreover, this correlation should be strong if it is to bear the weight of a causal link from revenue inequality to competitive imbalance. Second, we test directly whether any such causal link exists, in a statistical sense. In addition to performing the relevant tests for Major League Baseball (MLB), to sharpen our results we carry out similar tests for English soccer.

We find that the correlation between team performance and payroll is relatively weak in MLB from 1980 to the mid-1990s and robust thereafter. The correlation for English soccer is strong throughout the tested period, 1974-1999. Granger causality tests affirm that in English soccer the causality runs from payroll to performance and that in MLB the causality runs from performance to payroll during 1980-1994. The results for MLB during 1995-2000 are consistent with causality running in both directions.

We conclude by considering the institutional features of MLB and English professional soccer that may account for these statistical results. We argue that the restrictions on trading in player markets that are a recognized feature of baseball limit the scope for turning income into success and also enhance the opportunities for players to turn success into income. Nevertheless, the sharply growing revenue disparities in MLB since 1990 have reopened the opportunity to differentiate team performance through payroll. The presence of long-term contracts and restrictive labor market rules, however, seem to prevent the identification of unambiguous one-way causality.

By contrast, the well-established and accepted player markets of soccer leagues (not just in England but worldwide) ensure that players are paid a market rate for what they do. Not only are soccer clubs free to buy a better team in the market but the market worldwide is large enough to ensure that such a team can be assembled relatively quickly, and consequently spending determines success.

THE CORRELATION BETWEEN PLAYER SPENDING AND WINNING

Baseball

Playing talent is the principal input used by clubs to generate success on the field. In a perfectly competitive industry, we would expect that each player would receive his expected marginal revenue product in wages. Scully's (1974) seminal article suggested a direct test of the competitiveness of the market by comparing an individual player's wages with his estimated marginal revenue product based on the relationship between (a) playing success and team revenue and (b) player performance statistics and success. He found that marginal revenue products were substantially above player salaries, a finding accounted for by the operation of the reserve clause that granted team owners monopsony power.[1] The introduction of free agency from 1976 onward substantially undermined, if not eliminated, the monopsony power of the owners. Zimbalist (1992) employed a modified Scully method for baseball and found that salaries were on balance much closer to marginal revenue products, although there were substantial differences among different categories of players. In general, free agents appeared to earn in excess of their marginal revenue products (MRPs), whereas rookies continued to earn substantially less. This finding in itself can be taken as evidence that the market for playing talent does not function efficiently. In an efficient market with free agency, players offered less than their expected MRP would receive better offers from rival teams and move, whereas players whose salaries exceeded MRP would face either layoff or a pay cut. However, this conclusion is necessarily tentative, given the difficulties inherent in measuring MRP.

Quirk and Fort (1999) suggest another approach. They argue that under free agency, "A player will end up playing for the team for which he adds most revenue . . . and he will earn something between what he is worth to that team and what he would be worth to the team that places the second highest value on his services" (p. 81), and from this they conclude that "teams presumably pretty much get what they pay for" (p. 83). To test this proposition they then look at the correlation between the rank of regular-season winning percentages (i.e., highest, second highest, third highest, etc.) and the rank of player payroll cost by team averaged over the 7 seasons during 1990-1996. They find that for the American League the correlation coefficient is 0.509, whereas for the National League it is 0.135. Neither of these correlations is statistically significant. They conclude that payrolls "were essentially worthless in explaining the won-lost records in baseball (p. 86)." A related exercise conducted by Zimbalist (1992) reports a low correlation coefficient for baseball and concludes that "average team salary has been related only tenuously to team performance" (p. 96).[2]

This conclusion is striking because it challenges the idea that teams with larger revenue bases can successfully corner the best players in a free agency market by offering the highest salaries. There might be other mechanisms that enable wealthy teams to attract the best players. First, it might be that benefits in kind and other perquisites that do not appear in the accounting data underlying player salaries are the means by which the wealthy attract the talented, but this seems unlikely in an era of such remarkable salary and payroll inflation. Second, it might be that the quality of the coaching staff and player training facilities gives the wealthier teams the ability to extract more from players of a given talent. This also seems unlikely to explain all of the variation in performance, given that payroll itself constitutes such a large fraction of total costs (53% for the average club in 1999 according to the Blue Ribbon Panel, and even more for the median club). Third, it may be that players are attracted to the largest revenue markets because of the greater opportunities to earn endorsement and promotional income outside the club. This could imply that salaries need be no higher than (and may be slightly below) the alternative to attract a player to a large revenue market. Indeed, if this were the case, we might expect to find a negative correlation between success and club payrolls.

In this study, we first look at the relationship between payroll and performance, using pooled data for Major League Baseball (MLB) during the period 1980-2000. In particular, we focus on winning percentages in the regular season and payroll spending by each team relative to the average payroll spending of all teams for the season. If wealthy teams can buy success, we conjecture, then the most precise measure of their spending is the ratio rather than the rank. For example, given that luck still plays a part, then the team that spends the most is more likely to achieve the highest ranking if it spends 10 times the average rather than 5 times the average. Moreover, winning percentages are a more accurate measure of success than rank of winning percentages because a team with the season's highest winning percentage will generally be deemed more successful if it achieved this with a 0.65 rather than a 0.60 record.

Figure 1 is a scatter diagram for all clubs during all years in the data. The solid line is a linear regression line, and the figure indicates that the R^2 for this regression is about 0.24; in other words, spending relative to the average accounts for about 24% of the variation in yearly winning percentages—only a modest correlation. However, given that there are numerous factors that may influence a team's performance in a particular season, many of them purely random, a more reliable test of the effect of spending might be to consider those teams that overspend during the long term to see if they outperform the rest. To look at this, we averaged winning percentages for each team during the 21 years and averaged their annual spending relative to the average. Although this process of averaging may obscure a great deal of within-group variation, it gives a clear idea of the relationship between long-term spending and long-term success. The long-term average relationship is depicted in Figure 2.

Each dot on the graph represents a particular team (the New York Yankees, Florida Marlins, and Montreal Expos are labeled), and as before the regression line shows the linear relationship between the variables and the R^2 gives an indication of the degree of correlation.[3] What is striking about this chart is that the degree of correlation is much greater than in Figure 1, suggesting that during the longer term consistently high spending is associated with a high level of success.

A Comparison With English Soccer

The league structure of English soccer is somewhat different from that of MLB. The top division in England (called the Premier League) currently consists of only 20 teams, but at the end of each season the 3 worst performing teams are relegated or demoted to the immediately junior division (called the Football League First Division) and replaced by the 3 best performing teams in that division. An analo-

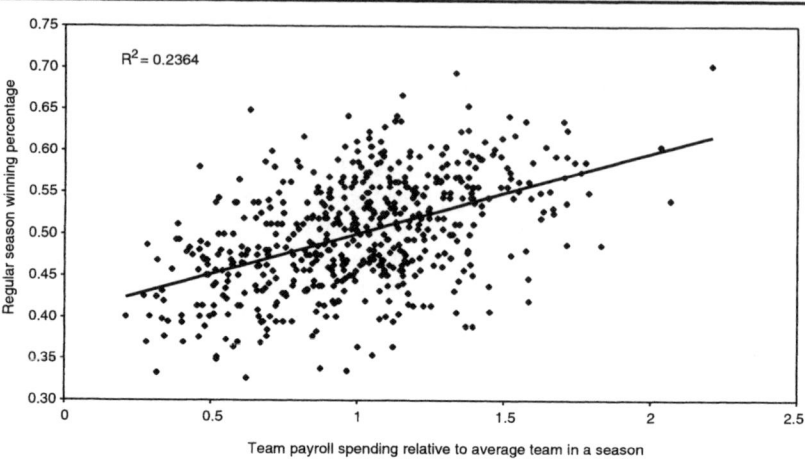

Figure 1:   Annual Payroll and Winning in Baseball: 1980-2000

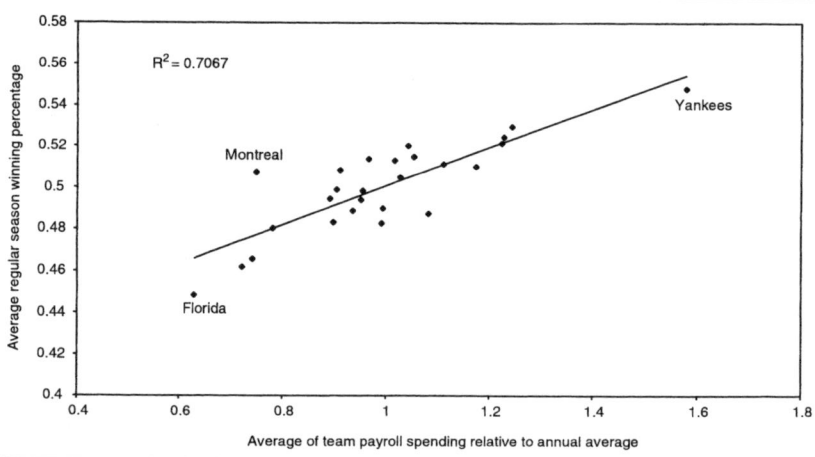

Figure 2:   Average Payroll and Average Winning Percentage: 1980-2000

gous relationship exists between the Football League's First and Second Divisions and its Second and Third Divisions. This system of promotion and relegation permits a significant degree of mobility among the 92 teams that participate in the four divisions, both in theory and in practice. Since 1987, there has also been a small amount of mobility at the bottom, as the worst performing team in the Third Division has been relegated to junior competition and replaced by the most successful lower league team. Thus, between 1987 and 1999 there were 99 teams appearing in the four divisions, of which only 5 were never either promoted or relegated. Of the teams, 32% played in only two different divisions, whereas 43% played in three and 12% managed to play in all four during the 12-year period.[4]

Given this degree of mobility, it is misleading to analyze the top division in isolation. Instead, we have used a balanced panel of 39 teams that were present in the leagues during the 26 seasons 1973-1974 to 1998-1999. These clubs provide a representative sample of all the divisions during the period. The promotion and relegation structure of league soccer renders the interdivisional comparison of winning percentages meaningless; therefore, some other measure of success needs to be adopted. Here we use league ranks measuring from the top of the Premier League (1) to the bottom of the Football League Third Division (92). Payroll costs[5] are taken from published company accounts and are again expressed relative to the average payroll of all teams for a season.[6] Figure 3 illustrates the relationship between league rank (transformed into the log odds of league rank) and spending relative to the average.

Although there are clearly a number of outliers at the top and bottom ends of the performance distribution, the overall correlation between performance and player spending seems much stronger for English soccer than for baseball, as indicated by the R^2 of 0.74. When we look at the relationship between payroll and success during 26 years for each of the clubs on average (see Figure 4), we similarly find a much closer correlation than we do in baseball.[7]

Before concluding from this that there is a genuinely closer correlation between payrolls and performance in soccer than in baseball, it is necessary to consider the relevant ranges of the data. There is both more variation in success and more variation in payroll spending in soccer than in baseball. Thus, the standard deviation in player payrolls (relative to the season's average) for the baseball data during the period 1980-2000 is 0.33, less than half that of the soccer data 0.76 (covering 1974-1999). The differences in performance are also much greater in soccer, given the much larger number of teams involved.

One way to compare like with like is to look at the winning percentages and salary variation of teams in the Premier League only. The standard deviation of payrolls for teams appearing in the Premier League is only 0.34, almost exactly the same as the standard deviation for MLB. The standard deviation of winning percentages is much larger for the Premier League (0.11) than for baseball (0.07). This is all the more striking because the much longer season in baseball (around 160 games compared to around 40 for the Premier League) would imply that the effect of variation due to chance would be much smaller in the former;[8] therefore, if payrolls did influence success systematically the effect should be more, not less apparent.

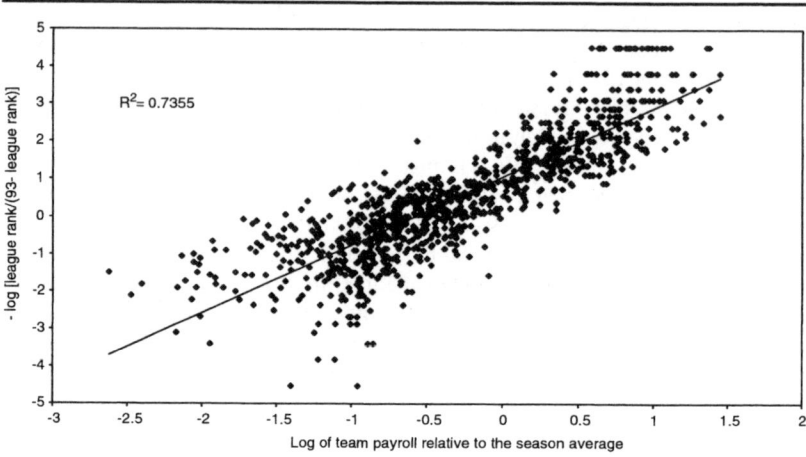

Figure 3:   Payroll and Winning in English Soccer: 1974-1999

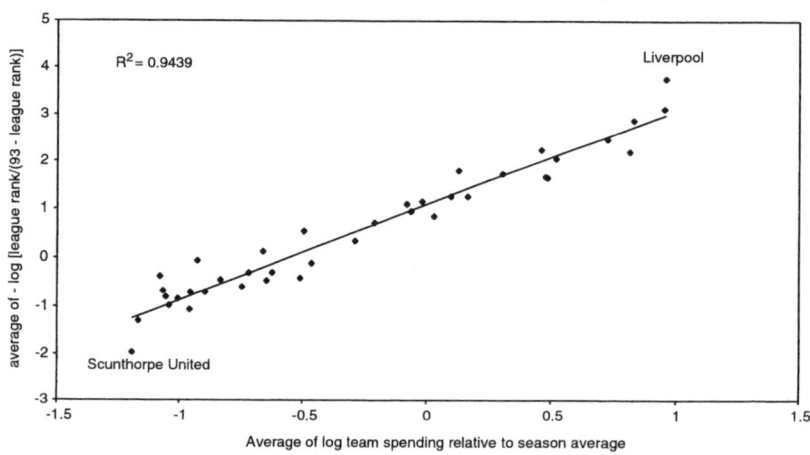

Figure 4:   Team Average Spending and Average League Position: 1974-1999

Figures 5 and 6 are the analogous charts for Figures 3 and 4, considering only top division soccer teams. In fact, by inspection, these charts now resemble Figures 1 and 2, respectively, rather closely.

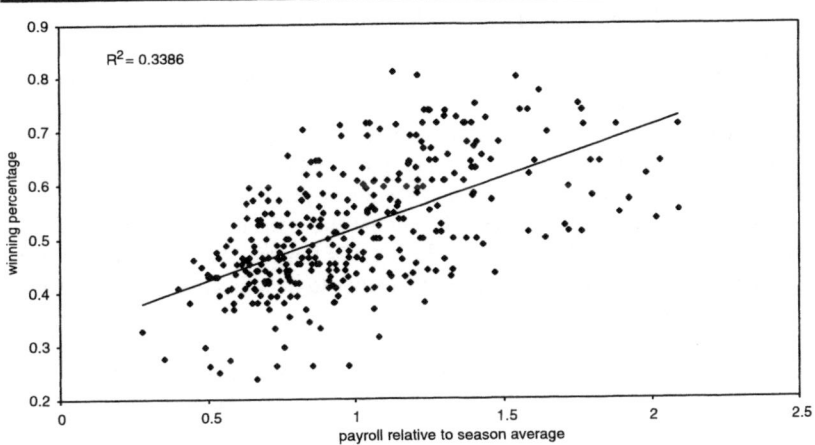

Figure 5: Winning Percentage and Payroll for Top Division Soccer Teams: 1974-1999

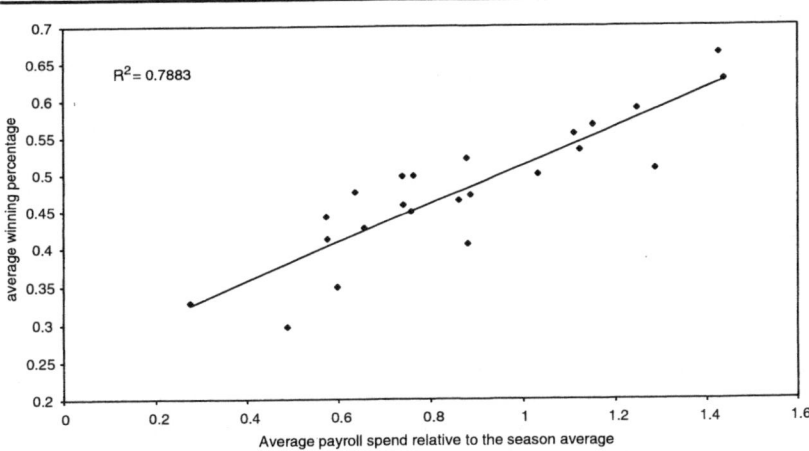

Figure 6: Team Average Spending in the English Top Division: 1974-1999

We can directly compare the implied relationship between winning percentage and relative payroll spending for MLB and the Premier League by looking at the simple regression equation for Figures 1 and 5:

$$\text{Win \% in MLB} = 0.404 + 0.097 \, \text{payroll/(average payroll)}$$

Win % in Premier League = 0.327 + 0.191 payroll/(average payroll).

In MLB, a team spending 50% of the average could expect a 0.453 winning percentage, whereas a team in the Premier League with similar underspending would only achieve a record of 0.423. Similarly, a team spending 50% more than the average in baseball could only expect a winning percentage of 0.550, whereas in the Premier League the team could expect a winning percentage of 0.614. Alternatively, a team spending two standard deviations above the mean would have a win percentage of .564 in MLB and .649 in the Premier League. Performance at the top level of English soccer seems much more sensitive to spending than performance at the top level of baseball.

The regression estimates above are highly significant at conventional levels—for both equations, the t-statistic on relative payrolls is more than 13. However, neither regression directly establishes causality from player spending to team performance.

SPENDING, PERFORMANCE, AND CAUSALITY

Background

The commonsense view is that you get what you pay for. Teams compete in the market for playing talent, bidding up salaries to the point where wages equal marginal revenue products, and therefore total payroll is a perfect predictor of performance. Moreover, in sports markets where players perform on a regular basis in front of large audiences, the usual hidden information and hidden action accounts of market failure are not plausible.

So, how might it come about that a causal relationship from pay to performance is not visible statistically? It might be that the mechanism works but only imperfectly, due to factors such as player complementarities, managerial talent, injuries, luck, poor judgement, and so forth. Too much noise might obscure the true underlying causal relationship. If the trading market is itself very thin, as it has become in baseball in the free agency era, then trades may fail to occur at efficient prices.

Prior to free agency, player trading was frequent—for example, Daly and Moore (1981) quote an average figure of nine trades per team per season between 1955 and 1964 and eight trades per team per season between 1965 and 1973. Eckard (2001) states that this amounted to 7.8% of all players in the period 1973-1975. Since then, however, player trading has much diminished, and the phenomenon of cash sales has more or less disappeared (Daly, 1992; Fort & Quirk, 1995). Hylan, Lage, and Treglia (1996) found that pitchers in the free agency era with 7 or more years of experience were less likely to move to another team than in the reserve era. Furthermore, although trades continue, the incidence of teams trading first-line players who are likely to have the greatest effect on the outcome of games and therefore win percentage has become even less frequent (Daly, 1992). Horrow (2001) reports that during 1951-1976 an annual average of 4.7 players per team moved to a different club via cash sales, trades, waivers, and other transactions, and during 1977-1994 that figure was 4.6.[9]

Although these market encumbrances may weaken the link between wages and performance, they do not explain why causation might run from performance to wages rather than wages to performance.

The explanation, in the case of baseball, may be associated with the long-term nature of the employment contract and the impediments to trading star players. The trading of top players in MLB is encumbered by two factors. First, since Commissioner Kuhn prohibited the use of substantial cash in player transactions in 1976, there is no clean or divisible mechanism for clubs to equalize the value of player trades.[10] MLB's young stars who have not yet earned free-agent status generally produce more value than they are paid. But unlike in European soccer, where cash is commonly used in a trade to fill the difference between a player's MRP and his salary, the best way for an MLB owner to extract surplus is to hold such a player until he becomes a free agent. Second, unlike English soccer, MLB free agent stars frequently have no trade clauses in their contracts.

Players on a winning team expect to be rewarded for the team's success. Thus, free agents on a winning team as well as players a year away from free agency often earn handsome salary increases, whereas the salary of other players does not respond to team performance in the short run. Many of these salaries were set years earlier while the player was at a different performance level.[11]

In English soccer the situation is quite different. Traditionally, players have been employed on relatively short-term contracts of between 1 and 5 years, and player trading is an important part of the operation of the league. Carmichael, Forrest, and Simmons (1999) report that, for example, 12.3% of players changed teams in the 1993-1994 season, which is not unusual. Moreover, the leading teams regularly trade their top stars in search of a better lineup, whereas players frequently express their ambition to play for a variety of clubs in a variety of leagues during their careers. Thus, English league teams spent just under $2 billion (gross) on player transfers during the seasons 1995-1996 to 1999-2000, an average of $400 million per season and equal to around 70% of total spending on player salaries (see *Annual Review*, 2001, p. 27).[12]

In English soccer, unlike MLB, young stars at the beginning of their careers have mobility similar to the established stars. Importantly, "no trade" clauses are virtually unheard of in English soccer. Soccer fans are more likely to complain if their team's owners do not go after the best players than they are to grouse that their team's players rapidly turn over. In a league where the teams themselves are mobile between divisions, mobility of personnel is accepted as part and parcel of the system. Players, in turn, always seek to move up in division, league, and team to maximize their experience and income. The concentration of a large number of teams in English soccer in relative geographic proximity to each other also makes it easier for players to move among clubs without upsetting their social lives. Hence, both for contractual and structural reasons there is much greater freedom in the labor market of English soccer than in MLB. This allows for a closer match between salaries and MRPs and for higher payroll outlays to be converted into performance success more readily. It also means that players are in much less of a position to bargain for any rents that accrue from unexpected success because players demanding unrealistic salaries (i.e., well in excess of their MRP) can be more readily traded.

Testing for Granger Causality

The problem of identifying economic causality from the statistical analysis of data series has long been recognized as a fundamental problem in econometrics. Causality in its most general sense is nebulous and nonoperational in a statistical sense. We might think, for instance, of future expectations causing things to happen now, which would suggest that the future in some way could cause the past. To make the concept of causality operational we need to define a precise concept that is clear, and this inevitably involves limiting the broad meaning of causality. In operational econometrics there are two broad definitions of causality currently being used: Granger causality and long-run (sometimes weak) causality. Long-run causality is only operational for models containing nonstationary variables. In this case we can divide the model's properties into two parts: the long-run determination of the system and the short-run adjustment. Long-run causality is defined only with respect to the long-run determination of the model. Granger causality focuses on any structural influence of one variable on another and is therefore operational in the case of stationary and nonstationary data.

Granger (1969) proposed an operational definition of causality between two or more variables in terms of the influence that one variable may have on another. Consider the case of two processes, x and y, and the information on them contained in their past behavior X_t ($X_t = x_{t-1}, x_{t-2}, \ldots x_{t-q}$) and Y_t ($Y_t = y_{t-1}, y_{t-2}, \ldots y_{t-q}$) for a suitable lag length q. y Granger causes x if Y_t provides additional information for the forecast of x_t above that provided by X_t. Granger causality is usually tested formally within the framework of a stationary vector autoregression (VAR). In this simple bivariate case, the test would involve the following system:

$$y_t = \alpha Y_t + \beta X_t + v_t$$

$$x_t = \chi Y_t + \delta X_t + \varepsilon_t,$$

where α, β, χ, and δ are conformably dimensioned vectors of parameters. The test of the hypothesis that x does not Granger cause y is given by the joint test that $\beta = 0$ and the test of the hypothesis that y does not Granger cause x is given by the joint test that $\chi = 0$. Because this procedure is carried out for a reduced form VAR, it is important to realize that two types of causality are actually being tested for at once. This is the possibility that (a) in the structural form of the model y is simultaneously caused by x or (b) in the structural form of the model y is caused by lagged values of x. This may be fully appreciated if we state the above system in structural form that allows for contemporaneous interactions:

$$y_t = a_{12}x_t + \alpha^* Y_t + \beta^* X_t + v_t$$

$$x_t = a_{21}y_t + \chi^* Y_t + \delta^* X_t + \varepsilon_t.$$

In matrix notation we can then write this system as

$$Az_t = BZ_t,$$

where $z = (y\ x)'$, $Z = (Y\ X)'$, and

$$A = \begin{pmatrix} 1 & -a_{12} \\ -a_{21} & 1 \end{pmatrix} \quad B = \begin{pmatrix} \alpha^* & \beta^* \\ \chi^* & \delta^* \end{pmatrix}.$$

The A and B matrices are the structural form parameters, and the parameters in the reduced form VAR model above are derived as the reduced form of this system $(A^{-1}B)$. So the test that $\beta = 0$ would be rejected if either $a_{12} \neq 0$ or if $\beta^* \neq 0$, that is, if in the structural form there is either contemporaneous causality from x to y or lagged causality.

Since the mid-1980s, a revolution has occurred in the analysis of time series data with the development of the concepts of stationarity and cointegration. These methods have led to the development of statistical tests that can reject hypotheses consistent with a particular direction of causality in the long run in isolation from the complete dynamic response. However, we will not pursue this here as subsequent testing of our data revealed it to be stationary. In team sports, as in much of industrial organization, one is often concerned with panel data rather than simple time series. In recent years, several researchers have begun to apply these techniques to the analysis of panel data (e.g., see Hall & Urga, 2000) and one interesting result is that a key feature determining how a panel should be treated is the source of the nonstationarity in the panel. If a nonstationary variable in the panel is driven by only one nonstationary common stochastic trend across the whole panel, this will affect the properties of standard panel estimators in an important way to considerably simplify the problem. In the case being considered here, payment costs are almost certainly nonstationary. But if this nonstationarity comes from only one source (the general rise in wages across all clubs), then this is the single source of nonstationarity and it may be removed by considering a relative payroll variable, which is what we use. It is theoretically possible, of course, that this transformation would not remove the nonstationarity from the data, and this would imply that more than one common stochastic trend underlies the complete panel. This is, of course, a testable hypothesis in terms of testing the relative payroll variable for stationarity. The conventional test of stationarity is a Dickey-Fuller test for a unit root. In the panel data context, our regression equation was

$$\Delta y_{i,t} = \alpha_i + \rho y_{i,\,t-1} + e_{i,t},$$
$$i = 1, 2, \ldots N, t = 1, 2, \ldots, T, \tag{1}$$

where the α_i are fixed effects. The distribution for the t-statistic on the ρ coefficients is asymptotically normal as the number of clubs goes to infinity; for a small sample it would be closer to a standard Dickey-Fuller distribution, so assuming a critical value close to 3 would be very conservative.

Note that for this analysis we have reverted to the full English League soccer database, not the restricted Premier League sample. One difficulty with the using the Premier League sample alone would be that due to relegation there is not in general a complete series for lagged winning percentage. In any case, from the point of view of testing for causality from wages to performance there is little sense in excluding more than two thirds of the data.

Table 1 establishes that all of the variables considered appear to be stationary. Our next step is to use a Granger causality test to examine the direction of causality. In this context, our regression equation is

$$y_{i,t} = \alpha_i + \beta_1 y_{i,\,t-1} + \beta_2 x_{i,\,t-1} + u_{i,t}, \tag{2}$$

where y_i is the dependent variable and x_i is the independent variable. A variable z can be said to Granger cause a variable w if the coefficient β_2 for the regression with w on the left hand side (LHS) is economically and statistically significant, whereas the coefficient β_2 for the regression with z on the LHS is economically and statistically insignificant.[13]

These results tell a very different story for baseball and soccer (see Table 2). In the baseball case, performance appears to Granger cause wages but wages do not Granger cause performance. In the English soccer case, wages Granger cause performance but performance does not Granger cause wages (the coefficient is very small and not significant at the 1% level).

From an economic point of view, the implication of the Granger causality test is that English soccer conforms to the efficiency wage model of sporting competition, whereas baseball does not over these time periods. If wages do not cause better performance in baseball, what does? In our model the only other explanatory variable is past success, which diminishes in effect over time. The fixed effects are also insignificant, so the statistical interpretation is that teams randomly achieve success from time to time; this success persists for a while (and is translated into higher wages) but eventually teams regress to the mean 0.50 winning record. Such an interpretation is not economic nonsense but does seem to be at odds with the per-

162 JOURNAL OF SPORTS ECONOMICS / May 2002

TABLE 1: Estimates of ρ

Dependent Variable	Coefficient for ρ	t-Statistic	Observation
Baseball winning percentage	−0.62	−15.57	527
Baseball relative payroll	−0.33	−9.81	527
Soccer logit of position	−0.34	−14.04	975
Soccer relative payroll	−0.059	−3.46	975

TABLE 2: Estimates of β_2: 1980-2000 for Major League Baseball and 1974-1999 for Soccer

Dependent Variable	Coefficient for β_2	t-Statistic	Observation
Baseball winning percentage	0.003	0.24	527
Baseball relative payroll	0.823	5.18	527
Soccer logit of position	0.372	5.13	975
Soccer relative payroll	0.018	2.19	975

ceived development of baseball and the sustained dominance of some teams. One possibility is that other explanatory variables might account for success, thus expanding the statistical model. Many such candidate variables (e.g., expenditures—including signing bonuses—on player development, the extent of ownership synergies with related businesses, and the depth of the pockets of the team owners) should be closely correlated with the ability to pay high salaries and hence to some degree have already been indirectly ruled out. Other variables, such as the intensity of fan support, might have an effect on success but are hard to measure directly. We experimented with the inclusion of local population variables for each team; these had no significant effect on our results, which may not be all that surprising because population tends to change only slowly and is thus similar to the fixed effects. Of course, if tradition itself was an explanation of long-run success, then the fixed effects would indeed be significant, which they are not. Within the Granger framework, the causal influences of success in MLB during 1980-2000 remain difficult to identify unambiguously or at least such influences are not readily quantifiable.

Testing for a Structural Break in Baseball

According to MLB's Blue Ribbon Panel Report, the situation in baseball has changed significantly since 1994, with differentials in economic status having a much greater effect than hitherto. More generally, the argument of a structural shift in the mid-1990s is premised on several factors. First, in 1994 baseball's new national television contract fell by more than 60%. At the same time, certain big market teams (such as the Yankees) were earning more than $40 million a year in unshared local media revenues, and the era of the new, big revenue–generating stadiums was ushered in by Camden Yards in 1992. With MLB's centrally distributed monies below $10 million per club, teams with a big market or new stadium found themselves with a rapidly growing revenue advantage. Whereas the revenue disparity between the richest and poorest team was around $30 million in 1989, by 1999 it was $164 million. Local revenues (including all stadium-related and local media income) in 1999 went from a high of $176 million for the Yankees to a low of $12 million for the Montreal Expos.

Second, the 1990s witnessed the emergence of new franchise owners who also own international communications networks or are attempting to build regional sports channels. These owners value their ballplayers not only by the value they produce on the field but what they produce for their networks. Presumably, when Rupert Murdoch signed 33-year-old Kevin Brown to a 7-year deal worth an average of $15 million annually, he was thinking about the News Corp's emerging influence via satellite television in the huge Asian market as well as his enhanced ability to prevent the formation of a rival Disney-owned regional sports network in Southern California. Similarly, when George Steinbrenner opened up his wallet for David Cone ($12 million in 2000) or Roger Clemens ($30 million for 2001-2002), he had in mind creating a new New York sports channel built around the Yankees. In these and other instances, the owners of baseball teams do not treat their teams as stand-alone profit centers; rather, the team is a cog in a larger corporate machine that is used to maximize the long-term profits of a conglomerate.

Third, baseball's expansion by four teams in the 1990s, although adding excitement to the game, by decompressing talent makes the star players stand out more and thereby makes it easier to buy a winning team.

Fourth, the selection of amateur players through the draft (introduced in 1965) had served as an important leveler. In the 1990s, however, the selection of amateurs began to favor the high-revenue teams, contributing to a greater imbalance on the playing field. Sharply growing revenue disparities across the teams came to be reflected in vastly different player development budgets across the teams. In 1999, for instance, the Yankees spent more than $20 million on their player development system, whereas the Oakland Athletics invested less than $6 million. This disparity allows the Yankees, by offering far more handsome signing bonuses, to have greater success in signing foreign players who come to the United States as free agents. It also makes it more difficult for the bottom revenue teams to sign their top draft picks of domestic players.[14]

The evidence presented in Table 3 provides prima facie support for a mid-1990s structural break. It shows simple year-by-year regressions of winning percentage on player payrolls.

From this table, it is apparent that in the 8 seasons between 1980 and 1992, payroll spending was significant at the 5% level only thrice, and never at the 1% level. In the 8 seasons between 1993 and 2000, payroll was always significant at the 5%

TABLE 3:   Estimated Equation: $Win\ Pct_i = \alpha + \beta\ Payroll_i + e_i$

Year	α	β	R^2	n
1980	.484	3.24 E-09	.006	26
	(11.1)	(0.38)		
1981	.464	5.66 E-09	.002	26
	(9.06)	(0.73)		
1982	.489	1.46 E-09	.005	26
	(13.31)	(0.34)		
1983	.491	9.87 E-10	.003	26
	(12.82)	(0.26)		
1984	.418	7.48 E-09*	.166	26
	(10.77)	(2.18)		
1985	.362	1.30 E-08	.149	26
	(5.26)	(2.05)		
1986	.460	3.41 E-09	.029	26
	(9.29)	(0.84)		
1987	.466	3.02 E-09	.022	26
	(9.65)	(0.74)		
1988	.393	9.37 E-09*	.181	26
	(8.12)	(2.31)		
1989	.389	7.89 E-09*	.232	26
	(9.10)	(2.69)		
1990	.460	2.30 E-09	.028	26
	(9.46)	(0.84)		
1991	.420	3.14 E-09	.151	26
	(10.44)	(2.07)		
1992	.470	9.45 E-10	.020	26
	(10.72)	(0.70)		
1993	.398	3.17 E-09*	.195	28
	(9.29)	(2.51)		
1994	.386	3.53 E-09*	.203	28
	(8.39)	(2.57)		
1995	.382	3.57 E-09**	.319	28
	(10.71)	(3.49)		
1996	.397	3.07 E-09**	.396	28
	(14.93)	(4.13)		
1997	.392	2.72 E-09**	.450	28
	(15.65)	(4.61)		
1998	.355	3.43 E-09**	.554	30
	(13.42)	(5.89)		
1999	.389	2.26 E-09**	.475	30
	(15.93)	(5.03)		
2000	.426	1.36 E-09**	.284	30
	(17.67)	(3.33)		

NOTE: *t*-statistics in parentheses.
*Two-tailed test, significant at 5%. **Two-tailed test, significant at 1%.

TABLE 4:   Estimates of β_2: 1980-1994 and 1995-2000

Dependent Variable	Coefficient for β_2	t-Statistic
Baseball winning percentage		
1980-1994	0.006	0.52
1995-2000	0.034	2.21
Baseball relative payroll		
1980-1994	0.864	5.38
1995-2000	0.583	2.87

NOTE: Number of observations = 527.

level and significant at the 1% in all but the first 2 seasons. This does seem to suggest that payroll spending may have become more important for success after the mid-1990s.

If this is so, we should also observe a structural break in our econometric model. To test for this we ran our Granger causality regressions to allow for slope coefficients to change in either 1994 or 1995. We found that there did appear to be a change and that the break was most plausibly fixed at the end of 1994. We report the relevant coefficients for the Granger causality tests in Table 4.

From this it is apparent that lagged wages in the performance regression have become statistically significant since 1994. At the same time, the wages regression shows that the effect of past performance has declined, although it is still significant. These results indicate that although it is still not possible to identify a unique causal relationship from wages to performance, since 1995 it has also become impossible to argue the reverse, that wages are determined by performance, because causality no longer appears to flow in a single direction.

It is useful, perhaps, to consider the full Granger causality regressions to observe more closely the apparent changes.

Prior to 1995, our two estimated relationships are

$$Wpc_{i,t} = 0.322 + 0.343 \ Wpc_{i,\,t-1}$$

$$Wages_{i,t} = \alpha_i + 0.532 \ wages_{i,\,t-1} + 0.864 \ Wpc_{i,\,t-1},$$

whereas since 1995 the relationships are

$$Wpc_{i,t} = 0.322 + 0.290 \ Wpc_{i,\,t-1} + 0.034 \ wages_{i,\,t-1}$$

$$Wages_{i,t} = \alpha_i + 0.674 \ wages_{i,\,t-1} + 0.583 \ Wpc_{i,\,t-1}.$$

Wages, as before, are expressed relative to the mean of all clubs in a given season. If these estimates represented a trend in the underlying parameters that drive success in baseball, the model would eventually come to resemble closely the efficiency wage system observable in soccer.

DISCUSSION AND CONCLUSIONS

The finding that player spending does appear, statistically, to cause improved performance in English soccer confirms not only the earlier research of Szymanski and Smith (1997) but also seems consistent with the more or less unfettered operation of the player market in soccer. Although baseball during 1980-1994 presents no evidence of Granger causality from wages to performance, there appears to be a shift in the mid-1990s. In our tests, since 1995 there is evidence that the causality between performance and payroll runs in both directions. If our measurement of expenditures on players and player development were more precise and complete, it is possible that the causal link from player costs to performance would become stronger.[15]

The cause of the differences in the way that the soccer and baseball markets operate are to be found in the institutional rules that govern them. Restrictive agreements that limit player spending, player mobility, roster sizes, the right to trade players, and so forth have made it less likely that teams can fully use their financial muscle to buy success in baseball. The absence of any of these restrictions in English soccer make it more likely that teams can buy success.

NOTES

1. Scully's (1974) general method has also been used to test for discrimination through the performance regressions. Limited evidence of salary discrimination has been found in baseball (see Kahn, 2000).

2. This finding is consistent with Major League Baseball's (MLB's) Economic Study Committee Report of December 3, 1992, and the staff analysis on which it is based. See, for instance, Section III of the *Major League Baseball Economic Study Committee, Staff Analysis*, December 1992.

3. Removing the Yankees from the regression reduces the coefficient of determination from .24 to .21 in Figure 1 and from .71 to .65 in Figure 2. Clearly, the Yankees are strong contributors to the pay-performance link, but the link is still healthy without them.

4. See Noll (2002 [this issue]) and Szymanski and Ross (2000) for a more detailed analysis of the promotion and relegation system.

5. Here, payroll refers to all club salaries and not just players. This figure now accounts for more than 50% of total costs. Transfer fees are not included. Transfer fees are best viewed as long-term investment and would require a compelling amortization scheme to be employed. In any event, because it is the most successful clubs that are the highest net transfer fee spenders, if this information were included it would only strengthen the measured pay-performance link in British soccer.

6. This data set, together with other accounting variables until 1997, can be found in Szymanski and Kuypers (1999).

7. It might be reasonably asked whether the improved fit for the soccer data is a result of the loglinear specification. Accordingly, we also tested the baseball data using logit and loglinear specifications; the closeness of fit was almost identical.

8. The "idealized" standard deviation of winning percentages in a league where each team has an equal chance of winning is $.5/\sqrt{m}$, where m is the number of matches in a season. For a 160-game season it would be 0.0395 and for a 40-game season it would be 0.0791. Thus, the actual standard deviation of the baseball winning percentages is 75% larger than the idealized, whereas for Premier League soccer it is only 40% larger.

9. Our own review of the Sporting News's *Baseball Guide* from 1960 through 2000 revealed the following pattern of diminished cash sales and trades. From 1960 through 1975 there were 518 cash purchases of players, representing 6% of all players in the major leagues at the time. During the 1980s there were 157 cash purchases, representing 2.4% of major leaguers, and during 1990-2000 there were 9 cash purchases, representing 0.1% of all major leaguers. In contrast, the share of players affected by trades went from 9.0% during 1960-1976 to 11.3% during 1977-2000. Hence, the overall movement of players from trades and cash sales fell from 15.0% during 1960-1976 to 12.2% during 1977-2000. The difference in the extent of cash trading in English soccer is striking. Sloane (1969) reports that in the 6 seasons between 1961-1962 and 1966-1967 more than 5% of professionals were traded for a fee every season. Because professional careers average 3 or 4 seasons in soccer, this implies a much higher degree of turnover than 6% during a period as long as 16 years (1960 to 1975). Moreover, evidence from Dobson and Gerrard (2000) suggests that turnover has increased. In the 4 seasons between 1990-1991 and 1993-1994, they found that on average 10.3% of professionals were transferred for a fee every season.

10. In June 1976, Commissioner Bowie Kuhn disallowed Charlie Finley's attempted sales of Joe Rudi and Rollie Fingers from the Oakland A's to the Boston Red Sox for $2 million and of Vida Blue from the A's to the New York Yankees for $1.5 million. Commissioner Kuhn set a rule of thumb that all trades involving more that $400,000 in cash had to be approved by his office. Today, the threshold for commissioner sanction is $1 million. According to the Sporting News's *Baseball Guide*, the last time a player moved teams as a result of a cash sale was in 1991.

11. Note that the correlation between success and payroll in baseball often results from the ability to hold a winning team together rather than the initial purchase of a winning team. The 2001 Yankees were composed mostly of players from their farm system or were acquired through trades. Of course, the Yankee farm system itself benefits from annual player development expenditures in excess of $20 million.

12. Although a high level of player mobility has always been an accepted part of the soccer system, until recently clubs were able to place some obstacles in the way of players wanting to move. Most notably, until 1995 clubs could demand a transfer fee for players moving to a new club even when their old contract had ended. The famous Bosman judgment of 1995 outlawed this kind arrangement within the European Union, as well as prohibiting restrictions imposed by national governing bodies on the number of foreign players permitted on a team. It is still too early to tell whether this ruling has further increased the mobility of players, but there has certainly been a considerable influx of foreign players into the English Premier League in recent years.

13. Davies, Downward, and Jackson (1995) and Dobson and Goddard (1998) investigated Granger causality between attendance and performance for the Rugby League and English soccer, respectively. In both cases they found mixed evidence.

14. This point is treated in more detail in Zimbalist (2001).

15. Another possible factor here is that for most years the baseball salary data in our study reflects end of year payroll, whereas for some years it reflects beginning of year figures. The effect of this is discussed (and illustrated for the National Hockey League) in Zimbalist (2002 [this issue]).

REFERENCES

Annual review of football finance. (2001). Manchester, UK: Deloitte & Touche.

Carmichael, F., Forrest, D., & Simmons, R. (1999). The labour market in association football: Who gets transferred and for how much? *Bulletin of Economic Research, 51*(1), 1-26.

Daly, G. (1992). The baseball players' market revisited. In P. Sommers (Ed.), *Diamonds are forever: The business of baseball.* Washington, DC: Brookings Institution.

Daly, G., & Moore, W. (1981). Externalities, property rights, and the allocation of resources in Major League Baseball. *Economic Inquiry, 29*, 77-95.

Davies, B., Downward, P., & Jackson, I. (1995). The demand for rugby league: Evidence from causality tests. *Applied Economics, 27*, 1003-1007.

Dobson, S., & Gerrard, B. (2000). Testing for monopoly rents in the market for playing talent: Evidence from English professional football. *Journal of Economic Studies, 27*(3), 142-164.

Dobson, S., & Goddard, J. (1998). Performance and revenue in professional league football: Evidence from Granger causality tests. *Applied Economics, 30,* 1641-1651.

Eckard, E. (2001). Free agency, competitive balance and diminishing returns to pennant contention. *Economic Inquiry, 39*(3), 430-443.

Fort, R., & Quirk, J. (1995). Cross subsidization, incentives and outcomes in professional team sports leagues. *Journal of Economic Literature, 33*(3), 1265-1299.

Granger, C. (1969). Investigating causal relations by econometric models and cross-spectral methods. *Econometrica, 37,* 424-438.

Hall, S., & Urga, G. (2000). New developments in the analysis of panel data sets. In Dahiya (Ed.), *The current state of business disciplines* (Vol. 2, pp. 537-564). Spellbound.

Horrow, R. (2001, October 25). *Baseball must find new, creative ways to market game.* Retrieved from www.sportsline.com

Hylan, T., Lage, M., & Treglia, M. (1996). The Coase Theorem, free agency, and Major League Baseball: A panel study of pitcher mobility from 1961 to 1992. *Southern Economic Journal, 62,* 1029-1042.

Kahn, L. (2000). The sports business as a labor market laboratory. *Journal of Economic Perspectives, 14*(3), 75-94.

Levin, R. C., Mitchell, G. J., Volcker, P. A., & Will, G. F. (2000). The report of the independent members of the commissioner's blue ribbon panel on baseball economics, Major League Baseball.

Noll, R. G. (2002). The economics of promotion and relegation in sports leagues: The case of English football. *Journal of Sports Economics, 3*(2), 169-203.

Quirk, J., & Fort, R. (1999). *Hard ball: The abuse of power in pro team sports.* Princeton, NJ: Princeton University Press.

Scully, G. (1974). Pay and performance in Major League Baseball. *American Economic Review, 64,* 915-930.

Sloane, P. J. (1969). The labour market in professional football. *British Journal of Industrial Relations, 7*(2), 181-199.

Szymanski, S., & Kuypers, T. (1999). *Winners and losers: The business strategy of football.* London: Viking.

Szymanski, S., & Ross, S. (2000). *Open competition in league sports.* Retrieved from http://papers.ssrn.com/paper.taf?abstract_id=243756

Szymanski, S., & Smith, R. (1997). The English football industry, profit, performance and industrial structure. *International Review of Applied Economics, 11*(1), 135-153.

Zimbalist, A. (1992). Salaries and performance: Beyond the Scully model. In P. Sommers (Ed.), *Diamonds are forever: The business of baseball* (pp. 109-133). Washington, DC: Brookings Institution.

Zimbalist, A. (2001). Competitive balance in Major League Baseball. *Milken Institute Review, 3*(1).

Zimbalist, A. S. (2002). Competitive balance in sports leagues: An introduction. *Journal of Sports Economics, 3*(2), 111-121.

Stephen Hall is in the School of Management at Imperial College in London.

Stefan Szymanski is a senior lecturer of economics in the School of Management at Imperial College in London.

Andrew S. Zimbalist is a professor of economics at Smith College in Northhampton, Massachusetts.

[14]

Journal of Sport Management, 2005, **19**, 143-169
© 2005 Human Kinetics Publishers, Inc.

A Resource-Utilization Model of Organizational Efficiency in Professional Sports Teams

Bill Gerrard
University of Leeds

The resource-based view explains sustainable competitive advantage as the consequence of an organization's endowment of unique and imperfectly replicable resources. Superior organizational performance, however, depends not only on the organization's resource endowment but also on the efficiency with which the resource endowment is used. In this article a resource-utilization model of a professional sports team is developed in which teams optimize the stock of athletic resources (i.e., playing talent), subject to ownership preferences, over sporting and financial performance. The resource-utilization model is used to analyze the factors influencing the team's current endowment of athletic resources and evaluate the efficiency with which teams utilize both their athletic and allegiance (i.e., fan base) resources to achieve sporting and financial targets. Empirical evidence is presented on the sporting and financial performance of English professional soccer teams in the FA Premier League over the period 1998–2002. It was found that the financial performance of teams is significantly affected by their ownership status.

Introduction

A recent development in sport management has been the application of the resource-based view (RBV) to sports and sports-related organizations (e.g., Amis, 2003; Amis et al., 1997; Mauws et al., 2003; Smart & Wolfe, 2000, 2003). The RBV approach focuses attention on the nature of the resources that create a sustainable competitive advantage for firms. Essentially, the RBV approach differentiates between general resources available to all firms in an industry and firm-specific resources that are unique to the individual firm and only imperfectly replicable by other competing firms. From the RBV perspective, it is the quantity and quality of the firm's endowment of firm-specific resources that explains superior organizational performance.

The author is with the Leeds University Business School, Maurice Keyworth Building, University of Leeds, LEEDS LS2 9JT, U.K.

Superior organizational performance, however, is likely to depend not only on an organization's resource endowment but also on the efficiency with which the resource endowment is utilized. Thus, a complementary line of enquiry is to ask how well organizations utilize their available resources. There are two aspects to the effectiveness with which organizations utilize their resources. First, in organizations characterized by a complex, multidimensional objective function with potential trade-offs between the different dimensions of organizational performance, organizational effectiveness requires that the size and composition of the available stock of resources be optimized relative to the organization's performance targets. Second, given the available stock of resources, organizational effectiveness also requires that the attainable level of performance outcome be maximized. The first aspect of organizational effectiveness represents *allocative efficiency*, whereas the second aspect represents *technical efficiency*. Technical efficiency is amenable to cross-sectional statistical analysis across organizations provided that organizational performance is controlled for differences in the resource endowment.

The objective of this study is to develop a resource-utilization model of professional sports teams in order to analyze the effectiveness with which teams utilize their resource endowment to achieve the maximum attainable levels of sporting and financial performance. A key argument is that professional sports teams face a potential trade-off between sporting and financial performance, but the team ownership (allocative) decision on the optimal mix of performance targets should not necessarily affect the technical efficiency with which both sporting and financial targets are pursued. Empirical evidence presented on organizational efficiency in English professional soccer teams, however, suggests that there is a link between ownership status and the technical efficiency of financial performance. In particular, it was found that those teams that are listed on the London Stock Exchange have lower wage costs, higher revenues, and better operating profit margins, *ceteris paribus*.

The plan of the article is as follows. The existing literatures on the RBV approach and organizational objectives and managerial efficiency in professional sports teams are reviewed. A theoretical resource-utilization model is developed and the conditions for allocative efficiency are derived. The performance trade-off is defined and graphically illustrated. The effects of technical inefficiency are then investigated. The following section sets out the empirical methodology to be adopted—performance ratio analysis and regression analysis. The data set is described and the empirical hypotheses to be tested are stated formally. The empirical results are then presented and discussed. The article concludes with a summary of the key findings, a discussion of the limitations of the present study, and the implications for future research.

Literature Review

The RBV approach emerged in the strategic management literature partly as a reaction to the more structuralist, economics-based approaches in which the strategic decisions of firms are seen as primarily driven by competitive forces. In particular, Porter (1980) identified five forces shaping corporate strategy: competitive rivalry, buyers, suppliers, substitutes, and potential entrants. The RBV approach (Barney, 1991; Grant, 1991; Lado & Wilson, 1994; Peteraf, 1993) is a much more firm-centered approach, identifying the firm-specific resources that enable individual firms to build and profitably exploit sustainable competitive advantage. The RBV approach focuses on those strategic resources (or competencies) that other firms can only replicate imperfectly, if at all.

Researchers in sport management have begun to adopt the RBV approach. For example, Amis, Pant, and Slack (1997) have applied the RBV approach to understanding sport sponsorship. Using two case studies, Amis et al. show that the RBV approach provides a useful framework for analyzing the critical factors determining the success or failure of a sport sponsorship relationship. Specifically, they argue that sport sponsorship can only generate a sustainable competitive advantage if the sponsor invests sufficient time and support to build a unique, imperfectly replicable sponsorship resource that complements the sponsor's other advertising and sponsorship resources. Smart and Wolfe (2000) also use the RBV approach to investigate the resources contributing to the sustainable competitive advantage of Pennsylvania State University's football program. Smart and Wolfe conclude that the program's competitive advantage is founded on "the history, relationships, trust, and culture that have developed within the program's coaching staff over many years. Such complex and interdependent organizational resources tend not to be subject to imitation" (p. 144). Both of these studies focus on the identification of the strategic resources that create competitive advantage. There is no direct attempt to determine the degree to which the strategic resources are utilized to maximize competitive advantage. The focus of the present study is to assess the efficiency with which organizations utilize strategic resources.

The nature of the organizational objective function in professional sports teams has been mainly addressed in the economics-of-sport literature. The standard assumption in the economic theory of the firm is profit maximization. A peculiar feature of the economics of professional team sports, however, is that owners might derive intrinsic value from sporting performance independently of the impact on profitability. This creates the possibility of the "sportsman-owner effect" (Vrooman, 1997) in which team owners aim for a level of sporting performance beyond that consistent with profit maximization. This performance trade-off is investigated formally in the resource-utilization model. Sloane (1971) first questioned the appropriateness of the profit-maximization assumption in the context of professional team sports. Sloane argued that professional soccer teams should be seen as utility maximizers subject to a financial viability constraint. Sloane proposed a multidimensional objective function in which team-owner utility depends on playing success, average attendance, the health of the league, and profits. Noll (1982) also recognized the possibility of alternative motivations for team owners. Noll suggested three alternative team-owner objective functions: (a) unconstrained maximization of games won; (b) profit maximization; and (c) maximization of victories subject to a minimum profit constraint. Apart from recognizing the possibility that team owners might set sporting performance targets inconsistent with profit maximization, however, none of the above studies explicitly discusses the factors that are likely to influence the ownership preferences over sporting and financial performance.

Of particular relevance to the present study is the common assertion that professional sports teams with shares publicly listed and traded in the stock market (hereafter referred to as "listed teams") are likely to be more oriented towards profit maximization. The basic rationale for the change in the organizational objectives after stock market flotation is the requirement of listed teams to create shareholder value for financial investors by generating additional profits (beyond that required to cover the cost of debt) with which to pay dividends. Hamil, Michie, Oughton, and Warby (2001), analyzing the impact of the stock market flotation of many leading professional soccer teams in the UK, argue that listed teams "take (undue) account of the interests of shareholders who have bought shares purely as a financial investment whilst ignoring the interests of supporter shareholders. The interests of non-supporter shareholders are often diametrically opposed to those of supporter shareholders" (p. 3). Conn (1997) and Horton (1997) also argue that there is an increased prioritization of financial performance by listed teams in English professional soccer. Very little empirical evidence, however, has been presented on whether or not listed teams put greater emphasis on financial performance. Indeed some have suggested that the highly competitive nature of the professional team sports industry ensures profit maximization irrespective of the ownership status of teams (see, for example, Szymanski & Kuypers, 1999). The present study investigates whether or not resource-allocation outcomes for listed teams differ significantly from those for nonlisted teams.

Previous studies of organizational efficiency in professional sports teams have concentrated exclusively on the technical efficiency of the coaching process (see Dawson, Dobson, & Gerrard, 2000, for a survey of the existing literature on coaching efficiency). From this perspective, professional sports teams are viewed as a sporting production function in which the output—team performance (i.e., wins or losses)—is produced from the input—playing talent—with individual player performance as an intermediate good. The coaching effect comprises both the *direct coaching effect* of transforming player performance into team performance and the *indirect coaching effect* of transforming "raw" playing talent into on-the-field player performance. The fundamental problem in any empirical investigation of coaching efficiency is the difficulty in controlling for the available stock of playing talent. In order to quantify total coaching efficiency, a measure of player quality is needed that is independent of player and team performance (Gerrard, 2001). Empirical studies have tended to investigate only the direct coaching effect using either player performance data (see, for example, Porter & Scully, 1982) or *ex post* proxy measures of player quality such as player wage costs, which suffer from potential endogeneity problems (see, for example, Szymanski & Kuypers, 1999).

Two studies of coaching efficiency attempt to control for the available stock of playing talent by using *ex ante* measures of player quality: the study by Fizel and D'itri (1996) of college basketball coaches and the study by Dawson et al.

(2000) of coaches in English professional soccer. Both of these studies focus only on the technical efficiency of sporting performance—how efficient teams are in achieving the maximum attainable sporting performance given the available stock of playing talent. The present study seeks to encompass these previous efficiency studies in a more general framework in order to consider both allocative and technical efficiency in professional sports teams with multidimensional objective functions (i.e., sporting and financial performance targets).

The Resource-Utilization Model of a Professional Sports Team

The resource-utilization model of a professional sports team consists of five basic relationships stated in a simple, but general, mathematical form: (1) the team-owner objective function; (2) the sporting production function; (3) the profit function; (4) the revenue function; and (5) the cost function. The initial formulation of the model assumes full technical efficiency so that performance levels are the maximum attainable given the available inputs. The impact of technical inefficiency will be investigated subsequently.

The team-owner objective function (1) can be stated as follows.

$$\text{Max } V_{it} = V(P_{it}, W_{it})$$

The team-owner objective function is the maximization of current ownership (financial and nonfinancial) value, V_{it}. The team is identified by subscript i and the time period by subscript t. Ownership value depends on both current financial profit, P_{it}, and current sporting performance, W_{it}. In order to simplify the theoretical exposition, a single-period model is assumed with current resource-allocation decisions determined only by the expected impact on current sporting and financial performance. A dynamic multiperiod model would require the value function, V, to be specified as a present value function in which current ownership value depends on both current and expected future sporting and financial performance.

The sporting production function (2) is stated in the following equation. It states the (full technically efficient) relationship between current team (sporting) performance and the available stock of playing talent, Q_{it}. The team's available stock of playing talent represents its current endowment of athletic resources, the principal short-term strategic resource in a professional sports team.

$$W_{it} = W(Q_{it})$$

The profit function (3) can be stated as follows.

$$P_{it} = R_{it} - C_{it}$$

Current profits are defined as the difference between current revenue, R_{it} and current costs, C_{it}. Equation 4 provides a simple representation of a team's revenue function.

$$R_{it} = R(W_{it}, F_{it})$$

Team revenue consists of match-day receipts (i.e., ticket sales, corporate hospitality, and other venue-related activities directly associated with the staging of team games), TV and other media revenues, merchandising, sponsorship, and other commercial activities. A team's current revenue depends primarily on its fan base, F_{it}, and its current sporting performance. A team's fan base is defined to include all fans with an affinity to the team, both economically active fans contributing to the team's current revenue streams, as well as passive fans that do not currently purchase goods and services from the team. The team's fan base determines the current size of its potential market and represents the team's current endowment of allegiance resources, the principal long-term strategic resource of a professional sports team. A team's fan base is largely a matter of history and geography. Fan affinity is determined primarily by the demographics of the team's local market and past sporting success. There is likely to be relatively little scope for an established team to significantly build its potential market in the short term. The extent to which a team can realize revenue from its potential market is crucially dependent on its current sporting performance. Winning teams tend to attract more fans to their games (as well as playing more games in elimination tournaments, such as end-of-season playoffs) and become more valuable as media and sponsorship properties.

The cost structure of a professional sports team is primarily driven by player salary costs particularly in an era of free agency in which star players have a high degree of bargaining power. A simple cost function (5) for a professional sports team takes the following form.

$$C_{it} = C(Q_{it}, W_{it})$$

Total current costs depend on the team's stock of playing talent and its sporting performance. The latter allows for performance-related pay such as win bonuses.

Equations 1–5 constitute the resource-utilization model. The team is treated as facing an optimization problem with two value drivers (i.e., sporting and financial performance) and two strategic resources (i.e., athletic and allegiance resources). The key resource-allocation decision is the optimal stock of playing talent because only the team's endowment of athletic resources can be significantly adjusted in the short term. Ultimately the team organization must solve the optimization problem of maximizing ownership value by choosing the appropriate level of playing talent. Given that the optimization problem of the team's hiring policy must be solved in advance of performance outcomes, team management must determine the hiring policy on the basis of expectations of the sporting production, revenue, and cost relationships. In order to simplify the theoretical model, it is assumed that team management has realistic (i.e., information-efficient) expectations of actual outcomes.

Substituting Equations 2–5 into Equation 1 and solving the optimization problem yields the following first-order condition for the maximization of team ownership value (6):

$$V_Q = V_P[\,P_R R_w W_Q + P_C(C_Q + C_w W_Q)\,] + V_w W_Q = 0$$

where V_Q represents the first derivative of the ownership value function with respect to the stock of playing talent, and so on. If a monetary metric is used to measure both financial and nonfinancial value (with no loss of generality), the first derivatives of the ownership value function with respect to profits, and the profit function with respect to revenue and costs, are unity by definition (i.e., $V_P = P_R = -P_C = 1$). Imposing this condition on Equation 6 and rearranging yields Equation 7.

$$(R_w + V_w)W_Q = C_Q + C_w W_Q$$

Equation 7 represents the condition for allocative efficiency in a professional sports team in which ownership value depends on both sporting and financial performance. The left-hand side of the equation shows the marginal benefit of acquiring additional athletic resources. The right-hand side of the equation shows the marginal cost of additional athletic resources. Allocative efficiency requires that marginal benefit equals marginal cost. The marginal benefit of additional athletic resources depends on three factors: (a) the marginal revenue generated from sporting performance, R_w; (b) the marginal ownership value derived directly from sporting performance, V_w; and (c) the marginal impact on sporting performance of additional athletic resources, W_Q. The marginal cost of additional athletic resources depends on three factors: (a) the increase in basic (i.e., nonperformance-related) player remuneration as the team increases its stock of playing talent, C_Q; (b) the increase in performance-related player remuneration as sporting performance improves, C_w; and (c) the marginal impact on sporting performance of additional athletic resources, W_Q. Decreasing marginal benefit and increasing marginal cost are sufficient to guarantee that the first-order conditions represent a maximum.

A special case is a profit-maximizing professional sports team in which sporting performance has no direct impact on ownership value (i.e., $V_w = 0$). In this case sporting performance has only an indirect value to team owners through the impact on financial performance. The optimality condition for a profit-maximizing team is given in Equation 8.

$$R_w W_Q = C_Q + C_w W_Q$$

For a profit-maximizing team, playing talent should be hired up to the point at which the marginal revenue from the expected improvement in sporting performance equals the marginal cost of higher basic and performance-related player remuneration.

Figure 1a and 1b provide a graphical solution of the optimization problem. The first diagram shows the marginal benefit and marginal cost of additional athletic resources. MB_P, the marginal benefit curve for a profit-maximizing team, shows the marginal revenue from additional athletic resources. It is assumed that the marginal revenue of additional playing resources is positive but declining. For a value-maximizing team in which the team owners derive direct benefit from sporting performance independently of the financial effects, the marginal benefit curve shifts outwards to reflect the additional source of ownership value. MB_V represents the marginal benefit curve of a value-maximizing team. The marginal cost curve, MC, shows that incremental player remuneration costs are increasing. (For expositional purposes, both marginal benefit and marginal cost are assumed to be linear functions of athletic resources.) The intersection of the marginal benefit and marginal cost curves represents the optimality point of allocative efficiency. The optimal stock of playing talent for the profit-maximizing team, Q_P, is lower than the optimal stock of playing talent for the value-maximizing team, Q_V. Thus, *ceteris paribus*, the profit-maximizing team has a lower level of sporting performance than the value-maximizing team. At the optimality point for the value-maximizing team, marginal cost exceeds marginal revenue implying that the team has lower profits than the profit-maximizing team. In other words, there is a performance trade-off: the value-maximizing team achieves better sporting performance at the expense of poorer financial performance.

Figure 1b shows the performance trade-off between sporting and financial performance for allocative-efficient teams that optimize the stock of athletic resources to maximize ownership value. The profit-maximizing team has sporting performance, W_P, and financial performance, P_P. The value-maximizing team has better sporting performance, W_V, but lower financial performance, P_V. This is what Vrooman (1997) has termed the "sportsman-owner effect." The performance frontier

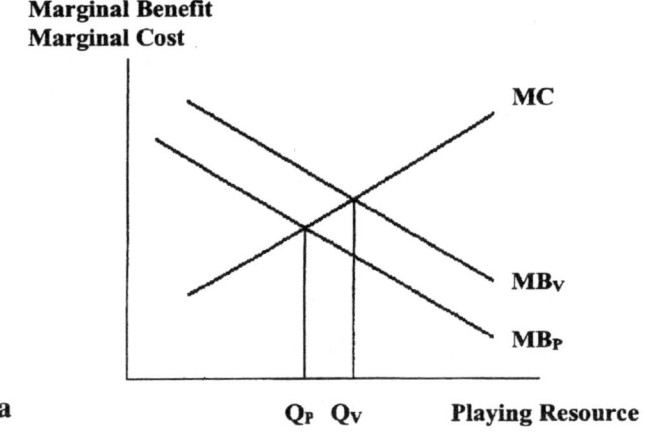

a

Figure 1a — **Full efficiency optimization in a pro sports team: the marginal benefit and marginal cost of additional athletic resources.**
Note. MB_P = marginal benefit curve for profit-maximizing team; MB_V = marginal benefit curve of value-maximizing team; MC = marginal cost curve; Q_P = optimal stock of playing talent for profit-maximizing team; Q_V = optimal stock of playing talent for value-maximizing team.

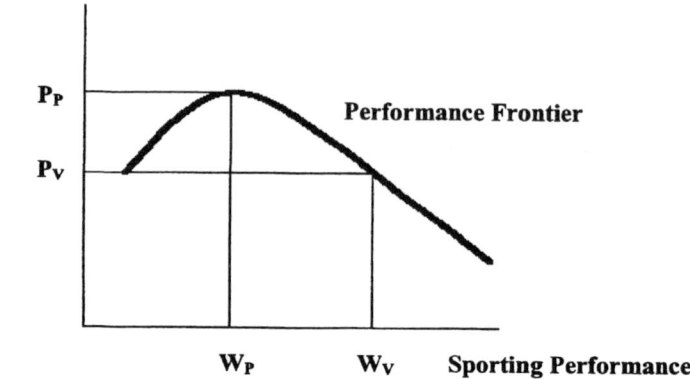

b

Figure 1b — Full efficiency optimization in a pro sports team: the performance trade-off between sporting and financial performance for teams that optimize athletic resources.
Note. W_P = sporting performance of profit-maximizing team; P_P = financial performance of profit-maximizing team; W_V = sporting performance of value-maximizing team; P_V = financial performance of value-maximizing team.

represents the maximum attainable combinations of sporting and financial performance given the team's current endowment of allegiance resources. The performance frontier shifts outward for teams with larger fan bases that are able to generate greater revenues from any given level of sporting performance.

  By construction, the performance frontier represents not only allocative efficiency but also full technical efficiency in the sense of maximum attainable performance from the resources utilized. The possibility of technical inefficiency can be introduced by rewriting the sporting production, revenue, and cost equations to include technical-efficiency parameters as follows:

$$(2a)\ W_{it} = e^W_{it} W(Q_{it})$$

$$(4a)\ R_{it} = e^R_{it} R(W_{it}, F_i)$$

$$(5a)\ C_{it} = (1/e^C_{it}) C(Q_{it}, W_{it})$$

where e^W, e^R, and e^C are the technical-efficiency parameters bounded by zero and unity with unity representing full technical efficiency. The technical-efficiency parameter in the cost function enters as a reciprocal reflecting that technical cost-management efficiency implies lower costs. Solving the optimization problem now yields the following optimality (i.e., allocative-efficient) condition.

$$(9)\ [e^R_{it}R_w + V_w)]e^W_{it}W_Q = (1/e^C_{it})[C_Q + e^W_{it}W_QC_w]$$

The optimizing outcome now depends on (technical) coaching efficiency, e^W, and (technical) managerial efficiency in generating revenue, e^R, and controlling costs, e^C.

The impact of technical inefficiency on the sporting and financial performance is shown graphically in Figure 2. The performance frontier shows the full technical-efficient combinations of sporting and financial performance. The average-efficiency benchmark shows combinations of sporting and financial performance attainable by teams operating with average technical efficiency.

The resource-utilization model of a professional sports team provides a framework for assessing the impact of ownership status on organizational performance. There are two possible impacts: the resource-allocation impact and the technical-efficiency impact. The resource-allocation impact relates to the choice of optimal outcome on the performance frontier. If listed teams put more weight on financial performance relative to sporting performance, then listed teams will set targets on the performance frontier closer to the profit-maximization outcome. This, in turn, implies that listed teams will tend to have a lower stock of playing talent, *ceteris paribus*. The technical-efficiency impact relates to whether or not the distance between the average-efficiency benchmark and the performance frontier is affected by ownership status. If the organizational behavior of listed teams leads to greater technical efficiency, then the observed average-efficiency benchmark will be closer to the performance frontier for listed teams compared with nonlisted teams. The distance between the performance frontier and the average-efficiency benchmark will also reflect the extent to which organizational structure and governance processes limit the principal–agent problem in teams in which there is a significant separation between ownership and control.

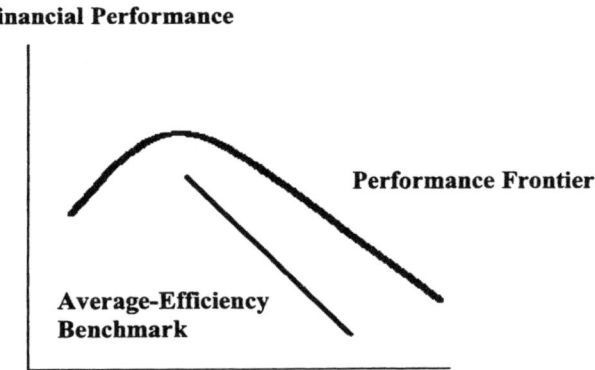

Financial Performance

Performance Frontier

Average-Efficiency Benchmark

Sporting Performance

Figure 2 — Average-Efficiency Benchmark

Methodology, Data, and Hypotheses

The empirical study has three objectives: to investigate the factors influencing the current stock of playing talent in professional sports teams; to identify whether or not professional sports teams face a performance trade-off; and to determine whether ownership status has an impact on organizational effectiveness in professional team sports. Two forms of analysis are used: performance ratio analysis and regression analysis. In the performance ratio analysis, two efficiency ratios are calculated: revenue efficiency and wage efficiency. The regression analysis is initially conducted using ordinary least squares (OLS) multiple regression. OLS multiple regression analysis can provide estimates of average-efficiency (i.e., benchmark) performance relationships across a sample of teams with the inclusion of control variables to allow for systematic differences between teams. In order to allow for the possible endogeneity of some of the control variables in the estimated performance relationships, instrumental variable (IV) estimation is also used. IV estimation is a two-stage estimation procedure that involves estimating reduced-form equations for the endogenous control variables and then using the predicted values in the subsequent estimation of the structural equations.

It should be noted that multiple regression analysis could not provide estimates of the full-efficiency performance frontier. Frontier estimation techniques are available, but these techniques are laden with assumptions and the empirical results can be highly sensitive to the particular frontier specification and estimation technique (see Dawson et al., 2000). Given the fragility of frontier estimation results, the parsimonious stochastic specifications implied by OLS and IV estimation are preferred. Future research should consider the robustness of the empirical results to the use of different estimation techniques.

The data set contains information on English professional soccer teams competing in the FA Premier League during playing seasons 1997/98–2001/02. Professional soccer in Europe is organized on a merit-hierarchy basis with teams being promoted and relegated among league tournaments on the basis of performance in the previous season. The FA Premier League is the highest level domestic league in England with games organized on a round-robin home-and-away basis. There are 20 teams in the league with every team playing 38 league games during the season: 19 home games and 19 away (i.e., on-the-road) games. Three points are awarded for a win and one point for a tied game. There is no sudden-death overtime procedure to resolve tied games. There is also no end-of-season playoff tournament. The teams finishing at the top of the FA Premier League qualify in the following season for one of two European-based tournaments (i.e., the UEFA Champions League or the UEFA Cup) organized by UEFA, soccer's governing body in Europe. The bottom three teams are relegated to the the the top division of the Football League (currently known as the Coca-Cola Championship) and replaced by three promoted teams from that league tournament (the top two teams plus the winner of a playoff tournament involving the teams finishing third to sixth).

The data set consists of playing records, player information, and financial results for all of the teams that appeared in the FA Premier League during seasons

1997/98–2001/02. The data is arranged on a team–season basis with a maximum possible 100 observations (20 teams per season for five seasons) covering 29 different teams. The playing records and player information have been collected from various editions of the *Rothmans Football Yearbook* (Rollin & Rollin, 1970-). The financial information has been collected from various editions of the *Deloitte & Touche Annual Review of Football Finance* (Boon, 1992-) with *pro-rata* adjustments in the four instances of other than 12-month reporting periods. All professional soccer teams in the UK are independently owned, limited companies and are legally required to produce audited annual accounts. The *Deloitte & Touche Annual Review of Football Finance* provides a summary extract of the published accounts of English professional soccer teams in the FA Premier League and the Football League. During the data period, three teams failed to publish full annual accounts because of insolvency proceedings (Crystal Palace, 1997/98; Derby County, 2001/02; Leicester City, 2001/02). Hence, the final data set contains 97 observations.

The performance ratio analysis uses two efficiency ratios: revenue efficiency (10), and wage efficiency (11), which are defined as follows.

Revenue Efficiency = Total Revenue/Average League Gate

Wage Efficiency = Total Wage Costs/League Points

Revenue efficiency represents the ability of a team to generate revenue per capita from its active fan base as measured by the average attendance at home league games. Wage efficiency represents wage costs per league point won. Teams that are more efficient can extract better sporting performance per dollar spent and will have lower wage costs per league point won. Both efficiency ratios are calculated relative to the league average each season.

The two performance ratios are used for purposes of exploratory data analysis to provide a first cut on whether there is any evidence of a relationship between organizational efficiency and ownership status. Student *t* tests are applied to determine whether ownership status has a statistically significant association with revenue efficiency and/or wage efficiency. The performance ratio analysis is purely exploratory in nature because it provides only a bivariate analysis of the relationship between organizational efficiency and ownership status with no control for other potential influences on the relationship such as the market size of teams. Performance ratios are useful summary outcomes that are indicative of key research questions. The very complexity of most input–output relationships in organizations, however, implies that performance ratio analysis seldom provides, on its own, definitive evidence on the underlying causal nexus.

In order to test specific hypotheses derived from the resource-utilization model, multiple regression analysis is applied to a system of five basic structural equations: (a) athletic resource endowment; (b) wage costs; (c) sporting performance; (d) revenue; and (e) profitability (i.e., financial performance). Alternative measures are used for the market size of the team and team playing quality. In addition, in order to allow for the endogeneity of variables within a system of simultaneous equations, IV estimation of the structural equations is undertaken, as well as OLS estimation of both structural and reduced-form equations. A total of 18 estimated regressions are reported with goodness-of-fit and diagnostic-test statistics. The final specifications of the estimated regressions are determined by a diagnostic-led specification search using the White test for heteroscedasticity and the Ramsey RESET test for model misspecification. Logarithmic and quadratic specifications are explored.

The data set contains 97 team–season observations of 11 variables: current sporting performance (PTSRATE), previous sporting performance (PREVPTS and PROMOTED), profitability (OPMARGIN), wage costs (RELWAGE), revenue (RELREV), team playing quality (TTQI, UTQI, and AVINTER), team fan base (AVGATE), and team ownership status (LISTED). In the final reported regressions, logarithmic specifications of wage costs and revenue are also used (lnRELWAGE and lnRELREV).

Current sporting performance, PTSRATE, is measured with respect to league performance only (to avoid comparability issues if performance in other domestic and European knockout tournaments is included). PTSRATE is defined as the total number of points achieved as a ratio of the maximum possible 114 points (38 games × 3 points maximum per game). Previous sporting performance is included as a control variable in all of the reported regressions to allow for the dynamic interdependencies of organizational performance over time including momentum and inertia effects. Two measures of previous sporting performance are used: (a) a binary variable, PROMOTED, that takes the value of unity (zero otherwise) if the team was promoted from the Football League at the end of the previous season; and (b) PREVPTS, defined as the number of league points achieved in the previous season.

Profitability, OPMARGIN, is defined as the operating margin (i.e., operating profits as a percentage of revenue) before player trading. Wage costs, RELWAGE, are measured as team employee wage costs relative to the league annual average in order to allow for inflation effects. Total employee wage costs include both playing and nonplaying staff because teams do not report player wage costs separately in their annual financial accounts. Total employee wage costs, however, are likely to provide a good proxy measure of player wage costs given that player wages are by far the largest component in team employee wage costs and the likelihood that nonplaying wage costs are proportional to playing wage costs. Revenue, RELREV, is also measured relative to the league annual average to allow for inflation effects. Annual team revenue includes all sales revenue from operations (i.e., match-day receipts, media income, sponsorship, merchandising, and other commercial activities) but excludes the proceeds from player trading (that are more appropriately treated as net asset investment rather than operating revenue).

The market size of the team depends on its potential fan base (i.e., allegiance resource endowment). In a spatially concentrated league such as the FA Premier League, it is impossible to adequately define local market boundaries. Several urban areas had two or more Premiership teams during the sample period—London (Arsenal, Chelsea, Tottenham Hotspur, West Ham United, and Wimbledon), Manchester (Manchester City and Manchester United), and Liverpool (Liverpool and Everton). Furthermore, travel distances between teams are relatively small by North American standards with the maximum distance between Premiership teams around 350 miles. Many of the Premiership teams have a significant fan base outside the immediate vicinity of their home stadium. Because the team's fan base is being used as a control variable to capture differences in market size, the active fan base is proxied by AVGATE, measured as the team's average Premiership league attendance per home game over the sample period. The sensitivity of the results to the use of this measure of market size is examined by using RELREV as an alternative proxy measure of market size.

One of the key determinants of sporting and financial performance is the team's athletic resource endowment. Measuring team playing quality is a notoriously difficult task (see Gerrard, 2001). The approach adopted in this study is to use several alternative measures of the team's athletic resource endowment in order to determine whether the empirical results are robust to measurement changes. Three team playing quality variables are defined. TTQI and UTQI are measures based on the playing quality index (PQI) methodology suggested by Gerrard (2001). An alternative measure of team playing quality is provided by AVINTER, defined as the average career number of full international appearances by the team's players weighted by league starting appearances in the current season. In addition, wage costs, RELWAGE, are also used as a proxy variable for the team's athletic resource endowment.

The PQI methodology suggested by Gerrard (2001) involves combining publicly available information on the player's current and career performance into a single index using a set of weights derived from a hedonic-pricing analysis of player transfer fees. The rationale of using weights derived from player transfer fees is that the transfer market represents a market for trading a complex, multidimensional commodity, namely soccer player quality. Hence, an econometric analysis of player transfer fees can reveal what types of current and career performance information about the player appear to be relevant to teams for determining player quality for trading purposes. Furthermore, econometric analysis can impute the weights attached to different types of relevant information by decomposing player transfer fees into a set of implicit (or hedonic) prices of the individual characteristics that constitute soccer player quality.

The formula for calculating PQI has been derived from an analysis of the data set of 1,350 English soccer player transfers used in the previously published econometric study by Dobson and Gerrard (1999). The estimated hedonic-pricing player-transfer-fee equation includes not only player characteristics but also controls for the divisional status of the buying and selling clubs and current trading conditions in the transfer market. Veteran-player effects are also controlled in order to eliminate any age-related bias for veteran players in the PQI formula. Transfer fees for veteran players decline more rapidly with age than playing performance because of the increased probability of retirement and, hence, decreased probability of teams realizing any future sell-on value.

Using the Dobson and Gerrard data set, the following formula for PQI has been derived:

$$(10)\ PQI = \exp(6.575 + 1.201APPRATE + 1.193GOALS1 + 0.410GOALS2 \\ + 0.478U21 + 0.478INTER)$$

where APPRATE is the starting appearance rate in the current season, GOALS1 is the career goal-scoring rate, GOALS2 is the goal-scoring rate in the current season, U21 is a binary variable for under-21 international recognition and INTER is a binary variable for full international recognition. The weighting system has been calibrated such that the mean PQI score is 100. Total team playing quality, TTQI, is the summation of the individual PQI scores. TTQI represents a measure of the total playing resource available to a team during the playing season. The utilized team quality index, UTQI, is measured as the summation of individual PQI scores weighted by the player's appearance rate. UTQI represents how much playing resource has actually been used by teams in league games during the playing season.

Team ownership status, LISTED, is defined as a binary variable with a value of unity (zero otherwise) for those teams listed on the London Stock Exchange including the Alternative Investment Market (AIM). There has been no change in team ownership status during the sample period with Nottingham Forest and Leicester City being the last Premiership teams to float on the London Stock Exchange in October 1997. Descriptive statistics for the nonbinary variables are provided in Table 1.

Table 1   Descriptive Statistics

Variable	Maximum value	Minimum value	Mean	Standard deviation	Coefficient of variation
PTSRATE	0.798	0.211	0.462	0.123	0.267
OPMARGIN	0.515	−0.371	0.067	0.148	2.204
TTQI	3,634.971	2,204.243	2,875.502	295.573	0.103
UTQI	2,174.118	1,076.775	1,593.313	230.024	0.144
RELWAGE	1.968	0.280	1.000	0.422	0.422
AVINTER	33.878	1.244	14.472	7.127	0.492
AVGATE	60,701	17,346	31,762	10,520	0.331
RELREV	3.313	0.376	1.000	0.600	0.600
PREVPTS	0.798	0.316	0.509	0.115	0.227

Note. PTSRATE = current sporting performance; OPMARGIN = profitability; TTQI = total team playing quality; UTQI = utilized team quality index; AVINTER = average career number of full international appearances by the team's players weighted by league starting appearances in the current season; RELWAGE = wage costs; RELREV = revenue; AVGATE= team fan base; PREVPTS = previous sporting performance.

The regression analysis is used to test seven specific hypotheses.

Hypothesis 1 (H1): The total team athletic resource endowment is positively related to team market size, *ceteris paribus.*

   Rationale: As team market size (i.e., allegiance resource endowment) increases, the performance frontier shifts out, allowing teams to invest in a larger stock of playing talent and aspire for better sporting performance for any target level of financial performance.

Hypothesis 2 (H2): The total team athletic resource endowment is lower for listed teams, *ceteris paribus.*

   Rationale: Listed teams tend to operate closer to the profit-maximization outcome on the performance frontier with a higher target level of financial performance and lower target level of sporting performance, implying lower investment in the stock of playing talent.

Hypothesis 3 (H3): Sporting performance is positively related to the utilized team athletic resource endowment, *ceteris paribus.*

   Rationale: As stated in Equation 2, sporting performance depends primarily on the stock of playing talent actually used in sporting contests.

Hypothesis 4 (H4): Team revenue is positively related to sporting performance, *ceteris paribus.*

   Rationale: As stated in Equation 4, team revenue is results-elastic with better sporting performance increasing match-day receipts by attracting more fans, as well as enhancing the value of the team's media and sponsorship properties.

Hypothesis 5 (H5): Team revenue is higher for listed teams, *ceteris paribus.*

   Rationale: Listed teams are more technically efficient in generating revenue as a consequence of higher financial performance targets.

Hypothesis 6 (H6): Financial performance is negatively related to sporting performance, *ceteris paribus.*

   Rationale: As represented by Equation 7, allocative efficiency implies that performance-optimizing teams face a trade-off between financial and sporting performance.

Hypothesis 7 (H7): Financial performance is better for listed teams, *ceteris paribus.*

   Rationale: Listed teams tend to be more technically efficient and, as a consequence, achieve better financial performance for any given endowments of athletic and allegiance resources.

Empirical Results

Performance Ratio Analysis

   The results of the *t* tests of the relationship between organizational efficiency and ownership status are reported in Table 2. Results are reported for revenue efficiency and wage efficiency for individual years, as well as the full sample

Table 2   Revenue and Wage Efficiency: Listed vs. Nonlisted Teams

Year	Revenue efficiency			Wage efficiency		
	Listed	Nonlisted	t test	Listed	Nonlisted	t test
1998	1.128	0.885	.046**	1.097	0.913	.146
1999	1.137	0.863	.033**	0.957	1.043	.284
2000	1.189	0.845	.014**	1.031	0.975	.320
2001	1.097	0.903	.065*	0.934	1.066	.161
2002	0.987	1.016	.418	0.983	1.021	.330
1998–2002	1.106	0.896	.000***	0.998	1.002	.468

Note: t test = p value of one-tailed t test of difference between means with unequal variances.
*Significant at 10% level; ** significant at 5% level; ***significant at 1% level.

period. In the case of revenue efficiency (i.e., revenue per capita), the mean efficiency score for listed teams is higher than the mean efficiency score for nonlisted teams in each individual year, 1998–2001. The difference between listed and nonlisted teams is statistically significant in each of these years. The only exception is 2002 when the mean revenue efficiency score for nonlisted teams was higher, but the difference is not statistically significant. For the full sample period, the mean revenue efficiency score for listed teams is 1.106 compared with 0.896 for nonlisted teams with the difference being significant at the 5% level. This implies that listed teams on average generate 23.4% higher revenue per capita than nonlisted teams.

In the case of wage efficiency (i.e., wage costs per league point), there is no evidence of any statistically significant difference in performance between listed and nonlisted teams. Over the full sample period, listed and nonlisted teams have almost identical mean wage efficiency scores.

Regression Analysis

The 18 estimated regression equations are reported in Tables 3–5. Regressions 1–6 in Table 3 provide estimated models of total athletic resources (TTQI) and wage costs (lnRELWAGE). Regressions 7–12 in Table 4 are estimated models of sporting performance (PTSRATE) and revenue (lnRELREV). Table 5 contains six alternative estimated regressions, 13–18, of financial performance (OPMARGIN). The majority of the reported regressions have insignificant diagnostic-test statistics, indicating no evidence of either heteroscedasticity or specification errors. Some misspecification in the form of heteroscedasticity remains in the wage costs regressions, 4–6, and revenue regressions, 11 and 12, indicating the likelihood of deficiencies in the control variables. Most of the other significant diagnostic-test statistics are associated with possible endogeneity effects and are eliminated by the use of IV estimation.

Table 3 Regression Results: Athletic Resources and Wage Costs (Regressions 1–6)

	1	2	3	4	5	6
Dependent variable	TTQI	TTQI	TTQI	lnRELWAGE	lnRELWAGE	lnRELWAGE
Estimation method	OLS	OLS	IV	OLS	OLS	IV
Independent variables						
constant	2297.6	2573.8	2531.1	9.0384	10.160	10.179
	(32.262)***	(56.327)***	(52.842)***	(66.045)***	(173.529)***	(171.740)***
AVGATE	0.018769			0.000031256		
	(8.841)***			(7.661)***		
RELREV		334.50	383.50		0.74737	0.82708
		(8.693)***	(9.219)***		(9.031)***	(9.350)***
lnRELREV						
PROMOTED	−144.04	−141.60	−120.51	−0.27855	−0.19524	−0.16121
	(−2.346)**	(−2.285)**	(−1.918)*	(−2.361)**	(−1.745)*	(−1.425)
LISTED	5.0386	−25.030	−43.939	−0.036176	−0.11050	−0.13602
	(0.117)	(−0.562)	(−0.970)	(−0.436)	(−1.396)	(−1.697)*
R^2	0.540	0.533		0.470	0.540	
S	204.81	206.38	208.17	0.394	0.367	0.369
F	36.341***	35.322***		27.512***	36.334***	
White test	1.439	0.875	0.969	2.606***	3.619***	3.483***
RESET test	0.872	1.274		3.808*	2.870*	

Note. t ratios in parentheses (two-tailed test); S = standard error of regression; F = test of overall significance of regression (F one-tailed test); White test for heteroscedasticity (F one-tailed test); RESET test for specification errors (F one-tailed test). PTSRATE = current sporting performance; PREVPTS and PROMOTED = previous sporting performance; OPMARGIN = profitability; RELWAGE = wage costs; RELREV = revenue; AVGATE = team fan base; LISTED = team ownership status; lnRELWAGE = logarithmic specifications of wage costs; lnRELREV = logarithmic specifications of revenue; TTQI = total team playing quality; UTQI = utilized team quality index; AVINTER = the average career number of full international appearances by the team's players weighted by league starting appearances in the current season; OLS = ordinary least squares; IV = instrumental variable.
*Significant at 10% level; **significant at 5% level; ***significant at 1% level.

Table 4   Regression Results: Sporting Performance and Revenue (Regressions 7–12)

	7	8	9	10	11	12
Dependent variable	PTSRATE	PTSRATE	PTSRATE	PTSRATE	lnRELREV	lnRELREV
Estimation method	OLS	OLS	IV	OLS	OLS	IV
Independent variables						
constant	−0.19861	0.10986	0.12684	0.084356	−1.7932	−1.8143
	(−3.719)***	(2.738)**	(3.040)***	(2.047)**	(−21.816)***	(−18.948)***
UTQI	0.00024500					
	(6.480)***					
RELWAGE		0.13186	0.17806			
		(4.437)***	(4.507)***			
AVINTER				0.0044544		
				(3.066)***		
PTSRATE					1.6646	1.7587
					(7.601)***	(5.682)***
AVGATE					0.000026628	0.000025919
					(10.379)***	(8.498)***

(continued)

Table 4 (*continued*)

	7	8	9	10	11	12
PROMOTED	-0.16375	-0.12089	-0.075930	-0.19500	-0.055947	-0.051673
	(-6.048)***	(-3.113)***	(-1.631)	(-6.013)***	(-0.970)	(-0.882)
PREVPTS	0.58417	0.44996	0.31218	0.65415		
	(7.038)***	(3.775)***	(2.186)**	(6.295)***		
LISTED	-0.0074858	0.017019	0.017920	0.016407	0.097103	0.096177
	(-0.508)	(1.082)	(1.124)	(0.994)	(2.428)**	(2.399)**
R^2	0.702	0.643		0.607	0.865	0.190
S	0.069	0.076	0.077	0.079	0.190	
F	54.29***	41.419***		35.489***	147.93***	
White test	1.422	0.463	0.530	0.800	1.758*	1.769*
RESET test	3.043*	0.010		1.004	0.001	

Note. t ratios in parentheses (two-tailed test); S = standard error of regression; F = test of overall significance of regression (F one-tailed test); White test for heteroscedasticity (F one-tailed test); RESET test for specification errors (F one-tailed test). PTSRATE = current sporting performance; PREVPTS and PROMOTED = previous sporting performance; OPMARGIN = profitability; RELWAGE = wage costs; RELREV = revenue; AVGATE = team fan base; LISTED = team ownership status; lnRELWAGE = logarithmic specifications of wage costs; lnRELREV = logarithmic specifications of revenue; TTQI = total team playing quality; UTQI = utilized team quality index; AVINTER = the average career number of full international appearances by the team's players weighted by league starting appearances in the current season; OLS = ordinary least squares; IV = instrumental variable.
*Significant at 10% level; **significant at 5% level; ***significant at 1% level.

Table 5 Regression Results: Financial Performance (Regressions 13–18)

	13	14	15	16	17	18
Dependent variable	OPMARGIN	OPMARGIN	OPMARGIN	OPMARGIN	OPMARGIN	OPMARGIN
Estimation method	OLS	OLS	OLS	OLS	IV	IV
Independent variables						
constant	0.25972 (1.646)	0.47790 (2.797)***	0.28582 (1.768)*	0.50844 (3.078)***	0.29376 (1.779)*	0.65566 (3.420)***
PTSRATE	0.29201 (1.931)*	0.051235 (0.763)			−0.14226 (−0.671)	−0.54789 (−2.031)**
UTQI			−0.000013453 (−0.162)	−0.000046035 (−0.586)		
TTQI	−0.00019030 (−2.871)***	−0.00022019 (−3.520)***	−0.00016600 (−2.190)***	−0.00020126 (−2.872)***	−0.00016275 (−2.331)**	−0.00021649 (−3.244)***
AVGATE	0.0000053537 (2.600)**		0.0000072413 (3.868)***		0.0000081066 (3.480)***	
RELREV		0.15860 (3.859)***		0.16981 (5.364)***	0.25315 (4.681)***	0.25315 (4.681)***
PROMOTED	0.080529 (1.996)**	0.075280 (1.940)*	0.069651 (1.707)*	0.072706 (1.741)*	0.064779 (1.526)	0.055809 (1.332)
LISTED	0.077453 (2.835)***	0.059536 (2.207)**	0.081236 (2.849)***	0.061927 (2.264)**	0.081587 (2.856)***	0.052359 (1.813)*
R^2	0.285	0.339	0.255	0.341	0.135	0.133
S	0.130	0.124	0.132	0.124		
F	7.238***	9.354***	6.244***	9.430***		
White test	1.517	1.274	1.655*	1.593*	1.292	0.901
RESET test	0.792	1.313	0.377	1.099		

Note. t ratios in parentheses (two-tailed test); S = standard error of regression; F = test of overall significance of regression (F one-tailed test); White test for heteroscedasticity (F one-tailed test); RESET test for specification errors (F one-tailed test). PTSRATE = current sporting performance; PREVPTS and PROMOTED = previous sporting performance; OPMARGIN = profitability; RELWAGE = wage costs; RELREV = revenue; AVGATE = team fan base; LISTED = team ownership status; lnRELWAGE = logarithmic specifications of wage costs; lnRELREV = logarithmic specifications of revenue; TTQI = total team playing quality; UTQI = utilized team quality index; AVINTER = the average career number of full international appearances by the team's players weighted by league starting appearances in the current season; OLS = ordinary least squares; IV = instrumental variable.
*Significant at 10% level; **significant at 5% level; ***significant at 1% level.

Total athletic resources: Regressions 1–3. The OLS Regressions 1 and 2 show that the team's market size, measured either by average league gate or revenue, is a highly significant determinant of a team's total stock of playing quality. This finding is confirmed by Regression 3, with revenue as the market size measure but using IV estimation to allow for the endogeneity of revenue. In all three regressions, promoted teams have significantly lower stocks of playing quality. Ownership status has no significant impact on the total stock of playing talent in any of the three regressions, and indeed, the estimated coefficients change sign depending on the specification of the market size variable.

Wage costs: Regressions 4–6. Wage costs are significantly positively related to team market size irrespective of the specification of the market size variable. The result is robust to endogeneity effects using IV estimation. Recently promoted teams have a lower level of wage costs, although the effect is insignificant for IV estimation. It is also found in all three regressions that listed teams have lower wage costs with this relationship significant at the 10% level for IV estimation when revenue is used as proxy for team market size.

Sporting performance: Regressions 7–10. All four regressions confirm the standard sporting production function model that team performance is highly significantly dependent on player quality. This result is robust to alternative measures of player quality—the utilized team quality index, wage costs, and international caps. Regression 9 shows that the result is also robust to the possible endogeneity of wage costs. The regressions are also consistent in finding that promoted teams perform significantly worse in the first season after promotion. All the regressions also show that league performance in the previous season is a highly significant predictor of current league performance. There is no evidence of any significant effect of ownership status on sporting performance, although the exact variable specification of player quality has an impact on the estimated relationship with listed teams found to have better sporting performance with *t* ratios near unity when wage costs or international caps are used to control for player quality. The UTQI specification in Regression 6, however, yields better goodness-of-fit properties for the estimated model.

Revenue: Regressions 11–12. The OLS and IV estimates of the revenue model provide very consistent results. There is a highly significant results-sensitive effect of sporting performance on revenue. The average league gate is also a highly significant determinant of revenue. Promoted teams have lower revenues but the effect is not statistically significant. Listed teams have higher revenues and this effect is significant at the 5% level in both the OLS and IV regressions.

Financial performance: Regressions 13–18. All of the reported regressions show very consistent results with the exception of the impact of sporting performance on financial performance. Regressions 13 and 14 provide OLS estimates of the structural model of financial performance showing a positive impact of league performance on the operating margin (and statistically significant if team market size is proxied by average league gate rather than revenue). The relationship between sporting and financial performance, however, is likely to be subject to considerable endogeneity, rendering OLS estimates of structural models subject to serious simultaneous-equation bias. Allowing for endogeneity either through the use of OLS estimation of reduced-form models in Regressions 15 and 16 or IV estimation of the structural models in Regressions 17 and 18 yields a consistently negative but generally statistically insignificant relationship between sporting performance and financial performance. The negative relationship between sporting and financial performance is statistically significant at the 10% level in Regression 18 with the IV estimation method and revenue as the proxy for team market size.

All of the other control variables show very consistent results in the estimated financial performance regressions irrespective of the estimation method and model specification. The total team quality index has a significant negative effect on operating margin in all of the reported regressions, providing clear evidence of the cost effect of increasing the total stock of playing talent. The team market size effect is also consistently positive and highly significant in all the regressions for both average league gate and revenue measures. Promoted teams have higher operating margins but the effect tends to be marginally insignificant after controlling for endogeneity effects. Ownership status has a consistent impact in all of the regressions with listed teams having a significantly higher profit margin.

Discussion

The principal empirical findings of this study can be summarized with reference to the seven hypotheses tested with data from the FA Premier League, seasons 1997/98–2001/02.

H1: The total team athletic resource endowment is positively related to team market size, *ceteris paribus*.

Team market size is a highly statistically significant determinant of total team athletic resources irrespective of variable definition (TQI and wage cost measures of athletic resources or average gate and revenue measures of market size) and estimation method (OLS or IV estimation).

H2: The total team athletic resource endowment is lower for listed teams, *ceteris paribus*.

There is some evidence that listed teams have lower athletic resources, *ceteris paribus*, but the effect is only statistically significant when athletic resources are measured by wage costs, team market size is measured by revenue, and endogeneity effects are allowed for by IV estimation. This suggests that the effect is largely a technical (cost) efficiency effect with listed teams seemingly able to acquire playing talent at lower unit cost. The efficiency effect is relatively large with Regressions 5 and 6 indicating efficiency gains for listed teams of 11–14%. By contrast, regressions 2 and 3 indicate that the reduction in team quality for listed teams is only around 1%, and the effect is statistically insignificant.

H3: Sporting performance is positively related to the utilized team athletic resource endowment, *ceteris paribus.*

Sporting performance is positively and highly significantly related to a team's stock of playing talent irrespective of whether measured by UTQI, wage costs, or international caps. Regression 7, using UTQI as the measure of team athletic resources, provides the highest goodness of fit, but this might be because of the use of current season information in the construction of the index.

H4: Team revenue is positively related to sporting performance, *ceteris paribus.*

Team revenue is highly results-elastic with league performance (measured by PTSRATE) being statistically significant at the 1% level. The IV estimate in Regression 12 implies that a 1% improvement in points won is associated with a 0.81% rise in revenues relative to the league average.

H5: Team revenue is higher for listed teams, *ceteris paribus.*

Listed teams have statistically significant higher revenues, *ceteris paribus*, even after allowing for possible endogeneity effects. This technical (revenue) efficiency effect is estimated to be 9.6% in Regression 12 after controlling for sporting performance, team market size, divisional promotion, and endogeneity effects.

H6: Financial performance is negatively related to sporting performance, *ceteris paribus.*

There is evidence of a performance trade-off between sporting and financial targets after controlling for endogeneity effects using either reduced-form or IV estimation. Regression 18, using IV estimation and measuring team market size by revenue, provides the strongest support for the performance trade-off. The estimated average effect of a 1% improvement in league performance (i.e., points won) is a decrease in the operating margin of 0.25%. This estimated effect is significant at the 5% level.

H7: Financial performance is better for listed teams, *ceteris paribus.*

All of Regressions 13–18 provide strong support for a highly statistically significant improvement in financial performance in listed teams relative to nonlisted teams, *ceteris paribus.* The effect is robust to alternative model specifications and estimation methods. The magnitude of the effect depends on the measurement of team market size. Using revenue measures of team market size yields an estimated effect of between 5.2 and 6.2%. The estimated effect rises to 7.7–8.2% if average league gate is used as the market size variable. The preferred estimate of the overall impact of stock market listing on financial performance is 5.2% based on IV estimation with team market size proxied by team revenue relative to league average.

Overall, the empirical evidence strongly supports the existence of a relationship between team ownership status and the financial performance of professional soccer teams in the FA Premier League. Although there is some evidence of a performance trade-off, there is no evidence to indicate that listed teams differ significantly in resource allocation or sporting performance. The empirical evidence indicates team ownership status has primarily a technical (not allocative) efficiency effect on financial performance. Listed teams have lower wage costs, higher revenues, and higher operating margins, *ceteris paribus*. It is this technical-efficiency gain in listed teams that has mitigated the effects of the performance trade-off on the resource-allocation decision. Increased financial efficiency has allowed listed teams to improve financial performance without any significant impact on the accumulated stock of playing talent and sporting performance.

The superior financial efficiency of listed teams highlights an important but often overlooked strategic resource in professional sports teams, namely, the stock of general (i.e., commercial) managerial resources. Allegiance resources (i.e., team market size), athletic resources, and coaching resources are all widely recognized as significant drivers of organizational performance in professional team sports, and the present study reinforces the importance of these strategic resources. It is also clear, however, that flotation on the stock market is associated with efficiency gains linked to wide-ranging organizational changes affecting business structures, governance processes, and managerial recruitment. In particular, listed teams are required to be more transparent in their commercial activities with stock market requirements for public disclosure of significant information pertaining to their commercial activities and future prospects. Shareholders in listed teams are, therefore, better able to monitor and assess organizational performance and, as a consequence, provide stronger incentives for management to maximize organizational efficiency. This, in turn, is likely to lead to listed teams assigning greater status and financial rewards to commercial management functions resulting in a greater propensity to recruit specialists with business experience outside the professional team-sports industry (i.e., the "suits"). In contrast, nonlisted teams face less pressure from investors to transform traditional organizational structures in which commercial management plays a subordinate role to the sporting functions managed by former players (i.e., the "shirts").

The causal relationship between flotation on the stock market and improved financial efficiency is complex and not necessarily unidirectional. Although stock market requirements and investor expectations undoubtedly act as a strong incentive to maximize organizational efficiency, it is also likely that there is a selection bias in the sense of teams with a more commercial orientation being more likely to seek and successfully achieve a stock market listing. In other words, the process of organizational change and improved financial efficiency associated with stock market listing might precede flotation and might even influence the decision. The empirical evidence indicates a strong association between team ownership status and financial efficiency but does not determine the direction of causality.

Conclusions, Limitations, and Future Research

The resource-utilization model of a professional sports team distinguishes between allocative efficiency (i.e., the optimal matching of an organization's resource endowment to its performance targets) and technical efficiency (i.e., the maximization of performance outcomes relative to an organization's resource endowment). The empirical evidence provides strong statistical support for an association between ownership status and financial efficiency among professional soccer teams in the FA Premier League. Although there is some evidence of a potential trade-off between sporting and financial performance, the financial-efficiency gains associated with stock market flotation have largely offset any potential negative resource-allocation effect on sporting performance. To date, the arguments of Conn (1997), Horton (1997), and Hamil et al. (2001) on the likely detrimental effects of stock market listing on sporting performance are not supported by the available evidence, although this resource-allocation effect might eventually prove significant once technical-efficiency gains have been more fully exhausted.

The principal limitation to the present study is the exploratory nature of the "macro" empirical analysis. Cross-sectional multivariate statistical techniques have been used to identify the systematic (i.e., nonlocal) drivers of organizational performance across teams and to determine the relative importance of systematic and organization-specific (i.e., local) performance drivers. Cross-sectional macro analysis, however, must be complemented by "micro" comparative case-study analysis that provides a detailed investigation of individual organizations. Microanalysis is necessary to understand the causal processes underlying observed differences in organizational performance, particularly the local, organization-specific drivers. Microanalysis is required to determine whether the differences in organizational performance are because of real behavioral differences or statistical anomalies arising from measurement errors and/or other data and estimation problems. Given the strong statistical evidence of the financial-efficiency gains associated with stock market flotation, detailed comparative case studies are urgently required for both listed and nonlisted teams to understand more fully the specific strategic and organizational changes associated with the shift to the public trading of shares in professional sports teams.

References

Amis, J. (2003). Good things come to those who wait: The strategic management of image and reputation at Guinness. *European Sport Management Quarterly*, **3**, 189-214.

Amis, J., Pant, N., and Slack, T. (1997). Achieving a sustainable competitive advantage: A resource-based view of sport sponsorship. *Journal of Sport Management*, **11**, 80-96.

Barney, J.B. (1991). Firm resources and sustained competitive advantage. *Journal of Management*, **17**, 99-120.

Boon, G. (Ed.). (1992-). *Deloitte & Touche annual review of football finance*. Manchester, UK: Deloitte Touche.

Conn, D. (1997). *The football business: Fair game in the '90s?* Edinburgh: Mainstream.

Dawson, P., Dobson, S., & Gerrard, B. (2000). Estimating coaching efficiency in professional team sports: Evidence from English association football. *Scottish Journal of Political Economy, 47*, 399-421.

Dobson, S., & Gerrard, B. (1999). The determination of player transfer fees in English professional soccer. *Journal of Sport Management, 13*, 259-279.

Fizel, J.L., & D'itri, M. (1996). Estimating managerial efficiency: The case of college basketball coaches. *Journal of Sport Management, 10*, 435-445.

Gerrard, B. (2001). A new approach to measuring player and team quality in professional team sports. *European Sport Management Quarterly, 1*, 219-233.

Grant, R.M. (1991). The resource-based theory of competitive advantage: Implications for strategy formulation, *California Management Review, 33*, 114-135.

Hamil, S., Michie, J., Oughton, C., & Warby, S. (2001). Recent developments in football ownership. In S. Hamil, J. Michie, C. Oughton, & S. Warby (Eds.), *The changing face of the football business* (pp. 1-10). London: Frank Cass.

Horton, E. (1997). *Moving the goalposts: Football's exploitation.* Edinburgh: Mainstream.

Lado, A.A., & Wilson, M.C. (1994). Human resource systems and sustained competitive advantage: A competency-based perspective. *Academy of Management Review, 19*, 699-727.

Mauws, M.K., Mason, D.S., & Foster, W.A. (2003). Thinking strategically about professional sports. *European Sport Management Quarterly, 3*, 145-164.

Noll, R.G. (1982), Major league sports. In W. Adams (Ed.), *The structure of American industry* (6th ed., pp. 348-387). New York: Macmillan.

Peteraf, M.A. (1993). The cornerstones of competitive advantage: A resource-based view. *Strategic Management Journal, 14*, 179-191.

Porter, M.E. (1980). *Competitive strategy.* New York: Free Press.

Porter, P. & Scully, G.W. (1982), Measuring managerial efficiency: The case of baseball. *Southern Economic Journal, 48*, 642-650.

Rollin, G., & Rollin, J. (Eds.). (1970-). *Rothmans football yearbook.* London: Headline.

Sloane, P.J. (1971). The economics of professional football: The football club as a utility maximiser. *Scottish Journal of Political Economy, 18*, 121-146.

Smart, D.L., & Wolfe, R.A. (2000). Examining sustainable competitive advantage in intercollegiate athletics: A resource-based view. *Journal of Sport Management, 14*, 133-153.

Smart, D.L., & Wolfe, R.A. (2003). The contribution of leadership and human resources to organisational success: An empirical assessment of performance in Major League Baseball. *European Sport Management Quarterly, 3*, 165-188.

Szymanski, S., & Kuypers, T. (1999). *Winners and losers: The business strategy of football.* London: Viking.

Vrooman, J. (1997). A unified theory of capital and labor markets in Major League Baseball. *Southern Economic Journal, 63*, 594-619.

Part III
Match Prediction and Betting Market Efficiency

[15]

Economica, **56**, 323-41

Information, Prices and Efficiency in a Fixed-Odds Betting Market

By Peter F. Pope and David A. Peel

Strathclyde Business School, Glasgow, and University College of Wales, Aberystwyth

Final version received 6 June 1988. Accepted 19 December 1988.

This paper examines the efficiency of the Association Football betting market in the UK. The notable features of this market are that the odds are fixed some time before matches occur and differ between bookmaking firms. Whilst there is some evidence of *ex post* inefficiency there did not appear to be profitable betting strategies that could have been implemented *ex ante* during the sample period.

INTRODUCTION

Evidence of inefficiencies in financial markets is now appearing with increasing regularity.[1] One response to such evidence is to question the testing methodology presently employed by the researchers. An example of such a response is Ball (1978), who questions the specifications of the expectations models typically employed in deriving measures of residual returns in market reaction studies. An alternative explanation of results consistent with market inefficiency is that market participants are capable of employing currently available information in an inefficient manner when forming their expectations. There does seem to be mounting evidence that this explanation is not as implausible as it might first appear in a world dominated by the efficient markets and rational expectations paradigms. For example, analyses of the expectations data provided by surveys of financial market participants have found evidence of inefficiency and bias in inflation expectations (Figlewski and Wachtel, 1980; Carlson and Parkin, 1975). Also, controlled laboratory experiments have suggested that individuals tend to make systematic subjective judgment biases (Tversky and Kahneman, 1978). Hence if individuals are thought to have inherent tendencies to form biased judgments, perhaps it is not so surprising that evidence consistent with judgmental bias is found at the market level. Whether such bias is exploitable is an empirical question lying at the heart of the definition of market efficiency.

This paper examines the efficiency of the betting market concerned with the outcomes of Association Football matches in the United Kingdom. Bookmakers offer odds against each of three possible outcomes of a football match: home team win, away team win and drawn match. The motivation for the analysis presented here is twofold. The first stems from our observation that the odds offered by different bookmakers on the same outcomes of specific matches vary. This suggests that, even if the choices of match and outcome on which a bet is to be placed are independent of the odds quoted (which clearly in general is unlikely to be the case), the bettor should not be indifferent towards the bookmaking firm with which a bet is placed. Although other factors, such as the credit facilities offered, the levels of maximum payouts, location and habit, are likely to be important determinants of a bettor's choice, *ceteris paribus* a rational bettor will prefer to place a bet on a given outcome with the bookmaker offering the most favourable odds on that outcome. As long as one bookmaker does not dominate the others by taking a uniformly lower margin on his book, it seems that, by combining bets on the different outcomes of a match with different bookmakers, a bettor may be able to reduce the size of his gamble (i.e. his exposure to risk) and/or reduce the size of his expected loss. Perhaps the most remarkable statistic highlighting the importance to bettors of divergent odds is that, on one occasion during our sample period, it was possible to place a combination of bets on the three outcomes of a match which *guaranteed* an arbitrage return of 12 per cent before tax and 2 per cent net of tax within a mater of hours. The return would have been risk-free assuming that the two firms of bookmakers involved in the strategy had accepted and honoured the bets. There are also numerous instances in our database where, in the absence of tax, positive risk-free profits could have been made.

The second source of motivation for this analysis stems from the *a priori* reasonable assumption that the bookmakers' posted odds reflect their expectations as to the various outcomes. The analysis will therefore provide further evidence from a previously unexamined and novel data source on the rationality of directly observed expectations of 'expert agents', in this case bookmakers.[2] In this respect, betting in a fixed odds market differs in at least two important respects from racetrack betting. First, the odds are not determined jointly by buyers and sellers, but rather are fixed unilaterally by each seller—the bookmaker—several days before matches take place. Interestingly, once posted, the odds offered are invariant to the volume of bets placed on various outcomes, or indeed to any news that might be received by the market. Whereas the analogy drawn in previous work has been between the betting market and the spot market in securities, here the betting market is closer to an options market where contingent claims are sold at prices fixed for a non-trivial interval of time. The odds offered represent the outcome-contingent returns.

In this paper we examine the efficiency of the fixed odds market described above. We do this by testing for the existence of *ex ante* profitable betting strategies based upon both observable biases in the odds set by bookmakers, and broader information sets including the odds set by competing bookmakers and a set of 'expert' forecasts published after the odds have been posted.[3] There is some weak evidence of bettors being able to exploit publicly available information in a profitable manner, the major impediment to systematic profits being a substantial tax wedge of 10 per cent.

The remainder of the paper is organized as follows. In Section I a brief review of the literature on betting market efficiency is presented. In Section II we set out a model of how odds might be set. In Section III the empirical characteristics of the data are explored. In Section IV we assess the efficiency of the market by examining whether profitable betting strategies exist. Finally, in Section V we set out the salient implications of our analysis in a brief conclusion.

I. Literature Review

Several recent studies have explored the analogy between securities markets and betting markets at the empirical level. In general, they have sought to test whether the odds (prices) established in betting markets reflect the true probabilities of occurrence of specific outcomes of events, usually horse races. The evidence suggests that there is a systematic tendency for the betting public to overbet on long-shots and to underbet on favourites (Rossett, 1971; Ali, 1979; Snyder, 1978; Asch *et al.*, 1984). The implication is that a betting strategy that selects favourites will generate higher returns (or lower losses), on average, than strategies involving bets on longer-priced horses. Taking into consideration the average track take of about 18 per cent causes such a strategy to give rise to an average 9 per cent net loss approximately (Hausch *et al.*, 1981, p. 1438). As win bets are placed on progressively longer-priced horses, however, the average loss increases, implying the existence of a *negative* risk premium in this market. This result may be explained either by the existence of inefficiency in the market, i.e. biased expectations, or by heterogeneous risk attitudes among bettors, some of whom act as risk-lovers (Hausch *et al.*, 1981; Asch *et al.*, 1984).

Recently, Hausch *et al.* (1981) have developed a profitable system based on the bias in the market's estimated probability of winning. The model they developed involves place and show bets and is based solely on the relationship between current odds. The existence of a successful system is interpreted as a form of technical analysis which demonstrates weak-form market inefficiency. Asch *et al.* (1984) also find a profitable strategy of place and show betting[4] on horses predicted as having high probabilities of winning, using a logit model based on observable betting patterns. Although they question whether their result provides evidence of an exploitable market inefficiency, their paper does provide a further example of a weak-form test of efficiency. Semi-strong form tests of efficiency would necessarily utilize a wider information set. An example of this type of test is Figlewski (1979), who finds, for the win pool, that bettors as a group seem to fully impound into the market odds the information contained in the publicly available forecasts produced by professional handicappers, although off-track bettors are less successful in this regard. Finally, Crafts (1985) reports evidence for Britain on the profitability of strategies based on the relationship between forecast and starting odds, finding that it is possible for expected losses to be reduced using publicly available information. He also concludes that the market offers insiders the opportunity for profitable exploitation of private information.

In a different market, Vergin and Scriabin (1978) have identified exploitable biases in the setting of pointspreads for betting on National Football League games in the United States. They find that strategies involving betting on the underdog team, betting against the previous week's biggest winner and betting on 'turnaround' teams and the strongest teams were all profitable. Also, they show that arbitrage possibilities exist, based on the differential pointspreads offered by different bookmakers, particularly in different cities. Combining syndicated betting with one of their strategies would, they claim, give rise to a profit margin in excess of 10 per cent.

II. MODEL DEVELOPMENT

It appears reasonable, *a priori*, to assume that a bookmaker will set odds that reflect his subjective probability estimate relating to each outcome and a margin. Because the odds are fixed and set some time before a match is played, in principle the bettor will have more information concerning 'form' than the bookmaker. This means that there is a risk for the bookmaker that some posted odds will be more favourable than those that would be set conditional upon the information set at the time a bet is placed. Consequently, the margin will reflect the expected variance of the new information which accrues after the odds are posted, the extent to which the bookmaker wishes to insure against the risk and a brokerage fee.

As an illustrative example, suppose that there are just two outcomes on which bets can be placed. At the time the odds are posted, each has a probability of 0·5; i.e. the bet is even money (1/1). It is known that after the odds are posted equally probable information signals may be received which will show *either* that the probabilities are 0·75 for outcome 1 and 0·25 for outcome 2, or *vice versa*. Symmetry requires the bookmaker to quote the same odds for the two outcomes. He knows that bettors will wait for the information and then bet on whichever outcome has a probability of 0·75. Therefore, if the bookmaker wants to earn a 10 per cent margin on turnover, odds of 0·85 (2/11 approximately) for each outcome must be quoted if the risk associated with new information is to be fully insured against.

In fact, the gross *ex post* margin (the summation of the implied probabilities across all outcomes minus unity) averages only approximately 7 per cent for our sample. To illustrate the impact on the quoted odds, if the true odds against each of three outcomes were 2/1 against (a situation of maximum uncertainty) a 7 per cent allocated equally across the three outcomes would change the odds to 9/5 for each outcome. Alternatively, a 7 per cent margin allocated entirely to one outcome would change the odds for that outcome from 2/1 to 3/2. The small size of the margin suggests that the perceived variance of new information arriving between the fixing of odds and the matches being played is relatively insignificant. However, it is possible that the perceived variance differs across matches and that as a consequence the margin varies. One plausible model is that the margin is related to the propensity for the bookmaker to be surprised, as measured (say) by the Theil (1967) entropy statistic. This was considered in our empirical tests, but no evidence was found that the margins were related to the potential surprise (or, conversely, the degree of uncertainty) associated with a match.

The research on horse-race betting referred to in Section I has generally calculated odds (and hence the betting market's consensus probability estimates) directly from data on the aggregate dollar value of bets placed on each possible outcome (winning horse) in a particular event (race). In the fixed odds market being considered here, the volumes of different bets are unobservable. Rather, the focus of attention is on the *implied* subjective probability estimates of the agents who independently set the odds—the bookmakers.

The quoted odds against outcome j of match i occurring can be expressed in terms of the return θ_{ij} on a one-unit stake if outcome j is realized. If a bet is successful, then, before tax, the bettor receives back $(1 + \theta_{ij})$ for every one unit staked. Betting tax is charged proportionately at 10 per cent of the initial stake, and this constitutes a considerable transaction cost to be covered by any successful trading strategy.

From the perspective of a bookmaker, the odds (ϕ_{ij}) are modelled as depending on the perceived probability of outcome j of event i occurring (p_{ij})

and a margin (λ_{ij}) in the following manner:

$$(1) \qquad \phi_{ij} = \frac{1}{(1 + \theta_{ij})} = p_{ij} + \lambda_{ij}$$

where ϕ_{ij} is the equivalent 'probability' contained in odds of $\theta_{ij} : 1$. Thus, if each of the three outcomes of a match were considered to be equally likely, if the bookmaker did not wish to earn any profit for providing his brokerage service, and if no new information were released after the odds were posted, then λ_{ij} would be zero and the odds offered against each outcome would be $2:1$, i.e. $\theta_{ij} = 2$, and $\phi_{ij} = p_{ij} = 0.333$, $j = 1, 2, 3$. In practice, the bookmaker is assumed to expect to earn a positive margin with $\lambda_{ij} > 0$ and $\phi_{ij} > p_{ij}$.

III. DATA CHARACTERISTICS

(a) The data set

The odds at which bets on the outcomes of Football League matches could be placed were obtained for the 1981/2 season. Betting coupons were collected each week from the local branches of each of four national chains of bookmakers (firms A, B, C and D). Over the same period, the forecasts made by professional tipsters in six national newspapers were also collected. The outcome of each match was recorded using the following convention: home team win, $j = 1$; away team win, $j = 2$; and drawn match, $j = 3$. A sample of 1291 league matches was found for which a complete set of data existed. The sample was then divided into two subsamples. The first subsample is used for the preliminary data analysis and for identifying possible biases in the quoted odds. It comprises the first 1066 matches which were held between weeks 1 and 32 of the season. The second subsample comprises the remaining 225 matches which took place in weeks 33–37 of the season. This subsample is used for the holdout sample testing of efficiency.

(b) Size and distribution of margins

The first step in the analysis is to examine the size and the distribution of the margins in the four bookmaking firms. A comparison between the mean value of the odds for each outcome, ϕ_j, and the proportion of the sample for which outcome j was realized, μ_j, provides some insight into possible differences between firms in the mean margins on specific outcomes, λ_j. From (1), the *ex post* mean value of λ_j can be expressed as

$$(2) \qquad \lambda_j = \phi_j - \mu_j.$$

Since μ_j is simply the proportion of matches in the sample for which outcome j is realized, we can compute the mean margins earned by the four firms on outcome j. Table 1 compares the mean values of λ for the four firms and also reports the values of the mean and standard deviation of the odds expressed as equivalent probabilities and the population frequencies of each outcome during the sample period. The posted probabilities are on average higher than the outcome frequencies for all firms and outcomes, and hence the average margins are uniformly positive although they are different across firms. Overall, the mean margins on the home win outcome (average 4·6 per cent) are consistently higher than for the away win (average 2·6 per cent) and draw outcomes (average 2·0 per cent). A noticeable feature of Table 1 is the consistently low standard deviations for the draw probabilities compared with the other two outcomes, the order of magnitude of this difference being approximately 4. This might suggest that little attempt is made to adjust the odds set against draw outcomes to reflect differing perceptions about the probability of this outcome. As will be discussed below, this behaviour could simply reflect a general inability to predict draw outcomes with any degree of reliability, in which case the unconditional (constant) probability might be the most appropriate basis for setting the odds.

The differences in average margins were subjected to formal significance tests using the paired t-test under the assumption that the populations are not independent. The results are reported in Table 2 for the six pairwise comparisons between firms. In this sample 47·75 per cent of matches turned out to be home wins, 24 per cent were away wins, and 27·7 per cent were drawn. In Table 1, the top panel shows that for the home win outcome ($j = 1$) the ranking of firms is $B < A < C < D$. However, the test statistics in Table 2 indicate that only firm D sets a statistically significant higher margin. For the away win outcome ($j = 2$) the centre panel in Table 1 shows that the firms are ranked $D < C < A < B$, but the test statistics in Table 2 show that the differences between the pairs C/D and A/C are not statistically significant. The bottom panel of Table 1 shows that for the draw outcome ($j = 3$) the firms are ranked $B < A < C < D$, and these differences are found to be significantly different in Table 2, with the exception of A/C.

The preceding analysis suggests that, if a bettor were operating a simple strategy of placing randomly selected bets with specific firms, only firm B ($j = 1$ and $j = 3$) and firm D ($j = 2$) ought to be used; on average, they offer the best value for these types of bets.

TABLE 1

ODDS AND MARGINS SUMMARY STATISTICS

	Firm			
	A	B	C	D
ϕ_1	0·5199	0·5162	0·5218	0·5344
σ_1	0·0955	0·0986	0·0953	0·0939
μ_1	0·4775	0·4775	0·4775	0·4775
λ_1	0·0424	0·0387	0·0443	0·0569
ϕ_2	0·2722	0·2805	0·2697	0·2646
σ_2	0·0808	0·0835	0·0829	0·0732
μ_2	0·2458	0·2458	0·2458	0·2458
λ_2	0·0264	0·0347	0·0239	0·0188
ϕ_3	0·2952	0·2905	0·2964	0·3043
σ_3	0·0209	0·0212	0·0209	0·0214
μ_3	0·2767	0·2767	0·2767	0·2767
λ_3	0·0185	0·0138	0·0197	0·0276

Notes: σ_j is the standard deviation of ϕ_j. No. of observations: 1066.

TABLE 2

PAIRED t-TEST FOR DIFFERENCES IN
MEAN RETURNS

	Firm		
	B	C	D
$j = 1$			
A	0·88	−0·06	−3·53[a]
B		−1·45	−4·36[a]
C			−3·07[a]
$j = 2$			
A	−2·34[b]	0·71	2·29[b]
B		3·00[a]	4·68[a]
C			1·51
$j = 3$			
A	5·15[a]	−1·33	−9·93[a]
B		−6·47[a]	−14·96[a]
C			−8·62[a]

[a] Significant t-statistic at the 1 per cent level. [b] Significant t-statistic at the 5 per cent level.

(c) OLS Analysis of inter-firm odds differences

In the previous section the focus of attention was the population means. However, it is also possible to obtain an estimate of any systematic differences in the odds offered by the four firms by conducting simple pairwise comparisons of the odds, by regressing the odds of one firm on the odds of another. Under the null hypothesis of no systematic differences between firms, the intercept should be indistinguishable from zero and the slope coefficient should equal unity. The results in Table 3 show that the hypothesis that the intercept term equals zero can be rejected in the majority of cases and the hypothesis that the slope equals unity can be rejected for all 18 pairwise comparisons. The results are particularly striking for the draw comparisons where the correlation is relatively low between firms, the coefficient of determination ranging from 0·50–0·69 compared with 0·84–0·90 for home wins and 0·85–0·90 for away wins. Also, the point estimate of the slope coefficient is generally relatively low for draw odds, ranging from 0·641–0·827. The results are highly suggestive that the four firms are employing different models in their odds-setting. Differences might be explained either by variations in the size of the margins (μ_{ij}) across firms, for which some evidence has already been presented in the previous sub-section, or by varying degrees of bias in the probability estimates (p_{ij}) underlying the odds.

(d) Intra-distribution bias

The evidence for horse-race betting presented in Hausch et al. (1981) and others points to varying degrees and directions of bias for various levels of the odds against a particular outcome. In particular, there appears to be a consistent pattern of bias in the tails of odds distributions. In an attempt to establish whether biases and/or differences in margins exist over different

TABLE 3

REGRESSION RESULTS FOR PAIRWISE COMPARISONS OF ODDS

Dep. var.	Const.	ϕ_B	ϕ_C	ϕ_D	R^2
$j = 1$					
ϕ_A	0·045 (0·005)	0·920 (0·009)			0·90
ϕ_A	0·039 (0·006)		0·921 (0·012)		0·85
ϕ_A	0·016 (0·006)		0·943	(0·012)	0·86
ϕ_B	0·020 (0·007)		0·951 (0·012)		0·85
ϕ_B	−0·003 (0·007)			0·972 (0·012)	0·86
ϕ_C	0·025 (0·007)			0·930 (0·013)	0·84
$j = 2$					
ϕ_A	0·015 (0·003)	0·917 (0·010)			0·90
ϕ_B	0·031 (0·003)		0·894 (0·011)		0·85
ϕ_A	0·001 (0·003)			1·026 (0·013)	0·86
ϕ_B	0·032 (0·003)		0·922 (0·012)		0·85
ϕ_B	0·000 (0·004)			1·060 (0·013)	0·86
ϕ_C	−0·007 (0·004)			1·048 (0·014)	0·85
$j = 3$					
ϕ_A	0·057 (0·005)	0·821 (0·017)			0·69
ϕ_A	0·050 (0·006)		0·827 (0·021)		0·58
ϕ_A	0·068 (0·006)			0·747 (0·019)	0·59
ϕ_B	0·054 (0·007)		0·800 (0·023)		0·53
ϕ_B	0·061 (0·006)			0·754 (0·020)	0·58
ϕ_C	0·101 (0·006)			0·641 (0·019)	0·50

Note: standard errors in parentheses.

ranges of odds in our data set, odds were grouped and the mean odds compared against the actual frequencies as before. The results are reported in Tables 4(a)-(d). The estimated standard errors (σ_e) are given by $\sigma = (S^2/N)^{1/2}$, where S^2 is the actual frequency sample variance. To quantify the importance of any potential bias, the *ex post* mean return (r) on all matches in a particular group was calculated. When the value of r is positive, the average returns to betting on the matches in the group was positive. If the bettor had been aware of the

TABLE 4

MEAN ODDS ACTUAL FREQUENCIES AND ACTUAL RETURNS

ϕ	n	$\bar{\phi}$	$\bar{\mu}$	σ	r	n_1	r_1
(a) Firm A							
$j = 1$							
<0·400	125	0·351	0·256	0·039	−0·244	42	−0·316
0·400–0·449	184	0·430	0·446	0·037	0·037	38	−0·076
0·450–0·499	59	0·474	0·559	0·065	0·176	23	0·009
0·500–0·549	218	0·517	0·445	0·034	−0·139	23	0·265
0·550–0·599	204	0·568	0·505	0·035	−0·111	33	−0·193
0·600–0·649	193	0·614	0·596	0·035	−0·026	43	−0·172
>0·650	83	0·678	0·566	0·055	−0·168	23	0·390
$j = 2$							
<0·150	35	0·139	0·143	0·060	0·029	12	−1·000
0·150–0·199	115	0·174	0·174	0·036	−0·009	20	−0·450
0·200–0·249	285	0·215	0·148	0·021	−0·324	43	0·392
0·250–0·299	265	0·266	0·313	0·029	0·175	47	−0·356
0·300–0·349	230	0·324	0·244	0·029	−0·251	43	−0·294
0·350–0·399	74	0·371	0·297	0·053	−0·196	18	−0·396
>0·400	105	0·435	0·419	0·048	−0·019	42	−0·034
$j = 3$							
<0·275	180	0·261	0·278	0·033	0·065	66	−0·428
0·275–0·299	360	0·288	0·294	0·024	0·023	75	0·241
0·300–0·3249	435	0·308	0·262	0·021	−0·148	84	−0·149
>0·400	91	0·333	0·275	0·047	−0·176	0	N/A
(b) Firm B							
$j = 1$							
<0·400	137	0·343	0·299	0·039	−0·107	42	−0·429
0·400–0·449	154	0·427	0·390	0·039	−0·086	32	0·047
0·450–0·499	109	0·473	0·431	0·048	−0·090	21	0·205
0·500–0·549	209	0·522	0·493	0·035	−0·050	39	−0·097
0·550–0·599	189	0·563	0·578	0·036	0·020	26	−0·319
0·600–0·649	190	0·617	0·542	0·036	−0·121	37	−0·030
<0·650	78	0·675	0·590	0·056	−0·125	28	0·340
$j = 2$							
<0·150	19	0·138	0·158	0·086	0·105	12	−1·000
0·150–0·199	106	0·178	0·170	0·037	−0·009	26	−0·366
0·200–0·249	295	0·217	0·139	0·020	−0·358	52	0·074
0·250–0·299	245	0·270	0·265	0·028	−0·008	39	−0·163
0·300–0·349	197	0·323	0·335	0·034	0·035	29	−0·478
0·350–0·399	88	0·373	0·273	0·048	−0·269	42	−0·235
>0·400	116	0·444	0·388	0·045	−0·121	42	−0·008
$j = 3$							
<0·275	224	0·260	0·281	0·030	0·085	43	−0·383
0·275–0·299	452	0·288	0·270	0·021	−0·060	86	0·090
0·300–0·3249	334	0·352	0·290	0·025	−0·056	96	−0·154
>0·400	56	0·334	0·232	0·057	−0·306	0	N/A
(c) Firm C							
$j = 1$							
<0·400	125	0·351	0·280	0·119	−0·185	36	−0·340
0·400–0·449	166	0·432	0·416	0·089	−0·038	48	−0·065
0·450–0·499	85	0·476	0·506	0·013	0·062	12	0·575
0·500–0·549	185	0·513	0·416	0·071	−0·187	32	−0·395

continued overleaf

TABLE 4—continued

ϕ	n	$\bar{\phi}$	$\bar{\mu}$	σ	r	n_1	r_1
(c) Firm C							
$j = 1$							
0·550–0·599	214	0·567	0·570	0·060	0·006	34	0·040
0·600–0·649	216	0·616	0·569	0·055	−0·076	40	−0·077
>0·650	75	0·678	0·533	0·086	−0·214	23	0·321
$j = 2$							
<0·150	28	0·139	0·214	0·567	0·536	13	−1·000
0·200–0·249	245	0·210	0·184	0·117	−0·133	41	−0·171
0·250–0·299	255	0·267	0·294	0·107	0·095	45	−0·017
0·300–0·349	200	0·231	0·270	0·068	−0·159	34	−0·217
0·350–0·399	62	0·373	0·258	0·150	−0·309	28	−0·420
>0·400	110	0·434	0·418	0·111	−0·023	37	0·075
$j = 3$							
<0·275	136	0·260	0·294	0·152	0·135	44	−0·307
0·275–0·299	352	0·287	0·270	0·083	−0·059	88	−0·131
0·300–0·3249	509	0·308	0·289	0·065	−0·061	93	0·013
>0·400	69	0·337	0·188	0·142	−0·435	0	N/A
(d) Firm D							
$j = 1$							
<0·400	86	0·356	0·302	0·145	−0·126	40	−0·423
0·400–0·449	130	0·418	0·354	0·101	−0·154	27	0·059
0·450–0·499	108	0·467	0·454	0·011	−0·032	32	−0·263
0·500–0·549	157	0·511	0·470	0·078	−0·079	24	0·629
0·550–0·599	290	0·566	0·538	0·052	0·051	45	−0·293
0·600–0·649	202	0·627	0·535	0·056	−0·148	36	−0·072
>0·650	93	0·682	0·538	0·076	−0·211	21	0·376
$j = 2$							
<0·150	15	0·138	0·133	0·659	−0·033	8	−1·00
0·150–0·199	130	0·172	0·139	0·178	−0·192	24	−0·771
0·200–0·249	287	0·211	0·167	0·106	−0·200	47	0·511
0·250–0·299	338	0·266	0·284	0·093	0·068	47	−0·664
0·300–0·349	140	0·326	0·329	0·124	0·019	41	−0·027
0·350–0·399	85	0·368	0·271	0·136	−0·266	29	−0·176
>0·400	71	0·427	0·409	0·141	−0·021	29	0·029
$j = 3$							
<0·275	92	0·254	0·348	0·198	0·371	21	−0·786
0·275–0·299	298	0·290	0·272	0·089	−0·062	84	−0·106
0·300–0·3249	518	0·313	0·245	0·061	−0·215	81	−0·170
>0·400	158	0·333	0·348	0·114	0·044	39	0·154

inherent biases *ex ante*, then the profit opportunities would have been exploitable. The last column presents the comparable return statistic for the holdout sample and can be interpreted as a test of a trading rule involving the placing of bets on all matches in a particular odds group.

Analysis of Tables 4(a)–(d) indicates that, for most groupings, the odds on average imply higher probabilities than the group population frequencies relating to particular outcomes. This is consistent with positive bookmaker margins and the absence of systematic profit opportunities. There is some evidence of *ex post* bias over the estimation period for each firm, this occurring when $\bar{\phi} < \bar{\mu}$ and $r > 0$. The bias seems to occur consistently in the lower tails of the distributions for $j = 2$ and $j = 3$ with the exception of firm D, which displays no bias for $j = 2$ over the period. However, the *ex ante* exploitability of this observed bias is called into question when the returns to betting on a portfolio of matches belonging to the biased odds groupings are examined over the 225-match holdout period. The values of r_1 associated with positive values of r are frequently negative, and a strategy of betting on all such matches would have yielded negative average returns. Hence, while there is evidence of *ex post* bias in the estimation sample, this does not appear to translate into a profitable strategy for our holdout sample.

IV. REGRESSION-BASED TESTS

(a) Linear probability model

Assume that bookmakers are able to form unbiased and efficient estimates of the probabilities of outcomes so that

$$(3) \qquad p_{ij} = p_{ij}^* + \varepsilon_{ij}$$

where p_{ij} is the probability estimate, p_{ij}^* is the true unobservable probability, ε_{ij} is the estimation error with $E(\varepsilon_{ij}) = 0$, and $E(\varepsilon_{ij} p_{ij}) = 0$ (an efficiency condition).

One assumption that might be made is that the posted odds ϕ are related to p in the following manner:

$$(4) \qquad \phi_{ij} = p_{ij} + z_{ij} + b_{ij}$$

where b is the brokerage free and z is the variable that reflects the impact of new information on the odds. The gross margin λ is therefore equal to $z + b$.

The properties of the probability estimates underlying the quoted odds can be subjected to empirical testing using the following procedure. From (3), expression (1) can be rewritten as

$$(5) \qquad \phi_{ij} = (p_{ij}^* + \varepsilon_{ij}) + \lambda_{ij}.$$

From expression (5),

$$(6) \qquad p_{ij}^* = \phi_{ij} - \lambda_{ij} - \varepsilon_{ij}.$$

This can be seen to be an example of the well-known linear probability model. Both λ and ε are unobservable. However, p_{ij}^* can be estimated by retrieving the fitted values from the following estimating equation:

$$(7) \qquad f_{ij} = \alpha_j + \beta_j \phi_{ij} + \nu_{ij}$$

where $f_{ij} = 1$ if outcome j of match i occurs, and 0 if outcome $k(k \neq j)$ of match i occurs, α_j, β_j are regression coefficients, and ν_{ij} is a stochastic error term. The distribution of f_{ij} will be as follows:

$$\Pr\{f_{ij} = 1\} = p_{ij}^*$$

$$\Pr\{f_{ij} = 0\} = (1 - p_{ij}^*).$$

Hence $E(f_{ij}) = p_{ij}^*$, and the model (7) can be interpreted as generating estimates of the true probability of outcome j of match i conditional on the odds quoted by a firm.

If a bookmaker's expectations are weakly efficient (so that $E(\phi_{ij}\nu_{ij}) = 0$) and the margin does not contain any component proportional to the odds, then β will not be significantly different from unity in estimates of (7).[5,6] A comparison of expression (6) reveals that any constant bias will manifest itself in the size of the estimated constant; i.e. $E(\alpha_j) = -\{E(\lambda_j) + E(\varepsilon_j)\}$. It follows that in general it may not be possible to distinguish between a firm that deliberately sets higher margins and a firm that sets a lower margin but systematically overestimates the true probability by a constant amount. However, if $\alpha_j > 0$, then it follows that there must be constant bias in the relation between the true and measured probabilities under the stated assumptions.[7]

One econometric issue that arises in connection with estimating expression (7) is that ordinary least squares (OLS) estimates of α_j and β_j, while being unbiased and consistent, will be inefficient owing to heteroscedasticity in the error term ν_{ij} (Judge *et al.*, 1985, p. 757). One solution to this problem is to employ the weighted least squares (WLS) procedure, where the weights $(1/s(\nu_{ij}))$ are based on the following estimate of the standard deviation of ν_{ij}:

$$(8) \qquad s(\nu_{ij}) = \hat{f}_{ij}(1 - \hat{f}_{ij})$$

where $\hat{f}_{ij}$ is the fitted value retrieved from the OLS estimate of (7). As long as $\hat{f}_{ij}$ lies within the unit interval, then $s(\nu_{ij})$ is defined. For the data examined here, this requirement was satisfied for all firms and for all outcomes.[8]

The weighted least squares results are reported in Table 5. It should be noted that the low R^2 statistics are to be expected when the dependent variable is binary. Using the upper bounds for correlation between binary outcomes and probabilistic predictions in Morrison (1972), we find, for example, that for the home outcome the upper bound on the R^2 is approximately $0{\cdot}036$. The results indicate that the intercept term α is not significantly different from zero and the slope parameter β is significant but not different from unity for the predictions of home and away wins for any of the bookmakers. These results suggest unbiasedness in the home and away odds-setting processes. On the other hand, the draw odds have no statistically significant predictive content for the draw outcome with generally only the constants being significant. This is not surprising, given the descriptive statistics in Table 1, which show that the variance of draw probabilities is very low relatively, implying that the independent variable in the linear probability model is close to being a constant for the draw outcome.

(b) Logit estimation of linear probability model

As a further check on the weighted least squares results, we re-estimated the model using logit analysis. The results are reported in Table 6. We compared the results using the following approximation relatings least squares (LS) to logit (LOG) estimates (Maddala, 1983):

$$\alpha_{LS} \approx 0{\cdot}5 + 0{\cdot}25\alpha_{LOG}$$

and

$$\beta_{LS} \approx 0{\cdot}25\beta_{LOG}.$$

We observe that the empirical results from the two methods give a consistent picture. Taken together, the results are consistent with the hypothesis that the

TABLE 5

WLS LINEAR PROBABILITY MODEL ESTIMATES

j	α	β	R^2
Firm A			
1	0·030	0·859	0·02
	(0·081)	(0·154)	
2	−0·006	0·922	0·01
	(0·044)	(0·163)	
3	0·388	−0·206	0·00
	(0·195)	(0·658)	
Firm B			
1	0·340	0·859	0·03
	(0·777)	(0·149)	
2	−0·013	0·921	0·01
	(0·044)	(0·158)	
3	0·314	−0·128	0·00
	(0·189)	(0·649)	
Firm C			
1	0·020	0·876	0·02
	(0·081)	(0·154)	
2	0·003	0·898	0·01
	(0·043)	(0·160)	
3	0·463	−0·629	0·00
	(0·187)	(0·627)	
Firm D			
1	0·053	0·794	0·02
	(0·086)	(0·158)	
2	−0·010	0·962	0·01
	(0·048)	(0·181)	
3	0·350	−0·239	0·00
	(0·197)	(0·645)	

Note: standard errors are in parentheses.

odds are set in a weakly efficient manner for the home and away outcomes and are devoid of information content for the draw outcome.

(c) Linear probability model results: implications for market efficiency

Weak form efficiency of expectations, that is orthogonality of forecast errors and the forecast, is a necessary but not sufficient condition for an efficient market, defined here in terms of the absence of a profitable trading rule. Hence, there seems to be opportunity to exploit the apparent inability of the bookmaking firms to predict draw outcomes if a forecasting model with predictive content can be found that will enable over-priced matches to be identified. However, as Jaffe and Winkler (1976) have shown, a trader possessing superior forecasting skills, reflected in a lower forecast error variance than 'the market', can still engage in optimal speculation against a market, even if it is 'efficient' in the sense that prices are unbiased. Hence, it is also of interest to examine whether the expected losses can be reduced or even turned into expected profits for home and away outcomes by using forecasts based upon other publicly available information. The tests of market efficiency reported below

TABLE 6

LOGIT LINEAR PROBABILITY MODEL
ESTIMATES

j	α	β
Firm A		
1	$-1 \cdot 934$	$3 \cdot 539$
	$(0 \cdot 353)$	$(0 \cdot 666)$
2	$-2 \cdot 428$	$4 \cdot 673$
	$(0 \cdot 259)$	$(0 \cdot 868)$
3	$-0 \cdot 664$	$-1 \cdot 005$
	$(0 \cdot 968)$	$(3 \cdot 271)$
Firm B		
1	$-1 \cdot 941$	$3 \cdot 578$
	$(0 \cdot 342)$	$(0 \cdot 649)$
2	$-2 \cdot 495$	$4 \cdot 762$
	$(0 \cdot 259)$	$(0 \cdot 840)$
3	$-0 \cdot 779$	$-0 \cdot 626$
	$(0 \cdot 940)$	$(3 \cdot 228)$
Firm C		
1	$-1 \cdot 988$	$3 \cdot 629$
	$(0 \cdot 356)$	$(0 \cdot 669)$
2	$-2 \cdot 375$	$4 \cdot 516$
	$(0 \cdot 250)$	$(0 \cdot 841)$
3	$-0 \cdot 275$	$-2 \cdot 316$
	$(1 \cdot 045)$	$(3 \cdot 525)$
Firm D		
1	-1.842	$3 \cdot 273$
	$(0 \cdot 367)$	$(0 \cdot 674)$
2	$-2 \cdot 410$	$4 \cdot 760$
	$(0 \cdot 273)$	$(0 \cdot 954)$
3	$-0 \cdot 562$	$-1 \cdot 312$
	$(0 \cdot 968)$	$(3 \cdot 176)$

Note: asymptotic standard errors are in parentheses.

are based on two strategies, the first exploiting only on the information contained in the set of odds, the second utilizing the additional information contained in the forecasts of the professional tipsters. The results of following each strategy are reported for the estimation period and the holdout sample period.

Strategy 1. The first strategy involved the use of a consensus forecast based only on the set of odds offered by the four firms in the sample. While the issue of the optimal combination of probabilities is one deserving of further attention, at this time we simply examine the predictive content of the geometric means, which are a more appropriate method of pooling forecasts than arithmetic means when forecast errors are *a priori* lognormal.

One empirical feature of our data is that the home and away probabilities are very highly correlated. The least-squares regression between the geometric means of the home probabilities (LHP) and the away probabilities (LAP) gives

$$LHP = 0.845 - 1.190 \, LAP \qquad R^2 = 0.99$$
$$(0.012) \, (0.005) \qquad n = 1066.$$

(Standard errors are in parentheses.)

In order to avoid multicollinearity, the home and away probabilities are not entered in the same equations. We experimented over the estimation period with a number of combinations of our explanatory variables—linear as well as non-linear transformations—employing binary logit. Not surprisingly, in light of the results reported earlier, we failed to find significant explanatory variables for the draw category ($j = 3$). The most interesting results obtained using logit analysis are as follows:

$$H01 = -2.03 + 3.71 \, LHP \qquad\qquad R^2 = 0.021$$
$$(0.36) \, (0.68)$$

$$A01 = -5.78 + 2.89 \, LAP + 12.91 \, LDP \qquad R^2 = 0.029.$$
$$(1.64) \, (1.37) \qquad (6.36)$$

Note: $H01$ is 1 if outcome is home win, 0 otherwise. $A01$ is 1 if outcome is away win, 0 otherwise. Standard errors are in parentheses.)

It appears that the mean draw probability has some predictive content, as does the mean away probability, in predicting away results. This finding gives support for the hypothesis that bookmakers do not employ information optimally in the odds-setting process. In other words, the probabilities do not meet the axioms required of rational expectations.

The overall explanatory power of the estimated models, as evaluated by Macfadden's coefficient of determination, shows an improvement over the firm-specific models reported in Table 6. This may have implications for the potential for a profitable betting strategy based upon the odds. In order to test the efficiency of the odds with respect to the information set comprising the pooled odds, we examine the margins to a strategy of betting on matches for which the predicted probability from the logit model exceeds the posted probability.[9,10] In the cases of home and away outcomes, and given the estimated coefficient values, this condition is satisfied for only a few outlying observations. Consequently, the strategy can be evaluated for the draw outcome only by using large samples. The amount staked for each bet (assumed to be placed singly rather than as part of a combination) is set equal to $\hat{p}_3 = (1 - \hat{p}_1 - \hat{p}_2)$, where $\hat{p}_i$ is the probability predicted for outcome j using the mean-odds models described earlier in this section.[11]

The results of adopting such a strategy compared with a strategy of betting on all matches in the relevant sample are shown in Table 7. They indicate that a substantial improvement in the mean value of the realized return could be achieved as a result of following this strategy relative to a strategy involving betting on each available match in the sample. Except for firm A, where the negative *ex post* average return in the estimation period is notable, there is a consistent improvement in margins if the strategy is followed. The results for the holdout sample are interesting because they suggest that the bettor can use *ex ante* identifiable rules which at least reduce the size of the post-tax loss on betting. Of course, there are many explanations of why people might bet at unfair odds, e.g. thrill, and as a consequence they might gain in expected

TABLE 7

REALIZED RETURNS—STRATEGY 1

Firm	Unconditional mean return	n	Mean returns on strategy 1
Estimate sample			
A	−0·077	244	−0·268
B	−0·038	325	0·085
C	−0·056	210	0·089
D	−0·081	117	0·353
Holdout sample			
A	−0·120	91	−0·114
B	−0·103	74	0·059
C	−0·097	68	0·054
D	−0·140	32	−0·550

utility terms from money-losing systems and not prefer bets with lower expected losses. Nevertheless, to the extent that the magnitude of the return is important to a bettor, these results are interesting.

Strategy 2. The second strategy we examined involves betting on the basis of the expert recommendations collected from the national newspapers. In an effort to reduce idiosyncratic noise in the forecast, we computed the consensus of the six forecasters (Beaver, 1981, p. 160).[12] In Table 8 we report the results of adopting this strategy. The results for the estimation sample suggest that there is little information in the tipsters' forecasts. There is a modest reduction in the average loss in most cases, but there is no prima facie evidence of *ex post* inefficiency. However, an inspection of forecast accuracy statistics calculated at various points during the estimation period suggested that forecasters learn over time, with accuracy improving considerably after a few weeks have elapsed. Therefore, it is possible that the strategy returns for this period are misleading. A check on the performance of the strategy over the second half of the estimation period confirmed this to be the case.

The results for the holdout sample are quite dramatic. Large negative unconditional margins are, with the exception of firm A, transformed into positive margins by following this strategy for each outcome. The improvement in profitability offered by this strategy suggests a substantial degree of incremental information in the consensus forecasts. However, except in the case of the firm D with away bets, the margins fail to exceed the 10 per cent transaction cost arising from the betting tax. Therefore, the standard trading rule criterion for identifying market inefficiency is not satisfied, since from the perspective of the bettor there appear to be few systematic positive net-of-tax returns to be earned. However, assuming that bets are going to be placed at the prevailing odds, and given that the bookmaker is responsible for paying the tax on all bets collected, there is still arguably a significant inefficiency in this market, because, *if* a bettor adopted this strategy, then not only would he substantially limit the size of his expected losses, but the bookmaking firm would also realize on-average losses after tax. In this sense, the market is semi-strong inefficient.

TABLE 8
RETURNS ON STRATEGY 2

	Firm j	Unconditional mean return	Recommended matches	Mean returns on recommendations
Estimation				
A:	1	−0·080	663	−0·070
	2	−0·043	156	−0·046
	3	−0·077	247	−0·072
B:	1	−0·074	663	−0·070
	2	−0·117	156	−0·122
	3	−0·038	247	−0·021
C:	1	−0·084	663	−0·077
	2	−0·078	156	−0·102
	3	−0·056	247	−0·035
D:	1	−0·103	663	−0·089
	2	−0·054	156	−0·024
	3	−0·081	247	−0·066
Holdout				
A:	1	−0·032	126	0·067
	2	−0·110	41	−0·185
	3	−0·120	58	−0·023
B:	1	−0·040	126	0·051
	2	−0·153	41	0·022
	3	−0·103	58	0·090
C:	1	−0·036	126	0·054
	2	−0·164	41	0·021
	3	−0·097	58	0·086
D:	1	−0·039	126	0·064
	2	−0·120	41	0·115
	3	−0·140	58	0·038

In light of the results obtained for strategies 1 and 2, the possibility of devising a hybrid strategy was examined. It is interesting to note that the number of matches satisfying both criteria simultaneously, i.e. having the predicted probability greater than the odds *and* having the relevant outcome forecast by the consensus tipster, is very low (between 1 and 9 for the draw outcome in the holdout sample). However, for the small number of matches, the average margins were 57, 95 and 105 per cent for A, B and C respectively. This is at least suggestive of more profitable trading rules existing than those reported above.

V. CONCLUSION

The betting market examined in this paper differs from those considered in previous work in the sense that prices are fixed by a firm and differ between firms. Hence, we are not necessarily observing a market view of the appropriate prices and probabilities attaching to particular events. The evidence indicates that certain types of bets are more favourably priced by some firms than by others. Moreover, there are systematic differences in the apparent odds-setting processes employed by the firms which suggest that pooling of information contained in the odds will lead to more efficient forecasts. However, these superior forecasts do not appear to be translatable into betting strategies that generate post-tax profits. Consequently, the fixed odds betting market appears to meet the arguably most important criterion for market efficiency, namely the absence of a trading rule that generates abnormal profits. However, we did find evidence that the posted odds, particularly for the draw outcome, do not fully reflect available information, conditional on our assumptions concerning the extraction of probabilities from the odds. Consequently, the odds do not seem to meet the axioms of rational expectations. The implication of this result is that bettors can find strategies that will reduce losses. This could be significant to individual bettors, depending on their utility functions.

ACKNOWLEDGMENTS

The authors acknowledge the invaluable research assistance provided by Simon Blackman and Dot Jones.

NOTES

1. For a recent review see Foster (1984).
2. See Holden, Peel and Thompson (1985) for a survey of other evidence on this topic.
3. The odds are typically based on information with a minimum seven-day lag. The tipsters' forecasts, which are in discrete form, are published between six and three days before matches.
4. A place bet has a positive return if the horse is first or second, and a show bet has a positive return if the horse finishes in the first three places.
5. If z varied with the perceived uncertainty of a match outcome (the expected value of new information being greater the more uncertain the match outcome (Theil, 1967)), then a link could occur between z and p since p could be a good linear approximation to the Theil measure of uncertainty in the observed range of odds. However, our earlier analysis demonstrated that there is a very weak correlation between gross *ex post* margins and a Theil measure of uncertainty. Inputting a Theil uncertainty measure in equation (7) as an additional independent variable did not have any significant impact on the results. It would appear that z can be regarded as independent of p.
6. The brokerage fee b could in principle contain a component that varies with p. This would occur if bookmakers perceived bettors to have a bias in favour of certain types of bets (e.g. the evidence on longshot bets in horse racing) and therefore to price-discriminate by taking higher markups on 'mug' bet longshots.
7. It can be seen that the proposed test (7) is similar to tests of efficiency in the forward exchange market where the risk premium is modelled as a constant.
8. Another econometric issue of relevance here concerns the treatment of outcomes as binary events. If expression (7) is estimated independently for each outcome $j = 1, 2, 3$, then no recognition is being given to the fact that the errors v_{ij} will be cross-correlated for different values of j since the restriction $\sum v_{ij} = 0, j = 1, \ldots, 3$, should apply. This will induce inefficiency into the single-equation WLS estimation. One approach to dealing with this problem is to use a set of identical regressors for each equation. However, in attempting to combine this approach with the WLS procedure by including the odds for two outcomes on the right-hand side of each equation in the system, severe multicollinearity was experienced.
9. It is straightforward to show that the expected value of a unit bet is positive if the predicted probability exceeds the posted probability.
10. It should be noted that because of reasons relating to copyright of the fixture list a combination bet must be placed which includes a minimum of five bets if a home is included or three otherwise. It follows that the profitability of any strategy involving single bets is a necessary but not sufficient condition for the existence of an implementable strategy.
11. The procedure of weighting of bets by the estimated probabilities was found to be marginally more successful than an equal-weighting strategy, but the results obtained for the latter approach are very similar to those reported.
12. In the event of two outcomes being equally recommended, the outcome with the highest unconditional probability of occurring was chosen as the consensus forecast.

REFERENCES

ALI, MUKTAR M. (1979). Some evidence on the efficiency of a speculative market. *Econometrica*, **47**, 387-92.

ASCH, P., MALKIEL, B. G. and QUANDT, R. E. (1984). Market efficiency in racetrack betting. *Journal of Business*, **57**, 165-75.

BALL, R. (1978). Anomalies in relationships between securities' yields and yield-surrogates. *Journal of Financial Economics* **6**, 103-26.

BEAVER, W. H. (1981). *Financial Reporting: An Accounting Revolution.* Englewood Cliffs, NJ: Prentice-Hall.

CARLSON, J. A. and PARKIN, M. (1975). Inflation expectations. *Economica*, **42**, 123-38.

CRAFTS, N. F. R. (1985). Some evidence of insider knowledge in horse race betting in Britain. *Economica*, **52**, 295-304.

FIGLEWSKI, S. (1979). Subjective information and market efficiency in a betting model. *Journal of Political Economy*, **87**, 75-88.

—— and WACHTEL, P. (1980). The formation of inflationary expectations. *Review of Economics and Statistics*, **63**, 1-10.

FOSTER, G. (1984). Capital market efficiency: definitions, testing issues and anomalies. In M. J. R. Gaffkin (ed.), *Contemporary Accounting Thought: Essays in Honour of Raymond J. Chambers*, pp. 151-80. Melbourne: Prentice-Hall.

HAUSCH, D. B., ZIEMBA, W. T. and RUBINSTEIN, M. (1981). Efficiency of the market for racetrack betting. *Management Science*, **27**, 1435-52.

HOLDEN, K. and PEEL, D. A. (1987). On testing for unbiasedness and efficiency of forecasts. UCW Aberystwyth Department of Economics, Discussion Paper No. 11.

—— and THOMPSON, J. (1985). *Expectations: Theory and Empirical Evidence.* London: Macmillan.

JAFFE, J. F. and WINKLER, R. L. (1976). Optimal speculation against an efficient market. *Journal of Finance*, **31**, 49-61.

JUDGE, G. G., GRIFFITHS, W. E., HILL, R. C., LUTKEPOHL, H. and LEE, T. S. C. (1985). *Theory and Practice of Econometrics*, 2nd ed. New York: John Wiley.

MADDALA, G. S. (1983). *Limited Dependent and Qualitative Variables in Econometrics.* Cambridge University Press.

MORRISON, D. J. (1972). Upper bounds for correlations between binary outcomes and probabilistic predictions. *Journal of the American Statistical Association*, **67**, 68-70.

ROSSETT, R. N. (1971). Weak experimental verification of the expected utility hypothesis. *Review of Economic Studies*, **38**, 481-92.

SNYDER, WAYNE N. (1978). Horse racing: testing the efficient markets model. *Journal of Finance*, **33**, 1109-18.

THEIL, (1967). *Economics and Information Theory.* Chicago: Rand McNally.

TVERSKY, A. and KAHNEMAN, D. (1978). Judgement under uncertainty: heuristics and biases. *Science*, no. 185, 1124-31.

VERGIN, R. C. and SCRIABIN, M. (1978). Winning strategies for wagering on National Football League games. *Management Science*, **24**, 809-18.

[16]

Appl. Statist. (1997)
46, *No. 2, pp.* 265–280

Modelling Association Football Scores and Inefficiencies in the Football Betting Market

By MARK J. DIXON† and STUART G. COLES

Lancaster University, UK

[Received November 1995. Revised September 1996]

SUMMARY
A parametric model is developed and fitted to English league and cup football data from 1992 to 1995. The model is motivated by an aim to exploit potential inefficiencies in the association football betting market, and this is examined using bookmakers' odds from 1995 to 1996. The technique is based on a Poisson regression model but is complicated by the data structure and the dynamic nature of teams' performances. Maximum likelihood estimates are shown to be computationally obtainable, and the model is shown to have a positive return when used as the basis of a betting strategy.

Keywords: Betting strategy; Expected return; Football (soccer); Maximum likelihood; Poisson distribution

1. Introduction

Betting on the outcome of football (soccer) matches has a long tradition in the UK, most popularly in the form of football pools, which typically involve the selection of matches that are thought to be those most likely to be a draw. A recently introduced type of betting, *fixed odds betting*, is also rapidly increasing in popularity. Bookmakers offer odds on the various outcomes of a match. The simplest version of this uses just the outcome of the match, in the sense of it being a win by either the team playing at home or the team playing away, or a draw. More complicated bets can also be placed on the score or on the half-time and full-time results. In making bets the challenge then is to find 'good bets', in which the considered probability of occurrence is higher than the corresponding probability determined by the bookmakers' odds, so that there is a positive expected return. Unlike in other types of betting, such as in horse-racing, the odds are fixed around one week before the matches are played. This allows a detailed comparison of the bookmakers' odds with estimated probabilities so that any perceived weaknesses in the bookmakers' specification can be exploited. Consequently, a statistical model that is capable of accurately predicting probabilities of the outcome of football matches has the potential to form the basis of a profitable betting strategy. This paper develops a model that meets this requirement.

†*Address for correspondence*: Department of Mathematics and Statistics, Lancaster University, Lancaster, LA1 4YF, UK.
E-mail: m.dixon@lancaster.ac.uk

0035-9254/97/46265

Various proposals have been made for modelling the outcome of football matches; these are reviewed in Section 2. For a betting strategy, however, probabilities must be estimated on a team-specific basis, so that the probabilities of the various match outcomes between two specific teams on a particular date can be calculated. This degree of resolution falls outside the scope of most of the published models. An exception to this is the model due to Maher (1982), that assumes independent Poisson distributions for the number of goals scored by each of the home and away teams, with means that are specific to each team's past performance. This forms the basis of our modelling approach. However, in attempting to derive a model which is not just a reasonable description of the data, but which also has the potential to provide better estimates of probabilities than the subjective estimates ascribed by bookmakers, we have had to modify and enhance this basic model structure. These modifications account for the fluctuating performance of individual teams and also enable the estimation of match outcomes for cup competitions in which teams from different leagues play one another. One consequence of these modifications is that simple equations for the maximum likelihood estimators are no longer available, but despite the high dimensionality of the model we show that maximum likelihood estimators are still available numerically. From the fitted model, the probabilities of the outcomes of each match are calculated and compared with the bookmakers' odds; this underlies the specification of a betting strategy which, using historical data, we show to have a positive return.

Section 2 reviews the literature discussing the use of statistical methodology in summarizing data from football matches. The data available to us are described in Section 3. Section 4 develops a statistical model, building on the basic model structure of Maher (1982). The application of the model to our assimilated data is described together with some sample results in Section 4. The utility of the model as the basis for a betting strategy is outlined in Section 5. Finally Section 6 suggests refinements which, we believe, would lead to further improvements in return.

2. Literature Review

Surprisingly few papers have examined the use of statistical techniques for modelling football data. American National Football League (NFL) football has received much more attention, but the differences between the two sports mean that modelling techniques for NFL football do not naturally transfer to association football.

Early references to statistical modelling of football data concentrate mainly on the distribution of the number of goals scored in a game. Moroney (1956) briefly examined this problem and suggested that, although the Poisson distribution provided an adequate fit to scores, improvements could be obtained by working with the negative binomial distribution. Reep *et al.* (1971) similarly examined the fit of the negative binomial distribution to scores from football matches and other goal scoring games. They concluded that 'chance dominates the game', finding no way of predicting outcomes within their class of models given the inherent noise in observed data. In contrast Hill (1974) applied a simple comparisons test for final league placings with expert predictions and demonstrated a significant correlation. A more sophisticated analysis of this type was by Fahrmeir (1994), who applied newly developed techniques for time-dependent, ordered, paired comparisons to German football data.

These points illustrate an apparent dichotomy: in the long run, it is not difficult to predict fairly accurately which teams are likely to be successful, but the development of models that have a sufficiently high resolution to exploit this long run predictive capability for individual matches is substantially more difficult. To our knowledge, the only paper that derives a model for football scores in a match between specific teams, accounting for the different quality of the teams involved, is that by Maher (1982). He obtained maximum likelihood estimates for a model in which the scores of the home and away teams in any game are independent Poisson distributions, with means modelled as functions of the respective teams' previous performances. This approach forms the basis of our model in Section 4.

With somewhat different applications in mind, several papers have looked at the effect of specific circumstances on team performances: Barnett and Hilditch (1993) applied standard nonparametric tests to see whether artificial pitches, subsequently banned in the English league, gave a significant advantage to the home team; Ridder *et al.* (1994) investigated the effect of the sending-off of a player on the outcome of a football match. Other papers have used statistical models to describe aspects of individual matches themselves: Chedzoy (1995) informally investigated times when goals are scored; Reep and Benjamin (1968) modelled the number and type of passing moves within a game; Clarke and Norman (1995) investigated the advantage of playing at home.

In relation to betting strategies, papers on the efficiency and exploitation of betting markets are numerous in the economics literature. Many papers address horse-racing and NFL football betting, and a few also consider betting on football matches, though little use of statistical methodology is made in these. Discussions of various betting markets can be found in Golec and Tamarkin (1991), Hausch *et al.* (1981) and, specifically in the context of football betting, Pope and Peel (1989).

3. Data

A wealth of information is available from each football match played. Obviously scores are recorded, but also the times of the goals, the goal scorers, the team's league position at the time of playing and so on. An individual team's performance in any particular game could also be affected by many external factors: newly signed players or the sacking of a manager for example. Though this information is also available, it is less easily formalized and its qualitative value subjective. Consequently, our model exploits only each team's history of match scores, which we have assimilated over a 3-year period, though the possibility of including other forms of data is investigated in Section 6.

The available data, which comprise 6629 full-time league and cup match results from the seasons 1992–93, 1993–94 and 1994–95, each consist of a home score and an away score. Data from 1995–96 are also available but are used as a validation sample to test the utility of the model subsequently when used as a basis for a betting strategy. The data from 1992 to 1995 provide accurate empirical estimates of various aggregated features. Table 1 gives the relative frequency, expressed as a percentage, of the scores from 0–0 to 4–4. Standard errors on the basis of an underlying multinomial model are shown in parentheses. Aggregating, the ratio of frequencies of home wins, draws and away wins is found to be 46:27:27. Thus, an empirical estimate of the probability of a randomly selected match resulting in a home win, for example,

TABLE 1
Empirical estimates of each score probability for joint and marginal probability functions†

Home goals	Away	Estimates of score probabilities (%) for the following numbers of away goals:				
		0	1	2	3	4
		33.4 (0.74)	36.4 (0.57)	19.5 (0.49)	7.9 (0.42)	2.1 (0.16)
0	22.1 (0.36)	8.2 (0.32)	7.4 (0.28)	4.5 (0.23)	1.4 (0.13)	0.4 (0.06)
1	33.0 (0.65)	10.3 (0.38)	12.7 (0.30)	6.4 (0.24)	2.7 (0.15)	0.6 (0.07)
2	24.5 (0.51)	8.2 (0.31)	9.1 (0.25)	4.8 (0.22)	1.9 (0.14)	0.5 (0.09)
3	12.6 (0.40)	4.2 (0.25)	4.5 (0.25)	2.3 (0.19)	1.2 (0.11)	0.4 (0.06)
4	5.3 (0.31)	1.6 (0.14)	1.8 (0.13)	1.1 (0.13)	0.6 (0.07)	0.1 (0.04)

†Standard errors are given in parentheses.

is 0.46. Because of the size of the database, these empirical estimates provide accurate estimates of random match probabilities. Our objective in later sections is to obtain estimates in matches which are not randomly selected but are team specific.

The assumption that the marginal distribution of random match scores is Poisson can be examined at this stage. Fitting a Poisson distribution to the aggregated home and away scores in Table 1 reveals that by any criterion the Poisson model is a near perfect fit to the aggregated score data. This gives some reassurance that the Poisson regression model developed in Section 4 is at least plausible for our data, despite concerns raised by other researchers about the general appropriateness of the Poisson assumption. A further assumption of the basic model in Section 4 is that the home and away scores are independent. To assess the validity of this assumption, Table 2 displays

$$\frac{\tilde{f}(i, j)}{\tilde{f}_H(i)\tilde{f}_A(j)}$$

for each home and away score (i, j), $i = 0, \ldots, 6$ and $j = 0, \ldots, 5$, where $\tilde{f}, \tilde{f}_H$ and $\tilde{f}_A$ are the joint and marginal empirical probability functions for home and away scores respectively. Bootstrap standard errors are given in parentheses. Table 2 suggests

TABLE 2
Estimates of the ratios of the observed joint probability function and the empirical probability function obtained under the assumption of independence between the home and away scores†

Home goals	Estimates of ratios for the following numbers of away goals:					
	0	1	2	3	4	5
0	111.5 (3.52)	92.0 (2.87)	103.4 (4.18)	82.1 (7.67)	96.4 (15.31)	96.8 (28.12)
1	93.7 (2.43)	105.7 (2.00)	99.3 (3.74)	103.7 (6.31)	86.9 (13.15)	108.3 (19.99)
2	99.6 (2.91)	101.7 (2.11)	99.2 (3.78)	97.4 (7.41)	95.9 (17.4)	106.7 (23.77)
3	100.3 (4.25)	98.5 (3.61)	91.8 (6.51)	116.6 (11.03)	139.8 (23.85)	75.4 (40.5)
4	91.0 (7.07)	93.8 (7.16)	108.6 (10.74)	138.0 (16.31)	111.7 (32.86)	90.4 (55.33)
5	94.1 (13.24)	102.3 (12.28)	114.3 (20.6)	73.3 (31.01)	120.8 (74.71)	130.4 (129.7)
6	139.1 (31.95)	49.1 (23.66)	146.4 (41.33)	45.3 (57.84)	174.1 (122.2)	—

†The numbers are multiplied by 100 for clarity. Standard errors are given in parentheses.

that the assumption of independence between scores is reasonable, except for the scores 0–0, 1–0, 0–1 and 1–1. Based on the estimates and errors alone, the score 0–3 seems to be significantly underestimated by the independence model. However, viewed within the context of all the other results, we regard this as due to sampling error. A modification of the independence assumption in the light of these observations is considered in Section 4.

4. Model and Inference

4.1. *Model Specification*
With the aim of developing a profitable betting strategy, various features are required of a statistical model for football matches. For example:

(a) the model should take into account the different abilities of both teams in a match;

(b) there should be allowance for the fact that teams playing at home generally have some advantage — the so-called 'home effect';

(c) the most reasonable measure of a team's ability is likely to be based on a summary measure of their recent performance;

(d) the nature of football is such that a team's ability is likely to be best summarized in separate measures of their ability to attack (to score goals) and their ability to defend (not to concede goals);

(e) in summarizing a team's performance by recent results, account should be taken of the ability of the teams that they have played against.

It is not practical to obtain empirical estimates of probabilities of match outcomes that account for all these constraints. Instead, we use a statistical model that structurally incorporates each of these features. Our basis is the model proposed by Maher (1982), with modifications to enable the inclusion of non-complete data sets, and data from different divisions simultaneously, and to allow for fluctuations in team performance.

The basic assumption of Maher's model is that the number of goals scored by the home and away teams in any particular game are independent Poisson variables, whose means are determined by the respective attack and defence qualities of each side. More explicitly, in a match between teams indexed i and j, let $X_{i,j}$ and $Y_{i,j}$ be the number of goals scored by the home and away sides respectively. Then

$$X_{i,j} \sim \text{Poisson}(\alpha_i \beta_j \gamma),$$
$$Y_{i,j} \sim \text{Poisson}(\alpha_j \beta_i), \tag{4.1}$$

where $X_{i,j}$ and $Y_{i,j}$ are independent, α_i, $\beta_i > 0$, $\forall i$, the α_i measure the 'attack' rate of the teams, the β_i measure the 'defence' rates and $\gamma > 0$ is a parameter which allows for the home effect. In fact, Maher (1982) included a more general model specification than this, allowing for separate home and away, and attack and defence parameters for every team. However, like Maher (1982), we have found model (4.1) to be an adequate simplification, though there are still assumptions in this model that would not be supported by detailed study of match data. The essential point is that, although details of the model may be inaccurate, the global structure should be

270   DIXON AND COLES

sufficiently accurate to enable the development of a betting strategy with a positive expected (and realized) return.

Some aspects of the model are easily improved on, however. Consider first the assumption of independence. Maher (1982) suggested the use of a bivariate Poisson family as an extension of the basic model, but this family is unable to represent the departure from independence for low scoring games that we identified in Section 3. Instead, we propose the following modification of model (4.1):

$$\Pr(X_{i,j} = x, \ Y_{i,j} = y) = \tau_{\lambda,\mu}(x, y)\frac{\lambda^x \exp(-\lambda)}{x!} \frac{\mu^y \exp(-\mu)}{y!} \tag{4.2}$$

where
$$\lambda = \alpha_i\beta_j\gamma,$$
$$\mu = \alpha_j\beta_i$$

and
$$\tau_{\lambda,\mu}(x, y) = \begin{cases} 1 - \lambda\mu\rho & \text{if } x = y = 0, \\ 1 + \lambda\rho & \text{if } x = 0, y = 1, \\ 1 + \mu\rho & \text{if } x = 1, y = 0, \\ 1 - \rho & \text{if } x = y = 1, \\ 1 & \text{otherwise.} \end{cases}$$

In this model, ρ, where
$$\max(-1/\lambda, \ -1/\mu) \leqslant \rho \leqslant \min(1/\lambda\mu, 1),$$

enters as a dependence parameter: $\rho = 0$ corresponds to independence, but otherwise the independence distribution is perturbed for events with $x \leqslant 1$ and $y \leqslant 1$. It is easily checked that the corresponding marginal distributions remain Poisson with means λ and μ respectively.

Another limitation of the model is that it is static—the attack and defence parameters of each team are regarded as constant through time. This issue will be considered in Section 4.3.

4.2. Model Inference

It follows from model (4.2) that with n teams there are attack parameters $\{\alpha_1, \ldots, \alpha_n\}$, defence parameters $\{\beta_1, \ldots, \beta_n\}$, the dependence parameter ρ and the home effect parameter γ to be estimated. To prevent the model from being over-parameterized, we impose the constraint

$$n^{-1} \sum_{i=1}^{n} \alpha_i = 1.$$

For the English league system, which comprises the Premier League and divisions 1–3 of the Football League, $n = 92$, so the model has 185 identifiable parameters.

Our basic tool of inference is the likelihood function. With matches indexed $k = 1, \ldots, N$, and corresponding scores (x_k, y_k), this takes the form, up to proportionality,

$$L(\alpha_i, \beta_i, \rho, \gamma; i = 1, \ldots, n) = \prod_{k=1}^{N} \tau_{\lambda_k, \mu_k}(x_k, y_k) \exp(-\lambda_k)\lambda_k^{x_k} \exp(-\mu_k)\mu_k^{y_k} \quad (4.3)$$

where

$$\lambda_k = \alpha_{i(k)}\beta_{j(k)}\gamma,$$
$$\mu_k = \alpha_{j(k)}\beta_{i(k)}, \quad (4.4)$$

and $i(k)$ and $j(k)$ denote respectively the indices of the home and away teams playing in match k. With complete data, in the sense of each team having played every other team equally often, and in the simpler case of independence between home and away team scores ($\rho = 0$), Maher (1982) obtained a system of linear equations whose roots are the maximum likelihood estimates. To achieve greater generality, we are restricted to direct numerical maximization of equation (4.3). The near orthogonality of many parameter combinations means that this is straightforward, despite the high dimensionality of the model.

In equation (4.3), teams from all four divisions are included in the likelihood. This has two consequences: firstly, the parameters for each team should reflect the relative quality of the different divisions and, secondly, the parameters will be estimable only if there is information from matches between teams of different divisions. Fortunately, because there is some mobility between the teams of different divisions at the start of a new season due to promotion and relegation, the issue of parameter identifiability is resolved. The situation is also helped by the inclusion of results from cup games which involve teams of different divisions playing each other. Then, because the parameters are calibrated across the divisions, the model can validly be used to estimate the probabilities of match outcomes involving teams of different divisions, as in cup games for example. These points are illustrated by Table 3, which shows the mean attack and defence parameters for teams in each division. As expected, the average attack and defence rating of teams increases with higher league status, as measured by increasing and decreasing mean values of α and β respectively.

4.3. *Model Enhancement*

A structural limitation of model (4.3) is that the parameters are static, i.e. teams are assumed to have a constant performance rate, as determined by α_i and β_i, over

TABLE 3
Mean attack and defence parameters for teams within each division

League	Mean attack parameter $\bar{\alpha}$	Mean defence parameter $\bar{\beta}$
Premier	1.38	0.68
Division 1	1.07	0.86
Division 2	0.83	1.14
Division 3	0.73	1.32

time. In reality, a team's performance tends to be dynamic, varying from one time period to another, and this behaviour should be incorporated in the model. In particular a team's performance is likely to be more closely related to their performance in recent matches than in earlier matches. In principle, this behaviour could be modelled by formalizing a stochastic development of the model parameters; this is considered in Section 6. In view of the dimensionality of the model, however, and since we shall always need to estimate the parameters at the fixed time point of making a bet rather than, say, forecasting ahead, we take a more simplistic approach here. Thus we assume that the parameters are, in a loose sense, locally constant through time and that historical information is of less value than recent information, and we determine parameter estimates for each time point t that are based on the history of match scores up to time t. Modifying equation (4.3) we construct a 'pseudolikelihood' for each time point t,

$$L_t(\alpha_i, \beta_i, \rho, \gamma; i = 1, \ldots, n) = \prod_{k \in A_t} \{\tau_{\lambda_k, \mu_k}(x_k, y_k) \exp(-\lambda_k)\lambda_k^{x_k} \exp(-\mu_k)\mu_k^{y_k}\}^{\phi(t-t_k)}$$

(4.5)

where t_k is the time that match k was played, $A_t = \{k: t_k < t\}$, λ_k and μ_k are as in equations (4.4) and ϕ is a non-increasing function of time. This represents a slight abuse of notation since the parameters α_i, β_i, ρ and γ are themselves time dependent.

Maximizing equation (4.5) at time t leads to parameter estimates which are based on games up to time t only. In this way, the model has the capacity to reflect changes in team performance. Moreover, varying the choice of ϕ allows historical data to be downweighted in the likelihood to a greater or lesser degree.

4.4. *Choice of Weighting Function ϕ*

There are various possible choices for the weighting function ϕ in equation (4.5). One possibility would be

$$\phi(t) = \begin{cases} 1 & t \leqslant t_0, \\ 0 & t > t_0, \end{cases}$$

in which case, at time t, all results within the last t_0 time units would be given equal weight in the inference. Instead, we work with the model

$$\phi(t) = \exp(-\xi t),$$

in which all previous results, downweighted exponentially according to a parameter $\xi > 0$, are included in the inference at time t. The static model (4.3) arises as the special case $\xi = 0$, whereas taking increasingly large values of ξ gives relatively more weight to the most recent results.

Optimizing the choice of ξ is problematic, since equation (4.5) defines a sequence of non-independent 'likelihoods', whereas we require ξ such that the overall predictive capability of the model is maximized. In fact, in subsequent sections, we restrict attention to the prediction of match outcomes rather than match scores. Therefore it is pragmatic to choose ξ to optimize the prediction of outcomes. First note that the probability of a home win in match k is estimated as

$$p_k^H = \sum_{l,m \in B_H} \Pr(X_k = l, Y_k = m) \tag{4.6}$$

where $B_H = \{(l, m): l > m\}$, and the score probabilities are determined from the maximization of model (4.5) at $t(k)$, the time of match k. Similar expressions hold for p_k^A and p_k^D, the probabilities of an away win and a draw respectively. Now define

$$S(\xi) = \sum_{k=1}^{N} (\delta_k^H \log p_k^H + \delta_k^A \log p_k^A + \delta_k^D \log p_k^D) \tag{4.7}$$

where, for example, $\delta_k^H = 1$ if match k is a home win and $\delta_k^H = 0$ otherwise, and p_k^H, p_k^A and p_k^D are the maximum likelihood estimates from model (4.5), with weighting parameter set at ξ. Considering only the outcomes, and not the scores, equation (4.7) is the analogue of a predictive profile log-likelihood. A plot of $S(\xi)$ against ξ, with time units taken to be half-weeks, is given in Fig. 1. The function is maximized at $\xi = 0.0065$, and all subsequent results are given with respect to this choice of ξ, though in fact the results are robust across a range of ξ-values.

4.5. *Parameter Estimates and Results*

The complete set of parameter estimates, obtained by maximizing equation (4.5) with $\xi = 0.0065$, at each time point t, gives a profile of each team's changing performance in terms of defence and attack abilities. Data from at least 60 half-weeks are required to estimate parameters accurately, so estimates are obtained for t ranging from 60 to 174. For brevity we show only a subset of the results (for the full set of results for the 1996 season, contact M. Dixon). Tables 4 and 5 give the

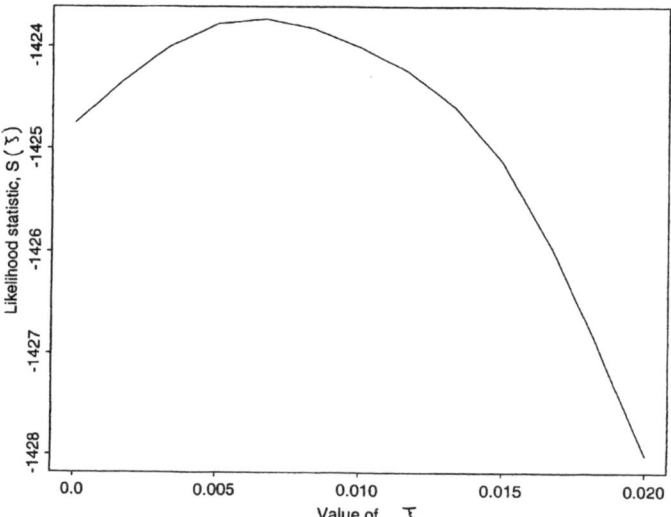

Fig. 1. $S(\xi)$ *versus* ξ: the maximum occurs at $\xi = 0.0065$

TABLE 4
*Maximum likelihood estimates and standard errors for the attack
and defence rate parameters, on August 5th, 1995, for Premiership
teams (in the 1995–96 season)*

Team	$\hat{\alpha}$	$se(\hat{\alpha})$	$\hat{\beta}$	$se(\hat{\beta})$
Arsenal	1.235	0.151	0.527	0.078
Aston Villa	1.278	0.178	0.649	0.086
Blackburn	1.730	0.209	0.534	0.082
Bolton	1.183	0.141	0.760	0.100
Chelsea	1.238	0.169	0.658	0.089
Coventry	1.115	0.164	0.699	0.094
Everton	1.177	0.169	0.667	0.091
Leeds	1.510	0.186	0.583	0.088
Liverpool	1.448	0.180	0.561	0.082
Manchester City	1.232	0.170	0.728	0.091
Manchester United	1.869	0.208	0.402	0.067
Middlesbrough	1.244	0.152	0.750	0.109
Newcastle	1.659	0.195	0.578	0.081
Nottingham Forest	1.460	0.170	0.658	0.095
Queen's Park Rangers	1.497	0.195	0.717	0.095
Sheffield Wednesday	1.387	0.179	0.698	0.091
Southampton	1.446	0.183	0.772	0.098
Tottenham	1.622	0.201	0.775	0.100
West Ham	1.192	0.169	0.649	0.087
Wimbledon	1.281	0.174	0.732	0.094

TABLE 5
*Maximum likelihood estimates and standard errors for the attack
and defence rate parameters on August 5th, 1995, for teams in
division 2 (in the 1995–96 season)*

Team	$\hat{\alpha}$	$se(\hat{\alpha})$	$\hat{\beta}$	$se(\hat{\beta})$
Blackpool	0.858	0.110	1.357	0.163
Bournemouth	0.681	0.096	1.095	0.139
Bradford	0.832	0.107	1.175	0.149
Brentford	0.967	0.115	0.900	0.129
Brighton	0.820	0.107	1.032	0.137
Bristol City	0.825	0.120	0.873	0.114
Bristol Rovers	0.917	0.113	0.965	0.138
Burnley	0.942	0.116	1.067	0.127
Carlisle	0.781	0.100	0.964	0.157
Chesterfield	0.764	0.099	1.024	0.160
Crewe	1.065	0.125	1.265	0.159
Hull	0.822	0.104	1.069	0.146
Notts County	0.985	0.132	0.979	0.120
Oxford	0.956	0.119	0.951	0.119
Peterborough	0.829	0.111	1.161	0.133
Rotherham	0.852	0.106	1.136	0.143
Shrewsbury	0.764	0.104	1.060	0.145
Stockport	0.945	0.115	1.040	0.136
Swansea	0.798	0.106	0.899	0.122
Swindon	1.160	0.154	1.091	0.120
Walsall	0.911	0.114	1.116	0.162
Wrexham	0.957	0.116	1.257	0.150
Wycombe	0.813	0.105	0.984	0.137
York	0.916	0.113	0.926	0.131

maximum likelihood estimates of the attack and defence parameters on August 5th, 1995, for teams which were in the Premier division and division 2 respectively in 1995–96. In addition, Fig. 2 shows the corresponding sequence of estimates of $\alpha(t)$ and $\beta(t)$ over time for three teams — the non-uniformity in these estimates suggests that teams' performances are genuinely dynamic. Also shown is the sequence of estimates of the home effect parameter $\gamma(t)$ which, as might be expected, remains nearly constant over time. The flat portion from $t = 82$ to $t = 90$ corresponds to the summer break in the football season. Furthermore, Table 6 gives a sample of matches and the maximum likelihood estimates of the outcome probabilities. The standard errors of the outcome estimates, particularly those of the draw probability estimates, are small relative to the standard errors of the attack and defence parameter estimates.

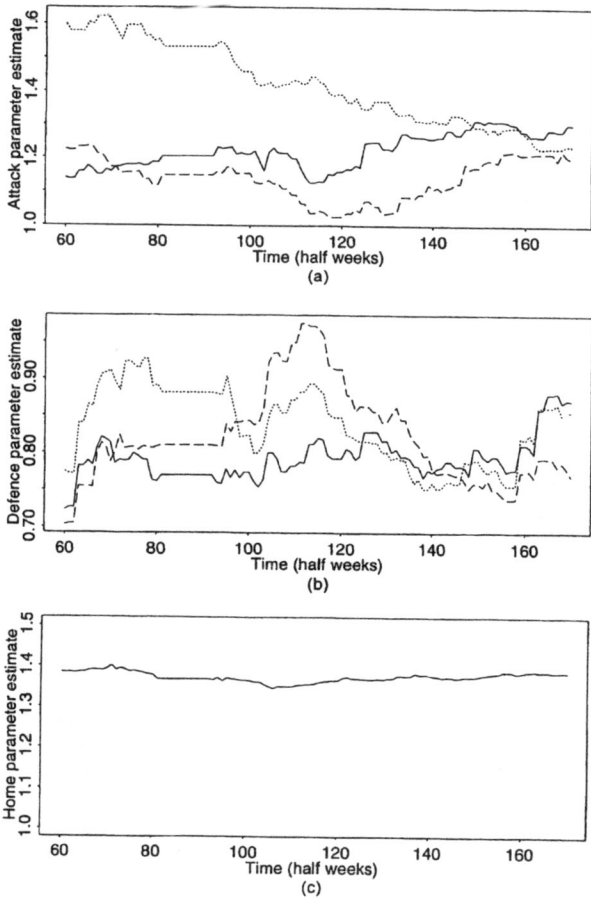

Fig. 2.   (a), (b) Time series of the maximum likelihood estimates of attack and defence rate parameters for Sheffield United (———), Norwich (··········) and Everton (– – –); (c) variation of the common home effect parameter with time

TABLE 6
Maximum likelihood estimates for match outcome probabilities†

Match	Maximum likelihood estimates for the following outcomes:		
	Home win	Draw	Away win
Arsenal *versus* Middlesbrough	0.535 (0.069)	0.280 (0.030)	0.184 (0.046)
Aston Villa *versus* Manchester United	0.214 (0.054)	0.291 (0.029)	0.495 (0.072)
Blackburn *versus* Queen's Park Rangers	0.615 (0.078)	0.221 (0.033)	0.164 (0.049)
Chelsea *versus* Everton	0.457 (0.075)	0.298 (0.030)	0.245 (0.057)
Liverpool *versus* Sheffield Wednesday	0.535 (0.076)	0.262 (0.031)	0.203 (0.052)
Blackpool *versus* Wrexham	0.428 (0.077)	0.240 (0.018)	0.332 (0.070)
Stockport *versus* Burnley	0.480 (0.077)	0.259 (0.024)	0.261 (0.062)
Newcastle *versus* Stoke	0.705 (0.073)	0.198 (0.042)	0.097 (0.034)

†The matches are a subset of the fixtures from August 19th, 1995, plus one other across-division match. Approximate standard errors are calculated using the delta method. Standard errors are given in parentheses.

5. Betting Strategy

How useful is the model derived in Section 4, when used as the basis for a betting strategy against odds provided by bookmakers? A detailed investigation into betting strategies for fixed odds football betting is given in Pope and Peel (1989) and Dixon and Pope (1996). Here we address the question by reference to a new set of results, corresponding to the 1995–96 season, for which we have both results and bookmakers' odds. We first use model (4.5), with $\xi = 0.0065$, at each new time point t to obtain current parameter estimates. Then, by comparing estimated result probabilities with bookmakers' odds for the following week, we determine which games are most advantageous to bet on. We then calculate the net return from such a strategy.

A typical set of bookmakers' odds for a particular match might be (8:13, 12:5, 4:1) for a home win, draw and away win respectively. Thus, in this example, a stake of 13 units on a home win would yield a profit of 8 units if that outcome occurred. Odds $o_1 : o_2$ transform to a probability p by using the formula

$$p = o_2 / (o_1 + o_2).$$

The above set of odds then corresponds to the set of probabilities (0.62, 0.29, 0.20), which has a sum of 1.11. This phenomenon is standard in betting markets: if the bookmakers are accurate in their probability specifications, they have an in-built 'take', corresponding to their expected profit, which in the above example is 11%. To win money from bookmakers, in the sense of having a positive expected return, requires a determination of probabilities which is sufficiently more accurate than those obtained from the odds in order to overcome the bookmakers' take. We first rescale multiplicatively the bookmakers' odds so that they sum to 1. Denote these probabilities for match k by b_k^H, b_k^D and b_k^A for a home win, draw and away win respectively, and similarly let $\hat{p}_k^H$, $\hat{p}_k^D$ and $\hat{p}_k^A$ be the corresponding maximum likelihood estimates for this match under model (4.5). Comparisons of the two sets of probability estimates for each of the result outcomes are given in Fig. 3 for each match in our database. Overall there is reasonable agreement between the probability assessments, but the variability in these plots indicates the potential for positive gain if our model probabilities are accurate.

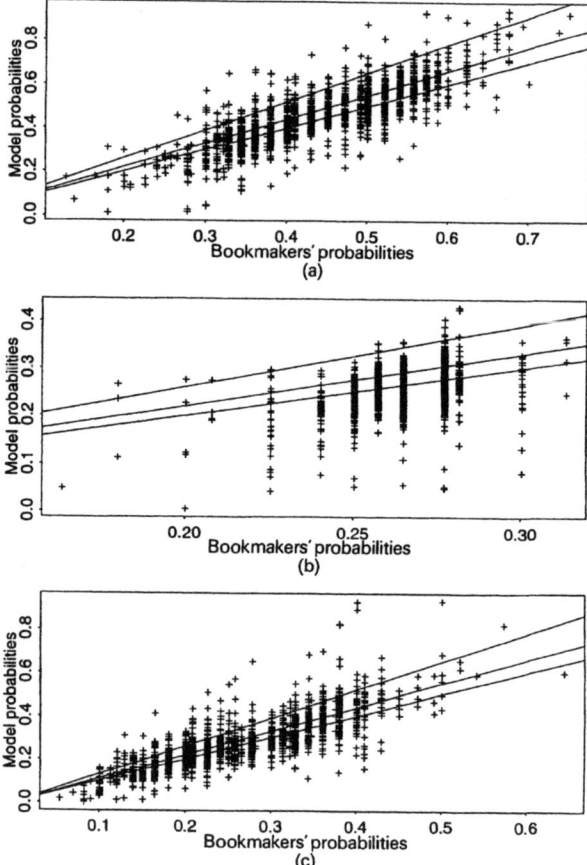

Fig. 3. Model probability estimates plotted against odds for all matches where odds were available: (a) home wins; (b) draws; (c) away wins

If the model probabilities were without error, then the expected gain from a unit stake bet on a home win, for example, is

$$E(G) = p_k^H / b_k^H - 1. \tag{5.1}$$

If b_k^H is the true probability then the expected gain will be 0.00, or -0.11 if the bookmakers' take is included. In reality neither p_k^H nor b_k^H is the true probability, but we obtain a positive return if our estimates are sufficiently more accurate than the bookmakers'.

From equation (5.1), a natural betting strategy for any particular game k is to bet on a home win, for example, if

$$\hat{p}_k^H / \hat{b}_k^H > r,$$

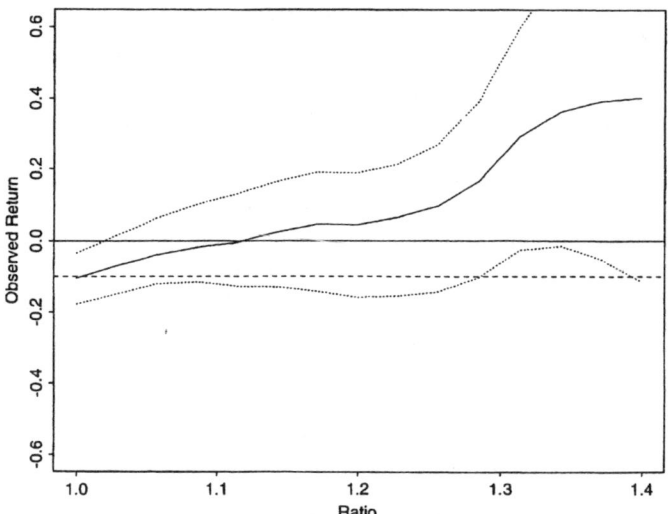

Fig 4. Observed mean return plotted against the ratio of model probabilities to bookmakers' probabilities (- - - -, return of −0.11, the expected return under random betting, which is due to the bookmakers' take of 11% for each match; ········, 90% bootstrap intervals): the mean return is calculated only when there are more than 10 sample values

where $\tilde{b}_k^H$ denotes the unscaled bookmakers' probability of a home win in match k, for some predetermined value of $r > 1$, with a corresponding strategy for bets on away wins or draws. Increasing r leads to a stricter betting regime, but consequently fewer bets. The effect of a range of different choices for r can be seen in Fig. 3, in which the line $\hat{p} = rb$ is plotted for $r = 1.0$, 1.1, 1.3. For a particular choice of r, points falling above that line correspond to matches on which this betting strategy would have led to a bet being placed on that particular outcome, with r as specified.

The success of this betting strategy can be assessed by calculating the observed return, if such a strategy had been adopted, given the match results which actually occurred. This is plotted as a function of r in Fig. 4, together with 90% confidence intervals obtained using the bootstrap. There is considerable variability in the plot which makes it difficult to draw definitive conclusions. However, with $r = 1.2$ our betting strategy leads to a return which is borderline significantly different from −0.11, the expected return under a random betting strategy due to the bookmakers' take, and has a positive expected absolute return for any $r > 1.1$. It is in this sense that we claim that the model and inference of Section 4 meet our stated objective of deriving a model for estimating football match outcomes which is the basis of a betting strategy with positive returns.

6.   Conclusions

Our aim has been to derive a method for estimating the probabilities of football results with the potential to achieve a positive expected return when used as the basis

MODELLING ASSOCIATION FOOTBALL SCORES   279

of a betting strategy against bookmakers' odds. Our basic model is simple — a bivariate Poisson distribution for the numbers of goals scored by each team, with parameters related to past performance — but refinements necessary to improve the realism and precision of the model make the associated inference a heavy computational burden. None-the-less, the computations are manageable and the resulting model is accurate in many respects.

Our betting strategy is equally simple: we bet on all outcomes for which the ratio of model to bookmakers' probabilities exceeds a specified level. For sufficiently high levels, we have shown that this strategy yields a positive expected return, even allowing for the in-built bias in the bookmakers' odds.

The simplicity of our model and the associated betting strategy is appealing. However, to improve further on the utility of our approach, we perceive that further modifications may be desirable. One possibility is to refine further the Poisson regression model. Stochastically updated parameters are a natural idea in this context, but the detailed implementation may be difficult. Smith (1981) considered a dynamic regression framework for simple Poisson models, but the generalization of these ideas to the scale of model (4.5) is not immediate. Broadening the scope of our model to incorporate additional covariate information is a second area for development. The quantitative value of such data is not always obvious, so such a development might need a Bayesian structure to exploit their subjective value. A third possibility is the betting regime. We have restricted attention so far to fixed odds bets of match *outcomes*. This leads to a betting strategy in which relatively few bets are actually placed. As bookmakers offer odds on specific match scores, the probabilities of which are also obtained from our model, a betting strategy based on match scores could be developed. More radically, there are several 'market-style' index betting options for football matches, where goal margins are bought and sold like commodities (e.g. Jackson (1994) and Dixon and Robinson (1996)); the implementation of our model for market strategies in such an option is a further possibility.

The lure of scientific improvement of our model and betting strategy, with the purely incidental by-product of winning money from the bookmakers, encourages us to build on the apparent success of the present model in the various ways discussed above.

Acknowledgements

We thank a referee and the Editor for comments on an earlier version of the paper and Jonathan Tawn for comments that helped to improve the handling of dependence between scores. We are grateful to many colleagues at Lancaster who helped to digitize football league data and bookmakers' odds. For entry of data and odds, we thank Simon Garside, Sara Morris, Mike Robinson and Pete Sewart. The data were obtained from Williams (1992, 1993, 1994), Hugman (1991) and *90-Minutes* weekly magazine. Odds were obtained from local branches of major UK bookmakers. We also thank Mike Robinson and Barry Rowlingson for writing some of the software used in the handling of data.

References

Barnett, V. and Hilditch, S. (1993) The effect of an artificial pitch surface on home team performance in football (soccer). *J. R. Statist. Soc.* A, **156**, 39–50.

Chedzoy, O. (1995) Influences on the distribution of goals in soccer. Private communication.

Clarke, S. R. and Norman, J. M. (1995) Home ground advantage of individual clubs in English soccer. *Statistician*, **44**, 509–521.

Dixon, M. J. and Pope, P. (1996) Inefficiency and bias in the UK football betting market. Submitted to *Mangmnt Sci.*

Dixon, M. J. and Robinson, M. E. (1996) A point process model for goal times in association football matches. Submitted to *J. Am. Statist. Ass.*

Fahrmeir, L. (1994) Dynamic-stochastic models for time-dependent ordered paired comparison systems. *J. Am. Statist. Ass.*, **89**, 1438–1449.

Golec, J. and Tamarkin, M. (1991) The degree of inefficiency in the football betting market. *J. Finan. Econ.*, **30**, 311–323.

Hausch, D. B., Ziemba, W. T. and Rubinstein, M. (1981) Efficiency of the market for racetrack betting. *Mangmnt Sci.*, **27**, 1435–1452.

Hill, I. D. (1974) Association football and statistical inference. *Appl. Statist.*, **23**, 203–208.

Hugman, B. J. (1991) *The Official Football League Yearbook.* Chichester: Facer.

Jackson, D. A. (1994) Index betting on sports. *Statistician*, **43**, 309–315.

Maher, M. J. (1982) Modelling association football scores. *Statist. Neerland.*, **36**, 109–118.

Moroney, M. J. (1956) *Facts from Figures*, 3rd edn. London: Penguin.

Pope, P. F. and Peel, D. A. (1989) Information, prices and efficiency in a fixed-odds betting market. *Economica*, **56**, 323–341.

Reep, C. and Benjamin, B. (1968) Skill and chance in association football. *J. R. Statist. Soc.* A, **131**, 581–585.

Reep, C., Pollard, R. and Benjamin, B. (1971) Skill and chance in ball games. *J. R. Statist. Soc.* A, **134**, 623–629.

Ridder, G., Cramer, J. S. and Hopstaken, P. (1994) Estimating the effect of a red card in soccer. *J. Am. Statist. Ass.*, **89**, 1124–1127.

Smith, J. Q. (1981) The multiparameter steady model. *J. R. Statist. Soc.* B, **43**, 256–260.

Williams, T. (1992) *Football Club Directory*. Exeter: Hamsworth Active.

——(1993) *Football Club Directory*. Exeter: Hamsworth Active.

——(1994) *Football Club Directory*. Exeter: Hamsworth Active.

[17]

Scottish Journal of Political Economy, Vol. 47, No. 1, February 2000
© Scottish Economic Society 2000. Published by Blackwell Publishers Ltd, 108 Cowley Road, Oxford OX4 1JF, UK and 350 Main Street, Malden, MA 02148, USA

THE FAVOURITE-LONGSHOT BIAS AND MARKET EFFICIENCY IN UK FOOTBALL BETTING

Michael Cain,* David Law** and David Peel***

ABSTRACT

It is shown that the individual fixed-odds betting market on UK football exhibits the same favourite-longshot bias as that found in horse-racing. The bias appears both in betting on results (home win, away win or draw) and in betting on specific scores, and there are certain trading rules which appear to be profitable. Poisson and Negative Binomial regressions are carried out to estimate the mean number of goals scored by a team in a match with given market odds for the various outcomes. Tables of odds for individual scores are derived and these appear to fit the actual outcomes far better than those of the bookmaker.

I INTRODUCTION

Thaler and Ziemba (1988) point out that wagering markets are, in one key respect, better suited to testing market efficiency and rational expectations than stock or other asset markets. This is because in wagering markets each asset or bet has a well-defined termination point at which its value becomes certain. As a consequence, there are none of the problems which arise in evaluating future dividends or fundamentals. Further, Thaler and Ziemba note that wagering markets have, *a priori*, a better chance of being efficient because the environment, namely of quick repeated feedback, is that usually thought to facilitate learning.

Given these characteristics, it is perhaps surprising to find that racetrack betting exhibits an anomaly called the favourite-longshot bias: favourites win more often than the subjective market probabilities imply, and longshots less often. Numerous researchers have documented this feature; see, for example, Ali (1977), Crafts (1985), Dowie (1976) and Figlewski (1979). Clearly, such a finding violates one or both of the usual definitions of market efficiency (see Thaler and Ziemba (*op. cit.*) since for strong form efficiency all bets should have equal expected value, and for weak form efficiency no bets should have positive expected value. A variety of explanations have been offered for this result. The

* University of Salford
** University of Wales, Aberystwyth
*** University of Wales, Cardiff

favourite-longshot bias has been explained in terms of risk-loving gamblers who know the correct chance of each horse winning a race but nevertheless prefer a lower-probability higher return bet; see for example, Weizman (1965) and Rosett (1965). Recently, Shin (1991, 1992, 1993) has provided an elegant explanation for the bias in markets where the odds are set by bookmakers. In his model, bookmakers are faced by a percentage of insiders, who know which horse will win, and outsiders whose preferences are distributed (without any bias) over all horses in the race. Shin demonstrates that the odds set by bookmakers in such circumstances have to be such as to raise enough revenue from outsiders to pay insiders their winnings, and consequently they have to exhibit a favourite-longshot bias.

The purpose in this paper is to examine whether the favourite-longshot bias found in horse-race betting appears also in another gambling market, namely the fixed odds betting market on UK football. Odds are fixed in the sense that, once they are declared by bookmakers a few days before the event, they remain fixed throughout the betting period until the event takes place. Two types of fixed odds bets are offered, and both are investigated in this paper. First, bookmakers set odds against the possible simple outcomes for a match: a win by the home team, a win by the team playing away from home and a draw, though punters must generally place combination bets, with a minimum of three matches if away wins or draws are selected, and five matches if home wins are selected. Second, conditional only on the quoted odds against a team winning or drawing, bookmakers offer odds against each possible score in the match. For example, in the 1991/92 season William Hill offered odds of 6, 8, 8 and 100 to 1 against a team winning with the particular scores of 1–0, 2–0, 2–1 and 6–2, respectively, in a match in which the quoted odds of the team winning were 4 to 6 against. Unlike betting on the simple outcome of a match, punters can bet on the score in a single match.

There are two particular sources of possible bias and inefficiency in this market. First of all, bookmaker odds against particular scores are determined by a simple rule of thumb, and depend only upon the quoted odds of a team winning or drawing, ie, where several teams playing at home have the same odds against winning their matches, bookmakers offer exactly the same odds against a particular score. Since one might expect that teams with the same chances of winning might differ dramatically in terms of whether their strength is in defence or attack, this feature of the market suggests potential inefficiency. A second key factor is that, whereas in horse racing and greyhound racing bookmakers can take account of the pattern of betting and vary their odds continuously during the betting period, betting is on a fixed odds basis in the football market; once posted, usually a few days before the event, the odds remain fixed. In this case, bookmakers are exposed to the danger that the relevant information set may change after their odds have been declared, for example, through the unexpected illness of key players or changes in the weather. Informed agents can utilise this information and are analogous to insider traders in other gambling markets. It would not be surprising if bookmakers protected themselves against this possibility, just as they would in the suspected presence of insider trading. Also, there are more obvious potential examples of insider information, including the possibility of players 'carrying injuries', or attempts to rig results by deliberate bad form. If this potential information asymmetry is thought by bookmakers to be important, they may be induced to set biased odds, so that the long-shot bets in this setting (ie, unusual scores such as 6–1, 9–0, or 8–8) will offer punters worse value than bets on favourites (ie, more likely scores such as 1–0, 1–1, or 2–0).

Pope and Peel (1989) examined the efficiency of the odds set against the home win, away win and draw outcomes in the 1981/82 football season, and concluded that the setting of odds appeared to be efficient, since there was no significant evidence of profitable betting strategies for punters, though they did not formally consider the favourite long-shot bias. As yet there has been no analysis of whether bookmaker odds against specific scores exhibit the favourite-long-shot bias, or whether this market is efficient.[1] That is the primary purpose in this paper.

The rest of the paper is structured as follows. In Section II we state our data sources and set out some stylised features of the data. In Section III we report formal regression results and in Section IV examine the relationship between predicted and actual odds, and whether a potentially profitable trading rule exists. The main conclusions are contained in Section V.

II THE DATA: STYLISED FACTS

Our data comprise the results of the 2 855 Football League matches played in the UK during the 1991/92 season, together with the associated odds against each simple outcome (home win, away win or draw) and against each score quoted by the bookmaker William Hill. Though our primary analysis is concerned with bookmaker odds against particular scores in matches, we analyse first the efficiency of the bookmaker odds against simple outcomes. For the full sample of matches there is some evidence of the favourite–longshot bias, as shown in the returns to bets at different prices in Table 1: bets on longshots generated substantially lower returns than bets on favourites, but there is no evidence of potentially profitable betting strategies on favourites.

In order to analyse the betting on scores, the total sample was divided into two sub-samples, one consisting of 2 000 matches for in-sample analysis and the other comprising 855 matches as a hold-out sample to test the robustness of any trading rules based on perceived inefficiencies in the odds-setting mechanism.

It seems plausible that a team with a high probability of winning (as indicated by low quoted odds) will score a large number of goals, on average, relative to a team with a low probability of winning, and also concede a relatively small

[1] Since this paper was completed, we have become aware of a related paper by Dixon and Coles (1997). Our paper differs in that the bookmaker's odds against scores are explicitly incorporated in the prediction of scores. Dixon and Coles develop a prediction model based on form attributes, which is then contrasted with the bookmaker's odds. They do not provide evidence on the favourite-longshot bias. A common feature of the papers is that bets appear to exist with potential positive expected value.

TABLE 1
Returns to a unit bet on match outcomes

Range of prices π_i	N	Returns
$0 < \pi_i \leqslant 0.2$	509	-0.155
$0.2 < \pi_i \leqslant 0.4$	5432	-0.109
$0.4 < \pi_i \leqslant 0.6$	2116	-0.101
$0.6 < \pi_i \leqslant 1$	598	-0.017
Total observations	8655	

Notes:
$\pi_i = 1/(1 + a_i)$, where a_i represents the odds against the home win, away win or draw.
N = number of possible bets in each category.

number of goals. This conjecture is reflected in the odds quoted against particular scores by William Hill. Table 2 shows the mean number of goals scored by the home and away teams for various ranges of prices of the home team winning.[2] The mean price of a win by the home team and by the away team is also shown. A prominent feature illustrated in the table is that the mean

TABLE 2
Number of home and away goals scored

Home-win price range	Mean home-win price	Mean home goals	Mean away goals	Mean away-win price	Maximum home goals	Maximum away goals	Number of matches
$0 < \pi < 0.3$	0.2288	0.8	1.96	0.5757	4	6	50
$0.3 \leqslant \pi < 0.34$	0.3231	0.9560	1.478	0.4713	3	5	46
$0.34 \leqslant \pi < 0.4$	0.3683	1.221	1.4378	0.4233	4	6	217
$\pi = 0.4$	0.40	1.4539	1.3191	0.3999	8	4	141
$0.42 \leqslant \pi < 0.43$	0.4210	1.2264	1.2075	0.3817	5	6	159
$\pi = 0.4444$	0.4444	1.3984	1.2941	0.3604	6	5	128
$0.45 \leqslant \pi < 0.46$	0.4545	1.4509	1.2745	0.3476	5	7	102
$0.47 \leqslant \pi < 0.48$	0.4762	1.4141	1.2020	0.3261	4	6	99
$\pi = 0.5$	0.50	1.4656	1.0920	0.3038	5	4	131
$0.52 \leqslant \pi < 0.53$	0.5238	1.8119	1.1966	0.2816	7	7	117
$0.54 \leqslant \pi < 0.55$	0.5454	1.5200	0.9694	0.2604	6	4	98
$\pi = 0.5555$	0.5555	1.6690	1.1550	0.2538	7	7	142
$0.57 \leqslant \pi < 0.58$	0.5789	1.6562	1.0000	0.2373	5	6	128
$\pi = 0.6$	0.60	1.6696	1.2615	0.2234	7	4	115
$0.61 \leqslant \pi < 0.62$	0.6190	1.9310	1.0198	0.2036	6	3	101
$0.63 \leqslant \pi < 0.64$	0.6363	1.8205	0.9480	0.1848	5	4	78
$0.65 \leqslant \pi < 0.66$	0.6521	1.6428	0.8570	0.1717	6	4	42
$\pi = 0.6667$	0.6667	1.6969	1.1515	0.1586	3	5	33
$0.69 \leqslant \pi < 0.7$	0.6923	2.2083	0.8333	0.1483	5	4	24
$0.7 \leqslant \pi$	0.7452	2.2650	0.5510	0.1217	6	3	49
All	0.4984	1.5180	1.1770	0.3103	8	7	2000

[2] The price of a home win, away win and a draw is, respectively, $\pi_i = 1/(1 + a_i)$, where a_i represents the odds against the home, away or draw.

number of goals scored by a team, whether playing at home or away, appears to rise essentially monotonically with its price (or probability) of winning. Table 3 reports the relative frequencies (f) and the corresponding odds $(1-f)/f$ of particular score outcomes, together with the mean home, away and draw prices, for the in-sample data. The key feature of this table is that different score outcomes show little apparent relationship to the draw prices (which remain approximately constant at about 0·3) whilst there is a clear tendency for higher score wins to be associated with higher prices (or probabilities) of winning. In Tables 2 and 3 there is evidence that the number of goals scored by each team, and the match outcome, are related to the prices or probabilities implied by the posted fixed odds.

Table 4 presents a contingency table of the score outcomes for the 2000 in-sample matches. To avoid small cell counts, aggregating the last 4 columns and the last 5 rows produces a 5×5 table with a χ^2 goodness of fit statistic of 21·76

TABLE 3
Relative frequency and odds of particular outcomes: corresponding mean home, away and draw prices

Sample 1–2000

Score H–A	Relative frequency	Mean home price	Mean away price	Mean draw price
0–0	0·0815	0·4862	0·3215	0·2999
1–1	0·1290	0·4973	0·3102	0·2997
2–2	0·0540	0·4917	0·3161	0·3008
3–3	0·0130	0·4913	0·3179	0·2996
4–4	0·0020	0·4994	0·3085	0·3043
1–0	0·1115	0·5058	0·3028	0·2983
2–0	0·0665	0·5403	0·2720	0·2945
3–0	0·0390	0·5377	0·2749	0·2937
4–0	0·0185	0·5836	0·2410	0·2852
5–0	0·0040	0·6000	0·2183	0·2882
2–1	0·0870	0·5123	0·2984	0·2979
3–1	0·0390	0·5508	0·2634	0·2932
4–1	0·0170	0·5478	0·2649	0·2950
5–1	0·0040	0·5174	0·2986	0·2940
6–1	0·0015	0·5522	0·2555	0·3019
3–2	0·0290	0·4941	0·3100	0·3019
4–2	0·0125	0·5084	0·3029	0·2993
5–2	0·0040	0·5466	0·2682	0·2902
0–1	0·0730	0·4700	0·3345	0·3026
0–2	0·0380	0·4667	0·3395	0·3014
0–3	0·0160	0·4372	0·3710	0·3024
0–4	0·0075	0·4303	0·3745	0·3006
0–5	0·0020	0·3079	0·5110	0·2864
1–2	0·0705	0·4629	0·3409	0·3027
1–3	0·0265	0·4428	0·3648	0·3030
1–4	0·0075	0·4892	0·3139	0·3033
2–3	0·0190	0·4820	0·3259	0·3009
2–4	0·0040	0·3832	0·4305	0·2972
2–5	0·0020	0·4727	0·3320	0·2987

30   MICHAEL CAIN, DAVID LAW AND DAVID PEEL

TABLE 4
Contingency table of score outcomes in-sample (2000 matches)

		Away goals							
		0	1	2	3	4	5	6	7
	0	163	146	76	32	15	4	1	0
	1	223	258	141	53	15	3	1	1
	2	133	174	108	38	8	4	2	0
Home	3	78	78	58	26	8	2	1	0
goals	4	37	34	25	9	4	0	1	3
	5	8	8	8	1	0	0	0	0
	6	1	3	3	1	0	0	0	0
	7	1	2	0	0	0	0	0	0
	8	0	0	0	0	1	0	0	0

with 16 degrees of freedom. The corresponding *p*-value of such an event is approximately 0·15, and hence it appears that the two classifications, the number of goals scored by the home team and the number scored by the away team, are independent in this sample.

III   NEGATIVE BINOMIAL REGRESSIONS

Since the early analysis of Moroney (1956) and Reep and Benjamin (1968), the Poisson and its generalisation, the negative binomial distribution, have been likely candidates for describing the goal-scoring process in football and the points-scoring process in other sports, though their potential importance in this area seems to have been ignored in the economics literature. The negative binomial probability function is given by:

$$p(x) = \frac{\Gamma(1/\alpha + x)}{\Gamma(1/\alpha)x!} \left[\frac{1}{1+\alpha\lambda}\right]^{1/\alpha} \left[\frac{\alpha\lambda}{1+\alpha\lambda}\right]^{x} \qquad x = 0, 1, 2, \ldots$$

for which the mean is $E(X) = \lambda$ and the variance $V(X) = \lambda[1 + \alpha\lambda]$.

The Poisson probability function is given by:

$$p(x) = \frac{e^{-\lambda}\lambda^x}{x!}, \qquad x = 0, 1, 2, \ldots$$

It can be shown that the Poisson distribution is a limiting case of the Negative Binomial distribution when the degree of dispersion, $\alpha \rightarrow 0$.

Moroney (1956) argued that the Poisson distribution should not be expected to give a perfect description of football scores, since it applied in cases where the expected mean value is constant from trial to trial, whereas the expected number of goals might vary between games with such factors as the quality of the opposing teams and weather conditions. He proceeded to show that a negative binomial distribution (which he called a 'modified Poisson' distribution) gave a better fit than the ordinary Poisson. Colwell and Gillett (1981) and

Pollard (1985) provided further empirical evidence that negative binomial distributions, with a constant mean derived from the ex-post number of goals scored by home and by away teams, provide parsimonious fits to the number of goals scored, in their analysis of 581 English football games played between 1972 and 1983.

We examined whether the negative binomial distribution provided a good fit to the number of goals scored by home and away teams in our sample of 2 000 matches; and we estimated two models.[3] The first model, a 'naive' benchmark, simply employs a constant, the *ex post* mean. The second model uses the home or away price as an additional explanatory variable.[4] The home scores turned out to be most parsimoniously described by a Poisson distribution, in which the mean and variance are not statistically different, whilst away scores are better represented by a negative binomial. This seems to imply that the expected goals scored by home teams are roughly constant from match to match, irrespective of their opposition, weather conditions, etc., whereas this is not so for teams playing away from home. The results are reported in Tables 5a and 5b and some summary statistics are given in Table 5c. Because the home and away prices are inversely, and highly, correlated ($r = -0.984$), each is an excellent proxy for the other. The draw prices show very little variation, so the home and away prices essentially sum to a constant. We experimented with the draw price but, not surprisingly, it did not provide any significant explanatory power. The key feature in the results is the high significance of the home and away prices in explaining the number of home and away goals scored.

TABLE 5a
Poisson regressions of home goals scored (SCH)

Dependent variable	Constant coefficient	Home-win price	Away-win price	χ^2 value
1. SCH	0.4174 (0.0181)			2072
2. SCH	−0.3857 (0.0892)	1.5819 (0.1689)		1988
3. SCH	0.9482 (0.0591)		−1.7573 (0.1913)	1992

Note:
Standard errors are in parentheses.
The expected number of goals scored = 1.5180.

[3] Using the Limdep 6.0 statistical package.

[4] Cain, Law and Peel (1996) have written a programme to adjust the prices for the degree of insider trading implied by the Shin model (available on request). These adjusted 'Shin probabilities' (SHINP) and price have a R^2 of near unity in a linear regression, as shown below, so that the bookmaker's price, and a constant, are excellent proxies for adjusted probabilities in the negative binomial regressions: $\pi_i = 0.027 + 1.026$ SHINP, $R^2 = 0.9994$.

32   MICHAEL CAIN, DAVID LAW AND DAVID PEEL

TABLE 5b
Negative binomial regressions of away goals scored (SCA)

Dependent variable	Constant coefficient	Home-win price	Away-win price	χ^2 value	α
1. SCA	0·1629 (0·0216)			2210	0·0840 (0·0281)
2. SCA	0·9397 (0·0958)	−1·5881 (0·1931)		2145	0·0566 (0·0262)
3. SCA	−0·3894 (0·0714)		1·7324 (0·0561)	2143	0·0561 (0·0261)

Note:
α is the degree of dispersion. The expected number of goals scored = 1·1770.

TABLE 5c
Summary statistics of prices in the sample of 2 000 matches

	Mean	Standard deviation	Maximum	Minimum
Home win	0·4984	0·1082	0·8570	0·1125
Away win	0·3103	0·0981	0·7143	0·0769
Draw	0·2989	0·0171	0·3478	0·1667

Note:
Sample correlation between home-win price and away-win price = 0·984.

Our empirical results are thus consistent with those reported in the early literature by Colwell and Gillett (1981) and Pollard (1985). Both home and away goals appear to be parsimoniously modelled by the negative binomial distribution, though in the case of home goals the Poisson, the special case of the negative binomial, is more parsimonious although the dispersion parameter has a small point coefficient. In fact, the Poisson provides in-sample fits for the away goals that differ only in the fourth decimal point from those given by the Negative Binomial distribution; consequently, the results are unchanged if the former is employed as a predictor rather than the latter.[5]

IV ODDS COMPILATION AND TRADING RULES

Given the independence of the number of home and away goals, we can use the estimates in Tables 5a and 5b to provide probabilities or odds against various scores, and compare these with those offered by the bookmaker. We therefore model the number of goals scored by the home team by a Poisson probability function, where, for particular home and away win prices, λ is estimated as the

[5] For example, the Poisson regression corresponding to regression 2 in Table 4b had a constant of 0·9399 and a coefficient on Home-win price of −1·5884, corresponding to negative binomial coefficients of 0·9397 and −1·5881. Clearly, whilst the dispersion parameter is significantly different from zero in our sample, its quantitative impact is negligible so that the negative binomial and Poisson distributions produce essentially the same mean forecasts.

mean number of home goals by equations 2 or 3 of Table 5a; and the number of goals scored by the away team is modelled by a negative binomial probability function, λ being estimated in this case by equations 2 or 3 of Table 5b.

In Tables 6a, 6b and 6c we set out some examples of the odds implied by the probabilities from the in-sample regressions compared to those offered by the bookmaker for various score outcomes, together with the bookmaker odds against winning (others are available on request). For instance, in Table 6a we report the odds against various score outcomes given by regression 2 from Tables 5a and 5b. There are a number of notable features in these tables. First, the odds offered by bookmakers against long-shot bets appear to be very poor;

TABLE 6a
Estimated fair odds (E) and bookmaker odds (B) against specific scores, given home win odds

Home win odds	1–0		2–0		2–1		3–1		3–2		5–0	
	E	B	E	B	E	B	E	B	E	B	E	B
1/6	9·1	10	6·7	8	11·1	14	12·8	10	40·2	66	24·0	12
1/5	8·7	9	6·7	7	10·7	12	12·8	9	38·8	50	27·1	14
1/1	8·2	6	11·2	8	10·3	8	21·5	14	38·2	28	216·3	100
2/1	11	7·5	19·2	12	13·6	10	36·9	25	50·8	28	793·6	100
3/1	13	9	26·8	20	16·7	14	51·7	33	62·6	33	1618·9	100

TABLE 6b
Estimated fair odds (E) and bookmaker odds (B) against specific scores, given away win odds

Away win odds	0–1		0–2		1–2	
	E	B	E	B	E	B
1/6	10·0	10	7·1	8	13·2	14
1/5	9·5	9	7·1	7	12·5	12
1/1	8·2	6	10·8	8	10·1	8
2/1	10·9	7·5	19·0	12	12·9	10
3/1	13·7	9	27·3	20	16·0	14

TABLE 6c
Estimated fair odds (E) and bookmaker odds (B) against a draw, given home win odds

Home win odds	0–0		1–1		2–2		3–3	
	E	B	E	B	E	B	E	B
1/6	25·6	16	15·0	12	35·0	35	174·4	50
1/5	23·8	16	13·8	12	32·7	35	162·6	50
1/1	12·7	7·5	7·4	5·5	18·6	14	96·4	50
2/1	12·4	7	7·4	5·5	18·8	14	99·4	50
3/1	13·1	7·5	8·0	5·5	20·4	14	108·3	50

34   MICHAEL CAIN, DAVID LAW AND DAVID PEEL

eg, for a home team with odds of 3 to 1 against winning, the bookmaker offered odds of 100 to 1 against a score of 5–0, whilst our estimated odds were 1 618·9 to 1. Second, for teams that are heavily odds-on to win, the bookmaker odds appear to offer potentially profitable betting opportunities for scores of 1–0, 2–0, 2–1 and 3–2. Thirdly, draws (not reported) appear not to offer profitable betting opportunities on the whole, with 3–3 draws being particularly poor bets. Fourthly, the odds offered against the away team winning by a particular score, or drawing, are generally worse than the corresponding odds offered against the home team. This is partly explained by the lower expected goals scored by an away team, compared to a home team with the same posted odds of winning.

In Tables 7a and 7b we report the average bookmaker odds and those implied by the recorded frequency of outcome for a sample of odds against the home and away teams winning (others are available on request). These tables broadly confirm the conclusions derived from Tables 6a–c. In particular, teams which are heavily odds-on to win, either at home or away, appear to offer profitable betting opportunities, though there are only a small number of matches in this

TABLE 7a
Mean bookmaker odds (B) and actual odds (A) against specific scores, given home win odds

		1–0			2–0			2–1		
N	OH	A	B	f	A	B	f	A	B	f
10	0⩽0·3	4	8	0·2	∞	7	0	4	7	0·2
442	0·3⩽0·67	7·7	6·5	0·115	9·1	6·5	0·099	8·4	7·5	0·106
485	0·67⩽1	8	6	0·111	10·5	7·5	0·057	13·3	7·5	0·07
619	1⩽1·5	7·6	6·5	0·116	20·3	9	0·046	8·7	8	0·103
358	1·5⩽2	8·2	7	0·109	21·4	11	0·045	12·3	10	0·075
96	⩾2	12·7	8	0·073	47·0	16	0·021	47	16	0·021

Note:
N = number of matches with OH in given range, OH = odds against home win, f = relative frequency of score, A = (1 – f)/f, B = Bookmaker's Odds.

TABLE 7b
Mean bookmaker odds (B) and actual odds (A) against specific scores, given away win odds

		0–1			0–2			1–2		
N	OA	A	B	f	A	B	f	A	B	f
14	0⩽0·67	6	6·5	0·143	6	6·5	0·143	6	8	0·143
43	0·67⩽1	13·3	6·5	0·070	9·8	7	0·093	3·8	7·5	0·209
285	1⩽1·5	10·9	6·5	0·084	20·9	8	0·046	8·8	6·5	0·102
534	1·5⩽2	8·9	7·5	0·101	19·5	12	0·049	10·4	10	0·088
464	2⩽3	14·5	8	0·065	22·2	14	0·043	13·1	12	0·071
502	3⩽4·5	15·7	9	0·060	32·5	20	0·030	20·8	14	0·046
215	⩾4·5	25·9	12	0·037	107	28	0·009	22·9	18	0·042

Note:
OA = odds against away win.

category. Good bets seem to be those on home teams winning 1−0, 2−0, 2−1 or 3−2 when the home win odds are no more than 0·3; or on away teams winning by the same scores when the away win odds are less than 0·2. The profitability of such bets for the initial sample of 2 000 matches is summarised in Table 8a, and the results for the hold-out sample of 855 matches are given in Table 8b. There were very few matches with short odds on the away team winning, and hence we considered a category of odds less than 0·67 rather than less than 0·2. Nevertheless, there is evidence that the setting of odds on particular scores is not efficient, particularly in the case of short-odds expected wins.

TABLE 8a
Winning bets

In-sample bets

N	OH	1−0		2−0		2−1		3−2	
		A	B	A	B	A	B	A	B
10	0≤0·3	4	8	∞	7	4	7	∞	50
442	0·3≤0·67	7·7	6·5	9·1	6·5	8·4	7·5	33	33

N	OA	0−1		0−2		1−2		2−3	
		A	B	A	B	A	B	A	B
14	0≤0·67	6	6·5	6	6·5	6	8	13	33

TABLE 8b
Winning bets

Out of sample bets

N	OH	1−0			2−0			2−1			3−2		
		n	A	B	n	A	B	n	A	B	n	A	B
18	0≤0·3	4	3·5	8	3	5	8	0					
211	0·3≤0·67										7	29·1	33

N	OA	0−1			0−2			1−2			2−3		
		n	A	B	n	A	B	n	A	B	n	A	B
8	0≤0·67	1	7	6	0			2	3	8	0		

Note:
n = number of winning bets; where n = 0, there were no out-of-sample scores in that category. A completely blank entry appears, e.g. for scores of 1−0, 2−0 and 2−1 when OH < 0·67, because in-sample results did not provide a potentially profitable trading rule, i.e. A > B.

36   MICHAEL CAIN, DAVID LAW AND DAVID PEEL

V Conclusions

There is great interest in gambling markets at present, and a number of anomalies exist that are intriguing for economists. This paper adds to the literature by the novel examination of the properties of the individual fixed odds betting market for the outcomes of football matches in the UK. The key result of the paper is that there appears to be a favourite-longshot bias, in that the odds offered by bookmakers for heavily odds-on teams seem to provide better bets for the punter than those of longshot bets, and that low scores (favourites) offer better bets than high scores (longshots). In addition, we found that the Poisson and Negative Binomial distributions appear to provide good descriptions of the goal-scoring processes, the mean number of goals scored being a function of the home or away team's posted odds of winning. The fixed odds offered against particular score outcomes do seem to offer profitable betting opportunities in some cases, but these are few in number.

Acknowledgements

The authors are grateful for some very helpful comments from two referees. Any remaining errors are the authors' own responsibility.

References

ALI, M. M. (1977). Probability and utility estimates by racetrack bettors. *Journal of Political Economy*, 85, 803–15.

CAIN, M., LAW, D. and PEEL, D. A. (1996). Estimating the incidence of insider trading in a betting market. *University Of Salford Discussion Paper 2*.

COLWELL, D. J. and GILLETT, J. R. (1981). Is goal scoring a Poisson process?. *The Mathematical Gazette*, 65, 30–2.

CRAFTS, N. F. R. (1985). Some evidence of insider knowledge in horse race betting in Britain. *Economica*, 52, 295–304.

DIXON, M. J. and COLES, S. G. (1997). Modelling association football scores and inefficiencies in the football betting market. *Applied Statistics*, 46, 265–80.

DOWIE, J. A. (1976). On the efficiency and equity of betting markets. *Economica*, 43, 139–50.

FIGLEWSKI, S. (1979). Subjective information and market efficiency in a betting model. *Journal of Political Economy*, 87, 75–88.

MORONEY, M. J. (1956). *Facts from Figures*. London: Penguin.

POLLARD, R. (1985). Goal-scoring and the negative binomial distribution. *The Mathematical Gazette*, 69, 45–7.

POPE, P. and PEEL, D. A. (1989). Information, prices and efficiency in a fixed odds betting market. *Economica*, 56, 323–41.

REEP, C. and BENJAMIN, B. (1968). Skill and chance in association football. *Journal of the Royal Statistical Society, Series A*, 131, 581–5.

SHIN, H. (1991). Optimal betting odds against insider traders. *Economic Journal*, 101, 1179–85.

SHIN, H. (1992). Prices of state-contingent claims with insider traders, and the favourite-longshot bias. *Economic Journal*, 102, 426–35.

SHIN, H. (1993). Measuring the incidence of insider trading in a market for state-contingent claims. *Economic Journal*, 103, 1141–53.

THALER, R. H. and ZIEMBA, W. T. (1988). Anomalies: parimutuel betting markets, racetracks and lotteries. *Journal of Economic Perspectives*, 2, 161–74.

Date of receipt of final manuscript: 18 May 1999.

[18]

ELSEVIER   International Journal of Forecasting 16 (2000) 317–331

www.elsevier.com/locate/ijforecast

Forecasting sport: the behaviour and performance of football tipsters

David Forrest*, Robert Simmons

Centre for Sports Economics, University of Salford, Salford M5 4WT, UK

Abstract

Professional advice is available in several forecasting contexts, such as share prices, sales and the weather. English newspaper tipsters offer professional advice on the outcomes of English and Scottish football (soccer) matches. Such advice could potentially inform selections of bettors in fixed odds or pools betting. This paper investigates the effectiveness of the guidance given by newspaper tipsters. Employing a sample of three tipsters and 1694 English league games, we find that tipster success rates are higher than would follow from random forecasting methods. We identify some differences between the processes by which actual results and tipster forecasts are determined. Likelihood-ratio tests imply that the tipsters fail adequately to utilise easily obtainable public information on teams' strength. Further tests show that only one of three tipsters appears to make successful use of other unspecified information relevant to game outcomes. A consensus forecast across the three tipsters appears to outperform any single tipster. © 2000 Elsevier Science B.V. All rights reserved.

Keywords: Football; Newspaper tipsters; Logit

1. Introduction

Professional advice on the outcomes of economic, political and other events is readily available in many settings. For example, independent forecasters may predict the aggregate inflation rate, sales, asset prices, outcomes of political elections and the weather. The judgements of forecasters may represent specialised, marketed advice or may be available as free advice in the media. This paper focuses on the

provision of free professional advice, published in newspapers, in order to guide the behaviour of bettors interested in the outcomes of football matches. Tipsters are a familiar adjunct to many betting markets. Some of those predicting National Lottery winning numbers claim psychic powers but one may presume that sports tipsters profess a more conventionally defined form of expertise. However, Makradakis, Wheelwright, and Hyndman (1998) summarised the literature on expert forecasts as follows: 'in nearly all cases where the data can be quantified, the predictions of the (statistical) models are superior to those of the expert' (p. 492). In this paper, we investigate the nature of tipster expertise and assess the effectiveness of the

*Corresponding author. Tel.: +44-161-295-3674; fax: +44-161-295-2130.

E-mail address: d.k.forrest@salford.ac.uk (D. Forrest).

0169-2070/00/$ – see front matter © 2000 Elsevier Science B.V. All rights reserved.
PII: S0169-2070(00)00050-9

318 D. Forrest, R. Simmons / International Journal of Forecasting 16 (2000) 317–331

guidance offered against a statistical model of actual football results.

Newspaper football tipsters are essentially involved in subjective probabilistic judgemental forecasting (Goodwin & Wright, 1993; Webby & O'Connor, 1996). Judgemental forecasting usually refers to the use of additional elements of judgement over and above techniques of time-series forecasting. Football tipsters offer definite selections of match outcomes which bettors might use in their selections. The selections offered are not probability-weighted. A football match has a well-defined termination point (at least in the eyes of bookmakers) and a well-defined outcome, in the form of either home win, draw (tie) or away win. Unlike most applications of judgemental forecasting, football tipsters do not apply formal statistical techniques to inform their predictions, relying instead on intuition. We can infer the tipster's implicit model, however, by regression analysis.

The information available to forecasters includes 'public' information, such as the league placings and form of the two competing teams, and 'private' information which is somewhat less tangible. Tipsters can use combinations of public and private information to make their selections. Hence, tipsters employ contextual information (information other than time-series patterns and general data on team performance) to make their selections. In this respect, the 'broken-leg cue' is important (Webby & O'Connor, 1996). This refers to unusual pieces of information which enter into a tipster's judgement over and above normal information. Here, the broken-leg cue has a literal meaning when injuries to key players may influence a tipster's prediction of a result.

Academic studies of sports tipster performance are limited in number and normally linked to tests of betting market efficiency. For example, Figlewski (1979) found that the forecasts of a group of newspaper tipsters (handicappers in American parlance) had considerable power in explaining the results of horse races in New York if no other variables were included in his regression equation but added nothing to a model containing betting odds. This finding supported the notion of market efficiency but said little about the performance of the tipsters themselves. Thus the failure of the tipsters' predictions to raise the explanatory power of an equation including (only) betting odds may have resulted (to take two possibilities) either from the tipsters being so respected that the odds responded so as to fully discount their selections or from the tipsters and bettors independently reaching the same conclusions from their reading of form (in a pari-mutuel betting market, odds are determined solely by the behaviour of the bettors). In the first case, one would regard the tipsters as truly expert and serving the function of aiding market efficiency but in the second, they would be judged inexpert because they know no more than the bettors themselves. Clarification of the issue would require the employment of objective data on the ability and form of each runner to check whether tipsters fully exploited the information and whether they added anything to it.

Bird and McCrae (1987) and Pope and Peel (1989) considered tipsters in the context of bookmaker rather than pari-mutuel betting markets, looking at horse racing in Australia and soccer in the United Kingdom, respectively. Each paper reported a simulation of bets being placed in accordance with the recommendations of a panel of newspaper experts. Neither found evidence for abnormal bettor returns (though there was some indication that experts' predictions became worth following towards the end of the football season). Again, the implication is that experts' selections contain the same information as betting odds. However, it would be interesting to know what sort of information was being captured and whether it was being exploited fully.

Goodwin and Corral (1996) adopted a more

D. Forrest, R. Simmons / International Journal of Forecasting 16 (2000) 317–331   319

comprehensive approach which included explicit consideration of the question of whether newspaper tipsters possessed information additional to that included in the form records. The application was to greyhound racing at the Woodlands dog track in Kansas City. Employing a likelihood-ratio test to distinguish between different logit models, they found that dummy variables indicating newspaper tips of the winner and runner-up in each race were statistically significant in the presence of a large number of variables representing information recorded in the greyhound formbook. Tipsters thus appeared to know something (perhaps intangible) not included in the readily obtainable public information. On the other hand, a similar test revealed that tipsters themselves did not fully exploit the public information.

The context of our paper is English professional soccer. Like Goodwin and Corral, we test whether newspaper forecasts contain information not in the form listings and whether the tipsters themselves fully exploit the listings. We go further by modelling the role of the various form data in determining the tipsters' forecasts and whether these tipsters give the appropriate weight to each type of form information. In addition, we consider alternative approaches to measuring the help tipsters give to their readers. Our contribution is novel in directly assessing what variables determine tipster predictions. Our methodology can be generally applied to situations where forecasters make judgements on outcomes which can be ordered.

2. Data

In 1925, *The People* became the first newspaper to include a column offering forecasts of soccer results (Sharpe, 1997). It took six decades for some of the more up-market newspapers to follow them but now all London-based national daily newspapers except the *Financial Times* carry a weekly guide for football bettors that includes an expert's forecast of the outcome of each match (home win, away win or draw). Tabloid and middle-market newspapers carry ancillary information on, for example, recent form and league standings and some newspapers offer 'expert analysis' in the form of supporting commentary on predicted match outcomes by their tipster. Resource constraints prevented our studying the performance of every newspaper tipster, so we selected three newspapers for analysis. They were chosen to be representative of the range of titles available: we required a broadsheet, a middle-market and a tabloid publication and thus adopted (in view of their availability in library archives to which we had access) *The Times*, the *Daily Mail* and *The Mirror*. Each of the three tipsters' columns produced forecasts of the outcome of every professional fixture rather than pick 'best bet' games.

We attempted to collect information pertaining to all matches played within the English professional league structure on Saturdays between December, 1996 and April, 1998 (The professional leagues are the FA Premiership and the three divisions of the Football League; Cup and Scottish League fixtures were excluded). However, we omitted August and September of 1997 from our data set because these were the first two months of a new season and there was therefore limited recent form information on the teams in each match. For each included fixture, we noted the forecasts of the three tipsters and collected the information, listed in bettors' guides in the *Daily Mail* and *The Mirror*, on the recent home and away performances of the home and away team, respectively. We also collected the summary statistics of each club's cumulative (current season) performance embodied in the weekly tables of league standings, also published on the newspapers' sports pages. A small number of games were omitted from our data set because we were unable to obtain

320   D. Forrest, R. Simmons / International Journal of Forecasting 16 (2000) 317–331

forecasts from all three tipsters (e.g. there may have been a production problem or strike at one of the newspapers). We were left with a data set of 1694 football matches.

3. Criteria for assessing performance

An examination of the success of the tipsters in forecasting the 1694 matches must be based on some benchmark level of performance which they would need to have exceeded for their employment to be judged worthwhile. What should they be expected to achieve? The answer depends on what sorts of bettors they are intended to help. We propose three levels at which they might give assistance and each requires different statistical tests to be performed.

The weakest test of tipster efficiency would be to check whether they offered any guidance to a bettor who would enjoy a gamble but who knows nothing about soccer. Such bettors would hope that, at a minimum, tipsters would call more matches correctly than would be expected to follow from randomly picking home wins, draws and away wins. In Section 4, we ask what 'random' selection would mean in this context and test the extent to which tipsters' forecasts are more accurate than a random method that we employ.

A second and higher level of guidance that tipsters could offer is to bettors who are aware of the significance of all the items of data printed in the newspaper guides but who have no taste or time for processing them themselves: they look to the forecaster to provide a single statistic (namely home, draw or away selection) that captures and summarises all this public information. In Section 5, we employ regression analysis to model how the experts process the public information and propose and implement tests of whether the processing is performed efficiently.

A yet higher level of expectation of tipsters

would be implied if one supposed that they should have access to relevant information that was either private or semi-public (in the sense of being too costly for ordinary bettors to purchase). An example of private information might be a training injury to a key player. An example of semi-public information might be that the attacking set-pieces of a high-flying team would be likely to be ineffective against an apparently weaker team because of the defensive style the latter employs (such a conclusion might require reviews of video evidence). If tipsters possess such information (and tipsters interviewed in Sharpe (1997, Ch. 4) claim to have access to news that the public does not hear), then in appropriate regression analysis tipsters' forecasts should be statistically significant in explaining the pattern of match outcomes even when all public listed information is included. In Section 6, we confront tipsters with this toughest test of their usefulness. Section 7 summarises the conclusion of the several approaches adopted in the paper.

4. Tipster picks versus random picks

In our data set, the proportions of matches called successfully by the three tipsters were:

Daily Mail	42.56%
The Mirror	41.09%
The Times	42.86%

Can these strike-rates be considered high or low? Would pure guesswork be likely to yield worse or better strike-rates? Since we are beginning with a weak test of tipster efficiency, we require an appropriately naïve strategy to provide a benchmark against which to make judgements.

One extremely simple strategy would be to call every match a home win, this being the most frequently occurring of the three outcomes. In our data set, 0.475 of matches played

D. Forrest, R. Simmons / International Journal of Forecasting 16 (2000) 317–331   321

were won by the home team, 0.281 were draws, and 0.244 were away victories. Therefore, always forecasting a home win would have yielded a 47.5% strike-rate, comfortably superior to that of any of the three tipsters.

This line of thought is no doubt unfair to tipsters. Their editors would scarcely pay them for providing a 100% home win list of forecasts each week and it would be of little use to bettors who could hardly dare hope for a betting market so inefficient as to yield a positive return to betting on the same outcome every time. The tipsters therefore produce a mixture of all three possible forecasts in each week's list of games. Indeed, an important function of tipsters is to provide guidance to bettors in the choice of draws in the pari-mutuel football pools game, and so tipsters must feel obliged to report some predicted draws.

What might be proposed as an alternative naïve strategy is to choose the outcome of each match at random within the constraint that the proportions of home wins, draws and away wins should correspond to the proportions found in real life results. These proportions are relatively stable over time. For simplicity, we use the proportions from our data set. If h, a and d are these proportions, then the strike-rate from such a strategy would have been $h^2 + d^2 + a^2 = 36.4\%$. All the tipsters outperformed this naïve random strategy.

Of course, it would be easy for those with little knowledge of soccer to pass this test, simply by moving some way towards selecting all matches as home wins. In fact, all three tipsters over-predicted homes relative to the frequency of home wins in real results; respectively, they called home wins in 0.563, 0.539 and 0.533 of games.

Suppose a prospective tipster has no expertise or no wish to make the effort required to use his expertise. Might he obtain as good a strike-rate as one of our experts by random forecasting within the constraint that he adopts the same win–draw–away proportions as the expert himself? If so, the efforts of the real-life expert might be judged wasted.

If one had allocated the forecasts of tipsters randomly across the 1694 matches, the strike-rate achieved would have been $h_i h + d_i d + a_i a$, where h_i, d_i and a_i are the proportions adopted by tipster i and h, d and a are the relative frequencies in real match outcomes. Depending on whether tipster i was the *Mail, Mirror* or *Times* expert, realised strike-rates would have been 38.3, 37.9, and 37.5%, respectively. In each case, therefore, the newspaper tipster achieved a higher strike-rate than would have resulted from random picking within the constraint of predicting the same proportion of each outcome as the tipster himself. To this extent, the achieved strike-rates indicate that some knowledge of soccer is embodied in the published forecasts.

This finding may be checked by regression analysis with the advantage that the statistical significance of the superiority of a tipster's forecasts over random selection could be assessed easily from a likelihood-ratio test. In Table 1, we report our first regression results. Because the three possible outcomes of a match follow a natural ordering, the ordered logit model (first proposed by Zavoina & McElvey, 1975) is appropriate. The dependent variable is match outcome (home = 0, draw = 1, away = 2) and tipster forecasts are embodied in dummy variables corresponding to draw and away predictions. An alternative approach to modelling soccer results, applied by Maher (1982) and Dixon and Coles (1997), is to assume that goals scored by opposing teams are each determined independently by a Poisson process. Our approach takes a different tack and explicitly models what tipsters do. We use our model of tipster predictions as a basis for an assessment of their performance. Tipsters are unlikely to use the Poisson process in making their selections, given the formidable computational requirements involved and their preference for intuition over formal modelling.

Table 1
Ordered logit regression analysis[a]

	(1) Daily Mail		(2) The Mirror		(3) The Times	
	Coefficient	Impact	Coefficient	Impact	Coefficient	Impact
Constant	−0.063	+0.016	−0.071	+0.018	−0.083	+0.021
	(1.02)		(1.12)		(1.27)	
Draw tip	0.252*	−0.063	0.348*	−0.087	0.329*	−0.082
	(2.26)		(3.25)		(2.80)	
Away tip	0.628*	−0.157	0.510*	−0.128	0.460*	−0.115
	(5.11)		(4.12)	(1.27)	(4.23)	
Log-likelihood	−1773.18		−1776.00		−1776.80	
Restricted log-likelihood	−1786.75		−1786.75		−1786.75	

[a] Dependent variable: match result; independent variables: tipster forecasts in the relevant newspaper; 'Impact' shows the marginal effect on home win; absolute t-statistics shown in parentheses; * indicates significance at the 5% level.

In the regression estimates of actual results in Table 1, the coefficients on both tipster dummies are significant in the equations for all three newspapers. The positive signs indicate that in every case, if the tipster calls a draw or an away win, this is associated with a lower probability of a home win occurring on the field. The model implicitly places each match on a scale ranging from 'home win extremely likely' to 'away win extremely likely' and, when a tipster calls other than a home win, the match is pushed along the scale from the home win end towards draw and away win. The marginal effects (calculated as in Greene, 1997) are interpreted as follows. Taking *The Times* as an example, if *The Times* expert predicts a draw, this lowers the probability that there will be a home win by eight percentage points. If his forecast is for an away win, this lowers the probability of a home win by 11 percentage points. However, it is worth noting that, even in the presence of tipsters' forecasts, the most probable outcome in every single match (regardless of tipster forecasts) remains a home win, reflecting the large magnitude of home advantage in English soccer.

In the equation for each tipster, the statistical significance of the newspaper forecasts may be assessed by comparing the log-likelihood function with that for a model in which the coefficients on the relevant variables are constrained to be zero. In a chi-squared likelihood ratio test, the test statistic is $2(L_F - L_R)$, where L_R is the maximised value of the log-likelihood function for the restricted model and L_F is that for the unrestricted model. The number of degrees of freedom is given by the number of restrictions imposed on the restricted model (here two). For our three equations, the test statistic values are 27.14, 21.50 and 19.88. The critical value is 5.99 at the 5% level. The hypothesis that there is no relevant information captured in the tipster's forecasts is therefore rejected decisively in all three cases. This confirms our conclusion that tipsters pass the weak requirement of knowing something. From the preceding analysis, it appears that they know enough for copying the forecasts of any one of them to yield more success than if one just guessed the outcomes of matches.

5. Tipsters and public information

We now inquire as to the source of tipsters' knowledge. The broadsheet newspapers such as *The Times* excepted, there is little variation

D. Forrest, R. Simmons / International Journal of Forecasting 16 (2000) 317–331   323

across newspapers in the choice of facts and figures displayed in the weekly bettor guides. Presumably, this reflects some consensus about what matters in the determination of the likely outcome of a soccer game. In Table 2, we report the results of ordered logit estimation of the relationship between each tipster's forecasts and the information that newspapers often present alongside tipsters' columns. Recent form is represented by variables (last five home and last five away) measuring the home team's performance in its last five home games and the away team's performance in its last five away games, as reported in the *Daily Mail*. Our measures were constructed by awarding two points for each win and one point for each draw so that the variables take values in the range zero to ten. The cumulative season-to-date home

Table 2
Ordered logit regression analysis[a]

	(1) Daily Mail		(2) The Mirror		(3) The Times		(4) Result	
	Coefficient	Impact	Coefficient	Impact	Coefficient	Impact	Coefficient	Impact
Constant	0.431	−0.104	0.485*	−0.119	0.810*	−0.199	0.278	−0.067
	(1.37)		(2.22)		(3.89)		(1.37)	
Last 5 home	−0.193*	+0.091	−0.139*	+0.067	−0.134*	+0.065	0.011	−0.005
	(5.97)		(4.40)		(4.21)		(0.38)	
Last 5 away	0.054	−0.025	−0.029	+0.014	−0.028	+0.014	−0.009	+0.004
	(1.95)		(0.99)		(1.03)		(0.37)	
Home goals ratio	−0.118	+0.025	−0.135	+0.029	0.075	+0.016	−0.152*	+0.033
	(1.40)		(1.59)		(0.92)		(2.26)	
Away goals ratio	0.912*	−0.099	1.000*	−0.110	0.301*	−0.033	0.337*	−0.038
	(7.82)		(7.80)		(2.29)		(2.87)	
Home lead 17+	−2.255*	+0.543	−3.236*	+0.795	−3.207*	+0.787	−0.287	+0.072
	(4.39)		(4.37)		(5.26)		(1.02)	
Home lead 13–16	−2.047*	+0.493	−3.315*	+0.814	−3.426*	+0.840	−0.928*	+0.232
	(5.27)		(5.52)		(6.49)		(4.01)	
Home lead 9–12	−1.624*	+0.391	−1.843*	+0.453	−2.061*	+0.506	−0.454*	+0.113
	(5.69)		(6.64)		(7.50)		(2.36)	
Home lead 5–8	−1.212*	+0.292	−1.242*	+0.305	−1.139*	+0.279	−0.260	+0.065
	(5.88)		(6.27)		(6.20)		(1.57)	
Home lead 1–4	−0.498*	+0.120	−0.773*	+0.190	−0.500*	+0.123	−0.301	+0.075
	(2.87)		(4.30)		(3.04)		(1.85)	
Away lead 5–8	0.487*	−0.117	0.581*	−0.143	0.311	−0.076	−0.137	+0.034
	(2.99)		(3.49)		(1.93)		(0.86)	
Away lead 9–12	0.902*	−0.217	1.347*	−0.331	0.606*	−0.149	−0.139	+0.034
	(4.78)		(7.15)		(3.39)		(0.77)	
Away lead 13–16	1.184*	−0.285	1.812*	−0.445	1.134*	−0.278	−0.137	+0.034
	(5.41)		(7.86)		(5.04)		(0.65)	
Away lead 17+	1.549*	−0.373	2.283*	−0.561	1.518*	−0.372	0.105	−0.026
	(4.65)		(7.15)		(5.08)		(0.39)	
Log-likelihood	−1332.22		−1262.02		−1442.25		−1758.63	
Count-R^2	0.638		0.658		0.596		0.479	

[a] Dependent variable: (1) to (3) tipster forecasts; (4) match results; independent variables: public listed information; 'Impact' shows the marginal effects on home win (dummy variables) or the standard deviation marginal effect on home win (continuous variables); absolute *t*-statistics in parentheses; * indicates significance at the 5% level.

and away performances of the two teams are captured by 'home goals ratio' and 'away goals ratio', in each case calculated by dividing goals scored by goals conceded. The relative all-round strength of the clubs measured over the season to date is embodied in the difference in their league positions. To allow for non-linearity, relative league position is entered via banding with a series of dummies such as 'home lead 13–16' (the current league position of the home team is between 13 and 16 places higher than the visiting team) and 'away lead 5–8' (the away team currently leads its hosts by between 5 and 8 places in the standings); the reference band is 'away 1–4', chosen because this was, by a small margin, the most frequently occurring grouping in the data set.

In Table 2, we also show for comparison the result of ordered logit estimation of an equation relating actual outcomes to all these team strength indicators. As one might expect, given the scope for matches to be decided by random on-the-field events, this equation is less well determined than those which model tipster selections, but it nevertheless serves the function of allowing a check on whether the items of data either emphasised or neglected by tipsters in fact matter in accounting for the actual pattern of game outcomes.

In an ordered logit model, interpretation of the size of coefficients (as opposed to their statistical significance) requires computation of marginal effects. In Table 2, in columns headed 'impact', we show for the binary variables the marginal effect on home win of the variable taking on the value of one rather than zero. For example, we estimate that if the home team has a lead of 1–4 places in the league standings, the probability that the *Daily Mail* columnist will call a home win is raised by 12.0 percentage points relative to the situation represented by the reference (or excluded) category of the away side enjoying a lead of 1–4 places. Of course, the model also permits calculation of marginal

effects on draws and away wins but, for conciseness, we omit these from the table.

The 'impact' shown in Table 2 in respect of the set of continuous variables (last five home, last five away, home goals ratio, away goals ratio) was obtained by taking the calculated marginal effect on home win and multiplying it by the standard deviation of the variable.

This 'standard deviation marginal effect' shows how the probability of a home win is affected when the value of the relevant variable is raised by one standard deviation from its mean. For example, in the estimates of actual results, the impact shown for 'away goals ratio' is -0.038. This implies that if the visiting team has an away goal ratio one standard deviation better than the mean away goal ratio (measured across all observations), then the probability of the home team winning is thereby lowered by 3.8 percentage points.

It is clear from Table 2 that tipsters give considerable implicit weight to our proposed indicators derived from data listed in newspapers. The coefficients on most of the variables are highly significant. However, they are not uniformly so and the following principal points emerge.

First, all three tipsters accord significance to the recent home performances of the home team while appearing not to take seriously the recent road record of the visiting club. Possibly they have in mind that home advantage stems in part from the home team's familiarity with the physical characteristics of its stadium and from the degree of crowd support from which it benefits (Courneya & Carron, 1992). The extent to which the team can exploit these advantages may be thought to be embodied in the recent results obtained at that stadium. The away team's recent away record will, on the other hand, relate to games at a variety of stadia where the physical dimensions, surface characteristics and crowd behaviour may be different in every case from the conditions to be en-

D. Forrest. R. Simmons / International Journal of Forecasting 16 (2000) 317–331   325

countered in the next fixture. For this or for whatever reason, recent away form appears not to be taken as relevant to the outcome of the next away trip.

Second, and by contrast, the season-long goal ratio variable is shown in Table 2 to have a significant effect on newspaper forecasts only in the case of the away club. The information selected as mattering as a summary of the away team's past performances has at least the advantage that it will be unaffected by whether the recent away games have been played on grounds with particularly idiosyncratic characteristics.

Inspection of the regression results for these variables in respect of real match outcomes indicates that recent form is in fact of little relevance whether it refers to the home or away team. The coefficients on home goals ratio and away goals ratio are, however, both highly significant and almost symmetric in their impact on the predicted outcome of a match. These variables measure cumulative form and are more reliable predictors of actual results given the difficulty in separating signal and noise when only a small number of matches are considered. The tipsters perhaps suggest an overly deterministic process where match results are seen to some extent as extrapolations of recent form. Note that these contrasts between the determination of tipster and actual results are unlikely to be explained by collinearity between the recent form and goals ratio variables which, from an inspection of the correlation matrix, appeared not to be unduly high (0.52 (last five home results and home goals ratio) and 0.25 (last five away results and away goals ratio)).

Another possible source of home advantage noted by Courneya and Carron (1992) is the travel fatigue and disruption to routine experienced by the away team. Clarke and Norman (1995) related the degree of home advantage to the distance between the two teams'

grounds. We experimented with the inclusion of distance in all the equations estimated in Table 2 but, while correctly (negatively) signed in the results equation, it was not statistically significant; nor did tipsters appear to give this information any weight. Distance was therefore omitted from the final estimated equations.

The third feature of interest in Table 2 is the large weight tipsters accord to relative league positions. The relevant coefficients are all highly significant in each of the three tipster equations. Furthermore, inspection of the marginal effects shows it to be almost uniformly true that each extra step on the spectrum from large away lead to large home lead raises sharply the probability of a home win being tipped. This faith in the guidance offered by the standings is not quite supported by the equation for actual match outcomes where substantial home leads certainly improve the chances of a home win but where the size of an away lead is not a useful predictor: the coefficients on the away lead bandings are all insignificant, showing no impact on the result relative to the base situation of a small away lead (away lead 1–4 being the reference banding in the specified equation). Relative to the statistical process determining actual results, it appears that the tipsters give undue weight to both small home team leads and to away leads. Indeed, the tipsters appear to make their predictions as if matches can be ranked according to a scale between large away lead (away win) and large home lead (home win). Actual results contain far more noise than this procedure would warrant; only large home leads, of 9–16 places, significantly affect the probability of a home win. A similar comparison appears in a study of the verdicts of the Pools Panel when matches are postponed (Forrest & Simmons, 2000).

There are then differences between the way tipsters model the relationship between outcomes and listed information and the way in which the information appears to matter in practice. This could of course raise a suspicion that tipsters might not be processing the information accurately. That in itself, one should note, would not necessarily bring about unsatisfactory overall performance by tipsters in that they may compensate by wise use of private information. For now, we shall analyse further the use they made of the public information.

Ordered logit estimation yields, for each observation, a fitted value of a continuous latent variable that is posited to underlie the discrete categories of the dependent variable that we actually observe. Predicted probabilities of each category occurring may then be obtained corresponding to each observation. In our case, we had, for each fixture, estimated probabilities for home win, draw and away win. In the calculation of count-R^2, the 'predicted outcome' is the category with the highest probability and this predicted outcome is then compared with observed outcome to obtain the proportion of observations 'explained'. Our regression equation on actual results in this sense 'explains' 47.9% of the observations. However, the figure cannot be taken too seriously. Though it is higher than the tipster strike-rates reported in Section 4 above, it is achieved only by 'predicting' that 96.5% of matches will be won by the home team. This reflects the substantial magnitude of home advantage in professional soccer since, notwithstanding the identification of several variables that might significantly pull the balance of advantage towards the away team, the single most probable outcome in almost every match remained a home win. As noted above, calling home win in almost every match is not an option for tipsters, so they cannot be expected to achieve strike-rates comparable with the proportion of observations 'explained' by the results regression equation.

As a first means of assessing the extent to which tipsters take adequate account of the patterns identified by regression analysis of

actual outcomes, we adopted the following procedure, described for the *Daily Mail* but applied in turn to *The Mirror* and *The Times* as well. Of the 1694 matches in the data set, the *Daily Mail* called 954 in favour of the home team; 417 were forecast to be draws; the away side was tipped in the remaining 323 fixtures. We sorted the 1694 observations according to how probable a home win was according to the estimated real-results regression equation; probabilities of a home win ranged from 0.789 to 0.117. Taking the *Daily Mail* tipster predictions as constraints, we allocated as 'home predictions' the 954 matches with the highest probability of a home win; we called draws for the next 417 fixtures ordered in descending order of probability of home win; and the residual 323 contests were termed 'away predictions'. Our allocations were then compared with on-the-field results. 44.0% of match outcomes were 'explained' by this procedure of using the regression equation but imposing the same home–draw–away distribution as in the *Daily Mail* data set. The corresponding figures for *The Mirror* and *The Times* were 43.4 and 43.6%, respectively. All these figures were higher than the tipster strike-rates recorded earlier, strengthening a suspicion that the newspaper experts were not modelling as successfully as they might the role of the data embodied in public information. Thus, even when imposing the constraint that the set of results had to have the same distributions of outcomes as the tipster's forecasts, the statistical model was still more successful than the expert.

Of course, it is possible that the supposed superiority of the regression-based 'forecasts' over the subjective forecasts is attributable to their having the advantage of being made ex post rather than ex ante. The findings therefore needed to be checked against out-of-sample forecasting performance. Accordingly, we collected a fresh sample which included all matches played in the English leagues on the 12

D. Forrest. R. Simmons / International Journal of Forecasting 16 (2000) 317–331   327

Saturdays from October 10 to December 26, 1998. However, missing copies in our newspaper archive (microfilm records were not yet available) limited our comparisons to 139 matches in the case of *The Mirror* and 262 in the case of the *Daily Mail* (as against 367 for *The Times*).

We followed our previous procedure, employing the regression equation estimated from our main sample (reported in Table 2 above) to generate sets of forecasts made within the constraint that our home–draw–away proportions had to match those found in the columns of the relevant newspaper tipster over the second sample period. *The Times* and *The Mirror* achieved slightly higher strike-rates than the corresponding regression-based forecasts. However, the average tipster strike-rate across the three newspapers (weighted by sample size) was again less than the regression strike-rate: 41.8% compared with 43.4%.

Given this evidence, we returned to our original sample to conduct a more formal test of whether tipsters made full use of public information. We re-estimated the equation relating actual results to public information but with the addition of dummy variables representing the picking out of a game as 'draw' or 'away win'

by the particular tipster. The results for each of the tipsters are exhibited as Table 3.

We again report our findings using the *Daily Mail* as reference point. In Table 1, we reported a regression of match results on *Daily Mail* tips. In Table 3, we regress match results on *Daily Mail* tips and on 13 variables representing public listed information. The model in the first regression is therefore nested within that used in the subsequent regression. Hence, nested hypothesis testing is appropriate. The log-likelihood value for the first equation (where the coefficients on the 13 public information variables are constrained to be zero) is compared with the log-likelihood value for the second (unrestricted) equation.

The quantity $2(L_F - L_R)$ is distributed as chi-squared with k degrees of freedom, where L_F and L_R are the log-likelihood values for the full and restricted models, respectively and k is the number of coefficients constrained in the restricted version. Here $2(L_F - L_R) = 35.64$. The critical value of chi-squared with 13 degrees of freedom (5% level) is 22.36. The restrictions are therefore decisively rejected: the 13 extra variables contribute information relevant to match outcomes that is not included in the *Daily Mail* tips. It appears that the *Daily Mail* tipster

Table 3
Ordered logit regression analysis[a]

| | (1) Daily Mail | | (2) The Mirror | | (3) The Times | |
	Coefficient	Impact	Coefficient	Impact	Coefficient	Impact
Constant	0.198	−0.049	0.197	−0.049	0.162	−0.040
	(0.96)		(0.96)		(0.78)	
Draw tip	0.046	−0.112	0.126	−0.031	0.143	−0.036
	(0.38)		(1.06)		(1.14)	
Away tip	0.142*	−0.088	0.175	−0.044	0.181	−0.045
	(2.50)		(1.14)		(1.43)	
Log-likelihood	−1755.36		−1957.78		−1757.45	

[a] Dependent variable: match results; independent variables: 13 public listed information variables and tipster forecasts; 'Impact' shows the marginal effect on home win; absolute t-statistics shown in parentheses; * indicates significance at the 5% level.

328   *D. Forrest. R. Simmons / International Journal of Forecasting 16 (2000) 317–331*

does not fully exploit all the information available in his own newspaper.

Results for *The Mirror* and *The Times* are similar. Test statistics in these cases were (respectively) 36.44 and 38.70. The formal tests therefore provide further support for our suspicion that there is some deficiency in the way in which each of the three tipsters employs the public listed information. This deficiency refers specifically to the role of variables which are widely publicised in newspapers and which add significantly to the explanatory power of our regression results in Table 2.

6. Tipsters and private information

Of course, any deficiencies in tipsters' processing of public information could be compensated if they were to employ insights attributable to their command of private information or semi-public information (information in principle in the public domain but not cheaply accessible or interpretable to non-specialists). In this section, we implement further nested hypothesis tests to illuminate this possibility. We are unable to ascertain what semi-public information the tipster may possess nor the effectiveness with which this information is processed. We can, though, assess whether extra insights offered, implicitly or explicitly, by the tipsters add explanatory power to the role of variables representing public information in our regression equation for actual results.

Consider the 'results' equation in Table 2 where match result is regressed on public information. This is a restricted version of the equation in Table 3 where match result is regressed on public information and on two dummy variables reflecting the *Daily Mail's* tips. Once again, we can test the restrictions. In this case, the test statistic is 6.54 against a critical value (2 degrees of freedom) of 5.99. The restrictions are therefore rejected and the

Daily Mail expert appears able to add to the ability of the public information to account for the pattern of match results. However, the values of the test statistic in similar procedures including *Mirror* and *Times* forecasts were 1.70 and 2.36, respectively, and one could not therefore reject the hypothesis that the conclusions in these newspapers provided no information supplementary to that captured in the public information variables (The regression of match results on tipster forecasts yielded significant coefficients (Table 1) but for *The Mirror* and *The Times* the coefficients became insignificant in the presence of public information variables (Table 3)). Inspection of *t*-statistics implies therefore that *Mirror* and *Times* tip dummies may contain no independent information. However, jointly assessing the significance of 'tip draw' and 'tip away' in the nested hypothesis test reported here is necessary because we know that public information plays a substantial role in determining tips (Table 2) and collinearity between tip dummies and public information variables could therefore account for the rejection of the former in *t*-tests where both sets of variables are present).

It is possible that a consensus of tipsters' forecasts might perform better than any one individual tipster. Some studies suggest otherwise. Clarke (1993) set up a computer program to predict Australian Rules scores and found that this yielded superior forecasts to individual and consensus tips, although some of the 'tipsters' appeared to be more concerned with newspaper publicity by means of 'controversial' selections than with more objective assessment. Clemen and Winkler (1985) examined the independence of a group of North American sports forecasters and found a correlation between forecasts of 0.8 which was equivalent to only 1.25 independent forecasts. In our context of soccer predictions, we might similarly anticipate a problem of correlated forecasts and consequent lack of independence between tips-

D. Forrest. R. Simmons / International Journal of Forecasting 16 (2000) 317–331   329

Table 4
Ordered logit regression analysis[a]

	(1)		(2)	
	Coefficient	Impact	Coefficient	Impact
Constant	0.002	0	0.094	−0.023
	(0.02)		(0.44)	
Home tip	−0.109	0.027	0.130	−0.032
	(0.84)		(0.89)	
Draw tip	0.283	−0.071	0.270	−0.067
	(1.86)		(1.76)	
Away tip	0.600*	−0.150	0.521*	−0.130
	(3.91)		(3.15)	
Log-likelihood	−1769.6		−1753.7	

[a] Dependent variable: match results; independent variables: (1) consensus tipster forecast; (2) consensus tipster forecasts and three public information variables as shown in Table 2; 'Impact' shows the marginal effect on home win; absolute t-statistics shown in parentheses; * indicates significance at 1% level.

ter selections, given the findings in Table 2. On the other hand, if each of the three tipsters captures unique insights then the consensus should outperform any individual forecast.

To test for the effectiveness of a consensus forecast, we identified cases where two or more of the three tipsters agreed on the outcome of a match. Thus, if any two tipsters call a draw we code the dummy variable, *draw tip* as 1, and similarly for *home tip* and *away tip*. The excluded category here is no consensus, i.e. three different selections by the tipsters. The regression results using this consensus forecast are shown in Table 4. As before, we test for whether the consensus fully exploits all the public information present in our performance variables. The likelihood ratio chi-squared test statistic is 32.62. Set against a critical value of 22.36 for 13 degrees of freedom, this suggests that the coefficients on the added public information variables are jointly significantly different from zero. Hence, the public information variables add extra explanatory power to the consensus forecast in the determination of actual results.

Does a consensus forecast yield explanatory

power over and above a regression of actual results on public information indicators only? Here, the likelihood-ratio test for addition of the three extra tipster dummy variables gives a chi-squared test statistic of 10.58. With a critical value for three degrees of freedom of 7.82, we cannot reject the hypothesis that the coefficients of the extra tipster variables are jointly significantly different from zero. Hence, we conclude that the consensus forecast adds something to our public information variables even though two of the tipsters considered on an individual basis do not.

7. Summary and conclusions

Our first statistical tests were concerned with whether the three newspaper tipsters sampled were able to predict more soccer games successfully than would someone employing a random process based on a very limited knowledge of soccer. All three tipsters passed these tests and therefore possessed some appropriate knowledge of soccer.

However, when we modelled the process by

which tipsters took into account the information on teams' strength featured on soccer betting pages in two of the newspapers, we noted some differences from the process by which the results themselves appeared to be determined. From the results of likelihood-ratio tests conducted after estimating equations regressing match results on individual tipster forecasts (with and without the items of public listed information), these differences seem to be sufficient for all three tipsters to be judged inadequate in their processing of public listed information.

Finally, we implemented likelihood-ratio tests designed to find whether the tipsters possessed enough independent information for their tips to remain statistically significant predictors of match results even in the presence of publicly listed data. Only one of the tipsters appeared to exploit such private or semi-public information. Hence, there is no overwhelming evidence here that the predictions of match results from our regression models are inferior to those made by the experts. This conclusion is consistent with the received wisdom on the effectiveness of expertise in forecasting, as summarised in Makradakis et al. (1998). As a caveat, we found that taking into account the presence of any consensus among tipsters could add to the effectiveness of regression forecasts based on public information. We conclude that while individual tipsters' guidance is better than no guidance, the expertise they can claim to offer is limited.

Acknowledgements

The bulk of the research assistance was carried out thoroughly by Joanne Lord whose role is duly acknowledged. We are also grateful to Pam Carroll and Daniel Eisen for additional help. The comments of two anonymous referees and an editor facilitated improvements in the paper. The usual caveat applies.

References

Bird, R., & McCrae, M. (1987). Tests of the efficiency of racetrack betting using bookmaker odds. *Management Science 33*, 1552–1562.

Clarke, S. R. (1993). Computer forecasting of Australian rules football for a daily newspaper. *Journal of the Operational Research Society 44*, 753–759.

Clarke, S. R., & Norman, J. M. (1995). Home advantage of individual clubs in English soccer. *Journal of the Royal Statistical Society Series D (The Statistician) 44*, 509–521.

Clemen, R. T., & Winkler, R. L. (1985). Limits for the precision and value of information from dependent sources. *Operations Research 33*, 427–442.

Courneya, K. S., & Carron, A. V. (1992). The home advantage in sports competitions: A literature review. *Journal of Sport and Exercise Psychology 14*, 13–27.

Dixon, M. J., & Coles, S. G. (1997). Modelling association football scores and inefficiencies in the UK football betting market. *Journal of the Royal Statistical Society Series C 46*, 265–280.

Figlewski, S. (1979). Subjective information and market efficiency in a betting market. *Journal of Political Economy 87*, 75–87.

Forrest, D. K., & Simmons, R. (2000). Making up the results: The work of the Football Pools Panel 1963–97. *Journal of the Royal Statistical Society Series D (The Statistician) 49*, 253–260.

Goodwin, B. K., & Corral, L. R. (1996). Bettor handicapping and market efficiency in greyhound pari-mutuel gambling. *Applied Economics 28*, 1181–1190.

Goodwin, P., & Wright, G. (1993). Improving judgemental time series forecasting: A review of the guidance provided by research. *International Journal of Forecasting 9*, 147–161.

Greene, W. H. (1997). Econometric analysis, 3rd ed, Macmillan, New York.

Maher, M. J. (1982). Modelling association football scores. *Statistica Neerlandica 36*, 109–118.

Makradakis, S., Wheelwright, S., & Hyndman, R. (1998). Forecasting methods and applications, 3rd ed, Wiley, New York.

Pope, P. F., & Peel, D. A. (1989). Information, prices and efficiency in a fixed-odds betting market. *Economica 56*, 323–341.

Sharpe, G. (1997). Gambling on goals: a century of football betting, Mainstream, Edinburgh.

Webby, R., & O'Connor, M. (1996). Judgemental and statistical time series forecasting: A review of the literature. *International Journal of Forecasting 12*, 91–118.

D. Forrest, R. Simmons / International Journal of Forecasting 16 (2000) 317–331   331

Zavoina, R., & McElvey, W. (1975). A statistical model for the analysis of ordinal level variables. *Journal of Mathematical Sociology 2*(Summer), 103–120.

Biographies: David FORREST is Lecturer in Economics, University of Salford. He has research interests in the economics of sport, the arts and gambling and in valuation issues in cost–benefit analysis. Recent outlets include *Oxford Economic Papers, Journal of the Royal Statistical Society, Journal of Transport Economics and Policy* and *Journal of Gambling Studies*.

Robert SIMMONS is Lecturer in Economics and Director of the Centre for Sports Economics, at the University of Salford. His research interests are in labour economics, economics of professional team sports and economics of gambling. He has published in *Economica, Bulletin of Economic Research, Applied Economics* and several other economics journals. He is a member of the Board of Editors of the *Journal of Sports Economics*.

[19]

The Statistician (2000)
49, Part 2, pp. 253–260

Focus on Sport

Making up the results: the work of the Football Pools Panel, 1963–1997

David Forrest and Robert Simmons

University of Salford, UK

[Received September 1998. Revised October 1999]

Summary. Since 1963, a panel of experts has determined for gambling purposes the results of soccer matches in Britain which were included in the football pools weekly game but which could not be played because of adverse weather. The paper models its behaviour and highlights differences between the factors which appear to influence the panel's predictions and those that matter to the outcomes of real games. Panel results are more predictable than real results and the paper offers a specific recommendation to the Pools Panel to render its judgments less predictable. The panel also appears to overemphasize the importance of the recent away form of the away team. An explanation for this systematic difference in the statistical estimates of Pools Panel and actual results is found in the home advantage literature in sports statistics.

Keywords: Football pools; Ordered logit; Pools Panel

1. The football pools

The Pools Promoters' Association Pools Panel (henceforth, the Pools Panel) is a very peculiar British sporting institution. Currently, the treble chance is the most popular of several games offered by the pools industry. This *pari-mutuel* game invites bettors to select eight matches from a weekly list of 49 games. If all eight selected matches are drawn (tied), the bettor wins a share in the jackpot prize; near misses are rewarded with lesser prizes. If any of the 49 games are postponed, the Pools Panel adjudicates on the outcomes solely for the purposes of pools betting.

The Pools Panel was initiated in January 1963 by the pools companies in response to the loss of revenue incurred through the cancellation of fixtures, and indeed abandonment of the pools game, on several Saturdays owing to the exceptionally severe winter of 1962–1963. In early January 1963, a Swedish pools company set a precedent by paying out prize money on the pools on the basis of allocating postponed matches outcomes determined by a random draw. The British Pools Panel followed a different approach. A panel was set up to determine the outcomes of postponed and abandoned matches which appeared on pools coupons. This panel comprised five experts, a mix of dignitaries and former players and referees, and a non-voting chairman. Its first meeting was on January 26th, 1963. In its earlier stages the panel met during Saturday afternoons when 30 or more matches were postponed, this being the number that had previously been sufficient to cancel the pools competition. Now, the Pools Panel adjudicates whenever even a single match on the pools coupon cannot take place for whatever reason.

Address for correspondence: David Forrest, Centre for Sports Economics, University of Salford, Salford, M5 4WT, UK.
E-mail: d.k.forrest@salford.ac.uk

0039–0526/00/49253

The integrity of any gambling medium is important for its survival. A loss of public confidence in the fairness of the betting process could lead to long-term loss of turnover. The industry may therefore hope that its appointed experts would seek to avoid controversy. If they do, their results will be more predictable than those of real life. However, this approach has its own problems. As early as February 1963, the *Daily Mirror*'s pools tipster, Longsight, pointed out that it was

> 'not only possible but comparatively easy for anyone who knew a lot about soccer to predict most of the results given to unplayed matches by the Panel on a Saturday'.

This greater predictability of panel outcomes could reduce individual prizes because more people each week would select the 'correct' results. This would lead to lower revenue for the pools companies as the expected reduced jackpot prize per winner would deter bettors from entering the pools competition.

Our analysis in this paper, based on 35 years of Pools Panel activity, shows Longsight's remarks to be prescient. We compare Pools Panel football match decisions with actual results and demonstrate the relatively greater predictability of the former. We also find systematic behavioural differences in the statistical processes which determine Pools Panel and actual results. The paper is structured as follows. Section 2 introduces our data set and presents some summary statistics. Section 3 sets out our proposed model and statistical methodology. Section 4 reports our results, drawing attention to key differences between the estimates of actual and invented results. Section 5 concludes with a precise recommendation for the future conduct of the Pools Panel.

2. The data

We collected from newspaper microfilm records samples of the real or manufactured results of (English) Football League and Scottish League fixtures scheduled between 1963 and 1997. There were three criteria for sampling matches:

(a) we only included Pools Panel verdicts on Saturdays when it turned out to predict the results of at least 10 matches;
(b) we only included actual match results on Saturdays where they coexisted with at least 10 Pools Panel verdicts;
(c) cup games were excluded.

This gave us matched samples of 1384 actual results and 1483 Pools Panel results. That the samples are from the same Saturdays is useful for our purpose of comparing what determined outcomes in the two categories because different factors may influence outcomes at different times of the year (for example, shock results may occur when the minds of weak teams are concentrated by end-of-season relegation struggles) and we would not therefore want a different pattern of dates for the sample of real results from that for the panel's results. Again, where 10 or more matches are postponed, it is likely that there are bad weather conditions over much of the country and the results of the matches that survived the weather may be affected by the marginal conditions in which they will have had to be played (and in which the postponed matches would also have had to be played if the referees had not called them off).

Table 1 displays the proportions of away wins, draws and home wins in our two samples. Draws are less represented in the panel than in the real matches data but so also are away wins. What is evident from Table 1 is that the panel stressed home advantage more than was justified by the record of results on the field. 52% of panel decisions favoured the home team but only 46% of home teams that played succeeded in securing a win. These percentages differ statistically at the 0.1% significance level.

Table 1. Outcomes (proportions) of real and panel matches, 1963–1997

Match	Away win	Draw	Home win
Real	0.24	0.30	0.46
Panel	0.21	0.27	0.52

Longsight (1963) laid particular emphasis on the predictability of the panel when a team had both home advantage and a lead over its opponent in the league standings. In his early assessment of the Pools Panel, after just 2 weeks, he pointed out that, where the home teams were at least 10 places higher in the league tables than the visitors, the panel always decided on a home win. It seems that this behaviour pattern became ingrained over the next 34 years of Pools Panel operation. We grouped matches according to the difference in the current league standings between the position of the home team and the position of the away team. For all bands where the home team occupied the higher league place, the panel called a home win very much more often than data on real matches suggested that they should.

3. An ordered logit model

The Pools Panel must form a judgment about where each game lies on a scale between 'away win certain' and 'home win certain'. Some games which it thinks likely to yield a home victory may be viewed as 'safer' calls than others for which a home win is nevertheless the most probable outcome. However, we do not observe which home win calls are regarded as close and which lie further towards the home win certain extreme because the announced predictions merely place each game in one of three categories: away win, draw or home win. Essentially, there is an unobserved (or latent) continuous variable (how far along the away–home scale the panel puts the individual match) but we observe only three categories of outcome.

An appropriate empirical methodology for a situation such as this is provided by the ordered logit model proposed by Zavoina and McElvey (1975). The model is specified as

$$y^* = \mathbf{b}'\mathbf{x} + \epsilon \qquad (1)$$

where y^* is the unobserved dependent variable (here the relative strength of the home team as judged by the Pools Panel) and $\mathbf{x}$ is a vector of explanatory variables (here those which affect Pools Panel behaviour); $\mathbf{b}$ is a vector of parameters to be estimated and ϵ is an error term.

There are three ordered measures of relative home team strength which map into three categories selected by the Pools Panel: away win, draw and home win. Then:

$$y = \begin{cases} 0 & \text{if } y^* \leq 0, & (2a) \\ 1 & \text{if } 0 < y^* < \mu, & (2b) \\ 2 & \text{if } \mu \leq y^* & (2c) \end{cases}$$

where μ is a threshold level to be estimated by the model. A set of ordered variables is constructed for categories of Pools Panel selection, where $j = 1, 2, 3$ indexes the categories of away win, draw and home win respectively and where $i = 1, \ldots, n$ represents individual fixtures. Hence, for a particular fixture i, we create the dummy variable

$$z_{ij} = \begin{cases} 1 & \text{if } y \text{ falls in the } j\text{th category}, & (3a) \\ 0 & \text{otherwise}. & (3b) \end{cases}$$

The basic principle of the ordered logit regression model is that the logit of the probability of each underlying outcome is estimated as a linear function of the independent variables and a set of threshold levels. For any fixture i, the probability of observing outcome j corresponds to the probability that the estimated linear function is within the range of the threshold levels estimated for the outcome:

$$\Pr(z_{ij} = 1) = \Pr(\mu_{j-1} < b_1 x_{1j} + b_2 x_{2j} + \ldots + b_k x_{kj} \leq \mu_j). \tag{4}$$

Maximum likelihood estimation, across a sample of fixtures, generates the vector of coefficients **b** along with the threshold levels μ_1 and μ_2. With three possible outcomes, μ_0 is taken as $-\infty$, μ_1 as 0 and μ_3 as ∞, leaving just $\mu_2 = \mu$ as the reported threshold level in the following tables. Estimates of **b** from any ordered response model are difficult to interpret. Consequently, following Greene (1997), we shall also compute the marginal effects of **x**, the vector of explanatory variables, on the three categories of Pools Panel outcome. Here, we propose ordered logit estimation but (unreported) ordered probit estimation gave similar results.

Our choice of explanatory variables was influenced by an announcement by the first chairman of the Pools Panel, Lord Brabazon, on the criteria that it would employ in reaching its decision on a match: the panel would take account of the two clubs' current league records (i.e. league standings), the recent home form and away form of the home and away team respectively and the clubs' goal averages (i.e. the ratio of goals scored to goals conceded). Corresponding data are published by most daily newspapers as part of their weekly guide for pools bettors and so presumably the panel's criteria reflect a consensus that these factors matter in the determination of outcomes of matches. Accordingly, we collected data for each fixture in our samples on

(a) the difference between the league position of the home team and the away team (DIFFPOS) and its square (DIFFPOS2) to allow for non-linearity,
(b) the proportion of its preceding six home matches that the home team had won (draws counting as half a win) (HOMEFORM),
(c) the proportion of its preceding six matches that the away team had won (draws counting as half a win) (AWAYFORM),
(d) for the home team, the ratio of goals scored at home so far that season to goals conceded at home in the same period (HOMEGOALRATIO) and,
(e) for the away team, the ratio of goals scored away so far that season to goals conceded away in the same period (AWAYGOALRATIO).

In addition to these variables, we experimented with some dummy variables but none had an estimated regression coefficient that was significant at the 5% level and they were all excluded from our reported analysis. These included dummy variables to represent the division of the English or Scottish league in which the fixture was scheduled, a dummy variable to represent fixtures taking place under revised league rules under which winning teams in actual matches were rewarded with 3 league points instead of 2 (1 point being awarded for a draw in either case) and dummy variables to represent different time periods.

Our experiments indicated that the panel was uninfluenced in its allocation of results by which division was being discussed, or by whether teams had an enhanced incentive to play for a win rather than a draw; nor did the panel reveal structural breaks in its behaviour.

4. Results

Table 2 displays the results from estimating our ordered logit model on the sample of Pools Panel verdicts. It also displays the corresponding marginal effects (calculated as in Greene (1997), pages

927–930). The marginal effects show how the probability of being in each Pools Panel category changes with a 1-unit increase in the value of the relevant explanatory variable. Without the computation of marginal effects, the sign of the coefficient on the variable would not allow us to conclude whether the probability of the middle category (a draw) is raised or lowered.

In Table 3 we show how the probability of being in each panel category is affected when the value of the relevant variable is raised by one standard deviation from its mean. Table 3 excludes the zero marginal effects obtained for DIFFPOS2. For example, consider the variable HOME-FORM with mean 0.609 and standard deviation 0.205. If the home form measure rises by one standard deviation from 0.609 to 0.814, all else equal, then the marginal effect derived from Table 2 shows that the probability that the panel selects a home win is raised by 8.0 percentage points. This is the 'standard deviation marginal effect'. In this case, the probability of a draw as well as that of an away win is also lowered.

The coefficients in our ordered logit equation are all of the expected sign and most are highly significant, with the exception of the squared difference in position. By contrast, when we experimented with a multinomial logit model, where the categories of result are not ordered, few of our variables were significant in explaining the Pools Panel's behaviour. The implication is that the Pools Panel indeed makes its judgments as if it is placing matches on a scale ordered from almost certain away win to almost certain home win with the draw as an intermediate case.

Our results demonstrate that our publicly available indicators used in press coverage of forthcoming matches are indeed taken into serious consideration by the Pools Panel. This is

Table 2. Pools Panel results: ordered logit estimation

Variable	Coefficient	Absolute t-statistic	Marginal effects			Variable mean	Variable standard deviation
			Away (0)	Draw (1)	Home (2)		
Constant	1.522	7.37†					
HOMEFORM	1.553	4.47†	−0.213	−0.175	0.388	0.609	0.205
AWAYFORM	−1.561	4.20†	0.214	0.176	−0.390	0.385	0.191
HOMEGOALRATIO	0.282	3.31†	−0.039	−0.032	0.070	1.607	0.962
AWAYGOALRATIO	−0.806	5.34†	0.111	0.091	−0.201	0.814	0.513
DIFFPOS	−0.584	6.59†	0.122	0.100	−0.222	0.582	8.471
DIFFPOS2	−0.001	0.92	0.000	0.000	−0.000	77.96	93.47
MU	1.573	20.41†					
% correct	59.5						
Sample size	1483						

†Significant at the 0.1% level.

Table 3. Pools Panel results: marginal effects from a one-standard-deviation change in explanatory variables

Variable	Standard deviation marginal effects		
	Away (0)	Draw (1)	Home (2)
HOMEFORM	−0.044	−0.036	0.080
AWAYFORM	0.041	0.034	−0.074
HOMEGOALRATIO	−0.038	−0.031	0.067
AWAYGOALRATIO	0.057	0.047	−0.103
DIFFPOS	1.033	0.847	−1.881

underlined by the count R^2 of the estimated equation which indicates that our model correctly predicted 59.5% of Pools Panel decisions. A contrasting naïve model might take the overall (panel) totals of away, draw and home decisions and allocate these at random among all the fixtures in the sample. This would result in a 38.5% success rate. Using a few widely available indicators of team strength therefore added substantially to our ability to predict panel decisions, compared with employing only a naïve model.

It is relevant to ask whether the model implicitly used by the Pools Panel resembles that which determines the outcomes of real matches. In Tables 4 and 5, we report the regression results, marginal effects and standard deviation marginal effects obtained from applying the same model used to represent the Pools Panel's behaviour to our sample of 1384 real matches. Although all variables apart from AWAYFORM and DIFFPOS2 have significant coefficients (at the 5% level), the model predicts less well in this new context. Only 48.2% of results are correctly predicted. Our estimates clearly demonstrate the greater predictability of Pools Panel outcomes over real results; the latter are simply noisier. There is still, however, enough relevance in the variables included for this to be sharply higher than the success rate (36.5%) that would follow from allocating results at random within the constraint that the proportions of outcomes in each category should match those in the sample.

It is not surprising that the model for predicting actual results has less predictive power. Panel members know that shock results happen but it is doubtful whether they have inside information

Table 4. Real results: ordered logit estimation

Variable	Coefficient	Absolute t-statistic	Marginal effects			Variable mean	Variable standard deviation
			Away (0)	Draw (1)	Home (2)		
Constant	1.129	5.49†					
HOMEFORM	0.852	2.70‡	−0.148	−0.064	0.212	0.619	0.217
AWAYFORM	−0.139	0.44	0.024	0.010	−0.034	0.385	0.239
HOMEGOALRATIO	0.110	2.08§	−0.018	−0.008	0.026	1.738	1.143
AWAYGOALRATIO	−0.699	4.58†	0.121	0.052	−0.174	0.783	0.444
DIFFPOS	−0.020	2.56§	0.003	0.002	−0.005	−0.454	8.773
DIFFPOS2	−0.000	0.03	0.037	0.016	−0.053	77.96	100.53
MU	1.415	22.45†					
% correct	48.2						
Sample size	1384						

†Significant at the 0.1% level.
‡Significant at the 1% level.
§Significant at the 5% level.

Table 5. Real results: marginal effects from a one-standard-deviation change in explanatory variables

Variable	Standard deviation marginal effects		
	Away (0)	Draw (1)	Home (2)
HOMEFORM	−0.032	−0.014	0.046
AWAYFORM	0.006	0.002	−0.008
HOMEGOALRATIO	−0.021	−0.009	0.030
AWAYGOALRATIO	0.054	0.023	−0.077
DIFFPOS	0.026	0.018	−0.044

which gives insight into where these may occur. Therefore, they are prone to base their judgments on criteria that are known in advance, such as the relative league positions of the teams before the games postponed.

Our estimates also suggest that, whereas there is symmetry in the treatment by the Pools Panel of the importance of the HOMEFORM and AWAYFORM variables, with almost exactly equal and opposite signed coefficients and marginal effects, the real match outcomes appear not to be influenced at all by AWAYFORM. Most newspapers, like the Pools Panel, think that the recent away form of the away club helps to predict outcomes (they print the data for each match) but our finding is that it does not.

A possible reason for the lack of significance of AWAYFORM in the actual results estimates lies in the various sources of home advantage in sports listed in a survey by Courneya and Carron (1992): these include the surface and dimensions of the playing area which differ between venues (home teams can adapt their playing style to exploit the peculiarities of their particular stadium), the adverse effect on the away team of the fatigue and disruption to routine that are associated with travel and the partisan nature of crowds which may influence players' performances or key refereeing decisions in matches to the advantage of the home side. Some recent statistical work on UK soccer by Clarke and Norman (1995) draws attention to home advantage being more important as the distance of travel between the grounds increases whereas Nevill *et al.* (1996) found that referees' decisions appeared to favour the home team to a greater extent in those divisions which attracted larger crowds. Given the various sources of home advantage, it is understandable why the recent home form of the home team is more relevant than the recent away form of the away team in predicting actual match outcomes. The away team's form in recent away matches will reflect a wide variety of venues and opposing home crowds. In contrast, the home team will have played its last six home games in the same stadium and probably before a crowd of similar size and partisanship. How well the players respond to these conditions will be embodied in the last six home results. The last six results at home may therefore have some informational content to aid in predicting the result of their next appearance in the same stadium. Recent away form is observed over more heterogeneous playing conditions and is less relevant although cumulative away form, in which longer-term average conditions are captured, may help to predict a team's performance as revealed by the significant coefficient on AWAYGOALRATIO.

Our ordered logit estimates show that Pools Panel decisions can be more easily predicted than can real outcomes. We have also shown that details of their implicit model may be flawed and their misguided faith in the relevance of recent away form is the most striking case in point. At the inception of the Pools Panel, Longsight (1963) claimed that its results would be more predictable than on-the-field results and that therefore the number of pools winners would increase (and the size of individual prizes consequently decrease). On the basis of our findings, he was correct to assert that it would be 'comparatively easy to anyone who knew a lot about soccer (or who used our model) to predict most of the results given to unplayed matches by the Panel'.

5. Conclusions

The first chairman of the Pools Panel effectively established its constitution by stating the factors that it would take into account in its decision-making on the outcomes of football games that could not be played because of weather conditions or other circumstances. The criteria matched those for which there appeared to be a consensus between journalists about their relevance for results of games. Our study shows that the panel has continued to employ these criteria through-out its life and has therefore followed its unwritten constitution. In doing so, it has avoided controversy. If it instead wished to simulate the process by which real results are generated, it would need to give less attention than it seems to do to certain factors such as the recent away form of the away team.

Our regression results show that actual game outcomes contain considerable noise whereas Pools Panel verdicts are much more predictable. Adding some random noise to the findings of the expert panellists, when fixtures are postponed, would simulate real life more closely and may now be acceptable to the pools companies, particularly in the face of severe competition from the UK National Lottery and growing forms of football betting such as fixed odds results betting and index betting.

We suggest that the Pools Panel should add some random noise to its verdicts to simulate real results more closely. Our ordered logit estimates gave an 11% difference between the prediction rates in the Pools Panel and actual results regressions (59.5% from Table 2 minus 48.2% from Table 4). To make the pools competition both less predictable and more interesting, and to simulate real results more closely, we would therefore suggest that the Pools Panel should introduce approximately 10% of 'wild' predictions into their results, to reflect better the unpredictable nature of real games.

Acknowledgements

We wish to thank Pam Carroll for her excellent research assistance. Stephen Drinkwater, David Percy and a referee provided helpful comments although they are not to be held responsible for the contents of the paper.

References

Clarke, S. R. and Norman, J. M. (1995) Home ground advantage of individual clubs in English soccer. *Statistician*, **44**, 509–521.

Courneya, K. S. and Carron, A. V. (1992) The home advantage in sports competitions: a literature review. *J. Sport Exercise Psychol.*, **14**, 13–27.

Greene, W. H. (1997) *Econometric Analysis*, 3rd edn. New York: Macmillan.

Longsight (1963) The Longsight column. *Daily Mirror*, Feb. 7th, 1963.

Nevill, A. M., Newell, S. M. and Gale, S. (1996) Factors associated with home advantage in English and Scottish soccer matches. *J. Sports Sci.*, **14**, 181–186.

Zavoina, R. and McElvey, W. (1975) A statistical model for the analysis of ordinal level variables. *J. Math. Sociol.*, **4**, 103–120.

[20]

Applied Economics, 2000, **32**, 1353–1363

Information and efficiency: an empirical study of a fixed odds betting market

TIM KUYPERS

University College London, UK
E-mail: tim.kuypers@cwcom.co.uk

The efficiency of the fixed odds betting market for football in England is investigated. It is the efficiency of how market participants utilize available information that is tested. A model of bookmaker behaviour is presented in which the bookmaker maximizes their expected share of the total amount bet. It is found that an expected profit maximizing bookmaker could set market inefficient odds. Several empirical tests using the ordered probit model with data on prices and publicly available information are carried out. Evidence of market inefficiency is identified offering profitable betting opportunities.

I. INTRODUCTION

There has been extensive debate in the literature about the efficiency of information markets, both financial markets and betting markets. This study investigates a particular form of betting, the fixed odds betting market.

Several studies have rejected the efficient market hypothesis for financial markets (see Figlewski and Wachtel, 1981). An explanation advanced for the inefficient market finding is that agents employ information in an inefficient manner. The extreme of this is Keynes' view that financial markets are dominated by unstable psychological factors or 'animal spirits'.

Betting markets have similar characteristics to financial markets but have advantages for empirical investigation of efficiency. Betting markets give detailed price and outcome information with a neatly specified time between purchase of the bet and the outcome of the event. Fixed-odds betting systems have only been modelled once before (Pope and Peel, 1990): the main focus of betting markets studies has been on pari-mutuel and starting price systems. The uniqueness of fixed odds betting is that odds are set several days in advance and do not move in response to betting before the event.

The particular fixed odds market that this paper looks at is English football that has a turnover in the UK of approximately £300m and is growing. The efficiency of fixed odds betting markets is used as an assumption in various papers investigating the demand for football (see Kuypers, 1996; Peel and Thomas, 1998) where odds have been used as measure of outcome uncertainty. This paper tests the validity of this assumption.

II. INFORMATION AND EFFICIENCY

The definition of efficient markets adopted is set out by Fama (1970) in his much referenced *Journal of Finance* article. Fama examines the stock market as an information market and not a service industry. Thus he defines an efficient market as a market whose prices fully reflect all available information. He distinguishes three forms of tests dependent on the information set utilized:

- 'weak' form tests using past prices only;
- 'semi-strong' tests using all publicly available information; and
- 'strong' tests using all information including any information over which certain groups have a monopoly.

In betting markets, weak form efficiency implies that no abnormal returns, either to the bookmaker or to the punter, can be achieved using just price information. Abnormal returns are defined as returns different from the bookmakers' take. For example, in the Tote pari-mutuel system the bookmakers' take is set by regulation at around 20%. If bookmakers were obtaining returns greater than 20% or punters were able to make returns better than −20% then this would imply that abnormal returns were being made.

1354   *T. Kuypers*

Table 1. *Betting market efficiency in the literature*

Study	Sport	Test	Inefficiency	Positive returns
Pari-mutuel				
Snyder (1978)	US horse	Weak	✓	✗
Ali (1977)	US harness	Weak	✓	✓
Asch *et al.* (1984, 1986)	US thoroughbred	Weak	✓	✗
Hausch *et al.* (1981)	? exotic bets	Weak	✓	✓
Figlewski (1979)	US horse	Semi-strong	✓	?
Quoted odds				
Dowie (1976)	UK horse	Strong	✗	✗
Crafts (1985)	UK horse	Strong	✓	✓
Johnson and Bruce (1992)	UK horse	Weak (?)	✗	✗
Cain *et al.* (1990)	UK greyhound	Semi-strong (?)	✓	✗
Gabriel and Marsden (1990)	UK horse PM vs Quoted	Semi-strong	✓	?
Pope and Peel (1990)	English football	Weak	✓	✗
Spread betting systems				
Zuber *et al.* (1985)	US football	Semi-strong	✓	✓
Sauer *et al.* (1988)	US football	Semi-strong	✗	✗
Gandar *et al.* (1988)	US football	Semi-strong	✓	✓
Dobra *et al.* (1990)	US basketball	Weak	✗	✗

Semi-strong efficiency implies that the incorporation of publicly available information should not improve on the accuracy of outcome predictions based on odds. Thus there should not be abnormal returns to a betting strategy utilizing odds and publicly available information for either the bookmaker or the punters.

Strong efficiency implies that no group in society, as a result of private information, can make abnormal returns.

Table 1 summarizes the investigation of betting market efficiency. As the table indicates the majority of the studies have focused on horse racing and there has been a distinct US bias. The results of these studies are mixed. Some studies find that betting markets are efficient, others that betting markets are inefficient and a minority find both inefficiency and profitable betting opportunities.

III. THE UK FOOTBALL BETTING MARKET

There are varying methods of betting on football in Britain. There are several specialist firms[1] that offer spread betting and bookmakers often quote odds on bigger games (especially televised games). However this study concentrates on the biggest form of football betting in Britain, via fixed odds coupons. These coupons offer betting odds on match results, the time and scorer of the first and last goal plus half-time scores.

In fixed odds betting the bookmakers produce a coupon three to four days before the football programme. The general coupon will contain odds for results and correct scores for each English and Scottish league match (or alternatively cup games if it is a cup weekend). The results bet offer odds for a home win, away win and draw. The correct scores odds are quoted in relation to the results odds regardless on which team you are betting. For example for any team whose odds to win the game are 4/5, the odds for a 3–0 win will always be 12/1. Thus free scoring teams and lower scoring teams are given the same odds. For the bigger games (e.g. live televised matches) often a single coupon will be produced which offers results odds, correct score odds and odds on the first/last player to score.

There are varying combinations of bets that are allowed. Single bets (i.e. bet on the result of a single game) are only usually allowed on televised matches. Trebles (simultaneously bet on the result of three matches) are allowed on approximately 30 matches usually including the Premier League, the First Division and Scottish Premier Division plus a handful of lower division games. Five-fold bets (simultaneous bets on the results of five matches) are allowed on any combination of English and Scottish matches. The odds on the same match for different categories of bet are identical. Singles and upwards are accepted on correct scores.

Once the odds have been set it is extremely rare that they will change before the kick off of the matches. This is where fixed odds betting is most different from both pari-mutuel systems and quoted odds systems, which reflect and react

[1] For example Sporting Index.

to the amount of money bet on each outcome right up to the start of the event.

IV. MODEL OF BOOKMAKERS' ODDS SETTING DECISION

Introduction

The bookmaking business can be looked at as both a service and an information market. Bookmakers are providing a service, i.e. the opportunity and facilities to place a bet, but also creating an information market similar to markets in stocks and shares. The price for each aspect of the business can be separated. The price for providing the facilities to bet is the bookmakers' take while the prices in the information market are the relative odds.

In pari-mutuel betting systems the bookmaker's take is a fixed percentage of the handle or total amount bet. In fixed price odds betting this is not true but the bookmakers' take can be estimated from the 'over-roundness' of the book.

The bookmaker's theoretical gross margin (over-roundness), assuming a balanced book and ignoring betting duty can be easily calculated. This is best illustrated by a simple example. In all matches the home team is the team whose ground the game is played on and is signified by coming first in the fixture. The odds on a Liverpool v Sheffield Wednesday match are 5/6 home win, 13/5 away win and 12/5 draw. A home win in this case is a Liverpool victory. For each outcome the percentage (amount bet required to win £100) is calculated as follows:

home win $100/(1 + 5/6) = 54.5$

away win $100/(1 + 13/5) = 27.8$

draw $100/(1 + 12/5) = 29.4$

The over-roundness of the book is then the sum of the percentages less 100: over-roundness $= (54.5 + 27.8 + 29.4) - 100 = 11.7$.

Thus if the book is balanced, that is, the bookmaker takes stakes on the three outcomes in the proportion 54.5: 27.8: 29.4 then the bookmaker will keep 11.7 whatever the outcome of the match. The bookmakers' return is then 11.7/111.7= 10.5% of the total stake (known as the handle).[2]

In football fixed odds betting the over-roundness of the book is remarkably constant at around 11.5% for all the major bookmakers. The average over-roundness in the sample of 3382 games is 11.5% with a standard deviation of only 0.34.

The second part of the price can be considered the relative odds or more properly the implied probabilities

derived from the odds. Assuming that the over-roundness of the book is fixed and is 11% the formula below translates odds into implied probabilities. The probabilities calculated are the 'percentage' calculations above but adjusted so as to sum to one. The formula is:

$$implied\ probability = \frac{1}{1.11(1 + odds)} \qquad (1)$$

The prices investigated in this study are the prices in the information market. No attempt is made to explain or investigate how the 11% over-roundness is set. It is assumed that it is a result of the competitive and regulatory processes. Efficiency of the football betting market is looked at in terms of the information market only.

Adopting Fama's (1970) terminology, the football betting market can be assumed to be weakly efficient if abnormal returns cannot be made using price information only (i.e. odds). Abnormal returns are defined as returns better than the bookmakers' take, thus in this case returns better than -11%. The market can be assumed to be semi-strongly efficient if prices reflect all publicly available information and thus no abnormal returns can be made using publicly available information. The market can be assumed to be strongly efficient if the implied probabilities reflect all publicly available information and no one group in society can use its private information to achieve abnormal returns.

The model

In the model it is assumed that bookmakers have no private information but are able to evaluate publicly available information as well as any other individual or organization. In football it is unlikely that there is a great deal of insider information: games are played in front of large audiences and reported widely in the media. The sort of private information that could be available would be information on an injured player that a club is keeping secret. It is unlikely that this sort of information would vest with the bookmakers and not the media. Another form of private information could be the knowledge that certain players are going to throw matches. Despite the recent high profile case[3] there is no evidence that this is widespread. The existence of this form of information does not however invalidate the assumption about the bookmaker's information set.

There are three decision points in the model. First, the bookmaker decides which odds to quote. Second, the punters decide on which outcome to bet and third, nature decides the outcome of the game. The bookmaker's decision process is modelled and thus will incorporate reaction

---

[2] For discussion of margins in different forms of gambling see The Royal Commission On Gambling (1978), Annex b.
[3] The Crown versus Messrs. Grobelaar, Fashanu and Segers, who were acquitted of match fixing.

functions for the punters' decision on which outcome to bet.

There are three distinct outcomes on which a punter can bet i.e. home win, away win and draw. These outcomes are denoted by use of the subscripts 1, 2 and 3.

Let H be the handle.

Let h_1, h_2, h_3 be the amount bet on each outcome. Thus the share of H on each outcome is defined as:

$$s_1 = \frac{h_1}{H} \quad s_2 = \frac{h_2}{H} \quad s_3 = \frac{h_3}{H} \tag{2}$$

Let the bookmaker's subjective probability that the result of the event be 1, 2 or 3 be represented by b_1, b_2 and b_3. By definition, $b_1 + b_2 + b_3 = 1$. Let the bookmaker's posted odds be denoted by o_1, o_2 and o_3. As we are assuming that the over-roundness of the book is 11% then:

$$\frac{1}{1 + o_1} + \frac{1}{1 + o_2} + \frac{1}{1 + o_3} = 1.11 \tag{3}$$

Let d be the implied probabilities from the odds i.e.:

$$d_1 = \frac{1}{1.11(1 + o_1)}, \quad d_2 = \frac{1}{1.11(1 + o_2)} \text{ and}$$

$$d_3 = \frac{1}{1.11(1 + o_3)} \tag{4}$$

By definition $d_1 + d_2 + d_3 = 1$.

The decision to enter the market has already been made. That is, the punters accept the bookmaker's price for offering his service (i.e. the over-roundness of the book). The model is only concerned with how punters spread their bets over the three outcomes. Thus the punters' reaction functions are only used to determine the share of the handle (i.e. s_i) which is bet on each outcome.

Throughout the model we are assuming that bookmakers know the appropriate punters' reaction function. Bookmakers are assumed to be risk neutral and as such are expected profit maximizers. The relaxation of this assumption and the introduction of tax are discussed later.

The bookmaker's expected profit is:

$$E(\Pi) = H - b_1[h_1 o_1 + h_1] - b_2[h_2 o_2 + h_2] - b_3[h_3 o_3 + h_3] \tag{5}$$

That is the bookmaker's expected profit is the handle less his subjective probability of each outcome multiplied by the payout for each outcome. Winning punters receive the odds multiplied by their stake ($h_i o_i$) and their stake returned (h_i).

Note: $h_i = H s_i$ and $o_i = \frac{1}{1.11 d_i} - 1$, substituting into Equation 5 gives:

$$E(\Pi) = H - b_1 \left[H s_1 \left(\frac{1}{1.11 d_1} - 1 \right) + H s_1 \right]$$

$$- b_2 \left[H s_2 \left(\frac{1}{1.11 d_2} - 1 \right) + H s_2 \right]$$

$$- b_3 \left[H s_3 \left(\frac{1}{1.11 d_3} - 1 \right) + H s_3 \right] \tag{6}$$

Note that $d_1 + d_2 + d_3 = 1$ and therefore $d_3 = 1 - d_1 - d_2$. Substituting into Equation 6 and re-arranging one arrives at:

$$E(\Pi) = H - \frac{b_1 H s_1}{1.11 d_1} - \frac{b_2 H s_2}{1.11 d_2} - \frac{b_3 H s_3}{1.11(1 - d_1 - d_2)} \tag{7}$$

The bookmaker wishes to maximize his expected profit by setting odds given the punters' reaction function. For ease of calculation Equation 7 contains implied probabilities (d) but not odds (o), the bookmaker's decision variable. The bookmaker maximizes profit by setting d (implied probability) which implicitly sets odds, as each d implies a unique odd.

It is assumed that the punter compares her subjective probability of an outcome with the odds. S/he will bet on outcomes that s/he believes are more likely than the odds suggest.

Thus, the share bet is a function of the implied probability from the bookmaker's odds and the distribution of punters' subjective probabilities over the three outcomes labelled P. Thus, $s_i = f(d_i, P)$.

Thus the bookmaker's expected profit function becomes:

$$E(\Pi) = H - \frac{b_1 H s_1(d_1, P)}{1.11 d_1} - \frac{b_2 H s_2(d_2, P)}{1.11 d_2}$$

$$- \frac{(1 - b_1 - b_2) H s_3(d_1, d_2, P)}{1.11(1 - d_1 - d_2)} \tag{8}$$

Differentiating with respect to d_1 and d_2 the bookmaker's decision variables:

$$\frac{\delta E(\Pi)}{\delta d_1} = \frac{b_1 H s_1(d_1, P)}{1.11 d_1^2} - \frac{\delta s_1(d_1, P)}{\delta d_1} \cdot \frac{b_1 H}{1.11 d_1}$$

$$- \frac{(1 - b_1 - b_2) H s_3(d_1, d_2, P)}{1.11(1 - d_1 - d_2)^2} - \frac{\delta s_3(d_1, d_2, P)}{\delta d_1}$$

$$\cdot \frac{b_3 H}{1.11(1 - d_1 - d_2)} = 0 \tag{9}$$

$$\frac{\delta E(\Pi)}{\delta d_2} = \frac{b_2 H s_2(d_2, P)}{1.11 d_2^2} - \frac{\delta s_2(d_2, P)}{\delta d_2} \cdot \frac{b_2 H}{1.11 d_2}$$

$$- \frac{(1 - b_1 - b_2) H s_3(d_1, d_2, P)}{1.11(1 - d_1 - d_2)^2} - \frac{\delta s_3(d_1, d_2, P)}{\delta d_2}$$

$$\cdot \frac{b_3 H}{1.11(1 - d_1 - d_2)} = 0 \tag{10}$$

In this model in order for the market to be efficient then $d_i = b_i$, i.e. implied probability from the odds = the bookmakers' subjective probability which is assumed the best possible subjective probability. Substituting this into Equations 9 and 10 and simplifying and rearranging:

$$s_1(d_1, P) = b_1 \left[\frac{\delta s_1(d_1, P)}{\delta d_1} + \frac{s_3(d_1, d_2, P)}{(1 - b_1 - b_2)} + \frac{\delta s_3(d_1, d_2, P)}{\delta d_1} \right]$$

(11)

$$s_2(d_2, P) = b_2 \left[\frac{\delta s_2(d_2, P)}{\delta d_2} + \frac{s_3(d_1, d_2, P)}{(1 - b_1 - b_2)} + \frac{\delta s_3(d_1, d_2, P)}{\delta d_2} \right]$$

(12)

Thus in order for the market to be efficient then the function that determines the shares evaluated at $d_1 = b_1$ and $d_2 = b_2$ must satisfy Equations 11 and 12 above. This is by no means necessarily the case and thus a situation can be envisaged in which the expected profit maximizing implied probabilities (in effect odds) are not equal to their subjective probability.

The simple numerical example below illustrates a case where an inefficient outcome can result. There is a single match Liverpool versus Manchester United. There are ten punters each betting 1 unit and following the same betting rule:

bet on outcome i such that:

$$i = \arg\max(p_i - d_i) \quad p_i \neq d_i \forall i$$
$$i = \arg\max(p_i) \quad p_i = d_i \forall i$$

(13)

That is bet on the outcome which maximizes the difference between their subjective probability (p_i) and the probability implied by the odds (d_i). If for each outcome the subjective probability equals the probability implied by the odds, bet on the most likely event.

Let us assume that there are two types of punters, six Manchester United (Man U) fans and four neutrals. The Man U fans believe that Man U have a better chance of winning the game than the bookmakers and have subjective probabilities $p_{1mu} = 0.4$, $p_{2mu} = 0.2$ and $p_{3mu} = 0.4$. The neutrals are of the same opinion as the bookmaker i.e. $b_1 = p_{1n} = 0.5$, $b_2 = p_{2n} = 0.2$ and $b_3 = p_{3n} = 0.3$.

Now assume that the bookmaker sets the market efficient level of odds ($d_i = b_i$) i.e. $d_1 = 0.5$, $d_2 = 0.2$ and $d_3 = 0.3$. Using Equation 13, all the Man U fans would bet on an away win, i.e. $i = 3$ and all the neutral fans on a home win $i = 1$. Thus the shares of the bet are $s_1 = 0.4$, $s_2 = 0$ and $s_3 = 0.6$. Thus Equation 7 becomes:

$$E(\Pi) = 10 - \frac{0.5*10*0.4}{1.11*0.5} - \frac{0.2*10*0}{1.11*0.2} - \frac{0.3*10*0.6}{1.11*0.3}$$

$$= 0.99$$

However the bookmaker could set odds to take account of the Man U supporters' bias. For example he could set odds such that $d_1 = 0.41$ $d_2 = 0.2$ and $d_3 = 0.39$. With these odds and using Equation 13, the punters would bet in an identical way to when the odds were efficient. Thus Equation 7 becomes:

$$E(\Pi) = 10 - \frac{0.5*10*0.4}{1.11*0.41} - \frac{0.2*10*0}{1.11*0.2} - \frac{0.3*10*0.6}{1.11*0.39}$$

$$= 1.45$$

Thus using the assumed punter reaction function, the bookmaker can increase his expected profit by setting market inefficient odds.

Related issues

In the model above it is assumed that the bookmaker is an expected profit maximizer implying risk neutrality. In the example above the bookmaker increases his expected profit by setting non-market efficient odds. However his/her actual profit will depend on the outcome of the match. There is another risk minimizing strategy that the bookmaker could adopt. If s/he always sets the odds such that the underlying probability equals his subjective probability (i.e. $d_i = b_i$) he would be guaranteed a return, whatever the outcome of the event of 0.0991H.

The bookmaker's decision can be represented in a payoff matrix (see Fig 1). If for example $s_1 > d_1$, $s_2 = d_2$ and $s_3 < d_3$, then the expected profit maximizing strategy will give a greater return to the bookmaker than the risk minimizing strategy only if the outcome of the game is a draw. An away win would leave the bookmaker's position unchanged and a home win would make him/her worse off.

Two further issues also need discussing, namely taxation and multiple bet restrictions. 'Taxation' is levied at 10% on all football bets.[4] Tax will not affect the share of money bet on different outcomes, however it might affect a punter's decision to enter the market. In the behavioural rule described earlier the variables that affect a punters decision on which outcome to bet are the odds and the punter's own subjective probabilities. The level of taxation does not affect either of these variables and can be seen as an addition to the charge for the bookmaker's service (overroundness). However, taxation will affect the level of returns required before the punter becomes profitable.

The second issue is multiple bets. As noted in Section III bookmakers often place restrictions on the number of games that make up a bet, for example often a minimum

[4] Reduced to 9% in 1996.

Bookmaker	Nature		
	Home win	Away win	Draw
'Risk Minimizing Strategy' $d_i = b_i$	0.0991H	0.991H	0.991H
Expected profit maximizing	$H - \dfrac{Hs_1}{1.11d_1}$	$H - \dfrac{Hs_2}{1.11d_2}$	$H - \dfrac{Hs_3}{1.11d_3}$

Fig. 1. *Payoff matrix*

treble is required. As with taxation multiple bet restrictions increase the over-roundness of the bet. For example on a triple bet if each of the matches has an over-roundness of 11% then the over-roundness on the triple will be $(1.11)^3 - 1 = 0.368 = 36.8\%$. The restriction on triple bets will not affect how the punter actually places her bet but might affect the decision to enter the market.

V. EMPIRICAL TESTS

Weak test of efficiency

A weak test of efficiency is to compare the subjective probability implied from odds with outcome probability. In an efficient market these would not be systematically different as this would allow profitable betting opportunities. This type of test has discovered long shot bias (i.e. more people bet on low probability high return combinations than on high probability low return bets) in pari-mutuel systems where lower odds categories have yielded positive returns (Synder, 1978).

The sample used is 3382 matches from the 1993–1994 and 1994–1995 in the four divisions of the English football league. Odds are grouped into 24 categories and the implied probability calculated using Equation 1 is compared with the outcome probability.

For example, there were 193 bets with odds of evens in the sample. Of these 193 bets 85 were correct (that is if the odds on a home win was evens and the result of the game was a home win then the bet was correct). Thus the outcome probability is $85/193 = 0.44$. This is then compared with the implied probability from the odds i.e. a probability of $1/[1.11(1+1)] = 0.45$.

The ability to make profits is tested by calculating the return on £1 (plus tax) placed on each bet in a given odds category. In effect this is testing a strategy of placing a bet on every outcome with a particular level of odds. The returns are then compared with the expected return to these strategies under the assumption of odds efficiency. The expected returns given an efficient market are calculated below:

Using the notation above

$$\text{odds } o_1, o_2, o_3 \quad \text{where} \quad \sum_{i=1}^{3} \frac{1}{1+o_i} = 1.115 \quad (14)$$

that is the assumed over-roundness of the book is 11.5% which as shown earlier is the case in practise.

Given the assumption that that the true probability of event i = the implied probability (from odds) of event $i = 1/(1.115(1 + o_i))$

Then the expected payout on a £1 bet on event i = expected probability * stake * odds

$$= \frac{1}{1.115(1+o_i)} * 1 * (1+o_i) = \frac{1}{1.115} = 0.8969$$

Thus the expected return without tax is the payout minus stake divided by the stake i.e. $(0.8969 - 1)/1 = -10.31\%$. The expected returns tax paid is again the payout minus stake divided by the stake i.e. $(0.8969 - 1.1)/1.1 = -18.46\%$

Table 2 sets out the implied probabilities, the odds from which these probabilities are derived along with the outcome probability and the return to a £1 bet tax paid. The odds are taken from the fixed odds coupons of a leading bookmaker (Ladbrokes) and the results taken from Rollin (1994, 1995).

For an efficient betting market implied probability (column a) would equal the outcome probability (column c) and the returns (column d) would equal −18%.

Figure 2 plots the outcome probability versus implied probability from the odds (columns c and a in the table). The 45 degree line represents where the outcome and implied probability are equal.

As can be seen the implied probability seems a good match with the outcome probability except around a probability of 0.5. In order to do a more formal test of whether the outcome probability equals implied probability a simple OLS regression was carried out. The estimated equation was: implied probability = b * outcome probability (see Table 3). The hypothesis that b = 1 (i.e. implied probability = actual probability) could not be rejected at the 95% confidence level. Thus the regression analysis backs up Fig. 2, there is no systematic bias.

The returns column in Table 2 shows that although there are returns that are better than the −18% there are no

Table 2. *Implied versus outcome probability*

(a) Implied probability	(b) Odds	(c) Outcome probabilities	(d) Returns (%)
0.68	0.335	0.651	−20.99
0.63	0.441	0.678	−11.20
0.59	0.527	0.649	−9.84
0.57	0.581	0.601	−13.60
0.55	0.638	0.547	−18.51
0.53	0.700	0.511	−20.99
0.51	0.766	0.488	−21.71
0.49	0.839	0.580	−3.13
0.47	0.917	0.502	−12.47
0.45	1.002	0.440	−19.84
0.43	1.095	0.425	−18.98
0.41	1.197	0.440	−12.06
0.39	1.310	0.397	−16.67
0.37	1.435	0.362	−19.90
0.35	1.574	0.338	−20.89
0.33	1.730	0.310	−23.09
0.31	1.906	0.315	−16.91
0.29	2.107	0.282	−20.41
0.27	2.337	0.280	−14.98
0.25	2.604	0.236	−22.71
0.23	2.917	0.215	−23.60
0.21	3.290	0.240	−6.47
0.19	3.742	0.201	−13.48
0.17	4.299	0.158	−23.70

Notes: (1) Implied probability as per Equation 1; (2) columns a and b are mid points of categories; (3) column d is return to a £1 bet tax paid on each outcome that is in the implied probability category.

Table 3. *Implied versus outcome probability regression*

Coefficient	0.97
t stat	74.74
R squared adjusted	0.92
95% lower limit	0.9463
95% upper limit	1.0002

positive returns. The higher returns directly correspond to the odds categories where the actual probability is higher than the implied probability. Thus in order for there to be a systematic bias in the returns there would have to be a systematic difference between the implied and outcome probabilities, a hypothesis rejected by the above analysis. Over all odds categories the return was −18.11%. Although in this sample the punter could achieve a return as high as −3%, there is no proof of a systematic bias.

Pope and Peel (1990) found that there was a systematic bias in draw odds. Table 4 sets out the average return to home bets, away bets and draws along with the highest and lowest returns to a particular level of odds in each outcome. This is calculated by placing a £1 on each bet that falls into the category from the sample. The results give no

Table 4. *Betting returns*

	Home	Away	Draw
Return to all odds categories Return %	−16.5	−22.4	−15.4
Return to a particular odds category:			
Highest	−2.5	+4	−4.5
Lowest	−47.6	−44	−23.4

support to Pope and Peel's assertion that there is systematic bias in the odds for draws. As a further check the regression analysis carried out above was repeated for home win, away win and draw odds separately. Table 5 shows that all three regressions could not reject the hypothesis that $b = 1$, i.e. implied equals actual probability.

Tests of semi-strong efficiency

Assuming an efficient market, it would not be possible for a punter to exploit publicly available information to achieve systematic abnormal returns. This section attempts to do just that, using ordered probit models and publicly available information, it tests the semi-strong efficiency of football betting markets by attempting to achieve abnormal returns.

Abnormal returns would at best be profitable returns, but are defined as better than the expected return of −18% (tax paid) reflecting the bookmaker's take as set out above. The dependent variable in these estimations is the result of the match, a home win= 0, a draw= 1 and an away win= 2.

The ordered probit was chosen to take account of the ordinal nature of the dependent variable. For example, if a very strong home team was playing a weak team then the most likely outcome would be a home win, then a draw then an away win. Reversing the teams' strengths you would most likely see an away win, then a draw then a home win. Thus there is a natural ordering of the outcomes that is best addressed by using the ordered probit model.

Throughout this section, as well as ordered probit models, ordered probit models adjusting for heteroscedasticity and ordered logit models were also estimated. However there was no evidence to reject the ordered probit. Neither the logit nor the ordered probit adjusted for heteroscedasticity performed better than the ordered probit, nor did they give significantly different results.

The basic model using ordered probit is:

$$y* = \beta'x + \varepsilon \qquad (15)$$

where $y*$ is the probability of the outcome and is unobserved. The x vector is made up of the explanatory variables. What is observed is the outcome of the game:

Outcome Probability

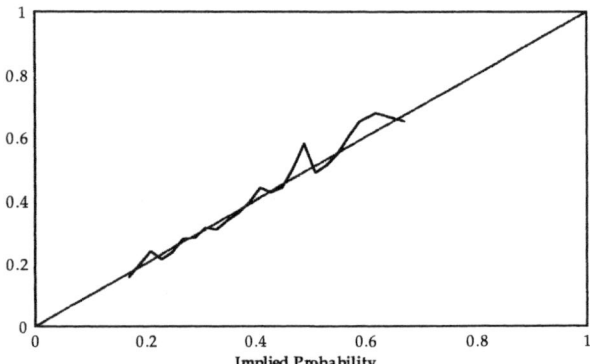

Fig. 2. *Implied versus outcome probability*

Table 5. *OLS outcome probability and implied probability*

	Home	Away	Draw
Coefficient	0.97	0.93	1.02
t stat	49.41	19.02	43.50
R squared adjusted	0.873	0.414	0.799
95% lower limit	0.934	0.822	0.971
95% upper limit	1.015	1.028	1.076

home win $y = 0$ if $y* \leqslant 0$ (16)

draw $y = 1$ if $0 < y* \leqslant \mu$ (17)

away win $y = 2$ if $\mu. \leqslant y*$ (18)

μ is unknown and is estimated along with β.

The predicted probabilities are

$$\text{Prob}(y = 0) = 1 - \Phi(\beta'x) \tag{19}$$

$$\text{Prob}(y = 1) = \Phi(\mu - \beta'x) - \Phi(-\beta'x) \tag{20}$$

$$\text{Prob}(y = 2) = 1 - \Phi(\mu - \beta'x) \tag{21}$$

In the ordered probit model information given by the estimated coefficients is limited. The marginal effects of the coefficients on the predicted probability of each outcome offer more insight. In this model the marginal effects are calculated as follows:

$$\frac{\delta \text{Prob}(y = 0)}{\delta x} = -\phi(\beta'x)\beta \tag{22}$$

$$\frac{\delta \text{Prob}(y = 1)}{\delta x} = (\phi(-\beta'x) - \phi(\mu - \beta'x))\beta \tag{23}$$

$$\frac{\delta \text{Prob}(y = 2)}{\delta x} = \phi(\mu - \beta'x)\beta \tag{24}$$

The data set used is for two English League seasons, 1993–1994 and 1994–1995. All four divisions are used giving 1733 match observations for 1993–1994 and 1649 match observations for 1994–1995.

The publicly available information variables are all derived from Rollin (1994, 1995). 'Difference in teams'' just refers to the value of the variable for the home team minus the value of the variable for the away team. The variables used were:

- difference in teams' average points per game over the season;
- difference in teams' cumulative points over the season;
- difference in teams' league position;
- difference in teams' average points over the last three games;
- difference in teams' average goal difference (goals scored minus goals conceded);
- difference in teams' cumulative goal difference;
- difference in teams' goal difference in the last three games;
- difference in teams' average weighted points in last three games. Points gained in away fixtures are weighted more than points gained in home fixtures as these are more difficult to obtain; and
- difference in points between the home team's cumulative points won in home matches and the away team's cumulative points won in its away matches.

As the variables described above increase they would be expected to increase the probability of a home win and decrease the probability of an away win. As the variable approaches 0 the probability of a draw would be expected to be greatest. The only exception is the difference in league position, as this increases the probability of an away win should increase and the probability of a home win decrease.

Models were estimated with four different combinations of explanatory data: odds only; all odds and performance data; performance data only; and performance data and selected odds. The model with odds only detected inefficiency but no profitable betting opportunities, neither the all odds and performance data nor the performance data only models gave evidence of inefficiency. The results of the selected odds and performance data is given in Table 6.

For each observation the predicted probability using the estimated coefficients and Equations 19–21 were calculated. In addition the implied probability from the odds was calculated using:[5]

$$\text{Prob outcome } i = \frac{\dfrac{1}{1 + odds_i}}{\sum_{1}^{i=3} \dfrac{1}{1 + odds_i}} \qquad (25)$$

A betting rule was then developed:

place £1 on the outcome of a particular match if:

Table 6. *Ordered probit: performance data and selected odds*

Variable	Coefficient	*t*-stat
Constant	− 0.231	− 3.469
Odds of an away win	0.133	5.417
diff in league position	0.057	17.564
μ	0.804	34.596
log likelihood	− 3363.494	

Note: Dependent variable = outcome of 3382 matches in the 1993–1994 and 1994–1995 seasons.

Marginal effects ... on the probability of a home win	
Constant	0.092
Away win odds	−0.053
Diff in league position	−0.023

on the probability of a draw	
Constant	−0.019
Away win odds	−0.011
Diff in league position	−0.005

on the probability of an away win	
Constant	−0.072
Away win odds	0.041
Diff in league position	0.018

[5] This is a refinement of Equation 1.

$$\text{Probability ratio} = \frac{\text{Predicted probability using model}}{\text{Implied probability from odds}}$$

$$> X \qquad (26)$$

The results are presented for different values of X. This betting rule could mean that a bet was placed on two outcomes in a particular game. An alternative rule could have been used to just place a bet on the maximum probability ratio in a given match if the probability ratio satisfied Equation 26. This is an alternate but not necessary a better betting rule.

Table 7 indicates that abnormal returns can be made. Indeed, using X's of 1.1 or above positive returns can be made. This implies that the betting market for football is not efficient.

The strategy above could not have been implemented because the model was estimated using data to which the betting strategy was then applied. In order to test the robustness of this result under more realistic conditions the data set was split into seasons. The model was estimated using 1993–1994 data and then the betting rule using these coefficients applied to the 1994–1995 season. The coefficient estimates and significance were all very similar to those estimated with the full sample described in Table 7. The results using these coefficients are contained in Table 8. As can be seen the returns are not as good but are still positive and thus abnormal, supporting the inefficiency of the betting markets.

The betting strategies described above are practical in that the models are tested on data not included in the estimation sample. There is one difficulty in implementing the strategy due to the restriction on single bets. The strategy assumes that single bets are allowed on all games and this is not the case. This has two implications: first in order to cover all possible outcomes, the weekly number of bet is increased; and second the over-roundness of the bet is increased, reducing profitability.

Table 7. *Betting returns using performance data and odds model*

	X			
	1.1	1.2	1.3	1.4
No bets (Max 3382)	3533	1681	1019	607
% bets correct	44	53	53	50
Return no tax (%)	16	31	36	44
Return tax paid (%)	6	19	24	31

Notes: Model estimated using both seasons (3382) and the betting rule applied to both seasons data.

1362   *T. Kuypers*

Table 8. *Betting returns using performance and odds 1994–1995*

	X			
	1.1	1.2	1.3	1.4
No bets (Max 1649)	1638	723	421	267
% bets correct	44	50	49	44
Return no tax (%)	18	36	44	45
Return tax paid (%)	7	23	31	32

Notes: Model estimated using 1993–1994 season data (1733 observations) and the betting rule applied to the 1994–1995 season (1649 observations).

Table 9. *Half time/full time combinations*

	Half Time	Full Time
1	home win	home win
2	home win	away win
3	home win	draw
4	away win	home win
5	away win	away win
6	away win	draw
7	draw	home win
8	draw	away win
9	draw	draw

IV. CONCLUSIONS

This study investigates the efficiency of fixed odds betting, the major form of betting on football in England. It provides both a model of bookmakers' behaviour and a test of the efficient market hypothesis.

The model of bookmaker behaviour shows that market inefficient odds are possible when the bookmaker maximises expected profit. The model indicates that if there is a bias in punters' expectations, perhaps due to team loyalty, then the bookmaker can take advantage of this by setting non-market efficient odds.

Empirical work on two seasons' data was carried to test whether inefficient odds were set in practice. The unique use of the ordered probit model does identify inefficiency and exploitable betting opportunities using both odds and publicly available performance data as explanatory variables. A betting rule is developed which in the seasons tested provides a positive post tax return. This is a practical outcome of the study, a profitable betting rule. However, as well as the transactions costs of monitoring the system there are complications in implementing the solution. There has been a move by bookmakers in seasons subsequent to the study to further restrict the bets they allow. Currently only a minority of games can be bet on outside five-fold (i.e. you must bet of the results of five games simultaneously). This restriction affects the bookmaker's take and complicates the implementation of the betting strategy.

For example taking Table 8 which looks at the results of a particular betting rule over season 1994–1995 and using a filter of 1.2 there are 723 bets which are recommended of which the rule predicts 50% correctly. In a season of 35 weeks this averages out at just over 20 matches a week forecasting correctly approximately 10 matches. If singles were allowed then this would amount to 20 bets, however to cover all possibilities with five-fold combinations this would require over 15 000[6] five-fold bets. Thus given that most bookmakers have a minimum bet of around £0.25

the average weekly expenditure becomes very large. The return using five-folds is also diminished by the extra over-roundness on multiple bets as described above.

An alternative option to overcome the restrictions would be to bet on half-time/full-time scores. The bookmaker allows bets predicting the score at half time and the score at full time. Thus there are nine combination of bet as shown in Table 9. In order to cover one prediction (e.g. a home win) three bets will be required (i.e. 1, 4 and 7). Thus the average number of weekly bets becomes 60, still large but much less than the five fold combinations. The over-roundness of these types of bets is around 20%, greater than single bets but much less than five-folds.

This is the first study to rigorously test the efficiency of a fixed odds market and discover the rare occurrence of both inefficiency and profitable betting opportunities. It provides evidence against the efficient market hypothesis and despite implementation difficulties gives a betting rule for punters to exploit.

REFERENCES

Ali, M. M. (1977) Probability and utility estimates for racetrack bettors, *Journal of Political Economy*, **85**, 803–15.

Ali, M. M. (1979) Some evidence of the efficiency of a speculative market, *Econometrica*, **47**, 387–92.

Asch, P., Malkiel, B. G. and Quandt R. E. (1984) Market efficiency in racetrack betting, *Journal of Business*, **57**, 157–75.

Asch, P., Malkiel, B. G. and Quandt R. E. (1986) Market efficiency in racetrack betting: further evidence and a correction, *Journal of Business*, **59**, 157–60.

Cain, M., Law, D. and Peel, D. A. (1990) Greyhound racing: further empirical evidence on a wagering market, University College of Wales Working Paper.

Crafts, N. F. R. (1985) Some evidence of insider knowledge in horse race betting in Britain, *Economica*, **52**, 295–304.

Dobra, J. L., Cargill, T. F. and Meyer, R. A. (1990) Efficient markets for wagers: the case of professional basketball wagering, in *Sportometrics* (Eds) B. Goff and R. D. Tollison. Texas A & M University Press, pp. 215–49.

Dowie, J. A. (1976) On the efficiency and equity of betting markets, *Economica*, **43**, 139–50.

[6] Calculated as $20!/(5! \ 15!) = 15504$.

Even, W. E. and Noble, N. R. (1992) Testing the efficiency in gambling markets, *Applied Economics*, **24**, 85–8.

Fama, E. F. (1970) Efficient capital markets: a review of theory and empirical work, *Journal of Finance*, **33**, 383–423.

Figlewski, S. (1979) Subjective information and market efficiency in a betting market, *Journal of Political Economy*, **87**, 75–88.

Figlewski, S. and Wachtel, P. (1981) The formation of inflationary expectations, *The Review of Economics and Statistics*, **LXIII**, 1–10.

Gabriel, P. E. and Marsden, J. R. (1990) An examination of market efficiency in British racetrack betting, *Journal of Political Economy*, **98**, 874–85.

Gandar, J. M, Zuber, R., O'Brien, T. and Russo, B. (1988) Testing rationality in the point spread betting market, *Journal of Finance*, **XLIII**, 995–1008.

Hausch, D. B. and Ziemba, W. T. (1985) Transactions costs, extent of inefficiencies, entries and multiple wagers in a racetrack betting model, *Management Science*, **31**, 381–94.

Johnson, J. E. V. and Bruce, A. C. (1992) Betting patterns in early and late races: an exploitable opportunity?, Discussion Papers in Accounting and Management Science, University of Southampton.

Kuypers, T. J. (1996) The beautiful game? An econometric study of why people watch English football, UCL Economics Department Discussion Papers, 96-01.

Lacey, N. J. (1990) An estimation of market efficiency in the NFL point spread betting market. *Applied Economics*, **22**, 117–29.

Peel, D. and Thomas, D. (1988) Outcome uncertainty and the demand for football: an analysis of match attendances in the English football league, *Scottish Journal of Political Economy*, **35**(3), 242–9.

Pope, P. F. and Peel, D. A. (1990) Information, prices and efficiency in a fixed-odds betting market, *Economica*, **56**, 323–41.

Rollin, J. (ed.) (1995) *Rothman's Football Yearbook 1995/1996*, Headline Publishing, London.

Royal Commission on Gambling (1978) *Final Report*. Cmnd. 7200. London, HMSO.

Sauer, R. D., Brajer, V., Ferris, S. P. and Marr, M. W. (1988) Hold your bets: another look at the efficiency of the gambling market for national football league games, *Journal of Political Economy*, **96**, 206–13.

Snyder, W. W. (1978) Horse racing: testing the efficient markets model, *The Journal of Finance*, **XXXIII**, 1109–18.

Thaler, R. H. and Ziemba, W. T. (1988) Pari-mutuel betting markets: racetracks and lotteries, *Journal of Economic Perspectives*, **2**, 161–74.

Zuber, R. A., Gandar, J. M. and Bowers, B. D. (1985) Beating the spread: testing the efficiency of the gambling market for national football league games, *Journal of Political Economy*, **93**, 800–5.

[21]

The Statistician (2002)
51, *Part 2, pp.* 157–168

Dynamic modelling and prediction of English Football League matches for betting

Martin Crowder,

Imperial College of Science, Technology and Medicine, London, UK

Mark Dixon

City University, London, UK

and Anthony Ledford and Mike Robinson

Man Investment Products Ltd, London, UK

[Received July 2001. Revised November 2001]

Summary. We focus on modelling the 92 soccer teams in the English Football Association League over the years 1992–1997 using refinements of the independent Poisson model of Dixon and Coles. Our framework assumes that each team has attack and defence strengths that evolve through time (rather than remaining constant) according to some unobserved bivariate stochastic process. Estimation of the teams' attack and defence capabilities is undertaken via a novel approach involving an approximation that is computationally convenient and fast. The results of this approximation compare very favourably with results obtained through the Dixon and Coles approach. We note that the full model (i.e. the model before the above approximation is made) may be implemented using Markov chain Monte Carlo procedures, and that this approach is vastly more computationally expensive. We focus on the probabilities of home win, draw or away win because these outcomes constitute the primary betting market. These probabilities are estimated for games played between any two of the 92 teams and the predictions are compared with the actual results.

Keywords: Attack and defence strengths; Football results; Poisson models; State space modelling

1. Team talk

Consider the match between team i (home) and team j (away) played at time t, in which the goals scored are x_{it} (by team i) and y_{jt} (by team j). According to the independent Poisson model, the probability of this result is

$$\{\exp(-\eta\alpha_{it}\beta_{jt})(\eta\alpha_{it}\beta_{jt})^{x_{it}}/x_{it}!\}\{\exp(-\alpha_{jt}\beta_{it})(\alpha_{jt}\beta_{it})^{y_{jt}}/y_{jt}!\}, \tag{1.1}$$

where α_{it} and α_{jt} represent the attack rates (strengths) of teams i and j at time t, β_{it} and β_{jt} their defence rates (weaknesses) and η is the home advantage factor. With increasing η, α_{it} and β_{jt}, more goals will tend to be scored by team i against team j; likewise, there will be more goals at the other end when $\alpha_{jt}\beta_{it}$ increases. Though the model describes goals scored by the

---

Address for correspondence: Martin Crowder, Department of Mathematics, Huxley Building, Imperial College of Science, Technology and Medicine, 180 Queen's Gate, London, SW7 2BZ, UK.
E-mail: m.crowder@ic.ac.uk

0039–0526/02/51157

teams, this is simply a route to estimating the probabilities of win, draw or lose for the primary football betting market.

Maher (1982) took the αs and βs to be constant over time, so each team is assigned a pair of fixed parameters, α_i and β_i. Dixon and Coles (1997) adjusted the model to reflect a dependence between x_{it} and y_{jt} at the lower end (when x_{it} and y_{jt} are both less than 2). Also, with prediction in mind, they tapered the likelihood function to give greater weight to more recent results. This is in recognition of the probable need to allow α_i and β_i to vary through time, not to be constrained to stay constant.

Recently, three papers have appeared with a theme that is similar to ours. Where we take the goals scored as the data, the observations in Knorr-Held (2000) and Koning (2000) comprise only the win, lose or draw results. In addition, their models are based on a single team strength, rather than separating attack and defence, and are based on thresholds in cumulative distribution functions, in the usual way for ordered categorical data. Both Knorr-Held (2000) and Koning (2000) derived point estimates for the parameters, Koning applying maximum likelihood and Knorr-Held using an extended Kalman filter together with an *ad hoc* method for a variance parameter.

Rue and Salvesen (2000) used a modified independent Poisson model, as proposed by Dixon and Coles (1997). They allowed for separate attack and defence strengths but incorporated these in a further-modified way that involves a psychological factor to reflect the overall difference in the opposing teams' strengths. Also, they truncated the numbers of goals at 5, so a score of 9–6 is interpreted as 5–5, for example. In a final modification, a mixture model was proposed in which the previously described form is mixed with a similar form based on average scores. There was no allowance for a home ground advantage, however.

In both Knorr-Held (2000) and Rue and Salvesen (2000) the team strength parameters were allowed to vary over time according to random walks with independent normal increments. This aspect is similar to our formulation, given in Section 3, but in other respects our treatment and aims are quite different from those of Knorr-Held and Rue and Salvesen.

2. Constraints on team behaviour

The αs and βs only appear in the likelihood function (1.1) in combinations $\alpha_{it}\beta_{jt}$. In consequence, there is a lack of identifiability; for example, the αs could be doubled and the βs halved without altering their products. A standard approach in such cases is to apply one or more constraints to the parameters. However, any such constraint has the undesirable effect of tying their values together in some way. Thus, if one team's (α, β) changes, as a result of some local event, say, other teams' (α, β)s must change to preserve the constraints, even though the event in question does not affect them. This consideration suggests that any particular set of (α, β)s does not itself necessarily constitute the 'true' team strengths: the values are merely the projections of the strengths onto the constraint surface along trajectories of constant likelihood.

It is not immediately obvious how many constraints will be needed on the (α, β)s to obtain identifiability, though it is clearly at least one because of the scaling ambiguity mentioned above. With m teams, there are $2m$ αs and βs, and $m(m-1)$ combinations $\alpha_i\beta_j$. Thus, with enough data, i.e. sufficient hypothetical replication of the matches, to fix the combinations, there are $m(m-1)$ equations in $2m$ unknowns. For example, with $m = 4$ this is 12 equations in eight unknowns, which would seem to imply inconsistency even without any constraints. However, the 12 equations are not necessarily independent, and we must identify the extent of this dependence to calculate the number of constraints required. It is shown in Appendix A.1 that a single constraint will suffice for identifiability.

We shall take the single constraint to be

$$\sum_{i=1}^{m}\log(\alpha_{it}\beta_{it}) = 0, \tag{2.1}$$

i.e. that the geometric mean of the $(\alpha_{it}\beta_{it})$ is 1. Note that $\alpha_{it}\beta_{it}$ is the average scoring rate of team i's attack against its own defence per game. Constraint (2.1) will be imposed by expressing the α_{it} and β_{it} in terms of a more basic set of unconstrained parameters. Let these underlying parameters be $\gamma_{it} = (\gamma_{\alpha_{it}}, \gamma_{\beta_{it}})^{\mathrm{T}}$, and take

$$\begin{aligned}
\log(\alpha_{it}) &= \gamma_{\alpha_{it}} - \bar{\gamma}_{t}, \\
\log(\beta_{it}) &= \gamma_{\beta_{it}} - \bar{\gamma}_{t},
\end{aligned} \tag{2.2}$$

where

$$\bar{\gamma}_{t} = (2m)^{-1}\sum_{j=1}^{m}(\gamma_{\alpha_{jt}} + \gamma_{\beta_{jt}}).$$

Thus, constraint (2.1) is automatically satisfied.

3. A stochastic process tactic

Dixon and Coles (1997) recognized the probable need for the αs and βs to vary over time. One way of tackling such a drift, alternative to theirs, is to model the processes explicitly. The changes over time may be small, for consistently performing teams, or larger, reflecting more substantial events, planned or not. We shall implement this by adopting an autoregressive AR(1) process for $\gamma_{it} = (\gamma_{\alpha_{it}}, \gamma_{\beta_{it}})^{\mathrm{T}}$:

$$\gamma_{it} - \gamma_{i0} = R(\gamma_{i, t-1} - \gamma_{i0}) + u_{it}. \tag{3.1}$$

Thus, the stochastic process moves in the γ-space, of $2m$ dimensions, and then, by equation (2.2), this is projected into the (α, β) space, of $2m - 1$ dimensions. In equation (3.1) R is a $2{\times}2$ matrix of autoregression parameters,

$$R = \begin{pmatrix} \rho_{\alpha\alpha} & \rho_{\alpha\beta} \\ \rho_{\beta\alpha} & \rho_{\beta\beta} \end{pmatrix},$$

the u_{it} are independent $N_2(0,\Sigma)$ innovations (independent of all previous outcomes and all other u_{jt}s) and γ_{i0} is a base-line value towards which γ_{it} is drawn if R is small in some sense (e.g. $\mathrm{tr}(R^{\mathrm{T}}R) < 1$, which ensures that $|Rx| < |x|$ for all x).

Because of the independence of the u_{it}, the γ_{it}-processes for different teams evolve over time independently of one another. However, dependence between the αs and βs for different teams is introduced via equation (2.2). These processes are not directly observable, but their effects are seen in the match results. Special cases of equation (3.1) include the following. If the γ_{i0} are all 0, the base-line attraction aspect is absent and the processes are purely autoregressive. If R and Σ are both diagonal the processes $\gamma_{\alpha_{it}}$ (attack) and $\gamma_{\beta_{it}}$ (defence) evolve independently. If $R = I$, the unit matrix, the γ_{it}-process is just a two-dimensional random walk with steps u_{it}. If $R = I$ and $\Sigma = 0$, the zero matrix, γ_{it} is constant over time as in the Maher (1982) model.

Even if we take the γ_{i0} that appear explicitly in equation (3.1) as 0 we still need to specify initial values because for $t = 1$ the formula involves γ_{i0}. These values can be defined with reference to the previous season's results, or perhaps as random effects from some suitable distribution, or retained as fixed effects parameters to be estimated.

An overall likelihood function can be constructed for matches up to and including time t as follows. The vector of unknown parameters is $\theta = (\eta, R, \Sigma)$, of dimension $1 + 4 + 3 = 8$. Let G_t comprise the goal results of all the matches played at time t, i.e. all the x_{it} and y_{jt} for i and j ranging over all the teams involved, and let Γ_t represent the set of unobserved γ_{it} at time t for these teams. Then

$$p(\Gamma_1, \ldots, \Gamma_t | \Gamma_0, \theta) = \prod_{s=1}^{t} p(\Gamma_s | \Gamma_{s-1}, \theta) = \prod_{s=1}^{t} \prod_{i} p(\gamma_{is} | \gamma_{i,s-1}, \theta) \qquad (3.2)$$

and

$$p(G_1, \ldots, G_t | \Gamma_0, \ldots, \Gamma_t, \theta) = \prod_{s=1}^{t} p(G_s | \Gamma_s, \eta) = \prod_{s=1}^{t} \prod_{ij} p(x_{is}, y_{js} | a_{is}, a_{js}, \eta) \qquad (3.3)$$

where $a_{is} = (\log(\alpha_{is}), \log(\beta_{is}))^{\mathrm{T}}$ and the product Π_{ij} in equation (3.3) is over all the games played at time s. It has been assumed in equation (3.3) that, given $(\alpha_{is}, \beta_{is}, \eta)$, the result (x_{is}, y_{js}) is independent of all others. Hence, the likelihood function for θ based on the matches up to time t, conditional on Γ_0, is

$$\begin{aligned}
L_t(\theta) &= p(G_1, \ldots, G_t | \Gamma_0, \theta) \\
&= \int p(G_1, \ldots, G_t, \Gamma_1, \ldots, \Gamma_t | \Gamma_0, \theta) \, \mathrm{d}\Gamma_1 \ldots \mathrm{d}\Gamma_t \\
&= \int p(G_1, \ldots, G_t | \Gamma_0, \ldots, \Gamma_t, \theta) \, p(\Gamma_1, \ldots, \Gamma_t | \Gamma_0, \theta) \, \mathrm{d}\Gamma_1 \ldots \mathrm{d}\Gamma_t \\
&= \int \prod_{s=1}^{t} \{ \prod_{ij} p(x_{is}, y_{js} | a_{is}, a_{js}, \eta) \prod_{i} p(\gamma_{is} | \gamma_{i,s-1}, \theta) \} \mathrm{d}\Gamma_1 \ldots \mathrm{d}\Gamma_t, \qquad (3.4)
\end{aligned}$$

using equations (3.2) and (3.3). The two core ingredients in the integrand of equation (3.4) are straightforward to compute: $p(x_{is}, y_{js} | a_{is}, a_{js}, \eta)$ is given as the Poisson product in expression (1.1) and $p(\gamma_{is} | \gamma_{i,s-1}, \theta)$ as the density of $N\{\gamma_{i0} + R(\gamma_{i,t-1} - \gamma_{i0}), \Sigma\}$, from equation (3.1). However, the dimension of the integration is $2mt$, m being the number of teams involved. For instance, with $m = 92$, the number of teams in the English Football League, and $t = 40$, roughly the number of games played in one season, $2mt = 7360$. This makes equation (3.4) difficult to deal with directly.

Markov chain Monte Carlo (MCMC) methods were initially applied to the present problem but, for brevity, they are not reported here. In short, a form of MCMC sampling was employed using a Gibbs-type method with the components, γ_{is} and γ_{js} of $(\Gamma_1, \ldots, \Gamma_t, \theta)$, being updated one at a time via the usual Metropolis acceptance formula. By virtue of the Markov property of the γ_{it}-processes, seen in equation (3.2), and of the dependence of (x_{is}, y_{js}) on $(\Gamma_1, \ldots, \Gamma_t, \theta)$ only through (a_{is}, a_{js}, η), γ_{is} and γ_{js} each appear in only three individual factors of the full posterior expression. Thus, a significant short-cut can be made in computing the acceptance probability for proposal values of γ_{is}. On this basis the computations for predictions for a single week become feasible. However, for comparisons over whole seasons, as required for the present study, the MCMC method is still too slow to be used routinely. For this reason a faster method was sought, and such an approach is described next.

4. An approximation

The model here is essentially a non-normal, non-linear state space model in which the states are the Γ_{it} and the observed quantities are the x_{it} and y_{it}. Many references have presented approximate methods for filtering and smoothing for such models, e.g. Kitagawa (1987), Carlin *et al.* (1992), Carter and Kohn (1994) and Shephard and Pitt (1997). Some of the methods proposed are based on numerical integration and others on simulation, but what they all have in common is the retention of the underlying model formulation. The approach to be outlined in this section differs in that the original model is replaced by a derived model that is easier to handle. The attitude here is that no model is likely to be 'true', however carefully constructed, and the only true worth of any model lies in its predictive performance: in the present context this is its ability to predict the outcomes of matches so that useful bets can be identified and placed.

It is shown in Appendix A.1 that, in consequence of equations (3.1) and (2.2), the $(\alpha_{it}, \beta_{it})$ process is given by

$$a_{it} - a_{i0} = R(a_{i,t-1} - a_{i0}) + (RJ - JR)(\gamma_{t-1} - \gamma_0) + u_{it} - (2m)^{-1} \sum_{j=1}^{m} Ju_{jt}, \qquad (4.1)$$

where $a_{it} = (\log(\alpha_{it}), \log(\beta_{it}))^{\mathrm{T}}$ and J is a 2×2 matrix of 1s. Note that

$$RJ - JR = \begin{pmatrix} \rho_{\alpha\alpha} + \rho_{\alpha\beta} & \rho_{\alpha\alpha} + \rho_{\alpha\beta} \\ \rho_{\beta\alpha} + \rho_{\beta\beta} & \rho_{\beta\alpha} + \rho_{\beta\beta} \end{pmatrix} - \begin{pmatrix} \rho_{\alpha\alpha} + \rho_{\beta\alpha} & \rho_{\alpha\beta} + \rho_{\beta\beta} \\ \rho_{\alpha\alpha} + \rho_{\beta\alpha} & \rho_{\alpha\beta} + \rho_{\beta\beta} \end{pmatrix}$$

$$= \begin{pmatrix} \rho_{\alpha\beta} - \rho_{\beta\alpha} & \rho_{\alpha\alpha} - \rho_{\beta\beta} \\ \rho_{\beta\beta} - \rho_{\alpha\alpha} & \rho_{\beta\alpha} - \rho_{\alpha\beta} \end{pmatrix}.$$

Thus, $RJ - JR$ is 0 if $R = I$, as for the random walk model. However, in that case equation (3.1) would represent a non-stationary autoregressive model. More generally, $RJ - JR$ is 0 if R is symmetric about both diagonals, i.e. $\rho_{\alpha\alpha} = \rho_{\beta\beta}$ and $\rho_{\alpha\beta} = \rho_{\beta\alpha}$, and a stationary autoregressive model obtains if $|R| < 1$, i.e. $\rho_{\alpha\alpha}^2 + \rho_{\beta\beta}^2 + \rho_{\alpha\beta}^2 + \rho_{\beta\alpha}^2 < 1$.

Suppose that $RJ - JR = 0$, and omit the $O_p(m^{-1})$ contribution in equation (4.1). Then we obtain an autoregressive model for the a_{it}:

$$a_{it} - a_{i0} = R(a_{i,t-1} - a_{i0}) + u_{it}. \qquad (4.2)$$

This model might have been adopted at the outset, but it does not incorporate the constraint explicitly. However, it can lead to a useful approximate approach as follows.

Note that equation (4.2) gives

$$p(a_{it}|a_{i0}, a_{i1}, \ldots, a_{i,t-1}) = \det(2\pi\Sigma)^{-1/2} \exp\{-\tfrac{1}{2}(a_{it} - m_{it})^{\mathrm{T}}\Sigma^{-1}(a_{it} - m_{it})\}, \qquad (4.3)$$

with

$$m_{it} = a_{i0} + R(a_{i,t-1} - a_{i0}). \qquad (4.4)$$

Also, the appropriate distribution for updating a_{it} and a_{jt}, as a result of the unobserved changes from time $t - 1$ together with the evidence from the match result (x_{it}, y_{jt}), is

$$p(a_{it}, a_{jt}|a_{i,t-1}, a_{j,t-1}, x_{it}, y_{jt})$$
$$= p(x_{it}, y_{jt}|a_{it}, a_{jt}, a_{i,t-1}, a_{j,t-1})\, p(a_{it}, a_{jt}|a_{i,t-1}, a_{j,t-1})/p(x_{it}, y_{jt}|a_{i,t-1}, a_{j,t-1})$$
$$= p(x_{it}, y_{jt}|a_{it}, a_{jt})\, p(a_{it}|a_{i,t-1})\, p(a_{jt}|a_{j,t-1})/p(x_{it}, y_{jt}|a_{i,t-1}, a_{j,t-1}), \qquad (4.5)$$

where $p(x_{it}, y_{jt}|a_{it}, a_{jt})$ is given by equation (1.1) and $p(a_{it}|a_{i,t-1})$ and $p(a_{jt}|a_{j,t-1})$ are given by equation (4.3); the denominator does not involve (a_{it}, a_{jt}).

We seek some summary of the information in equation (4.5) that will enable us to avoid the integration in equation (3.4). A natural suggestion is to adopt, for the updated versions of a_{it} and a_{jt}, their maximum probability estimators based on equation (4.5); see, for example, Fahrmeir and Kaufman (1991) and Fahrmeir (1992). These are derived in Appendix A.2 as

$$a_{it} = m_{it} + \Sigma r_{ijt},$$
$$a_{jt} = m_{jt} + \Sigma r_{jit}, \qquad (4.6)$$

where

$$r_{ijt} = (x_{it} - \eta \alpha_{it} \beta_{jt}, y_{jt} - \alpha_{jt} \beta_{it})^{\mathrm{T}}$$

is the vector of 'Poisson residuals', i.e. the discrepancies between the home and away goals and their expected values; r_{jit} is just r_{ijt} with the components interchanged. The updated version of a_{it} is thus expressed as its autoregressive mean m_{it} plus an adjustment Σr_{ijt}, to take account of the match result, and likewise for a_{jt}. Unfortunately, however, r_{ijt} itself involves the components of a_{it} and a_{jt}, so equations (4.6) give a_{it} and a_{jt} implicitly. An iterative solution, described in Appendix A.2, has been implemented and works reasonably well. At least one solution to equations (4.6) exists because the probability density (4.5) must have at least one maximum. If teams i and j do not play at time t, the appropriate updating distribution is just $p(a_{it}, a_{jt}|a_{i,t-1}, a_{j,t-1})$. On the same basis as above, this leads to the reduced updating formulae

$$a_{it} = m_{it},$$
$$a_{jt} = m_{jt}. \qquad (4.7)$$

We now propose that the updating formulae (4.6) and (4.7) be adopted in place of equation (4.2) as the formal model for $(\alpha_{it}, \beta_{it}, \alpha_{jt}, \beta_{jt})$. In effect, the $(\alpha_{it}, \beta_{it})$ become interlinked stochastic processes driven by the innovations (x_{it}, y_{jt}) with initial values $(\alpha_{i0}, \beta_{i0})$ and parameter set $\theta = (\eta, R, \Sigma)$. In equation (4.2) the $(\alpha_{it}, \beta_{it})$ evolve independently over time and information would just be gathered about their progress from the match results. Now, in equations (4.6) and (4.7), the processes $(\alpha_{it}, \beta_{it})$ are actually driven by the match results and are thereby interdependent.

The nature of the approximation made in this section can be described as follows: the original process (4.1) has been replaced by the approximation (4.2), and then equation (4.2) has been replaced by a different, but closely related, process.

A likelihood function based on this scheme can be constructed for the matches up to and including time t as

$$L_t(\theta) = p(G_1, \ldots, G_t|A_0, \theta) = \prod_{s=1}^{t} p(G_s|G_1, \ldots, G_{s-1}, A_0, \theta),$$

where $A_t = (a_{1t}, \ldots, a_{mt})$. Assume that $(G_1, \ldots, G_{s-1}, A_0)$ and $(A_0, \ldots, A_{s-1})$ are equivalent, i.e. that expression (4.6) has a unique solution for a_{it} and a_{jt}. Then,

$$p(G_s|G_1, \ldots, G_{s-1}, A_0, \theta) = p(G_s|A_0, \ldots, A_{s-1}, \theta)$$
$$= \int p(G_s|A_0, \ldots, A_s, \theta) \, p(A_s|A_0, \ldots, A_{s-1}, \theta) \, \mathrm{d}A_s$$
$$= p(G_s|A_0, \ldots, A_{s-1}, A_s = M_s, \theta) = p(G_s|A_s = M_s, \theta) \qquad (4.8)$$

because, according to equations (4.7), $p(A_s|A_0, \ldots, A_{s-1}, \theta)$ is concentrated at the single point $A_s = M_s$, where M_s is the complete set of m_{is}-values for all the teams. Hence,

$$L_t(\theta) = \prod_{s=1}^{t} p(G_s|A_s = M_s, \theta) = \prod_{s=1}^{t} \prod_{ij} p(x_{is}, y_{js}|a_{is} = m_{is}, a_{js} = m_{js}, \theta), \qquad (4.9)$$

where Π_{ij} is the product over all the matches played at time s and $p(x_{is}, y_{js}|a_{is} = m_{is}, a_{js} = m_{js}, \theta)$ is given by equations (1.1) and (4.4). Note that $L_t(\theta)$ in equation (4.9) is implicitly conditioned on Γ_0 because the m_{i1} depend on the a_{i0}. This likelihood function is very simply computed, unlike that in equation (3.4).

5. Prediction

Because of the steadily accruing information on the a_{it} we might hope that predictions would become more useful as time goes on. However, the inherent variability of low count Poisson variables limits the attainable accuracy of forecasting match results. Even if the model were correct, and the parameters precisely known, there would still be considerable uncertainty in the predictions.

For prediction one step ahead, the relevant distribution is $p(G_t|G_1, \ldots, G_{t-1}, \Gamma_0)$. This gives the probabilities of various scores (x_{it}, y_{jt}) for particular games, and so the probabilities of home or away wins can be computed. It may be evaluated as

$$p(G_t|G_1, \ldots, G_{t-1}, \Gamma_0) = \int p(G_t|G_1, \ldots, G_{t-1}, \Gamma_0, \theta) \, p(\theta|G_1, \ldots, G_{t-1}, \Gamma_0) \, d\theta, \qquad (5.1)$$

where $p(\theta|G_1, \ldots, G_{t-1}, \Gamma_0)$ is the posterior distribution of θ given the match results up to time $t-1$.

For the approximation method we have, from equation (4.8),

$$p(G_t|G_1, \ldots, G_{t-1}, \Gamma_0, \theta) = p(G_t|A_t = M_t, \theta),$$

which is given by equations (1.1) and (4.4). Provided that $p(\theta|G_1, \ldots, G_{t-1}, \Gamma_0)$ is sufficiently peaked, the integral (5.1) can be well approximated by a plug-in estimate, $p(G_t|A_t = M_t, \theta = \hat{\theta}_{t-1})$, where $\hat{\theta}_{t-1}$ is the maximum likelihood estimate based on $(G_1, \ldots, G_{t-1}, \Gamma_0)$. The integral could be evaluated by simulation, e.g. by MCMC sampling from the posterior, but we have not pursued this alternative because our focus is on a computational approach that avoids MCMC methods: see the discussion in Section 7.

6. Full results round-up

The methods described above were applied to the Football Association League fixtures over the years 1992–1997, and home win, draw and away win probabilities were calculated accordingly. It is these probabilities that are of chief concern in the primary betting market. Some summary statistics examining the performance of each approach were evaluated and are now presented.

Table 1 shows summaries of the actual outcomes given the most likely predicted outcome for the approximation method and the Dixon and Coles (1997) model. If a model is performing well then the elements in the leading diagonal of these tables should dominate. In practice though, since a draw is so seldom predicted as the most likely outcome, only the results for a home win and an away win are of significant interest. The two approaches appear to have roughly the same predictive ability for home wins (in the first row of the table), with just under 50% of games

Table 1. Comparison of predicted and actual outcomes

Most likely predicted outcome	Approximation results for the following actual outcomes:			Dixon–Coles results for the following actual outcomes:		
	Home win	Draw	Away win	Home win	Draw	Away win
Home win	0.48	0.28	0.24	0.49	0.28	0.23
Draw	—	—	—	0.33	0.33	0.33
Away win	0.33	0.28	0.39	0.33	0.31	0.36

predicted as home wins actually resulting in home wins. For away wins, the methods perform less well, with the approximation method slightly better.

The indicators examined above, although informative, are prone to considerable variability since, for example, a home win could be the most likely outcome for any probability greater than $\frac{1}{3}$. As an alternative, consider the predictive ability of each method when only strong favourites are considered. Table 2 gives a summary of the empirical outcomes conditional on strong favourites, 'strong' in the sense that the predicted probability is 0.5 or more. Again, for both home and away wins the two approaches perform very similarly.

Tables 1 and 2 provide summary information averaged over the entire time horizon of the study. Of potentially greater interest is the performance of the approaches through time: do the methods become better at predicting the outcomes of games as time goes on? Fig. 1 depicts a quantity that is related to this issue, namely, a rolling predictive likelihood defined as

$$\mathrm{RPL}(s, t) = -N(s, t)^{-1} \sum_{r=s}^{t} \sum_{ij} \log\{\mathrm{pr}(o_{ijr})\},$$

where o_{ijr} denotes the outcome of the match between teams i and j played at time r, Σ_{ij} denotes summation over those games and $N(s, t)$ denotes the total number of games played at times $s, s+1, \ldots, t$; $\mathrm{pr}(o_{ijr})$ is the predicted probability of outcome o_{ijr}. A good performance is indicated by a small value of this statistic. Fig. 1 shows a plot, for each method, of $\mathrm{RPL}(t - 69, t)$ versus t; the window length, 70 time periods, is roughly one season. The Dixon–Coles method starts poorly but improves rapidly and betters the approximation around week 210. However, the approximation, which is a more general, likelihood-based approach, is at least competitive throughout.

7. Conclusion

The purpose of the work described here is to develop a fast computational approach for predicting the results of football matches with a view to betting in the primary market on win, draw

Table 2. Comparison of predicted and actual outcomes

Approximation	0.51	0.43
Dixon–Coles	0.52	0.49

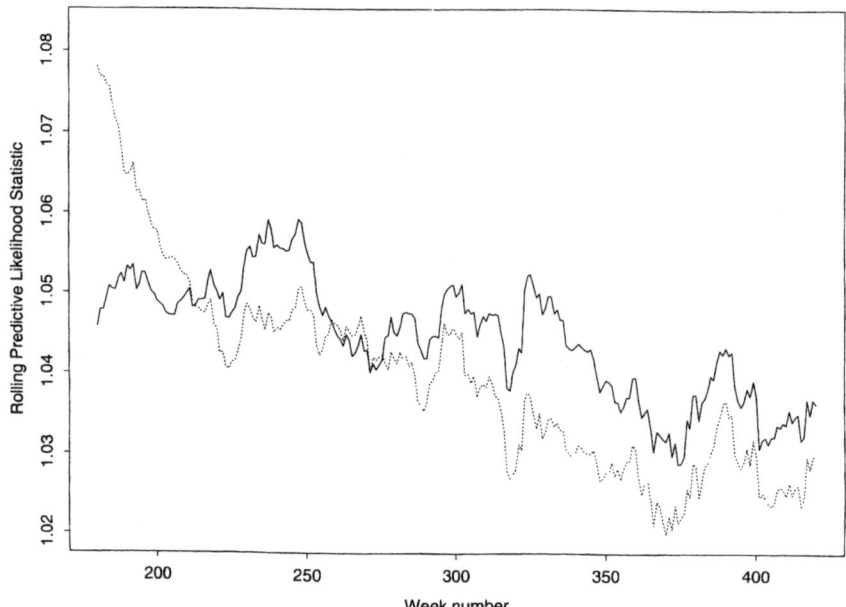

Fig. 1. Rolling predictive likelihood statistic for the Dixon–Coles method (· · · · · ·) and the approximation
(———)

or lose outcomes. For this, a novel method has been developed in which the original stochastic process model is replaced by an approximation that yields more tractable computation than MCMC methodology in this case, but which does not lose too much predictive power. The approximation method clearly has wider potential for tractable computations in the context of non-linear state space models.

Acknowledgements

We thank the Joint Editor and referees for their helpful comments.

Appendix A

A.1. The identifiability constraint

Suppose that $\alpha_i \beta_j$ is fixed as $\exp(\nu_{ij})$, i.e. $\log(\alpha_i) + \log(\beta_j) = \nu_{ij}$. Then the whole set of equations can be written as $Ax = \nu$, where x is the $2m \times 1$ vector

$$(\log(\alpha_1), \ldots, \log(\alpha_m), \log(\beta_1), \ldots, \log(\beta_m))^{\mathrm{T}},$$

ν is the $m(m-1) \times 1$ vector of ν_{ij}s and A is the appropriate $m(m-1) \times 2m$ incidence matrix. With $m = 4$, for instance,

166 *M. Crowder, M. Dixon, A. Ledford and M. Robinson*

$$A = \begin{pmatrix} 1\,0\,0\,0 & 0\,1\,0\,0 \\ 1\,0\,0\,0 & 0\,0\,1\,0 \\ 1\,0\,0\,0 & 0\,0\,0\,1 \\ 0\,1\,0\,0 & 1\,0\,0\,0 \\ 0\,1\,0\,0 & 0\,0\,1\,0 \\ 0\,1\,0\,0 & 0\,0\,0\,1 \\ 0\,0\,1\,0 & 1\,0\,0\,0 \\ 0\,0\,1\,0 & 0\,1\,0\,0 \\ 0\,0\,1\,0 & 0\,0\,0\,1 \\ 0\,0\,0\,1 & 1\,0\,0\,0 \\ 0\,0\,0\,1 & 0\,1\,0\,0 \\ 0\,0\,0\,1 & 0\,0\,1\,0 \end{pmatrix}.$$

The identifiable parametric functions are the elements of Ax, and so the number of independent identifiable functions is rank(A). Thus, the appropriate number of constraints will be $2m - \text{rank}(A)$. We can determine the dimension of the kernel of A quite easily by seeing that the only solutions of $Ay = 0$ are y-vectors proportional to $(1, \ldots, 1, -1, \ldots, -1)$; this can be checked for the example with $m = 4$ given above, and thence generalized. Note that this y-vector corresponds to adding a constant to each $\log(\alpha_i)$ and subtracting the same constant from each $\log(\beta_i)$, which amounts to precisely the rescaling of the αs and βs referred to in Section 2. Thus, dim$\{\ker(A)\} = 1$, so rank(A) $= 2m - 1$ and so only a single constraint is needed.

The implications of the autoregressive model (3.1) for the αs and βs defined by equation (2.2) are as follows. We have

$$\begin{pmatrix} \log(\alpha_{it}) \\ \log(\beta_{it}) \end{pmatrix} = \begin{pmatrix} \gamma_{\alpha it} - \gamma_t \\ \gamma_{\beta it} - \gamma_t \end{pmatrix} = \gamma_{it} - (2m)^{-1} \sum_{j=1}^{m} J\gamma_{jt},$$

where J is a 2×2 matrix of 1s. Hence,

$$\begin{pmatrix} \log(\alpha_{it}) - \log(\alpha_{i0}) \\ \log(\beta_{it}) - \log(\beta_{i0}) \end{pmatrix} = \gamma_{it} - \gamma_{i0} - (2m)^{-1} \sum_{j=1}^{m} J(\gamma_{jt} - \gamma_{j0})$$

$$= R(\gamma_{i,t-1} - \gamma_{i0}) + u_{it} - (2m)^{-1} \sum_{j=1}^{m} J\{R(\gamma_{j,t-1} - \gamma_{j0}) + u_{jt}\}$$

$$= R(\gamma_{i,t-1} - \gamma_{i0}) - (2m)^{-1} \sum_{j=1}^{m} RJ(\gamma_{j,t-1} - \gamma_{j0})$$

$$+ (2m)^{-1} \sum_{j=1}^{m} (RJ - JR)(\gamma_{j,t-1} - \gamma_{j0}) + u_{it} - (2m)^{-1} \sum_{j=1}^{m} Ju_{jt}$$

$$= R \begin{pmatrix} \log(\alpha_{i,t-1}) - \log(\alpha_{i0}) \\ \log(\beta_{i,t-1}) - \log(\beta_{i0}) \end{pmatrix} + (RJ - JR)(\gamma_{t-1} - \gamma_0) + u_{it} - (2m)^{-1} \sum_{j=1}^{m} Ju_{jt},$$

which is equation (4.1).

A.2. Equations and numerical solution for the approximation method

Equation (4.6) is derived together with a suggested numerical method of solution. The relevant part of the logarithm of equation (4.5) is

$$M = -\gamma\alpha_{it}\beta_{jt} + x_{it}\log(\gamma\alpha_{it}\beta_{jt}) - \alpha_{jt}\beta_{it} + y_{jt}\log(\alpha_{jt}\beta_{it})$$
$$- \tfrac{1}{2}(a_{it} - m_{it})^{\mathrm{T}}\Sigma^{-1}(a_{it} - m_{it}) - \tfrac{1}{2}(a_{jt} - m_{jt})^{\mathrm{T}}\Sigma^{-1}(a_{jt} - m_{jt}),$$

and this has derivatives as follows:

$$\frac{\partial M}{\partial \alpha_{it}} = -\gamma \beta_{jt} + \alpha_{it}^{-1} x_{it} - \alpha_{it}^{-1} [\{\log(\alpha_{it}) - m_{it1}\}\Sigma^{11} + \{\log(\beta_{it}) - m_{it2}\}\Sigma^{12}];$$

$$\frac{\partial M}{\partial \beta_{it}} = -\alpha_{jt} + \beta_{it}^{-1} y_{jt} - \beta_{it}^{-1} [\{\log(\beta_{it}) - m_{it2}\}\Sigma^{22} + \{\log(\alpha_{it}) - m_{it1}\}\Sigma^{12}];$$

$$\frac{\partial M}{\partial \alpha_{jt}} = -\beta_{it} + \alpha_{jt}^{-1} y_{jt} - \alpha_{jt}^{-1} [\{\log(\alpha_{jt}) - m_{jt1}\}\Sigma^{11} + \{\log(\beta_{jt}) - m_{jt2}\}\Sigma^{12}];$$

$$\frac{\partial M}{\partial \beta_{jt}} = -\gamma \alpha_{it} + \beta_{jt}^{-1} x_{it} - \beta_{jt}^{-1} [\{\log(\beta_{jt}) - m_{jt2}\}\Sigma^{22} + \{\log(\alpha_{jt}) - m_{jt1}\}\Sigma^{12}];$$

here, m_{it1} and m_{it2} are the components of m_{it}, and the Σ^{jk} are the elements of Σ^{-1}. On equating these derivatives to 0, and rearranging, we obtain

$$\{\log(\alpha_{it}) - m_{it1}\}\Sigma^{11} + \{\log(\beta_{it}) - m_{it2}\}\Sigma^{12} = x_{it} - \gamma \alpha_{it}\beta_{jt},$$

$$\{\log(\alpha_{it}) - m_{it1}\}\Sigma^{12} + \{\log(\beta_{it}) - m_{it2}\}\Sigma^{22} = y_{jt} - \alpha_{jt}\beta_{it},$$

$$\{\log(\alpha_{jt}) - m_{jt1}\}\Sigma^{11} + \{\log(\beta_{jt}) - m_{jt2}\}\Sigma^{12} = y_{jt} - \alpha_{jt}\beta_{it},$$

$$\{\log(\alpha_{jt}) - m_{jt1}\}\Sigma^{12} + \{\log(\beta_{jt}) - m_{jt2}\}\Sigma^{22} = x_{it} - \gamma \alpha_{it}\beta_{jt}.$$

These equations may be 'solved' to give

$$\{\log(\alpha_{it}) - m_{it1}\}\{\Sigma^{11}\Sigma^{22} - (\Sigma^{12})^2\} = \Sigma^{22}(x_{it} - \gamma \alpha_{it}\beta_{jt}) - \Sigma^{12}(y_{jt} - \alpha_{jt}\beta_{it}),$$

$$\{\log(\beta_{it}) - m_{it2}\}\{\Sigma^{11}\Sigma^{22} - (\Sigma^{12})^2\} = -\Sigma^{12}(x_{it} - \gamma \alpha_{it}\beta_{jt}) + \Sigma^{11}(y_{jt} - \alpha_{jt}\beta_{it}),$$

$$\{\log(\alpha_{jt}) - m_{jt1}\}\{\Sigma^{11}\Sigma^{22} - (\Sigma^{12})^2\} = -\Sigma^{12}(x_{it} - \gamma \alpha_{it}\beta_{jt}) + \Sigma^{22}(y_{jt} - \alpha_{jt}\beta_{it}),$$

$$\{\log(\beta_{jt}) - m_{jt2}\}\{\Sigma^{11}\Sigma^{22} - (\Sigma^{12})^2\} = \Sigma^{11}(x_{it} - \gamma \alpha_{it}\beta_{jt}) - \Sigma^{12}(y_{jt} - \alpha_{jt}\beta_{it}).$$

Using the identity $(\Sigma^{-1})^{-1} = \Sigma$, in component form, these equations yield equations (4.6):

$$\log(\alpha_{it}) = m_{it1} + \Sigma_{11}(x_{it} - \gamma \alpha_{it}\beta_{jt}) + \Sigma_{12}(y_{jt} - \alpha_{jt}\beta_{it}),$$

$$\log(\beta_{it}) = m_{it2} + \Sigma_{12}(x_{it} - \gamma \alpha_{it}\beta_{jt}) + \Sigma_{22}(y_{jt} - \alpha_{jt}\beta_{it}),$$

$$\log(\alpha_{jt}) = m_{jt1} + \Sigma_{12}(x_{it} - \gamma \alpha_{it}\beta_{jt}) + \Sigma_{11}(y_{jt} - \alpha_{jt}\beta_{it}),$$

$$\log(\beta_{jt}) = m_{jt2} + \Sigma_{22}(x_{it} - \gamma \alpha_{it}\beta_{jt}) + \Sigma_{12}(y_{jt} - \alpha_{jt}\beta_{it}).$$

For numerical solution we first reduce these four equations to two, by adding the first and fourth, and the second and third, to obtain

$$\log(\alpha_{it}\beta_{jt}) = m_{it1} + m_{jt2} + (\Sigma_{11} + \Sigma_{22})(x_{it} - \gamma \alpha_{it}\beta_{jt}) + 2\Sigma_{12}(y_{jt} - \alpha_{jt}\beta_{it}),$$

$$\log(\alpha_{jt}\beta_{it}) = m_{it2} + m_{jt1} + 2\Sigma_{12}(x_{it} - \gamma \alpha_{it}\beta_{jt}) + (\Sigma_{11} + \Sigma_{22})(y_{jt} - \alpha_{jt}\beta_{it}).$$

We now have two non-linear equations in the two quantities, $\alpha_{it}\beta_{jt}$ and $\alpha_{jt}\beta_{it}$, so an iterative scheme for solution is called for. The first attempt was one in which the right-hand sides contained the previous estimates, but the successive values tended to oscillate. This suggested that convergence could be accelerated by updating the estimates as the average of the current and previous values, and this scheme was found to work quite well. The technique bears a strong resemblance to Aitken's δ^2 acceleration method (Dixon (1974), section 7.6). Once the process has converged, the previous set of equations is used to compute α_{it}, β_{it}, α_{jt} and β_{jt} separately.

168   *M. Crowder, M. Dixon, A. Ledford and M. Robinson*

References

Carlin, B. P., Polson, N. G. and Stoffer, D. S. (1992) A Monte Carlo approach to nonnormal and nonlinear state-space modeling. *J. Am. Statist. Ass.*, **87**, 493–500.

Carter, C. K. and Kohn, R. (1994) On Gibbs sampling for state space models. *Biometrika*, **81**, 541–553.

Dixon, C. (1974) *Numerical Analysis*. London: Blackie.

Dixon, M. J. and Coles, S. G. (1997) Modelling association football scores and inefficiencies in the football betting market. *Appl. Statist.*, **46**, 265–280.

Fahrmeir, L. (1992) Posterior mode estimation by extended Kalman filtering for multivariate dynamic generalised linear models. *J. Am. Statist. Ass.*, **87**, 501–509.

Fahrmeir, L. and Kaufman, H. (1991) On Kalman filtering, posterior mode estimation and Fisher scoring in dynamic exponential family models. *Metrika*, **38**, 37–60.

Kitagawa, G. (1987) Non-Gaussian state-space modelling of nonstationary time series (with discussion). *J. Am. Statist. Ass.*, **82**, 1032–1063.

Knorr-Held, L. (2000) Dynamic rating of sports teams. *Statistician*, **49**, 261–276.

Koning, R. H. (2000) Balance in competition in Dutch soccer. *Statistician*, **49**, 419–431.

Maher, M. J. (1982) Modelling association football scores. *Statist. Neerland.*, **36**, 109–118.

Rue, H. and Salvesen, Ø. (2000) Prediction and retrospective analysis of soccer matches in a league. *Statistician*, **49**, 399–418.

Shephard, N. and Pitt, M. K. (1997) Likelihood analysis of non-Gaussian measurement time series. *Biometrika*, **84**, 653–667.

Part IV
International Perspectives

[22]

The Statistician (2000)
49, *Part 3, pp.* 419–431

Balance in competition in Dutch soccer

Ruud H. Koning

University of Groningen, the Netherlands

[Received August 1999. Revised April 2000]

Summary. We estimate an ordered probit model for soccer results in the Netherlands. The result of a game is assumed to be determined by home ground advantage and differences in quality between the opposing teams. The parameters of the model are used to assess whether the balance in competition in Dutch professional soccer has changed over time. Contrary to popular belief, we find that the balance has not changed much since the mid-1970s.

Keywords: Balance in competition; Home advantage; Ordered probit model; Professional soccer

1. Introduction

Professional soccer is a big business today. Broadcasting rights for 4 years have been sold in England for approximately US $1 billion, a typical sponsor contract for a top European team is valued at US $6 million (yearly) and the annual salary of a top striker is rumoured to be US $6 million. Demand, as measured by attendances in stadiums or numbers of spectators watching live broadcasts, has increased as well in recent years. In other words, the soccer business is becoming a major amusement industry (Economist, 1997).

The two main reasons for interest in a particular soccer game, or in any sports contest, are the quality of the play in absolute terms and the uncertainty about the outcome. The home games of weak teams are usually sold out when the top teams visit. Strong teams tend to win their games but sometimes they are taken by surprise by a weaker team. Most soccer *aficionados* can recall stories about a leader of a league who lost unexpectedly against a team that was at the bottom of the league. In fact, soccer results are more random than the results of games in other sports as only a few goals are scored each game and chance may be quite influential in determining the outcome. (The relationship between predictability and scores in different sports has been examined by Stefani (1983).)

Schemes such as sponsorship contracts, proceeds from the lucrative Champions League competition (a European competition in which only a selected number of teams participate), merchandizing and television rights allow wealthy teams to lure players away from poorer teams, even to sit on the substitutes' bench. As a result, weak teams are concerned that an increasing inequality in the income distribution of clubs leads to a decrease in the odds of beating strong teams. Poorer teams used to receive revenues from transferring players with great talent to top teams, but this source of income has vanished after the Bosman ruling. (According to the Bosman ruling by the European Court of Justice, a soccer player from the European Community is a free agent after his contract has expired.) This income could be used to improve training facilities for

Address for correspondence: Ruud H. Koning, Department of Econometrics, University of Groningen, PO Box 800, 9700 AV Groningen, the Netherlands.
E-mail: r.h.koning@eco.rug.nl

0039–0526/00/49419

weaker teams or to increase the quality of the team by hiring players. The increased demand for top players across Europe has sent salaries sky high with obvious repercussions for the salary demands of mediocre players in average teams. These developments may cause a breakdown in balance in competition between teams and hence may decrease interest in soccer in the long run. Some weaker teams use these arguments to call for a redistribution of the proceeds of the sale of television rights (both of the national competitions and of the Champions League).

This paper examines the development of the balance in competition in Dutch professional soccer. Our aims are modest: we shall measure the balance in various ways, and we shall discuss its development over time. The structure of the paper is as follows. Section 2 discusses some theory on balance in competition. In Section 3 we develop a simple statistical model that can be used to analyse soccer results. The balance in competition and its evolution over time are discussed in Section 4. We end with some conclusions and directions for further research in Section 5.

2. Theory

Sports contests are interesting when there is not much difference in the quality of the contenders. As Quirk and Fort (1992), page 243, put it:

> 'One of the key ingredients of the demand by fans for team sports is the excitement generated because of uncertainty of outcome of league games. ... In order to maintain fan interest, a sports league has to ensure that teams do not get too strong or too weak relative to one another so that uncertainty of outcome is preserved.'

In fact, this is cited as the reason why some sports organizations in the USA are exempted from anti-trust regulation. Two teams engage in a joint production when they play a game. The outcome and the quality of the game are the good that is sold to the public. The public is worse off when the outcome of a game is easily predicted than if the game is tight. Therefore, collusion between teams to increase the quality of the game may be in the public's interest. This view neglects the absolute quality of the play. In fact, one of the important instruments to maintain balance in competitions in the USA is the inverse draft system, where lower ranked teams can pick talented new players before higher ranked teams can. In soccer leagues, there is no such balancing regulation.

According to the view cited above, an important task for sport bodies like the Union of European Football Associations or the Dutch Soccer Association is to maintain balance in competition because it is needed to ensure long-term interest in the league. The instruments that are available to achieve balance are limited, however. In the Netherlands, a court has decided in a preliminary ruling that individual teams are the owners of the broadcasting rights and not the organizing body. Each team can therefore sell its broadcasting rights individually and take the proceeds of this transaction. An implicit subsidy from wealthy teams to poor teams by the organizing body, to maintain balance, is no longer possible. Moreover, in contrast with baseball and football in the USA, gate receipts are not split between both teams. This may favour teams with big stadiums, even though a completely balanced competition is played (each pair of teams meets twice, once at each venue). In addition, there are no salary caps, either for the teams in total or for individual contracts in European soccer.

Balance in competition and regulations that intended to change it have been studied in the American context but not in the context of European soccer. Neumann and Tamura (1996) studied the balance in the National Football League in the USA. It is measured as the spread of parameters in a non-linear regression model. These parameters capture the quality of the teams. Bennett and

Fizel (1995) examined the effect of telecast deregulation on balance in competition in US college football. They measured it by comparing actual performances in a league with the performances that would be found if all teams were of equal strength (an approach developed by Noll (1991) and Scully (1989)). Empirical results have also been published in Quirk and Fort (1992). They measured the long-term development in five American professional sports leagues. They measured the balance by comparing the percentages of wins or losses for each league for each year with the percentages we would expect to find if all teams were equally strong. Each of the five leagues that they analysed showed a significant imbalance, though the imbalance in both baseball leagues has been decreasing in the last 20 or 30 years.

In the American literature, balance is usually defined as a win percentage of 50%. Such a definition is not useful for soccer, because of the prevalence of draws (unless we consider a draw to be a half-win). Draws are quite common in soccer. Over the period from 1956–1957 to 1996–1997, 26% of all league games ended in a draw, 48% ended in a win by the home team and the remaining 26% ended in a win for the away team. We define a soccer league to be in perfect balance for a certain year if the probability that any team wins a home game does not vary with the opponent or with the team. We assume that the home ground advantage is equal for each team, so in a balanced competition two teams would have equal probability of winning if the game were played on a neutral ground. In a balanced competition the probability that a team wins its home game may exceed the probability of a loss of a home game because of the home advantage. This definition allows for home advantage that changes over time, while the league is still in complete balance.

3. A model to analyse soccer results

3.1. The statistical model

In this section we propose a simple statistical model to analyse the outcome of soccer games. The model is an extension of the model of Neumann and Tamura (1996) in that we allow for an advantage for the home team. The strength of team i in the league is measured by a single parameter α_i. This parameter is independent of the opponent and venue of the game, and it is assumed to be constant during the season. If we assume that team i plays at home and team j is the away team, the difference in strength is $\alpha_i - \alpha_j$. To allow for unmeasured characteristics (i.e. those not captured by α), chance events during a game that influence the score etc., we assume that the outcome of the game is determined by the random variable D_{ij}^*:

$$D_{ij}^* = \alpha_i - \alpha_j + h_{ij} + \eta_{ij}, \qquad i, j = 1, \ldots, 18, \quad j \neq i. \tag{1}$$

In equation (1), h_{ij} is the home ground advantage of team i over team j which is assumed to be normally distributed with mean h. η_{ij} is a mean 0 random variable that captures other determinants of the result of the game. If D_{ij}^* is positive, team i is stronger than j, and D_{ij}^* is negative if team j is stronger than i. We do not observe the actual difference in strength; we only observe the outcome of the game. In fact, we observe whether team i has won, has played a draw or lost against team j. The latent difference in strength is transformed into an observed outcome of the game by

$$D_{ij} = \begin{cases} 1 & D_{ij}^* > c_2', \\ 0 & c_1' < D_{ij}^* \leq c_2', \\ -1 & D_{ij}^* \leq c_1' \end{cases} \tag{2}$$

with $D_{ij} = 1$ if team i wins, $D_{ij} = 0$ if team i plays a draw and $D_{ij} = -1$ if team j (the away team) wins the game. If we assume that h_{ij} and η_{ij} in equation (1) are independent normally distributed ($\epsilon_{ij} = h_{ij} + \eta_{ij} \sim \mathcal{N}(h, \sigma^2)$), then the probabilities of the possible outcomes of a game are

$$\Pr(D_{ij} = 1) = 1 - \Phi\{(c_2 - \alpha_i + \alpha_j)/\sigma\},$$

$$\Pr(D_{ij} = 0) = \Phi\{(c_2 - \alpha_i + \alpha_j)/\sigma\} - \Phi\{(c_1 - \alpha_i + \alpha_j)/\sigma\}, \quad (3)$$

$$\Pr(D_{ij} = -1) = \Phi\{(c_1 - \alpha_i + \alpha_j)/\sigma\}$$

with $\Phi(\cdot)$ the standard normal distribution function and $c_1 = c_1' - h$ and $c_2 = c_2' - h$.

The statistical model in equation (2) allows for a constant home ground advantage. Consider two (hypothetical) teams of equal strength so that $\alpha_i - \alpha_j = 0$. The probability that the home team wins is $1 - \Phi(c_2/\sigma)$ and the probability that the home team loses is $\Phi(c_1/\sigma)$. These two probabilities are not constrained to be equal. In fact, we would expect that $\Phi(c_1/\sigma) < 1 - \Phi(c_2/\sigma)$ and this is confirmed by the results of our estimation. The existence of a home advantage can be examined formally by testing the hypothesis $c_1 = -c_2$.

It is not possible to identify all the parameters of this model. First, we need to fix the location of the quality parameters α. We impose the identifying restriction $\Sigma_i \alpha_i = 0$ so that the parameters α can be interpreted as deviations from a hypothetical average team with quality 0. A positive α_i implies that the quality of team i is better than average; a negative α_i implies the opposite. In addition, we fix the scale of the model by imposing the standard normalization $\sigma^2 = 1$.

Model (3) resembles models used by Clarke and Norman (1995), Stefani (1980) and Kuk (1995) to model soccer results. In Stefani (1980) and Clarke and Norman (1995), the dependent variable is the goal difference, and their models are estimated by least squares techniques. By using the least squares method, the dependent variable is assumed to follow a normal distribution. However, the observed goal difference takes only integer values with a limited range. They allow home ground advantage to vary between teams. The model in Kuk (1995) resembles the model above in that the dependent variable is the result of the game (and not the goal difference), and that an ordered probit model is used to derive the probability that a game is won, drawn or lost. In his model, the quality of a team differs between home and away games, and the home advantage varies between teams and over games. He estimated his model by using methods of moments using only the final ranking at the end of the season. An alternative approach could be based on Poisson-like models for the exact score in a game; see for instance Maher (1982), Dixon and Coles (1997) and Dixon and Robinson (1997). The reason that we prefer the ordered probit model is the simplicity of model (2): the quality of each individual team is captured by a single parameter. Moreover, this model allows for a simple separation between the measurement of quality of the teams and home advantage. In addition, the values that the dependent variable take are consistent with the stochastic specification of the model. Poisson-like models are usually more complex and have more parameters. For instance, in Maher (1982) at least two parameters per team had to be estimated and these parameters are difficult to interpret. Maher also assumed that the numbers of goals scored by the home team and the away team in a particular game are statistically independent. This may be too strong an assumption. He also assumed that games are mutually independent, an assumption that we shall make as well.

3.2. Description of the data and estimation results

The parameters were estimated by using the complete history of the Premier League of professional soccer in the Netherlands. (The data were obtained from Michael Koolhaas (private correspondence) and http://www.noord.bart.nl/~kammenga/soccer.) Organization of the competition as we know it today was introduced in the 1955–1956 season. In the 1962–1963, 1963–1964, 1964–1965 and 1965–1966 seasons only 16 teams participated in the Premier League. In all the other seasons 18 teams participated. Rules for relegation to the first division have changed over time. In the last few seasons the team finishing last was relegated automatically to the first division. The teams ranked 16 and 17 had to play additional games against teams in the first division. However, in earlier seasons, the teams finishing in the 17th and 18th places were relegated without having to play additional games. In total, 54 different clubs have played in the Premier League since the start of the competition in 1955–1956. Each year a couple of new teams entered the competition, either because of mergers or because of promotion. (A list of all the relevant mergers is given in Appendix A.) In each season, any combination of two teams meet twice: once at each venue. Therefore, a competition with 18 teams consists of 306 games; in total the data set comprises 12155 games. However, data from only 179 games are recorded from the 1996–1997 season.

We begin by estimating the parameters α_i, c_1 and c_2. It is assumed that the quality of the teams (measured by α_i) and the home advantage (measured by c_1 and c_2) were constant during the history of professional soccer. We use these results to calculate an all-time ranking of Dutch soccer teams by pooling the data over all seasons. The parameters were estimated by maximization of the log-likelihood function

$$l(\theta) = \sum_\tau \sum_{(i,j)\in\mathscr{T}_\tau} [I_{(D_{ij}=1)} \ln\{1 - \Phi(c_2 - \alpha_i + \alpha_j)\} + I_{(D_{ij}=0)} \ln\{\Phi(c_2 - \alpha_i + \alpha_j) - \Phi(c_1 - \alpha_i + \alpha_j)\}$$

$$+ I_{(D_{ij}=-1)} \ln\{\Phi(c_1 - \alpha_i + \alpha_j)\}]. \qquad (4)$$

In this equation, τ is the index indicating the season and $\mathscr{T}_\tau$ is the index set of teams playing in the Premier League in season τ. The point estimates and their standard errors are given in Table 3 in Appendix A. The ordering of the parameters α_i indicates an all-time ranking. The best three teams have been Ajax (0.963), Feyenoord (0.750) and PSV Eindhoven (0.735), and the teams performing least well have been Dordrecht (−0.581), Fortuna SC (−0.498) and SVV (−0.433). This ranking is not necessarily equal to the standard ranking in which two or three points are awarded for each win and one for a draw. Teams that are relegated during some seasons do not earn any points in this ranking and would be at the bottom of the standard ranking. In our approach, there are no observations on a team if it does not participate in the Premier League during a season. Hence, the estimated α_i of a team that has participated in the Premier League for two seasons only can exceed the estimated α_i of a team that has played in the Premier League for, say, three seasons, if that first team played well during these two seasons. Indeed, we find that the teams with least points are not those with the smallest α_i: these are Fortuna SC, SHS and Alkmaar.

Second, we estimate the parameters for each year. This approach allows for variation in team-specific quality over time. Fig. 1 presents estimates of the home advantage. Detailed information on the individual estimates for each year is available on request. Home advantage is measured as the difference between the probability that the home team wins if both teams are of equal quality (i.e. $\alpha_i = \alpha_j$) and the probability that the away team wins. The circles depict the probability that the home team wins and the triangles the probability that the away team wins. If there had been no home advantage both sets would coincide (apart from sample variation). However, we see that there is a clear home advantage which has increased markedly during the second half of the 1960s to 33% in 1970–1971. Since the early 1970s, the probability that the home team wins against an opponent of equal strength is approximately 45–50%. The corresponding probability for the away team appears to have increased since then from approximately 15% to 20%. Therefore, home

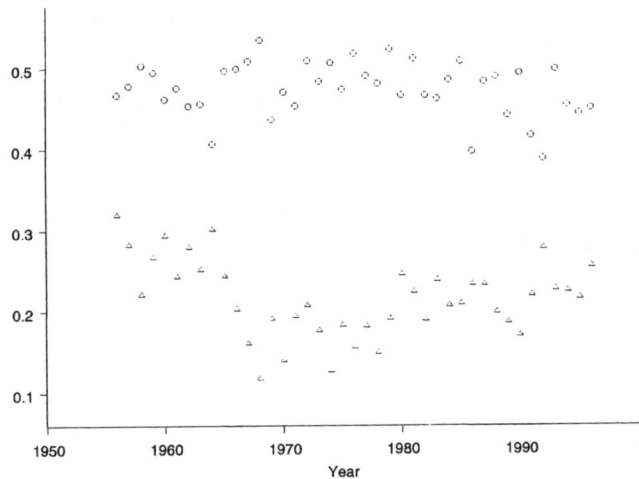

Fig. 1. Probabilities of winning of home (O) and away (△) games when the teams are of equal strength

advantage decreased over that period. Indeed, over the 1990–1996 period, home advantage averaged 21% compared with 31% in the period 1970–1975. Home advantage in the league varies from year to year. This was also found by Clarke and Norman (1995). A test of whether $c_1 = -c_2$ is rejected at any reasonable level of significance for all years.

In Table 1, we present some summary statistics of the estimation results for each year. For each season we list the strongest and the weakest teams, and the standard deviation of the estimated α_is. Instead of giving the point estimates for the α_i-parameters, which are difficult to interpret, we give a transformation of these estimates. If team i has quality α_i in a given year, then the probability that this team wins a home game against the hypothetical team with quality 0 is $1 - \Phi(\alpha_i - c_2)$. This probability is given in the third and fifth columns of Table 1, where $\pi_{(n)}$ denotes the probability that the worst team in a given year beats the average team in a home game. $\pi_{(1)}$ is calculated similarly for the best team in that year. We have set $c_2 = 0.060$, the value obtained when estimating the model for the whole sample period. Hence, the variation in the probabilities reflects variations in quality, not changes in home advantage.

Note that the maximum likelihood estimate for an α_i would diverge to $-\infty$ if a team loses all its games during a season or to ∞ if a team wins all its games. No such teams are to be found even though Ajax came close in the 1971–1972 season by losing only one game, drawing in a mere three games and winning all the other games.

3.3. Specification tests

The model used in the previous sections is estimated by using maximum likelihood. The parameters are estimated inconsistently if the distributional assumption of normality is not correct. We tested whether we should reject the assumption of normality against the more general alternative that the distribution of the error terms belongs to a member of the Pearson family of distributions (for details of the test statistic we refer to Glewwe (1997) and Weiss (1997)). Members of the Pearson family include the normal, t- and Γ-distributions. Essentially, we test

Table 1. Best and worst team for each year

Year	Worst team	$\pi_{(n)}$	Best team	$\pi_{(1)}$	Standard deviation
1956	eindhoven	0.259	ajax	0.714	0.320
1957	den bosch	0.260	sc enschede	0.679	0.273
1958	shs	0.212	sparta	0.755	0.412
1959	sittardia	0.196	ajax	0.735	0.363
1960	noad	0.212	feyenoord	0.776	0.386
1961	rapid jc	0.263	feyenoord	0.730	0.308
1962	volewijckers	0.112	psv	0.700	0.399
1963	blauw-wit	0.265	dws	0.706	0.362
1964	nac	0.335	feyenoord	0.747	0.270
1965	heracles	0.297	ajax	0.867	0.466
1966	willem ii	0.143	ajax	0.863	0.537
1967	sittardia	0.212	ajax	0.898	0.529
1968	fortuna sc	0.175	feyenoord	0.894	0.628
1969	svv	0.144	ajax	0.918	0.600
1970	az	0.128	feyenoord	0.904	0.739
1971	volendam	0.168	ajax	0.959	0.725
1972	den bosch	0.179	ajax	0.931	0.678
1973	groningen	0.233	feyenoord	0.865	0.595
1974	wageningen	0.261	psv	0.852	0.520
1975	excelsior	0.216	psv	0.810	0.501
1976	de graafschap	0.273	ajax	0.794	0.429
1977	telstar	0.165	psv	0.795	0.443
1978	vvv	0.134	ajax	0.841	0.539
1979	haarlem	0.323	ajax	0.749	0.352
1980	wageningen	0.257	az	0.888	0.486
1981	de graafschap	0.122	ajax	0.852	0.552
1982	nec	0.259	ajax	0.887	0.514
1983	ds79	0.163	feyenoord	0.860	0.560
1984	pec zwolle	0.200	ajax	0.813	0.446
1985	heracles	0.123	psv	0.896	0.550
1986	excelsior	0.223	psv	0.894	0.484
1987	ds79	0.138	psv	0.877	0.476
1988	veendam	0.306	psv	0.808	0.370
1989	haarlem	0.167	ajax	0.736	0.403
1990	nec	0.292	psv	0.812	0.440
1991	vvv	0.120	psv	0.875	0.576
1992	fortuna sc	0.252	feyenoord	0.792	0.467
1993	cambuur	0.233	ajax	0.820	0.409
1994	dordrecht	0.238	ajax	0.914	0.556
1995	go ahead eagles	0.197	ajax	0.872	0.550
1996	az	0.237	psv	0.795	0.422

whether the third moment of ϵ is 0 and the fourth moment of ϵ is 3. The test statistic was calculated for each year that the model was estimated. The null hypothesis of normality was not rejected in any season at a 5% level of significance. This conclusion is not at odds with the Poisson assumption that is often made when analysing soccer scores. The score difference is estimated by summing over a large number of Poisson-distributed scores, and hence in the limit it can be approximated by a normal distribution. Clarke and Norman (1995) also found that the residuals were approximately normally distributed when they estimated a model similar to equation (1) by least squares.

We tested whether or not restrictions on the parameters could be imposed. First, for each year all estimated α_i were found to be jointly significantly different from 0. Second, the hypothesis that the home advantage is constant over time had to be rejected. We also rejected the hypothesis that the quality of a given team does not vary over time.

If we assume that the quality parameters α_i remain constant over time, it is possible to test for variation in the variance of the error term in model (2). We imposed this restriction, and re-estimated the model for the period from 1991–1992 to 1996–1997 with unrestricted variances. We could not reject the null hypothesis that the variance of ϵ_{ij} is constant over time.

4. Empirical evidence of balance in competition

In this paper we measure the balance in competition in three different ways.

(a) If the standard deviation σ_P of the number of points in the final ranking of a competition is small, there is not much spread in the points gained at the end of the season and the competition has been tight.

(b) Since α_i is the extent to which team i is better than a hypothetical team with quality 0, it is natural to measure the balance in competition by the total deviation from average quality, $\Sigma_i \alpha_i^2$. This is proportional to the standard deviation σ_α of the quality parameters of the statistical model of the previous section. Again, if this number is small, the quality of the teams does not vary much.

(c) The concentration ratio CR_K is defined as the number of points obtained by the top K teams divided by the number of points that they could have gained. If there are J teams in a competition the team winning the competition could have obtained $2W(J-1)$ points where W is the number of points awarded for a game won. We denote the number of points obtained by the kth-best team by $P_{(k)}$. The concentration ratio is formally defined as

$$CR_K = \sum_{k=1}^{K} P_{(k)} \Big/ KW(2J - K - 1), \tag{5}$$

the number of points actually obtained by the K best teams divided by the maximum number of points that they could have obtained. If the concentration ratio is high, the top K teams did not lose many points to weaker teams.

These three measures are to some extent 'static' as they refer to balance *within* a particular season. An advantage of the second measure compared with the first measure is that it does not require that the season be complete. The concentration ratio is not a measure of balance in the whole competition; it applies to the quality of the top teams. This measure is interesting though as it is commonly believed that the gap between top teams and the rest has increased over time. It is not possible to address this issue with the first two measures.

The first two measures are not completely equivalent: a crucial drawback of σ_P as a measure of balance in competition is that it is not invariant under changes in home advantage. As our statistical model separates home advantage and team quality, σ_α does not suffer from this drawback. Moreover, in the 1995–1996 season the number of points obtained for a win was raised from 2 to 3. In contrast with the standard deviation of the number of points, the standard deviation of the α_i is invariant to changes in the number of points awarded for a win or a draw. Finally, we can estimate the α_i and their standard deviations even if a season is not finished completely. Note that σ_P and σ_α may rise if the average scoring frequency of all teams increases. In this case, skilled teams accumulate more wins whereas less skilled teams accumulate more losses, leading to more dispersion in the point and quality distributions. This is of little practical importance as goal scoring does not vary much over the years.

Estimates of σ_P and σ_α are graphed in Fig. 2. The standard deviation of the α_i varies between

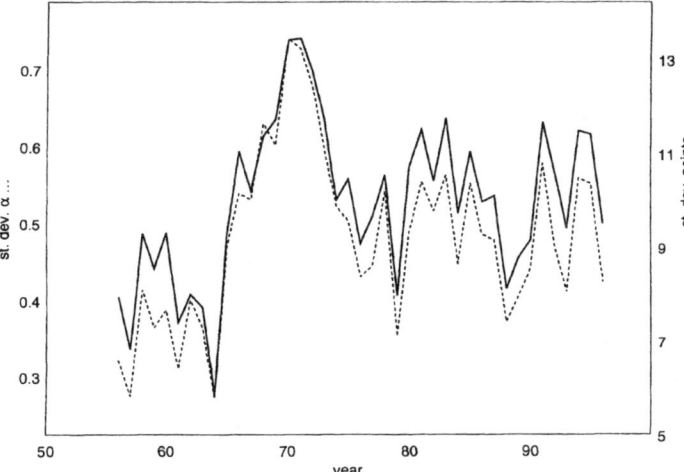

Fig. 2. Standard deviations of the estimated α_i ($\cdots\cdots$) and of the numbers of points (———)

0.25 and 0.75, and the standard deviation of the number of points varies between 5.9 and 13.5. To interpret the level of σ_P and σ_α we have simulated two hypothetical competitions and calculated σ_P and σ_α for each simulated competition. In the first competition, each team is equally strong and has a 50% probability of winning a home game, a 25% probability of playing a draw and 25% of losing a home game. For this case, the average value of σ_P is 4.92, and the average value of σ_α is 0.20.

In the second simulation the probabilities are the same, except for three strong teams. These three strong teams win games against each of the remaining 15 weaker opponents with 90% probability (and a 5% probability of a draw and a 5% probability of a loss). In this second case, the average value of σ_P is 9.87, and the average value of σ_α is 0.46. Therefore, a competition with three strong teams and 15 identical weaker teams gives the same values for σ_P and σ_α as we find in Fig. 2.

The balance in competition has not changed systematically from the early start of professional soccer in 1955 until the mid-1960s. We then see a marked decrease between 1965 and 1970 followed by an increase in between 1970 and 1976. Coincidentally (or not) it was in the period 1966–1970 that Dutch professional soccer caught up with the best teams in Europe. Ajax was the first Dutch finalist in a European tournament in the spring of 1969 and Feyenoord was the first Dutch winner in a European tournament in 1970. Dutch (and European) soccer was dominated by Ajax from 1970 until 1973, a period when the balance in competition in Dutch soccer increased sharply.

From the mid-1970s to the end of the century there is no clear trend in the balance in competition. One year, competition is tighter than in another year, but no clear trends are discernible from the data. The spread from year to year is considerable; years with a tight competition are interspersed with years with a one-sided competition. This is especially noteworthy because it was feared in the early 1980s that competition would become less tight because of shirt sponsorship which in Dutch soccer has been allowed from the 1981–1982 season onwards. At first, it seemed that criticism of shirt sponsorship was justified, since in the 1981–

1982 season two teams could not find a sponsor at all. This was only temporary though: even amateur teams now have shirt sponsors. Some teams have had better sponsoring deals than others, resulting in a more unequal distribution of income. This increase in income inequality is claimed to lead to a decrease in balance in competition. However, we do not find any evidence for this hypothesis. Less successful teams use the same arguments as those used against shirt sponsorship to oppose television contracts that give a larger share of the revenue to more successful teams. According to them, an unequal distribution of television revenues will lead to an unequal distribution of quality and this leads to a decrease in general interest in soccer. However, the balance in competition has not decreased significantly since the introduction of shirt sponsorship. In fact, shirt sponsorship may have enabled most semiprofessional players to become full professionals and this may have increased the overall quality of soccer.

To examine the robustness of our results, we have estimated two other models. First, we estimated the quality parameters of the teams by using the model of Clarke and Norman (1995). In this model the dependent variable was the difference in goals scored, and the parameters were estimated by using least squares. In the second model, the ordered probit structure of equation (3) was retained, but two additional categories were added. The dependent variable now makes a distinction between a win (or loss) by a three-goal difference (or more). In both cases, the variation in the estimated quality parameters was examined, and it turned out that the results were very similar to those in Fig. 2. Hence, our conclusions about the development of the balance in competition are robust with respect to the statistical model used.

As a third indicator of the balance in competition, we look at the concentration ratios for the first and fourth place. The results are given in Fig. 3. Qualitatively, we see the same picture as in the previous graphs: until the mid-1960s the top team in each year captured only 75% of the number of points that it could have obtained at the end of the season. This percentage increases during the second half of the 1960s, to a maximum of 94% for the top team in 1971–1972. Then an increase in the balance of competition sets in, followed by an irregular period with no clear trends. The picture is slightly different for the top four teams: a slight upward trend of the

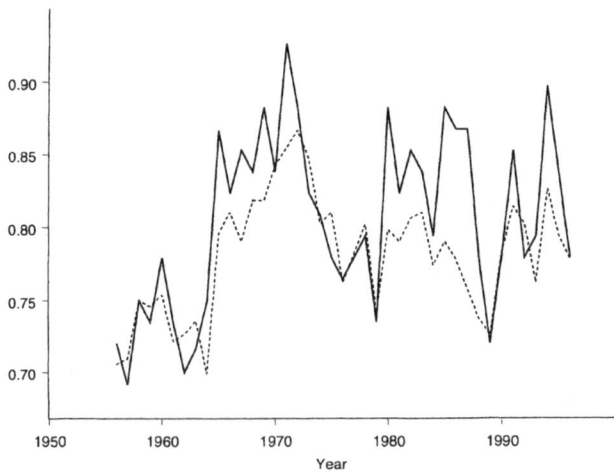

Fig. 3. Concentration ratios for the first and fourth places: ———, first place; ··········, fourth place

concentration ratio during the 1980s and 1990s is visible. (CR$_4$ exceeds CR$_1$ in a particular year if the number of points obtained by the teams that end second, third and fourth does not differ much from the number of points obtained by the team that ended first (i.e. if $P_{(2)} + P_{(3)} + P_{(4)} > (45/17)P_{(1)}$). This happens in 13 seasons.) Contrary to common opinion and despite the slight upward trend, the value of CR$_4$ is not high when compared with typical values encountered during the 1960s.

5. Conclusion

In this paper we have discussed the balance in competition in Dutch professional soccer. We used a simple model to estimate the quality of the teams participating in the Premier League. We find that the balance decreased markedly during the second half of the 1960s and increased during the first half of the 1970s but that there has been no clear trend since. We also find that the introduction of shirt sponsorship did not lead to a noticeable significant decrease in the balance. These conclusions are borne out by three different measures of balance and hence are not sensitive to model specification.

This paper provides only a starting-point for a more structural economic analysis of the balance in competition. The 'superstar' model of Rosen (1981) may provide insight into why an increase in income inequality that may have taken place did not lead to a decrease in the balance of competition. Another issue to be resolved is to examine whether the lack of recent trends in the balance of competition is specific to Dutch soccer or whether it is a more international phenomenon.

Acknowledgements

The author thanks Marco Haan, Peter Hopstaken, Bas van der Klaauw, Geert Ridder, seminar participants at the University of Mannheim, Concordia University, Queen's University and participants at the Statistische Dag and the European Economic Association meeting in Berlin for helpful discussions and comments. The exposition and the content of the paper have benefited from detailed comments by three referees.

Appendix A: Estimation results of the complete model

In this appendix we discuss the construction of our data set and give estimation results of the model with the α_i constant during the sample period. First, in Table 2 we give a list of mergers in Dutch professional soccer. (The list is based on information provided in Verkammen and Vermeer (1994).) Some teams have played under several names. For instance, FC Dordrecht changed its name in 1979 to DS '79 and in 1990 again to Dordrecht '90. In other cases, professional soccer teams merged with other professional soccer teams (for example, in 1991 Dordrecht '90 merged with SVV to form SVV/Dordrecht '90 which changed its name again in 1992, reverting to Dordrecht '90). We have treated each team that resulted from a merger as a new team, so we distinguish between DS '79 (a predecessor of Dordrecht '90 that played in the Premier League in 1987–1988) and Dordrecht '90 that resulted from a merger with SVV. In the same vein, FC Amsterdam before 1974 is considered to be a different team from FC Amsterdam after the year when it merged with De Volenwijckers.

In Table 3 we give the estimation results of the model estimated over the period 1956–1996 in which all parameters are constant over time. The number of cases is 12155, and the mean log-likelihood is -0.980507.

430   R. H. Koning

Table 2. Mergers in Dutch professional soccer†

Year	New team	Merged teams
1958	DWS	Amsterdam, *DWS*
1962	Roda JC	*Roda Sport*, Rapid JC
1963	Telstar	*Stormvogels*, *VSV*
1965	Twente	SC Enschede, *Enschedese Boys*
1967	AZ	Alkmaar, *Zaanstreek*
1967	Den Bosch	*Den Bosch*, *Wilhelmina*
1967	Xerxes/DHC	*DHC*, Xerxes
1968	Fortuna SC	Fortuna '54, Sittardia
1970	Utrecht	Dos, Elinkwijk, *Velox*
1971	Den Haag	ADO, Holland Sport
1972	FC Amsterdam	DWS, Blauw Wit
1974	FC Amsterdam	FC Amsterdam, De Volenwijckers
1991	Dordrecht '90	*Dordrecht '90*, SVV

†Teams in italics have never played in the Premier League.

Table 3. Estimation results of the full model

Team	$\hat{\alpha}$	Standard deviation	Team	$\hat{\alpha}$	Standard deviation	Team	$\hat{\alpha}$	Standard deviation
ado	0.322	0.032	fortuna 54	0.159	0.029	shs	−0.546	0.174
ajax	0.951	0.031	fortuna sc	0.009	0.022	sittardia	−0.212	0.040
alkmaar	−0.219	0.043	go ahead eagles	0.057	0.028	sparta	0.262	0.029
amsterdam	0.034	0.033	graafschap	−0.046	0.030	svv	−0.443	0.047
az	0.215	0.032	groningen	0.123	0.021	telstar	−0.082	0.033
blauw-wit	0.023	0.031	haarlem	−0.032	0.032	twente	0.389	0.028
cambuur	−0.297	0.040	heerenveen	0.105	0.041	utrecht	0.127	0.023
de graafschap	−0.446	0.054	helmond	−0.446	0.044	veendam	−0.255	0.038
den bosch	−0.067	0.022	heracles	−0.192	0.051	vitesse	0.252	0.031
den haag	−0.002	0.025	holland	0.031	0.031	volendam	−0.050	0.021
dordrecht	−0.335	0.050	mvv	0.048	0.032	volewijckers	−0.353	0.035
dos	0.156	0.019	nac	0.045	0.033	vvv	0.004	0.021
ds79	−0.829	0.113	nec	−0.085	0.029	wageningen	−0.356	0.045
dws	0.141	0.023	noad	−0.235	0.040	willem ii	−0.047	0.022
eindhoven	−0.283	0.057	pec zwolle	−0.103	0.041	xerxes	0.212	0.085
elinkwijk	−0.136	0.051	psv	0.724	0.029	xerxes/dhc	0.272	0.116
excelsior	−0.236	0.039	rapid jc	0.111	0.020	c_1	−0.721	0.012
fc amsterdam 1	0.280	0.049	rkc	0.107	0.019	c_2	0.060	0.010
fc amsterdam 2	−0.152	0.026	roda jc	0.267	0.034			

References

Bennett, R. W. and Fizel, J. L. (1995) Telecast deregulation and competitive balance: NCAA Division I football. *Am. J. Econ. Sociol.*, **54**, 183–199.

Clarke, S. R. and Norman, J. M. (1995) Home ground advantage of individual clubs in English soccer. *Statistician*, **44**, 509–521.

Dixon, M. J. and Coles, S. G. (1997) Modelling association football scores and inefficiencies in the football betting market. *Appl. Statist.*, **46**, 265–280.

Dixon, M. J. and Robinson, M. E. (1997) A birth process for association football matches. Lancaster University, Lancaster.

Economist (1997) Golden goals. *Economist*, May 31st, 63–65.

Glewwe, P. (1997) A test of the normality assumption in the ordered probit model. *Econometr. Rev.*, **16**, 1–19.

Kuk, A. Y. C. (1995) Modelling paired comparison data with large numbers of draws and large variability of draw percentages among players. *Statistician*, **44**, 523–528.

Maher, M. J. (1982) Modelling association football scores. *Statist. Neerland.*, **36**, 109–118.

Neumann, G. R. and Tamura, R. F. (1996) Managing competition: the case of the national football league. University of Iowa, Iowa City.

Noll, R. G. (1991) Professional basketball: economic and business perspectives. In *The Business of Professional Sports* (eds P. D. Staudohar and J. A. Mongan), pp. 18–47. Chicago: University of Illinois Press.

Quirk, J. and Fort, R. D. (1992) *Pay Dirt*. Princeton: Princeton University Press.

Rosen, S. (1981) The economics of superstars. *Am. Econ. Rev.*, **71**, 845–858.

Scully, G. W. (1989) *The Business of Major League Baseball*. Chicago: University of Chicago Press.

Stefani, R. T. (1980) Improved least squares football, basketball, and soccer predictions. *IEEE Trans. Syst. Man Cyber.*, **10**, 116–123.

———(1983) Observed betting tendencies and suggested betting strategies for European football pools. *Statistician*, **32**, 319–329.

Verkammen, M. and Vermeer, E. (1994) *Om 't Spel en de Knikkers*. Bilthoven: Mundt.

Weiss, A. A. (1997) Specification tests in ordered logit and probit models. *Econometr. Rev.*, **16**, 361–391.

[23]

The Determinants of Football Match Attendance Revisited

Empirical Evidence From the Spanish Football League

JAUME GARCÍA
Universitat Pompeu Fabra

PLÁCIDO RODRÍGUEZ
Universidad de Oviedo

An attendance equation is estimated using data on individual games played in the Spanish First Division Football League. The specification includes as explanatory factors: economic variables, quality, uncertainty and opportunity costs. The authors concentrate the analysis on some specification issues such as controlling the effect of unobservables given the panel data structure of the data set, the type of functional form, and the potential endogeneity of prices. The authors obtain the expected effects on attendance for all the variables. The estimated price elasticities are, in general, smaller than one in absolute value but are sensitive to the specification issues, in particular, the endogeneity of prices.

T he analysis of the determinants of attendance at professional team sports events is one of the topics that has received most attention in the empirical literature of the economics of sports.[1] The usual approach is the estimation of a demand equation, which is either linear or can be linearized, including as explanatory factors the usual economic variables (prices and income) and the sectoral variables that try to capture the heterogeneity of this type of good (a match). This has been done using different types of data sets, depending on data availability and the objectives of the study.[2]

AUTHORS' NOTE: *We are very grateful to César Rodríguez, Joaquín Lorences, and the participants in a seminar at the University of Oviedo for their comments on earlier stages of this work, and also to an anonymous referee for comments on the previous version of this article. Special thanks are also due to the Liga Nacional de Fútbol Profesional for providing the data used in this article. The first author wishes to express his gratitude for financial support from DGESIC Grant No. PB98-1058-C03-01. The second author wishes to thank FUNCAS for its financial support. The usual disclaimer applies.*

JOURNAL OF SPORTS ECONOMICS, Vol. 3 No. 1, February 2002   18–38
© 2002 Sage Publications

Most of the studies do not pay too much attention either to econometric specification issues or to the economic implications of the results. With respect to the latter point, not all the articles include prices as an explanatory factor and not many take into account the interpretation of the price elasticities obtained and try to rationalize it. Articles by Heilmann and Wendling (1976); Ferguson, Stewart, Jones, and Le Dressay (1991); Salant (1992); Marburger (1997); and Boyd and Boyd (1998) are among those that try, in the context of a profit maximizing behavior for the professional teams, as assumed in El Hodiri and Quirk (1971), to give a theoretical explanation for the usual empirical finding of a price elasticity of less than one. This finding can also be explained in a context where teams have objective functions other than profits, as proposed by Sloane (1971).

In this article, we try to bring new evidence from European football[3] to bear on this empirical issue making use, for the first time in this literature, of a data set corresponding to the Spanish Football League, one of the most important and highly regarded in Europe. We use a complete data set with observations of economic and sectoral variables for all the matches played in the Spanish First Division League during the seasons 1992-93 to 1995-96, which allows us to specify an attendance equation that is more detailed in terms of the explanatory variables than in previous studies. We use the panel data structure to control for some unobservables to estimate price elasticity consistently while also taking into account the possible endogeneity of prices. Our empirical results show that price elasticities are underestimated in absolute value when not taking into account the last issue. We also analyze the incidence of the specification of the functional form in the estimated elasticities. Finally, we also evaluate the importance of the different groups of variables in explaining attendance.

The article is organized as follows. In the next section, we present the specification of the empirical model, followed by a discussion of the estimation results. The article ends with a summary of the main conclusions.

MODEL SPECIFICATION

Model and Variables

We specify and estimate a fairly standard demand equation distinguishing, among the explanatory factors that have an effect on attendance, the following groups of variables: economic variables, variables proxying the expected quality of the match, those measuring the uncertainty of the result, and those capturing the opportunity cost of attending a match.

The basic data set comes from the information received by the Liga Nacional de Fútbol Profesional from each club about the number of people attending each match and the prices charged. The sources and the descriptive statistics of the variables are presented in Table A1 in the appendix.

20   JOURNAL OF SPORTS ECONOMICS / February 2002

The endogenous variable is the (log)number of tickets sold for a match (attendance), not including those for children and season tickets.[4] Among the economic variables we include: prices, measured by the price of the cheapest ticket[5] deflated by the Consumer Price Index; real income per capita in the province of the team playing at home; and the population in the province of the home team, which is distributed when there are two or more teams in a province according to the number of season ticket holders corresponding to each team. We expect a negative effect for prices and a positive one for both income (i.e., a normal good) and population.

The expected quality of the match can be measured by what we call ex ante quality, that is, the quality of both teams at the beginning of the season, independent of performance previous to the match and by those variables proxying the most recent performance of both teams (current quality). In the first group, we include the budgets (in real terms) of both teams because they depend, among other things, on the salaries of the players, which should proxy their productivity;[6] the number of players who have played for their national team (internationals); two dummies for those matches where the away team is either Barcelona or Real Madrid, historically the two most important teams in Spain; a dummy for those games of special interest because of historical or regional rivalry; and, finally, a dummy indicating whether season ticket holders have to pay to attend the match (Club's Day match), a usual practice of most Spanish clubs. This is an indicator of the club's expectation about the quality (or interest) of the game.

Among the variables capturing the recent performance of both teams we include:[7] the number of home team wins in the past three games; the result (as the difference between goals scored for and against) of the most recent game played by the home team; the home team's current position in the league; the number of goals scored in the past match at home by the home team; a dummy for the away team not having lost a game out of the past four; and two dummies for the home team having the value one if the latter has no chance of winning the championship or of leaving the relegation zone. We expect all variables increasing quality to have a positive effect on attendance.

With respect to uncertainty we distinguish, as it is done in Kuypers (1996), between match and seasonal uncertainty.[8] We use as measures of match uncertainty a quadratic form of the difference between the league positions of the home and the away teams previous to the match and a dummy equal to one if the home team is between three positions ahead and five positions behind the away team. To measure seasonal uncertainty with respect to winning the championship, we have chosen the second indicator proposed by Kuypers (1996), which is the product of the number of games left before the championship is decided and the number of points the team trails behind the leader, being equal to zero when there is no possibility of the team's winning the championship. Uncertainty increases attendance, and in the particular case of the measure of seasonal uncertainty, we expect a negative sign because the higher the uncertainty, the smaller the value of the indicator we have defined.

Finally, we include a set of variables that capture the opportunity cost of attending a football match. We model the effect of weather conditions with dummy variables that correspond to the following situations: no rain, high temperature; no rain, low temperature; and rainy days, which is the omitted dummy. We expect that the better the weather is, the higher the attendance will be. The second factor has to do with the game's being televised. Because in Spain football games are televised by both public and private channels, in the latter case only for subscribers, we define two different dummies depending on which channel is broadcasting the match. The omitted group corresponds to matches not televised. We expect that televising games will reduce attendance, especially if the match is televised by a public channel.

The day of the match also has to play a role in determining attendance. Specifically, if a match is played on a weekday rather than on the weekend, attendance should decrease.[9] We model this variable by means of a dummy.

Finally, we include the distance between the towns of both teams as a way of capturing the demand that comes from away team supporters. We give special consideration to the case of Tenerife, located on the Canary Islands, by including two dummies: one for Tenerife playing at home and the second one for Tenerife playing away. We expect distance to have a negative effect on attendance.

Econometric Specification

Given the panel data structure of our data set, the variables included in the demand equation can have different sources of variability. There is time variation because the observations correspond to games played during four seasons (1992-93 through 1995-96)[10] from September through May/June. On the other hand, there is variation depending on the teams that correspond to each observation (home and away teams). Consequently, we use three subindices to identify each observation. They refer to the season (t), the home team (i), and the away team (j), with four types of explanatory variables in terms of the sources of variation. We have a set of variables, included in the vector X_{ijt}, which vary in all three dimensions as also happens with the endogenous variable Y_{ijt}. Variables that refer to prices,[11] the difference between the two teams' current league positions, weather conditions, a match's being televised, a match's not being played on the weekend, and a Club's Day match are included in this group. The second group of variables, included in the vector Z_{it}, is made up of those variables that vary depending on the season and the home team. Variables such as income, population, the home team budget, the home team's result in the most recent game played, the number of wins by the home team in the past three games, Kuypers's measure of uncertainty for the home team with respect to the championship, and those variables referring to the home team's not having any chance of winning the championship or leaving the relegation zone belong to this second group. The third one includes variables such as the away team's budget, the number of internationals, and the away team's having not lost a match out of the past four, which show variation depending on the away team and the season. They are included in the vector V_{jt}. Finally, in the fourth group there are the variables, included in vector W_{ij}, which simultaneously depend on both teams playing the match. Variables capturing historical and local rivalries and the distance between the cities of the two teams are in this group. Note that there is, in fact, a fifth dimension of variation because some of the variables in Z_{it} and V_{jt} show variation across different games of a particular season, whereas others are constant through the season.

On the other hand, we can control for the presence of unobservables that can also have different sources of variation and whose omission in the specification and estimation of the model can cause inconsistency of estimates to the extent that they are correlated with the regressors. We consider home team effects (α_i), away team effects (η_j), and season effects (τ_t), apart from the usual disturbance term (u_{ijt}).

Consequently, the general specification of the model has the following form:

$$Y_{ijt} = X_{ijt}'\beta + Z_{it}'\gamma + V_{jt}'\delta + W_{ij}'\theta + \alpha_i + \eta_j + \tau_t + u_{ijt}, \tag{1}$$

where β, γ, δ, and θ are the vectors of parameters. In the empirical model, we do not take into account the unobserved away team effects because we consider that the explanatory variables related to the visitor capture the basic effects, specifically, those dummies that refer to a particular away team (Barcelona, Real Madrid, and Tenerife).[12]

Equation 1 is estimated by ordinary least squares (OLS),[13] which for consistency requires the unobserved effects to be uncorrelated with the explanatory variables. We also take the usual approach to controlling for these effects by including dummy variables for the home team and the season effects. Finally, we also transform the model by taking a special type of "differences." Specifically, we subtract from each variable the value of the observation corresponding to the previous match played at home by the home team in that season.[14] This transformation eliminates both the home team effect and the season effect but also eliminates those variables that show only this kind of variation (Z_{it}). The latter elimination does not happen when using the within group transformation.

On the other hand, we do not estimate the model by generalized least squares (Balestra & Nerlove, 1966) because, contrary to what happens with other panel data sets, the individual dimensions (the number of teams) are, in some sense, small. Consequently, when we specify a model with more explanatory variables than teams in the data set, as happens in our empirical model, we cannot obtain an estimate of the variance of the home team effects. Nor can we use Hausman's test for the null of home team effects' being uncorrelated with the explanatory variables. Note too that we can compare the specification in Equation 1 with that of those models estimated using data (averages) on seasons rather than data on games (e.g., Jones, Schofield, & Giles, 2000). This amounts to transforming our model by averaging variables for each home team in each season.

Finally, the price variable has potential problems of endogeneity as is usual in demand analysis. This could explain, apart from data availability, why most of the empirical studies do not include it but, in fact, estimate a kind of reduced form model. Because, in analyzing Spanish football clubs' optimization behavior, we are interested in estimating price elasticity consistently, we estimate the model by Instrumental Variables (IV), instrumenting the price variable using the value predicted from a reduced form equation. We include in this (log)price equation as explanatory variables all the variables, apart from prices, which appear in the attendance equation. We also include variables that refer to performance in the previous season (the final league positions of both home and away teams and dummies for either team's being in the second division in the previous season) and the number of tickets that can be sold (capacity). These variables allow us to identify the demand equation.

EMPIRICAL RESULTS

In this section, we present the main results of the specification and estimation of an attendance equation for Spanish football with special attention to the estimates of the price elasticities and their interpretation and to the contribution of each group of variables to explaining attendance.

General Results

We estimated different versions of Equation 1 in which the endogenous variable (attendance) is always in logs, using 1,580 observations. The results are reported in Table 1. First, we consider the equation linear in price and income variables, both in logs (Column 1), and we compare it with a more general specification based on a cubic polynomial for these two variables (Column 2). We also control for the potential correlation between home team and season effects and the regressors by including the corresponding dummies (Column 3), our preferred specification. We compare the last specification against a nonnested one where the price and income variables are not in logs and have a cubic profile (Column 4). We also estimate the preferred specification by applying OLS to the model transformed by taking differences as defined above (Column 5). Finally, we estimate the preferred specification by instrumenting the price variable (Column 6). The results of these estimations are reported in Table 1.

Results presented in Column 2 show that the model with cubic polynomials both in (log)prices and (log)income better fits the attendance equation than does the standard model linear in logs (Column 1).[15] All the coefficients in both models have

TABLE 1: Estimates of the Attendance Equation

	1		2		3		4		5		6	
	Coefficient	t-Statistic	Coefficient	t-Statistic	Coefficient	t-Statistic	Coefficient	t-Statistic	Coefficient	t-Statistic	Coefficient	t-Statistic
Economic variables												
Log(price)	-0.630	10.04	-8.984	3.21	-14.017	5.30			-12.879	4.88	-48.781	3.08
Log(price)**2			2.831	2.90	4.697	4.98			4.289	4.53	16.095	3.00
Log(price)**3			-0.310	2.76	-0.529	4.76			-0.478	4.27	-1.783	2.94
Price							-0.136	4.79				
Price**2							0.004	4.43				
Price**3 (divided by 1,000)							-0.047	4.64				
Log(income)	0.513	4.93	1,980.4	4.84	-1,652.1	1.20					-1,935.0	1.32
Log(income)**2			-212.5	4.90	171.46	1.17					201.17	1.29
Log(income)**3			7.600	4.96	-5.945	1.14					-6.984	1.27
Income							-0.004	3.36				
Income**2							0.267	2.75				
Income**3							-5.920	2.38				
Log(population)	0.247	5.05	0.342	6.81	0.026	0.28	-0.019	0.21	-0.033	0.59	-0.034	0.34
Ex ante quality												
Budget (h)	0.017	8.12	0.013	6.09	-0.010	1.14	-0.012	1.35			-0.016	1.75
Budget (v)	0.014	3.03	0.014	3.11	0.014	3.41	0.013	3.17			0.014	3.25
Number of internationals (v)	0.015	2.41	0.016	2.51	0.015	2.81	0.015	2.85			0.016	2.89
Away team Barcelona	0.455	2.07	0.428	1.99	0.407	2.06	0.445	2.24	1.328	20.01	0.462	2.19
Away team Real Madrid	0.275	1.27	0.271	1.28	0.264	1.37	0.302	1.56	1.172	17.40	0.300	1.49
Rivalry	0.491	5.79	0.450	5.34	0.453	5.50	0.438	5.22	0.420	5.53	0.496	2.27
Club's Day match	0.217	2.85	0.190	2.44	0.197	2.53	0.193	2.44	0.166	2.49	0.246	2.27
Current quality												
Number of wins in the past 3 games (h)	0.047	1.95	0.044	1.93	0.028	1.38	0.031	1.53	0.017	0.75	0.036	1.59
Score past game (h)	0.046	4.54	0.043	4.32	0.040	4.49	0.041	4.53	0.034	4.08	0.040	4.41
Goals past game at home (h)	0.045	3.20	0.046	3.32	0.038	3.11	0.037	3.08	0.048	4.40	0.038	3.12
Standings (h)	-0.008	1.39	-0.005	0.91	-0.016	2.88	-0.015	2.62	-0.036	4.90	-0.018	2.15

24

No defeat in past 4 games (v)	0.119	2.66	0.099	2.27	0.103	2.58	0.115	2.86	0.027	0.56	0.125	3.04
No chance to win the championship (h)	−0.215	3.91	−0.218	4.01	−0.160	3.17	−0.163	3.20	−0.052	0.55	−0.159	2.79
No chance of leaving relegation zone (h)	−1.162	4.25	−1.074	3.92	−1.011	4.40	−1.035	4.47	−0.577	0.77	−1.101	4.31
Uncertainty												
Difference in league positions (h−v)	0.022	6.12	0.022	6.19	0.021	6.79	0.021	6.67	0.034	12.17	0.022	5.14
Difference in league positions**2 (h−v)	0.001	3.61	0.001	3.78	0.001	3.35	0.001	3.25	0.000	1.19	0.001	2.74
Closeness of league positions	0.098	2.30	0.088	2.15	0.047	1.31	0.050	1.37	0.055	1.59	0.046	1.25
Uncertainty of championship (h)	−0.001	5.85	−0.001	6.08	−0.001	3.54	−0.001	3.81	0.000	0.27	−0.001	3.04
Opportunity cost												
No rain, hot	0.374	6.22	0.355	5.94	0.303	5.49	0.305	5.50	0.269	5.49	0.307	5.48
No rain, cold	0.334	5.61	0.325	5.48	0.270	4.90	0.273	4.95	0.246	5.08	0.271	4.88
Televised by public channels	−0.427	5.78	−0.458	6.57	−0.464	7.26	−0.459	6.93	−0.425	8.18	−0.454	6.59
Televised by a private channel	−0.321	4.79	−0.323	5.22	−0.318	5.69	−0.318	5.62	−0.344	7.28	−0.330	5.48
Not played on the weekend	−0.235	4.01	−0.233	3.99	−0.216	4.00	−0.220	4.10	−0.245	4.99	−0.239	4.28
Distance	−0.525	6.86	−0.503	6.69	−0.497	6.74	−0.496	6.63	−0.521	7.60	−0.501	6.37
Home team Tenerife	0.327	4.06	0.451	5.59	0.955	6.48	0.939	6.27			0.878	5.18
Away team Tenerife	−0.507	5.34	−0.494	5.24	−0.492	5.79	−0.491	5.76	−0.546	7.42	−0.498	5.71
Constant	0.667	0.46	−6137.7	4.77	5337.2	1.24	30.78	5.26			6270.3	1.36
Home team effects	No		No		Yes		Yes		No		Yes	
Season effects	No		No		Yes		Yes		No		Yes	
R^2	0.6252		0.6489		0.7270		0.7229		0.4776		0.7121	

NOTE: h = home team; v = away team. N = 1,580; endogenous variable is log(attendance). In Model 4, the quadratic and cubic terms of income are divided by 10^6 and 10^{12}, respectively, and the cubic term of the price variable by 10^3. The distance variable is measured in thousands of kilometers.

25

the expected sign, and almost all of them are significant at a 5% level. Additionally, the estimates do not differ very much between the two specifications except for the price and income variables.

The income elasticity (η_Y) obtained from the model in Column 2 is

$$\eta_Y = 1980.4 - 425*\log(\text{INCOME}) + 22.8*[\log(\text{INCOME})]^2,$$

which is in the interval $[-0.137, 5.373]$ evaluated at the values of the observations of our sample. This means that although elasticity has a quadratic form, the relevant values for our sample are basically positive; that is, attendance is a normal good. In fact, in the simplest specification of Column 1, the estimated constant income elasticity, which is the coefficient of (log)income, is positive and significant.

All variables proxying ex ante quality have the expected positive sign. The coefficients of the budget variables are very similar (statistically the same), with the effect on attendance of a match's being played by "rival" teams found to be more important than the fact that either Barcelona or Real Madrid are the away team. This could be explained by the fact that its effect is captured through the budget variables. In fact, when defining the budget variables in logs, the coefficients of the dummies corresponding to Real Madrid and Barcelona become significant, but the fit of the model is worse than that of the corresponding model reported in Table 1. Additionally, the number of internationals playing for the away team also has a positive effect on attendance.[16]

Scoring an additional goal either in the past match or in the past match at home and having an extra victory in the past three games have a similar effect on attendance, as shown in Column 2. On the other hand, the fact that the away team is unbeaten in the past four games also increases attendance. The other three variables included in this group proxying current quality (current interest) of the match produce some problems when we interpret their effects because they may also proxy the uncertainty of the match and of the season. In particular, those games in which the home team has no chance of either winning the championship or leaving the relegation zone have ceteris paribus smaller attendance.[17]

Given that there is no information available for betting odds on Spanish football for the period under consideration, we cannot use this variable to proxy the uncertainty of the outcome by means of either the predicted probability of winning a game, as in Peel and Thomas (1988, 1997) and Knowles, Sherony, and Haupert (1992), or the evenness of the contest, as in Forrest and Simmons (2001). Instead, we use a quadratic form in the difference of league positions, which is consistent with measuring maximum uncertainty when the difference in league positions compensates home advantage. We would expect a negative sign for the quadratic term and a positive one for the linear term, but in all cases we estimate a positive sign for the quadratic term. There are some identification problems when using league positions to proxy uncertainty and also quality as mentioned above. We also included a dummy defined in terms of the closeness of the league positions that is not significant in our preferred models (3 and 6), although correctly signed. Consequently, no definite conclusions about the effect of the uncertainty of the outcome can be obtained because there is no information available to measure properly this variable. On the contrary, the variable measuring the uncertainty of the championship for the home team has the expected positive effect, although it has a negative coefficient given the way in which this variable has been defined, as mentioned in the previous section.

Poor weather conditions discourage people from attending football matches because they are played outdoors: the better the weather conditions, the higher the attendance. This negative effect is also obtained for the distance variable. On the other hand, games shown live on television and those not played on the weekend show significantly lower attendance. This effect is more important when matches are televised on a public channel to which everybody has free access, rather than on private channels to which access is by subscription.[18] Previous empirical evidence in this literature was not very conclusive about the effect of televising a match.[19] Specifically, for a team with an attendance for a nontelevised game equal to the sample mean (3,772), attendance will decrease by 1,386 spectators (36.74%)[20] if the match is televised by a public channel and by 1,042 (27.62%) if it is televised by a private channel.

When we include dummies to control for the home team and season effects (Column 3), the pattern of the effects we mentioned above does not change in either sign or significance, except for a few cases that correspond to variables that show variability only in the home team and season dimensions. This is the case with the budget variable and the income variable, whose parameter estimates are not significant although they are not signed as expected. The explanatory power of the model increases substantially by including these controls.[21]

We also estimated a model (Column 4) that, although similar, has a different functional form for the price and income variables (not in logs). The choice of the specification in Column 3 is confirmed by means of the J test (Davidson & MacKinnon, 1981) for the null that the model in Column 3 rather than the model in Column 4 is the true one. When running a regression of log(attendance) on the variables included in Model 3 plus the predicted (log)attendance from Model 4, the t-statistic for the coefficient of that predicted (log)attendance is 1.22, whereas when considering Model 4 as the null and using the same type of test, the t-statistic is 4.20. Consequently, we choose the specification in Model 3 as our preferred specification in terms of the functional form and the set of explanatory variables to be included.

Results seem to be quite robust to different transformations of the model to control for the home team and seasonal effects. In Column 5 we present the results corresponding to the OLS estimates of the model transformed using the special type of differences we mentioned above. This implies that those variables with no variation within a season will cancel out as happens with the home team and season effects. The most relevant change is the higher significance of the effect of Barcelona or Real Madrid being the away team. The explanation may be that these variables are, in some sense, capturing the ex ante quality of the away team measured by the budget and the number of international variables in the previous specification.

Finally, we estimate the preferred version (Column 3) of the attendance equation by correcting the possible endogeneity of prices. As mentioned above, we estimate a reduced form equation for log(prices) using all the variables included in the demand equation plus additional instruments to identify the demand equation. The instruments refer to previous season standings and the fact of being in the second division the past season for both home and away teams. They capture the information the clubs have at the beginning of the season when grouping the games in terms of the potential interest for the spectators. We also include all the variables in the attendance equation because the final decision about prices is taken considering the expected attendance. The results of the estimation of this price equation are presented in Table A2 of the appendix. We must point out the significance of both teams' finishing positions in the previous season in explaining prices. Whereas the higher the away team's position, the higher the price charged, we find the opposite effect for the home team's position.

From these equations, we calculate predicted (log)prices that are used instead of the observed price variables in the demand equation in a kind of nonlinear two-stage least squares estimator as proposed by Amemiya (1983). The results of this estimation are presented in Column 6 of Table 1 and are very similar to those obtained in Column 3, except for the magnitude of the coefficients of the price variables. Nevertheless, when testing for the endogeneity of prices by means of introducing the residual of the price equation as an additional regressor in the demand equation (Smith & Blundell, 1984), the estimated parameter has a t-statistic of 5.93, rejecting the null hypothesis of exogeneity of the price variable.[22]

Price Elasticities

One of the objectives of this article has to do with analyzing the sensitivity of the estimated price elasticities to different assumptions of our model, in particular, the functional form and the exogeneity of prices. As we stated before, the model with a cubic profile for (log)prices (Column 3) was preferred to the linear version (Column 1). This has important implications in terms of the price elasticities because the linear model implies a constant elasticity, whereas for the cubic version the elasticity will vary with prices.

The estimated price elasticity for the linear model is –0.63, statistically different from a unit elasticity that would be the value in a context of clubs acting as profit maximizers and costs not depending on attendance in a standard monopolistic model. When estimating the more general model with a cubic profile, the price elasticity (η) becomes

TABLE 2:   Descriptive Statistics of the Estimated Price Elasticities

	Mean	Max.	Min.	10%	25%	50%	75%	90%	% ($\eta < -1$)
Model 3	−0.295	−3.947	−0.116	−0.571	−0.321	−0.178	−0.124	−0.120	5.19
Model 6	−0.968	−14.100	−0.352	−1.713	−1.049	−0.542	−0.407	−0.368	27.91

$$\eta = -14.017 + 9.394 \log(PRICE) - 1.587 \, [\log(PRICE)]^2.$$

In the first row of Table 2 we present the descriptive statistics of the estimated elasticities for the sample used in the estimation. The mean is even smaller in absolute value (−0.295) than the estimated elasticity for the linear model, and only 5.19% of the observations have elasticity greater than 1 in absolute value. In fact, the value for the first decile (−0.571) is also smaller in absolute value than the estimated elasticity for the first model.

When taking into account the possible endogeneity of prices, the estimated price elasticity changes substantially with respect to the previous results. It becomes

$$\eta = -48.781 + 32.190 \log(PRICE) - 5.349 \, [\log(PRICE)]^2.$$

As shown in the second row of Table 2, the mean of the estimated elasticities is almost 1 in absolute value (−0.968), with a larger range of variation and a higher percentage of observations with elasticities greater than 1 in absolute value (27.91%) as compared with the previous model. Consequently, although in both cases most of the observations correspond to clubs working in the inelastic part of the demand curve, the pattern is significantly different after taking into account price endogeneity. It is also relevant to point out that when estimating a (log)linear version of our specification by IV, price elasticity becomes insignificant.

In Table 3, we present the average of the estimated price elasticities for each team for the two versions (OLS, IV) of our preferred specification (Models 3 and 6). We could distinguish different groups of clubs depending on these values. As pointed out by a referee, variation in price elasticity across clubs is to be expected as clubs have different degrees of local monopoly power, depending on the availability of substitutes in their areas.

The results in the first column of Table 3 show that all clubs have average price elasticities below 1 in absolute value. In fact, out of 27 clubs there are only 2 with a price elasticity greater than 0.5. These elasticities are statistically different from 1. The results in the second column (the model with prices instrumented) show that out of 27 clubs there are 11 with average price elasticities higher than 1 in absolute value. By means of a Wald test we cannot reject for all clubs the null hypothesis of a unit elasticity, but this result very much depends on the high covariances of the esti-

TABLE 3:   Average Price Elasticities for Each Team

	Price Elasticity	
Team	Model 3, Table 1	Model 6, Table 1
Albacete	−0.2679	−0.7778
Athletic de Bilbao	−0.1729	−0.5067
Atlético de Madrid	−0.1598	−0.5097
Barcelona	−0.2875	−0.9236
Betis	−0.4142	−1.1625
Burgos	−0.2154	−0.6844
Cádiz	−0.2898	−1.1038
Celta	−0.2179	−0.7875
Compostela	−0.3934	−1.1198
Deportivo de La Coruña	−0.1978	−0.6277
Español	−0.2208	−0.6863
Logroñés	−0.3250	−0.9137
Lleida	−0.5441	−1.6093
Mérida	−0.3696	−1.3574
Osasuna	−0.2774	−0.9976
Oviedo	−0.3377	−0.9498
Racing de Santander	−0.1577	−0.5391
Rayo Vallecano	−0.3320	−1.0726
Real Madrid	−0.7358	−2.7388
Real Sociedad	−0.1891	−0.5503
Salamanca	−0.2464	−0.6676
Sevilla	−0.3290	−1.1294
Sporting de Gijón	−0.2407	−0.7758
Tenerife	−0.3002	−1.1486
Valencia	−0.3041	−1.0355
Valladolid	−0.2964	−0.9421
Zaragoza	−0.3748	−1.3269

mated parameters of the cubic profile when using IV. Finally, when comparing both models, the pattern of the distribution of the clubs is similar in both cases but, as was stated above, the elasticities are smaller in the case of the OLS estimation. This underestimation of the price elasticity when not taking into account the endogeneity of prices is consistent with the expected positive correlation of those unobserved factors affecting both prices and attendance.

Consequently, results from Model 3 agree with the empirical evidence on esti-mated price elasticities for professional team sports events, whereas those from Model 6 seem to give some support for a nearly elastic or elastic demand for a sig-nificant proportion of clubs. As mentioned in the introduction, this evidence can be rationalized either in a context of profit maximization under different modifications of the standard model or in a context where a club's objective function has argu-ments other than profits.[23] On the other hand, price elasticities can be underesti-

TABLE 4: Significance of Each Set of Explanatory Variables

	Model Without Home Team and Season Effects				Model With Home Team and Season Effects			
	SSR	K	r	F Test	SSR	K	r	F Test
Basic model	604.07	33			469.68	61		
Set of excluded variables								
Economic variables	731.62	26	7	46.63	513.83	54	7	20.39
Ex ante quality	774.20	26	7	62.20	621.20	54	7	69.96
Current quality	658.22	26	7	19.80	514.87	54	7	20.86
Home team quality	641.53	28	5	19.17	488.63	56	5	12.25
Away team quality	626.50	30	3	19.14	490.73	58	3	22.66
Uncertainty	646.07	29	4	26.87	493.39	57	4	19.16
Opportunity cost	715.08	25	8	35.51	529.55	54	7	27.64
Home team effects					596.98	36	25	16.46
Season effects					482.58	58	3	13.89

NOTE: SSR = residual sum of squares; K = number of parameters; r = number of restrictions. The basic models are those in Columns 2 and 3 of Table 1 for the models without and with effects, respectively.

mated as a consequence of the omission of other components of total cost of attendance, like transport costs, for which we do not have information in our data set.

Although the estimated model does not allow us to identify which theoretical framework applies to the Spanish case, the recent transformation of the Spanish clubs into limited companies seems to support an explanation for our results based on maximizing an objective function more general than a profit function.[24]

Contribution of Each Group of Variables to Explaining Attendance

A final aspect we wish to evaluate is the contribution of each group of variables we included in our model to explaining attendance. We do this by performing F tests for the null hypothesis of the coefficients of each group of variables separately being equal to zero. In fact, in using the F test, we are comparing the average reduction on the residual sum of squares by each additional estimated parameter included in a particular group of variables against the average reduction when including all the variables. This gives us a measure of what group of variables most reduces the residual sum of squares when the number of extra parameters to be estimated is taken into account.

In Table 4, we present the results of this exercise for two models: that without a home team and season effects (Model 2 in Table 1) and that with those effects (Model 3 in Table 1). Clearly, in both cases the group of variables capturing ex ante quality of the two teams is the group with the highest effect on attendance. On the other hand, when controlling for the unobserved effects the effect of the economic

32   JOURNAL OF SPORTS ECONOMICS / February 2002

variables has substantially reduced, in particular, that of income. The group of variables proxying the opportunity costs of attending a match is the second most important group in explaining attendance ahead of home team effects.

Finally, we wish to comment on the importance of home and team quality variables because of the implications on the effect of revenue sharing on competitive balance when the absolute value of a game affects attendance (Késenne, 2000). Our results do not show that home team quality (budget, number of wins in the past three games, current league position, number of goals scored in the past match at home, and result of the past game) has a larger effect on attendance than away team quality (budget, number of internationals, and no defeat in the past four games). In fact, when including in the away team quality variables the dummies corresponding to either Barcelona or Real Madrid as visitors, the effect of the away team quality is clearly higher than that of the home team. So, the necessary conditions for revenue sharing having an effect on competitive balance do not seem to be satisfied.

CONCLUSIONS

In this article we have estimated an attendance equation for the Spanish Football League using data on the individual games played during the seasons 1992-93 to 1995-96. We concentrated our attention on specification issues. We have included all the types of variables (economic and sectoral) proposed in the literature as explanatory factors in this kind of demand equations. Additionally, we have given attention to the functional form of the equation and the potential endogeneity of prices, specifically, with respect to their implications for estimated price elasticities. We also have employed the panel data structure of our data set to control for the effect of unobservables potentially correlated with the regressors.

As is usual in this literature, we estimated price elasticities that, in general, are less than one in absolute value, but these estimates show substantial differences depending on the functional form and consideration of the potential endogeneity of prices. In fact, when this last issue is taken into account, results seem to support a nearly elastic demand for a significant proportion of clubs.

At the same time, we have measured the contribution of each group of explanatory factors on explaining attendance, concluding that those variables related to ex ante quality of the two teams are those with the highest explanatory power.

As the sample period corresponds precisely to the initial stages of most Spanish football clubs' roles as limited companies, future research needs to extend the sample period in attempting to characterize their economic behavior more accurately. This would permit a more detailed analysis of the effect of televising football matches on attendance, given that the pay-per-view option could be included in the analysis.

APPENDIX
TABLE A1: Descriptive Statistics and Sources

Variable	Mean	SD	Source
Attendance	3,772.59	5,101.24	LNFP
Economic variables			
Price[a]	2,047.53	662.16	LNFP
Income[a]	1,292.86	277.44	BBVA
Population[b]	1,089.36	1,058.43	BBVA
Ex ante quality			
Budget (h)[a]	1,790.54	1,736.59	LNFP
Budget (v)[a]	1,776.39	1,727.63	LNFP
Number of internationals (v)	11.85	4.90	Dinámico[c]
Away team Barcelona	0.0487		
Away team Real Madrid	0.0487		
Rivalry	0.0468		
Club's Day match	0.0563		LNFP
Current quality			
Number of wins in the past 3 games (h)	0.9127	0.8255	
Score past game (h)	−0.4025	1.7253	
Goals past game at home (h)	1.0887	1.1477	
Standings (h)	10.7006	6.0825	
No defeat in past 4 games (v)	0.1587		
No chance of winning the championship (h)	0.1791		
No chance of leaving relegation zone (h)	0.0089		
Uncertainty			
Difference in league positions (h-v)	0.3329	8.2663	
Closeness in league positions	0.3006		
Uncertainty of championship (h)[d]	180.719	143.969	
Opportunity cost			
No rain, hot	0.5361		Dinámico
No rain, cold	0.3627		Dinámico
Televised by public channels	0.1006		LNFP
Televised by a private channel	0.0987		LNFP
Not played on the weekend	0.0715		LNFP
Distance	544.447	268.072	Road map
Home team Tenerife	0.0494		
Away team Tenerife	0.0487		

NOTE: LNFP = Liga Nacional de Fútbol Profesional; BBVA = Fundación BBVA, *Renta Nacional de España y su Distribución Provincial*; and *Dinámico* = football yearbook; h = home team; v = away team.
a. These variables are expressed in real terms (1991 *pesetas*). Income in thousands of pesetas and budgets in millions of pesetas.
b. Population is in thousands.
c. We also used information from Sarmiento (1994).
d. This is based on Kuypers (1996) measure.

TABLE A2: Estimation of a Price Equation (Reduced Form)

Variable	Coefficient	t-Statistic
Previous season standings (h)	0.007	3.37
Previous season standings (v)	–0.004	2.32
Previous season in Second Division (h)	0.017	0.48
Previous season in Second Division (v)	–0.036	1.31
Log(capacity)	–0.035	1.34
Economic variables		
Log(income)	–228.83	0.36
Log(income)**2	22.221	0.33
Log(income)**3	–0.711	0.30
Log(population)	0.036	0.67
Ex ante quality		
Budget (h)	0.100	0.22
Budget (v)	0.009	0.06
Number of internationals (v)	0.003	1.20
Away team Barcelona	0.131	1.55
Away team Real Madrid	0.107	1.29
Rivalry	0.142	4.14
Club's Day match	0.138	4.42
Current quality		
Number of wins in the past 3 games (h)	0.010	0.97
Score past game (h)	–0.001	0.23
Goals past game at home (h)	0.004	0.79
Standings (h)	–0.012	4.34
No defeat in past 4 games (v)	0.012	0.62
No chance of winning the championship (h)	–0.038	1.85
No chance of leaving relegation zone (h)	–0.150	2.17
Uncertainty		
Difference in league positions (h-v)	0.005	3.93
Difference in league positions**2 (h-v)	–0.000	1.15
Closeness in league positions	0.002	0.15
Uncertainty of championship (h)	0.270	2.62
Opportunity cost		
No rain, hot	0.022	1.04
No rain, cold	0.003	0.13
Televised by public channels	–0.023	0.79
Televised by a private channel	–0.036	1.53
Not played on the weekend	–0.032	1.52
Distance	–0.042	1.33
Home team Tenerife	–0.225	3.29
Away team Tenerife	–0.015	0.48
Constant	781.12	0.39
Home team effects	Yes	
Season effects	Yes	
R^2	0.5052	

NOTE: h = home team; v = away team. Endogenous variable is log(price). The distance variable is measured in thousands of kilometers. The uncertainty for the title variable is measured in thousands.

NOTES

1. See Schofield (1983); Cairns, Jennett, and Sloane (1986); Cairns (1990); and Downward and Dawson (2000) for surveys of this literature.

2. See Rodríguez (2001) for a recent survey of the empirical specification issues related to the estimation of attendance equations.

3. See Szymanski and Smith (1997), Szymanski and Kuypers (1999), and Hoehn and Szymanski (1999) for complete analysis of the British football industry.

4. The attendance of season ticket holders will be explained by a different model where some variables, in particular the economic variables, will not play any explanatory role. See Rodríguez (2001) for some preliminary results for this type of attendance in the Spanish Football League. Evidence for the English Football League from Simmons (1996), using season data for individual clubs, suggests that "casual" spectators are more price-sensitive than season ticket holders.

5. This form of measuring the price variable has been used previously in the literature. See Jennett (1984), Borland (1987), Borland and Lye (1992), and Falter and Pérignon (2000), among others. We prefer this to the usual average ticket price, as in this manner we avoid the inclusion of the endogenous variable (attendance) in the definition of the price variable. On the other hand, this is almost equivalent to the use of a constructed average ticket price using each class of seat's share of stadium capacity as proposed by Coffin (1996). This is because there is almost proportionality among the prices of the different types of seats, and their share of stadium capacity has not changed substantially in the period under consideration.

6. As far as we know, Falter and Pérignon (2000) is the only article in the literature on attendance at professional team sporting events that includes this type of variable in a demand equation.

7. We report the variables included in the final specification. Other variables proxying the same effects have been included in previous estimations, not reported here but available on request.

8. See Cairns (1988) for a complete discussion of how to model uncertainty in these demand equations.

9. We have also considered the possibility that the scheduling of a match might have an influence on attendance but the estimated effect was not significant.

10. Each team played 38 matches each season, except in 1995-96 when they played 42 matches.

11. Most of the clubs have more than three different prices during the season. In fact, the proportion of the total price variation in each season due to within-club variation represented 51.4% in the 1992-93 season, 53.9% in 1993-94, 56.5% in 1994-95, and 53.0% in 1995-96 when considering the cheapest price.

12. Some studies have shown a tendency to control for the unobserved component corresponding to each fixture in a particular season, as in Baimbridge, Cameron, and Dawson (1996) and Carmichael, Millington, and Simmons (1999), whereas other studies include dummies for the initial and final games of the season, as in Peel and Thomas (1988) and Wilson and Sim (1995). In our study, when attempting to control for this effect, we did not obtain significant estimates.

13. These estimates would be inconsistent if clubs were capacity constrained. In our sample, only 3.4% of the observations correspond to this situation. Results obtained estimating a Tobit model do not differ significantly from those presented here.

14. This is the usual approach when transforming a dynamic model for panel data previous to its estimation by Instrumental Variables or Generalized Method of Moments.

15. The F statistic for testing the null hypothesis of a linear specification against the alternative of a cubic one is 26.92, rejecting this null at a 5% significance level ($F_{4, 1,550} = 2.37$). When fitting a polynomial of fourth order all the coeffcients of the (log)price variables become not significant because of collinearity problems.

16. We have not included the number of internationals of the home team in the final specification because it was wrongly signed when included, unless we eliminated the budget of the home team as a explanatory variable.

36   JOURNAL OF SPORTS ECONOMICS / February 2002

17. We considered the possibility of including a dummy variable for the home team having won the championship, but in three out four of the seasons included in the sample the champion was not known until the final game was played and in the remaining season the championship was won one game before the end. For this reason, we decided not to include it in the model as this dummy would have the value one for only a single observation.

18. In these seasons, the pay-per-view system was not still available in Spain.

19. For U.S. professional football, Welki and Zlatoper (1994) found that games that are blacked out for local television are more poorly attended; for English football, Kuypers (1996) did not find a significant effect for this variable; and for Major League Baseball, Bruggink and Eaton (1996) obtained different effects for games televised on a local free channel and on premium cable. Negative effects of television on baseball attendance were found in Demmert (1973). Baimbridge, Cameron, and Dawson (1996) argue that the net effect of television on attendance is indeterminate.

20. Note that we cannot interpret the coefficients of the dummies for a match being televised as a rate of increase of the endogenous variable because they are not small rates. The figures calculated above are not based on this approximation.

21. The F statistic for testing the null hypothesis of not including these controls is 13.16, rejecting this null at a 5% significance level ($F_{33, 1.518} = 1.46$).

22. Given the cubic profile for prices, we also introduced the square and cubic residuals of the price equation in the demand equation, with the coefficents of the linear and quadratic terms being significant.

23. See Fort (2000) for a comparison of European and North American sports in terms of team objectives.

24. This transformation took place in 1992 and all the clubs were involved with the exception of Athletic of Bilbao, Barcelona, Osasuna, and Real Madrid. Before 1992, all football clubs were nonprofit associations.

REFERENCES

Amemiya, T. (1983). Nonlinear regression models. In Z. Griliches & M. D. Intriligator (Eds.), *Handbook of econometrics, volume 1* (pp. 333-389). Amsterdam: North-Holland.

Baimbridge, M., Cameron, S., & Dawson, P. (1996). Satellite television and the demand for football: A whole new ball game? *Scottish Journal of Political Economy, 43*, 317-333.

Balestra, P., & Nerlove P. M. (1966). Pooling cross section and time series data in the estimation of a dynamic model: The demand for natural gas. *Econometrica, 34*, 586-612.

Borland, J. (1987). The demand for Australian rules football. *Economic Record, 63*, 220-230.

Borland, J., & Lye, J. (1992). Attendance at Australian rules football: A panel study. *Applied Economics, 24*, 1053-1058.

Boyd, D. W., & Boyd, L. A. (1998). The home field advantage: Implications for the pricing of tickets to professional team sporting events. *Journal of Economics and Finance, 22*, 169-179.

Bruggink, T. H., & Eaton, J. W. (1996). Rebuilding attendance in Major League Baseball: The demand for individual games. In J. L. Fizel, E. Gustafson, & L. Hadley (Eds.), *Baseball economics: Current research* (pp. 9-31). Westport, CT: Praeger.

Cairns, J. A. (1988). *Uncertainty of outcome and the demand for football* (Discussion Paper No. 88-02). Department of Economics, University of Aberdeen.

Cairns, J. A. (1990). The demand for professional team sports. *British Review of Economic Issues, 12*, 1-20.

Cairns, J. A., Jennett, N., & Sloane, P. J. (1986). The economics of professional team sport: A survey of theory and evidence. *Journal of Economic Studies, 13*, 3-80.

Carmichael, F., Millington, J., & Simmons, R. (1999). Elasticity of demand for rugby league attendance and the impact of BskyB, *Applied Economics Letters, 6*, 797-800.

Coffin, D. A. (1996). If you build it, will they come? Attendance and new stadium construction. In J. L. Fizel, E. Gustafson, & L. Hadley (Eds.), *Baseball economics: Current research* (pp. 33-46). Westport, CT: Praeger.

Davidson, R., & MacKinnon, J. (1981). Several tests of model specification in the presence of alternative hypotheses. *Econometrica, 49,* 781-793.

Demmert, H. G. (1973). *The economics of professional team sports.* Lexington, MA: Lexington Books.

Downward, P., & Dawson, A. (2000). *The economics of professional team sports.* London: Routledge.

El Hodiri, M., & Quirk, J. (1971). An economic model of a professional sports league. *Journal of Political Economy, 79,* 1302-1319.

Falter, J. M., & Pérignon, C. (2000). Demand for football and intramatch winning probability: An essay on the glorious uncertainty of sports. *Applied Economics, 32,* 1757-1765.

Ferguson, D. G., Stewart, K. G., Jones, J.C.H., & Le Dressay, A. (1991). The pricing of sports events: Do teams maximize profit? *Journal of Industrial Economics, 39,* 297-310.

Forrest, D., & Simmons, R. (2001). *Outcome uncertainty and attendance demand in sport: The case of English soccer.* Retrieved from www.aems.salford.ac.uk/salgroup

Fort, R. (2000). European and North American sports differences (?). *Scottish Journal of Political Economy, 47,* 431-455.

Heilmann, L., & Wendling, W. R. (1976). A note on optimum pricing strategies for sport events. In R. E. Machol & S. P. Ladany (Eds.), *Management science in sports* (pp. 91-99). Amsterdam: North-Holland.

Hoehn, T., & Szymanski, S. (1999). The Americanization of European football. *Economic Policy, 28,* 203-240.

Jennett, N. (1984). Attendance, uncertainty of outcome and policy in the Scottish League Football. *Scottish Journal of Political Economy, 31,* 176-198.

Jones, J.C.H., Schofield, J. A., & Giles, D.E.A. (2000). Our fans in the north: The demand for British Rugby League. *Applied Economics, 32,* 1877-1887.

Késenne, S. (2000). Revenue sharing and competitive balance in professional team sports. *Journal of Sports Economics, 1,* 56-65.

Knowles, G., Sherony, K., & Haupert, M. (1992). The demand for Major League Baseball: A test of the uncertainty of outcome hypothesis. *American Economist, 36,* 72-80.

Kuypers, T. (1996). *The beautiful game? An econometric study of why people watch English football* (Discussion Paper in Economics No. 96-01). University College London.

Marburger, D. R. (1997). Optimal ticket pricing for performance goods. *Managerial and Decision Economics, 18,* 375-381.

Peel, D., & Thomas, D. (1988). Outcome uncertainty and the demand for football: An analysis of match attendances in the English Football League. *Scottish Journal of Political Economy, 35,* 242-249.

Peel, D., & Thomas, D. (1997). Handicaps, outcome uncertainty and attendance demand. *Applied Economics Letters, 4,* 567-570.

Rodríguez, P. (2001). *Análisis económico de la demanda de entradas en el fútbol español* [Economic analysis of attendance in Spanish football]. Doctoral dissertation, Universidad de Oviedo, Spain.

Salant, D. J. (1992). Price setting in professional team sports. In P. M. Sommers (Ed.), *Diamonds are forever: The business of baseball* (pp. 77-90). Washington, DC: The Brookings Institution.

Sarmiento, M. (1994). *Selección española de fútbol: Sus hombres, uno a uno* [Spanish national football team: Their men one by one]. Madrid, Spain: Fundación del Fútbol Profesional.

Schofield, J. A. (1983). Performance and attendance at professional team sports. *Journal of Sports Behaviour, 6,* 196-206.

Simmons, R. (1996). The demand for English League Football: A club-level analysis. *Applied Economics, 28,* 139-155.

Sloane, P. J. (1971). The economics of professional football: The football club as a utility maximizer. *Scottish Journal of Political Economy, 17,* 121-146.

38   JOURNAL OF SPORTS ECONOMICS / February 2002

Smith, R., & Blundell, R. (1984). An exogeneity test for a simultaneous equation Tobit model with an application to labour supply. *Econometrica, 54,* 679-685.

Szymanski, S., & Kuypers, T. (1999). *Winners and losers.* London: Viking.

Szymanski, S., & Smith, R. (1997). The English football industry: Profit, performance and industrial structure. *International Review of Applied Economics, 11,* 135-153.

Welki, A. M., & Zlatoper, T. J. (1994). US professional football: The demand for game-day attendance in 1991. *Managerial and Decision Economics, 15,* 489-495.

Wilson, P.R.D., & Sim, B. (1995). The demand for semi-pro league football in Malaysia 1989-91: A panel data approach. *Applied Economics, 27,* 131-138.

Jaume García is a professor of economics at the Universitat Pompeu Fabra in Barcelona, Spain. He received his undergraduate degree from the University of Barcelona and his M. Sc. (Econometrics and Mathematical Economics) and Ph. D. (Economics) degrees from the London School of Economics and Political Science. His fields of specialization are microeconometrics, labour economics, health economics, and sports economics.

Plácido Rodríguez is a lecturer in economics at the Universidad de Oviedo in Salamanca, Spain. He is a doctor of economics and licentiate on laws. He has served as President of Real Sporting de Grijón, a First Division soccer club, and is a member of AIES.

[24]

Measuring the Efficiency of Spanish First-Division Soccer Teams

MANUEL ESPITIA-ESCUER
LUCÍA ISABEL GARCÍA-CEBRIÁN
University of Zaragoza, Spain

The aim of this article is to measure the efficiency of the professional soccer teams that play in the Spanish First Division in their activity of converting attacking moves during the match into sporting success. The timeline of the study is the three seasons from 1998 to 2001. To that end, we apply the data envelopment analysis (DEA) methodology, taking as input variables the players used, attacking moves, the minutes of possession of the ball, and the shots and headers; as output, we considered the number of points achieved. Our main conclusion is that the efficient teams in the activity analyzed do not always correspond with those that finished highest in the league at the end of the season.

Keywords: *efficiency; data envelopment analysis; Spanish soccer teams*

The professional soccer teams that comprise the Spanish First Division are, in their majority, the star product of the institutions of which they form a part. Many of these institutions also have soccer teams that play in lower leagues, as well as basketball teams and other professional team sports that represent a broad and varied offering for their shareholders and season ticket holders alike. Furthermore, the great majority of them take the legal form of corporations (more specifically, under the Spanish company law system, *sociedades anónimas deportivas*). In the near future, some of these companies will be quoted on the Spanish stock market, as is already the case with some soccer clubs operating in other European countries. We are, therefore, dealing with entities that can be analyzed and studied from the point of view of economics and are using the tools of analysis that are provided by this discipline. In this sense, these entities carry out a productive process in which the productive factors are essentially human resources. These resources take the form of a team, which during the working week generates and perfects skills that are

AUTHORS' NOTE: *The authors wish to express their thanks to GECA Sport for its collaboration in supplying the data used in this article. They are also grateful to Emili Grifell and Alberto Lafuente for their helpful observations on its content.*

JOURNAL OF SPORTS ECONOMICS, Vol. 5 No. 4, November 2004   329–346
DOI: 10.1177/1527002503258047
© 2004 Sage Publications

330   JOURNAL OF SPORTS ECONOMICS / November 2004

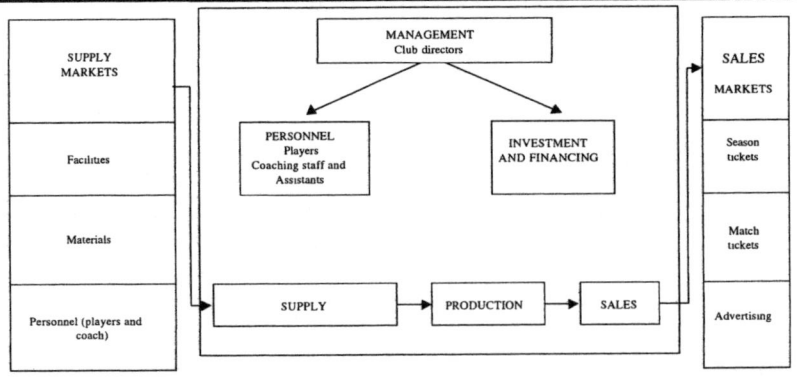

Figure 1:   The Fandel (1991) Functional Model of the Firm Adapted to the Case of Soccer
             Teams

made effective in competition against another team during the time that is represented by the match.

If we start from a very simple characterization of firms, their activity can be explained by reference to criteria of effectiveness and efficiency. *Effectiveness* is the achievement of the objectives set by the unit under analysis that, in the case of firms, is generally the maximization of profits. These profits are obtained through the sale of a product that these firms have manufactured. For its part, firm efficiency analyzes the use of the productive resources in the production of the good sold in the market, with a unit being considered as efficient when it does not waste its resources in carrying out its activity. In summary, an effective firm is that which achieves its objectives with greater precision, which means that it has carried out the appropriate activities to reach those objectives. On the other hand, an *efficient firm* is one that has not wasted resources, which means that it has carried out its activity in an appropriate manner in the process of obtaining its products, independent of the achievement of its objectives.

Figure 1 presents the functional model of a firm proposed by Fandel (1991), adapted to the case of soccer teams. Here, we can note that the supply markets provide these organizations with the installations, fundamentally those required for training purposes, physical preparation, and the match. They also provide the materials and the playing staff, which represents the most important part of the supplies not only by virtue of the cost assumed by the signing of players but also because soccer teams can be considered as service-sector firms. On the other hand, the sales markets are understood as those in which the firms offer the product obtained from their activity to obtain income. In the case of professional soccer teams, this income is obtained through the sale of match tickets and annual season tickets[1] as well as through advertising revenue. To maximize this income, the team has to offer an exciting spectacle and beat its rivals, all of which can be equated to the production (using its resources) of the product-service that is sold in the market. Therefore, in the ambit with which we are concerned in this article, efficiency will consist of not wasting the resources available in the course of the sporting competition.

From an economic point of view, the objective of soccer teams would be the maximization of their profit, whose expression, taking into account the above considerations, could be written in the following form:

$$B_t = I_t - C_t(r_t)$$

where:

B_t is the profit of the entity in season t,
I_t is the income in season t,
C_t are the costs in season t, and
r_t are the resources used in playing the matches over the course of the season t.

In turn, the income in period t would be a function of the sporting results achieved in the seasons prior to t (A_t), which will themselves depend on the resources that have historically being used prior to period t (R_t). Thus, the income can be expressed in the following form:

$$I_t = I_t[A_{t-1}(R_t)]$$

Using this expression of profit for the case of a soccer club, we can confirm that for a given period, the income is fixed in that it depends on the previous sporting results. Thus, an alternative to maximize profits would be to reduce the use of resources in such a way that the costs would be nil or as low as possible. In reality, however, no one would opt for such an approach because the nonuse of resources would lead to bad sporting results, which would have a negative repercussion on the income of the subsequent seasons. Therefore, given the interrelation between the sporting results and the profits of subsequent seasons, and to not compromise the income of those subsequent seasons, the appropriate approach would be to maximize the sporting results in each season. This must, however, be achieved in such a way that resources are not misused so as to not increase the costs of the season under consideration to an unnecessary extent. Therefore, the maximization of the profit of soccer clubs rests on the efficiency with which they execute the matches throughout the season or, equivalently, on the absence of waste in what is their productive activity.

Against this background, in this article, we set out to measure the efficiency of the professional soccer teams that play in the Spanish First Division, taking the 1998-1999, 1999-2000, and 2000-2001 seasons as the time span for the analysis. To that end, we apply the data envelopment analysis methodology. In the next sec-

332 JOURNAL OF SPORTS ECONOMICS / November 2004

tion, we present the results obtained from the calculation of this efficiency. Before doing so, however, we first offer a brief description of both data envelopment analysis and the input and output variables that will be considered as representative of the production function of soccer teams and that are used to make the efficiency calculations. The identification of the most efficient teams will allow us to offer recommendations aimed at reducing waste in the use of resources. The final section closes the article with a summary of the main conclusions.

THE EFFICIENCY OF THE PROFESSIONAL SOCCER TEAMS PLAYING IN THE SPANISH FIRST DIVISION

In the empirical part of this article, we will use deterministic nonparametric frontiers. *Frontier functions* measure efficiency with respect to the best observations and correspond to optimization processes. Within these types of models, we can find a number of different approaches, which have been summarized by Førsund, Lovell, and Schmidt (1980). Deterministic nonparametric frontiers do not consider a specific functional form for the frontier; rather, they are formed through linear programming techniques, such as the envelopment of the observed values.[2] Firms lying on the frontier established in this way are considered as efficient. The use of this type of frontier has given rise to the methodology known as data envelopment analysis.

As Farrell (1957) indicates, the most significant aspect of this method is not the graphical representation of the isoquant but rather the mathematical formulation shown in the following linear programming problem:[3]

$$\text{Min } \lambda_1 \qquad \text{P.1}$$
$$\text{s.t.} \quad u \leq z\,U$$
$$\lambda_1 x \geq z\,X$$
$$z \in R_k^+$$

where

λ_1 is the overall technical efficiency index considering an orientation toward input (a unit is technically efficient if it is not possible to reduce the use of one of its factors without increasing the use of any other resource or without reducing the amount of any product),

u is the vector that represents the amounts of the m products produced by the firm,

U is the k.m matrix that represents the amount of the m products for the k firms in the sample,

x are the amounts of the n productive factors used by the firm whose efficiency is being measured,

X is the k.n matrix of the amounts of the n productive factors used by the firms in the sample, and z is a vector of parameters that determines combinations of factors and products observed.

Given the formulation of the problem that serves for the efficiency calculation by way of data envelopment analysis, λ_1 is the value of the overall technical efficiency of each unit studied in comparison with the other units of the sample, so that when $\lambda_1 = 1$, the firm being analyzed lies on the isoquant and it is impossible to obtain its production vector with a radial reduction of all its resources. If a given unit has a value of λ_1 lower than one,[4] it is not considered as efficient, given that it could obtain the same quantity of the final product by reducing the quantities of resources consumed in a proportion $(1-\lambda_1)$.

Until now, we have worked under the assumption of constant returns to scale. It is, however, possible to relax this hypothesis to consider the case of variable returns to scale. In such cases, it is possible to measure the efficiency of each firm not only with respect to all the firms in the sample but also with respect to firms of a similar size. The mathematical formulation that allows us to measure such efficiency takes the form:

$$\text{Min } \lambda_2 \qquad\qquad \text{P.2}$$
$$\text{s.t.} \quad u \leq z\,U$$
$$\lambda_2\, x \geq z\, X$$
$$\Sigma\, z_i = 1$$
$$z \in R_k^+$$

where λ_2 is the value of the so-called purely technical efficiency. The scale efficiency is therefore the value of the quotient λ_1/λ_2 and measures the losses in efficiency due to a wrong choice of firm size.

Table 1 presents a sample of articles that have been dedicated to evaluating team and sports performance using economic tools. From a study of this table, we can first note the wide variety of sports that have been studied. We can also appreciate that the units of analysis taken by the various articles differ, with this being related to the particular sport in question. Thus, in the case of baseball, when interaction between players is reduced, the different works have taken the individual as the unit of study. As regards the other sports, however, it is performance of the team that is considered. Furthermore, in those cases in which the aim is to evaluate the coach, information is taken relative to the whole of the team, due to the difficulty of presenting separately the contribution made by each individual to the global result obtained by the team.

Secondly, as regards the variables[5] taken by the different studies to measure the inputs and outputs, we should note that practically all these use some proxy variable of the sporting results obtained as a measurement of the product. With respect to the variables that represent the factors used, however, we can observe a much greater variety, although they can fundamentally be grouped into two different categories:

TABLE 1: A Review of the Literature on the Evaluation of Team Sports Activities From an Economic Viewpoint

Article	Sport	Unit of Study	Objective of the Article	Variables		Methodology
				Input	Output	
Anderson and Sharp (1997)	Baseball	Batters	To create, on basis of DEA, a new measurement to evaluate batters	Plate appearances	Walks Singles Doubles Triples Home runs	Deterministic nonparametric frontier
Carmichael and Thomas (1995)	Rugby	Team	Formulation of production function	Tries Goals Drops (all of them, for and against)	Percentage of matches won during the season	Average function of production (evaluates efficiency)
Carmichael, Thomas, and Ward (2000)	Soccer	Performance of each team in the match	Obtaining a production frontier	Game variables Characteristics variables of teams If the match was played on the ground of the team being studied	Result of the match (differences between goals in favour and goals against)	Average function of production (does not evaluate efficiency)
Dawson, Dobson, and Gerrard (2000a)	Soccer	Coach (taking data from the team)	Testing the robustness of the estimation of the efficiency of the coach	Talent of the players	Percentage of matches won with respect of those played Idem corrected for draws Percentage of points over maximum possible (Alternative measures)	Stochastic frontier
Dawson, Dobson, and Gerrard (2000b)	Soccer	Coach (taking data from the team)	Provide estimations of technical efficiency for a panel of coaches	Quality of the team	Proportion of matches won in relation to number played	Stochastic frontier

	Sport	Unit of analysis	Objective	Inputs	Output	Method
Fizel and D'Itri (1997)	Basketball	Coach (taking data from the team)	Construct a measurement of the efficiency of the coach to apply it to the analysis of the relationship between the replacement of the coach and the performance of the teams	Talent and abilities of the players; Potential of the opposition	Percentage of matches won	Deterministic nonparametric frontier
Hadley, Poitras, Ruggiero, and Knowles (2000)	American football	Team during the league	Analysis of the performance of the team with respect to its potential	Variables that reflect a defensive and offensive performance	Percentage of matches actually won with respect to those forecasted	Deterministic statistical frontier
Hofler and Payne (1997)	Basketball	Team	Evaluation of the performance of the team with respect to its potential	Field goal percentage; Free throw percentage; Offensive rebounds; Defensive rebounds; Assists; Steals; Turnovers	Number of matches won in the season	Stochastic frontier
Mazur (1994)	Baseball	Player	Offer a ranking of players	Identical for all players	Performance of batter; Performance of pitcher	Deterministic nonparametric frontier
Schofield (1988)	Cricket	Team	Estimate production functions	Performance of players; Inherent abilities of player	Percentage of matches won during season; Percentage of maximum points achieved	Average function of production (does not evaluate efficiency)
Scully (1994)	Baseball, basketball, and American football	Team	Study the relationship between performance of coaches in a team and the efficiency of its management	Offensive and defensive abilities	Percentage of matches won	Deterministic statistical frontiers and stochastic frontier

(continued)

TABLE 1 (continued)

336

Article	Sport	Unit of Study	Objective of the Article	Variables		Methodology
				Input	Output	
Sueyoshi, Ohnishi, and Kinase (1999)	Baseball	Player	Complement results obtained from application of DEA to identify best player	At bats Double plays	Singles Doubles Triples Home runs Runs batted in Steals Sacrifices Walks	Deterministic nonparametric frontier (in combination with other measurement of performance)
Zak, Huang, and Siegfried (1979)	Basketball	Team	Estimation of the production frontier to determine the potential of the team and the determinants of its performance	Field goal Free throw Offensive rebounds Defensive rebounds Assists Personal fouls Steals Turnovers Location	Ratio of final results	Parametric Deterministic frontier

TABLE 2: Relevant Data on the Soccer Teams that Formed the Spanish First Division

League Season 1998-1999	Points Achieved	Goals Scored	Attacking Moves	Players Used	Minutes of Possession	Shots and Headers Made
Maximum value	79	87	5227	31	1149	514
Minimum value	27	27	4468	19	851	342
Average	52	50	4798.15	24.55	956.55	418.2
Standard deviation	13.51	15.25	164.61	2.70	77.72	52.65
League champions (Barcelona)	79	87	4706	25	1126	504
Bottom-placed club (Salamanca)	27	29	4909	26	978	383

League Season 1999-2000	Points Achieved	Goals Scored	Attacking Moves	Players Used	Minutes of Possession	Shots and Headers Made
Maximum value	69	70	5162	32	1215	611
Minimum value	28	33	4697	22	852	462
Average	51.4	49.95	4954.7	25.9	963.2	514.45
Standard deviation	10.1	9.49	124.67	2.88	76.03	42.42
League champions (Deportivo)	69	66	5015	23	983	556
Bottom-placed club (Sevilla)	28	42	4914	32	947	481

League Season 2000-2001	Points Achieved	Goals Scored	Attacking Moves	Players Used	Minutes of Possession	Shots and Headers Made
Maximum value	80	81	5080	30	1176	637
Minimum value	39	40	4288	23	914	399
Average	52.05	54.75	4594	25.75	1002.55	518
Standard deviation	12.5	11.92	179.63	2.19	63.81	62.55
League champions (Real Madrid)	80	81	4783	23	1115	614
Bottom-placed club (Numancia)	39	40	4684	26	954	510

those that make reference to the skills or talent of the players and those that refer to their activity on the field of play during the game. Furthermore, some studies not only take into account the variables corresponding to the team being studied but also consider amongst the inputs those relative to the opposing team, making the assumption that these have an influence on the result obtained.

Some data relative to the soccer teams that formed the Spanish First Division in the seasons 1998-2001 are set out in Table 2.

From a reading of this table, we can appreciate that the average of the variables considered takes similar values in the seasons in question. If, however, we focus

338   JOURNAL OF SPORTS ECONOMICS / November 2004

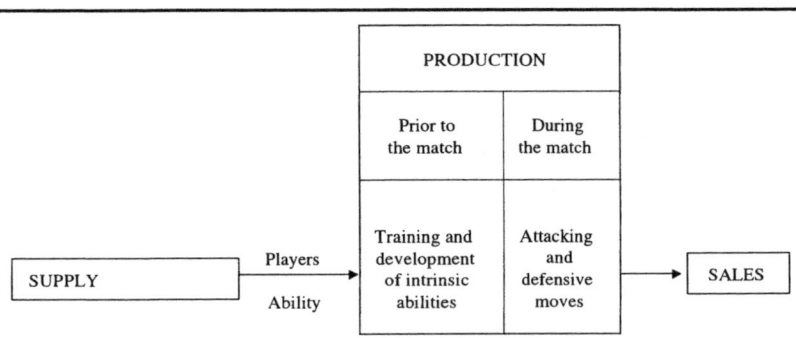

Figure 2:   Breakdown of the Production Function in Soccer Teams

exclusively on the performance of the league champions, we can note that although in the 1998-1999 and 2000-2001 seasons there is a similar behavior in that, save for the number of shots made, the remaining variables take comparable values, the champions of the 1999-2000 season scored significantly fewer goals, made more attacking moves, and had fewer minutes of possession. Note the differences exhibited by the values corresponding to the 1999-2000 league champions and, more specifically, the fact that with a higher number of attacking moves, the number of goals scored was lower and, furthermore, that the total points was lower than that achieved by the champions of the other seasons. All this allows us to confirm that the style of play during the 1999-2000 season was more defensive than that of the other seasons analyzed.

As regards the productive process of these teams, Schofield (1988), Carmichael and Thomas (1995), and Carmichael, Thomas, and Ward (2000) consider a recursive system in which the success of the team depends on the performance of the players during the game, and this, in turn, depends on both their abilities[6] and the work of the coach, as reflected in Figure 2. Therefore, if this is applied to the production function of soccer teams, we can consider that such a function is made up of two different components, each with its own inputs and outputs:

> In the first part, we can consider the abilities of the players (e.g., sporting talent, physical condition and form, and experience) together with the work of the coach (e.g., work during training sessions, tactics, and lineup) as the inputs to obtain a result: the performance during the match, that is, attacking and defensive moves against the opposing team.
> In the second part, we take as inputs the attacking and defensive moves (the results of the first component), which are transformed into success during the matches, in such a way that they can be considered as output.

Our analysis of the efficiency of the professional soccer teams playing in the Spanish First Division in the 1998-1999, 1999-2000, and 2000-2001 seasons focuses on the second of the above-mentioned components of the production function. On the basis of the results obtained when applying both the concept of economic efficiency, as well as one of the possible methods that allow this to be calculated in empirical applications, it is possible for us to draw a number of conclusions and make various recommendations on the nature of the play executed during the matches. To that end, we have taken as input variables the number of players used, the number of attacking moves, the number of minutes during which the teams had possession of the ball, and the number of shots and headers, all of them throughout the length of the season. The noninclusion of defensive moves is due to the fact that in carrying out this work, we have taken the data on the complete season, during which all the teams play each other twice, in such a way that the influence of the opponents is homogeneous for all the sample. As output, we have taken the number of points achieved throughout the season, following the recommendations of Dawson, Dobson, and Gerrard (2000a). These authors place emphasis on the soccer games that end in a draw and, therefore, conclude that a measurement based solely on a team's victories would not reflect all its results. It is possible to think that, when taking the number of goals scored, the problems highlighted by these authors would be avoided. From Table 2, however, we can note that the league champions are not necessarily the team that has scored the most goals (e.g., the case of Deportivo in the 1999-2000 season), nor is it the case that the bottom-placed club is the one that has scored the fewest number (illustrated by Salamanca and Sevilla in the 1998-1999 and 1999-2000 seasons, respectively). Furthermore, the difference between goals scored and goals conceded for a complete season is an aggregate value that does not adequately represent the situation of win, draw, or loss that is produced in each match and that, in summary, is what leads to the final league positions. On the basis of all of the above, it is considered that the variable that best represents the output is the number of points obtained.[7]

The results obtained from the resolution of the linear programming problems P.1 and P.2 applied to the values of the sample, and analyzed and taking the data on a season-by-season basis, are set out in Table 3, 4, and 5. Furthermore, Table 6 presents the efficiency values of the soccer teams that comprise the Spanish First Division when taking the values corresponding to the three seasons in question as a joint sample.[8]

Although, in the three seasons analyzed, the team that won the league is efficient, from the results obtained when giving separate consideration to the data corresponding to each season, we can note the lack of coincidence between the teams that filled the leading positions in the end-of-season league tables and those that are the most efficient. Thus, in the 1998-1999 season, the Real Madrid soccer club, which is not efficient, was classified in the league table above a team (that is, Mallorca). Furthermore, there are teams that are classified in a worse position but are nevertheless more efficient. In the 1999-2000 season, this tendency is even more marked, given that the Alavés soccer club is, together with the league champions, the only team that can be regarded as efficient, and yet it occupies fifth position

TABLE 3:   Efficiency and Results Corresponding to the 1998-1999 Season

Team	Overall Technical Efficiency	Purely Technical Efficiency	Scale Efficiency	Position in the Table
Alavés	0.64	1	0.64	16
At. Madrid	0.63	0.87	0.73	13
Ath. Bilbao	0.97	1	0.97	7
Barcelona	1	1	1	1
Betis	0.72	0.97	0.74	11
Celta	0.95	1	0.95	5
Deportivo	0.90	0.96	0.94	6
Español	0.95	1	0.95	8
Extremadura	0.65	1	0.65	17
Mallorca	1	1	1	3
Oviedo	0.71	1	0.71	14
Racing	0.63	0.92	0.68	15
Real Madrid	0.84	0.96	0.87	2
Real Sociedad	0.79	0.99	0.80	10
Salamanca	0.39	0.93	0.42	20
Tenerife	0.48	0.95	0.51	19
Valencia	0.98	1	0.98	4
Valladolid	0.71	0.98	0.72	12
Villarreal	0.58	1	0.58	18
Zaragoza	0.87	0.97	0.89	9

in the league table. In the last of the seasons analyzed, however, the teams filling the three highest positions in the league at the end of the season can, in turn, be regarded as efficient. Furthermore, we can note that the teams that finished level on points are not equal as regards their efficiency value.

Secondly, from the results presented in Tables 3, 4, and 5, pay attention to the fact that scale inefficiency is an important component in overall technical inefficiency, given that around half the teams present purely technical efficiency. When we find that some efficient team is exceeded in terms of points gained by less efficient teams, we have two different situations: one in which these better classified but inefficient teams present purely technical efficiency (e.g., Barcelona, Valencia, and Zaragoza during the 1999-2000 season), and one in which they are not even efficient from the purely technical point of view (e.g., Real Madrid in the 1998-1999 and 1999-2000 seasons). In this sense, we should particularly note the case of Villarreal in the 1998-1999 season, when this team was relegated to a lower league but nevertheless presented a value of purely technical efficiency equal to one.

As regards the values obtained when considering jointly the data corresponding to each of the three seasons, we can note that for the teams competing in the 1999-2000 season, there was a fall in both their overall technical efficiency and their pure technical efficiency in comparison with the values obtained in the individual analy-

TABLE 4:   Efficiency and Results Corresponding to the 1999-2000 Season

Team	Overall Technical Efficiency	Purely Technical Efficiency	Scale Efficiency	Position in the Table
Alavés	1	1	1	6
At. Madrid	0.56	0.94	0.59	19
Ath. Bilbao	0.78	0.98	0.79	11
Barcelona	0.99	1	0.99	2
Betis	0.68	0.99	0.69	18
Celta	0.81	0.98	0.82	7
Deportivo	1	1	1	1
Español	0.75	0.98	0.76	14
Málaga	0.75	0.99	0.75	12
Mallorca	0.84	1	0.84	10
Numancia	0.75	1	0.75	17
Oviedo	0.73	0.98	0.74	16
Racing	0.70	1	0.70	15
Rayo Valleca	0.88	1	0.88	9
Real Madrid	0.91	0.97	0.93	5
Real Sociedad	0.76	1	0.76	13
Sevilla	0.45	0.99	0.45	20
Valencia	0.96	1	0.96	3
Valladolid	0.83	0.97	0.86	8
Zaragoza	0.97	1	0.97	4

sis of each season. Thus, no team in that particular season presents an overall technical efficiency equal to one, and only one of them (Numancia) achieves the pure technical efficiency equal to one. This would suggest that the activity carried out by Spanish First-Division football teams during the matches of the 1999-2000 season did not reflect the efficient use of resources when compared to the previous and subsequent seasons.

CONCLUSIONS

In this article, we have measured the efficiency of the professional soccer teams playing in the Spanish First Division in their activity of converting attacking moves during the match into sporting success. To that end, we have taken the time span of the three seasons from 1998-1999 to 2000-2001 and have applied data envelopment analysis (DEA) methodology, dividing the values obtained for overall technical efficiency into purely technical efficiency and scale efficiency. Given that the number of observations for each season is not particularly large, we have considered each of the three seasons both separately and as a joint sample, with our aim being to determine whether the results obtained might have been affected by this situation.

TABLE 5: Efficiency and Results Corresponding to the 2000-2001 Season

Team	Overall Technical Efficiency	Purely Technical Efficiency	Scale Efficiency	Position in the Table
Alavés	0.74	1	0.74	10
Ath. Bilbao	0.70	1	0.70	12
Barcelona	0.82	0.99	0.83	4
Celta	0.82	1	0.82	6
Deportivo	1	1	1	2
Español	0.72	1	0.72	9
Las Palmas	0.72	1	0.72	11
Málaga	0.87	1	0.87	8
Mallorca	1	1	1	3
Numancia	0.56	0.96	0.58	20
Osasuna	0.77	1	0.77	15
Oviedo	0.58	0.94	0.61	18
Racing	0.54	0.95	0.57	19
Rayo Vallecano	0.74	1	0.74	14
Real Madrid	1	1	1	1
Real Sociedad	0.64	0.99	0.64	13
Valencia	0.87	0.99	0.87	5
Valladolid	0.63	0.98	0.64	16
Villarreal	0.84	1	0.84	7
Zaragoza	0.57	0.96	0.59	17

Although the individual efficiency values we have obtained could be interpreted as the quotient between the amount of resources that a team should use to be efficient and the amount actually used, two fundamental and general results have emerged. First, we have noted that the efficient teams in the activity analyzed do not always correspond with those that finished highest in the league at the end of the season. If we view the management of sports clubs as the management of business organizations, this result implies that well-classified but inefficient teams could have achieved the same sporting results with less resources when executing their play or could have improved their results with the same resources that they have used. In other words, soccer competitions are a type of activity in which, because the sporting results come first (the victory in each match and as a consequence the number of points gained during the complete season) independent of the amount of resources used, a team can be effective without being efficient and, furthermore, it is the former that is rewarded.

Secondly, the importance of scale inefficiencies makes it clear that we are dealing with an activity that gives rise to variable returns to scale and, therefore, the size of each team is a factor to be taken into account when evaluating its efficiency.

In this article, the calculation of efficiency has been applied to one of the activities carried out by football clubs, namely the playing of matches during a league

TABLE 6:   Efficiency of the Total Sample

Team	Season	Overall Technical Efficiency	Purely Technical Efficiency	Scale Efficiency
Alavés	98	0.64	1.00	0.64
At. Madrid	98	0.62	0.87	0.72
Ath. Bilbao	98	0.96	1.00	0.96
Barcelona	98	1.00	1.00	1.00
Betis	98	0.73	0.98	0.74
Celta	98	0.94	1.00	0.94
Deportivo	98	0.90	0.96	0.93
Español	98	0.94	1.00	0.94
Extremadura	98	0.65	1.00	0.65
Mallorca	98	1.00	1.00	1.00
Oviedo	98	0.71	1.00	0.71
Racing	98	0.63	0.92	0.68
Real Madrid	98	0.84	0.95	0.88
Real Sociedad	98	0.80	0.99	0.80
Salamanca	98	0.39	0.94	0.42
Tenerife	98	0.48	0.94	0.51
Valencia	98	0.97	1.00	0.97
Valladolid	98	0.71	0.98	0.73
Villarreal	98	0.58	1.00	0.58
Zaragoza	98	0.85	0.97	0.88
Alavés	99	0.87	0.95	0.92
At. Madrid	99	0.55	0.90	0.61
Ath. Bilbao	99	0.77	0.95	0.81
Barcelona	99	0.81	0.97	0.84
Betis	99	0.60	0.92	0.66
Celta	99	0.77	0.94	0.82
Deportivo	99	0.98	0.99	0.99
Español	99	0.74	0.97	0.76
Málaga	99	0.70	0.95	0.74
Mallorca	99	0.76	0.94	0.81
Numancia	99	0.73	1.00	0.73
Oviedo	99	0.62	0.91	0.69
Racing	99	0.66	0.97	0.68
Rayo Vallecano	99	0.82	0.97	0.84
Real Madrid	99	0.82	0.91	0.89
Real Sociedad	99	0.74	0.98	0.76
Sevilla	99	0.41	0.92	0.45
Valencia	99	0.94	0.97	0.97
Valladolid	99	0.76	0.91	0.83
Zaragoza	99	0.92	0.99	0.94
Alavés	00	0.66	1.00	0.66
Ath. Bilbao	00	0.66	0.99	0.66
Barcelona	00	0.82	0.99	0.83
Celta	00	0.81	1.00	0.81
Deportivo	00	0.95	0.95	1.00

(continued)

TABLE 6 (continued)

Team	Season	Overall Technical Efficiency	Purely Technical Efficiency	Scale Efficiency
Español	00	0.72	1.00	0.72
Las Palmas	00	0.67	1.00	0.67
Málaga	00	0.82	0.99	0.83
Mallorca	00	1.00	1.00	1.00
Numancia	00	0.57	0.95	0.60
Osasuna	00	0.62	0.99	0.62
Oviedo	00	0.58	0.94	0.61
Racing	00	0.54	0.95	0.57
Rayo Vallecano	00	0.64	0.96	0.67
Real Madrid	00	1.00	1.00	1.00
Real Sociedad	00	0.61	1.00	0.61
Valencia	00	0.87	0.98	0.89
Valladolid	00	0.59	0.95	0.62
Villarreal	00	0.84	0.99	0.85
Zaragoza	00	0.58	0.96	0.60

season, which has allowed us to evaluate the style of play executed by reference to the concept of efficiency. Thus, for example, given that during the 1999-2000 season a more defensive style of play was used and, from the point of view of efficiency, the results were worse, it could be recommended that more offensive tactics be used with the aim of saving resources.

Bearing in mind the forthcoming appearance of these corporations (or *sociedades anónimas deportivas*) on the Spanish stock market, and their subsequent management and evaluation as business organizations, the results of this article highlight the fact that, at least up to now, the economic objective (maximization of profits or minimization of costs) has been second in importance to the sporting objectives that, in this ambit, are the match and league results. This has been the case because the boards of directors have been responsible to their season ticket holders, who naturally wish to see their teams perform well in all the competitions they enter. It is to be expected that when these entities are converted into corporations, and their boards of directors become subject to the criteria of owners who search for a return on their investments, profit will become the objective. This search for maximum profit will necessarily imply the elimination of waste in the use of resources and, as a result, efficiency will be converted into a useful criterion with which to evaluate the activities of professional soccer teams.

NOTES

1. A distinction can be drawn with respect to the sales and profits of firms and their equivalent in the case of soccer teams, namely that in the latter case, the income of one year will depend on the results obtained by the team during the previous season.

2. In the literature on the measurement of efficiency, there is an open debate on whether the calculations should be made by way of deterministic nonparametric frontiers or stochastic frontiers. The most significant drawback of the former is that they do not allow us to distinguish between the effects of the random errors and the inefficiency. Their advantages, however, such as the fact that there is no need to specify a production function, together with the possibility of calculating the technical efficiency of multiproduct units using physical units to measure the variables and, finally, the more intuitive approach, are such that we have chosen to adopt this technique in our study.

3. The approach to the various problems considered in this article is based on that presented by Färe, Grosskopf, and Logan (1985) and also used by Berg, Førsund, and Jansen (1989); Hausman and Neufeld (1991); Ley (1991); Prior (1991); and Grifell, Prior, and Salas (1992). Alternative approaches can, however, be found in Farrell (1957); Seitz (1971); Charnes, Cooper, and Rhodes (1981); and Banker, Charnes, and Cooper (1984).

4. If the overall technical efficiency is measured with an orientation to the input, λ_1 can never present values higher than one in the solution of problem P.1.

5. Table 1 does not present a detailed list of all the inputs and outputs taken or used in the different studies; rather, in the majority of cases, the variable that appears in the table is composed of a group of variables.

6. Here we should note that this division of the productive process coincides with the classification given to the input variables in the studies referred to in Table 1.

7. The data used in this article have been kindly supplied by GECA Sport.

8. In all the calculations, we have confirmed that the efficient teams (that is, those whose values of λ_1 and λ_2 are equal to one) do not present positive slacks.

REFERENCES

Anderson, T. R., & Sharp, G. P. (1997). A new measure of baseball batters using DEA. *Annals of Operations Research, 73*, 141-151.

Banker, R. D., Charnes, A., & Cooper, W. W. (1984). Some models for estimating technical and scale inefficiencies in data envelopment analysis. *Management Science, 30*(9), 1078-1092.

Berg, S. A., Førsund, F. R., & Jansen, E. S. (1989). Bank output measurement and the construction of best practice frontiers. Working paper 1989/6. Norges Bank.

Carmichael, F., & Thomas, D. (1995, September). Production and efficiency in team sports: An investigation of rugby league football. *Applied Economics, 27*(9), 859-869.

Carmichael, F., Thomas, D., & Ward, R. (2000, January-February). Team performance: The case of English premiership football. *Managerial and Decision Economics, 21*(1), 31-45.

Charnes, A., Cooper, W. W., & Rhodes, E. (1981). Evaluating program and managerial efficiency: An application of data envelopment analysis to program follow through. *Management Science, 27*(6), 668-697.

Dawson, P., Dobson, S., & Gerrard, B. (2000a, September). Estimating coaching efficiency in professional team sports: Evidence from English association football. *Scottish Journal of Political Economy, 47*(4), 399-421.

Dawson, P., Dobson, S., & Gerrard, B. (2000b, November). Stochastic frontiers and the temporal structure of managerial efficiency in English soccer. *Journal of Sports Economics, 1*(4), 341-362.

Fandel, G. (1991). *Theory of production and cost.* Berline: Springer-Verlag.

Färe, R., Grosskopf, S., & Logan, J. (1985). The relative performance of publicly-owned and privately-owned electric utilities. *Journal of Public Economics, 26*(1), 89-106.

Farrell, M. J. (1957). The measurement of productive efficiency. *Journal of the Royal Statistical Society,* Series A, *120*(3), 253-281.

Fizel, J. L., & D'Itri, M. P. (1997, June). Managerial efficiency, managerial succession and organizational performance. *Mangerial and Decision Economics, 18*(4), 295-308.

Førsund, F. R., Lovell, C. A. K., & Schmidt, P. (1980). A survey of frontier production functions and of their relationship to efficiency measurement. *Journal of Econometrics, 13*, 5-25.

Grifell, E., Prior, D., & Salas, V. (1992, September). Eficiencia de empresa y eficiencia de planta en los modelos frontera no paramétricos: Aplicación a las cajas de ahorros en España, 1989-1990. Paper presented at the Congress VIII Jornadas de Economìa Industrial, Madrid, Spain.

Hadley, L., Poitras, M., Ruggiero, J., & Knowles, S. (2000). Performance evaluation of National Football League teams. *Managerial and Decision Economics, 21*, 63-70.

Hausman, W. J., & Neufeld, J. L. (1991, August). Property rights versus public spirit: Ownership and efficiency of V.S. electric utilities prior to rate-of-return regulation. *The Review of Economics and Statistics, 73*(3), 414-423.

Hofler, R. A., & Payne, J. E. (1997, August). Measuring efficiency in the National Basketball Association. *Economic Letters, 55*(2), 293-299.

Ley, E. (1991). Eficiencia productiva: Un estudio aplicado al sector hospitalario. *Investigaciones Económicas*, 2nd period, *15*(1), 71-88.

Mazur, M. J. (1994). Evaluating the relative efficiency of baseball players. In A. Charnes, W. W. Cooper, A. Y. Lewin, & L. M. Seiford (Eds.), *Data envelopment analysis: Theory, methodology and application* (pp. 369-391). Boston: Kluwer Academic Publishers.

Prior, D. (1991, September). Los modelos frontera en la evaluación de la productividad. Paper presented at the I Congreso Nacional de ACEDE, Universidad de Alcalá de Henares, Spain.

Schofield, J. A. (1988, February). Production functions in the sports industry: An empirical analysis of professional cricket. *Applied Economics, 20*(2), 177-193.

Scully, G. W. (1994, September-October). Managerial efficiency and survivability in professional team sports. *Managerial and Decision Economics, 15*(5), 403-411.

Seitz, W. D. (1971). Productive efficiency in the steam electric generating industry. *Journal of Political Economy, 79*, 878-886.

Sueyoshi, T., Ohnishi, K., & Kinase, Y. (1999, June). A benchmark approach for baseball evaluation. *European Journal of Operational Research, 15*(3), 429-448.

Zak, T. A., Huang, C. J., & Siegfried, J. J. (1979). Production efficiency: The case of professional basketball. *Journal of Business, 52*(3), 379-392.

Manuel Espitia-Escuer is professor in the Economics and Business Department of the University of Zaragoza, Spain. His fields of research are firm efficiency and business and financial strategy, and his teaching is focused on management.

Lucía Isabel García-Cebrián is associate professor in the Economics and Business Department of the University of Zaragoza, Spain. Her research and teaching are focused on operations, efficiency analysis, and the regulation of public utilities.

Name Index